LATER MEDIEVAL FRANCE

Later Medieval France

THE POLITY

P. S. Lewis

Macmillan
LONDON · MELBOURNE · TORONTO
St Martin's Press
NEW YORK
1968

© P. S. Lewis 1968

Published by

MACMILLAN & CO LTD

Little Essex Street London W C 2

and also at Bombay Calcutta and Madras

Macmillan South Africa (Publishers) Pty Ltd Johannesburg

The Macmillan Company of Australia Pty Ltd Melbourne

The Macmillan Company of Canada Ltd Toronto

St Martin's Press Inc New York

Printed in Great Britain by

ROBERT MACLEHOSE AND CO LTD

The University Press, Glasgow

Library of Congress catalog card no. 68–10531

Contents

MAPS

TABLE

Preface

SOME time between 30 November 1404 and 23 November 1407 Christine de Pisan completed her *Livre du corps de policie*.[1] 'Princes ... knights and nobles, and ... all the people universally ...' she argued, 'should be in a single polity, as a proper living body is, according to the rule of Plutarch, who, in an epistle which he sent to the emperor Trajan, compares the commonwealth to a body having life ...'.[2] Plutarch's epistle to Trajan, the *Institutio Traiani*, which was probably invented by John of Salisbury,[3] was a popular medieval text, though those who used it tended to make their own glosses upon the original. Jean Juvenal des Ursins, archbishop of Reims in the mid-fifteenth century, saw 'the commonwealth ... like a body compaginated of several members, of which the king is the head, the officers of justice the members, as *baillis* and *prévôts* the eyes and ears, the wise counsellors the heart, the knights and nobles the hands and the labourers and merchants the feet'.[4] A hundred years or so earlier Guillaume de Deguileville had grafted the idea onto the statue of Nebuchadnezzar[5] and thus made even more of a morality out of it.[6] This version, too, seems to have been popular;[7] but the concept on its own had, as we shall see, enough capacity for being moralised over.

[1] S. Solente, 'Dates de deux ouvrages de Christine de Pisan', in *Bibl. Ec. Chartes*, XCIV (1933) 422.

[2] E. Nys, *Christine de Pisan et ses principales œuvres* (Brussels, 1914) p. 56.

[3] H. Liebeschütz, 'John of Salisbury and Pseudo-Plutarch', in *J. Warburg and Courtauld Inst.* VI (1943) 33–9; A. Momigliano and H. Liebeschütz, 'Notes on Petrarch, John of Salisbury and the *Institutio Traiani*', in ibid. XII (1949) 189–90.

[4] '... la chose publique ... comme ung corps compagine de plusieurs membres, dont le roy cest le chef, les officiers de justice les membres, comme baillis et prevostz les yeulx et oreilles, les sages conseilliers le cuer, les chevaliers et nobles les mains et les laboureux et marchans les piez' ('Verba mea auribus percipe, Domine', Bibl. nat. MS fr. 2701, fo. 88r–v).

[5] Daniel ii 31–45.

[6] *Le Pelerinage de l'ame*, ed. J. J. Stürzinger (Roxburghe Club: London, 1895) pp. 236–71.

[7] Cf. D. M. Bell, *Etude sur Le Songe du Vieil Pèlerin de Philippe de Mézières* (Geneva, 1955) p. 109.

This book is an attempt to describe in modern terms, and without the moralising, the *corps de policie* of later medieval France. Essentially it deals with the question of power. For 'the power process is not a distinct and separable part of the social process, but only the political aspect of an interactive whole. It is, in fact, only the political aspect of the social process in its entirety.'[1] Such a book must necessarily represent, in its selection of material and in its presentation, the attitude of its author; both to the society he is attempting to revivify, and to the way in which that revivification can be communicated. It must necessarily represent a simple essay upon that society; and to a large extent an interim report upon it too. Taken as such it may, perhaps, not need too much apology. That such a report may be made is due to the work at the frontiers of many scholars, including its author. The burden of gratitude he must owe them is very great; as is that which he must owe to those colleagues at home and abroad who have contributed, some in ways perhaps unknown to them, to the formation of this book.

P.S.L.

All Souls College, Oxford

[1] H. D. Lasswell and A. Kaplan, *Power and Society. A Framework for Political Enquiry* (Yale, 1950) p. xvii.

Author's Notes

Acknowledgements

MY thanks are due to the Royal Historical Society, the Institute of Historical Research, the Society for Medieval Languages and Literature and the Past and Present Society for their permission to re-use material which first appeared in 'War-propaganda and Historiography in Fifteenth-century France and England', in *Trans. Roy. hist. Soc.* ser. 5 xv (1965) 1–21; 'Decayed and Non-feudalism in Later Medieval France', in *B. Inst. hist. Research,* XXXVII (1964) 157–84; 'Jean Juvenal des Ursins and the Common Literary Attitude towards Tyranny in Fifteenth-century France', in *Medium Aevum,* XXXIV (1965) 103–21; and 'The Failure of the French Medieval Estates', in *Past & Present,* XXIII (1962) 3–24.

References

I have given references only to the sources of quotations, to those of particular points of detail and to selected illustrative material. It is impossible in a book of this kind, unless the text is to float high upon a deep sea of footnotes, to give anything like a complete bibliographical coverage for each topic raised; much that has gone into the making of this book cannot therefore be referred to. I have reproduced in the notes the original text only of these pieces of material not to be found in print elsewhere. The edition by R. H. Lucas of Christine de Pisan, *Le Livre du corps de policie* (Geneva, 1967) appeared too late for me to be able to use it. Most of the abbreviations used in the notes should be self-evident; for those in references to periodicals I have followed the current conventions of the *Bibliographie annuelle de l'histoire de France.*

Money

The money of account in later medieval France was the familiar *l*[*ivre*], *s*[*ou*] and *d*[*enier*], either *t*[*ournois*] or, less commonly, *p*[*arisis*]; the latter was rated from the mid-fourteenth century 25 per cent higher than the former. The actual coins in use, which themselves varied in bullion content, had different values in terms of money of account, which varied as the government 'cried' them. The rate at which English and French moneys exchanged depended not only upon the 'cried' value of the coin, but also upon its intrinsic value in terms of bullion and upon its actual condition (new, or worn, or clipped).

But to give some rough idea of contemporaries' notions of the comparative value of *livres tournois* and pounds sterling some instances may be cited. The English noble was first minted in 1344 to run at 6s. 8d. sterling and deliberately at twice the value of the French *écu*, selling in London at 3s. 4d. (A. E. Feavearyear, *The Pound Sterling* (Oxford, 1931) p. 28). As far as the gold content of the coins is concerned this ratio was roughly right (ibid. p. 348; A. Blanchet and A. Dieudonné, *Manuel de numismatique française*, II (1916) 248). In 1337 the *écu d'or* ran at 20 s.t.; in 1343 it had been cried up to 56 s.t., but returned, now slightly alloyed, to 25 s.t. in 1349. The *écu* still ran at this figure in 1360, when the conversion figure for the payment of Jean II's ransom was again fixed at 2 *écus* to the noble. The weight of the noble had been reduced, but so had the fineness of the *écu*; so again the proportion in terms of gold was roughly right ('The Ransom of John II, King of France, 1360–1370', ed. D. M. Broome, in *Camden Miscellany*, XIV (Camden Third Series, 37: 1926); Feavearyear, op. cit. p. 29; Blanchet and Dieudonné, op. cit. pp. 255–6). In 1414 the unfortunate maître Jean Fusoris was given 100 nobles in payment of 200 *écus*, but a changer in Paris would give him only 167 *écus* for them ('Le Procès de maître Jean Fusoris', ed. L. Mirot, in *M. Soc. Hist. Paris*, XXVII (1900) 234). The ratio between the *écu* and the noble was, since 1411, in terms of gold content, about 1·8 : 1 (Feavearyear, op. cit. p. 35; Blanchet and Dieudonné, op. cit. p. 270); but if Fusoris' coins were clipped or worn, a ratio of about 1·6 : 1 is understandable. He did in fact complain and was given his second term of payment of 100 nobles in 'good' coins ('Le Procès', p. 247). In 1414 the *écu* ran at 22s. 6d.t. Some time in the 1450s William Worcester estimated that 9 *l.t.* were equal to a pound sterling (*Letters and Papers Illustrative of the Wars of the English in France during the Reign of Henry the Sixth*, ed. J. Stevenson (Rolls Series) II, part 2 (1864) [534], [546], [551]). The ratio in the gold content of the *écu* and the noble was again about 2 : 1; but the *écu* now ran at 27s. 6d. t. at most (Feavearyear, op. cit. p. 36; Blanchet and Dieudonné, op. cit. p. 288). On the cried value of the coins this would give 8l. 5s. t. to the pound sterling. But as the example of Fusoris' difficulties shows, conversion figures were treacherous.

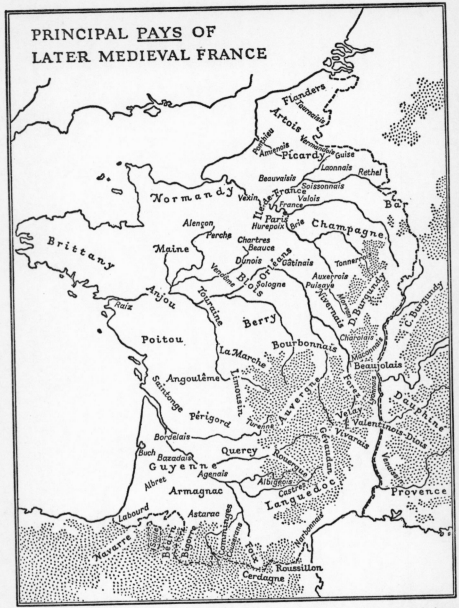

PRINCIPAL PAYS OF
LATER MEDIEVAL FRANCE

Flanders
Artois
Tournaisis
Ponthieu
Amienois
Vermandois
Picardy
Guise
Laonnais
Rethel
Beauvaisis
Soissonnais
Bar
Vexin
Ile-de-France
Valois
Paris
France
Hurepoix
Brie
Champagne
Normandy
Alençon
Perche
Chartres
Beauce
Dunois
Gâtinais
Tonnerrois
Maine
Vendôme
Blois
Orléans
Auxerrois
Puisaye
Brittany
Touraine
Sologne
Nivernais
Morvan
D. Burgundy
C. Burgundy
Anjou
Berry
Charolais
Raiz
Mâconnais
Bourbonnais
Beaujolais
Poitou
La Marche
Forez
Lyonnais
Angoulême
Limousin
Auvergne
Dauphiné
Saintonge
Turenne
Velay
Valentinois-Diois
Périgord
Gévaudan
Vivarais
Venaissin
Bordelais
Rouergue
Buch
Bazadais
Quercy
Provence
Guyenne
Agenais
Albigeois
Languedoc
Albret
Castres
Armagnac
Labourd
Astarac
Narbonnais
Navarre
Soule
Béarn
Bigorre
Comminges
Couserans
Foix
Roussillon
Cerdagne

Selection and nomenclature are based primarily on Gilles Le Bouvier (see below, p. 2, n. 3). For further detail see, for instance, G. du Fresne de Beaucourt, *Hist. de Charles VII*, II (1882) *carte* (by A. Longnon).

I

Some Conditions of Life

France; the pays *and local feeling*

WHAT was France in the later middle ages? Both the idea and the
reality varied.[1] For Gilles Le Bouvier, Berry herald, in the mid-fifteenth
century, the kingdom was bounded by the sea from Sluys in Flanders to
the border of Navarre; thence its frontier ran along the Pyrenees to
Narbonne; and it was again confined by the sea to Aigues-Mortes.
From the Mediterranean its eastern border followed the Rhône and the
Saône northward to Lorraine; then the frontier followed the Meuse to
Hainaut and Liège, and finally the Escaut to the North Sea.[2] His view,
though suffering from abbreviation, was far from inaccurate; and it had
behind it an official tradition based upon a hazy impression of the treaty
of Verdun of 843.[3] But there is some evidence that an older tradition of
the frontiers of Gaul (to which Gilles Le Bouvier indeed half subscribed)
led Louis XI as dauphin in 1444 and throughout his life as king to
argue that France ran eastward to the Rhine.[4] And in reality the frontier
of 'France', in a looser sense, outdistanced Gilles Le Bouvier's definition.

[1] For meanings of the word 'France' other than that of the kingdom, see
'Du Nom de France et des différents pays auquel il fut appliqué', in *Annuê
hist. Soc. Hist. France* (1849) pp. 152–68.
[2] *Le Livre de la description des pays*, ed. E. T. Hamy (Rec. de voyages et de
docs pour servir à l'hist. de la géog. 22: 1908) pp. 31–2.
[3] A. Longnon, 'Les Limites de la France et l'étendue de la domination
anglaise à l'époque de la mission de Jeanne d'Arc', in R. *Questions hist.* XVIII
(1875) 446, 463–4.
[4] Op. cit. p. 52; G. du Fresne de Beaucourt, *Hist. de Charles VII*, v.
(1888) 35; L. Caillet, *Etude sur les relations de la commune de Lyon avec Charles VII
et Louis XI (1417–1483)* (Lyon, 1909) p. 227. Cf. M. Lugge, *'Gallia' und
'Francia' im Mittelalter* (Bonn, 1960) pp. 208 ff.

If at the western end of the Pyrenees Béarn (at least *de facto*)[1] and Basse-Navarre escaped the sovereignty of the king of France, and if the frontier from the North Sea to Pontailler on the Saône followed Gilles' roughly sketched boundary only intermittently, at each end of the Mediterranean littoral the effective boundaries of the kingdom could be wider. In the west, Roussillon and Cerdagne became temporarily part of France in 1463; and in the south-east the effective frontier overleapt the Alps onto the Italian side. Dauphiné, acquired by 1349, remained imperial territory and nominally in the hands of the king's eldest son; and to it was joined by 1434 Valentinois-Diois, already a possession of the crown and for which homage had been done before the Valois came to the throne. Farther north, other seigneuries, formally imperial, were under French control; and in 1481 Provence was acquired by Louis XI.

But if areas theoretically not under the king of France's sovereignty were effectively under his control, areas which were, were effectively not. Clearly, until 1453, the fluctuating areas under English domination during the Hundred Years War escaped it; in the Pyrenees the chance of accepting an alternative sovereignty was occasionally taken — as it was at times in the north, in Brittany, in the Low Countries and in Burgundy. The limit of the kingdom of Bourges, the kingdom of Charles VII in 1429, was very clearly not the limit of the kingdom of France, let alone that of a greater entity. An account of the arrival of Jeanne d'Arc recorded at Albi describes the English as holding 'all the *pays* of Normandy and of Picardy except Tournai, [the *pays*] of Beauvaisis, of Maine and of Artois, of Brie, of Beauce and all Champagne, Paris and all *la dolsa Franssa*, the *pays* of Hainaut and of Cambrésis, up to the river Loire', let alone what they held in the south-west.[2] The effective boundaries of the kingdom thus tended to a greater or less degree to be different both from those of theoretical sovereignty and indeed from those of geography.

Some sense of the latter was not lacking in fifteenth-century France. The configuration of the country was described in the middle of the century by Gilles Le Bouvier.[3] His account indeed was not unlike that

[1] P. Tucoo-Chala, *La Vicomté de Béarn et le problème de sa souveraineté des origines à 1620* (Bordeaux, 1961) pp. 79–107.

[2] *Procès de condamnation et de réhabilitation de Jeanne d'Arc*, ed. J. Quicherat (Soc. Hist. France) IV (1847) 301.

[3] Op. cit. pp. 30 ff.

sketched by Michelet four hundred years later. Gilles' patriotic eulogising can be discounted; his ethnographical observations were less extreme than his successor's; but, like Michelet's, his picture is of a France much diversified in geography, broken up essentially into *pays*, each with a considerable local identity, of soil and climate and population. But the *pays*, a sentimental, legal, political unit, was not created wholly by geography. The geography of the duchy of Burgundy, or of Berry, or of Brittany was far from undiversified. Nor did the *pays* base itself upon even the strongest of ethnic distinctions: Breton was not the language of all Bretons, and Basque did not create a nation. The identity of each *pays* in the later middle ages had been created by more accidental forces than these. Nature proposes and man disposes.[1] It was the social and legal development of the past which had created the 'countries' of France; and the political immunity which their territorial magnates had enjoyed — and which some to a greater or less extent still enjoyed — which had engendered a wider regional cohesion.[2] The particularism of the *pays* is, if only sentimentally, far from extinct today. The departmentalisation of France did not destroy the Béarnais and create the Bas-Pyrénéan; and the schoolchild in Saône-et-Loire still chants that it is proud to be a Burgundian.

Not that the term *pays* was confined in the later middle ages to those areas later thought of as 'provinces'.[3] For Gilles Le Bouvier, for instance, it was clearly both a 'political' and a 'geographical' term; and it could be applied to ecclesiastical circumscriptions, to feudal entities, to administrative areas, to simple districts which one wished to distinguish from others, like 'haut pays' and 'bas pays'. It could be applied to larger areas, to half the kingdom like the 'pays de Languedoil', to the whole of the kingdom, the 'pays du roi'. One cannot interrogate the term too closely for its precise meaning and emotional significance to the inhabitants of the *pays* of later medieval France. But it is safely enough used to label those areas which had accreted an identity, and

[1] C. Higounet, 'La Géohistoire', in *L'Hist. et ses méthodes*, ed. C. Samaran (1961) p. 73.
[2] O. Martin, *Hist. de le coutume de* . . . *Paris*, I (1922) 32 ff.
[3] G. Dupont-Ferrier, 'Le Sens des mots "patria" et "patrie" en France au Moyen âge et jusqu'au début du xviie siècle', in R. *hist.* CLXXXVIII–CLXXXIX (1940) 89–104; B. Guenée, 'Etat et nation en France au Moyen âge', in R. *hist.* CCXXXVII (1967) 17–30.

which were, in the fourteenth and fifteenth centuries, natural social and political units. As such we shall see them in action as, say, the basic areas for regional representative institutions; but we shall also see them as areas not wholly sure of their political cohesion, areas in which a more local consciousness was not wholly avoided. The development of a preparedness to co-operate amongst 'large-scale communities'[1] is an intrinsic element in the development of wider political loyalties; and in some areas of France at some times this preparedness seems woefully to have been lacking. And if the *pays* themselves were uncertain of their *contrées*', their towns', or even of their inhabitants' adhesion, so might the kingdom to a greater extent be uncertain of the adhesion of the *pays*.

Communications and communication

We must begin, therefore, with this concept of a France highly regional in mentality; a concept offered us by Gilles Le Bouvier no less than by Michelet and by Vidal de La Blache. Clearly barriers existed. In 1443 the town of Millau sent a message to the dauphin Louis by the local Carmelite prior; the letter was actually put into his hand, but he was unable to read it 'because it was written in our tongue' and neither could his secretary.[2] Yet Gilles Le Bouvier, who commented upon the singularity of Breton, did not comment upon romance; and it seems difficult to imagine that a reasonably quick-witted person could not have made, at least in an emergency and on paper, some headway into 'nostra lenga'. To René d'Anjou, who spoke German and possibly English as well as Provençal, Italian and Spanish,[3] it might have seemed less unfamiliar. And if the majority found difficulty with a minority language, the minority must have found less difficulty with the more 'standard' French of the north. It has even been alleged that a romance-speaker from Auvergne would have had as much trouble in being understood by a romance-speaker from the high Pyrenees than would

[1] F. Cheyette, 'Procurations by Large-scale Communities in Fourteenth-century France', in *Speculum*, XXXVII (1962) 18–31.
[2] *Docs sur la ville de Millau*, ed. J. Artières (Arch. hist. Rouergue, 7: Millau, 1930) p. 314.
[3] A. Lecoy de La Marche, *Le Roi René*, II (1875) 191–2.

have had a French-speaker from the north.[1] Presumably the consuls of Rodez could understand the account of the Estates-general of Tours which was read aloud to them in 1468 in straightforward French.[2] The question perhaps turned on social status, on occupation, on mobility. In the Netherlands, where the language problem was possibly more acute, it was a clear advantage to be bilingual if one hoped to hold office: Jean de Lannoy thought his son should not be allowed to forget his Netherlandish, and Jan van Dadizeele was sent from Flemish Flanders at the age of twelve to Lille and Arras to learn French.[3] For those who needed to understand French more than very occasionally — and these are the people in whom we are primarily interested — it was clearly only common sense to have learned it.

But now we have come to the question of communication, to the removing of those barriers of local consciousness. We know comparatively little about the means of physical communication, the roads of later medieval France;[4] and contemporaries seem to have had no map to guide them before the sixteenth century. It seems clear that the Roman road system, based upon Lyon, was gradually replaced throughout the period of the Capets by another system, based upon Paris, which perhaps used only exceptionally the Roman network. Although the Roman idea of the 'public road' seems to have merged insensibly into the medieval idea of the 'royal road', medieval roads — though far from being, perhaps, as bad as they have sometimes (literally) been painted — lacked the solidity of their predecessors. But no-one seems

---

[1] P. Salies, *Etudes sur le notariat toulousain au Moyen âge* (Albi, 1959) p. 15.

[2] Arch. com. Rodez, BB 3, folios 50r ff.

[3] C. A. J. Armstrong, 'The Language Question in the Low Countries: The Use of French and Dutch by the Dukes of Burgundy and their Admin.', in *Europe in the Late Middle Ages*, ed. J.R.Hale, J.R.L.Highfield and B. Smalley (1965) p. 404; cf. R. Vaultier, *Le Folklore pendant la guerre de Cent ans d'après les lettres de rémission du Trésor des chartes* (1965) p. 8 n [2]. For a Breton boy learning French in the mid-fifteenth century, see *Le Procès de Gilles de Rais. Les Documents*, ed. G. Bataille (1965) p. 361.

[4] J. Hubert, 'Les Routes du Moyen âge', in *Les Routes de France depuis les origines jusqu'à nos jours*, ed. G. Michaud (Colloques des Cahiers de civilisation, 1: 1959) pp. 25–56. For an example of recent work, see R.H. Bautier, 'Recherches sur les routes de l'Europe médiévale. (i) De Paris et des foires de Champagne à la Méditerranée par le Massif central', in *B. philol hist. Com. Travaux hist. sci.* (1960) pp. 99–143; '(ii) Le Grand Axe routier est-ouest du Midi de la France, d'Avignon à Toulouse', in ibid. (1961) pp. 277–308.

to have complained about them, except, perhaps, when the comparatively light maintenance they required was interrupted by military manœuvres; and no-one seems to have been tempted over-much by the possibilities of water transport.[1] The number of miles which could be covered in a day naturally varied with the form of transport, with the nature of the terrain, with the purpose of the journey, with its length.[2] In England in 1482 a messenger-service carrying urgent news for Edward IV and served by strict relays is alleged to have covered 200 miles in two days.[3] But for more ordinary travellers the figure was lower: while it was possible to cover just over 50 miles a day, it in fact required 'a real effort' to keep up a speed of 30–33 miles a day, 'especially several days in succession', and most journeys were probably made at a rate of between 20 and 30 miles a day, a speed at which, in a mixed group of horse and foot, the latter seem easily to have kept up with the party.[4] The organisation of a service for speedy and certain communication in France — a relay or post system — seems to have been the work of Louis XI; 1479 has been offered as the date of the establishment of a *controleur-général* of *chevaucheurs*, who are to be found throughout our period.[5] Times over the routes Tours–Amiens and Tours–Bordeaux, some 190–220 miles, are alleged to have been 20–24 hours. If one used this service — which one did clandestinely — one's messages need not have suffered much, compared even with today's times. But such post-haste was admittedly exceptional. On the other hand, few medieval messages probably merited a greater speed in transit than that achieved by an ordinary horseman, even accompanied by a servant on foot. Frenetic speed was sometimes necessary;[6] but very often it was not.

[1] M. N. Boyer, 'Roads and Rivers: their Use and Disuse in Late Medieval France', in *Medievalia et Humanistica*, XIII (1960) 68–80.

[2] Y. Renouard, 'Information et transmission des nouvelles', in *L'Hist. et ses méthodes*, pp. 110–17.

[3] C. A. J. Armstrong, 'Some Examples of the Distribution and Speed of News in England at the Time of the Wars of the Roses', in *Studies ... F. M. Powicke* (Oxford, 1948) p. 439.

[4] M. N. Boyer, 'A Day's Journey in Medieval France', in *Speculum*, XXVI (1951) 597–608.

[5] R. Gandilhon, 'Louis XI, fondateur du service des postes en France', in R. *hist.* CLXXXIII (1938) 37–41; E. Vaillé, *Hist. gén. des Postes françaises*, I (1947) 149–75, II (1949) 5–37.

[6] Armstrong, 'Some Examples', p. 429.

What sort of 'communication', in a different sense, ran along the roads? Louis XI, for instance, wanted intelligence: when a *chevaucheur* was established at Lyon in 1481, it was to permit the king 'to know about and to have news of several neighbouring countries, like Provence, Savoy and Dauphiné'.[1] But the transit of information was not a one-way matter. 'We are always anxious to inform our good and loyal subjects properly of the things which occur affecting our honour and felicity, and those of our kingdom,' explained Louis XI in a circular letter in 1470; not only, presumably, because (as he wrote to the inhabitants of Péronne in 1465) 'we know that you will be glad to hear our good news', but also because (as another letter shows) the image of his government had to be maintained.[2] But this kind of news-letter (though perhaps not its self-eulogistic preamble) was of a type familiar enough at least from the beginning of the previous reign.[3] Information was eagerly enough received: in 1471 the council of Reims recruited two foot-messengers 'so that the news shall always be known' of the royal army.[4] But information from the crown could at least be edited. And the formal letter was not the only way of spreading the right material. Itinerant *chansonniers* could be licensed 'to go about a kingdom to sing and recite songs, verses and stories concerning the good news and occurrences which have happened to us and which happen each day to our advantage and that of our lordship'.[5] Preachers could be dispatched, like the friar Pierre Nicolas to Normandy, 'to preach and to admonish the people to remain loyal towards [their]...lord [the king] and to resist those who wish to harm him'.[6] In Troyes in 1439 friar Liénart Breton 'commended the cause of the king our lord and of his lordship most notably in all his preachings, and exhorted the people to love him and to remain in good and true obedience to him'.[7] And

[1] Gandilhon, op. cit. pp. 40–1.
[2] *Lettres de Louis XI*, ed. J. Vaesen and E. Charavay (Soc. Hist. France) IV (1890) 152–3, II (1885) 309, III (1887) 143; cf. H. Sée, *Louis XI et les villes* (1891) pp. 191–7.
[3] See, for example, Beaucourt, op. cit. I (1881) 461–2.
[4] Sée, op. cit. p. 191.
[5] C. Samaran, 'Chanteurs ambulants et propagande politique sous Louis XI', in *Bibl. Ec. Chartes*, C (1939) 233.
[6] R. Gandilhon, *Politique économique de Louis XI* (Rennes, 1940) p. 99.
[7] F. Bibolet, 'La Participation du clergé aux affaires municipales de la ville de Troyes aux xive et xve siècles', in *M. Soc. acad. Aube*, C (1943–5) 69.

with the introduction into France in 1470 of printing the organisation
of persuasion became perhaps easier. The only piece of incunable
political ephemera which appears to survive for the reign of Louis XI is
the printed treaty of Arras of 1482, probably produced in the last year of
his reign.[1] The *doléances* of the Estates-general of 1484, the government's
replies and some of the speeches were, as Thomas Basin noticed,
apparently 'published and disseminated everywhere';[2] the pamphlet ran
into two editions at least.[3] And from 1488 the government's use of the
printing press seems to have developed: the right 'good news' about
especially the Italian campaign in 1494-5 was scattered about the
country.[4] Thereafter its development as a means of controlled communication was unbroken;[5] but of communication, of course, not
necessarily on one side.

But it was not only the pedlars of printed ephemera, the messengers
and the propagandists, official and unofficial, whom one found on the
roads in later medieval France. Their business or their employment
brought members of every social group and of all levels of society
temporarily or permanently out of their original locality. The urge to
seek better land, better employment or, in the turmoil of war, mere
safety uprooted the peasant: 'a very great mobility of people from place
to place, a stirring-up of populations: these are the characteristics of the
rural world of the end of the Middle Ages'.[6] But the mental effects of
migration were perhaps much less: the 'foreigners' became assimilated,
conformed to local attitudes; their children were as local as the local
children. Only the vagabond — and vagabondage was, at least from the

---

[1] *Rec. de pièces hist. imprimées sous le règne de Louis XI*, ed. E. Picot and H.
Stein (Soc. des bibliophiles françois) *Texte* (1923) pp. 286–99.

[2] *Hist. des règnes de Charles VII et de Louis XI*, ed. J. Quicherat (Soc. Hist.
France) III (1857) 200.

[3] Jean Dupré, ?1484; Antoine Caillaut, ?1484.

[4] J. P. Seguin, 'L'Information à la fin du xve siècle en France. Pièces
d'actualité imprimées sous le règne de Charles VIII', in *Arts et Traditions
populaires*, IV (1956) 309–30, V (1957) 46–74.

[5] J. P. Seguin, *L'Information en France, de Louis XII à Henri III* (Geneva,
1961).

[6] J. Glénisson and J. Misraki, 'Désertions rurales dans la France médiévale',
in *Villages désertes et hist. écon., xie–xviiie siècle*, ed. F. Braudel (1965) p. 286.
Cf. R. Fossier, 'Remarques sur les mouvements de population en Champagne
méridionale au xve siècle', in *Bibl. Ec. Chartes*, CXXII (1964) 177–215.

fourteenth century, a social problem — broke free permanently from the ties of locality. Freer perhaps than the peasant migrant were those who had moved in search of a training and who might move again to a career in still a third locality. Notaries, for instance, created by the *capitouls* of Toulouse, had arrived in the city from all over the Midi; and they scattered themselves back in different places from those of their origin, allegedly 'a powerful element in the diffusion of ideas, of habits, of practice and above all of language'.[1] Budding advocates, for instance, left the *bailliage* of Senlis in search of a university education at Paris and, as the standard of their profession rose in the fifteenth century, went on to Orléans or even further for a qualification in civil law.[2] Newcomers to the legal societies of the *bailliage* made them in the second half of the fifteenth century 'a melting pot in which mingled mentalities come from every social, professional and geographical horizon'.[3]

The search for an education, for training, for a career might be thought to have offered a wider perspective to those who pursued it. It was a pursuit, on the whole, for the rich; the poor student was not wholly excluded, but he was, it is argued, rare in the university of Paris in the fifteenth century.[4] Of those students from the *bailliage* of Senlis at Paris, one in four perhaps was the son of a noble, one in four the son of a bourgeois notable; half were the sons of advocates and officers in the *bailliage*. The interest of the last group in the virtues of university education is perhaps sufficiently obvious. But the idea might be acceptable to the well-to-do for a considerable number of reasons. Sheer culture should not perhaps be underestimated. Gilles de St.-Simon, *chambellan* and *maître d'hôtel* to the constable Richmond, *chambellan* of the king, *bailli* of Senlis from 1439 to 1477, a military man, provided in his will that his three sons should be kept at their books until 'each one of them knows and understands his Latin'. That rather rebarbative text, the *Songe du Verger*, was not only bought in manuscript in 1453 by Jean d'Orléans comte d'Angoulême; the printed edition of 1492 seems to have been acquired by Guillaume Giroult, 'merchant and keeper of the

[1] Salies, op. cit. pp. 13–19.
[2] B. Guenée, *Tribunaux et gens de justice dans le bailliage de Senlis à la fin du Moyen âge* (1963) pp. 188 ff.
[3] Ibid. p. 392.
[4] Ibid. p. 191.

mint of Tours', fairly soon after it was published.[1] But education was perhaps not primarily valuable as a thing in itself. As at any time a degree meant preferment, especially, in the later middle ages, a degree in law: in the civil service, in the Church. Outside Paris and Montpellier the provincial universities of France were dominated by the faculties of law; the older schools of Angers and Orléans long remained without any other faculty; of the new universities of the fifteenth century Caen was originally purely legal and Bourges mainly so. Statistical evidence of the growth of legal study, or even of growth in the number of students matriculated in all university faculties, is largely lacking; but its influence will haunt us in our investigation of later medieval French society.

Peregrination in search of a career was, of course, hardly a new thing in the later middle ages. The military and the clerical had long sought their fortunes abroad; and so had the merchants. It would perhaps be rash to assert that their activity had radically increased. But that of civil servants, ecclesiastical and lay, clearly had; and with it increased the activity of all who had to deal with them. The interference of regional or central powers in the life of local groups naturally sent their members flocking to regional or central offices, to negotiate, to protest, to intrigue. The business of litigation brought men to regional centres and (before the establishment in the fifteenth century of regional Parlements) further to Paris, to appear in the courts in person or at least to discuss their cases with their lawyers. At the beginning of 1393 maître Raymond Queu went 'into France for the town [of St.-Jean-d'Angély], to our lord the king, to have the privileges of the town confirmed, and to notify him of the miseries of the *pays*, and to ask for a renewed grant of the *souchet*, and to carry out several other things necessary for the affairs of the town and to appear in the Parlement of our lord the King'.[2] In June 1396 the town empowered sire Aymeri Seignouret, 'proctor of the commune', not only to pursue favours about the king and his council, but also to pursue 'before the officers of the *Chambre des comptes*, before the *généraux élus sur le fait des aides pour la guerre*' and elsewhere any grants

---

[1] P. S. Lewis, 'War-propaganda and Historiography in Fifteenth-century France and England', in *Trans. Roy. hist. Soc.* ser. 5 xv (1965) 5.

[2] *Reg. de l'échevinage de St.-Jean-d'Angély*, ed. D. d'Aussy, 1 (Arch. hist. Saintonge Aunis, 24: 1895) 386.

the king in fact made.[1] The whole business of taxation produced a whole new set of motives for long and painful journeys, especially, perhaps, for the agents of towns.

Similar to them might be those journeys which took reluctant local delegates to distant meetings of representative institutions. There, too, they would meet the civil servants, royal commissioners to regional Estates, the greater officers at more general assemblies. The gyrations of the civil servants themselves were incessant. From the royal entourage, from the central courts and the central financial offices, commissions went into the country on legal, financial and administrative business. In the country the local civil servants went about their business and from the country they in turn visited the centre. Pierre Scatisse, *trésorier* of France and *général des aides* in Languedoc, recorded in an expense-account the journeys he had made in the service of the duke of Anjou, Charles V's lieutenant in Languedoc, 'and to see to things necessary for the conduct of the war' between 14 April 1369 and 3 December 1374; each year he crossed and re-crossed the length of Languedoc on this business alone.[2]

But it was only Anjou who, in this record, 'went into France'. Magnates had, apart from those others whose profession it was to travel, the greatest mobility. Statistical evidence is again hard to come by; but the itineraries, say, of Philippe *le hardi* and Jean *sans peur*, the first Valois dukes of Burgundy, for example, give high figures for restless movement.[3] The kings of France themselves were to a greater or less extent rarely still; the itineraries of Philippe VI and of Louis XI show each an 'indefatigable traveller'.[4] Both business and pleasure took the king and his greater subjects in circuits around their estates or on longer journeys through the kingdom; and with them went their entourages, more or less magnificent.

[1] Ibid. II (ibid. 26: 1897) 11–12. Cf. 'Le Journal des dépenses d'un notaire de Périgueux en mission à Paris', ed. A. Higounet-Nadal, in *A. Midi*, LXXVI (1964) 379–402.

[2] F. Ménard, *Hist. . . . de la ville de Nismes*, II (1751) 'Preuves', 2–7.

[3] *Itinéraires de Philippe 'le hardi' et de Jean 'sans peur', ducs de Bourgogne*, ed. E. Petit (Docs inéd. sur l'hist. de France: 1888). For the movements of Guy I de Châtillon comte de Blois between February 1319 and April 1320, see G. Tessier, 'Une Cour seigneuriale au xive siècle', in *Annu.-B. Soc. Hist. France* (1941) pp. 56 ff.

[4] R. Cazelles, *La Société politique et la crise de la royauté sous Philippe de Valois* (1958) pp. 403–4; *Lettres de Louis XI*, XI (1909) viii.

Wider horizons were provided, therefore, for a considerable number of at least the more important inhabitants of later medieval France. For some of them they were not bounded by the frontiers of the kingdom. Gilles Le Bouvier put together his *Livre de la description des pays* 'because many people in different nations and countries delight and take pleasure, as I have done in time past, in seeing the world and the different things that are in it, and because many people want to know about it without going out into it, and because others do want to see it for themselves, to go about and to travel . . .'.[1] The motive of travel simply 'to see the country' should not be despised.[2] Others had less pleasurable business abroad. Ambassadors and their trains had perforce to see the world. But it was perhaps, besides more esoteric trade, pilgrimage and crusade that took men on their wildest journeys. Pilgrimage took Ogier VIII d'Anglure in 1395–6 to the Holy Land, Nompar II de Caumont in 1419–1420 and Bertrandon de La Broquière in 1432–3, an unknown author there and to Mount Sinai, Cairo and Alexandria in the early 1420s.[3] Crusade took Gaston III Fébus comte de Foix to eastern Prussia in 1357–8, a group of minor Poitevin seigneurs in 1363–4 and the fallen Jacques Cœur to Chios in 1456.[4] The travels of Ghillebert de Lannoy in the first half of the fifteenth century encompassed the western world.[5] Crusade, too (though indirectly), took the officers of Guy VI de La Trémoille on an odyssey to Hungary, Italy, Turkey and the court of the Sultan, searching for their master after the débâcle of Nicopolis in 1396.[6]

---

[1] p. 29.

[2] In 1461 Robert de Balsac had, according to Louis XI, 'grant desir et affection d'aler veoir le monde' and to take military occupation abroad (*Lettres de Louis XI*, II 183).

[3] *Le Saint Voyage de Jhérusalem du seigneur d'Anglure*, ed. F. Bonnardot and A. Longnon (Soc. des anciens textes français: 1878); *Voyaige d'oultremer ou Jhérusalem par le seigneur de Caumont, l'an mccccxviii*, ed. A. E. L. de La Grange (1858); *Le Voyage d'outremer de Bertrandon de La Broquière*, ed. C. Schéfer (Rec. de voyages et de docs pour servir à l'hist. de la géog. 12: 1892); H. Moranvillé, 'Un Pèlerinage en Terre Sainte et au Sinaï au xvᵉ siècle', in *Bibl. Ec. Chartes*, LXVI (1905) 70–106.

[4] P. Tucoo-Chala, *Gaston Fébus et la vicomté de Béarn* (Bordeaux, 1960) pp. 74–8; C. Higounet, 'De La Rochelle à Torun: aventure de barons en Prusse et relations économiques (1363–1364)', in *Moyen Age*, LXIX (1963) 529–40; Beaucourt, op. cit. V (1890) 131.

[5] *Œuvres*, ed. C. Potvin (Louvain, 1878) pp. 8–178.

[6] *Les La Trémoille pendant cinq siècles*, ed. L. de La Trémoille, I (Nantes,

His tailor, Daniel de La Court, was away for seven months or more and went as far as Lesbos. He discovered Guy VI had died at Rhodes, and the body was fetched by Pierre Valée, who had been to Pera to look for the missing magnate. It was a far cry from keeping the mint in Troyes.

Conservatism and pessimism

But though some of these travellers wrote up their experiences, it is difficult to assess their impact upon their readers. Even Gilles Le Bouvier remained convinced, at least patriotically, that the 'kingdom of France . . . is the finest, the most pleasant, the most gracious and the best proportioned of them all'.[1] His views would have pleased the French herald in that (for a French piece) curiously unvenomous *Débat des hérauts d'armes*.[2] It cannot be argued that the travellers (or the travellers' tales) contributed towards giving their contemporaries a consciousness of a wider unity. Nor perhaps can it be argued that they had developed much of a consciousness of the unity of France, or that a sense of community had grown up in the country. Admittedly, under war conditions, a consciousness of the existence and of the needs of another *pays* might be forced upon one. At the king's command an Auvergnat might be led to think of, and subvent, Flanders, or a Norman, Guyenne. Pressure of taxation might lead at least to a plea for uniformity in sharing its burden throughout the country. But this attitude might still be thought to have sprung from a determination to preserve one's own rights against a neighbour's advantage; and it might still seem to have remained that charity began at home.[3] A request was made to the Estates of Rouergue in 1443, for instance, for money to drive the English out of a place in Quercy. The town council of Millau decided that 'the *pays* should not help them by as much as one denier, because they don't help us in our necessity'.[4] The council's attitude

1890) 76 ff.; *Guy de La Trémoille et Marie de Sully, Livre de comptes, 1395–1406*, ed. L. de La Trémoille (Nantes, 1887) pp. 104 ff.

[1] Op. cit. p. 30.

[2] *Le Débat des hérauts d'armes de France et d'Angleterre*, ed. L. Pannier and P. Meyer (Soc. des anciens textes français: 1877).

[3] G. Dupont-Ferrier, 'Où en était la formation de l'unité française aux xve et xvie siècles?', in *J. Savants* (1941) pp. 113–15.

[4] *Docs sur la ville de Millau*, pp. 312–13.

towards the main request for 15,000 livres 'to help to support the charges and to pay the wages of the soldiery on the frontiers' was that the *pays* should give 'the least sum that it can and that the longest possible term should be taken to pay it'. Rouergue may have been a particularly independent or benighted place; but regional powers that were enlightened seem on the whole to have been few.

When taxation came into the argument the deputies to the Estates-general of 1484 still went for each other's throats in defence of the regions they represented.[1] That cosmopolitan René d'Anjou was at least persuaded by his Angevin subjects in the mid-fifteenth century to demand tax remission for them, even though it might be said that 'it would be a precedent and have repercussions throughout the kingdom'.[2] The answer to that, it was thought, was 'that amongst all the *pays* and *contrées* of the kingdom, that of Anjou, all in all, has thoroughly merited and deserved to receive this favour, and even a greater one'. It was René's duty to defend his subjects in the *pays*; like a loyal attorney he made out a case for them against other lords'. Charles VII's reaction was to send commissioners into Anjou, Poitou, Touraine and Berry to see if in fact the case was a good one, 'because the king would wish to maintain equality amongst all the *pays* of his kingdom'. It was the king, as judge, who thought of the common good. The inhabitants of the *pays* of the country, litigants before him, were naturally advocates of their own interests.

It would be unreasonable to expect them to have thought of anything else.[3] In some sense it was the king alone who was the sole inhabitant of all France, the king who, like Louis XI, thought of having 'one weight, one measure, one ell and one currency' throughout the kingdom;[4] and one custom. The last 'would not have been possible', it has been argued,

---

[1] J. Masselin, *Journal des Etats généraux de France tenus à Tours en 1484*, ed. A. Bernier (Docs inéd. sur l'hist. de France: 1835) p. 458.

[2] P. Marchegay, *Arch. d'Anjou*, II (Angers, 1853) 305–39; H. Bellugou, *Le Roi René et la réforme fiscale dans le duché d'Anjou au milieu du xve siècle* (Angers, 1962).

[3] Cf. M. Rey, *Le Domaine du roi et les finances extraordinaires sous Charles VI, 1388–1413* (1965) pp. 369–70. But see below, pp. 167–8.

[4] R. Gandilhon, 'L'Unification des coutumes sous Louis XI', in R. *hist.* CXCIV (1944) 319. Unification also appealed to men of letters (P. Viollet, *Hist. des institutions politiques et admin. de la France*, II (1898) 207–8).

'without a complete overturning of mental structures'.[1] But already in the *bailliage* of Senlis from the mid-fifteenth century the influence of the custom of Paris was, through the attraction which the *Châtelet* as a court had for local litigants and their lawyers, beginning to provide common ground in the customs of Senlis, Clermont and Valois.[2] The process towards a common law was a long one; but it had begun. If the ultimate foundation of the countries of France is to be found in the spontaneous recognition of common attitudes in a common custom, in 'the feeling of following identical practices',[3] then only a change in mental attitude could produce a common consciousness; a change in mental attitude accepted because it was advantageous for oneself, not forced upon one because it was advantageous for someone else.

A dominant mental attitude was thus, it may be argued, of immunity; of the preservation of particular rights and privileges against those who in their own or indeed in a general interest might attack them, rights and privileges to be defended against 'novelty' as René d'Anjou defended the rights and privileges of his apanage in 1449–52. It was to the verities of the past, to the prerogatives of his predecessors, not to the possible verities of the future that he looked; novelty was synonymous with illegality. In that essentially static political society change was undesirable. Reform meant the proper working of an existing political system, not its alteration. The *status quo* had an infinite moral force;[4] the number of letters of non-prejudice the king was expected to issue in protection of the future interests of his subjects — against the precedent an action of his taken against them and for one time admitted might provide — testify to its extent. René d'Anjou objected in the mid-fifteenth century to Charles VII's grants of taxation taken on their lands to 'several barons and knights' of Anjou.[5] René had such a grant himself, and they cut down his profit, he claimed, considerably. 'Also,' he complained, 'it's a thing that didn't happen to . . . [René's] predecessors.' He would be 'most happy', on the other hand, if Charles wished to make such grants, 'provided it was without prejudice . . .'; for such

[1] Guenée, *Tribunaux et gens de justice*, p. 494.
[2] Ibid. pp. 497–500.
[3] Martin, op. cit. p. 36.
[4] Cf. J. Huizinga, *Le Déclin du Moyen âge* (1932) p. 46.
[5] Marchegay, op. cit. pp. 310, 322, 328.

grants 'might have considerable consequence'. The future had always to be moulded on the interest of the past.

That it was a society dominated by its past, clinging to the remnants of the present, was the view of at least some of the members of the society of later medieval France. 'We are diminished in age,' thought Philippe de Commynes, 'and . . . the life of man is not as long as it was, nor his body as strong . . . we are enfeebled of all faith and loyalty one to another.'[1] 'The example of our forebears' was the wisest guide to conduct. Even though by their actions they changed the nature of the monarchy, it was to the past that the minds of 'reformers' turned in the fourteenth century; to the reign of St.-Louis, an age ever more golden as the years went by.[2] In the fifteenth century Jean Dubois thought Charles VII should meditate upon the life and habits of his ancestor; Robert Blondel thought he should defend his crown and his people 'by the holy laws and praiseworthy customs of good St.-Louis'.[3] *Laudatores temporis acti*, these men of letters reflected views that seem to have been at least fashionable. The appeal to the past, to immunities secured in the past, was the automatic defence against the hazards of the present; 'because . . . to show by experience past matters properly conducted must encourage one and urge one to put order in present matters, if they are dealt with in a confused and disordered way'.[4]

Religion and the occult

That matters were indeed confused and disordered seems to have been clear enough again to at least some of the members of the society of later medieval France. An essential pessimism was at its least a dominant literary convention: the groans of the poets Eustache Deschamps and Jean Meschinot are only too easy to hear.[5] But Gerson,

[1] *Mémoires*, ed. J. Calmette and G. Durville, 1 (Classiques de l'hist. de France au Moyen âge, 3 : 1924) 129.

[2] R. Cazelles, 'Une Exigence de l'opinion depuis St.-Louis: la réformation du royaume', in *Annu.-B. Soc. Hist. France* (1962–3) pp. 91–9.

[3] N. Valois, 'Conseils et prédictions adressés à Charles VII, en 1445, par un certain Jean Du Bois', in ibid. (1909) pp. 237–8; R. Blondel, *Œuvres*, ed. A. Héron (Soc. Hist. Normandie) 1 (Rouen, 1891) 470.

[4] Marchegay, op. cit. p. 305.

[5] Against this it is, of course, necessary to set a more robust attitude to life

too, thought he lived in the senility of the world and that Antichrist was at hand; and in Paris in 1446 they thought he had arrived in the person of the inordinately talented Fernan de Cordova.[1] The prospect presented of the world in the *Art de bien vivre et bien mourir*, published by Antoine Vérard at the end of the century, must at least have been in accordance with a general taste. It offered no hope of the earthly development of mankind, no hope of progress; humanity could only become worse and with fifteen signs the end would come.[2] Man's only hope was in God.

With an intensity of feeling, man concentrated upon Him.[3] The icons of the faith were constantly before his eyes.[4] Their artists' treatment of them became more and more realistic; and in religious drama, which had contributed largely to the process, God and the company of the saints walked before his eyes. Essentially it was upon pain that one dwelt in the later middle ages: upon the dolour of the Passion, upon the dolour of man. Through the intervention of the saints, of the Virgin, of Christ, through the infinite mercy of God, one hoped in the end to attain that infinite felicity of light and music long before one's eyes on earth and to avoid the infinite dolour of a hell in the fifteenth century more and more realistically depicted. For hell in this sense was a fifteenth-century thing.

Even Gilles sire de Rais, who confessed in 1440 to the sexual murder of many children and to the invocation of demons, believed that through his perpetual veneration of the Church his soul was saved from the devil.[5] 'Be certain', he told his sorcerer François Prelati, 'that provided you have good patience and hope in God, we shall see

exhibited, for instance, in *Les Cent Nouvelles Nouvelles*, ed. F.P. Sweetser (Geneva, 1966).

[1] L. Thorndike, *A Hist. of Magic and Experimental Science*, IV (Columbia, 1934) 115; *Journal d'un bourgeois de Paris, 1405–1449*, ed. A. Tuétey (Soc. Hist. Paris: 1881) pp. 381–2.

[2] (1492) sigs k i[r] ff. Cf. W.W. Heist, *The Fifteen Signs before Doomsday* (Michigan, 1952).

[3] The most recent concise discussion of later medieval French religious sentiment is to be found in E. Delaruelle *et al.*, *L'Eglise au temps du Grand schisme et de la crise conciliaire* (Hist. de l'Eglise ... fondée par A. Fliche et V. Martin, 14: 1962–4) pp. 723–835.

[4] E. Mâle, *L'Art religieux de la fin du Moyen âge en France*, 5th ed. (1949).

[5] *Le Procès de Gilles de Rais. Les Docs*, ed. G. Bataille (1965) pp. 269–70, 281, 387–9.

one another again in the great joy of Paradise'; and on the scaffold he
promised the same glory to the accomplices of his homicides and
sodomies. The faith of this canon of St.-Hilaire-de-Poitiers, this founder
of the great chapel of the Holy Innocents at Machecoul, this companion
as marshal of France of Jeanne d'Arc, reveals in its most lurid light the
later medieval psychomachy, the conflict of the soul. In the Rohan book
of hours the corpse lies stiff amongst the bones; while in middle air the
angel and the demon dispute his soul, from the angeled empyrean God
the Father looks down in infinite compassion: 'for your sins you shall
do penance; on the day of judgement you shall be with Me'. Secure in
this faith, the great of the fifteenth century — and the not so great —
could contemplate with comparative equanimity the image of dissolution.[1]

Too detailed an investigation of the intellectual and emotional
foundations of the faith would go beyond the boundaries of this study.[2]
It is necessary perhaps only to consider the extent to which it was
implicit in the minds of later medieval Frenchmen and the extent to
which the fear of God and their own consciences might rule their
actions. That the doctors of the Church felt it necessary to regulate their
most intimate activities is abundantly clear from, for instance, Johann
Nider's *De morali lepra* or Gerson's *Tractatus de confessione mollitiei*.[3] With
printing, a third force joined those of the preacher and the confessor.
One of its first effects was to multiply the works of popular piety.[4]
Already xylographic techniques had brought precept to the people; and
the second half of the fifteenth century saw the publication of a large
number of moral treatises. For one great historian they provide the
foundation of the modern conscience.[5] And to another they help at
least to bear witness to the depth of the religious sentiment of later
medieval Frenchmen.[6]

[1] J. Porcher, *The Rohan Book of Hours* (1959) pl. 8. But cf. A. Teneti, *La Vie
et la mort à travers l'art du xve siècle* (Cahiers des Annales, 8 : 1952).

[2] See, again, Delaruelle *et al.* op. cit. pp. 601–879.

[3] J. Hansen, *Quellen und Untersuchungen zur Geschichte des Hexenwahns und der
Hexenverfolgung im Mittelalter* (Bonn, 1901) pp. 423 ff; *Gersonii opera*, ed. E. du
Pin, II (Antwerp, 1706) cols 453–5.

[4] L. Febvre and H. J. Martin, *L'Apparition du livre* (1958) pp. 378–83.

[5] Mâle, op. cit. p. 307.

[6] Febvre and Martin, op. cit. p. 383.

That they were not enough is, of course, equally clear. Later medieval Frenchmen were far from being saints. Sexual behaviour was hardly limited to the narrow path prescribed by Nider. The violent tenor of later medieval life is if anything only too much described by a modern writer.[1] The precise extent to which human passion was repressed by implicit faith is impossible to define; and so is the precise extent to which human action was initiated by it. Equally problematical is the extent to which men were prepared for intellectual or emotional reasons to renounce a part or the whole of orthodox faith. Heretics are not hard to find in later medieval France; but traces of heretical organisation are more difficult to discover. Clearest, perhaps, is the case of the Vaudois in the high mountains of Dauphiné, an old sect, which desired to return to the simplicity of primitive Christianity and which was periodically prosecuted by the Church which it denied; and which found, through his dislike of the archbishop of Embrun, a protector in Louis XI.[2] Traces can be found of the activity of the Brethren of the Free Spirit.[3] The views alleged by Froissart to be held by Jean de Bétisac of Beziers in 1389[4] might be assimilated to those of the Cathars, those great heretics considered to have been long extinct in Languedoc. The views alleged by the Religieux de St.-Denis to be held by Hugues Aubriot in Paris in 1381[5] have a curious affinity with those of contemporary English Lollards. Simple madmen appear, like Thomas of Apulia, who preached in Paris in 1388 under Joachimist influence that he was the envoy of the Holy Ghost.[6] A declaration of his insanity saved him from the stake. But there are traces also of those whose heretical or irreligious views seem at least to have been tolerated: in Paris in 1484 Jean Laillier seems to have held a large number of heretical tenets, and, about a century earlier, the humanist circle around Jean de Montreuil and the Cols included Ambrogio de' Migli, an Italian secretary, whose complete

---

[1] Such as J. Huizinga, *Le Déclin du Moyen âge* (1932) pp. 9–38.

[2] J. Marx, *L'Inquisition en Dauphiné. Étude sur le développement et la répression de l'hérésie et de la sorcellerie du xive siècle au début du règne de François Ier* (Bibl. Ec. Hautes Etudes, 206: 1914).

[3] H. C. Lea, *A Hist. of the Inquisition of the Middle Ages*, II (1888) 123–4, 126–7.

[4] *Œuvres*, ed. Kervyn de Lettenhove, XIV (Brussels, 1872) 59–70.

[5] *Chron.* ed. L. Bellaguet (Docs inéd. sur l'hist. de France) I (1839) 102–4.

[6] Lea, op. cit. p. 129.

B

atheism was apparently suffered, though Jean de Montreuil rejoiced at his conversion.[1] And some of the heretics who suffered did so because their heresy provided an excuse for a condemnation impossible to justify upon its real grounds. Bétisac, thought Froissart, would not have suffered from the administrative charges against him alone. Let alone those whose faith was through ignorance and superstition possibly erroneous, how many people of heretical views in fact escaped the penalties of heterodoxy? Amongst a number of perhaps not very eccentric views, François Garin thought in 1460 that the clergy should all be married, that a great part of them should be disbanded 'to earn their living another way', their incomes appropriated by princes to relieve the people, and that nunneries were unnatural. Garin's naturalism was, for a merchant of Lyon — and one who thought that too much reading of 'beaux livres' was not a good thing for merchants — perhaps rather remarkable.[2] But the *Roman de la Rose*, whose second author, Jean de Meun, 'blames young people who give themselves into religion because, he says, they naturally always try to get out of it' (as Gerson put it in refuting him), was, despite its eminent critics, a popular fifteenth-century text.[3]

But there was a windier side of revelation than mere heresy, however extreme. The unknown could present itself in more bizarre forms, which, according to the attitude of mind of its beholders, were more or less credible. Few men in the later middle ages seem to have been ready to reject the fascination of divination and sorcery. Effective at primarily the bottom end of the social scale, amongst those whose perception of the true faith was in any case more or less bizarre, the concept of witchcraft had by the end of the fifteenth century taken a firm hold. It had developed from ordinary sorcery and ancient superstition from the mid-fourteenth century.[4] Though it would be unwise to ignore

[1] Ibid. pp. 142–3; A. Coville, *Gontier et Pierre Col et l'humanisme en France au temps de Charles VI* (1934) pp. 117–38.

[2] *Complainte et enseignements*, ed. D[urand] de L[ançon] (1832) folios xij^v–xiij^r, xxxij^v–xxxiv^r.

[3] Coville, op. cit. p. 197; E. Langlois, *Les Manuscrits du Roman de la Rose* (Lille, 1910) pp. 2 ff; G. de Lorris and J. de Meun, *Le Roman de la Rose*, ed. E. Langlois (Soc. des anciens textes français) I (1914) 41 ff, 49 n 1.

[4] Lea, op. cit. III (1888) pp. 492 ff; cf. H. R. Trevor-Roper, 'The European Witch-craze of the Sixteenth and Seventeenth Centuries', in *Religion, the Reformation and Social Change* (1967) pp. 90–192.

the existence of social pressures which might create 'witch-hunts' and of psychopathic delusions which might provide a 'subjective reality', as a system it was to a great extent the invention of those in the Church who were determined to stamp it out: without their scholastic definition and their missionary zeal it would never have existed. By a process of torture and leading questions the perfect idea of the witches' sabbath was created; some of the interrogated were, perhaps, only too ready to confess. At the end of the fourteenth century the *Songe du verger* discussed still only the night-riders of Diana;[1] but from about 1400 the drearily erotic routine, already adumbrated from about 1335 in the Inquisition courts in southern France,[2] began to be confessed to in both ecclesiastical and secular courts in the north. The old canonical view that such ideas were a mere illusion of the devil, upheld by the author or authors of the *Songe du verger*,[3] was still the view of some men, in the Church and in the world, in the fifteenth century;[4] but God's protectors had begun to acquire their authority. During the witch-hunt in Arras in 1459–60 maître Jacques Dubois, dean of Notre-Dame d'Arras, was heard everywhere declaring that a third of Christianity were witches; there was an international conspiracy which already included bishops and cardinals and which, if it could find a king or a great prince as a leader, would overthrow the world; and he and his coadjutors were fully convinced of the new view that all sorcerers should be burned.[5] The danger of the conspiracy was, fortunately, not wholly appreciated by some who had to deal with such attitudes: by Philippe *le bon* duke of Burgundy, by the Parlement of Paris, by ecclesiastics concerned with its repercussions in Paris, in Amiens, in Tournai. But Arras was not the only witch-hunt in the 1450s in France.[6]

[1] ed. J. L. Brunet, in *Traitez des droits et libertez de l'Eglise gallicane*, II (1731) 241 ff.

[2] Hansen, op. cit. pp. 449 ff.

[3] ed. Brunet, loc. cit.

[4] Lea, op. cit. III 524, 534.

[5] J. du Clercq, *Mémoires*, ed. J. A. Buchon, *Chron. d'E. de Monstrelet*, XIV (Coll. des chron. nationales françaises: 1826) 15–17. The idea that a third of the world had joined forces with the occult was not new: cf. *Le Roman de la Rose*, IV (1922) lines 18428–30.

[6] See, for instance, Hansen, op. cit. pp. 559–61, for an outbreak in Marmande in 1453.

The old view — that sorcery was simply a heresy whose adherents might recant and live — melted away; though in France the jurisdiction the Parlement had over such cases helped to delay the inflation of witchcraft. When belief in the efficacy of malediction was so strong, when a cross word from an aggrieved old woman, followed by some misfortune, was sufficient proof of sorcery, fodder for the zealous or the frightened might indeed comprise a third of Christendom. When superstitious peasants turned from self-help — peasants in Torcy in Normandy about 1455 simply assaulted the local sorcerers in order to make them remove their malisons[1] — to the courts, when the *Malleus maleficarum* joined papal bulls in the mid-1480s as the foundation of the courts' jurisprudence, the juggernaut was well on the way downhill. For not much attention, again, seems to have been paid to simple sorcery[2] by the Church before the second half of the thirteenth century.[3] With the development of the Inquisition it began to prey on men's minds, and from the early fourteenth century it was vigorously suppressed by both ecclesiastical and secular courts. As in the particular case of witchcraft later, oppression inflated an innate superstition. Such codification of magic practices as the articles of the theology faculty of the university of Paris published in 1398 helped again to formalise — and popularise — the dim attitudes of the past. Superstition became damnable.

But powerful men were not wholly prone to listen to the fulminations of Parisian theologians. This was not so much because they took a rational view of such delusion and thought it negligible; on the contrary, it was because they implicitly believed in its use. Raymond seigneur de Coarraze had a familiar demon called Harton, whom he had enticed from an aggrieved Catalan clerk who had sent Harton to torment him; he flew faster than the wind and was much appreciated as a news service by Gaston Fébus comte de Foix. He spoke excellent Gascon. Unfortunately he vanished away after Raymond de Coarraze had made him angry by setting his dogs onto him when he had

---

[1] Ducange, *Glossarium*, s.v. Sortiarius. Cf. Marx, op. cit. p. 39; R. Vaultier, *Le Folklore pendant la guerre de Cent ans d'après les lettres de rémission du Trésor des chartes* (1965) pp. 39, 229 ff.

[2] Lea, op. cit. III 379 ff.

[3] Though this impression may be due to lack of evidence.

manifested himself one day as an outsize, though undernourished, sow. Gaston Fébus seems later to have had another friendly sprite of his own, who told him the sad news of the battle of Aljubarotta. The chronicler Froissart seems to have been far from upset at either demon; and neither was his informant.[1] Raymond de Coarraze was luckier than the psychopath Gilles de Rais, for whom François Prelati conjured his demon Barron in vain.[2] One of the difficulties about sorcery was that its only cure was counter-sorcery — even the author or authors of the *Songe du verger* approved of holy amulets as enchantment against the enchantments of the Enemy[3] — and sorcerers as counter-sorcerers were alleged to have flourished, though equally unlawful in the eyes of the theologians.[4] Belief in sorcery ran through society from top to bottom; the authors of the *Malleus maleficarum* were insistent upon the protection afforded wizards by the great.[5]

Sorcery had a common ground in divination with astrology — a term effectively, in this period, interchangeable with astronomy. Some kinds of divination, it was argued in the *Songe du verger*, involved the intervention of demons.[6] Others did not; but most were not approved of by the authors of the *Songe*. Upon astrology itself they passed the orthodox judgement, produced long before by, for instance, John of Salisbury and Thomas Aquinas: its decisions upon 'necessary' things were lawful, its apparent decisions upon 'accidental' things damnable as the inventions of the Enemy, the denial of the free will of man and of God's freedom to alter man's will. And even upon 'necessary' things the judgements of astrologers were liable to be fallacious: upon the weather, for instance. 'The principal purpose of astrology', thought the authors of the *Songe*, 'is not to make judgements about the future, but its principal purpose is because it gives knowledge of our Creator.'[7]

---

[1] J. Froissart, *Chron.* ed. L. Mirot (Soc. Hist. France) XII (1931) 170–81. For the demons in Dauphiné in the fifteenth century, see Marx, op. cit. pp. 32 ff.

[2] *Le Procès de Gilles de Rais*, pp. 291 ff.   [3] ed. Brunet, op. cit. pp. 238 ff.
[4] Lea, op. cit. III 507–8.

[5] ed. M. Summers (London, 1948) p. 151. For the prevalence of the belief at the other end of the social scale, see L. Celier, 'Les Mœurs rurales au xve siècle d'après les lettres de rémission', in *B. philol. hist. Com. Travaux hist. sci.* (1958) p. 417.

[6] ed. Brunet, op. cit. pp. 220 ff.   [7] ed. Brunet, op. cit. p. 246.

'Pure' astrology was the proper end of the study of the stars by princes. 'Applied' astrology, if not plain heresy, was liable to discover only remote or general causes and good astrologers who were not fatally prone to make mistakes were on the whole few.

But princes had their own views on the matter. No learned astrologer — and the great learning of the better astrologers was indisputable — felt the breath of serious persecution upon him in later medieval France before Simon de Phares in the last decade of the fifteenth century; and even he had the enjoyment, with the return of his patron Charles VIII from the Italian wars, of slandering those who had prosecuted him[1] in his *Recueil des plus célèbres astrologues*.[2] That work testifies to the popularity of astrological divination amongst the princes of the later middle ages. For an astrologer, by accurate consideration of the stars, could cast one's 'nativity'; could do a 'revolution' upon that nativity for particular years; could question the stars about particular matters, in 'interrogations' and 'elections'. Astrologers could predict from the conjuncture of the planets great mortalities, floods and minor changes in the weather. Astrologers could define the particular influence of the stars upon one's particular complexion of humours and so be essential for one's health. Medicine and astrology went hand in hand; the faculty of medicine of Paris was for a long time the faculty of medicine and astrology;[3] and it was not until an attack by Jean Gerson upon a doctor of medicine of Montpellier in 1428 that a theologian thought it necessary to assail astrological therapy.[4] Thomas de Pisan conjured with astrological magic the English out of France for Charles V with considerable success. Under a proper constellation five hollow human figures were made of lead, named for the king of England and four captains; they were labelled with astrological characters and names and filled with earth from the middle and the four corners of France. At the right astrological moment they were buried in the places the earth had come from, face downwards and with their hands behind their backs, with incantations for the annihilation of the persons they represented and the expulsion of the English and their adherents; 'and within a few months all the said

---

[1] L. Thorndike, *A Hist. of Magic and Experimental Science*, IV (Columbia, 1934) 550 ff.
[2] ed. E. Wickersheimer (1929).　　[3] Thorndike, op. cit. pp. 142.
[4] Ibid. pp. 122 ff.

companies had fled from the realm'.[1] Such valuable activities could not be abandoned for the sterner ways advocated by the more severe of the theologians. And some theologians were far from being fellow-travellers with astrology. Pierre d'Ailly thought hopefully that God had established astrology and theology in harmony by eternal law;[2] and even Gerson, whose views were attacked by d'Ailly and who thought that the world was senile and delirious,[3] went farther towards accepting the virtues of astrology than Nicole Oresme[4] and the *Songe du verger* a generation before. When so much of the physical world was unknown, it needed a very hard head indeed boldly to close one's mind to speculation.

An accusation of sorcery was admittedly another charge that could be added to the misdemeanours of a fallen politician. It was possibly the charge of sorcery alone which enabled Charles de Valois to do Enguerran de Marigny to death in 1315; on the administrative charges against him he might simply have been banished.[5] In 1358 the future Charles V accused Charles de Navarre of planning to employ against him the sorcery of his 'physician or astrologer', Dominic.[6] That unfortunate anticlerical Hugues Aubriot was accused *inter alia* in 1381 of the seduction of young virgins with the help of sorcerers.[7] But in the fifteenth century such cases seem harder to find in France than in England.[8] It was not that the politically important neglected the possibilities of the occult. Jean duc d'Alençon had his nativity cast by maître Michel Bars, to know why fortune had been so against him; he was provided with an astrological talisman to give him charm, as well as to protect him from a number of diseases, and a powder which, applied in various ways, detected enemies and gave in dreams perfect intelligence of important question.[9] Jean II duc de Bourbon had in his service the celebrated Conrad Heingarter, 'excellent in philosophy, most

[1] Ibid. II (Colombia, 1947) 802.   [2] Ibid. IV 112.   [3] Ibid. IV 115 ff.

[4] G. W. Coopland, *Nicole Oresme and the Astrologers. A Study of his 'Livre de divinacions'* (Liverpool, 1952).

[5] J. Favier, *Enguerran de Marigny* (1963) pp. 213–16.

[6] Froissart, *Œuvres*, ed. Kervyn de Lettenhove, VI (Brussels, 1868) 478.

[7] *Chron. du religieux de St.-Denis*, I 102.

[8] Jean Petit's denunciation in 1408 of the assassinated Louis d'Orléans included allegations of sorcery (E. de Monstrelet, *Chron.* ed. L. Douët-d'Arcq (Soc. Hist. France) I (1857) 223 ff).

[9] G. du Fresne de Beaucourt, *Hist. de Charles VII*, VI (1891) 43–4.

wise and expert doctor of medicine, subtle and profound astrologer',[1] who composed for him a commentary upon the *Quadripartitum* of Ptolemy and in 1477 an astrological treatise upon his health.[2] But neither in disfavour was accused of using his servants for political purposes.

The greatest use of astrologers was presumably for interrogations and elections. According to Simon de Phares 'maître Laurens de Richemond . . . gave the election to Jean de Villiers to enter Paris by night; and in the day for this reason the way was found to have the keys by Pierre Fefavre, who stole them from under his father's pillow. . . .'[3] This slightly garbled version of the Burgundian capture of Paris in 1418[4] is still accurate enough to tempt one to believe in maître Laurens' part in it. The counsels of astrologers are thick in the pages of Simon de Phares' *Recueil*.[5] Maître Germain de Tibouville, in Barbazan's company with the dauphin, gave excellent advice and was posted by the dauphin to John Stuart, constable of the Scottish army in France. Maître Olivier Chantemerle, a former pensioner of the duke of Burgundy, carried out elections for Charles d'Orléans. Messire Jean de Bregy, chevalier, astrologer at Charles VII's court, was most experienced in particular judgements. Maître Florant de Villiers, a man of subtle intelligence, was in Dunois' retinue. At Lyon Louis de Langle set up a consulting-room for interrogations and predicted the battle of Formigny in 1450 for Charles VII (Jean d'Alençon consulted him too).[6] The Benedictine Jean de Thonoyon or Thonon was in the service of the *bailli* of Beaujolais and did for him several excellent judgements and elections for the war; he predicted the siege of Marcigny-les-Nonnains precisely as it happened. The same kind of military prognostication could be distilled from Simon de Phares for the fourteenth century: Bertrand du Guesclin — whose wife was a trained astrologer and whose rise had been predicted from the prophecies of Merlin and the stars by an English captain in Brittany — had in his company maître Yves de Saint Branchier, expert in elections of proper days to fight the enemy or to refrain from doing

[1] S. de Phares, op. cit. p. 264.
[2] Thorndike, op. cit. IV 357–85. Heingarter, admittedly, was not likely to have lent himself to sorcery.
[3] Op. cit. p. 248.   [4] Beaucourt, op. cit. I (1881) 32.
[5] pp. 250–1, 254, 254–5, 255–6, 258, 262.
[6] Thorndike, op. cit. IV 555.

so;[1] and so could the same kind of questioning of the stars for more private purposes.

It is, of course, again impossible to determine precisely to what extent men's actions were governed by their astrologers' readings of the constellations. According to Simon de Phares, Charles V, that patron of Oresme, ruled his life by their predictions;[2] but Simon de Phares is perhaps a biased witness. And even he admits that in other cases the advice of astrologers was ignored, albeit mistakenly.[3] In Gerson's view the opinion of astrologers should be weighed against that of other experts; but this may be evidence of how much greater weight others might give to their views.[4] The great in France seem to have consulted astrologers enough.[5] And not only the great: both Louis de Langle and Simon de Phares kept at Lyon 'open office to respond to and judge upon all questions and interrogations' in the mid- and later-fifteenth centuries.[6] The rising lawyer Jean I Jouvenel in Paris early in the fifteenth century recorded the hours of the births of his children, perhaps for the purpose of drawing their nativities.[7] And why should men consult astrologers, unless they felt they might in some circumstances act upon their opinions?

Economic difficulties

Equally a dominant characteristic of this later medieval world, it may be argued, was its insecurity. A fundamental economic malaise has been detected in the activity of French land-owners, lay and ecclesiastical, of French merchants, of French labourers. Its periodicity and its causes

---

[1] Op. cit. pp. 224, 225–6, 229.

[2] Ibid. pp. 228–9. His view, naturally enough, was shared by Thomas de Pisan's daughter Christine (*Le Livre des fais et bonnes meurs du sage roy Charles V*, ed. S. Solente (Soc. Hist. France) II (1940) 16).

[3] Op. cit. pp. 208, 221, 226, 230–1.   [4] Thorndike, op. cit. IV 119.

[5] S. de Phares, op. cit. pp. 211 ff *passim*.

[6] Ibid. pp. 257–8.

[7] L. Battifol, *Jean Jouvenel, prévôt des marchands de la ville de Paris (1360—1431)*, (1894) pp. 317–24. I have throughout allowed Jean II his adoption of the form 'Juvenal', while retaining for his brothers Guillaume and Jacques (who used the form 'Juvenel') and for his brother Michel the form used by their father. For the problem of the addition of 'des Ursins', see below, p. 177 n 5.

B2

have been discussed. In that of Toulouse,[1] for instance, three patterns of difficulty may be detected. First, there were brief crises of a few months, some associated with epidemics, some with dearths, some with monetary troubles, some with military activity. Second, these crises fitted into a broader rhythm. There was a first general period of 'calamities' in the fourteenth century, with a rapid series of crises in 1343–8, 1355–9, 1361–2, 1374–6 and 1381–3. This was followed by a calm period in which there was peace, no important dearth, and no significant epidemic. Finally, there was a second period of crises, in 1415–21, 1425–8, 1430–3, 1438–42, which ended with the epidemic of 1451. This rhythm, it is argued, was imposed by external, 'accidental', forces. The third pattern is more fundamental: it is of a general stagnation of the Toulousain economy from 1350 to 1450. There was no movement in prices in the period, no movement in investment, no movement of population to fill the gaps created by epidemics, general regression. Toulouse thus presents a picture of 'a stagnant economy with sharp "accidents" '. Its inhabitants maintained their affection for rich food and fine cloths; but it became more difficult for them to assuage it. Neither the demographic pattern of the town nor its production was sufficient. In this sense there was decline in Toulouse in the later middle ages.

What was its cause? At this stage the argument becomes admittedly hypothetical. Not so much the war, it is argued; not so much monetary instability; but a growth crisis in the rural society of Toulousain. Disequilibrium between demographic pressure and a food supply provided by rudimentary agricultural techniques produced, from the beginning of the fourteenth century, a series of famines and, in an undernourished community, 'an astonishing expansion of epidemics'. The town found both its own food supply and its market in its rural hinterland. In order to adapt to this new environment it 'ruralised' itself. This period of disorientation came to an end about the middle of the following century, when there were signs of a new equilibrium in the urban milieu.

The pattern of difficulties elsewhere has been analysed: in the area of Paris throughout the fourteenth and fifteenth centuries, for instance, on the estates of St.-Martin de Tournai up to 1350, in the barony of Le

[1] P. Wolff, *Commerces et marchands de Toulouse (vers 1350–vers 1450)* (1954) pp. 627 ff.

Neubourg in the fifteenth century, in Forez, in Sologne and in Bordelais; in the manufacturing towns of the Low Countries; in the commerce of Normandy.[1] Varying weight is given by the authors of these analyses and of others to the different factors which, in each particular place, contributed to the economic conjuncture. One must, as elsewhere, recognise the importance of local nuances, local contradictions to an apparently general pattern;[2] and it would perhaps be unwise to attempt to put them into any order of general importance.

But to begin with population movement.[3] It seems clear that plague after 1348 was responsible for drastic falls in population. At Givry near Chalon-sur-Saône, where the parish register survives, between 5 August and 19 November 1348 there were 615 deaths from a population of 1500–1700: a 38–43 per cent mortality, where there had been one of about 2 per cent in the previous ten years.[4] In the meridional towns of Albi and Castres there was again a 50 per cent disappearance rate, if not a 50 per

[1] G. Fourquin, *Les Campagnes de la région parisienne à la fin du Moyen âge* (1964); A. d'Haenens, *L'Abbaye St.-Martin de Tournai de 1290 à 1350* (Louvain, 1961); A. Plaisse, *La Baronnie du Neubourg* (1961); I. Guérin, *La Vie rurale en Sologne aux xive et xve siècles* (1960); E. Fournial, *Les Villes et l'économie d'échange en Forez aux xiiie et xive siècles* (1967); R. Boutruche, *La Crise d'une société. Seigneurs et paysans du Bordelais pendant la guerre de Cent ans* (1947); E. Coornaert, *La Draperie-sayetterie d'Hondschoote (xive–xviiie siècles)* (1930) and *L'Industrie de la laine à Bergues-St.-Winoc* (1930) (cf. 'Draperies rurales, draperies urbaines. L'Evolution de l'industrie flamande au Moyen âge et au xvie siècle', in *R. belge Philol. Hist.* XXVIII (1950) 59–96); M. Mollat, *Le Commerce maritime normand à la fin du Moyen âge* (1952).

[2] Cf. J. Heers, *L'Occident aux xive et xve siècles. Aspects écon. et sociaux* (Nouvelle Clio, 23: 2nd ed. 1966) pp. 108–10; R. D. Ware, 'Discussion [of H. A. Miskimin, "Monetary Movements and Market Structure — Forces for Contraction in Fourteenth- and Fifteenth-century England"]', in *J. econ. Hist.* XXIV (1964) 494–5. Such a contradictory pattern may be seen in Flanders and Brabant in the fifteenth century (R. van Uytven, 'La Flandre et le Brabant, "Terres de promission" sous les ducs de Bourgogne?', in *R. Nord,* XLIII (1961) 281–317).

[3] E. Carpentier and J. Glénisson, 'La Démographie française au xive siècle', in *Annales,* XVII (1962) 109–29. The total population of France in 1328 has been estimated at just under 12,250,000 (F. Lot, 'L'Etat des paroisses et des feux de 1328', in *Bibl. Ec. Chartes,* XC (1929) 297); but with M. Perroy (*Hist. gen. des civilisations,* ed. M. Crouzet, IV *Le Moyen Age* (1955) 406) one might well find this hard to believe.

[4] R. Mols, *Introduction à la démographie historique des villes d'Europe du xive au xviiie siècle,* II (Louvain, 1955) 433.

cent death rate; in Millau it was rather less.[1] There is evidence, say from Toulouse, say from Reims, of the continued effect of plague and other disease upon the urban population, possibly for the following century.[2] But it is also possible that there is evidence of falling population before the Black Death of 1348, for instance in Millau and in parts of Provence.[3]

Perturbations following upon the 'corn crisis' of 1315–17, which allegedly 'smote all the lands from the Pyrenees to the plains of Russia and from Scotland to Italy' may also seem evident.[4] So might those of other, local crises.[5] More difficult a question is the possibility of disequilibrium in the supply of bullion in western Europe. Shortage of gold and silver due to the vagaries of the bullion trade with the Orient and of bullion production within Europe led, it has been argued, to an imbalance, which in turn forced governments both to tamper with their own currencies and to engage in 'monetary wars' with those of their neighbours.[6] An absolute shortage of bullion was responsible for the fallen prices of the period, which were a cause of trade recession, pessimism and retrenchment. Equally difficult a question is possible

[1] G. Prat, 'Albi et la peste noire', in A. Midi, LXIV (1952) 15–25; P. Wolff, 'Trois Etudes de démographie médiévale en France méridionale', in Studi . . . A. Sapori, I (Milan, 1957) 493–503. The social incidence of plague was of course variable: see, for instance, R. Cazelles, 'La Peste de 1348–1349 en Langue d'oïl. Epidémie prolétarienne et enfantine', in B. philol. hist. Com. Travaux hist. sci. (1962) pp. 293–305.

[2] Wolff, Commerces et marchands, pp. 68 ff; P. Desportes, 'La Population de Reims au xve siècle', in Moyen Age, LXXII (1966) 463–509.

[3] Wolff, 'Trois Etudes', pp. 502–3; E. Baratier, La Démographie provençale du xiiie au xvie siècle (1961) 80–1, 120. The movement in Provence was far from even.

[4] H. S. Lucas, 'The Great European Famine of 1315, 1316 and 1317', in Speculum, v (1930) 343–77; d'Haenens, op. cit. pp. 121–3. But see G. Duby, 'Le Grand Domaine de la fin du Moyen âge en France', in Première Conférence internationale d'hist. écon., Stockholm, mcmlx. Contributions, communications (1960) p. 340; Fourquin, op. cit. pp. 191–202; M. Larenaudie, 'Les Famines en Languedoc aux xive et xve siècles', in A. Midi, LXIV (1952) 27–39.

[5] See, for instance, Fournial, op. cit. pp. 265 ff.

[6] M. Bloch, 'Le Problème de l'or au Moyen âge', in Annales d'hist. écon. et sociale, v (1933) 1–34; A. Girard, 'Un Phénomène écon.: la guerre monétaire (xive–xve siècles)', in Annales d'hist. sociale, II (1940) 207–18; R. H. Bautier, 'L'Or et l'argent en Occident de la fin du xiiie siècle au début du xive siècle', in C. R. Acad. Inscript. (1951) pp. 169–74; W. C. Robinson, 'Money, Population and Econ. Change in Late Medieval Europe', in Econ. Hist. R. ser. 2 XII (1959–60) 63–76; Miskimin, op. cit. pp. 470–90.

secular variation in the weather of western Europe.[1] And more imponderable is the question of mental attitudes, of human reaction to events, of human success and failure.[2]

But one factor in the creation of local economic conjunctures and of insecurity itself bulks obviously very large in later medieval France. The war and the political situations which lay behind it dominated the life of most Frenchmen for most of the fourteenth and fifteenth centuries.

War

A thirty-six-year-old apostolic notary in Cahorsin in the later fourteenth century claimed that all his life he had never seen anything in the diocese but war.[3] In a number of other parts of France as well as his, warfare was, for a considerable amount of the time, a dominant condition of life. The instruments of arbitration[4] were comparatively weak. The pope, the emperor and other persons of influence might attempt to prevent international conflict; the king of France within his kingdom might attempt to prevent the open warfare of his subjects with each other. None was wholly successful. The sanctions which the arbitrators might impose were clearly ineffective. Those which might be applied in the international field were primarily moral; those in the national field primarily physical. Behind neither group lay an authority sufficient to make it effective. The pope or the emperor might themselves be suspected of partiality towards the enemy;[5] the king of France, as judge in his own cause, might reasonably be thought by an aggrieved

[1] G. Utterström, 'Climatic Fluctuations and Population Problems in Early Modern Hist.', in *Scandinavian Econ. Hist. R.* III (1955) 3–47.

[2] See, for instance, d'Haenens, op. cit. pp. 97 ff.; Coornaert, *Bergues-St.-Winoc*, pp. 101–4; cf. Duby, op. cit. pp. 341–2.

[3] H. S. Denifle, *La Désolation des églises, monastères et hôpitaux en France pendant la guerre de Cent ans*, II (1899) 827.

[4] F. L. Ganshof, *Le Moyen Age* (Hist. des relations internationales publiée sous la direction de P. Renouvin, I : 1953) pp. 291–5, 301–2.

[5] For example, see E. Déprez, *Les Préliminaires de la guerre de Cent ans. La Papauté, la France et l'Angleterre (1328–1342)* (1902) p. 144; J. H. Wylie and W. T. Waugh, *The Reign of Henry the Fifth*, III (Cambridge, 1929) 17, 35; J. G. Dickinson, *The Congress of Arras, 1435* (Oxford, 1955) pp. 130–1.

subject in conflict with him hardly as impartial as the office of king required him to be. Neither the moral nor the physical sanction of the king of France was sufficient to deter a magnate of his kingdom from engaging in prosperous rebellion against his anointed sovereign. The forces which held 'France' together as a political concept were far from robust. The sovereignty in principle of the ruler had to be imposed in practice: the unity of the country depended upon the efficacy of the ruler in maintaining his authority over his greater subjects. Throughout the fourteenth and fifteenth centuries both in France and in England civil war was dangerously near the surface. In England civil war did not threaten to tear the country apart; in France it might. When magnates on the frontiers of the kingdom began to rule their domains by the grace of God,[1] the cracks in the tenuous surface were showing. Magnates in central France had, like their English colleagues, little chance of territorial independence; but in the far west, and on the frontier of the empire, and on the frontier of the Pyrenees the plaster on the surface of unity was clearly thin.

English rights and French supporters

The warfare endemic in later medieval France was the product of the real disunity beneath the theoretical sovereignty of the king of France over the whole of his kingdom: essentially of the opposition to him of powers which did not wish to fade into nothing in the rising sun of the united monarchy.[2] The struggle of the duke of Aquitaine, king of England, with the king of France was an example essentially of the resistance of a territorial magnate to the extension in practice of a sovereignty which he could not gainsay in theory. As such it was first a legal matter. The legal position was fairly clear. By the beginning of the fourteenth century the kings of England had recognised the sovereignty

[1] See below, pp. 188–9.
[2] Cf. P. Wolff, 'Un Problème d'origines: la guerre de Cent ans', in *Hommage à Lucien Febvre*, II (1953) 141–8; J. Le Patourel, 'Edward III and the Kingdom of France', in *History*, XLIII (1958) 184–5, 'The Plantagenet Dominions', in *History*, L (1965) 305–6, and 'The King and the Princes in Fourteenth-century France', in *Europe in the Late Middle Ages*, ed. J. R. Hale, J. R. L. Highfield and B. Smalley (1965) pp. 155–83.

of the kings of France over each of their continental possessions. In all cases except one that sovereignty was of immemorial standing. In the case of Gascony it dated from the treaty of Paris in 1259; for Gascony before the treaty had arguably been an allod, land held of no superior lord.[1] In 1259[2] Henry III, in return for peace and financial subvention, recognised it held of Louis IX. Over Normandy, Anjou, Maine, Touraine, Poitou, the king of England renounced his rights. His continental possessions were reduced in law as in fact to the duchy of Aquitaine; and in parts of the duchy his rights remained far from clear. But the greatest source of danger for the duke of Aquitaine lay in his recognition of the sovereignty of the king of France over Gascony. That the change in the status of the *pays* was worth what he had paid for it was abundantly clear to St.-Louis.[3] The continental possessions of the king of England were now clearly held by homage of the king of France. Their inhabitants could appeal from the decisions of the courts of Aquitaine to those of the ultimate sovereign. The right of the king of France over this new part of his kingdom was clearly defined; it remained only for his officers to make it effective.

But the king of England was himself a sovereign, emperor in his kingdom; and his actions as sovereign might imperil his position as vassal. Was he, for instance, to abstain as king of England from international action to the detriment of his suzerain in France? This would make a mockery of his sovereignty. But as king of England he was in a comparatively powerful position to resist the king of France over matters upon which there might legitimately be conflict between an admitted sovereign and his admitted vassal. That the power of the last Capetians and of the Valois fell short of their pretensions was cruelly demonstrated by the long resistance of the duke of Aquitaine. For nearly two centuries the unity of the kingdom was threatened by the disruptive attraction so great a satellite had for those elements of it themselves threatening disruption.

But the conflict between the duke of Aquitaine and the king of France had by then long surpassed the legal wrangles of vassal and

[1] P. Chaplais, 'Le Traité de Paris de 1259 et l'inféodation de la Gascogne allodiale', in *Moyen Age*, LXI (1955) 121-37.

[2] M. Gavrilovitch, *Etude sur le traité de Paris de 1259* (Bibl. Ec. Hautes Etudes, 125: 1899) pp. 18-38.

[3] Chaplais, op. cit. pp. 124 ff.

sovereign. These themselves had lasted for nearly a century after 1259.[1] A number of the loose ends left by the treaty of Paris had been tied up by the end of the century; but basic problems remained. Most basic was the question of jurisdiction. The duke of Aquitaine, formerly sovereign of Gascony, had a duty to protect the customs of his subjects; and these might conflict with the king of France's views of the rights of subjects. Beyond lay the question of appeal from Aquitaine into France: litigants eager for a decision in their favour were disinclined to consider the political effects of their actions, and the king's courts were hardly tender towards the 'rights' of his rival. The pressures that could be seen later in the legal dealings of kings of France with their more over-mighty subjects were already all too visible in Aquitaine in the decades before full-scale war broke out. The question of the legislative powers of king and duke again reflected the nature of the conflict between them as one over definitions, over the establishment of practical limits to a sovereignty that was from Philippe IV's reign at least in theory infinite.[2]

In this struggle against a shadow the duke of Aquitaine was naturally on the defensive. The attempts of the king of England peaceably to maintain rights he considered his against the onslaughts of the French were very considerable. The two major ruptures between the countries were both caused by French initiative, in 1294 and in 1324;[3] on both occasions the king of France considered the duke of Aquitaine had failed in his duty and confiscated his duchy. But conflict between the kings of England and of France did not turn simply on matters of jurisdiction. There was a natural reluctance on the part of the former to do homage to the latter: a reluctance which contributed to the second breach and the subsequent war of St.-Sardos. The question of the nature of the homage stipulated in 1259 was not settled until 1331.[4] There was the question of the restoration of land confiscated after St.-Sardos, in 1327.[5] The questions raised by the treaty of Paris in 1259

[1] Gavrilovitch, op. cit. pp. 49–104; P. Chaplais, 'Le Duché-pairie de Guyenne: l'hommage et les services féodaux de 1259 à 1303', in *A. Midi*, LXIX (1957) 5–38, and 'de 1303 à 1337', in *A. Midi*, LXX (1958) 135–60.

[2] P. Chaplais, 'La Souveraineté du roi de France et le pouvoir législatif en Guyenne au début du xive siècle', in *Moyen Age*, LXIX (1963) 449–69.

[3] Gavrilovitch, op. cit. pp. 105–11.

[4] Ibid. pp. 49–53.   [5] Déprez, op. cit. pp. 38 ff.

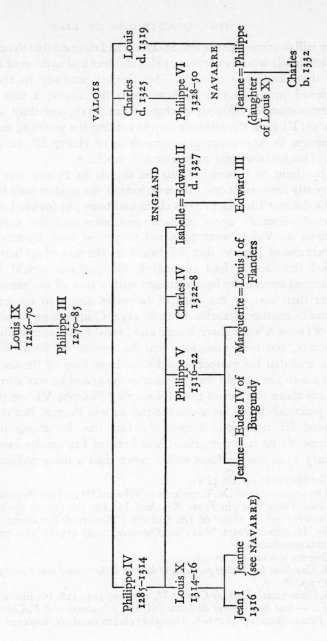

THE LINE OF ST-LOUIS

were still in some sense open. St.-Louis had claimed that the concessions he then made would give peace to his children and to those of Henry III;[1] but they were not enough. The English attitude to the problem hardened progressively, perhaps from the 1290s; a new policy of confrontation developed, perhaps from 1317, certainly after 1330. Edward III took the ultimate step in forcing the position, in becoming sovereign in Aquitaine: great-grandson of Henry III, he denied the title of king to the great-grandson of Louis IX.[2]

The claim of Edward III to the throne of France was legally an eminently reasonable one.[3] He was, indeed, the nearest male heir in 1328 to the defunct Charles IV. His claim had been put forward in 1328 and rejected primarily upon political grounds;[4] and the supporters of Philippe de Valois were prepared to pay at least lip-service to the Frenchness of France. But if Edward, as the son of an heiress herself denied the crown, had succeeded, his position would have been threatened eventually by a claimant with a title of the same kind, but better than his: by the sons of heiresses closer to the crown than Edward's mother, Isabelle. Born in 1332, Charles king of Navarre, the son of Louis X's daughter Jeanne and Louis' first cousin Philippe comte d'Evreux, was fully conscious that 'he was of the fleurs-de-lis on all sides, and that his mother would have been king of France if she had been a man', as he told the Parisians in 1358; and he was also conscious that his claim was better than Edward's.[5] Philippe VI was in 1328 the best practical choice, let alone the fact he was French. But the claim of Edward III remained, despite the fact that by doing homage to Philippe VI he had recognised him king of France. Its invocation in January 1340 was perhaps rather more than a mere political pretext.

[1] Gavrilovitch, op. cit. p. 41.

[2] The arguments of Dr. Templeman ('Edward III and the Beginnings of the Hundred Years War', in *Trans. Roy. hist. Soc.* ser. 5 II (1952) 69–88) seem to me outweighed by those of Dr. Cuttino ('Historical Revision: the Causes of the Hundred Years War', in *Speculum*, XXXI (1956) 463–77) and Dr. Chaplais (cited above).

[3] Déprez, op. cit. pp. 27–37.

[4] R. Cazelles, *La Société politique et la crise de la royauté sous Philippe de Valois* (1958) pp. 48–57.

[5] R. Delachenal, *Hist. de Charles V*, 1 (1909) 325, 418. He did not however press it — but see *Lettres de Louis XI*, ed. J. Vaesen and E. Charavay (Soc. Hist. France) VIII (1903) 276–7. The other claims need not however concern us.

Not only did it solve the question of Aquitaine, but it gave a legitimacy to the actions of Edward and his allies; a legitimacy perhaps more than a moral coating upon a bitter pill of policy. In a God-fearing age it was important to have God on one's side: and God was on the side of right. Chandos herald's image of the perfect prince was made to say before the battle of Poitiers

> Father, as thou art true God, true man,
> Deign by thy most holy name
> Me and my folk to protect from harm,
> Because, true God in Heaven on high,
> You know that my right is good.[1]

The part of God in the war was ever at the back of men's minds: He might for a time allow the unrighteous to triumph; but the righteous won in the end.[2] If the assumption of the title of France was a pious fraud, it was a fraud in which many people, perhaps even many of the English leaders,[3] believed implicitly. *Dieu et mon droit* had some real content: under this device one did not fight unjustly.

It was clear to the realistic soldier Sir John Fastolf in 1435 that that right should be maintained. If Henry VI should renounce his title to the French, he thought, 'it might be said, noised and deemed in all Christian lands where it should be spoken of, that not Harry the king nor his noble progenitors had, nor have, no right in the crown of France and that all their wars and conquest have been but usurpation and tyranny'.[4] But the kings of England were far from consistent in the pursuit of their right: a fact which French propagandists were eager to point out.[5] In fact, they were often prepared to settle for less. The pressure of events conditioned the use to which their just claim to

---

[1] *Life of the Black Prince*, ed. M. K. Pope and E. C. Lodge (Oxford, 1910) p. 38.

[2] It could be argued — for instance by Edward III in 1340 — that the righteous had a duty to pursue their right in conformity with God's will (Le Patourel, 'Edward III and the Kingdom of France', p. 176).

[3] Ibid.; for the attitude of Henry V, see E. F. Jacob, *The Fifteenth Century* (Oxford, 1961) pp. 122–4.

[4] P. S. Lewis, 'War-propaganda and Historiography in Fifteenth-century France and England', in *Trans. Roy. hist. Soc.* ser. 5 xv (1965) 8.

[5] Ibid. p. 13.

France was put.[1] When Edward III made formal claim to the French throne in October 1337, it was against a background of French interference in Scotland and in Guyenne — the duchy had been confiscated yet again in May; and when he assumed the title and arms of France in January 1340, he did so partly in order to seduce the Flemings.[2] Some twenty years later Edward arranged to renounce his title in return for an enlarged holding in the south-west and the concession by the king of France that all his continental possessions were held in full sovereignty. But in fact the renunciations provided for in the treaty of Brétigny and in the treaty of Calais of 1360 were never made;[3] and when the war began again nine years later the English claim to the throne was unimpaired.

It continued to lie behind the more practical negotiations for a return to the Brétigny settlement (though the English were perhaps at times prepared to go even further)[4] which continued as the war dragged on through the reigns of Richard II and Henry IV; and it gained increasing prominence as Henry V gained ground in France after his invasion in 1415. In 1419 it emerged as a practical proposition;[5] and by the treaty of Troyes in 1420 Henry became the heir of Charles VI of France. But Charles survived him; and it was his son, Henry VI, the child of Charles' daughter Catherine, who became ruler of the double monarchy in title and the ruler of a considerable area of France in practice. The title to the throne was maintained throughout the negotiations which led up to the congress of Arras in 1435; and it was not until 1444 that the English council once more contemplated its renunciation in return

[1] Cf. Le Patourel, 'Edward III and the Kingdom of France', pp. 173–89, and 'The Treaty of Brétigny, 1360', in *Trans. Roy. hist. Soc.* ser. 5 x (1960) 19–39.

[2] The political conjuncture which produced the actual beginning of the war is discussed exhaustively by Wolff, 'Un Problème d'origines', and by Cuttino, op. cit.

[3] 'Some Documents regarding the Fulfilment and Interpretation of the Treaty of Brétigny, 1361–1369', ed. P. Chaplais, in *Camden Miscellany*, xix (Camden Third Series, 80: 1952) 5–8.

[4] J. J. N. Palmer, 'The Anglo-French Peace Negotiations, 1390–1396', in *Trans. Roy. hist. Soc.* ser. 5 xvi (1966) 81–94, and 'Articles for a Final Peace between England and France, 16 June 1393', in *B. Inst. hist. Research*, xxxix (1966) 180–5, provides the latest (if not, perhaps, the last) word on the subject.

[5] P. Bonenfant, *Du Meurtre de Montereau au traité de Troyes* (Brussels, 1958) pp. 32 ff.

for peace and territorial concessions.[1] But in fact it was the English who ceded Maine in 1448 and who were finally driven from France by 1453. The king of England was still in possession of his title; and wars and rumours of wars in pursuit of it survived the century.

The nature of the English rights in France was thus a dual one: the English king was rightful king of France, but he might be prepared to forgo his right in return for the concession by his rival of sovereignty over extended continental possessions: under Henry V, over Normandy, Touraine, Maine, Anjou, Brittany, Flanders, Beaufort, Nogent and half Provence as well as the ancient duchy of Aquitaine. For the Valois rulers of France the first claim was inadmissible and the second conceded only under duress. But the possible rectitude of the English rights provided for those who might disagree with their French king justification for discussion with their English one.[2] From the very beginning there had been French magnates eager to invite the kings of England to descend upon their rightful inheritance.[3] In this sense the war between England and France had the aspect of an internecine conflict in which other internecine rivalries merged. If the Valois had had more than a factitious claim to the throne of England,[4] the same pattern might have obtained there. The concept of national unity may have appealed to the sentimental and to the propagandists in France of the Valois line; but it did not appeal to those whom the Valois slighted, or to those who hoped for greater advantages from the Plantagenets.

It was this acceptance of the English claims that made them dangerous. In the political allegory *Audite celi que loquor*, written by Jean Juvenal des Ursins in 1435, a battered and woebegone France deplored before her proud adversary England, 'the disaffection of some of those who speak my tongue, who mocked at the idea of supporting me and,

---

[1] Dickinson, op. cit. pp. 143 ff; *Letters and Papers Illustrative of the Wars of the English in France*, ed. J. Stevenson (Rolls Series) 1 (1861) 151; Jacob, op. cit. p. 475. For the background to the change of attitude, see C.T. Allmand, 'The Anglo-French Negotiations, 1439', in *B. Inst. hist. Research*, XL (1967) 1–33.

[2] Cf. Le Patourel, 'Edward III and the Kingdom of France', pp. 180 ff.

[3] P. Chaplais, 'Un Message de Jean de Fiennes à Edouard II et le projet de démembrement du royaume de France (janvier 1317)', in *R. Nord*, XLIII (1961) 145–8; Le Patourel, 'Edward III and the Kingdom of France', pp. 186 ff.

[4] Lewis, 'War-propaganda and Historiography', p. 14.

under the colour of vengeance and foolish error, and blind of true knowledge and understanding, have allied with you; and they persist in it without appearance of repentance because of obstinacy, envy, hatred and miserable shame'.[1] A long and distinguished line of the foolish and vengeful stretched backwards to the beginning of the war. Robert d'Artois, deprived, he claimed, unjustly of his inheritance in the county,[2] was long seen by the French propagandists[3] as the evil genius who had urged Edward III to action in the 1330s. Jean de Montfort, threatened with much the same kind of injustice *vis-à-vis* his inheritance of the duchy of Brittany, turned to Edward in 1341.[4] Geoffrey d'Harcourt's revolt in 1343 again should be seen against a background of a series of judicial slights to the Harcourt family; and there were other rebels in the north-west in the 1340s than the Harcourts.[5] Charles de Navarre, that prince of the fleurs-de-lis on both sides, intrigued incessantly with the English from the early 1350s. The problem of loyalty was to remain with the Valois throughout the later middle ages and beyond. Few magnates were immune from the temptation to rebel; and many in their rebellion were not immune from alliance with the 'enemy'. It was essentially this almost permanent condition of civil war in later medieval France which allowed the English their most significant success in the years between 1420 and 1450. The great conflict which developed as the reign of the midsummer madman Charles VI turned the century led both sides, 'Armagnacs' and 'Burgundians', with some reticence from 1411 onwards to court Henry IV and Henry V of England;[6] and it was the murder of Jean *sans peur* duke of Burgundy by

---

[1] '. . . la separacion daucuns de ma langue quilz derissent me soustenir & avecques toy sont alyes, soubz umbre de vengence et folle erreur par avuglement de vraye congnoiscence & entendement; et y persistent sans appercevance de repentence par le moyen de obstinacion, envie, haine et honte maulvaise' (Bibl. nat. MS fr. 5022, fo. 29ʳ).

[2] Cazelles, op. cit. pp. 75 ff.

[3] For instance, by Jean de Montreuil (*La Cronique martinienne* (1502?) folios 263ᵛ–264ʳ); by Jean Juvenal des Ursins ('Traictie compendieux de la querelle de France contre les Anglois', Bibl. nat. MS fr. 17512, folios 6ᵛ ff); and by the author of the treatise 'Pourceque pluseurs' (*Pretensions des Anglois à la couronne de France*, ed. R. Anstruther (Roxburghe Club: London, 1847) pp. 24–25).

[4] Cazelles, op. cit. pp. 140 ff.   [5] Ibid. pp. 146 ff.

[6] J. H. Wylie, *Hist. of England under Henry the Fourth*, IV (1898) 36–40, 54–87; Wylie and Waugh, op. cit. I (Cambridge, 1914) 415 ff.

the Armagnacs at Montereau in 1419 that made possible the settlement of Troyes the following year — as it was the reconciliation of his successor Philippe *le bon* with Charles VII, the French king of France dispossessed by his father in 1421, in the years between 1429 and 1435 which was the predisposing cause of the final failure of the English in France. But the hopefully treacherous magnate did not disappear in 1453. The symbiosis between discontented French princes and the English pretenders to France continued, dangerous — like the relationship between Edward IV and Charles *le téméraire* duke of Burgundy which ended in the English invasion of 1475 — or merely comic — like the intrigues of Jean duc d'Alençon in the 1450s.[1] The *mécontent* Charles duc de Bourbon was still ostensibly to be moved by consideration of the English title to the French throne in 1522.[2]

In 1417 Charles de Bourbon's great-grandfather, Jean I duc de Bourbon, a prisoner in England, prepared to submit to Henry V. A report of his interview with him once survived in Henry's own hand.

> The duc de Bourbon desired to speak with me; and so he did: and these were his words in substance that follow; saving that he spoke French.
>
> 'My lord, since God sent us into your hands, there have been many ways moved; and for the most part, at all times, you have desired that we should know you for rightful king of France, seeing that your right is great; wherefore many of us, before this, have sent into France, to seek and to have more full knowledge of your right than any of us had before our taking: and, of truth, thereof we had more knowledge than ever we had before; and, for myself, I dare well say, for I know more than ever I did of your right. Also, my lord, I have heard you desire to have certain lordships and lands, &c, as spoken by you and by your subjects; and, if you might have those, that, for reverence of God, &c, and for the good of peace, you would freely of your will renounce the right you have now in the crown of France, to him that now occupies it, and to his heirs, as form must be made on both the sides: the which I, duc of Bourbon, think as for your part, a great

---

[1] J. Calmette and G. Périnelle, *Louis XI et l'Angleterre* (1930) pp. 164 ff; G. du Fresne de Beaucourt, *Hist. de Charles VII*, VI (1891) 38–63, 179–98.

[2] *Letters and Papers Foreign and Domestic, Henry VIII*, III, part 2, p. 1091, no. 2567 and p. 1321, no. 3154.

and reasonable offer, that ought not to be refused by him, that you call your adversary. . . . If this be denied by your adversary we have acquitted ourselves, and especially I, duc of Bourbon; and then I shall haste me to you . . . and when I come into your presence, as with God's grace I will not fail, I promise you, by the faith of my body, to do you homage as to my sovereign lord, rightful king of France; and I shall show your right so clear to all men that it shall be well known that I do but as I ought; and that he that does not the same as I shall, does harm to his honour.'[1]

How much should one doubt these words? The circumstances under which they were spoken[2] might well bring them into disrepute. But Jean I de Bourbon was not the only descendant of St.-Louis who might in return for liberty have conceded more than was in the interest of his kinsman the king of France: Jean's father, Louis II de Bourbon, had been amongst those four princes of the fleurs-de-lis who in 1362 were prepared to grant Edward III more than the French council wished him to have.[3] And he was not the only descendant of St.-Louis who might in return for advantage admit, albeit with some reluctance, the claims of St.-Louis' other descendant, the king of England. Rights and advantages, principle and interest were mingled in these men's minds; it would probably be unwise overmuch to try to disentangle them. It might be argued that the kings of England and their French adherents argued their interests disguised as principles, that political realities were harder than these virtuous discussions of right. But it remains that it was in terms of right that their arguments and their minds were cast; and without reference to them one cannot fully describe the activities of the men who were the leaders of the Hundred Years War.

Warfare

The formal pattern of the war was imposed by that question of rights. The king of England claimed the throne of France. Alter-

[1] *Foedera*, ed. T. Rymer, IV, part 2 (The Hague, 1740) pp. 190–1.

[2] Wylie and Waugh, op. cit. III 39–41; A. Leguai, 'Le Problème des rançons au xve siècle: la captivité de Jean 1er, duc de Bourbon', in *Cah. Hist.* VI (1961) 41–58.

[3] Delachenal, op. cit. pp. 339 ff.

natively, he claimed his inheritance in France to hold in full sovereignty. Admission of these claims might be forced upon his opponent by a number of other means than by mere military activity. Negotiation between the rivals might render force unnecessary; arbitration might impose a settlement. The soldiery in the fields are only the simplest element in the war to grasp. Behind the activity of armies lay the activity of the diplomats. And the pattern of the conflict widened not only in this sense; it also widened as the principal contestants sought allies, as the quarrel of the kings of England and of France became embroiled in the secular and ecclesiastical politics of other European forces. But with this political imbroglio we are hardly concerned.

War in the fourteenth century was effectively one of short military campaigns set against a constant background of negotiation. In September 1339 Edward III made a plundering incursion through Cambrésis and Vermandois into Thiérache; in June 1340 he won a naval battle at Sluys and followed it up with a second campaign on land towards St.-Omer and towards Tournai. During the first campaign Philippe VI had offered a formal battle and then, to the accompaniment of English cries of cowardice, declined it; during the second it was Edward who, having offered formally to fight, refused to do so when the French offered to stake the question of the title to the throne upon the outcome of the battle. The first stage of the war ended with the truce of Espléchin on 25 September 1340; as far as the war aims of the English government were concerned it had brought them only a useful alliance with the Flemish towns in rebellion against their count and perhaps a diversion of French interest from the Gascon frontier. The north and the south-west remained theatres of war, the first intermittently, the second almost permanently. In the south-west, French pressure developed; but the English found in the Breton succession-dispute the opportunity again to create a diversion of French military strength northward, as well as an adherent in Jean de Montfort on the English case to the sovereignty of France. Once more, in the autumn of 1342, a major battle might have been fought, near Vannes; again it was avoided and the second stage of the war ended with the truce of Malestroit in January 1343. Gascony became again the centre of conflict. At first the English had considerable success; but French counter-pressure by 1346 placed the English in the south-west in the need of assistance from home. Edward III may well have planned his expedition for the relief of Gascony; but for a number of reasons it ended up as another invasion in the north. Edward landed in Normandy and headed northward towards his Flemish allies. This time the great armies did meet; and in the evening battle at Crécy-en-Ponthieu the French, imprudently attacking the English with old-fashioned tactics and the sun in their eyes, were thoroughly defeated. Edward III continued northward and besieged Calais; the town's capitulation on 4 August 1347 provided him with a strategic *pied-à-terre* in the north, and he promptly stocked it with English colonists. Soon the Flemish alliance collapsed; and by 1354 Edward was engaged in negotiations for a general truce. Although an army was sent to Calais in October 1355 it returned without venturing further.

Meanwhile the local war in Brittany and in Gascony had continued. From Bordeaux, Edward prince of Wales mounted heavy raiding-parties into the profitable east and north. Returning from a *chevauchée* to the Loire in the autumn of 1356, his army encountered the French under Jean II near Poitiers. The English were at some disadvantage; but the French had not yet learned fully how to deal with English tactics in a major battle. Once more they were defeated; and, what was worse, the king of France fell into the hands of his rival's son. A truce was arranged for two years, and negotiations began with the captive. But pressure had still to be brought on the French: in the winter of 1359–60 Edward mounted a great campaign in the north with disappointingly little success. In 1360 he was ready to treat for rather less that he might have done.

The treaties of Brétigny and of Calais were not, as we have seen, in any way a final solution. In 1369 the war began again. In Brittany and in Gascony the local war went very much against the English; the armed raids of Sir Robert Knolles in 1370 and of John duke of Lancaster in 1373 had little political effect. The truce of Bruges in 1375 brought this episode to an end. In 1380 it was the turn of Thomas earl of Buckingham to lead a *chevauchée* in France; but by 1386 the French could threaten to invade England. From the truce of 1389 the war cooled even further; and in 1396 the unwarlike Richard II made a truce for twenty-eight years with the French and married Charles VI's daughter. Richard's demise had little effect upon English activity and not very much upon that of the French. There was some fighting around Calais and some movement in 1403–7 towards the investment of Gascony. Henry IV was too busy preserving his English throne to long overmuch for his French one; the princes of France were too concerned to oppose each other to oppose overmuch the English in France. It was not until a war party in England, to which Henry's heir adhered, persuaded him to take advantage of those princes' appeals for help that English forces once more crossed the Channel. Henry's army sent to support the Burgundians in 1411 adventured as far as Paris; the army sent to support the Armagnacs in 1412 got much farther before it was bought off and retired to Gascony. When Henry V came to the throne in 1413 the English possessions in France remained those in English possession in the early 1370s: Calais in the north, and in the south-west Bordeaux and its hinterland, Dax, Bayonne and the *pays* of Labourde and Soule.

Henry's first campaign in France in 1415 added the town of Harfleur in Normandy, a second Calais, to the list; and the bad battle-management of the French added, as Henry's depleted army moved northward through Artois, the name of Agincourt to the list of English set-piece victories. The pattern of alternating military and diplomatic activity had continued from the fourteenth century; but with Henry V's second campaign in 1417 the pattern began to change. The English forces began now to invest Normandy: Caen, Alençon, Mortagne, Bellême, Falaise had all fallen to them by February 1418. The diplomatic negotiations continued; but in the intervals of truces the conquest of Normandy steadily continued. In January 1419 Rouen fell; in July Pontoise. The murder of Montereau drove Philippe *le bon* duke of Burgundy, whose late father had been as steadily investing the area around Paris, into the arms of Henry V. Between 1419 and 1420 the consolidation of the English holdings continued. The treaty of Troyes made the conquest of territory in the obedience of the dispossessed dauphin Charles obligatory upon the true *héritier* of France; and it continued to be obligatory upon his son, Henry VI king of France and England. Despite disaster at Baugé in 1421 the Anglo-Burgundian advance continued. In the east at Cravant on the Yonne in 1423 the French were again defeated. In the west at Vernueil in 1424 their defeat laid the way open for the English occupation of Maine and Anjou.

It remained to invest the Loire salient and force the Armagnacs back to the Massif central.

The key to the Loire line was Orléans. In 1429 the siege of Orléans failed; the English were defeated at Patay, and Charles was swept northward with Jeanne d'Arc, whose 'false enchantments and sorcery' may well have contributed to English demoralisation at the siege,[1] for unction at Reims. Philippe *le bon*, who had from the beginning been less than wholeheartedly English, began, at this sign of divine will, to think once more of being, however half-heartedly, French. 1426 saw, in fact, the greatest extension of English conquest in the north. In the south-west, spasmodic fighting had continued during the ten years; and spasmodic fighting continued in the deep military no-man's-lands around the possessions of the king of France and England for nearly thirty years. It was a period of local wars, of truces, of embassies, after 1429. In 1435 Philippe *le bon* crossed, at Arras, formally to the French side. In 1444 the first of the general truces between England and France was arranged; in 1447 the English surrendered Maine, and in 1448 the English captains defending it were persuaded to give it up. In 1449, on a pretext as flimsy as its real background was perhaps dangerous to him,[2] Charles VII began the reconquest of Normandy. It was over very quickly; and the reconquest the following year of Guyenne took almost as little time. But it was not until 1453 that the inhabitants of Bordeaux, loyal to the core to the 'petit roy Godon', were finally as rebels defeated with the failure of an English expeditionary force which had come to their aid, at Castillon-la-Bataille.

The nature of the Englishness of Gascony and the nature of the Englishness of those parts of the north under English obedience in the fifteenth century are topics which will concern us later. For Frenchmen outside those areas, apart from the fact that it raised similar questions of conscience, the war took on the aspect of a more or less intermittent blight. For the sum of the disorders produced by the war was far greater than that produced merely by the movements of the grand armies. Each major stage of the greater conflict was accompanied by

[1] *Procès de condamnation et de réhabilitation de Jeanne d'Arc*, ed. J. Quicherat (Soc. Hist. France) v (1849) 136–7. Cf. G. Lefèvre-Pontalis, 'La Panique anglaise en mai 1429', in *Moyen Age*, vii (1894) 81–96.
[2] See below, p. 233.

an epidemic of minor local conflicts, each potentially productive of innumerable troubles for the local inhabitants;[1] and these had their origin partly in the nature of later medieval warfare itself.

By the time Edward III claimed the throne of France the 'feudal' army, if it had ever been of any use for such an enterprise as that upon which he was about to embark, had long been supplanted in England by methods of raising troops in a way far more rational than that prescribed by custom. The war was fought by paid professionals. The alien adventurers who joined his army with their companies clearly deserved this title; but it belonged no less to the English captains who made their fortunes abroad, to the English nobility who maintained their fortunes in land with the profits of a career in arms, and even to the rank and file raised in England in the fourteenth century by the conscription of the commissioners of array: they seem to have gone abroad eagerly enough.[2] In France customary obligations were more resilient.[3] But though the *ban* and *arrière-ban* provided the bulk of the army in time of crisis at least until the 1420s, its actual conditions of service differed little from those of royal companies retained from the beginning of our period more formally; and with the development of those companies into 'permanence' by the 1440s — a development already foreshadowed in the later fourteenth century — the feudal host was eclipsed.[4] And — though the distinction between 'professional' and 'amateur' should again be avoided — the crown could again recruit 'free' companies, whose livelihood depended most clearly upon making war pay. The profit of prowess in arms derived primarily from the defeat and ransom of one's opponent; and the rules of the game, the law of arms, had an international validity.[5] The practices of chivalry infused an iron reality; but its hard outlines were dominant. The professional was in the game to make a living; that interest took

[1] P. C. Timbal, *La Guerre de Cent ans vue a travers les reg. du Parlement (1337–1369)* (1961) p. 105.

[2] The subject is admittedly an obscure one; but see H. J. Hewitt, *The Organization of War under Edward III* (Manchester, 1966) p. 37.

[3] F. Lot and R. Fawtier, *Hist. des institutions françaises au Moyen âge*, II *Institutions royales* (1958) 517 ff; Timbal, op. cit. pp. 7–71.

[4] Monsieur Philippe Contamine will soon illuminate this obscure field.

[5] Timbal, op. cit. pp. 305–74; M. H. Keen, *The Laws of War in the Late Middle Ages* (1965).

precedence over any sentiment of fighting for a cause. Bertrand du Guesclin is alleged to have told Charles V to take care to pay his troops: 'badly is he served', he added, 'who doesn't make due payment'.[1]

Their profit the companies of the fourteenth and fifteenth centuries took as they found it. They were paid; they had the possibility of acquiring ransoms; they had the possibility of plunder. Their captains profited from payments made to avoid particular areas or to surrender captured fortresses.[2] English captains and some of their subordinates profited during the fifteenth century from estates and office in northern France;[3] and the captains profited throughout from a formalised taxation system upon the gains of war of their subordinates.[4] Business partnerships were established by the smaller men for the sharing of the profits and the risks of war, moulded in the chivalric practice of brotherhood in arms.[5] That there were risks — principally the ransom of one's own person — is abundantly clear.[6] The duchesse d'Alençon, whose husband had already paid a ruinous ransom to the English, was loth to let him go to war in 1429; she was reassured by Jeanne d'Arc, who promised to return him in one piece.[7] But, as the captured Talbot told Alençon after the battle of Patay, it was the fortune of war;[8] and the military were determined to make as much as they could while their luck held. Clearly the armies had an overwhelming interest in war. But not everyone's heart stirred like Froissart's to the banners waving in the wind.[9] Those who paid for the adventures and the fortunes of the soldiery held different views. The French nobility, complained the clerical author of the *Complainte sur la bataille de Poitiers*:

[1] *Chron. de Bertrand du Guesclin par Cuvelier*, ed. E. Charrière (Docs inéd. sur l'hist. de France) II (1839) 135.

[2] See, for instance, A. Thomas, *Les Etats provinciaux de la France centrale sous Charles VII*, I (1879) 149 ff; Timbal, op. cit. pp. 283–304.

[3] See, for instance, K.B. McFarlane, 'The Investment of Sir John Fastolf's Profits of War', in *Trans. Roy. hist. Soc.* ser. 5 VII (1957) 91–116, and 'A Business-partnership in War and Admin. 1421–1445', in *Engl. hist. R.* LXXVIII (1963) 290–310.

[4] Keen, op. cit. pp. 137–55.

[5] Timbal, op. cit. pp. 269 ff; McFarlane, 'A Business-partnership', pp. 290–3.

[6] See below, pp. 211–12.

[7] *Procès de condamnation et de réhabilitation de Jeanne d'Arc*, ed. J. Quicherat (Soc. Hist. France) III (1845) 96.

[8] Ibid. p. 99.   [9] *Chron.* ed. S. Luce (Soc. Hist. France) V (1874) 195.

For their great greed and not to conquer honour
Have made this arrangement with [the enemy]:
'Don't let's kill one another — let's keep the war going —
Pretend to be captured — we'll gain a lot that way.'
And through this greed they've many great gifts acquired
From the English, who have revealed it all,
And on their faces you could see
That by treason they'd betrayed their king.[1]

This rather extravagant commentary upon the mores of the military did nothing to change anybody's outlook. The public interest, though it struggled to emerge,[2] was overwhelmed by the private interest of the armies which fought the war.

This interest thus survived the political, public interest of the two kings. Edward III, for instance, had agreed in the treaty of Brétigny to evacuate fortresses held by his troops; but it was still necessary for the French in 1361 to ransom five in Basse-Normandie held by Henry duke of Lancaster for twenty thousand *écus d'or* and possible for the representative of his executors to argue in the Parlement of Paris in 1366 that such a treaty between kings could not prejudice the private interest involved. The Parlement accepted his argument:[3] the right of the military to what they had captured was justifiable under the law of arms. And if the interest of the soldiers lay alongside or even overwhelmed that of the kings in whose names they fought the war, so the armies survived in being after the quarrels of those kings were formally settled. If they were unemployed by the rulers, they could still employ themselves. The loyalties of the true *routiers*, the men who had no other livelihood than the profession of arms, many of them foreign both to France and to England, had always been to the captains who had recruited them; and they proceeded, both after the treaty of Calais in 1360 and after the treaty of Arras in 1435, to live off the country in the

[1] 'Complainte sur la bataille de Poitiers', ed. C. de Beaurepaire, in *Bibl. Ec. Chartes*, ser. 3 II (1851) 261.
[2] In his memorandum of 1435, for instance, Sir John Fastolf stressed the need for the English commanders not to 'raunsone, appatise, ner favour no contre nor place that thei passe thorough for no singuler lucre nor profite of themsilfe; but that thei doo and execute duely that that thei come fore' (*Letters and Papers Illustrative of the Wars* II, part 2 (1864) [580]).
[3] Timbal, op. cit. pp. 456–62.

only way possible to them. In the fourteenth century the most formidable of them, like Arnaud de Cervole, the notorious *Archiprêtre*, dominated from captured castles whole areas in which they were effectively immune from judicial process.[1] Their interest was in war; that interest under the law of arms might even be protected in the courts. The only thing to do with such companies — as indeed with any later medieval army, friendly, enemy or free — was to pay them to stay clear of one; the only thing to do with a nest of soldiers *apatisant*, ransoming, from a neighbouring stronghold was, if possible, to pay them to go away. At times the garrisons scattered through a region for its own defence seemed to the defended little better than an enemy; though compensation could be demanded in the courts for unjust prises of goods and foodstuffs — if the garrison commander were not too important. And the needs of local defence still weighed upon townsmen and country-dwellers. For both there was watch-service in the local place of refuge; for those whose refuge was a seigneurial castle or a town there was as well a contribution towards its upkeep. The destruction of castles which could not be defended and might fall to the enemy and of buildings which encumbered the defences of towns brought tribulation to their owners. And in a number of other minor ways as well[2] as in clearly the major way — through taxation for the war — the conflict brought tribulation to those who had no interest in it other than that inculcated by patriotism.

French merchants captured in Normandy in 1417 successively by English, Burgundians and French said that the Burgundians treated them worse than the English, and that the French were more cruel than Saracens.[3] All armies, enemy, free or friendly, had much the same aims; the interests of the soldiery weighed heavily upon those of the noncombatants. As far as that part of it formally under the control of the king of France was concerned, the matter was one of bringing 'discipline to the soldiery'; the only effective way in which *routiers* and the more independent-minded of the domestic troops could be kept in check — apart from exporting them abroad[4] — was by others bribed with

---

[1] Ibid. pp. 470 ff, 486 ff.   [2] Ibid. pp. 105 ff.

[3] *Journal d'un bourgeois de Paris, 1405–1449*, ed. A. Tuétey (Soc. Hist. Paris: 1881) p. 83.

[4] Both Charles V and Charles VII attempted to do this (Lot and Fawtier, op. cit. II 523–4).

regular employment and pay not to behave like them. The feudal host proved itself in 1362 utterly incapable of dealing with the free companies.[1] Although Jean II and Charles V had attempted to reconstruct an army based upon the company system and governed by a stringent system of muster and review, their successor seems to have lost the initiative to acquire a professional army; and it was left to Charles VII in 1445 to create the royal companies of the *gens d'ordonnance*.[2] Thereafter his contemporaries seem agreed that the greater depredations ceased.[3] But warfare and disorder did not end in France with the last battles of the war with England and with the evaporation of the last companies. Frenchmen were quite as prepared to fight each other as to fight the Goddams. The companies that a magnate such as Jean duc de Berry had recruited to fight the English and to defend his apanage were presumably equally useful to him in the internecine conflict of Armagnacs and Burgundians; as, indeed, was the feudal host of his apanage, which was ready to follow him against the anointed king of France.[4] Some fifty years later Jean II duc de Bourbon could still call out his vassals in Forez[5] against Louis XI.

The aims of the soldiery in civil war were naturally the same as their aims in 'national' war. It was a matter for comment if an army behaved well in a modern sense. 'It isn't too big,' wrote Guillaume Cousinot of Louis XI's army in Bourbonnais during the civil war of the Public Weal in 1465,

> only twelve or fourteen thousand soldiers — and I don't think anyone's seen anything like it: it's so well disciplined, both in battle and on the road, and it doesn't harm anyone. No farm

[1] Delachenal, op. cit. II 319–20.

[2] J. M. Tourneur-Aumont, *La Bataille de Poitiers (1356) et la construction de la France* (1940) pp. 107–28; P. Contamine, 'Batailles, bannières, compagnies. Aspects de l'organisation militaire française pendant la première partie de la guerre de Cent ans', Actes du colloque international de Cocherel ... 1964, in *Les Cahiers vernonnais*, IV (1964) 27 ff; Lot and Fawtier, op. cit. II 523 ff; Beaucourt, op. cit. IV (1888) 387–404.

[3] P. S. Lewis, 'Jean Juvenal des Ursins and the Common Literary Attitude towards Tyranny in Fifteenth-century France', in *Medium Aevum*, XXXIV (1965) 115–16.

[4] R. Lacour, *Le Gouvernement de l'apanage de Jean, duc de Berry* (1934) pp. 275–6, 313–14.

[5] Letters of 27 April 1465, in Arch. nat. P 1402¹, cote 1225.

labourers run away, nor any churchman, nor merchant; and everybody's here in the army, it's just like Paris, except that the billets aren't as good, and that as far as victuals are concerned some pay for them, some don't: you've never seen such a well-behaved war. You won't hear of a woman raped, or of a church pillaged, or of a man taken — if it isn't in the towns one has to take by assault, or if he isn't a soldier — or of a horse stolen, or of a man robbed.[1]

Nor was disorder confined to that engendered by the more spectacular of the civil conflicts, like the quarrel between Armagnacs and Burgundians, like the Praguerie of 1440,[2] like the war of the Public Weal. The 'policies' of the nobility, especially perhaps on the wilder fringes of the country, could 'extend' themselves very rapidly into warfare. Although, as we shall see, the kings of France had long made some attempt to restrict private warfare in the country, they could not forbid it utterly, even in law; and for the powerful and the lawless such restriction as there was was cheerfully ignored. The great quarrel of the houses of Armagnac and Foix stretched over centuries; and there were other quarrels that were fought out in the foothills of the Pyrenees. From these the gamut of commotion ran downwards to the occasional violence of neighbours. Few seem to have been immune from its temptations: rival clerks for benefices besieged each other with artillery,[3] and knives flew rapidly into hands in tavern arguments.

The aftermath of the greater conflicts was peopled by such figures as the one on the road in Berry at the beginning of Lent 1465, 'dressed like a soldier, in a short hard leather jacket, with a great sword hung round his neck and a little cloak and a small mace trussed up with it, and a dagger in his belt and a salmon in a sort of pack in his hand (he'd stolen the salmon that day from a fishmonger in Le Blanc)'.[4] The

[1] A. M. Chazaud, 'Une Campagne de Louis XI. La Ligue du Bien public en Bourbonnais (mars–juillet 1465)', in *B. Soc. Emulation Allier*, XII (1870) 176.

[2] Beaucourt, op. cit. III (1885) 115–42.

[3] See, for instance, N. Valois, *Hist. de la Pragmatique sanction de Bourges sous Charles VII* (1906) p. xlix n 7.

[4] *Rec. des docs concernant le Poitou contenus dans les reg. de la Chancellerie de France*, ed. P. Guérin, XI (*1465–1474*) (Arch. hist. Poitou, 38: Poitiers, 1909) 33.

control of such heroes and the elimination of their habits depended
upon the policing power of the crown via its local agents; and this in
turn depended upon the ability of the crown to control its agents. The
question of public order was thus intimately linked to the whole
question of royal influence over its officers and over local seigneurial
powers; and, like these, it was a question far from solved by the end of
the fifteenth century.

War economy

How did the warfare epidemic in later medieval France affect the
livings of its inhabitants? Admittedly contemporaries blamed the
wickednesses of the military for the miseries of the world.[1] But one
must allow for the mortalities of the plague endemic in later medieval
France in assessing the part played by warfare in the permanent going
out of cultivation of the land. When only five *bonnes gens* were left in
Vignolles parish in the early fifteenth century because of 'the mortalities
and the war which have lasted a long time and which still continue',
they decided to go and live in Bordeaux;[2] and their estimate of the
causes of depopulation was probably a reasonable one. Nothing is more
difficult than the attempt to assess precisely the damage war caused to
agriculture. The destructions were immense, but their intensity varied
from region to region and within each region from place to place. They
were considerable in the north of France, in the north-west, in Agenais
and in Quercy; but Béarn and Alsace were completely spared. War
damage in other areas was graded in between these extremes. Within
each area, ravaged villages were mixed up with those that escaped.
There were so many nuances that in the present state of local research
it is impossible accurately to appreciate the over-all effect of the
devastations upon the economy.[3]

[1] H. S. Denifle, *La Désolation des églises, monastères et hôpitaux en France
pendant la guerre de Cent ans* (1897–9) *passim*.

[2] R. Boutruche, *La Crise d'une société. Seigneurs et paysans du Bordelais pendant
la guerre de Cent ans* (1947) p. 517.

[3] R. Boutruche, 'La Dévastation des campagnes pendant la guerre de
Cent ans et la reconstruction agricole de la France', in *Mélanges 1945*, III

The effect of warfare on trade is easier to estimate. Deliberate attempts at economic warfare were few and not really very successful. Edward III put an embargo on English wool in order to bully the Flemings.[1] Charles VII and Louis XI made some half-hearted attempts to stop English merchants coming to Bordeaux after its capture in 1453; the latter was possibly more successful at a land embargo on foodstuffs for Flanders in order to starve out Charles *le téméraire*, though he failed utterly to cut off Charles' credit with the Medici bank, which was happily financing both sides.[2] The effects of war were accidental: effectively, in organised or disorganised piracy on land or sea. Wasn't it fun, said (according to Froissart) the old *routier* Aimerigot Marchès, to ride about the country 'when ... we could find in the fields a rich abbot or a rich prior or a rich merchant or a mule train from Montpellier, Narbonne, Limoux, Fougas, Béziers, Carcassonne or Toulouse, loaded with cloth of gold or silk, or from Brussels or Montivilliers ... or spices coming from Bruges or other merchandise from Damascus and Alexandria? All was ours, or ransomed at our will. Every day we had more money.'[3] No wonder trade suffered. In mid-fourteenth century Montauban, the merchant Barthélémy Bonis gave it up and went in for money-lending, and, eventually, by foreclosing, for the safer perils of land-ownership.[4] But his colleagues in Montauban were not, on the whole, as discouraged as he — though the tendency to invest in land was a normal one, as we shall see. Trade was still possible. The great land-routes shifted across Europe to avoid the war areas; convoys, letters of safe-conduct and, to a certain extent, marine insurance could

Etudes historiques (1947) 127–63. Cf. V. Chomel, 'Droit de patronage et pratique religieuse dans l'archevêché de Narbonne au début du xvᵉ siècle', in *Bibl. Ec. Chartes*, cxv (1957) 70–84.

[1] H. S. Lucas, *The Low Countries and the Hundred Years War* (Ann Arbor, 1929) p. 586.

[2] E. Carus-Wilson, 'The Effects of the Acquisition and of the Loss of Gascony on the English Wine Trade', in *B. Inst. hist. Research*, xxi (1946–8) 145–54; Y. Renouard, 'Les Conséquences de la conquête de la Guienne par le roi de France pour le commerce des vins de Gascogne', in *A. Midi*, lxi (1948–9) 15–31; A. Gandilhon, *Politique écon. de Louis XI* (Rennes, 1940) pp. 362 ff.

[3] *Œuvres*, ed. Kervyn de Lettenhove, xiv (Brussels, 1872) 164.

[4] C. Cugnasse, 'Activité écon. et milieu humain à Montauban au xivᵉ siècle, d'après le reg. de Barthélémy Bonis', in *A. Midi*, lxix (1957) 219 ff.

reduce the perils of the deep. But these could do no more than mitigate the endemic damage of military and political activity. Very properly could the belligerent be accused, as the herald of France accused the English in the *Débat des hérauts d'armes* about 1456: 'you hinder', he said, 'the trade of all Christendom'.[1] When Robert Winnington captured the whole Bay Fleet of 110 ships in 1449 there was some truth in the accusation.[2]

But the effect of the war was not limited to such direct action. There was also the more indirect effect of the cost of war. It is difficult to give precise figures; but it seems undoubted that the expenses of the military placed a strain on the financial structure of the country waging the war. Taxation was the most obvious burden. By 1356 it could be said that 'since the wars began, the people of France have been much burdened, and ceaseless exactions have been made from them, by means of *gabelles*, impositions, subsidies, tenths, thirtieths, loans, prises of corn, of wine, of horses, of carts, and other things, and none of them paid for'.[3] Already at the end of the previous century the chronicler of St.-Magloire had complained

> One thing I'm all too certain of,
> That in France and in Champagne,
> There's no-one that doesn't complain
> Of the taxes that are taken
> On corn and wine and merchandise . . .[4]

and in the following century Sir John Fortescue thought that 'because the commons there, though they have grumbled, have not rebelled (nor are they bold enough to rebel), the French kings have each year since then set such charges upon them, and so increased those charges that the commons are so impoverished and undone, that they may not live . . . Truly they live in the most extreme poverty and misery, and yet they live in one of the most fertile kingdoms in the world.'[5] In France it was

[1] ed. L. Pannier and P. Meyer (Soc. des anciens textes français: 1877) p. 26.
[2] *Studies in English Trade in the Fifteenth Century*, ed. E. Power and M. M. Postan (1933) pp. 127–8.
[3] 'Journal des Etats généraux réunis à Paris au mois d'octobre 1356', ed. R. Delachenal, in *Nouvelle R. hist. Droit*, XXIV (1900) 432.
[4] ed. N. de Wailly and L. Delisle, in *Rec. des historiens des Gaules et de la France*, XXII (1865) 85.
[5] *The Governance of England*, ed. C. Plummer (Oxford, 1885) p. 114.

only the peasantry and the lesser bourgeoisie who paid direct taxes. The *populaires*' purse, thought Alain Chartier's knight in 1422, 'is like the cistern which has gathered and is gathering the waters and the gutters of all the wealth in the kingdom'.[1] Admittedly some peasants may have been getting richer; but it is doubtful that the shift was really sufficient to provide an economic argument for soaking the class least able to protect itself. There might, admittedly, for their lords be other profits of war to redress the balance of government exaction. The hazards of war might have their advantages. Ransoms, plunder and grant of captured territory might increase the wealth of conquering heroes and — in the persons of their kings — of conquering governments. But here it is clear that the balance of booty payments ran mainly one way: from France to England. The ransom of Jean II, which was fixed at 3,000,000 *écus d'or* (and well over a third of which was actually paid), was only the most spectacular of the payments which were sent sadly into England.[2]

One government expedient in France to raise money provides a whole problem on its own. The question of monetary mutation is linked inextricably with the question of the later medieval bullion supply. There were possibly four motives for monetary mutation, each more or less indirectly, perhaps, caused by bullion shortage.[3] The first was the need to adjust the coinage to changes in the market value of gold and silver. The second was the need to combat accidental devaluation caused by wear, clipping, counterfeiting and Gresham's Law. The action of the last — of the dictum that bad coinage drives out the good — was clearly understood and almost as clearly formulated at least as far back as the thirteenth century;[4] and it was caused primarily by devaluation in neighbouring countries. The third motive was the need to increase the amount of specie in circulation. The fourth motive, which some contemporaries insisted and some economic historians still

---

[1] *Le Quadrilogue invectif*, ed. E. Droz (Classiques français du Moyen âge: 2nd ed. 1950) p. 34.

[2] 'The Ransom of John II, King of France, 1360–1370', ed. D. Broome, in *Camden Miscellany*, XIV (Camden Third Series, 37: 1926). Cf. K. B. McFarlane, 'England and the Hundred Years War', in *Past & Present*, XXII (1962) 9–11.

[3] M. Bloch, *Esquisse d'une hist. monétaire de l'Europe* (Cahiers des Annales 9: 1954) pp. 75–6.

[4] Ibid. p. 62.

insist was the prime motive,[1] was the desire on the part of governments to make a fiscal profit at the mints, through their legitimate seigneurage charges and through their arguably illegitimate opportunities of embezzling the coinage. Certainly the mint profits could be pretty large; Oresme was probably exaggerating when he argued that 'no tallage can be heavier, more general or more severe' than monetary mutation; but still the mint profits in one accounting-term brought Philippe VI of France 522,028 *livres parisis* in 1349, and in 1419–20 mint profits in Burgundian France rose to 1,053,326 *livres tournois* over twenty months.[2] But these summits were in the two great periods of mutations in France, which lasted roughly from 1340 to 1360 and from 1415 to 1435. Though evidence is largely lacking, the big profits were probably confined to these. And the government, too, had an interest as a *rentier* on the side of those who wanted a hard, stable currency.

It was quite clear whom, if they were unwary, monetary mutation hit. Alain Chartier's knight's peasants got cistern-pursed, 'for the devalued state of the currency has effectively cut down for them the amount they have to pay us in dues and rents' amongst other things;[3] and it is difficult to better the percipient if overbearingly high-minded Oresme's views of the consequences of devaluation for the innocent.[4] Evidence for almost all he said is comparatively easy to find. In Toulouse in 1419–22 the settlement and arrangement of contracts, the proper collection of revenues and the normal method of accounting were violently disturbed; there was a clear tendency to abandon money as a means of payment and to despair and riot at any sign of monetary mutation.[5] But as far as economic development as a whole was concerned these tribulations, though severe, were of an essentially short term; and there were those more wise in the ways of the world who were determined to fly in the face of Oresme and his authority Aristotle and

[1] For instance, H. van Werveke, 'Currency Manipulation in the Middle Ages: the Case of Louis de Male, Count of Flanders', in *Trans. Roy. hist. Soc.* ser. 4 XXXI (1949) 115–27; R. Cazelles, 'Quelques Réflexions à propos des mutations de la monnaie royale française (1295–1360)', in *Moyen Age*, LXXII (1966) 267 ff.

[2] *De Moneta*, ed. C. Johnson (London, 1956) p. 32; F. Lot and R. Fawtier, *Hist. des Institutions françaises au Moyen âge*, II *Institutions royales* (1958) 236, 269.

[3] Op. cit. p. 34.   [4] Op. cit. pp. 33–5.

[5] P. Wolff, *Commerces et marchands de Toulouse (vers 1350–vers 1450)* (1954) pp. 332–4, 344–7.

at least diminish the consequences of ups and downs in the coinage. The seigneurs of Haut-Dauphiné pegged their rents to the tolerably stable florin of Florence; and when in 1417–18 even it became unstuck they seem to have been able to revalue the tariff in order to compensate for its devaluation.[1] Barthélémy Bonis, in the unstable period of the 1340s and 1350s, first kept in a third column of his accounts the day-to-day exchange rate in money of account; and then, having found that this was fictitious and unstable, he worked out his accounts in florins or some other hard currency.[2] The same sort of thing was done in the royal administration itself after the devaluation of 1351: like the urban administration of Toulouse in the 1430s, it was forced to put 'le pris de l'or a la monnoye', to account roughly in terms of gold.[3] In the abbey of St.-Martin de Tournai they had already in 1278 seen the danger of monetary instability to cash rents and had pegged them not to the legal value of money but to the merchant value; and so the abbey's money rents were sheltered from monetary fluctuations. When a later abbot, Gilles li Muisis, wrote the much quoted triplet,

> Money and the currency are most obscure things,
> They keep on going up and down and no-one knows why,
> If you want to win you lose however hard you try,

he seems to have been demonstrating in his dotage his inability to understand something which his abbey during his own administration had in fact understood perfectly well. There were reasons for an economic depression at St.-Martin in the mid-fourteenth century. They were taxation, war damage and the mismanagement of Gilles' predecessors. At least in the flare-up of prices at Tournai in the 1340s due to devaluation the abbey's receipts did not suffer.[4]

Admittedly the mint officers of France were made to swear to keep a devaluation 'secretly, without mentioning it to anyone, or letting

---

[1] V. Chomel, 'La Perception des cens en argent dans les seigneuries du Haut-Dauphiné aux xive et xve siècles', in *Rec. . . . C. Brunel*, I (1955) 255–71. Cf. for 'indexation' in Forez, E. Fournial, *Les Villes et l'économie d'échange en Forez aux xiiie et xive siècles* (1967) pp. 382 ff.

[2] Cugnasse, op. cit. p. 218.

[3] Wolff, *Commerces et marchands*, p. 345 n 171.

[4] A. d'Haenens, 'Les Mutations monétaires du xive siècle et leur incidence sur les finances des abbayes bénédictines: le budget de St.-Martin de Tournai de 1331 à 1348', in R. *belge Philol. Hist.* xxxvii (1959) 317–42.

anyone know in any way at all';[1] but there was much that could not be kept secret from the average intelligent merchant. 'When the prince does not announce beforehand the date and the scheme of the mutation which he means to make,' wrote Oresme, 'some persons, by their own cunning or through their friends, secretly foreknow it, and buy up merchandise with the weak money to sell again for the sound, get rich quickly, and make an excessive and undue profit against the lawful course of normal trade, at which St. Augustine is amazed and much marvels.'[2] Certainly the espionage system of the international bankers seems to have been highly developed;[3] and the reaction of lesser people and of prices can be plotted fairly accurately. In Tournai in the 1340s, in Toulouse in the early 1420s prices soared up after devaluation with very little delay.[4] It seems clear that in France the effect of devaluation — if not of revaluation — was to cause an almost immediate price-fluctuation.[5]

Again it is difficult to strike a balance. Some people suffered; others did not. One should probably not overestimate the short-term deleterious effect of devaluation, great though this may have been — or seemed. In the long term, devaluation may have helped to keep prices as buoyant as they were.[6]

'National sentiment'

The assessment of the true effect of warfare upon the economy of France in the later middle ages is thus difficult to arrive at. And equally difficult is an assessment of the moral effect of the war upon French society.[7] Much, for instance, has been written about the development of

[1] Bloch, op. cit. p. 67.   [2] Op. cit. p. 34.

[3] R. de Roover, *L'Evolution de la lettre de change, xive–xviiie siècles* (1953) pp. 56–7.

[4] D'Haenens, 'Les Mutations monétaires', graph at p. 342; Wolff, *Commerces et marchands*, graph xiii b.

[5] Cf. H. A. Miskimin, *Money, Prices and Foreign Exchange in Fourteenth-century France* (Yale, 1963).

[6] For instance, in Toulouse (Wolff, *Commerces et marchands*, pp. 429–30).

[7] Cf. J. Heers, 'Difficultés écon. et troubles sociaux en France et en Angleterre pendant la guerre de Cent ans: le problème des origines', Actes ... de Cocherel, pp. 47–53.

'national sentiment' in later medieval France. That Jeanne d'Arc, a member of the last class to have an interest in the war, should have been so insistent that Charles VII was 'true heir of France and king's son'[1] might be seen as evidence of the penetration of patriotic feeling deep into society. But was she really characteristic in this of her class or of the classes above hers? To what extent did the war contribute towards giving the society of later medieval France a greater sense of its own identity?

Clearly the victories of Charles VII gave some reality to the claims of the king of France to sovereignty over the whole of his kingdom. Some, like the inhabitants of Bordeaux, who had to be conquered twice, in 1451 and in 1453, found them hard to swallow.[2] For others conviction came an easier way. The inhabitants of Bayonne were convinced by a miracle.

> Today 20 August [wrote the comte de Dunois to Charles VII in a letter sedulously published by its recipient] at seven in the morning, the time the city of Bayonne had promised to yield, as the king's troops entered to take possession of it, in the sky (which at the time was clear and sparkling) there appeared within a cloud a white cross, to the right of the city on the Spanish side. The cross, without moving, stayed there for the space of an hour; and some said that at the beginning there was on the cross a shape like a crucifix crowned with a crown of blue, and that the crown turned into a fleur-de-lis, at which everyone much marvelled. The inhabitants of the town were appalled to see such marvels and they hastened to remove the badges with the red crosses which they had on their gates and towers. More than a thousand men saw the cross; and all those who saw it, French, Spanish and Navarrese, said they'd never seen anything like it.[3]

[1] *Procès de condamnation et de réhabilitation de Jeanne d'Arc*, ed. J. Quicherat (Soc. Hist. France) III (1845) 103.

[2] In 1453, thought the author of the *Chron. du Mont-St.-Michel*, 'les bourgois de Bordeaulx . . . n'estoient pas encor bons françois' (ed. S. Luce (Soc. des anciens textes français) I (1879) 60).

[3] G. du Fresne de Beaucourt, *Hist. de Charles VII*, v (1890) 52 n 1, from Bibl. nat. MS fr. 5028, fo. 183ᵛ: 'Sensieut la coppie des lettres du miracle de Bayonne et qui y advint.' The text ends: 'Plus de mille hommes ont veu ladicte croix; et dient tous ceulx qui lont veu, tant Franchois, Espaignois que Navarrois, que jamais navoient veu chose samblable.'

After the recovery of Normandy and of Guyenne Charles VII was prompt to give credit where credit was due: processions and masses were ordered, 'such as it is usual to perform in such cases, when Our Lord has bestowed such very great favours upon us and upon our kingdom'.[1] Victory, the clear emanation of the divine Will, was probably enough to convince many of the justice of the French cause — as the coronation of Charles VII at Reims may have convinced many of the justice of his title to the throne. But on the far side of superstition murkier views lay. ' "The king is king" ', said (in 1457) an ancient inhabitant of Auvergne, Jean Battifol of Bialon, 'who had drunk so much that because of the wine and also because of old age he didn't know what he was saying', ' "but it's not his place to be king, because when he was born, he didn't bear the royal mark, he didn't have the fleur-de-lis [on his back] like a proper king." '[2] Here at least was one stalwart who was not convinced by Jeanne d'Arc.

Quantitative evidence of the loyalty of Frenchmen to their French king is difficult, though not impossible, to find. Few Frenchmen, probably, would have liked to have been thought of as English *eo nomine*. There were exceptions in the south-west: according to Froissart, the Gascon towns repulsed the advances of the duc de Bourbon in 1399 with the sensible argument that 'if the French ruled over us, they'd [tax us unmercifully] . . . so it's better for us to be English, as we were born such, for they treat us freely and liberally, rather than in the subjection of the French'.[3] Independence, at least, if not positive anglophilia, was evinced by the Gascons. But they had at least the English to fall back on in their resistance to the French government. Frenchmen in other parts of the country had no such resort. But it was not for them necessarily a matter of denying their French king and embracing their English one, though this was the view that the propagandists of the former hoped to inculcate in them. The Plantagenet pretenders to the throne did, after all, descend from St.-Louis as clearly as did the Valois tenants of it. One could accept Edward III and his descendants without stopping being French; indeed, the English parliament needed reassurance both under

---

[1] Beaucourt, op. cit. v 38, 52–3.
[2] A. Thomas, 'Le "Signe royal" et le secret de Jeanne d'Arc', in R. *hist.* CIII (1910) 280 n 2.
[3] *Œuvres*, ed. Kervyn de Lettenhove, XVI (Brussels, 1872) 216–17.

Edward and under his great-grandson Henry V that under the double monarchy Englishmen would not stop being English.[1]

St. Bridgit of Sweden had in a notorious revelation decreed that Philippe VI should adopt Edward III as his heir[2] — as in fact Charles VI adopted Henry V. Until He showed His hand in the mid-fifteenth century neither God nor the saints could be said positively to be on the side of the Valois. Reasonable, as well as interested, doubt could exist on the question of the Plantagenet claim; and one does not have to look very far for the doubtful. In July 1346 a bourgeois of Compiègne was cut up like butcher's meat because he said that the kingdom 'belonged better' to Edward III than to Philippe VI.[3] At Les Andelys in Normandy a Jean de Lyons spent from 1347 to 1353 in prison for arguing that Edward should be king of France, because his touch for the king's evil was so much more efficacious than his French rival's.[4] Into the making up of men's minds in the fourteenth and fifteenth century went so many elements. Some, as we shall see, were reflected in contemporary propaganda. But to get at those minds is a much more difficult matter.

In September 1431 Jean Donnillet, a tailor of Notre-Dame-de-Cenilly, was being helped out of the gate of Coutances by two of his neighbours 'who were taking him home, holding him up under the arms, because he couldn't stand up or walk straight because of the enormous load of wine he had on board', when he said to the porters on the gate that although he'd been captured twice by the Armagnacs he still loved Charles VII more than Henry VI. This treachery he repeated to the lieutenant of the town and to the *vicomte* of Coutances. When he woke up in jail the following morning, unable, so he said with a certain degree of credibility, to remember a thing of what had happened, he declared tearfully to the jailer that he loved Henry VI more than

---

[1] J. H. Wylie and W. T. Waugh, *The Reign of Henry the Fifth*, III (Cambridge, 1929) 266.

[2] E. Colledge, '*Epistola solitarii ad reges*: Alphonse of Pecha as Organiser of Birgittine and Urbanist Propaganda', in *Mediaeval Stud.* XVIII (1956) pp. 32–3; J. H. Wylie, *Hist. of England under Henry the Fourth*, IV (1898) 36–7; Wylie and Waugh, op. cit. I (Cambridge, 1914) 440.

[3] *Les Grandes Chron. de France*, ed. J. Viard (Soc. Hist. France) IX (1937) 269–70.

[4] R. Cazelles, *La Société politique et la crise de la royauté sous Philippe de Valois* (1958) p. 204.

Charles VII.[1] What is one to make of this story? *Veritas* does not necessarily appear *in vino* — or, for that matter, *in sobrietate* either. There is a considerable amount of evidence which arguably illustrates the patriotic resistance offered by the French to the occupying English;[2] and Sir John Fastolf stated quite flatly in 1435 that the French people 'of nature love' Henry VI's 'adversary more than him'.[3]

Patriotic French literature is very far from lacking.[4] 'They are', wrote one author about 1419 with venom of the English, 'a race of people accursed, denying virtue and justice, ravishing wolves, proud, pompous, deceitful hypocrites without conscience, tyrants and persecutors of Christians, who drink and swallow down human blood, like birds of prey who live by robbery at the expense of their simple and well-disposed neighbours.'[5] The pride and wickedness of the English, who 'in the last hundred years . . . have killed and have had killed more Christians than all the other nations put together', and who killed even their kings, were stressed; 'when I see', wrote Jean de Montreuil about 1411, 'that they desire nothing so much as to destroy and lay waste this kingdom (which God forbid) and that they engage in war to the death with all their neighbours, I regard them with such abomination and hatred that I love those who hate them and hate those who love them'. 'Whenever I come to something which concerns the English', wrote

[1] *Chron. du Mont-St.-Michel*, 1 300–1.
[2] See, for instance, G. Lefèvre-Pontalis, 'La Guerre de partisans dans la Haute-Normandie (1424–1429)', in *Bibl. Ec. Chartes*, LIV (1893) 475–521, LV (1894) 259–305, LVI (1895) 433–508, LVII (1896) 5–54, XCVII (1936) 102–30; A. Plaisse, *La Baronie du Neubourg* (1961) pp. 309–17.
[3] *Letters and Papers Illustrative of the Wars of the English in France*, ed. J. Stevenson (Rolls Series) II, part 2 (1864) [577].
[4] For the use of the word *patria* see G. Dupont-Ferrier, 'Le Sens des mots "patria" et "patrie" en France au Moyen âge et jusqu'au début du xviie siècle', in R. *hist.* CLXXXVIII–CLXXXIX (1940) 89–104; B. Guenée, 'Etat et nation en France au Moyen âge', in R. *hist.* CCXXXVII (1967) 17–30; F. de Monte-Belluna, 'Tragicum argumentum de miserabili statu regni Francie (1357)', ed. A. Vernet, in *Annu.-B. Soc. Hist. France* (1962–3) 123; A. Bossuat, 'Jacques de Comborn, évêque de Clermont, et son secrétaire. Notes sur l'humanisme en Auvergne au xve siècle', in *Rec. . . . Clovis Brunel*, 1 (1955) 161.
[5] A. Bossuat, 'Les Origines Troyennes: leur rôle dans la littérature hist. au xve siècle', in *A. Normandie*, VIII (1958) 196. For this text, see Lewis, 'War-propaganda and Historiography in Fifteenth-century France and England', in *Trans. Roy. hist. Soc.* ser. 5 XV (1965) 10 n 6.

Noel de Fribois in 1459, 'I can't control my pen.' The image of a France 'all dishevelled, torn, squandered, wasted and undone, accompanied by tribulation, affliction, impatience, discontent, division, the dissimulation of humility and hope, and the abandonment or forgetting of things past and of those possible to accomplish' was invoked to persuade those inconscient of it; the 'good, true Frenchmen of the kingdom' were exhorted to think of the fleurs-de-lis. Before the English occupation of Normandy Jean de Montreuil was certain that 'no-one, please God, from the greatest to the smallest, would wish to allow or agree or not resist to the last that an Englishman as ruler or king should lord it in France'; later writers were perhaps less confident. But others than he could be found who followed him in thinking that after the English 'had tormented the French enough, they'll be tormented and punished themselves, and France will be left to the French'.[1]

But these writers were the propagandists of the Valois side; and the quantity of their output seems to indicate at least that there was a need for it.

> All the natives of Normandy [complained an anonymous versifier]
> Who've joined up with your party,
> Are traitors, I've no doubt of it,
> The great as well as the small.[2]

Christine de Pisan was quick to seize upon the moral consequences of the mission of Jeanne d'Arc and the coronation at Reims for those who had neglected too easily the claims of the dauphin Charles:

> And you, snotty-nosed rebels [she wrote],
> Who've sided with the English,
> Can't you see it would have been better
> To have taken the right road and not the wrong
> And become simply [their] serfs?
> Watch out that more doesn't happen to you,
> You've blown too hot already,
> And remember that an end must come.
> Can't you see, blind people,
> That God has seizin here?[3]

---

[1] Lewis, 'War-propaganda and Historiography', pp. 2-3.
[2] *Rec. de chants hist. français*, ed. Leroux de Lincy, I (1841) 326.
[3] 'Je, Christine, qui ay plouré', ed. J. Quicherat, in *Procès de ... Jeanne d'Arc*, v (1849) 17.

But their blindness lasted another twenty years.

Few stones were left by the propagandists in their efforts on behalf of the Valois. The writers around Charles V strove to enhance the image of the king of France. With the political consequences of this we will deal later; but it was at this time that the legend of the miraculous descent of the fleurs-de-lis was concocted, at this time that the supernatural element crept into the legend of the oriflamme, at this time that the more extreme writers got close to canonising the king of France *ex officio* in his lifetime.[1] The sacerdotal quality of the true king of France was heavily emphasised (at the same time as was his inability to alienate royal rights) in the coronation *ordo* of Charles V.[2] The whole development of the *roi très-chrétien* theme took on almost a political aspect. The mysteries and miracles of the house of France were not thus redecorated entirely to discredit the Plantagenets; but they certainly had the aim of forcing the rectitude of the Valois upon their subjects. And certainly in opposition to that rectitude were the murderous tendencies of the English kings; the remote history of the past was sifted to provide other examples than that of Henry IV. The Plantagenets were clearly unfitted to be *rois très-chrétiens*.[3]

'God is not pleased with treason';[4] or with murder either. But the propagandists were not only intent upon appealing to the patriotic and religious sentiments of their audience; they appealed also to their reason. The authors of a considerable number of treatises attempted to convince their readers of the truth about the English pretensions.[5] The war began with a manifesto from Edward III, to be fixed upon church doors in the kingdom he claimed.[6] It was not until after the treaty of Calais that French propaganda got fully under way. Nicole Oresme was allegedly 'of the clerks then alive the one whom ... King Charles [V] employed the most in writing against the English and the Navarrese, as one can see if one looks at his writings': these were probably his

[1] See below, pp. 81–4.   [2] See below, p. 96 n 2.

[3] Lewis, 'War-propaganda and Historiography', p. 13, and 'Jean Juvenal des Ursins', p. 103.

[4] *Rec. de chants hist. français*, I 326.

[5] Lewis, 'War-propaganda and Historiography', pp. 10–12.

[6] *Foedera*, ed. T. Rymer, II, part 4 (The Hague, 1740) 64; A. Guesnon, 'Docs inéd. sur l'invasion anglaise et les Etats au temps de Philippe VI et de Jean *le bon*', in *B. philol. hist. Com. Travaux hist. sci.* (1897) pp. 221–2.

commentaries upon Aristotle's *Politics*. But he may well have had a hand in the composition of the *Songe du verger*, which dealt with the English claims in a number of its chapters.[1] From the beginning of the fifteenth century the treatises fall thick upon the ground. A literary tradition of argument developed, based ultimately upon the diplomatic documents of the fourteenth century and upon the records of a more remote past. The barrier to female succession, the inconsistency of the English claims, the impossibility of the Troyes settlement blocked the English claim to the throne; the non-fulfilment of the treaty of Calais and the French king's inability to alienate his sovereignty blocked the English claims under that treaty. The actions of Charles V in 1369 and of Charles VII in 1449 in beginning the war again were demonstrated legal; and a number of authors carried the war into the enemy's territory and declared the king of France true king of England.

But that their countrymen needed to be persuaded of these things was only too clear to the authors of these treatises. There was also the foreigner to consider: both sides were careful to inform influential foreign powers of the truth.[2] But in general the English seem to have produced far less propaganda of a serious kind than the French. The initiative was in their hands and God apparently on their side for a considerable part of the time; it was those in France who might collaborate with them that needed persuasion — though it may well have been loyal Frenchmen, anxious like the readers of advertisements after their purchases to be confirmed in their views, who in fact bought the products of the propagandists. They certainly appealed to a wide spectrum of society.[3] But it was the collaborators whom the writers of the treatises sought perhaps primarily to convince. For when one has accounted for the propagandists, and accounted for the loyal patriots in the *maquis* of Normandy and their not-so-disinterested criminal friends, one is still left with a vast number of Frenchmen to whom the quarrel of the kings of France and of England was not a matter of black and white but a very neutral shade of grey indeed.

[1] Lewis, 'War-propaganda and Historiography', p. 9.

[2] See, for instance, E. Déprez, *Les Préliminaires de la guerre de Cent ans. La Papauté, la France et l'Angleterre (1328-1342)* (1902) pp. 226 ff; *The Reg. of Henry Chichele archbishop of Canterbury*, ed. E.F. Jacob, 1 (Oxford, 1943) xxxv-xxxvi.

[3] Lewis, 'War-propaganda and Historiography', pp. 5-6.

More or less eager *collabos* can of course be found. The inhabitants of Bordeaux, a number of Gascon seigneurs, some of the inhabitants of Rouen, the ambassadors of the Estates of Normandy, some of the inhabitants of Paris in the fifteenth century, some of the inhabitants of the west in the fourteenth, clearly for one reason or another supported the English.[1] The attitude of Jean Marcel, merchant and money-changer of Rouen, cannot be glossed over. Under the English occupation he advanced money to the English; under the liberation he advanced money to the French. In order to bribe the duke of Somerset in 1449 to alter the face value of '*blancs* at ten *deniers* each' to his advantage he 'lent [him] upon security ... three thousand of them to make an English war-payment'; a little over six years later he reported to the tribunal engaged in rehabilitating Jeanne d'Arc that most people present at the stake had thought her unjustly condemned.[2] In five sergeantries of the *vicomté* of Carentan seventy of the ninety-five tenants in possession before the occupation were still there in 1426; and they or their children were probably still there after the revelations of Jeanne d'Arc, and still there after the recovery of Normandy by Charles VII. Those who emigrated were a majority of the greater seigneurs and a minority of the lesser ones.[3] At this, the land-owner

[1] C. Samaran, 'Quelques aspects des rapports franco-anglais en Guyenne et Gascogne à la fin de la guerre de Cent ans', in *A. Midi*, LXV (1953) 21–34; *Rouen au temps de Jeanne d'Arc et pendant l'occupation anglaise*, ed. P. Le Cacheux (Soc. Hist. Normandie: Rouen, 1931) pp. cxij, cxxvij–cxxx; *Lettres de rois, reines et autres personnages*, ed. A. Champollion-Figeac (Docs inéd. sur l'hist. de France) II (1847) 423 ff; A. Longnon, *Paris pendant la domination anglaise (1420–1436)* (Soc. Hist. Paris: 1878); *Rec. des docs concernant le Poitou*, III *(1348–1369)* (Arch. hist. Poitou, 17: Poitiers, 1886) IV *(1369–1376)* (ibid. 19: Poitiers, 1888) *passim*.

[2] M. Mollat, 'Un "Collaborateur" au temps de la guerre de Cent ans. Jehan Marcel, changeur à Rouen', in *Annales*, I (1946) 35–42.

[3] A. Dupont, 'Pour ou contre le roi d'Angleterre (les titulaires de fiefs à la date du 2 avril 1426 dans les sergenteries de St.-Lô, Le Hommet, Ste.-Marie-du-Mont, La Haye-du-Puits et Ste.-Mère-Eglise, dépendant de la vicomté de Carentan)', in *B. Soc. Antiq. Normandie*, LIV (1957–8) 164–6. Much the same thing seems to have happened in the vicomté of Orbec (H. de Frondeville, *I: La Vicomté d'Orbec pendant l'occupation anglaise*; *II: Compte de Jean Le Muet vicomte d'Orbec pour la St.-Michel 1444* (Etudes lexoviennes, 4: Caen, 1936) 80) and in the barony of Le Neubourg (Plaisse, op. cit. pp. 304–5).

level, patriotism clearly followed interest. Yet, even so, compromise was possible. Families split to avoid the consequences of over-much devotion to the true king of France. In 1427 the children of Guillaume d'Estouteville, 'so-called seigneur de Torcy, our rebel and enemy', were granted a considerable amount of property by Bedford's government to provide for their upkeep and education.[1] Jean de Roffignac remained loyal to Charles VII and kept his family's property in Limousin; he sent his son Guiot to take the oath to Henry VI and preserve the family's property in Nivernais. Loyalty across the Franco-Burgundian frontier was even more ambiguous. Two Châteauvillain brothers served happily on opposing sides. In 1427 the English confiscated the property of Georges de La Trémoille, the 'favourite' of Charles VII, and gave it to his brother Jean de La Trémoille seigneur de Jonvelle. The brothers were on the best of terms.[2] When the civil war set brother against brother and father against son, one must be careful to discover what precisely this meant to them.

When Charles VII in 1437 closed the 'alley . . . called Glatigny' on the Ile de la Cité — abandoned by a company of prostitutes for grander streets alongside — on behalf of Jacques Jouvenel des Ursins so that he could extend the house of Jean I Jouvenel, it was in recompense for the service of the Jouvenels 'who, to keep their loyalty towards us, abandoned one and all the property and goods they had in Paris; they left the town in 1418 at the same time as we left it, and have always remained and still remain in our obedience'.[3] But not all those who might be the king's servants betrayed such loyalty to him. In 1445 Jean Juvenal analysed the men who might be called to the council for his brother Guillaume, chancellor of France.

> There's a singular thing which one has to watch out for in this kingdom [he wrote]. The past has been pretty amazing and there've

[1] *Actes de la Chancellerie d'Henri VI concernant la Normandie sous la domination anglaise*, ed. P. Le Cacheux (Soc. Hist. Normandie) II (Rouen, 1908) 179, 352–3.

[2] A. Bossuat, 'Le Rétablissement de la paix sociale sous le règne de Charles VII', in *Moyen Age*, LX (1954) 143–4.

[3] L. Battifol, *Jean Jouvenel, prévôt des marchands de la ville de Paris (1360—1413)*, (1894) pp. 308–11. The rue de Glatigny was alternatively known as the 'val d'amours' in 1460 (Bibl. nat. Pièces originales 1593, doss. Jouvenel, no. 46).

been people with different views. Some, for instance, have always been in the king's party without flinching, and have abandoned their lands and lordships, and one can properly call them good and loyal Frenchmen ... Our ... father ... said often that he'd go and find his bread in beggary sooner than be on the side of the enemies of his sovereign lord. ... Others have held the side of monsieur de Bourgogne, on the pretext of the death of the late duke Jean, but they never had any love for the English, except in so far as they helped them; and since the peace made with him[1] they've shown themselves and show themselves still to have good and loyal hearts towards the king and the enemies of his enemies. Others — the third group — have shown themselves in their hearts and otherwise true and perfect Englishmen, more almost than the English natives of England; and they were conquered against their will and liking, and in spite of themselves, and it's only the fear of losing their goods and property that stops them being with the English. And one must still believe that their hearts and loyalties are with the enemy, whatever face they put on it and however diligent they are against them.[2]

The tensions engendered by the civil war complicated the problem. In 1422 Jean Ladvertit, canon of Ste.-Ragon-de-Poitiers, was accused in the Parlement sitting in that town of 'having said that the country is better off under the subjection of the English than it is at present. He

---

[1] The treaty of Arras in 1435.

[2] 'Y a une chose singuliere de quoy on se doit fort garder en ce royaume. Le temps passe a este moult merveilleux et y a eu gens de diverses ymaginacions. Les ungs, cestassavoir, ceulx qui ont tenu le party du roy tousjours, sans flechir, et habandonne leurs terres et seignouries, et les peut on bien nommer bons et loyaulx Francois. ... Nostre ... pere ... disoit souvent que il yroit avant querir son pain en ung bisac que estre et demoure avec les ennemis de son souverain seigneur. ... Les aultrez ont tenu le parti de monsr. de Bourgongne, soubz umbre de la mort du feu duc Jehan, mais ne avoient amour aucune aux Anglois, si non en tant quilz sen aidoient; et depuis la paix faicte avecques mondit sr. se sont monstrez et monstrent avoir bon et loyal courage au roy et aux ennemis de ses ennemis. Les aultrez et troisiemes se sont monstrez tenus en courage et aultrement vrais et parfais Anglois, plus a peine que les Anglois natifs dAngleterre, et se sont reduitz contre leur gre et voulente et malgre eulx, et se neust este pour doubte de perdre leurs biens meubles et immeubles ilz feussent avecques les Anglois. Et encores est a croirre que leurs cuers et courages sont avecques les ennemis, quelque semblant que ilz facent ou diligences a lencontre de eulx.' ('A, a, a, nescio loqui quia puer ego sum', Bibl. nat. MS fr. 2701, fo. 43ᵛ.)

said that . . . the regent was only a child and that one could make him say anything one wanted to . . . he was astonished that he called himself regent.'[1] All the trouble began, thought Jean Ladvertit, with Louis d'Orléans. The duke of Burgundy should be regent. Should, he had asked his hearers, one pretend to be pleased with someone who had murdered one's father? He also said the Parlement of Poitiers was 'nothing'. This can hardly have pleased Jean I Jouvenel, second president in the court, or his son Jean II, advocate there.[2]

The 'anti-Parlement' of Paris displayed a considerable amount of formal affection for the invader.[3] Its members behaved towards the king of France and England exactly as they had done towards his predecessor and as they were to do towards his successor: they opposed the king when they felt such opposition was in the interest of the crown. They did their narrower duty; they ignored the broader duty the partisans of the Valois waved before them. The maintenance of such normality was the aim of Bedford's government in France.[4] Even though such anomalous institutions as the council of Rouen might be maintained they were staffed by 'renegade Frenchmen'.[5] The university of Caen owed its existence to the English; under the English the long-lost 'liberty' of the Estates of Normandy was recovered and not lost again.[6] But for the fact that it was English, there was a great deal to be said for Bedford's government in France. The considerable number of Frenchmen that accepted it can hardly be blamed for doing so.

The evidence of Thomas Basin is perhaps the most convincing here.[7]

[1] '. . . davoir dit que le pais est plus aise en la subjection des Anglois quil nest de present. Dist que monsr. le regent nestoit que un enfant et que pour une fouace on lui feroit dire ce que on vouldroit. Item sesbahissoit comment se disoit regent.' (Arch. nat. X^{1}A9197, fo. 28^r.)

[2] Ibid. folios 1^r, 21^r ff *passim*.

[3] A. Bossuat, 'Le Parlement de Paris pendant l'occupation anglaise', in R. *hist.* CCXXIX (1963) 19–40.

[4] Cf. C. A. J. Armstrong, 'La Double Monarchie France–Angleterre et la maison de Bourgogne', in *A. Bourgogne*, XXXVII (1965) 81–112.

[5] B. J. H. Rowe, 'The Grand Conseil under the Duke of Bedford', in *Essays . . . H. E. Salter* (Oxford, 1934) 207–34.

[6] H. Prentout, *Les Etats provinciaux de Normandie*, 1 (M. Acad. nat. Sci. Arts Caen, NS 1: Caen, 1925) 142–55; B. J. H. Rowe, 'The Estates of Normandy under the Duke of Bedford', in *Engl. hist.* R. XLVI (1931) 551–78.

[7] *Hist. de Charles VII*, ed. C. Samaran, 1 (Classiques de l'hist. de France au Moyen âge, 15: 1964) 104–14, 196–226, 11 (ibid. 21: 1944) 52–6, 104–6.

To this son of a bourgeois of Caudebec-en-Caux, to this bishop of Lisieux under English rule, Bedford was able and just. The areas of France under English control were pillaged by English troops, by those who 'said' they fought for the French side, and by 'brigands' who lived in the woods, some of whom did so out of hatred of the English, but others of whom did so out of baseness, greed or because they were on the run. The English tried to put the brigands down; but, despite their zeal and skill, they were unable to do so while the English occupation lasted. It was for this reason a 'priest' — possibly Basin himself — had, with some understandable diffidence, told some English the only real remedy was for them to go home. The brigands attacked the English above all, and the English succeeded in executing a large number of them and of those who harboured them. But the French peasantry came to hate the English for their own pillaging, especially after Bedford's death. In 1434 the English armed the Norman peasants against all those who pillaged them, brigands, French and English: the last were to be handed over to justice. Not unnaturally they felt aggrieved and oppressed the Normans even more. A revolt against one of them, Richard Venables, led to a massacre, and Venables was executed by Bedford; but people thought that as atonement this was hardly enough.

The brigands tried to stir up the peasantry to revolt as a cover for their own treason. Revolts in Bessin and in the Val de Vire failed, and the English issued a general amnesty. With the English rejection of the treaty of Arras in 1435, dislike of them increased and with it tension. After the defeat of Arundel at Gerberoy and the fall of Dieppe to them, French pillaging in the pays de Caux, added to the pillaging of the English themselves there, led to a peasant revolt: the French persuaded 'the simple and innocent' to liberate themselves, but the peasants were again defeated, at Caudebec. The English and the French continued to oppress Basse-Normandie; the peasants there had a 'natural' love of the Valois king of France, but he, too, failed to protect them and 'dissimulated' the misdeeds of his partisans. After the truces in 1444 anarchy increased; the inhabitants of the country had henceforth very little sympathy for the English; and this state of affairs finally detached them from them, because the English didn't keep them in peace. Finally the French, who had been kept English only by fear, flocked to their natural lord in 1449–50 — urged on the more because he promised them security.

But had Bedford succeeded in keeping the peace, what would have happened then to their natural love for Charles VII? In Basin's view those who kept the flame of resistance alight were at least as troublesome as those who tried to extinguish it. The bourgeois of Paris, too, it will be remembered, reported in 1417 that those who had been captured in turn by them all would rather be captured by the English than by the Burgundians and by the Burgundians than by the French.[1] At least Bedford tried to reduce the disorder left by military activity in the occupied areas. The evidence of Thomas Basin hardly argues that all the brigands executed in Normandy were loyal maquisards. A very considerable number of them were brigands and nothing more; even the French would have executed them — for they, too, had 'brigands' in areas under their control, whom no-one is likely to label 'patriots' wholesale. Open enemies of the English in Normandy who had never taken an oath to Henry VI were, in principle at least, when captured by them to be treated as prisoners of war. Admittedly those who had taken such an oath suffered as traitors; and admittedly to recognise men who preyed upon the English out of re-awakened loyalty to Charles VII rather than as a cover for simpler brigandage as traitors 'suggests a cold-blooded straining' of the law. But it is difficult to see upon what principle otherwise the legality of Henry VI's title could be asserted; or, indeed, upon what principle Bedford could have attempted to repress the pillaging which so oppressed the Normans.[2]

One need not deny the existence of partisan guerrillas loyally keeping a resistance alive under the occupation. But one must probably reduce their numbers; and one must probably reduce in a number of cases the patriotic fervour of their motives. The crucial question remains that of the attitude towards loyalty and loyalists of the rest of the population. Again one need not deny that the brigands had their supporters. But it seems clear also that they inspired a real terror amongst the peasantry. Near Gisors in 1424 'an assembly of the common folk of the country' was made 'to hunt out the brigands'; in the same area in 1432 they

[1] See above, p. 50.
[2] B. J. H. Rowe, 'John Duke of Bedford and the Norman "Brigands" ', in *Engl. hist. R.* XLVII (1932) 583–600.

attacked clear partisans of the French.[1] The whole tone of Thomas
Basin's evidence seems to indicate that the Norman peasantry wished a
plague upon both the houses, of Plantagenet and of Valois. Would they
indeed have praised a government which kept the peace and administered
well, as they execrated a government which failed to keep order? This
was precisely the distinction made by Jean Juvenal des Ursins, whom
no-one could call a traitor, but who warned Charles VII that the virtues
of English rule — and this even about 1440 — might make Charles'
subjects go over to the English. Bishop of Beauvais, he stressed the
loyalty of his people who had been 'English' only because of the
treachery of his predecessor:

> but if [he wrote] we were in the hands of the enemies we should
> be governed in justice and discipline like the other lands they've
> conquered. And your people can easily find a king; but you
> won't find a people when you want to. . . . All the *pays* which
> have shown their loyalty towards you are like a desert; and their
> reduction has been the cause of their destruction. You should be
> warned that your enemies, who know the tyrannical behaviour
> which your men follow, and know too that it is to your subjects a
> thing almost insupportable, thinking that the loss of their goods
> which they endure and the tyranny under which they live might
> be the cause of making your . . . subjects leave your obedience
> (for it's said in common proverb that 'he who loses his goods
> loses his wits') try to pervert them, talking and getting others to
> talk to particular individuals, sometimes with soft words, some-
> times with threats, actual ones which they carry out, trying to get
> them day and night, making them offers as big as can be.[2]

[1] *Actes de la Chancellerie d'Henri VI*, 1 (Rouen, 1907) 93, II 209. Cf. Rowe,
'John Duke of Bedford and the Norman "Brigands" ', p. 589 n 1.

[2] '. . . se estions es mains des ennemis nous serions gouvernes en justice &
polic[e] comme les autres des terres quilz ont conquises. Et finera bien ton
peuple de roy; mais tu ne fineras pas de peuple quant tu vouldras. . . . Tous
les pais qui ont monstre leur loyaulte envers vous sont comme en desert; et a
este leur reduction cause de leur destruction. Et est a advertir que voz
ennemis, qui congnoissent la tirannise que faisoient voz gens, et encore
congnoissent que cest a voz subgetz chose comme insuportable, cuidans que
la perte de leurs biens quilz faisoient et la tirannie que on leur faisoit peussent
estre cause de faire departir vosdiz subgetz de vostre obeissance (car on dit en
commum proverbe que "qui pert le sien il pert le sens") essaient a les
pervertir, en parlant et faisant parler a aucuns particuliers, aucunesfois par
doulceur, aucunesfois par menaces executees et reeles, en essayant a les

They even tried to seduce Jean Juvenal, not into treachery but at least into neutrality, with the promise of security; but he and his town stood firm — despite the advice of local gentlemen who thought he should give in. There was, it might be argued, in his view again not much in the motives of his subjects of patriotism; but much of a desire for peace.[1]

And as far as Gascony was concerned the onus of proof was on the liberator. The Gascons, thought Thomas Basin, were much attached to the English, for they had under them had too long an independence.[2] And the French occupying forces there, too, had their brigands to contend with. In February 1454 one of them was being interrogated under torture by French commissioners in Bordeaux. He had made it clear that he did not want to be French, but it could hardly be said that he burned with a patriotic conviction of the right of Henry VI to the throne of France. 'Asked why he hadn't gone off to England since he didn't want to be French, he replied that he didn't want to go there because he wouldn't like drinking beer.'[3] If Bernard Georges was being flippant under these circumstances he had little respect for the grander trappings of patriotism; if he was being serious his political horizon was, to say the least, limited.

Nor, with the liberation, did the virtuous triumph and the traitorous languish. The exodus from Gascony was limited: the names are known of some two hundred Gascon émigrés in England in the thirty years after 1453, of whom only forty were noble.[4] The settlement which the

prendre de jour et de nuyt, en leur faisant offres tant amples que on povoit.' ('Loquar in tribulacione spiritus mei', Bibl. nat. MS fr. 5022, fo. 3ʳ⁻ᵛ.)

[1] Cf. (for a slightly earlier period) 'Rôles normands et français et autres pièces tirées des archives de Londres par Bréquigny', in M. Soc. Antiq. Normandie, XXIII (1858) no. 1376 — redated by R. A. Newhall, The English Conquest of Normandy 1416–1424 (Yale, 1924) p. 274 n 25.

[2] Op. cit. II 160–2, 184; though seditious views could be found here too (Lettres de rois, pp. 444–7).

[3] 'Emquis pourquoy il ne sen est ale en Angleterre puisquil ne vouloit estre Francois, dit quil ne vouloit point y aler, pourcequil ne saroit boyre godalle' (Bibl. nat. MS fr. 6963, fo. 27ᵛ).

[4] A. Peyrègne, 'Les Emigrés gascons en Angleterre (1453–1485)', in A. Midi, LXVI (1954) 113–28. For Englishmen in the Vexin who, having married French wives, took oaths to Charles VII after the English débâcle and had their spouses' property restored to them, see A. M. Tattegrain, 'Le Vexin français sous la domination anglaise', in Positions des thèses de l'Ec. Chartes (1937) p. 163.

liberators made with the liberated as the English were driven from France was far from unfavourable to those who had taken advantage of English rule or who had simply accepted it as normal. A considerable number of problems was raised by the existence of rival governments. Not the least of these was the question of settlement of right to property granted after confiscation by either side in the heat of the struggle for loyalties.[1] Restitution was made to the dispossessed who returned with the victorious 'roi de Bourges'; but it was restitution of property in its present state rather than in the state in which it had been when they had been dispossessed of it. A flood of lawsuits which dealt with the complication of rights to property which might have changed hands many times between occupation and liberation took up the time of the Parlement of Paris to the end of Charles VII's reign. The Parlement had to deal not only with the normal hatreds engendered by a lawsuit, but also with the residual hatreds of a civil war. As an amalgam of the loyalist Parlement of Poitiers and the 'English' anti-Parlement, it strove manfully in the face of a muddle of conflicting legislation about restitutions to create peace and union amongst ex-Armagnacs and ex-Burgundians. The old party titles were outlawed: the ex-Burgundian Pierre II l'Orfevre got into considerable trouble for calling the counsellors of the Parlement 'you Armagnacs'. Forgetfulness was what the government hoped for; that those who had found themselves loyalists and traitors should have no 'reason to remember one against another the evils and misfortunes done and perpetrated during the wars and divisions'. Eventually forgetfulness came. But it was a forgetfulness not of ideological differences, but of purely material ones tricked out in a garb of patriotism and loyalty: a garb by which those who made the settlement were perhaps careful not to become too impressed.

If material differences thus gave some practical reality to the difference between those who accepted English rule and those who did not, such material differences could be settled without involving a question of loyalty. A few who, like the informer Pierre Rousseau, had been too compromised by his association with the expelled English safely to remain French departed across the Channel; merchants whose business lay with the English followed their customers; but for the most part the subjects of the ci-devant king of France and England had, like Bernard

[1] Bossuat, 'Le Rétablissement de la paix sociale', pp. 137–62.

Georges, no taste for *godale*. The war was one which the non-military classes disliked, military manœuvre by the soldiery on whatever side: in return for peace they would put up with any ruler capable of giving it. 'If a prince appeared who was powerful enough and wanted to maintain and do justice', thought Jean Juvenal des Ursins, 'even if he was a Saracen, it's to be feared that, like enraged and senseless people, they would put themselves in his obedience."' They had no interest in the war; they were not, it may be argued, to be stirred by propaganda into a resistance movement. A primitive xenophobia might be evoked by contemplation of the beer-swigging English soldiery; but it is difficult to see how their consciousness of being French was enhanced by the privations they suffered from anybody's army in anybody's cause.

Yet at certain crucial moments a consciousness of nationality might be forced on them. Before the reoccupation of Paris in 1436 Jeannette Roland had got engaged to Wexford pursuivant. Despite pressure she refused to give him up; and he in turn appealed to the Parlement. The Parlement made its decision with a wholly unaccustomed rapidity: 'the court', it said, 'will not allow . . . Jeannette to go off with . . . Wexford and become English while the war goes on between the king [of France] and the English'.[2] Though this was in the heat of the liberation. Twenty-odd years later René d'Anjou could relate in the *Livre du Cuer d'Amours espris*[3] that his great-uncle Jean duc de Berry had as a hostage in England for his father Jean II 'been so fiercely burned in the flames of love by an English lady, servant of the god of love' that he there and then adopted his badge of the Wounded Swan which he used until his death in 1416.

But arguably the permanence of victory made valid in a sense for the French the 'national sentiment' the propagandists had so long asserted. The struggle between the kings of England and of France had always been more than one over inheritance rights, set against a background of

---

[1] 'Et se il venoit prince aiant puissance qui voulsist tenir et faire justice & fust ung Sarrasin, il est doubte que comme gens furieux et sans entendement ilz ne se meissent en son obeissance.' ('Loquar in tribulacione spiritus mei', Bibl. nat. MS fr. 5022, fo. 25ʳ.)

[2] A. Bossuat, 'L'Idée de nation et la jurisprudence du Parlement de Paris au xvᵉ siècle', in R. *hist.* CCIV (1950) 54–61.

[3] ed. T. de Quatrebarbes, *Œuvres complètes du roi René*, III (Angers, 1846) 117.

legal conflict between a magnate and his sovereign; it was one between two sovereigns, and it could never have been settled finally except in terms of a 'national' war. Such a confrontation of the two countries thus conceived as a whole was bound to force men to think in terms of 'French' and 'English', to produce a semblance of 'national sentiment'; and the emotional propagandists hastened to fan the flames of patriotism and xenophobia. In their search, too, for material in the past their more cerebral colleagues emphasised far more than the chroniclers could an historical consciousness of the identity of the two countries. They forced their readers towards an historical perspective of that identity; they reinforced with reason the promptings of sentiment. To this extent at least the propagandists of the Valois cause contributed to the formation of a national mentality in the fifteenth century.[1]

[1] Cf. B. Guenée, 'Etat et nation en France au Moyen âge', in R. *Hist.* CCXXXVII (1967) 17–30.

2

Kings, Courtiers, Councillors,
Civil Servants

Legitimacy

YET those who had won had won. Victory made valid the anger and
the lies; the fleur-de-lis in the bellies of the French[1] was given a respectable ancestry; and in the quiet of victory the uncommitted in France
could contemplate the historical justification for the Valois resistance to
the Plantagenets. The crisis was over for the true kings of France. But
anxiety might still remain. In April 1478 Louis XI, in negotiation with
the English, might still dispatch Guillaume Cousinot, as his father had
dispatched Jean Juvenal des Ursins, into the *Trésor des chartes* and the
Chambre des comptes to 'draw up excellent, notable, great and ample
memoirs and instructions thoroughly to establish ... [Louis XI's]
rights' and to counter the English claims to the crown of France and to
Normandy and Guyenne; and still in the early years of Charles VIII's
reign the need for such memorials was stressed in official circles.[2]

But it was not only the ancient enemies that had to be feared. The
abbot of St.-Michel in Thiérache got into trouble in 1460 for having
said, while chattering away, that 'all the right that the ... English
claimed to have in ... [the] kingdom and especially in the duchy of
Normandy came about "because once a widowed queen of France
married a butcher from Paris or from Reims who was called de Valois"'.[3]
Admittedly 'divisions' had existed long before the disputed succession

---

[1] P. S. Lewis, 'War-propaganda and Historiography in Fifteenth-century
France and England', in *Trans. Roy. hist. Soc.* ser. 5 xv (1965) 21 n2.

[2] Ibid. pp. 16–17; *Lettres de Louis XI*, ed. J. Vaesen and E. Charavay (Soc.
Hist. France) VII (1900) 31–3.

[3] A. de Reilhac, *Jean de Reilhac*, III (1888) 78.

of 1328.[1] But the question of legitimacy had put, it may be argued, the whole nature of the Valois monarchy in doubt. There were first the legal problems. One had arisen in 1316 with the deaths of Louis X and of Jean I, the last Capetian to succeed in direct line from his father.[2] It was by no means legally clear that Louis' daughter, Jeanne, should be disinherited of the crown in favour of her uncle Philippe. It was by no means legally clear that the acquisitions of the crown over the past two hundred years should not be distributed amongst the male collaterals of Jean I, the future Charles IV and Edward II of England as well as Philippe V. The succession of 1328 provided another legal problem. The disinheriting of the dauphin Charles by his father in 1421 provided a third. Was the Valois king true king of France? This was a moral problem — a problem clearly felt by the abbot of St.-Michel but also by old Jean Batiffol of Bialon,[3] and one which, in a period when, as we shall see, the king was a sacerdotal figure it would be unwise to deride. And the legal and moral questions provided at least an excuse for legitimate rebellion: the question of the succession thus enhanced the political problem of the kings of France, the problem of making real the hopeful claims of sovereignty.

The Valois had thus to be justified. We have already touched upon some of the justifications.[4] The fortune of war gave the literary adherents of the line their most immediate problem. The capture of Jean II at Poitiers in 1356 was a blow which had naturally to be parried. The author of the *Tragicum argumentum de miserabili statu regni Francie*[5] argued that the king's capture gave him immortal glory, even though it left the country, by a wonderful contradiction, both with a head and headless. The author of the *Complainte sur la bataille de Poitiers*,[6] too, praised the king for his stand; but he dealt with the problem of the headless kingdom rather more dramatically.

[1] Cf. G. A. Knowlson, *Jean V, duc de Bretagne et l'Angleterre (1399–1442)* (Arch. hist. Bretagne, 2: Rennes, 1964) pp. 3–4.

[2] P. Chaplais, 'Un Message de Jean de Fiennes à Edouard II et le projet de démembrement du royaume de France (janvier 1317)', in R. *Nord.* XLIII (1961) 145–8.

[3] See above, p. 61.

[4] See above, p. 65.

[5] ed. A. Vernet, in *Annu.-B. Soc. Hist. France* (1962–3) pp. 134, 136.

[6] ed. C. de Beaurepaire, in *Bibl. Ec. Chartes*, ser. 3 II (1951) 262.

When the king saw himself taken, he said from great constance [he wrote]
'This is Jean de Valois and not the king of France!
Many shields will be broken and many a lance
Ere with ransom the French king your coffers enhance.'

With this deliberate scission of his two bodies, the private and the public, Jean II was made to save the second while the first was taken. But his captor, Edward prince of Wales, and his rival, Edward III, were careful to honour Jean de Valois as king. Nevertheless, to turn defeat into glory was no mean achievement. The myth (if it was one) seems to have spread rapidly: as early as 12 December 1356 Jean II could afford to be modest about the 'praise and honour' which, he had heard, the Parisians were according him for his part in the battle.[1]

Some fifty years later, after the recovery of Jean II's losses by means far from spectacularly honourable, Jean de Montreuil could wonder whether it would not have been better for Jean II to have run away — and Philippe VI from Crécy too.[2] In the fifteenth century other arguments appear. The proofs of legitimacy tended now to conflate with the proofs of submission. Jean Juvenal des Ursins argued in the early 1430s that the king should be loved and honoured because he was in some special way beloved of God, who by giving him victory had declared him true king of France.[3] Others adduced the mission of Jeanne d'Arc.[4] Robert Blondel exhorted the French to recognise the dauphin Charles as their lord

For his safety is our safety,
And his ruin is our loss.[5]

The very misfortunes of France reinforced the image of the saviour of France. And in their efforts to claim legitimacy for the Valois and to claim obedience in the midst of civil war for the king of France, the men of letters created or enhanced the various elements of an idea of a ruler effectively untouchable by man.

[1] R. Delachenal, *Hist. de Charles V*, II (1909) 50–1.
[2] *Opera*, ed. E. Ornato, I, part 1, *Epistolario* (Turin, 1963) 327.
[3] P.S. Lewis, 'Jean Juvenal des Ursins and the Common Literary Attitude towards Tyranny in Fifteenth-century France', in *Medium Aevum*, XXXIV (1965) 105 n 15.
[4] For instance, Robert Blondel (*Œuvres*, ed. A. Héron (Soc. Hist. Normandie) I (Rouen, 1891) 460).
[5] Ibid. p. 82.

Myths of kingship

What was the king? He was human, certainly; but around an often all too human frame an unearthly light had by the end of the middle ages developed. The king was far more than man alone. He was anointed with a chrism itself the subject of a miracle.[1] Unction had first been used at the coronation of Pepin in 751 in an attempt to legitimise an usurpation. Already by the ninth century the legend of the *sainte ampoule* had been developed, possibly already quite deliberately by those around the king. The oil for Clovis' baptism had, it was thought, been held up on its way to the cathedral in Reims; a dove (or, from the tenth century, an angel) descended from heaven with a phial for St.-Rémy, which was afterwards either inexhaustible or miraculously refilled for each coronation. The significance of royal unction was considerable. 'Because of the holy unction with the chrism', wrote Nicolas de Clamanges to Henry VI king of France and England, 'kings should be made holy in the Christian religion in the likeness of priests';[2] and Pierre Masuyer, bishop of Arras, had thought in 1380 that 'the king ... has not only temporality but divinity too, because he is anointed'.[3] Bishops, too, were anointed; and at his coronation, in the later fifteenth century, if not before, the king's tunic was 'to be in the fashion of a tunic that a sub-deacon wears when he serves at mass'; his mantle was to be 'raised on the left, as one raises the chasuble of a priest'.[4]

The christological tradition at once removed the king from other men; and the necessities of the Gallican controversy reinforced the schism. 'A king is verily like a prelate,' wrote Jean Juvenal des Ursins with the latter in mind in the mid-fifteenth century; 'you, my sovereign lord, are not simply a layman but a prelate of the church, the first in your kingdom after the pope, the right arm of the church'.[5] But it was during the course of the fourteenth century, and especially in the reign of Charles V, that what became the stock position in the fifteenth

[1] M. Bloch, *Les Rois thaumaturges* (1961) pp. 224 ff.
[2] *Opera omnia* (Leiden, 1613) p. 350.
[3] F. Cheyette, 'La Justice et le pouvoir royal à la fin du Moyen âge français', in R. *hist. Droit*, 4 ser. XL (1962) 391.
[4] *Arch. admin. de la ville de Reims*, ed. P. Varin (Docs inéd. sur l'hist. de France) II, part I (1843) 570n, 572n; cf. Bloch, op. cit. p. 482.
[5] Lewis, 'Jean Juvenal des Ursins', p. 104.

century was developed. It was quite clear by the 1390s that the king was, in Gerson's words, '*très-chrétien*' (an adjective which became almost a formal title and which distinguished the king of France from other Christian kings less favoured of God), 'king by miracle consecrated, king spiritual and priestly'.[1] From the Bible terms like 'priestly kingship' and 'royal priesthood' were culled; and Jean Golein, in a treatise on the coronation written under Charles V, could argue that the significance of the putting on of the royal robes by the anointed king was 'that he relinquishes the worldly state which previously he held to take that of the religion royal'.[2] Little extra touches were made: in the coronation order of Charles V the king wears for the first time gloves;[3] the parallel with the episcopate was thus reinforced. And already from the reign of Philippe VI — another king who needed what support he could get — the king of France took communion in both kinds;[4] his priestly nature could not be clearer.

Strictly speaking a king's coronation was simply a blessing upon a king already created; but popular feeling seems to have been that a king was hardly a proper king without coronation and unction.[5] And unction conferred another element in the miraculous image of the king. To the man of letters Golein, mixed consecration and royal race gave the ruler ability to touch for scrofula, the king's evil; though for others this thaumaturgic power had a more mysterious origin 'which is hidden from us' and 'cannot be investigated by man'.[6] Charles V, again, was the first king expressly to state that he touched for the evil by virtue of unction;[7] and his entourage was prepared to go to embarrassing lengths in its discussion of this royal attribute. In his preface to his translation of St. Augustine's *Civitas dei* Raoul de Presles told Charles V 'you have such a virtue and power, which is given and attributed to you by God, that you perform miracles in your own lifetime'; an opinion shared at the time by Etienne de Conty and a century later by the French clergy in council.[8]

By this time Clovis himself was thought to have participated in the miracle, as he did in a number of peripheral legends again enhanced

---

[1] Bloch, op. cit. p. 213. [2] Clamanges, op. cit. p. 350; Bloch, op. cit. p. 483.
[3] Ibid. p. 204. [4] Ibid. p. 205. [5] Ibid. pp. 217–21.
[6] Ibid. pp. 136 n 1, 224. [7] Ibid. p. 135.
[8] Ibid. pp. 92 n 1, 136 n 2; J. Combet, *Louis XI et le Saint-Siège* (1903) p. 258.

under Charles V.[1] There had been lilies on the arms of France since
Philippe-Auguste; about 1350 the legend arose that they appeared
miraculously on Clovis' shield; he won the ensuing battle of Tolbiac
and became a Christian. The story was picked up by Raoul de Presles;
it was later modified in its details but the definitive version had appeared
round about 1400. The oriflamme was in origin simply the banner of
St.-Denis; it became a royal banner after Philippe I's reign and a legend
developed around it; but the supernatural element in the story was
again the work of Charles' entourage. Now the tattered scarlet silk
originated as a flaming lance in the hand of Charlemagne (or, in the
fifteenth-century version, Clovis), appearing to the emperor of
Constantinople in a dream; an angel explained that he would save the
emperor's estates from the Saracens.[2]

These, then, were the legends of the royal line of France, conveniently
rehearsed by Guillaume Cousinot at the Estates-general of 1468: 'the
benefits and graces granted [the crown] . . . by God, such as the *sainte
ampoule*, the fleurs-de-lis, the oriflamme, the curing of the king's evil . . .'[3]
They supported a crown 'singularly decorated with grace and celestial
prerogative', a royal line which ran resoundingly from king Clovis and
St.-Charlemagne and St.-Louis to Charles VIII.[4] In this succession
Louis IX held a special place. As the descendants of the elected Hugh
Capet tried to attach themselves to the line of Charlemagne, so Philippe
de Valois stressed his attachment to that of St.-Louis, 'from whose
stock we are recognised as descending'.[5] His ancestor St.-Louis' memory
was engraven on the heart of Charles V as 'the flower, the ornament,
the light and the mirror, not only to our royal race, but to all Frenchmen;

---

[1] P. S. Lewis, 'Two Pieces of Fifteenth-century Political Iconography.
(a) Clovis touches for the King's Evil', in *J. Warburg and Courtauld Inst.*
XXVII (1964) 317–19; Bloch, op. cit. pp. 229–36.
[2] For a variant version see C. J. Liebman, Jr, 'Un Sermon de Philippe de
Villette, abbé de Saint-Denis, pour la levée de l'oriflamme (1414)', in
Romania, LXVIII (1944–5) 458–9.
[3] Lewis, 'Jean Juvenal des Ursins', p. 105.
[4] Ibid.; J. Masselin, *Journal des Etats généraux de France tenus à Tours en 1484*,
ed. A. Bernier (Docs inéd. sur l'hist. de France: 1835) p. 663.
[5] C. Devic and J. Vaissete, *Hist. gén. de Languedoc*, X (Toulouse, 1885)
'Preuves', col. 933; R. Cazelles, *La Société politique et la crise de la royauté sous
Philippe de Valois* (1958) pp. 96 ff, 164.

his memory shall be blessed until the end of time . . . his life shall be our education'.[1]

This, then, was the line of whose representative Jean de Terre-Vermeille went so far as say that he 'is God on earth'.[2] But there were other ways of proving the majesty of the king. 'A king', thought Gerson, for instance, 'is not only a private person, but also a public power, created for the safety of all the commonalty, as from the head descends and spreads life throughout the whole body.'[3] The idea, derived ultimately from John of Salisbury,[4] that the king was the head of a *corpus mysticum* of which the various groups in society were the members was a popular one. It, and the concept of the king's two bodies[5] touched upon here by Gerson, served again to place the king beyond the normal pale of humankind.

Sovereignty and tyranny

From the concept of the *corpus mysticum* Jean de Terre-Vermeille at the end of Charles VI's reign could argue that a man's duty to his head and lord *qua* subject supervened upon that *qua* vassal.[6] The same distinction was used to practical effect by Louis XI in his dealings with the duke of Brittany.[7] But it was hardly new in the fifteenth century. Already at the beginning of the fourteenth century there was a clear doctrine in the minds of royal lawyers of sovereignty.[8] The idea that the king was emperor in his kingdom[9] derived from the century before.

---

[1] *Rec. gén. des anciennes lois françaises*, ed. F. A. Isambert *et al.* v (n.d.) 419.

[2] Lewis, 'Jean Juvenal des Ursins', p. 104.   [3] Ibid. p. 106.

[4] *Policraticus*, ed. C. C. J. Webb, 1 (Oxford, 1909) 282–4. Cf. H. Liebeschütz, 'John of Salisbury and Pseudo-Plutarch', in *J. Warburg and Courtauld Inst.* VI (1943) 33–9.

[5] E. Kantorowicz, *The King's Two Bodies* (Princeton, 1957).

[6] Lewis, 'Jean Juvenal des Ursins', p. 106 n25.

[7] B. A. Pocquet du Haut-Jussé, 'Une Idée politique de Louis XI: la sujétion éclipse la vassalité', in *R. hist.* CCXXVI (1961) 383–98.

[8] P. Chaplais, 'La Souveraineté du roi de France et le pouvoir législatif en Guyenne au début du xive siècle', in *Moyen Age*, LXIX (1963) 450–2.

[9] A. Bossuat, 'La Formule, "Le Roi est empereur en son royaume". Son Emploi au xve siècle devant le Parlement de Paris', in *R. hist. Droit*, ser. 4 XXXIX (1961) 371–81; R. Feenstra, 'Jean de Blanot et la formule "Rex

It was important not so much in repelling the pretensions of the
emperor of the Holy Roman Empire or of the pope to universal
dominion, as in repelling the claims of princes inside the kingdom that
the king was only *primus inter pares*. In the christological tradition, as we
have seen, the king had always been more than that; but it had become
increasingly clear that the king's legal position too was imperial. To the
lawyers of Philippe IV his authority was without appeal; his appeal
court was the final court. His authority was shared with no-one; the
peers of France were each other's peers, not the king's. His sovereignty
was imprescriptible and inalienable; it was monarchic power *par
excellence*, power to which feudal barriers were nothing, power exercised
over all the subjects of the kingdom: power to legislate, power to
judge, power to control.

The concept of such sovereignty thus preceded our period; but
during our period it was incessantly in the minds of those who accepted
and so created the image of the king-emperor. The king was made the
noblest Roman of them all. Jean Juvenal des Ursins called Charles VII
'emperor, victorious, august'.[1] 'All emperors', thought the *premier
Président* of the Parlement of Paris in 1498, '. . . have much respect for
their senates and sovereign courts . . . as had Octavian, Hadrian,
Trajan . . .'[2] The assertion of the overriding sovereignty of the king
was constantly on the lips of the kings' advocates in the Parlement. In
1491 the king's proctor-general argued that discussion by others'
advocates of royal authority should be forbidden; it was sacrilege to
discuss it, 'for the authority of the king is much greater than the
advocates could express it and it is not subject to the opinions of the
doctors who have tried to talk about it'.[3]

In the same way the king could be regarded as above the law. It was
clear to Charles V in 1374 that the prince was *legibus solutus*.[4] Although

Franciae in regno suo princeps est" ', in *Etudes . . . Gabriel Le Bras*, II (1965)
885–95.
   [1] '. . . empereur, victorieulx, auguste . . .' ('Verba mea auribus percipe,
Domine', Bibl. nat. MS fr. 2701, fo. 86ʳ).
   [2] P. Imbart de La Tour, *Les Origines de la Réforme*, 2nd ed. 1 (Melun, 1948)
41 n 1.
   [3] R. Delachenal, *Hist. des avocats au Parlement de Paris, 1300–1600* (1885)
pp. 203–7.
   [4] *Ordonnances des rois de France de la troisième race*, VI, ed. D. Secousse (1741) 29.

the *Livres de Jostice et de Plet*, composed about the mid-thirteenth century, could argue that 'the prince is not above the law, but the law is above the prince; which gave him such privilege as he had',[1] the text is doubtful; and though Beaumanoir a little later thought that the king should act and make law only 'by very great counsel' his emphasis on conciliar restraint was very much less than that imposed upon the king by Bracton in England.[2] In the fourteenth and fifteenth centuries it was generally agreed that the king should conserve the laws. As Pierre Salmon wrote to Charles VI at the beginning of the fifteenth century, 'the virtue and worth of a king is assessed when he keeps his laws and ordinances and makes others keep them; and one sees a king in default in the matter when they are not well kept, and when the king hasn't the eye or the mind to keep them and see that they're well kept'.[3] The idea of immutability of the positive laws was an old one; and so was the idea that the king should submit to them. Jean Courtecuisse could be both a common lawyer and an Aristotelian when he argued in 1413 that 'once a law is made and provided that it is reasonable, the prince cannot, nor must he in good practice break it or go against it; for, as Aristotle says in the fifth book of the *Politics*, "Princes are lords of things not provided for by the laws, but of the laws themselves they are not" '.[4] Gerson thought the king should obey the law in imitating the submission of Christ; Jean Meschinot that he should do so in anticipating the chilly equality of the grave:

> Lords, you are not of other coin
> Than the poor common people;
> Make yourselves subject to the law,
> For certainly you will die like one
> Of the very poorest.[5]

Jean Juvenal des Ursins, too, thought that a king submitted to the laws.[6] 'Suppose . . .' he wrote, 'that . . . [the prince] is above the law;

---

[1] ed. P. N. Rapetti (Docs inéd. sur l'hist. de France: 1850) p. 6.

[2] *Coutumes de Beauvoisis*, ed. A. Salmon (Coll. de textes pour servir à l'étude et à l'enseignement de l'hist.) II (1900) 257; S. J. T. Miller, 'The Position of the King in Bracton and Beaumanoir', in *Speculum*, XXXI (1956) 276 ff.

[3] *Les Demandes faites par le roi Charles VI . . . avec les réponses de Pierre Salmon*, ed. G. A. Crapelet (1833) p. 32.

[4] Lewis, 'Jean Juvenal des Ursins', p. 107.   [5] Ibid. pp. 107–8.

[6] Ibid. p. 108.

for it is a great thing to be a king or a prince. But it is a still greater thing to submit the kingdom to good practice and to the laws. . . . I do not wish to say that the emperor or the king should be confined by or subject to the laws, so that he is unable when it seems proper to him to do the opposite and alter and change the laws. . . . But he should not do so without just and reasonable cause and provided that he wishes, as he should, to submit to the laws; for otherwise it might be called a tyrant's action and not a king's . . .' 'There may be many around princes', he wrote, 'who persuade them to maintain that it is quite licit for a prince to do as he will, and that his will is held to be law, since *what pleases the prince has the power of law.* Alas! They should attribute this power to that which a true prince should do, in such a way that this will cannot be attributed to the will of a tyrant.' The same distinction was made by the *premier Président* of the Parlement of Paris in 1527: 'We know well that you [the king] are above the laws and that the laws or ordinances cannot constrain you. . . . But what we mean to say is that you do not wish, nor should you wish to do all that which you could, only that which is good and equitable.'[1] The will of the prince is a true will only when it is good. Otherwise it is the will of a tyrant. The distinction is perfectly clear.

Resistance and obedience

It was a distinction which appeared equally clearly when theorists considered, in terms of christological or of *corpus mysticum* doctrines, the question of obedience and resistance. Resistance to a king so clearly favoured by God was naturally sacrilege; this was accepted by Gerson in 1405 as well as by Jean de Terre-Vermeille in 1420.[2] Treason acquired this added stigma: resistance to royal command, it was thought in the Parlement in 1490, was 'to fall into sacrilege and the crime of *lèse-majesté*'.[3] Yet divine right did not presuppose despotism. It could be argued, as Jean Juvenal des Ursins argued, that the vicariate of God implied a number of duties. Like many medieval arguments the theory of sacerdotal kingship could be turned inside out. 'Who, coming from the

---

[1] G. Zeller, *Les Institutions de la France au xvie siècle* (1948) p. 80.
[2] Lewis, 'Jean Juvenal des Ursins', p. 105.
[3] Imbart de La Tour, op. cit. p. 39 n2.

house of God, would in pride make God his enemy?' asked Nicolas de Clamanges; and Robert Blondel, through St.-Louis, warned Charles VII to 'remember well that this most noble kingdom is amongst all kingdoms most especially made and governed by divine ordinance and not by human disposition. And when it pleases God he may, for some hidden cause, take away the government from one person, if he is unsuitable, and give it to another who will profit the kingdom more.'[1] 'Do not forget', he wrote, 'the most worthy mystery of your coronation, in which you swore and promised to give freedom to your people, and that your oath should be carried out by you for the safety of your soul; for otherwise you must fear that that Sovereign, Emperor of heaven and earth, in whose hand are all kingdoms of the world, including yours, should in sudden vengeance turn the sword of his wrath upon you, if you should be ungrateful for the great benefits he has done you.' Jean Juvenal said much the same thing at considerably greater length.[2] 'God Paradise to tyrants denies', wrote Jean Meschinot:[3] the wrath of God in heaven, even the wrath of God on earth, were things with which to threaten a prince. But how far was one justified in advancing the hand of God?

The theory of the *corpus mysticum* equally could be treated ambivalently. Jean de Terre-Vermeille, in the midst of civil war, could use it to argue for almost a Hobbesian degree of obedience by the members of the body politic to the head and single will: rebellion was unnatural.[4] But, again, obligations and threats could be derived from the anthropomorphic idea. If, argued Gerson some years before civil war actually broke out, 'by the teaching of nature all the members of a true body risk themselves for the safety of the head, so must true subjects in a mystical body for their lord . . . on the other hand, the head should keep in order and govern the other members, because otherwise all is destroyed; for head without members may not endure'.[5] Therefore the ruler has

---

[1] Op. cit. p. 350; Blondel, op. cit. pp. 461, 472.
[2] 'Verba mea auribus percipe, Domine', Bibl. nat. MS fr. 2701, folios 86[v] ff.
[3] Lewis, 'Jean Juvenal des Ursins', p. 106.
[4] Ibid.
[5] Ibid. pp. 106–7. 'Quant prince demande plus au peuple que il ne pueut fournir', wrote Christine de Pisan about the same time, 'et que peuple murmure contre prince & se rebelle par desobeissance, tel discort perist tout ensemble; et pour ce conclus que union daccord est la conservation de tout

natural obligations to the subjects; if rebellion was unnatural so was tyranny.

> The prince is governor and head [wrote Jean Meschinot]
> Of the members of the body politic;
> It would do very grievous harm
> If he became paralytic
> Or wished to hold to a way oblique.
> In the position for which he's made
> All is lost unless he does things well.[1]

For Jean Juvenal des Ursins, too, the head had as much need of the body as the body had of the head. 'You', he said to the king, 'are the soul of the commonwealth; and never did the soul destroy the body, but always the body the soul. . . . You are also head of this body; and would it not be great tyranny if the head of a human creature should destroy the heart, hands and feet? Then must the head perish . . .' This has a true Gersonian ring.[2] But once more we are on the brink of discussing resistance; and had not in England in 1326 the text *Caput meum doleo* been used to preach resistance?[3]

What should one do with a tyrant? Gerson dealt with the problem in his sermon *Vivat rex* in 1405.[4] Two allegorical figures, Dissimulation and Sedition, were let in to have their say. 'You must temporise, I tell you. You must dissimulate . . .' said Dissimulation. 'Alas!' said Sedition, 'where are now the worthy and valiant champions of the commonwealth, who for the public good once risked their bodies and livelihood against the tyrants? . . . Where are now such persons to deliver this kingdom from miserable oppression? They must put into action what Seneca said, that there is no sacrifice as pleasing to God as the death of a tyrant.' But, thought Gerson, 'dissimulation suffers from timidity, sedition from temerity, discretion holds the right royal road, without

---

ledit corps de la policie' ('Le Livre du corps de policie', British Museum, Harleian MS 4410, fol 56ᵛ).

[1] Lewis, 'Jean Juvenal des Ursins', p. 107. The same view appears in Christine de Pisan's *Livre du corps de policie*: 'est il necessaire pour bien gouverner le corps de la policie publique que le chief soit sain, cestassavoir vertueux, car sil estoit malade tout sen sentiroit' (British Museum, Harleian MS 4410, fo. 2ʳ).

[2] Lewis, 'Jean Juvenal des Ursins', p. 107.

[3] *Chron. Galfridi Le Baker*, ed. E. Maunde Thompson (Oxford, 1889) p. 23.

[4] Lewis, 'Jean Juvenal des Ursins', pp. 108–9.

going off to the right towards dissimulation or to the left towards sedition'. But in what direction did this right royal road run? In Gerson's case with a rather uneasy course distinctly leftwards. Admittedly he argued that, since all power came from God, resistance was sacrilege, especially against the king of France, whose power had especial divine approbation; but he also quoted (and under the stern eye of Discretion) 'it is lawful to repel force by force', and he did argue that resistance was legitimate. Subjects should try first to cure the ruler; immediate tyrannicide would be madness; sedition, 'popular rebellion without rhyme and reason . . . is often worse than tyranny'; care should be taken that the results of resistance are not worse than its causes. 'There is a marvellous need of great discretion, prudence and temperance in getting rid of tyranny; the wise philosophers should be consulted, the jurists, the legists, the theologians and also men of great natural prudence and great experience'; and one should be really sure that the tyrant is subverting the whole commonwealth and not simply indulging in a few tyrannical eccentricities. But, on the whole, tyrants did seem to come to unpleasant ends; they should take care to use more reason and, like Theopompus, accept a more limited and more durable seigneury.

But very few writers in fifteenth-century France were as firm on the subject as Gerson. None dealt with the question of tyrannicide specifically in relation to a sovereign. Jean Petit defended it in his notorious justification of Jean *sans peur*'s murder of Louis d'Orléans in 1407; and after Jean *sans peur*'s own demise at Montereau, Jean de Terre-Vermeille on the Armagnac side argued (on rather slender grounds) that 'any inhabitant of the kingdom may kill a notorious tyrant engaged upon destroying the commonwealth, as he would kill any enemy'. But such a tyrant was only a ruler with a title in Terre-Vermeille's eyes unjust.[1] After bright revolutionary days at the first decade or so of the century, discretion totters miserably rightwards towards dissimulation; the right royal road becomes royal indeed. During the war of the Public Weal in the 1460s Jean Meschinot could argue for a rather crude resistance:

[1] E. de Monstrelet, *Chron.*, ed. L. Douët-d'Arcq (Soc. Hist. France) I (1857) 178–242; A. Coville, *Jean Petit. La Question du tyrannicide au commencement du xvᵉ siècle* (1932) pp. 133–68; F. Schoenstedt, *Der Tyrannenmord im Spätmittelalter* (Berlin, 1938) pp. 1 ff; Lewis, 'Jean Juvenal des Ursins', p. 109. Robert Blondel was prepared to accept the tyrannicide of Jean *sans peur* and urge (again on the slenderest grounds) that of Henry VI (op. cit. pp. 125, 317).

Kings are bound —
To what duty? To nourish peaceably —
Who? Their subjects. If they don't? Let them fall![1]

Thomas Basin had been involved in the war and, having burned his boats, he, too, could afford to be uninhibited. He saw in the revolt a noble cause betrayed by ignoble behaviour; and some years after the war he justified, on not very comprehensive grounds, the right of subjects to coerce a tyrant.[2] Given his hatred for Louis XI his views were a model of Gersonian discretion; and, however faintly, the old Gersonian battle-cry of *vim vi repellere licet* was heard once more in France.

But it caught no echo. The articulate members of the late fifteenth-century generation as a whole did not want to resist. Though they pointed to the customary awful warnings of scripture, antiquity and even recent history, though they fulminated against tyranny, they refused to justify action against it. The king should be left to God was the normal reaction in the fifteenth century to the question of resistance.[3] For Jean Juvenal des Ursins, revolts such as the war of the Public Weal were 'forbidden and prohibited, and to commit the crime of treason'; and he was prepared to use arguments similar to Jean de Terre-Vermeille's against such unnatural behaviour.[4] The loyal obedience of the oppressed people was glorified. The need to deride the English claim to the throne of France and the need to justify submission came together in the common literary attitude towards the regicidal proclivities of the English.[5] With some prurience the men of letters considered the holocaust of martyred monarchs: twenty-two, twenty-six of them, or indeed, one author thought towards the end of the fifteenth century 'all their kings, almost, have . . . been killed, down to the present day, either by the common people or by their close relatives'.[6] 'No-one', thought the chancellor of France at the Estates-general of 1484, 'can find in the faithful people of France such disloyalty, such

[1] Lewis, 'Jean Juvenal des Ursins' p. 113.
[2] *Hist. de Louis XI*, ed. C. Samaran, I (Classiques de l'hist. de France au Moyen âge, 26: 1963) 177 ff.
[3] Lewis, 'Jean Juvenal des Ursins', p. 110.   [4] Ibid. p. 113.
[5] Lewis, 'Two Pieces of Fifteenth-century Political Iconography. (b) The English Kill Their Kings', pp. 319–20.
[6] Lewis, 'Jean Juvenal des Ursins', p. 103 n 2.

stigmata of crime.'[1] And if a king should say, thought Commynes, that 'my subjects are indeed so good and loyal that they refuse me nothing I ask of them; I am more feared and obeyed and served than any prince on earth by subjects who bear all evils and all harshnesses more patiently and feel their grudges less' this would be 'great praise to him and the very truth'.[2]

The duke of Anjou, thought Guillaume the *juponnier*, the doublet-maker, 'overcome with wine' in Orléans on 29 December 1384, 'is dead and damned, and the king St.-Louis with him, and all the others. . . . *Estront, estront de roy et de roy!* We have no king but God! Do you think they've got rightfully what they've got? They tax me and tax me, and it hurts them because they can't have everything that belongs to us. What's the king got to do, taking what I earn with my needle away from me? I'd rather the king was dead, I'd rather all kings were dead than have my son have a pain in his little finger.'[3] This was a much more understandable reaction to rapacious government. About the same time an inhabitant of Rabastens-de-Bigorre called Charles VI 'king of *merde*, king of figs'.[4] Such men might not appreciate 'the most worthy status of the high crown of France', which, according to Christine de Pisan, Charles V intended to impress upon his successors by the 'royal ceremony' of an impressive cortège upon the high road[5] and also, presumably, upon the bystander. Atheists in this world of the royal religion thus certainly existed. 'God knows what . . . [the people] say of you,' Jean Juvenal des Ursins told Charles VII about 1440, 'they say, "Where is our king?"; and some say that they cry to God vengeance on you yourself.'[6] God was naturally on their side, 'for the poor people are ordained by God to be judges of those who do them wrong, and God does not save them'. The example of the subtraction of obedience from the pope at the turn of the previous century was one which might be

[1] Masselin, op. cit. p. 38.

[2] *Mémoires*, ed. J. Calmette and G. Durville, II (Classiques de l'hist. de France au Moyen âge, 5: 1925) 218–19.

[3] *Choix de pièces inéd. relatives au règne de Charles VI*, ed. L. Douët d'Arcq (Soc. Hist. France) I (1863) 59.

[4] Devic and Vaissete, op. cit. IX (Toulouse, 1886) 910 n 3 (=p. 911).

[5] *Le Livre des fais et bonnes meurs du sage roy Charles V*, ed. S. Solente (Soc. Hist. France) I (1936) 51.

[6] Lewis, 'Jean Juvenal des Ursins', p. 111.

followed in a general subversion.[1] But here, at least, there was no denial of kings wholesale; and in fact the general conservatism of the later middle ages seems to have affected the *menu peuple*, the small people, as much as the great. How many, even if they did not share fully in the myth of christological kingship, in the myth of the natural head, in the lawyers' idea of sovereignty, how many were prepared to hear with happy approbation Charles VII praised in the *Mistère du siège d'Orléans* by the Maid herself, so clearly favoured of God:

> Obedience all we owe to him;
> He is our king, the well-obeyed,
> He is our prince and our sovereign.
> It would be bad if we had failed him,
> Nor should we ever put from our minds
> That he is the king by right divine?[2]

Nor were great nobles in their seditions anxious to change the established order of things. They were rebels; but they were hardly revolutionary.

> Members [Robert Blondel had written] put yourselves in array
> To give succour to your head;
> Defend your noble king
> Who suffers such great misfortune.[3]

The great misfortune of the Valois had thus indeed, 'by a wonderful contradiction', created for them a high image of regality. Already at the end of the fourteenth century the danger of over-stressing divinity had been perceived. Jean Golein criticised Raoul de Presles for his views on the miraculous in Charles V's touching for the king's evil, 'so that those who come after, in time to come, less subtle and less experienced in knowledge or sound in opinion than is my ... lord, shall not derive from it the occasion of vain glory, or think themselves saints performing miracles'.[4] But to too many of those whose business it was to gild the tarnished image of Valois kingship such considerations do not seem to have occurred.

---

[1] Ibid. p. 112 n 57.
[2] ed. F. Guessard and E. de Certain (Docs inéd. sur l'hist. de France: 1862) pp. 779–80.
[3] Op. cit. p. 83.   [4] Bloch, op. cit. p. 489.

Bridles for the king

In such a welter of divinity it is hardly surprising that the contemporary theory of the sovereignty of the people[1] sank almost without a trace. Earthly monarchy came from men, thought the knight in the *Songe du verger* trenchantly;[2] but this straightforward statement was deprived of much of its force by being diluted with the christological theory. Gerson might let slip in *Vivat rex* the view that 'kings and princes were created in the beginning by the common agreement of all';[3] but he laid far more emphasis upon the king's spiritual aspect. Only once, it seems, was the scholastic theory of popular sovereignty really proclaimed in France: by the far from disinterested Philippe Pot, agent for the Beaujeu in the Estates-general of 1484.[4] 'Histories teach,' he argued, 'and I learned from my seniors, that in the beginning kings were made by the suffrage of the sovereign people. . . . How can flatterers attribute all power to the prince, when it is in part made by the people?' But Philippe Pot's object was clearly to argue that the assembly *qua* sovereign people should choose the government of the regency — and choose it in the Beaujeu interest;[5] and his argument was far from being accepted by his fellow-members of the Estates. Their recourse was to the less clearly formulated body of notions about their position and about the king's, derived ultimately from precedent, which might have some claim to be considered as 'fundamental laws'.

Such matters as the succession to the throne, the inalienability of the *domaine*, consent to taxation and the preservation of local and group privileges acquired around themselves in the course of time a body of doctrine which might or might not be respected in practice. The question of the succession was naturally complicated by the English claim to the throne of France. The exclusion of women derived, not from the Salic Law (which was first invoked in its aid in the reign of

[1] A. Lemaire, *Les Lois fondamentales de la monarchie française d'après les théoriciens de l'Ancien régime* (1907) pp. 29–35, 45–54, 63–70.

[2] J. L. Brunet, in *Traitez des droits et libertez de l'Eglise gallicane*, II (1731) 79–80.

[3] *Sermon fait devant le roy Charles sixiesme* (the sermon *Vivat rex* of 1405) (1505 ?) sig. c ii^r.

[4] Masselin, op. cit. pp. 146–8.

[5] H. Bouchard, 'Philippe Pot et la démocratie aux Etats généraux de 1484', in *A. Bourgogne*, XXII (1950) 33–40.

Jean II), but from custom, possibly tendentiously argued in the cases of the succession to Louis X and to Philippe V, and hardened by the *fait accompli* of their successors and the arguments of English lawyers.[1] Custom, again, was the foundation of the right of the eldest son to succeed to the throne. The arguments of Jean de Terre-Vermeille again confirmed and hardened the theory; by the time it reached Jean Juvenal des Ursins it seems to have been accepted that 'the king cannot prejudice the heir of his body, nor alienate or deliver the kingdom into the hand of another'.[2] From this theory it could be argued, as it was argued by Terre-Vermeille (against the pretensions of the duke of Burgundy and in defence of the rights of the dauphin to the regency when Charles VI was incapacitated), that the eldest son had an automatic right in the kingdom on the death, deposition, madness or absence of the king;[3] and the arrangements of the treaty of Troyes added, from Charles VII's point of view, force to his argument. And from a wider background of ideas the theory of the inalienability of the *domaine* could take shape. Jean Juvenal des Ursins argued that 'the king has only a kind of administrative right and the usufruct, which he enjoys for his life alone'.[4] Again a general theory was made precise and hardened firmly by political events. The question of peace with England constantly raised the cognate problem of the partition of the kingdom; it could be argued 'with a great deal of vigour' by Jacques Jouvenel des Ursins at the Estates of Orléans in 1439 that 'since the king was only a simple usufructuary of the crown, he could not alienate the least part of his

---

[1] Lemaire, op. cit. pp. 42–5, 54–62; Cazelles, op. cit. pp. 51–2; *Joannes de Terra Rubea contra rebelles suorum regum* (Lyon, 1526) fo. 15ᵛ. For the problem of the origin of the use of the Salic law in the debate between England and France, see P. Viollet, 'Comment les femmes ont été exclues, en France, de la succession à la couronne', in *Mémoires de l' Acad. Inscript.* xxxiv, part 2 (1895) 125–78; R. E. Giesey, 'The Juristic Basis of Dynastic Right to the French Throne', in *Trans. Am. philosophical Soc.* NS LI (1961) 17–20.

[2] '. . . et ne peult le roy prejudicier a son heritier descendant de sa cher ne aliener ou baillier le royaulme en aultre main que a celle auquel il doit venir par succession hereditale' ('Traictie compendieux de la querelle de France contre les Anglois', Bibl. nat. MS fr. 17512, fo. 12ᵛ).

[3] Terre-Vermeille, op. cit. fo. 21ʳ.

[4] '. . . et a proprement parler le roy ny a que une maniere de admin[i]stration et usage pour enjoyr sa vie durant tant seulement' ('Traictie compendieux', fo. 12ᵛ).

domaine without the consent of his Estates'.[1] But such grand views were not necessarily universally accepted. Both Jean and Guillaume Jouvenel des Ursins were present at the Estates of 1468; but neither of them, nor any other member of the assembly, produced the view to so alarming a ruler as Louis XI. The question was the alienation of Normandy in apanage to Charles of France. Louis had summoned the meeting to provide legal cover for his withdrawal of the duchy, which he had been forced to grant to his brother in the war of the Public Weal. But the only argument which seemed acceptable besides those of expediency was that article of the coronation oath in which the king swore not to alienate the goods of the crown: an article perhaps less confiningly useful to a king who wished to break his engagements.[2]

Arguably the fact that the Estates-general of the kingdom were consulted about the problem at all was a tacit proof for the view that they had to be consulted: but a wider problem is raised here. The basis of all 'fundamental laws' was custom, made more or less precise by the views of theorists. But how was custom preserved? Was it, as Jacques Jouvenel des Ursins thought in 1439, preserved by a representative assembly? It could be argued, in defence of his view that kings had consulted assemblies about alienations of crown land, that the Estates of Languedoil had been consulted in 1359 during the negotiations of the treaty of Brétigny; but there is very little evidence otherwise, and it is too much to make consent by the Estates to partition of the kingdom a 'fundamental law'. For in fact the accepted idea of the representative assembly was much less advanced than this. It could be argued, as it was argued on equally specious — or valid — historical evidence by Philippe Pot at the Estates-general of 1484, as we have seen, that the

---

[1] J. Garillot, *Les Etats-généraux de 1439* (Nancy, 1947) p. 15, from a now lost harangue quoted by Legrand.

[2] Arch. com. Rodez, BB 3, folios 53r, 56r, 59v, 63r. The idea of the precept at least may go back to Philippe VI (O. Martin, *L'Assemblée de Vincennes de 1329 et ses conséquences* (Rennes, 1909) pp. 122–3). An oath against alienation of the rights of the crown was certainly part of Charles V's *ordo* (*The Coronation Book of Charles V of France*, ed. E. S. Dewick (H. Bradshaw Soc. 16: 1899) col. 12). But the general concept was in the air in the thirteenth century (C. T. Wood, *The French Apanages and the Capetian Monarchy, 1224–1328* (Harvard, 1966) p. 19). For the broader aspects of the problem see P. N. Riesenberg, *Inalienability of Sovereignty in Medieval Political Thought* (Columbia, 1956).

assembly should choose the council during a regency.[1] But this was an extreme view. Jean de Terre-Vermeille, for instance, denied the Estates (along with the pope and the 'civil body of the kingdom') any right to change the fundamental law of primogeniture.[2] And the same difficulty, the same conflict of views, appeared at every point in the discussion of the place of the assembly in the kingdom. The reasons for this must occupy us considerably later on. But it is enough to say now that rules concerning the unity and inalienability of sovereignty and the *domaine* and the exclusive right of the eldest son to succession and regency were almost entirely non-controversial. Kings could agree with them; subjects could agree with them. They had a reasonable chance of becoming immutable and of being laid up in heaven. Other hopeful rules were not so successful.

The existence of the Estates themselves, as well as of their function as guardians of liberties, privileges and customs, was still a matter for dispute. The doctrine that 'what touches all should be approved by all' could be heard in France; but so could the view that 'it is treason to talk of assembling Estates; it is to diminish the power of the crown'.[3] Indeed, the existence of the Estates themselves was but one of the body of liberties and privileges protected by custom. By the fourteenth century France was a mass of liberties and immunities granted or usurped by individuals and by communities: by towns, by classes, by provinces, by the kingdom itself. The clearest to see quickly are those enshrined in the charters of Philippe IV's reign and in those of 1315–16. In the latter the general aim was to abolish novelties and to get back to the good reign of St.-Louis; economic and financial questions have a large place, especially monetary matters: but an attempt was made to restrict taxation only in Normandy and in Picardy. There were military clauses and clauses dealing with the land law. Various fiscal and administrative matters were brought up; so were the affairs of the officers concerned with them, the administration of justice and general questions of the feudal relations of the king and his vassals.[4] But though it was generally thought that the king ought to respect the privileges of his subjects, many betrayed a certain nervousness about the matter; the

[1] Masselin, op. cit. pp. 148 ff. [2] Op. cit. fo. 30ʳ.
[3] See below, pp. 361–2; Commynes, op. cit. II 219.
[4] A. Artonne, *Le Mouvement de 1314 et les chartes provinciales de 1315* (1912).

world was so very uncertain. The town of Millau in Rouergue may
stand as an example. The privileges of Millau had been granted by the
king of Aragon in 1187; they had afterwards been confirmed by the
king of France; but despite their having them regularly confirmed at
changes in sovereignty and accessions of monarchs the Millavois had
fairly frequently in the fourteenth and fifteenth centuries to fight off the
importunities of royal commissioners raising taxes in the south-west.[1]
Privileges were invaluable; the documents enshrining them were
protected with care; but once granted they did not, like a talisman,
protect the recipients for evermore. It was a matter of constant conflict,
a matter of constant balancing of interests on either side. The under-
currents of politics local and national were never stilled. The rights of
the privileged could only be momentary.

But rights and privileges had a legal content. For Claude de Seyssel
at the beginning of the sixteenth century the king of France was
restrained by three forces.[2] The first was religion. The third was 'police',
established ordinances for the conservation of the kingdom which the
king did not try to contravene — and if he did he was not obeyed. The
second was 'justice': the Parlements, thought Seyssel, 'have been
instituted principally . . . in order to bridle the absolute power which
the kings were wishing to use'. Seyssel recognised that acceptance of
such restraint was the characteristic of the 'good' king: Jean Juvenal's
'true prince' some sixty years earlier, the virtuous ruler of the *premier
Président* of the Parlement of Paris a decade or so later, or, as Seyssel put
it, the 'good king', the *très-chrétien*, the 'father of the people', the 'well-
beloved'.[3] The problem of the tyrant still remained: a ruler who
'wanders beyond the three barriers and wishes to act by unbridled
will . . . is . . . reputed bad, tyrannical, cruel and intolerable; and he
incurs the hatred of . . . his subjects'. It cannot be argued, therefore, that
Seyssel was describing what the king of France did do; like his
predecessors who preached to the monarch, he was describing what he
ought to do.

---

[1] *Docs sur la ville de Millau*, ed. J. Artières (Arch. hist. Rouergue, 7: Millau
1930) *passim*.

[2] *La Monarchie de France*, ed. J. Poujol (1961) pp. 113–20.

[3] Ibid. p. 143. The idea of such submission had appealed also to Gerson
(*Opera*, ed. E. du Pin, II (Antwerp, 1706) col. 279).

But it would be perhaps unwise to assume that the French kings of the later middle ages were in this question of 'justice' necessarily consistently tyrannical. It may well be argued that the Parlements, with their self-confidence and their body of jurisprudence, provided an effective, impersonal 'justice',[1] which even an intemperate king might find tedious to pervert. Louis XI is alleged to have been thoroughly tyrannical in his dealing with the Parlement of Paris.[2] Certainly he was prepared to order it to show favour to particular litigants before it.[3] But the tone of at least one of his letters to it, written in 1480, seems to indicate that the Parlement still needed bullying.[4] The court could ultimately be forced to submit; but it might be a long battle on each occasion. And litigants might still find that the Parlement had submitted without prejudice to their opponents' claims;[5] their case might be reopened when the pressure lifted. And it might perhaps be unwise, too, to assume that the high declarations of royal rights which the *gens du roi* produced with such regularity necessarily inhibited further discussion of the case in question. It might need considerable courage even discreetly to challenge them; but when an opposing advocate began his pleading with the protestation 'that he did not intend or wish in what he said in any way to derogate the king's authority, pre-eminence and prerogatives, but . . . that he wished to augment and increase them with all [his] . . . power', this did not mean that he intended to abandon his case — any more than did that former king's advocate in the Parlement of Poitiers, Jean Juvenal des Ursins, when he employed those cliché phrases in lip-service before he assailed the tyrant monarch in his political treatises.[6]

---

[1] F. Cheyette, 'La Justice et le pouvoir royal à la fin du Moyen âge français', in R. *hist. Droit*, ser. 4 XL (1962) 373–94.

[2] F. Lot and R. Fawtier, *Hist. des institutions françaises au Moyen âge*, II *Institutions royales* (1958) 351–2. He was not, of course, the first to interfere in the Parlement — see F. Aubert, *Le Parlement de Paris de Philippe le bel à Charles VII*, I (1887) 190 ff; G. Ducoudray, *Les Origines du Parlement de Paris et de la justice aux xiii*e *et xiv*e *siècles* (1902) pp. 1018 ff; E. Maugis, *Hist. du Parlement de Paris de l'avènement des rois Valois à la mort d'Henri IV*, I (1913) 372.

[3] See, for instance, *Lettres de Louis XI*, ed. J. Vaesen and E. Charavay (Soc. Hist. France) VIII (1903) p. 165.

[4] Ibid. pp. 183–5.   [5] Ibid. VI (1898) 273 n 1.

[6] R. Delachenal, *Hist. des avocats au Parlement de Paris, 1300–1600* (1885)

But there was a further check to the unbridled will of the king, which was recognised by Claude de Seyssel: 'good counsel', taken by 'all the wisest princes in the world on everything of importance'.[1] The need to take counsel — or the need for a council — was again part of the theorists' stock-in-trade. 'The king', thought Gerson, 'should not only ask for counsel, but believe it and carry it out. . . . A king without prudent counsel is like the head of a body without eyes, without ears and without nose.'[2] 'Will anyone tell me, I beg you, who is the prince or king who was ever so wise that he presumed to govern his kingdom with his single wit alone?' asked Guillaume Fillastre in 1468.[3] The counsel of others was clearly necessary to a ruler; and in so far as it formed his views his will was not his own. For practical, as well as moral, reasons, royal power was rather less than limitless. And as that power spread outward from the king, from the council throughout the kingdom, so it became weakened by the incompetence, the private interests, the wickednesses of those who were the king's agents. It was essentially that weakness that the men of letters of the fifteenth century called tyranny; a tyranny of inefficiency, of insufficient, rather than of over-much, royal power. The king tacitly allows the misdeeds of others: 'he who can prevent evil being done and does not do so', thought Jean Juvenal des Ursins, 'only gives favour to tyrannies'.[4] Gerson had seen the same fault in the unfortunate Charles VI: 'You, prince: you don't commit these evils, it's true; but you put up with them. Take care that God does not give judgement justly against you, saying, "I don't punish you: but if the devils of hell torment you I shan't stop them"; then you'd be for it.'[5] 'Never have such horrible and detestable tyrannies been committed in the kingdom as have been in your time,' Jean Juvenal wrote to Charles VII in the 1450s, 'and they've all been let go

p. 207; J. Juvenal des Ursins, 'Verba mea auribus percipe, Domine', Bibl. nat. MS fr. 2701, fo. 97ᵛ.

[1] Op. cit. pp. 133–4.
[2] P. S. Lewis, 'Jean Juvenal des Ursins and the Common Literary Attitude towards Tyranny in Fifteenth-Century France', in *Medium Aevum*, XXXIV (1965) p. 119.
[3] Ibid.
[4] Ibid. p. 114. For a similar theme in Philippe de Villette, see Liebman, op. cit. pp. 461–2.
[5] Lewis, 'Jean Juvenal des Ursins', p. 119.

in dissimulations, abolitions and remissions.'[1] With the king's agents we must deal later. But the civil service was not the only part of government in which, in Jean Juvenal's view, tyrannical acts occurred. They were occasioned by the army; they were occasioned by taxation.

'Tyranny': the army and taxation

In practice Charles VII in his later years and Louis XI had a permanent army. In principle from 1439 the right to raise troops was the king's alone. Attempts had been made since the tenth century by the Church, by other groups in society and finally by the king to limit private warfare; it was completely forbidden for the first time by St.-Louis in the mid-thirteenth century. He was not obeyed: Philippe IV and his successors were forced on the whole to be less rigorous and to adopt temporising expedients in order to try to extinguish it. Charles V, for instance, recognised the right to private war of nobles when both agreed to fight; he prohibited it absolutely only when one party was ready to go to law.[2] As long as the right existed it was impossible to prohibit private armies; and the desire of nobles to maintain it seems to have waned only during the long course of the Hundred Years War. But the war itself produced a cognate problem. If private warfare was banned during hostilities with England, this was only in order that the nobility should lead their private companies[3] against the enemy rather than against each other. Such companies could be as efficient as any; and they were only too necessary for the safety of the kingdom. But when their main *raison d'être* had largely disappeared in the later 1430s they could also be a danger to the safety of the kingdom. The depredations of the soldiery, as we have seen, were a constant complaint: Nicolas de Clamanges in 1408, the reformers of 1413, Jean Juvenal des Ursins in 1433–40 were much agitated by them.[4] The main purpose of

[1] Ibid.

[2] R. Cazelles, 'La Réglementation royale de la guerre privée de St.-Louis à Charles V et la precarité des ordonnances', in R. *hist. Droit*, ser. 4 XXVIII (1960) 530–48.

[3] For those of Jean duc de Berry, see R. Lacour, *Le Gouvernement de l'apanage de Jean, duc de Berry* (1934) pp. 274–6.

[4] J. Gerson, *Œuvres complètes*, ed. P. Glorieux, II (Tournai, 1960) 116–23; *L'Ordonnance cabochienne*, ed. A. Coville (Coll. de textes pour servir à l'étude et

the great ordinance of 1439[1] was to deal with military misdeeds; but in repressing them the king effectively deprived in principle all his subjects of any right to possess a private army except by his permission. It became treason to raise a company for war; and although patently very many nobles committed it in the latter part of Charles' reign and in that of his successor, the formal prohibition remained.

In 1445 the *compagnies d'ordonnance* were formed.[2] Fifteen captains were chosen; each had under his command 100 *lances* of men chosen by himself; each *lance* consisted effectively of four or five fighting men; and muster-and-review was to be carried out by royal marshals. The companies were to be distributed, at *lance* level, to regional stations — 130 *lances* to Poitou, for instance, 60 to Saintonge — and billeted upon the inhabitants, who could pay, through regional assemblies, a composition tax instead, the *taille des gens d'armes*. A year later the system was extended to Languedoc, which received 500 *lances*. The companies were supplemented about the same time by the territorial organisation of the *francs-archers*, which, despite Louis XI's attempts at reform, could hardly be regarded as much more than ludicrous; to some extent still, by the pale shadow of the feudal *ban* and *arrière-ban*; and the king had his artillery.[3]

In suppressing the disorders of the 1440s the measures of Charles VII seem to have been successful. By 1445–6 Jean Juvenal des Ursins was prepared to admit that pillaging had ceased and by the 1450s to say that the soldiery, for fear of the king, did not now commit misdeeds.[4] In this he agreed with Mathieu d'Escouchy, with Jacques du Clercq and with Georges Chastellain; and even with the author of the hostile *Livre des trahisons de France*.[5] A considerable number of letters of abolition for

à l'enseignement de l'hist.: 1891) pp. 172–5; Lewis, 'Jean Juvenal des Ursins', p. 115.

[1] G. du Fresne de Beaucourt, *Hist. de Charles VII*, III (1885) 384–416.

[2] Ibid. IV (1888) 387–99; Lot and Fawtier, op. cit. II 524–6.

[3] Beaucourt, op. cit. IV 400–4; Lot and Fawtier, op. cit. II 526–35; L. Caillet, *Etude sur les relations de la commune de Lyon avec Charles VII et Louis XI* (Lyon, 1909), pp. 154–6, 229–37; A. Gouron, 'Le Ban et l'arrière-ban d'après les sources languedociennes', in *XVIIe et XVIIIe Congrès Fédér. hist. Languedoc* (1953–4) pp. 87–100; P. Contamine, 'L'Artillerie royale française à la veille des guerres d'Italie', in *A. Bretagne*, LXXI (1964) pp. 221–61.

[4] Lewis, 'Jean Juvenal des Ursins', pp. 115–16.

[5] Beaucourt, op. cit. IV 395–6.

military misdemeanour testifies to pressure upon the soldiery in Poitou in 1446.[1] But Thomas Basin could still complain about its misdemeanours in 1461, and the troubles of Louis XI after 1465 again brought up the question of its discipline.[2] Complaint about pillaging and royal action against both *gens d'ordonnance* and others continued to the end of the reign.[3]

The tyranny of the army was thus seen in its disorder — and in its expense. It was costly and troublesome. In the 1450s Jean Juvenal des Ursins, like Thomas Basin in 1461, thought that it ought to be abolished on grounds of expense and general uselessness (though he saw the danger of trouble if the *compagnies d'ordonnance* were all let loose unpaid).[4] It was not that he saw it as a prop of despotism; he was much more concerned with the fact that the soldiery in leisure gave themselves over to 'every vice, like whoring, gluttony, dicing and wearing thin shirts'.[5] Thomas Basin, when he came to write his history of Charles VII in the 1470s, may have had some feeling that the army was a danger to liberty; but it was perhaps more as an example of what tyrants did, in taxing the people for such an unruly and unnecessary body, than as an actual instrument of their tyranny.[6] And certainly to Jean Juvenal it was its inefficiency rather than its efficiency and the king's lack of control over it rather than his using it as a ready weapon of oppression that constituted its danger to the people.

[1] *Rec. des docs concernant le Poitou contenus dans les reg. de la Chancellerie de France*, ed. P. Guérin, VIII (*1431–1447*) (Arch. hist. Poitou, 29: Poitiers, 1898) 217 ff.

[2] *Hist. des règnes de Charles VII et de Louis XI*, ed. J. Quicherat (Soc. Hist. France) III (1857) 253–4; Arch. com. Rodez, BB 3, fo. 60ʳ; Lewis, 'Jean Juvenal des Ursins', p. 116.

[3] *Rec. de chants hist. français*, ed. Le Roux de Lincy, I (1841) 378; *Lettres de Louis XI*, V (1895) 101–3, IX (1905) 330–40.

[4] 'Verba mea auribus percipe, Domine', folios 96ʳ–97ʳ; Basin, op. cit. ed. Quicherat, III 253–7.

[5] Lewis, 'Jean Juvenal des Ursins', p. 116.

[6] *Hist. de Charles VII*, ed. C. Samaran, II (Classiques de l'hist. de France au Moyen âge, 21: 1944) 25 ff. But cf. the view of Christine de Pisan at the beginning of the century: 'encore aultre office doivent avoir les gens darmes: cest ainsi que le bon chien rameine la brebiz qui se fourvoie, doivent ilz, si voient gent de commune qui par creinte ou paour ou par aucune mauvaise volente se vueullent rebeller & rendre a ladverse partie ou eulx y donner, les ramener a droit chemin soit par menaces ou par eulx en prendre bien garde' ('Le Livre du corps de policie', British Museum, Harleian MS 4410, fo. 9ᵛ).

It was certainly expensive enough. Eleven days before he died Louis XI warranted the roll of payments assigned to the companies of *gens d'armes* for the year 1 January–31 December 1482.[1] It came to 735,394 *livres tournois* for the nineteen companies, for three smaller groups and for the costs of administering them. With the effectively permanent army came effectively permanent taxation. The simplest starting point for the history of royal taxation in France is the reign of Philippe IV. There was, of course, a pre-history of taxation; but only from his reign were taxes taken with a regularity sufficient to cause consistent protest and to bring about some machinery to assuage it. The most successful tax of the reign was one which had its origin in a specious claim by the crown to the service of all its subjects, whosoever men they were. An earlier and equally specious claim that the crown had the right to take the property of any of its subjects in time of evident necessity for the defence of the realm[2] had failed as the basis of a system of taxation, even though nobles had been exempted, apparently on the grounds of their personal military service; its enduring product was a handy crop of theoretical justifications and legal arguments for an (at the time) entirely impractical piece of sovereign 'right' for the crown. Unable to tax universally as the king of England taxed, unable even to tax with a quiet exemption for nobles, the government of Philippe IV was forced back on the redemption of military service as a basis for taxation. Those who did not want to serve in the army 'for the defence of the realm' had to buy their way out;[3] and this fiction remained the foundation of the French system of direct taxation for the rest of the middle ages. The hundredth of 1295 brought in eventually some 350,000 *livres parisis*; the subsidy of 1304 produced well over 700,000 *livres tournois*.[4] Very little restriction was put on the king's power of taxation by the charters of 1315–16;[5] and taxes 'for the defence of the realm' continued. Little information survives about the revenue they produced. As the war with England developed, so did the French

[1] Bibl. nat. MS fr. 26098, no. 2020.

[2] J.R. Strayer, 'Defense of the realm and royal power in France', in *Studi ... Gino Luzzatto*, I (Milan, 1949) 289–96.

[3] J.R. Strayer and C.H. Taylor, *Studies in Early French Taxation* (Harvard 1939) pp. 43 ff.

[4] Lot and Fawtier, op. cit. pp. 230–1 (1304 was a year of bad currency).

[5] Artonne, op. cit. pp. 105 ff.

government's need of money. Taxes of various kinds were taken in various localities.[1] In 1341 a tax on salt, the *gabelle*, was introduced: its early career was chequered, but its life was to be long.[2]

All these taxes were regarded as temporary expedients to raise money for an exceptional situation; all, it was hoped, would be 'done away with for ever' when the crises ended.[3] But they continued. By 1356 it could be thought that 'since the wars began, the people of France have been much burdened, and ceaseless exactions have been made from them, by means of *gabelles*, impositions, subsidies, tenths, thirtieths, loans, prises of corn, of wine, of horses, of carts, and other things, and none of them paid for'.[4] The ceaseless exactions went on. The ransom of Jean II was fixed by the treaty of Brétigny at 3,000,000 *écus d'or*. As a feudal aid it did not in principle need the consent of the kingdom; but it imposed an intolerable burden upon it. A further tax 'for the defence of the ... kingdom'[5] was put on from 1363; and these continued, with variation, until Charles V's death. Two types of main tax were now current: the direct *fouages* put on in 1363, and the indirect *aides*[6] on consumables put on for the ransom in 1360. Amongst the latter were the *gabelle* of salt, which was applied very unevenly over only part of the kingdom. It is clear that the government now relied upon extraordinary revenue to meet other expenses than those incurred because of the war. The revenues of the *domaine* were not wholly negligible; but the king's 'ordinary' expenses could no longer be met out of the king's ordinary income.[7] Taxation was in to stay.

On his deathbed in 1380 Charles V, 'wishing to relieve [the people] to some degree of the taxes imposed upon them', abolished the *fouages*; and

---

[1] G. Dupont-Ferrier, *Etudes sur les institutions financières de la France à la fin du Moyen âge*, II *Les Finances extraordinaires et leur mécanisme* (1932) 2–161.

[2] Ibid. pp. 97–129.

[3] *Ordonnances des rois de France de la troisième race*, II, ed. E. J. de Laurière (1729) 239.

[4] 'Journal des Etats généraux réunis à Paris au mois d'octobre 1356', ed. R. Delachenal, in *Nouvelle R. hist. Droit*, XXIV (1900) 432.

[5] *Arch. admin. de la ville de Reims*, ed. P. Varin (Docs inéd. sur l'hist. de France) III (1848) 273.

[6] The term *aide* was also used in the later middle ages to describe all taxes, indirect and direct (Dupont-Ferrier, op. cit. pp. 2–22).

[7] M. Rey, *Le Domaine du roi et les finances extraordinaires sous Charles VI, 1388–1413* (1965) pp. 36–9, 61, 91.

the government of his son was forced by the mob reluctantly to abolish the remaining taxes.[1] 'However,' wrote Jean Juvenal des Ursins, 'the princes and dukes, realising that the *domaine* was impoverished and that its revenues were not enough for urgent and necessary things, assembled together a number of the most important Parisians; and they agreed to a subsidy of twelve *deniers* in the *livre*'; but the manœuvre was unsuccessful.[2] The government's attempt to re-establish the *aides* and the *gabelle* at the beginning of 1382 led to widespread rioting; but its repression after the victory of Roosebeke against the Flemings enabled the government to bring them back permanently.[3] In 1384 began a series of 'exceptional' direct *tailles*.[4] In 1413 even the Cabochian reformers allowed that 'half of all the revenue of taxation should be employed on the war, and the other half and the revenue from the *domaine* on the other businesses'.[5] But this first period of permanent taxation was brought to an end by Jean *sans peur*'s abolition of the *aides* in 1418; and his rival, the dauphin Charles, could not but follow suit in the area of France under his control. But taxation, in one form or another, continued in both Anglo-Burgundian and French France in the 1420s; and by 1436 all was as it had been in the reign of Charles VI.[6]

There still remained those who thought the king should live of his own. Jean Juvenal des Ursins in the 1440s thought that to use extraordinary revenue for purposes other than the war was to 'deceive the people and the commonwealth . . . it's plain robbery, one might even say treason against the king and the public weal of this kingdom'; those who profited 'ought to be thought publicly bigger thieves than those who hold people up in a wood. . . . History tells of people who've had their heads cut off for less.'[7] But such strong views were far from practical; and the *commun* of the Estates-general of Tours in 1484

[1] *Mandements et actes divers de Charles V*, ed. L. Delisle (Docs inéd. sur l'hist. de France: 1874) p. 948; H. A. Miskimin, 'The Last Act of Charles V: the Background of the Revolts of 1382', in *Speculum*, XXXVIII (1963) 433–42; F. Chatillon, 'Charles V *nummularius* et l'abolition des fouages', in R. *Moyen Age latin*, XX (1964) 112–43.

[2] *Hist. de Charles VI*, ed. Michaud and Poujoulat (Nouvelle coll. des mémoires, 2: 1857) p. 343.

[3] L. Mirot, *Les Insurrections urbaines au début du règne de Charles VI (1380–1383)* (1905); Rey, op. cit. pp. 164 ff.

[4] Ibid. pp. 324 ff.　[5] *L'Ordonnance cabochienne*, p. 70.　[6] See below, pp. 341–2.

[7] P. Viollet, *Hist. des institutions politiques et admin. de la France*, III (1903) 467.

thought that, in order to pay for 'the upkeep of the king and queen', for government, embassies and the army, 'first of all the revenue of the *domaine* should be used. And if it is insufficient, the people of France has always been ready, and is set to help the king in all the ways considered by the members of the three estates.'[1]

From 1439 taxation was *de facto* permanent in France, in the same way as the army was *de facto* permanent; though its incidence and its forms naturally varied from time to time and from place to place. And in the same way as the king claimed the monopoly of raising troops, so he claimed the monopoly of raising taxes. The right of the greater seigneurs to take subventions from their men had much the same ultimate foundation as the king's. But already in 1278 the count of Brittany was prevented by the Parlement of Paris from taking a tax in Rennes;[2] but with the development of royal taxation this kind of control weakened. By 1412 it was again in the air: in this year the king's proctor in the *Cour des aides* could argue that 'the king can impose *tailles* and *aides* upon his kingdom, as emperor, for its safekeeping and defence; and it is unlawful for any seigneur, whoever he may be, to take any tax what-soever without royal permission'; and this remained the doctrine of the court.[3] The ordinance of 1439 proclaimed it generally; but it was not fully enforced until the sixteenth century, and in any case royal permission, though possibly grudgingly, continued to be granted.

And one should perhaps be chary of seeing in the apparent affluence of the Valois kings of France too much possibility of autocracy. Admittedly the yields of taxation could be high; and the *domaine* was not wholly negligible. The income of the *aides* and *gabelles* about 1390 has been estimated at 2,000,000 *livres tournois*; the *tailles* between 1384 and 1412 varied between 1,000,000 *livres tournois* and below 300,000. To these should be added the figures for local *aides* and clerical tenths. In good years under Charles VI the *domaine* receivers might send 300,000 *livres tournois* to Paris.[4] 'Charles VII', thought Commynes, 'never raised more than 1,800,000 *francs* a year, and king Louis, his son, was raising

[1] J. Masselin, *Journal des Etats généraux de France tenus à Tours en 1484*, ed. A. Bernier (Docs inéd. sur l'hist. de France: 1835) p. 678.

[2] *Les Olim*, ed. Beugnot (Docs inéd. sur l'hist. de France) II (1842) 118.

[3] Dupont-Ferrier, op. cit. p. 42; cf. Rey, op. cit. p. 166 n4.

[4] Rey, op. cit. pp. 100, 262, 404, and *Les Finances royales sous Charles VI. Les Causes du déficit, 1388–1413* (1965) pp. 9–10.

at the time of his death 4,700,000 *francs*, without the artillery and other things like that'; and if one includes in those figures *domaine* receipts and makes some allowances he was not so very far wrong.[1] Yet even so one should be careful not to inflate too much the power of these kings simply because they seem to have been rich. In the reign of Charles VI — the only one for which we have a thorough financial study — fraud deprived the monarch of part of his revenues; and grants of taxation to the privileged greatly reduced the figure of his net profits.[2] Such grants went back to the reign of Philippe IV;[3] the agreement of the greater magnates had its price. And, during the long civil war, support for the Valois cause, too, had to be bought, with pensions, with grants, with gifts.

> Alas, poor *aides* [wrote Jean Juvenal des Ursins in 1445], go you to the war! But the allowances and pensions of the lords of the blood of France and the officers. . . . I can't think what the reason is why they should have them: they're relatives of the king, *ergo* they should have that with which the king should make war against his enemies. There isn't anyone nowadays who doesn't want to have a pension — the constable, the marshals, the *sénéchaux*, the *baillis*, the captains of particular places — above their ordinary wages. If every seigneur in his *pays* wanted to take the taxes levied on his lands and have pensions there'd be nothing left for the king.[4]

Misappropriation of taxation, Jean Juvenal thought by the 1450s, was to 'subsidise all sins and the devils of hell and to make war upon God, upon the Virtues and upon the Commandments'.[5] The question of resumption came into his arguments then and in 1468, as it had into those of the reformers of 1413, of Thomas Basin in 1461 and as it was to come into those of the Estates-general of 1484;[6] but the pensions

---

[1] Commynes, op. cit. II 220; R. Gandilhon, *Politique écon. de Louis XI* (Rennes, 1940) pp. 293–5.

[2] Rey, *Les Finances royales*, p. 10.   [3] Strayer and Taylor, op. cit. p. 47.

[4] Lewis, 'Jean Juvenal des Ursins', pp. 114–15. In 1422 the Lyonnais tried to make a grant in men-at-arms 'et non point en argent, pour ce que aucuns le despendent autrement que au prouffit dudit seigr.' (*Reg. consulaires de la ville de Lyon*, ed. M. C. and G. Guigue, I (Lyon, 1882) 351).

[5] Lewis, 'Jean Juvenal des Ursins', p. 115.

[6] Ibid.; *L'Ordonnance cabochienne, passim*; Basin, op. cit. ed. Quicherat, III 254; Masselin, op. cit. p. 676.

remained. In 1484, when the government wanted to grant 900 of them, the chancellor Guillaume de Rochefort's justification of the system was that

> as long as the king is a minor [as Charles VIII was in 1484] he has to keep everyone's affection, and not put anyone out. How do you think that a great number of people, and especially those who received formerly very large pensions, would take it if one deprived them of them entirely and refused them even a little one? It simply can't be done: they must be kept to their faith and duty with rewards and benefits. You want the king to imitate Charles VII, as if he were his age! But Charles VII governed the commonwealth by himself and his own counsel. Charles VIII because of his age cannot do this; he is forced to rely upon the assistance of others, to perform many things through other people, and to trust the whole administration of the kingdom to those loyal to him.[1]

Pace the chancellor, his argument could equally well apply to Charles VIII's grandfather; it could also apply to Charles VIII's father and to his ancestors, kings of France, back to at least the mid-fourteenth century.[2] They could not ignore the claims of patronage; and that very weakness contributed to those actions which Jean Juvenal des Ursins came close to stigmatising as those of a tyrant and not of a king.

We shall deal later with what the great got from the crown. But a glance at one of the very few surviving fifteenth-century budgets[3] shows that even Louis XI might feel the pinch. In February 1470, when Guyenne was in the hands of his brother Charles as an apanage, Louis' financial people estimated his net income at (in figures rounded off to the nearest thousand) some 1,854,000 *livres*. Military expenditure on the *gens d'armes* and the artillery came to 907,000 *livres*; on garrisons 17,000; on the captains-general of *francs-archers* 3000 and on the captains of the *arrière-ban* 6000; on musterers 1000. The households came to 327,000; the civil service to 98,000. The pensions of the princes of the blood (without such things as the grant of the revenues of *greniers*) came to 326,000 *livres*; the pensions of the members of the order of St.-Michel and of courtiers to 221,000; other miscellaneous pensions and gifts to

---

[1] Ibid. p. 386.   [2] See below, pp. 214 ff.

[3] Bibl. nat. MS fr. 20485, folios 89^r–90^v. Cf. J. Vaesen, 'Catalogue du fonds Bourré à la Bibl. nat.' in *Bibl. Ec. Chartes*, XLV (1884) 158.

94,000. There was a deficit of some 147,000 *livres tournois*.[1] The king had his army; he had his civil servants; he bribed the great. But it was, in this year, to say the least a strain. They had paid the expenses of the *gens d'ordonnance* and of the artillery, of the things concerning the king, and those he had specifically ordered to be paid, said his *gens de finances*, and they had kept the remainder; would he please tell them which accounts they were to pay?

The final responsibility was the king's. God on earth, fountain of justice, commander of the army, usufructuary of the kingdom; but was sacrilege non-existent, was the king's justice final, did his army obey him, did he indeed enjoy the revenues of the kingdom? A Valois king in the later middle ages was far from the empyrean in which his propagandists put him. Although he appeared to rule the game his wits were constantly stretched to keep the upper hand. And, although God may have given him authority, God might not have provided him, poor human, with wits enough.

Kings as men: Philippe VI to Louis XI

Of the king's two bodies, the public body and the private, the second was certainly human enough. The first three Valois monarchs were, on the whole, fairly normal. Philippe VI as the first tenant of a disputed throne did very far from badly. 'It's a reasonable thing to do, to change one's mind,' he said at the end of his reign;[2] and this ability to trim may to some extent explain his apparent inactivities as it might explain those of his descendant Charles VII. But he behaved like a king: he was active in leading his army; he was known for his vigour and his boldness.[3] He was thought by some to be precipitate in his behaviour: the author of the *Chronique des quatres premiers Valois* thought he was 'a fearfully hasty man';[4] but most obloquy seems to have fallen on Jeanne of Burgundy, his wife. 'The queen', Robert d'Artois is alleged to have

[1] It would have been covered by the revenues of Guyenne (H. Stein, *Charles de France* (1921) p. 382).

[2] R. Cazelles, *La Société politique et la crise de la royauté sous Philippe de Valois* (1958) p. 45.

[3] J. Froissart, *Chron.* ed. S. Luce (Soc. Hist. France) 1 (1869) 302–3.

[4] ed. S. Luce (Soc. Hist. France: 1862) p. 15.

said, 'was a she-devil'; and although some of the slander heaped upon
her can probably be discounted, 'the wicked lame queen . . . who
behaved as king and had those who thwarted her will destroyed'
certainly acquired an unenviable reputation. 'Wicked indeed and
dangerous was this queen of France, the mother of king Jean,' wrote
Froissart, 'and she died a sudden death.'[1] Her son is supposed to have
taken after her: he, too, had rather a bad press, though admittedly the
worst of it (he 'was the worst and cruellest king who ever lived, and he
was moreover the son of the queen of Burgundy, who never liked
Normans') appears in the fifteenth-century chronicle of the Norman
Pierre Cochon: not a very trustworthy source.[2] In the *Complainte sur la
bataille de Poitiers* he appears as the paragon of military regality:

> If everyone else had been as valiant as he
> Beaten and made villeins the English would be[3]

but the balance of the clerical author of the *Complainte* is also suspect.
The actual behaviour of the king could only too easily be assimilated by
the public image.

Charles V, his successor, has perhaps suffered from the adulation of
Christine de Pisan. Certainly for her 'this very true Christian', 'very
devout and very catholic' king[4] was almost without reproach. Illness
had made him unwarlike (though Christine's defence of his valour is
not very convincing),[5] but otherwise he was a model prince. Perhaps he
was wiser even than Christine knew. But she could point out, as we
have seen, that his apparent love of ceremonious progresses 'was not
simply indulgence, but in order to keep, maintain and give example to
his successors in time to come that in solemn order should be held and
conducted the most worthy status of the high crown of France, to

---

[1] 'Chron. parisienne anonyme de 1316–39', ed. A. Hellot, in *M. Soc. hist.
Paris*, XI (1884) 159; *Chron. des quatres premiers Valois*, p. 17; Froissart, op. cit.
I 303.

[2] Ibid. III (1872) 249; P. Cochon, *Chron. normande*, ed. C. de Beaurepaire
(Soc. Hist. Normandie: Rouen, 1870) p. 75.

[3] ed. C. de Beaurepaire, in *Bibl. Ec. Chartes*, ser. 3 II (1851) 262.

[4] *Le Livre des fais et bonnes meurs du sage roy Charles V*, ed. S. Solente (Soc.
Hist. France), I (1936) 94.

[5] Ibid. pp. 131–3; cf. pp. 120–2.

which all sovereign magnificence is due, pertains and must be paid':[1] certainly, as we have seen, Charles' entourage was prepared to gild it. Never angry, always moderate, imbued with political tact and loved by all,[2] he, too, was a paragon, but of the peaceful arts. The recovery of France during his reign was an undoubted tribute to his virtues; but one should not be carried away cloud-borne into Christine's apotheosis. If Christine could argue that Charles was so well behaved a king 'that he acquired the universal love of every person, and so he should have, for he did wrong to no-one', others might think differently. If he 'was obeyed, honoured, feared and loved, as a good prince should be',[3] this did not necessarily mean that he was chary of riding roughshod over the *menu peuple*, whom Christine, if she did not despise them, at least thought should be kept in their place. About June 1382, two years after his death, one of them, Raoulet Mathei, when rather drunk, wished that Charles had died ten years earlier: for then the taxes would have been remitted ten years earlier.[4] This was hardly a display of affection; even if it was a tacit acknowledgement of his prowess as ruler.

The brother of Charles' wife, Louis II de Bourbon, died a melancholic, and Jeanne de Bourbon herself lost 'her wits and her memory' for a while at the age of thirty-five in 1373.[5] In her child Charles VI the weakness of the line of St.-Louis came out to the full. Charles was every inch a king. Above average height, robust, broad-chested, fresh-faced and fair-haired, he loved tournaments and was alleged to excel in military exercises. He was friendly, good-tempered and generous.[6] But the old Adam and rather more did come out in this juvenile prodigy. Carnal appetites (though never causing scandal or dishonour to a family and never violently satisfied) reminded the Religieux de St.-Denis of the former; and his refusal to wear the now old-fashioned robes

[1] Ibid. p. 51; cf. The *'Livre de la paix'* of Christine de Pisan, ed. C. C. Willard (The Hague, 1958) p. 72.

[2] *Le Livre des fais*, I 48–9, II (1940) 28–9, 31.   [3] Ibid. II 31.

[4] *Choix de pièces inéd. relatives au règne de Charles VI*, ed. L. Douët-d'Arcq (Soc. Hist. France) I (1863) 99–100. For Christine's views on the lower orders, see The *'Livre de la paix'*, pp. 128 ff, and below, pp. 267, 289.

[5] A. Brachet, *Pathologie mentale des rois de France: Louis XI et ses ascendants* (1903) pp. cxxxii, 600 ff; *Chron. des quatres premiers Valois*, p. 244.

[6] *Chron. du religieux de St.-Denis*, ed. L. Bellaguet (Docs inéd. sur l'hist. de France) I (1839) 562 ff.

thought suitable for a king, his delight in disguising himself as a Bohemian or a German and his insistence in taking part in tournaments after having received unction upset the Religieux and probably others.[1] He seems, in fact, to have been a rather retarded youth. In 1392 he went off his head. In April he had had, probably, typhoid fever at Amiens. His convalescence from this had probably been insufficient, and during it he appeared very excitable: an expedition undertaken against Pierre de Craon in Brittany was probably a product of this excitability. At the beginning of August, on his way westward, he began to behave very peculiarly. On 5 August, possibly affected by alcohol, possibly affected by sunstroke, he went raving mad in the forest of Le Mans, after a slight shock, and killed four men before his sword broke and he could be tied up. A week later he had recovered; but he was not himself until November or December. In June 1393 he was mad again, this time until January 1394; and thereafter the attacks repeated one another with monotonous regularity: his madness became the king's 'usual malady'.[2]

Mania, mental confusion, depression have all been disentangled in Charles' syndrome. Even in the lucid periods the king was mentally unstable. At some times in them his grip failed: his attention, his memory and his will would wander. At other times he kept his wits about him and could be active in affairs. It was, therefore, possible for him to act independently as king; but he was a prey to those around him, great and small. No-one seriously seems to have thought of deposing him, though Pierre Salmon made dark forebodings to him on the analogy of the fate of Richard II of England.[3] The incapacity of the king did not diminish the prestige of the crown, though it could be grumbled in 1398 by one of his subjects that 'we've got enough to do and put up with all this taxation; the king is mad and off his head and

---

[1] Ibid. p. 566.

[2] Charles' insanity is discussed by Brachet — who reprints most of the relevant evidence (op. cit. pp. 621 ff) — and by J. Saltel, *La Folie du roi Charles VI* (Toulouse, 1907) and E. Dupré, 'La Folie de Charles VI roi de France', in R. *Deux Mondes*, LX (1910) 835–66. For the periodicity of the attacks, see *Chron. du religieux de St.-Denis, passim*; for their being accepted as 'usual', ibid. IV (1842) 250, 320.

[3] *Les Demandes faites par le roi Charles VI ... avec les réponses de Pierre Salmon*, ed. G. A. Crapelet (1833) pp. 97–100.

monsieur le duc d'Orléans is young and likes playing dice and whoring';[1] nor did it affect his government's being able to tax by arbitrary will.

Isabeau of Bavaria, Charles' wife,

> was pretty and gracious enough
> Without a quarter or a moiety
> Of [her husband]'s very great beauty,
> For she was short and brown-coloured.[2]

Other writers could be more unkind. Reason, in the *Songe veritable*, said

> You, lady Isabeau, the queen that
> Is enveloped in horrid fat[3]

and her ill looks, as well as the virtues and vices of the Wittelsbachs and the Viscontis, were passed on to son and grandson. It will never be known for certain if the tares of the Valois were passed on to Charles VII by Charles VI. Louis XI once told the Neapolitan ambassador that Isabeau 'was a great whore' and that Charles VII was supposed to be descended from her and Charles VI ('who was a fool') 'but that he did not know whose child he was'; and allegedly Charles VII had enough doubts about his paternity until they were supposedly assuaged by Jeanne d'Arc.[4] But there is little real reason to suppose that Charles VII could not have been the son of his putative father, and indeed, in those much-quoted words of the saint, 'true heir of France and king's son'.[5] But the mixture of Valois, Wittelsbach and Visconti, though it produced eccentrics, also produced kings of high ability.

He was thin, wrote Chastellain of Charles VII, with feeble legs and a most peculiar walk; 'his face was pallid, but good-looking enough, his speech good and very pleasing and subtle, not very high-pitched. His demeanour was attractive and gracious.' Mutability, distrust and envy were his principal failings, but his virtues, 'obviously by the labour of

---

[1] *Choix de pièces inéd.* I 153.

[2] 'Le Pastoralet', ed. Kervyn de Lettenhove, in *Chron. relatives à l'hist. de Belgique sous la domination des ducs de Bourgogne* (Coll. des chroniques belges) II (Brussels, 1873) 578.

[3] ed. H. Moranvillé, in *M. Soc. Hist. Paris*, XVII (1890) 296.

[4] Brachet, op. cit. pp. 82 ff; *Procès de condamnation et de réhabilitation de Jeanne d'Arc*, ed. J. Quicherat (Soc. Hist. France) IV (1847) 278–81.

[5] G. du Fresne de Beaucourt, *Hist. de Charles VII*, I (1881) 4 n3; *Procès*, III (1845) 103.

God', made him 'glorious above many of his predecessors'.[1] He undoubtedly had a number of not very important neuroses, the best documented of which is anthropophobia; but his physical health seems to have been good until the late 1450s.[2] Remarkable diagnoses of mental instability have been produced in order to explain his alleged inactivity in the 1420s and early 1430s. But there seems little real reason to go much beyond Chastellain's analysis of Charles' character. To the Burgundian chronicler the king, far from robust, far from bellicose, was never a man to do things for himself. He relied on others; but he was capable in the end of leading them and not being led by them. The very vice of changeableness led to a fairly rapid turnover of 'favourites'; the aspirant could be played off against the sitting tenant. In the end the government was made up of 'bits and pieces of different people all assembled up and sewn together', who worked effectively for the public good as well as for their own and eventually threw the English out of France. By this time Charles was so expert in managing this kind of government that he was able, victorious, to choose the best man for a particular job, 'one at the wars, another in the financial departments, another in the council, another running the artillery'. 'Eventually, since he had an expert knowledge of the individuals and since he had everything under his eye, misdeeds as well as virtuous ones, it became so dangerous to be in his entourage that no-one, however great he was, had the faintest idea where he stood; and so everybody watched their step very carefully, in case, if they put a foot wrong, they should be caught on the hop.'[3] It hardly seems necessary to think in terms of morbid psychology or to introduce Jeanne d'Arc in the role of psychotherapist[4] to understand, in the same way as Chastellain understood, Charles' behaviour in the difficult years 'when he suffered much misfortune and was much oppressed by his enemies, so that even the last boundaries of the kingdom were taken away from him'; in the difficult years 'when his luck was scanty indeed and his spirits were embittered by many different troubles and new adversity every day . . .'[5] They were enough to depress anyone. But when the troubles were over, the king came into his own: the almost universal adulation of chroniclers

---

[1] *Œuvres*, ed. Kervyn de Lettenhove, II (Brussels, 1863) 178–9.
[2] Brachet, op. cit. pp. 63 ff.   [3] Op. cit. II 183–4.
[4] Brachet, op. cit. pp. 87–8.   [5] Op. cit. II 179.

followed him to the grave.[1] Only those who thought with Jean Juvenal des Ursins that he had, perhaps, succeeded from his own point of view only too well in being a king might have had doubts.

We know more about the personality of Charles' successor, Louis XI, than about any of his predecessors'.[2] If he did nothing else, Louis had an infinite capacity for arousing hatred; it was with fear and imprecation that men remembered him. More than any of his predecessors he seems to have had a curious need and a capacity for self-expression in his words and in his actions. Italy and the ways of Italians fascinated him; deceit delighted him.[3] A Burgundian writer christened him the universal spider.[4] He could be both sentimental and ruthless,[5] entranced with his own wickedness and indignant that he might be thought wicked,[6] confident towards God and man and stricken with fear or remorse towards them.[7] He did not appear, or dress, or speak like a king;[8] yet 'he was the most terrible king who ever was' and even the trees trembled before him.[9] It was little wonder that an Italian ambassador

[1] Beaucourt, op. cit. VI (1891) 445–50.

[2] Louis has collected as much clinical curiosity as his father and grand-father; see, for instance, as well as Brachet, op. cit. pp. xvii–cxx, L. Ipcar, *Louis XI et ses médecins* (1936).

[3] *Dépêches des ambassadeurs milanais en France sous Louis XI et François Sforza*, ed. B. de Mandrot and C. Samaran (Soc. Hist. France) I (1916) 341, 362, III (1920) 327, IV (1923) 156.

[4] J. Molinet, 'Souffle, Triton', in *Œuvres de G. Chastellain*, op. cit. VII (Brussels, 1865) 209. But cf. ibid. pp. 207, 209 n 1.

[5] A. Gandilhon, 'Contribution à l'histoire de la vie privée et de la Cour de Louis XI (1423–1481)', in *M. Soc. hist. Cher*, ser. 4 XX (1905) 352–4; *Dépêches des ambassadeurs milanais*, I 137, 197; *Procédures politiques du règne de Louis XII*, ed. R. de Maulde (Docs inéd. sur l'hist. de France: 1885) p. 915 (cf. *Dépêches des ambassadeurs milanais*, II (1919) 35–6, 139).

[6] Ibid. III 325 ff, 380, 381 ff, IV 21 ff, 26, 29–30, 74, 237.

[7] Ibid. I 53, 337, 361, II 217, 251, III 169, 217, 223, 254–5; 'Dépêches de Nicolas de Roberti, ambassadeur du duc de Ferrare auprès du roi Louis XI, 1478–80', ed. G. Périnelle, in *Mél. Archéol. Hist. Ecole fr. Rome*, XXIV (1904) 147–8, 175; P. de Commynes, *Mémoires*, ed. J. Calmette and G. Durville, I (Classiques de l'hist. de France au Moyen âge, 3: 1924) 68, II (Classiques, 6: 1925) 292; A. Gandilhon, op. cit. pp. 355 ff.

[8] T. Basin, *Hist. des règnes de Charles VII et de Louis XI*, ed. J. Quicherat (Soc. Hist. France) III (1857) 165–7, 177–8, 193; Commynes, op. cit. I 138; *Dépêches des ambassadeurs milanais*, II 162–3; 'Dépêches de Nicolas de Roberti', p. 149. Cf. A. Gandilhon, op. cit. pp. 340–5.

[9] *Procédures politiques*, p. 978.

in 1462 said that he came out in a sweat from head to foot when he was summoned by Louis XI.[1] Yet he could be extremely friendly;[2] 'he knew how to be pleasant when he wanted to', even at his most crotchety;[3] he was pathologically fond of animals, especially dogs and singing-birds;[4] his love of hunting came second only to his love of the business of kingship and international politics and sometimes even got in the way of it.[5] Even his deepest calumniator did not deny that he was highly literate; even a rather critical Italian thought in 1479 that he cited the best authors.[6] He shocked everyone by an extreme and even endearing informality.[7] The Italian ambassadors, not used to such things, seemed constantly chasing miles after him to some 'extremely miserable little peasant's shack' in the woods.[8] He liked eating in taverns and with his rather peculiar friends in town.[9] He had a cruel sense of humour;[10] he could be unwittingly or wittingly cruel;[11] he lacked justice of mind and he lacked loyalty,[12] he liked adversity and he disliked concord.[13] He 'intended to be sovereign'; he 'did not wish to share his kingdom'.[14] He would and could never be beaten; he would never accept for long the will of others imposed upon him. Only rarely did he think himself wrong; and then not for long. 'Perhaps',

[1] *Dépêches des ambassadeurs milanais*, I 238.   [2] Ibid. I 235, 243.

[3] *Lettres et négociations de P. de Commynes*, ed. Kervyn de Lettenhove, I (Brussels, 1867) 286.

[4] *Dépêches des ambassadeurs milanais*, II 323, 374, III 21; 'Dépêches de Nicolas de Roberti', pp. 159–60; J. de Roye, *Journal*, ed. B. de Mandrot (Soc. Hist. France) I (1894) 220; Basin, op. cit. III 178–9; A. Gandilhon, op. cit. in *M. Soc. hist. Cher.* ser. 4 XXI (1906) 44 ff.

[5] See, for instance, *Lettres . . . de Commynes*, I 257 ff, III (Brussels, 1874) 9.

[6] A. de La Borderie, 'Jean Meschinot, sa vie et ses œuvres, ses satires contre Louis XI', in *Bibl. Ec. Chartes*, LVI (1895) 289; *Lettres . . . de Commynes*, I 258.

[7] See, for instance, *Dépêches des ambassadeurs milanais*, I 100, 160, 255, 337, 360, II 139, 151, 309; 'Dépêches de Nicolas de Roberti', p. 146; *Lettres . . . de Commynes*, I 224; Basin, op. cit. III 167, 179–80.

[8] *Dépêches des ambassadeurs milanais, passim; Lettres . . . de Commynes*, I 232 (cf. III 81).

[9] Ibid. I 224; *Dépêches des ambassadeurs milanais*, II 151, 274; 'Dépêches de Nicolas de Roberti', p. 149.

[10] *Dépêches des ambassadeurs milanais*, II 35–6; Basin, op. cit. III 193.

[11] *Dépêches des ambassadeurs milanais*, II 88.   [12] Ibid. II 139–40, IV 286.

[13] Ibid. II 306. Cf. Commynes, op. cit. I 225.

[14] *Dépêches des ambassadeurs milanais*, III 188, II 204.

he said to his doctors on the point of death, 'I am not as ill as you think.'[1] But he was, and he died.

Amongst the welter of voices deposing upon the character of Louis XI in the divorce trial of Louis XII in 1498 only one had the courage to speak, however misguidedly, for the king now dead some fifteen years. Jean de Châteauneuf, servant, counsellor, *chambellan* and pensioner of Louis XI from the war of the Public Weal until his death, had a healthy respect for his late master's memory. He had been 'so prudent, discreet and efficient a prince that, because of the great sense and intelligence and efficiency that he had, he was feared by all the lords princes of his kingdom of France who lived in his time'; and he was fearfully hard on those who disobeyed his will.[2] Of Louis' energy, except perhaps in his last years, there can be no doubt. There is plenty of evidence for his military prowess, though he disliked the strains war caused. He was apt, perhaps, to be unintelligent and incautious in his dealings with men: he disrespected their views and their feelings; and one suspects that he had little real imagination about the way in which such lesser beings worked.[3] He was afraid of them by nature, thought Commynes; those of whom he was not afraid he insulted to their faces, those of whom he was afraid behind their backs.[4] He thought flattery and money[5] would suffice to repair the damage done by neurotic insensitivity; they bought many, but they did not buy all. Only in the last years of his reign, when he had beaten those he could not buy, did he have peace; but it was a peace in which he was anguished by anxiety for his body and for his soul.[6] The Italian ambassadors thought at one time he was not as clever as Edward IV of England; Commynes, at another, that he was.[7] Though he tried to be infallible,[8] he was not; though in his early years as king at least 'he thinks every-

---

[1] Commynes, op. cit. II 316.   [2] *Procédures politiques*, pp. 1069–70.

[3] Despite the views of Commynes (op. cit. I 130) on Louis' ability to handle men, the impression one derives of it through the Milanese ambassadors' eyes is hardly flattering.

[4] Commynes, op. cit. I 68; Basin, op. cit. III 193.

[5] See, for instance, Commynes, op. cit. I 67, 142, 241; *Dépêches des ambassadeurs milanais*, III 106, 118, 146, 378, IV 10, 25 ff, 36, 58–9.

[6] Commynes, op. cit. II 274 ff.

[7] *Dépêches des ambassadeurs milanais*, II 300 [1464]; Commynes, op. cit. II 239 [1477].

[8] *Dépêches des ambassadeurs milanais*, I 137.

thing out in his brain, which he seems to have right at the top of his head', he was, as the Milanese ambassador Petrasancta pointed out after he had ruled sixteen years, 'only flesh and bone too';[1] no man, even in the power and isolation of the office of the king, could rule entirely on his own. The utter loneliness of such sovereignty was more than flesh and bone could stand. The king was forced to rely on others. He was forced to rely upon those around him: upon his courtiers and upon his councillors.

Court

Immoderately anxious to taste the heady joys of the wider world the infant Louis II de La Trémoille begged his father in the 1470s to let him go to court. 'The King's court', his panegyrist Jean Bouchet had him say, '. . . is the school of all that is honourable, frequented by the people of worth, from whom one learns to live in civility, and how to acquire not only the riches of the world, but also the incorruptible treasures of honour.' His father thought differently. 'The court', he began, 'is an ambitious humility, a crapulous sobriety, a lubricious chastity, an enraged moderation . . .': the list continued.[2] But Bouchet was borrowing on Louis I's behalf from a well-established convention; even some of his paradoxes had appeared a century before in Alain Chartier's *Curial*.[3] The horror of the court seemed only too describable.

> The court [thought Jean Meschinot] is like a sea whose waves
> Are pride and envy; storms from which
> There is hardly any rescue;
> And slander causes many wrecks;
> Wrath leads to strife and excess
> Which swamp the ships that sail that sea;
> Treachery there is manifest;
> Sail somewhere else for your fun.[4]

[1] Ibid. 1 100; *Lettres . . . de Commynes*, III 8.
[2] *Panégyric du chevallier sans reproche*, ed. Michaud and Poujoulat (Nouvelle coll. des mémoires, 4: 1854) pp. 414–15.
[3] ed. F. Heuckenkamp (Halle, 1899) pp. 23, 27.
[4] *Les Lunettes des princes* (1505) sig. m vi^r.

The court was corrupt. 'The abuses of the court and the habits of courtiers are such', thought Alain Chartier, that no-one ever lasts there without being corrupted, or rather, no-one ever even manages to rise there without being corruptible.'[1] The court was nerve-racking.

> The court is the nursemaid of those who by fraud or pretence train themselves to extract from each other words with which to persecute them, so that to others' disadvantage they can enter into the favour of those who have power [at court] to help people or to harm them and who much prefer false reports [of people] to true ones. If you have office at court you have to be equipped to fight to keep it; because if you have anything there, others will want to take it from you; and you won't escape without a quarrel with someone who will contrive some way of deceiving you, and you will be in torment how to resist it; and when you've used all your energy, your time and your money defending yourself, some newcomer to court will supplant you in the state of grace and perhaps deprive you of it. And so you'll lose to your great pain what took you so much labour to acquire; or if you do manage to keep it, you'll scarcely ever be free of the fear that he or someone else envious of you won't set about taking it away from you.[2]

But despite all this literary authority on his father's side the younger Louis de La Trémoille stood firm. 'It is better for my character', he said bravely, 'to put it through the perilous flame of the court, the purgative of the ignorance of those who live a private life, than to remain dividing my time between idleness, listlessness, gluttony, the pleasures of the flesh and the freedom to do ill, all of which lie in wait for human senses.'[3] Moths could not resist that candle.

This gloomy picture of the court did not derive its authority wholly from a literary convention. 'Those who know how to dissimulate are thought more highly of at court and last longer there than other people', thought Alain Chartier.[4] Jean Juvenal des Ursins in 1445 advised his brother the new chancellor of France 'not to think to resist the will of those who will be at court, because that will only finish you and have you put out. It's better to have patience and dissimulate and be the cause in the end of making less trouble, since one can't do any good

---

[1] Op. cit. p. 7.   [2] Ibid. pp. 19–21.
[3] Bouchet, op. cit. p. 416.   [4] Op. cit. p. 7.

otherwise, by being too firm and losing one's job. This was what messire Arnaud de Corbie used to do.'[1] Jean Juvenal seems to have been right about Arnaud de Corbie's capacity for political survival;[2] and certainly Guillaume Jouvenel des Ursins lasted long enough, though he was mildly shipwrecked in the stormy passage of 1461–5. The court was nerve-racking; the court was corrupt; but no-one save the men of letters would have it any different. While the courtier kept his nerve, his skill and his place, there was too much to be gained: not only the 'incorruptible treasures of honour' but also, and far to be misprized, the 'riches of the world'.

The court is rarely dignified by the label 'institution'.[3] Yet in some sense it was the most vital political institution. Its absurd formalities — and even in the fifteenth century they could be pretty absurd[4] — should not blind us to the fact that it was in court that real power lay. The absurdities of precedence and reverence themselves had some point. It was all very well for Alain Chartier to bewail that 'although we count highly amongst the joys of courtiers the reverence shown them, it still remains that there is nothing more vain than to glorify in honour received more from pretence than from a true desire and done by an honourer who often in his heart despises the honorand'.[5] But to suggest that dignities should not be maintained was morally shocking. Snobbish dame Aliénor de Poitiers was upset at the informality of the dauphin Louis at the court of Burgundy; but Louis' informality as king also surprised the Milanese ambassador Malletta in the early 1460s.[6] However much people knew what the realities of politics were, they did not like to be reminded of them. The formalities of the court provided

[1] P. S. Lewis, 'Jean Juvenal des Ursins and the Common Literary Attitude towards Tyranny in Fifteenth-century France', in *Medium Aevum*, XXXIV (1965) 109 n 42 (the word 'bout' in the fifth line of this note should read 'bont'); the text ('A, a, a, nescio loqui quia puer ego sum', Bibl. nat. MS fr. 2701, fo. 46ᵛ) continues '... et ceste maniere tenoit messire Arnault de Corbie'.

[2] M. Rey, *Les Finances royales sous Charles VI. Les Causes du déficit, 1388–1413* (1965) p. 581.

[3] But cf. for this point G. Zeller, *Les Institutions de la France au xviᵉ siècle* (1948) p. 94.

[4] See, for instance (primarily on the court of Burgundy), Aliénor de Poitiers, 'Les Honneurs de la Cour', ed. La Curne de Ste.-Palaye, in *Mémoires sur l'ancienne chevalerie*, nouv. éd. II (1781) 183–282.

[5] Op. cit. p. 17.   [6] Op. cit. pp. 208 ff; see above, p. 117 n 7.

some mental security in the midst of its torments. They provided, too, a framework for an otherwise structureless power-complex of influence and favour. For this was what the court really was.

However much the personal power of the king might formally be shackled, it was still in the person of the king that ultimate power lay. Without the king the whole of politics was non-existent. It was unthinkable in later medieval France that a new myth could be invented to inform political being; not even in Flanders could a republican soul replace effectively a monarchic one. And the king was not only, as it were, an inanimate *raison d'être* for politics; he was — if he were at least sane — a busy political person. The 2000-odd letters of Louis XI[1] that survive testify at least to the breadth of his activity, if they do not show it necessarily very different from that of his father. The actions that the king could take in matters effectively of personal advantage to individuals were very considerable. From a refusal to pardon the death sentence of a duke to the grant of a place in the guard of the Grosse Tour of Bourges to an elderly and legless archer, the 'patronage' of the crown held its sway over the lives and livelihoods of its subjects.[2] But, mere flesh and bone, the king could not exercise alone this great weight of favour. His entourage was only too eager to help him.

Who was at court? It was, according to Alain Chartier, a tremendous hurly-burly. 'They're always knocking at the rich man's doors,' he complained, 'in high palaces there is constant noise and murmur, in great places there are the great crowds which press hard around one. The hall of a great prince is usually foul and hot with people's breath, the usher hits those who are inside with his staff, some force their way in by pushing and others struggle to resist them.'[3] The impression given by the Milanese ambassadors to the court of Louis XI is of a quieter place, but no less an exciting one. To court came the magnates of France; to court and the *maîtres des requêtes* of the household came humble petitioners. Here might be found the officers of state, the heads of departments, the counsellors — and the courtiers. For the essence of the court was the royal household: that domestic organisation which *mutatis mutandis* provided for the everyday life and for the magnificence of the aristocracy from the king, the queen, the princes of the blood

---

[1] ed. E. Charavay, J. Vaesen and B. de Mandrot (Soc. Hist. France: 1883–1909).
[2] *Lettres de Louis XI*, VI (1898) 210–11, V (1895) 243.   [3] Op. cit. p. 21.

downwards. To describe it adequately would need as much space as Olivier de La Marche devoted to limning in 1474 for Edward IV of England the 'establishment of the household' of Charles *le téméraire*, 'which was for a duke great and magnificent'.[1] More important is it to remember that its multifarious offices provided the places for the courtiers; though court titles could be merely honorific. The courtier was essentially a grand domestic.

The business of politics national or international was carried on in the midst of a magnified, formalised family life; men had their lives to lead as well as their business to do. At court they all gossiped and joked and intrigued in a pleasanter sense: a Venetian ambassador couldn't understand why he was being sent packing, he hadn't interfered with the internal politics of the kingdom or made love to any of the king's *mignonnes*.[2] In this domestic world the king was at his most human. 'Very reverend father in God,' wrote Louis XI to Jean Jouffroy, bishop of Arras, in 1462, 'I received this morning, as I was getting up, the letters you sent me ... written at Florence ... together with a note from our Holy Father the pope, written in his own hand, to which I've replied, dictating it word by word on the spot, while I was dressing ... and if it isn't well done you must forgive me, because you know I'm no writer.'[3] In this domestic world the king was at his most vulnerable. In England in 1479, when John III Paston wanted Edward IV to take 'my service and my quarrel together', he thought that 'Sir George Brown, Sir James Radcliff and others of my acquaintance which wait most upon the king and lie nightly in his chamber will put to their good wills'.[4] Sir Georges and Sir Jameses could be found across the Channel too. The king was permanently under siege by those around him on behalf of their clients: 'while he was getting up, in his closet, at eight o'clock in the morning', after Mass, after his lunch, after his siesta, strolling in the fields around Vincennes, after dinner, even at three o'clock after midnight.[5] It was the need to beat one's opponents for

---

[1] ed. H. Beaune and J. d'Arbaumont, in *Mémoires d'Olivier de La Marche* (Soc. Hist. France) IV (1888) 1–94, 154. See M. Rey, *Les Finances royales sous Charles VI. Les Causes du déficit, 1388–1413* (1965) pp. 19 ff.

[2] *Dépêches des ambassadeurs milanais* II 152.   [3] *Lettres de Louis XI*, II (1885) 41.

[4] *The Paston Letters*, ed. J. Gairdner, VI (Edinburgh, 1904) 28–9.

[5] G. Dupont-Ferrier, *Etudes sur les institutions financières de la France à la fin du Moyen âge*, I *Les Elections et leur personnel* (1930) 75; G. Mollat, 'Le Roi de

priority in the gift of an office which drove the king's suppliants to their greatest importunity. But for less desperately urgent matters the assistance of the courtiers was equally vital. It was with such informality that the 'institutional activity' of the court took place. Those who had the ear of the king shared to some extent in his power.

In the early years of Louis XI, for instance, it was Jean de Montauban, the admiral of France, who was 'all with the king', and the marshal Armagnac, and Josselin du Bois, the *bailli* of the Montagnes d'Auvergne and *maréchal des logis*, 'who was the most accepted and the most familiar in speaking to the king'.[1] By 1465 Armagnac was 'the other king'.[2] In the later 1470s it was to monsieur d'Argenton, to Commynes himself that men applied and to whom the king 'talked often and highly confidentially', as he used to do to 'those who were nearest to him'.[3] The list of those who influenced Louis could be and has been much lengthened; their crimes have been described.[4] Already in 1527 Jean Bouchet argued that he had been 'handled by a barber, by an impostor and faithless bishop'.[5] But it may be wondered if the collaborators of Louis XI were really any different from those of his father.[6] No member of a king's entourage was in the game for some anachronistic concept of public service. The king's servants were in his service for what they could make out of it. According to an early sixteenth-century genealogy the great fortune of Antoine de Dammartin had been founded because 'he came at a good time, and started early, and was the *mignon* of King Charles'.[7] The sins of a Guillaume de Champeaux or a Georges de La Trémoille[8] were, it may be argued, at least not very far from the normal

France et la collation plénière (*pleno jure*) des bénéfices ecclésiastiques', in *Mémoires présentées par divers savants à l'Acad. Inscript.* XIV, part 2 (1951) 219–20.

[1] *Dépêches des ambassadeurs milanais*, I 337, 356, II 209, 356, 364–5, III 30.

[2] Ibid. III 42.

[3] Commynes, op. cit. II 40.

[4] E. Lavisse, *Hist. de France*, IV, part 2 (1902) 332 ff; P. Champion, *Louis XI*, II (1927) 215–30.

[5] Bouchet, op. cit. p. 415. They were Olivier Le Dain and Jean Balue.

[6] R. Doucet, 'Le Gouvernement de Louis XI', in R. *Cours et conférences*, XXIV (1922–3) 737–46.

[7] H. de Chabannes, *Preuves pour servir à l'hist. de la maison de Chabannes*, *Supplément*, I (Dijon, 1915) 50.

[8] C. Devic and J. Vaissete, *Hist. gén. de Languedoc*, X (Toulouse, 1885) 'Preuves', cols 2185–7; Beaucourt, op. cit. II (1882) 274–5.

peccadilloes of the great servant; they are known because their authors fell or felt it prudent to confess. They contributed, of course, to the prevalent 'default of justice'; but in that world they were normal and it does little good to bewail them.

The court, varied in its social construction, cut across the formal hierarchy of power based upon rank. Its work and its privileges fell to the professionals; though the great could be professionals too. The sons of princely houses, such as the constable Richmond or as Charles d'Anjou comte du Maine, were not excluded by the eminence of their families from the joys of political pre-eminence. But if the magnates had an undoubted right to rule and if many of them in fact did rule, the political careerist also had his chance. The career of Pierre II de Brézé[1] shows how he took it. His family was obscure. He rose through military prowess and the patronage of the Anjou family; in 1437 he became *sénéchal* of the duchy and in the same year a royal councillor; in 1441 he became royal *sénéchal* of Poitou. From 1443 to 1449, perhaps in some obscure alliance with Agnès Sorel, dame de Beauté, the king's mistress, he was 'the premier and most intimate councillor of the king, through whom everything is done'.[2] He seems to have played a preponderant part in dealings with Lorraine, with England, with military reform. In 1445 he eclipsed even his patron, Charles d'Anjou. Around him burst the mines of his enemies, who included his old employers and the dauphin Louis, tirelessly plotting from the safety of Dauphiné; but, supported by the duke of Brittany and the comte de Foix, he survived until Agnès' death in 1450. From 1451 he was 'en disponibilité',[3] as *grand sénéchal* of Normandy dealing with all aspects of the duchy's affairs, far from disgrace — though rarely at court. After the accession of Louis XI[4] he was imprisoned, his life perhaps in danger; but slowly, from 1462, he seems to have recovered his influence; in 1464 he became

[1] P. Bernus, 'Essai sur la vie de Pierre de Brézé (vers 1410–1465)', in *Positions des thèses de l'Ec. Chartes* (1906) pp. 7–17; G. Dupont-Ferrier, *Gallia regia* (1942–61) nos. 3727, 12880 *bis*, 16229, 17603, 17918, 17935, 19710.

[2] Beaucourt, op. cit. IV (1888) 208 n 8.

[3] P. Bernus, 'Le Rôle politique de Pierre de Brézé au cours des dix dernières années du règne de Charles VII (1451–61)', in *Bibl. Ec. Chartes*, LXIX (1908) 304.

[4] P. Bernus, 'Louis XI et Pierre de Brézé (1440 à 1465)', in *R. Anjou*, NS LXIII (1911) 241–89, 355–71.

again *grand sénéchal* of Normandy. In 1465 he was killed in his prime on the royal side at the battle of Montlhéry.

Offices, pension, gifts from Estates, gifts from the crown to him and his wife, the title of comte de Maulevrier, were the more obvious of the private profits of power which fell to Pierre de Brézé; but there were as well for this man who had flown so high, for whom Georges Chastellain wrote the best of his minor works[1] and an epitaph after his death,

> The gallant, the good, the valiant knight,
> The wise man, the glorious speaker . . .
> Messire Pierre, surnamed de Brézé,
> *Grand sénéchal*, comte de Maulevrier,[2]

there were as well the purer joys of public power, of handling 'the great weight of royal business, in war and in peace, and in the affairs of other regions and provinces', of being one of the 'two figures bent over [a table], leaning on their elbows in close council', deciding 'many high businesses, which were carried out gloriously'.[3] In the exercise of personal royal power it was inevitable that the king should have predilections for particular coadjutors. To label them 'favourites' is to underestimate their claim and to overestimate the claim of the princes of the blood to share in the government of the country — undoubted though that claim may in theory have been.

Council

For who were the king's councillors? They were, thought Guy Coquille in the sixteenth century, admittedly 'some born, others made. . . . The born councillors are the princes of [the king's] . . . blood and the peers of France, lay and ecclesiastic. The "made" councillors are the great officers of the crown.'[4] The king's council, like those of lesser men, had its magnate element and its civil-service element. The

---

[1] G. Pérouse, *Georges Chastellain. Etude sur l'hist. politique et littéraire du xve siècle* (Acad. royale de Belgique, Lettres &c. ser. 2 VII: Brussels, 1910) p. 80.

[2] *Œuvres*, ed. Kervyn de Lettenhove, VII (Brussels, 1865) 73.

[3] G. Chastellain, 'Déprécation pour messire Pierre de Brézé', in ibid. p. 41.

[4] 'Institution au droit français', in A. Loysel, *Institutes coutumières*, ed. A. M. Dupin and E. Laboulaye, I (1846) 3.

princes and their advocates were at times vocal on behalf of their right to share in the government of the country. In 1442 the magnates demanded 'that the king should summon the princes of his blood to deal with the great affairs of the kingdom more than any other people, and it is most proper that he should do this, seeing the great interest they have [in the kingdom]; and that this is what used to be done by the *très-chrétien* kings of France his progenitors.' 'The king', Charles VII replied, 'has never dealt with any important matter without the knowledge of these lords or of a majority of them, and it is still his intention not to do a whit differently.'[1] Interest and precedent could be reinforced by the fashionable clichés of political argument. In 1413 Guillaume Signel, *juge* of Nîmes, made on behalf of the princes an 'important statement' on the theme *Oculi mei semper ad Dominum.* 'In this statement he demonstrated that the king, who is head of the body of princes, cannot have true and complete government without its members, or the members without the head, and how amongst them the eyes, which watch over all the other members, are so necessary that without eyes the head is nothing, nor without head the eyes.'[2] The great were the king's natural counsellors.

But others took a different view.

> Alas! sire, [wrote Jean Juvenal des Ursins in 1440] I don't wish at all to say that your relatives don't behave well and loyally towards you; but there is amongst them a very considerable amount of envy, which causes a number of troubles, and when you've put them out [of your entourage] it'll all cease. Send them against the enemy and find a way of paying them; and when you take into account what those who are around you have for their upkeep you'll be able to provide for the frontiers. This is what the good king Charles [V] your ancestor used to do; for he had none of his brothers near him and when they came to see him he used to give them some thousand *écus* to go back again.[3]

[1] E. de Monstrelet, *Chron.* ed. L. Douët d'Arcq (Soc. Hist. France) VI (1862) 39–40.

[2] G. Cousinot, *Chron.* ed. Vallet de Viriville (1859) p. 148.

[3] 'Helas, sire, je ne veulx mie dire que voz parens ne soient bons & loyaulx envers vous; mais entre eulx a tresgrans envies, dont viennent plusieurs inconveniens, et quant voz les aurez mis hors tout cessera. Envoies lez sus les ennemis et trouvez moyen de les souldoyer; et quant vous mectrez ce que ont ceulx qui sont autour de vous pour leurs estas vous entretendrez les

Thirty years earlier the university of Paris, too, had demanded the banishment from court of princes.[1] But this was rather a radical view. If the magnates did not appear in the council this may have been that they had been 'overlooked': the duc de Berry complained in 1410 that nobody was summoning him to it,[2] the duke of Burgundy complained in 1417 that the commonwealth was 'dissipated and despoiled by people of low station [and] of unknown birth'.[3] But such snobbery from a magnate who ought to have been well aware from experience of his own administration of the value of the low-born work-horse civil servant smacks of polemic. In fact such demands as those of 1442 were exceptional;[4] and so was over-much attendance of the princes in council. From the thirteenth century the 'born councillors' had effectively eschewed the day-to-day drudgery of counselling. The work was done by the courtiers and by the civil servants.

If it is hardly helpful to denigrate the first as favourites, to comment upon the 'very humble' origins[5] of the second is about as relevant as commenting on the origins of modern senior civil servants. Nor perhaps, it may be argued, is it very safe to make, on the basis of an analysis of the surviving council minutes for March to June 1455,[6] too firm statements about the pre-eminence through assiduity of the civil servants. Three months' worth of material may hardly be an effective sample. And even if it were, a crude counting of attendances is hardly an assessment of influence. Some matters were far more important than others. The question of a resignation *in favorem* of the office of proctor of the Inquisition at Carcassonne could safely be left to the four most

---

frontieres. Et ainsi faisoit le bon roy Charles vostre ayeul; car il navoit nulz de ses freres pres de luy et quant ilz le venoient veoir il leur donnoit quelque mil escus pour eulx en retourner' ('Loquar in tribulacione spiritus mei', Bibl. nat. MS fr. 5022, folios 10ᵛ–11ʳ).

[1] *Chron. du religieux de St.-Denis*, ed. L. Bellaguet (Docs inéd. sur l'hist. de France) IV (1842) 372.

[2] Ibid. p. 286.

[3] Vallet de Viriville, 'Mémoire sur les institutions de Charles VII', in *Bibl. Ec. Chartes*, XXXIII (1872) 15.

[4] N. Valois, *Etude hist. sur le Conseil du Roi* (1886) p. lxxxi.

[5] N. Valois, *Le Conseil du roi aux xivᵉ, xvᵉ et xviᵉ siècles* (1888) p. 152. But cf. Valois, *Etude hist.* p. cvi.

[6] ed. Valois, *Le Conseil du roi*, pp. 231–323; or perhaps, for that matter, for those surviving from 1483–5 (ibid. pp. 160–75).

hard-working councillors, Guillaume Jouvenel des Ursins, chancellor of France, Richard-Olivier de Longueil, bishop of Coutances, Etienne Lefèvre and François Hallé. The question of the Scottish embassy brought in the king himself, the counts of Maine, Nevers, Richmond, Foix, La Marche, Albret, Dunois and Sancerre, as well as a clutch of lesser courtiers and the inevitable civil servants.[1] That they were the men who did most of the work is hardly to be doubted. But that the magnates had lost all influence over 'high matters' is more debatable. A king with a taste for ruling by himself might take less notice of his brothers, his uncles or his cousins than one incapable of such independence; the magnate hey-day was the reign of Charles VI. But not even Louis XI could exclude the great completely from his council — though he is alleged to have tried his best to do so.[2]

And it was assumed by Jean Juvenal des Ursins that the king's council might not be wholly his. 'Indeed', he wrote in 1445, 'I've seen ignorant young men, without wisdom, prudence, justice of mind, reasonableness or experience, made *maîtres des requêtes* of the king's household ... and of the king's great council at the request of particular lords; and all they care about is pleasing the people who put them there.'[3] If the magnates were not there, at least their servants may have been. Guillaume Jouvenel was instructed on the means to circumvent such conciliar unwisdom. 'For this reason', his brother told him, 'I've seen that the king went off into a little closet, and the people one wanted were called in there secretly. That worthy man the late monsieur de Trèves especially used to have this done, and when there were matters which had to be kept secret, too.'[4] Jean Juvenal assumed equally that

[1] Ibid. pp. 288–9, 264–7.
[2] R. Doucet, 'Le Gouvernement de Louis XI', in R. *Cours et conférences* XXIV (1922–3) 740.
[3] 'En verite, jay veu que a la requeste de seigneurs particuliers on faisoit maistres des requestes de lostel du roy [*lacuna in MS*] et du grant conseil du roy jeunes gens ignorans, ausquelz il ne chaloit mais ques ilz pleussent a ceulx qui les y mettoient, sans sapience, prudence, justice ne raison ne experience.' ('A, a, a, nescio loqui quia puer ego sum', Bibl. nat. MS fr. 2701, fo. 43ʳ.)
[4] 'Pour ceste cause jay veu que le roy sen partoit et sen venoit en ung petit retraict, et la on appelloit secretement ceulx que on vouloit. Et specialment le bon homme feu monsr. de Treves le faisoit faire, et mesmement en matieres que on devoit tenir secretes.' (Ibid. fo. 43ᵛ.)

there were matters which might have to be concealed from the council: 'at the end of the council,' he wrote, 'if any things turn up which mustn't be revealed and which must be kept thoroughly secret, you should mention them privately to the king and find out what he wants to do about them'.[1] In the same way 'there'll be no harm, when you have some troublesome problem which affects the king or the common-wealth very closely, in taking counsel with the king himself, finding out his opinion and giving him yours, and asking him to think of those with whom he wants to finish the matter off, and to summon them himself directly. And again, if the king or you wish to discuss something which some people perhaps might be afraid to give their opinion on in public, it's a good idea to ask each person about it privately, to find out what they think and why.'[2] 'A king without prudent counsel' may have been, as Gerson thought, 'like the head of a body without eyes, without ears and without nose';[3] in actual operation the council was less conveniently anthropomorphic.

The fifteenth-century *Grand Conseil* suffered at times, in Jean Juvenal's eyes, from a number of the familiar tares of a committee. 'I've seen several things come up for discussion at the same time so that they got in the way of each other and the meeting broke up with nothing decided . . .' 'I've seen some of the people on the council chattering and prattling away to each other and not listening to what was being dealt with, which was to make a mockery [of the council] — they ought to have been punished. And although in the council one ought never to interrupt a speaker, unless it's the king or the chancellor that does so, nevertheless some people trying to be clever do so, which is in effect to

---

[1] '. . . a lissue du conseil, se aucunes choses non a reveler et a tenir bien secretes vous seurvenoient, appart en devez parler au roy et advertir pour savoir son plaisir' (ibid. fo. 42^{r-v}).

[2] '. . . ny auroit point de mal, quant vous aurez aucune chose perplexe qui touche fort le roy ou la chose publique, de vous conseiller au roy mesmes et savoir son advis et luy dire le vostre, et que il advise ceulx que il vouldra avoir a conclurre la chose, et que luy mesmes les appelle. Et encores se le roy ou vous voulez avoir conseil daucune chose que aucuns apoir craindroient a dire publiquement, cest bien fait de le demander a chacun appart et de savoir leur ymaginacion et qui les meut.' (Ibid. fo. 43^{v}.)

[3] P. S. Lewis, 'Jean Juvenal des Ursins and the Common Literary Attitude towards Tyranny in Fifteenth-century France', in *Medium Aevum*, XXXIV (1965) 119.

despise the king and his chancellor.'[1] The self-seekers, the ditherers, the eager expressers of opinions were all to be found;[2] and the unconscionably fluent. 'Alas!' wrote Jean Juvenal. 'There's an awful lot of fine talking going on in this kingdom, and there are some soldiers and others who put all their efforts and creative faculties into speaking their words well, better almost than an advocate [in a law court], giving their counsel in a sort of flattering way, presuming to please rather than to advise.'[3] Whom had he in mind? Jean comte de Dunois, in 1445 on the brink of returning to court, 'one of the finest speakers of French that ever was in France'?[4] Or the risen Pierre de Brézé, 'the glorious speaker'?

This sense of familiarity is reinforced by the exordium of Bertrand de Beauvau seigneur de Précigny's contribution to the council of 3 June 1455. He 'said that he hadn't heard about the matter till now, and so he didn't really know what to say about it. Still, as far as he could understand . . .' he began; and uninformed though he was, he carried monsieur de Montsoreau and monsieur de Maupas with him.[5] The council was essentially intimate; not as intimate perhaps as the court — though the two might at times be hard to distinguish — but essentially a world in which the force of personality was paramount. The king might disagree with his council. He might according to Jean Juvenal have to be wooed out of an unreasonable opinion by a tactful chancellor.[6] But he could not do without his counsellors, 'without whose help he

---

[1] 'Jay veu mettre plusieurs choses en deliberacion que lune empeschoit laultre et sen partoit on sans riens conclurre . . .' 'Jay autresfoys veu que quant on estoit au conseil les ungs caquetoient et parloient et ne entendoient aux matieres que on traictoit, qui estoit une grant irrision et dont on deust avoir fait punicion. Et combien que au conseil on ne doye point interrumpre la parolle de celluy qui dit son oppinion si non le roy ou son chanceillier, toutevoie aucuns, tendans faire les bons varles, le font, qui est en effect contempner le roy et son chanceillier.' ('A, a, a, nescio loqui quia puer ego sum', folios 42ʳ, 43ʳ.)

[2] Ibid. folios 44ᵛ, 45ʳ.

[3] 'Helas! En ce royaume on a fort use dune maniere de beau parler, et y a plusieurs hommes darmes et aultres qui mettent entente toute et ymaginacion a bien prononcer leurs parolles mieulx a paine que ung advocat, en conseillant par une maniere de flaterye, en cuidant plus complaires que conseiller.' (Ibid. fo. 44ᵛ.)

[4] J. Chartier, Chron. de Charles VII, ed. Vallet de Viriville, II (1858) 105.

[5] Valois, Le Conseil du roi, pp. 292–3.

[6] 'A, a, a, nescio loqui quia puer ego sum', fo. 44ʳ.

should do nothing, since in his [private] person he acknowledged all the infirmities that other men have'.[1] The actual institutional framework in which he sought advice should perhaps not be made too rigid. Those who are assisted by committees can still take the advice of individual members of them outside their meetings; they can take the advice of those who may not even be members of them. The council was the formal expression of the king's need for close assistance; matters were delegated to it to be reduced to a state in which the king could, if necessary, deal with them. Some matters, thought Jean Juvenal, 'might well be dealt with sometimes without the presence of the king'; the 'decision' could be reported to him, to see if it pleases him. Other matters had to be dealt with in his presence.[2] But, as we have seen, Jean Juvenal did not regard the council as the be-all and end-all of counsel. It was much too flexible for that. And it was in that flexibility that the 'glorious speakers' had their chance to have 'greater power around the king', to have 'more influence with him than other people'.[3]

Administration, central and local

The whole complex of 'court' and 'council', of the greater 'departments of state' and the more notable offices in the country needs to be thought of as a whole. In function the council was omnicompetent. There was nothing with which it by royal authority could not deal. The administration of justice and of finance was dealt with by two divisions of the council which had developed a life of their own under St.-Louis, the Parlement and the *Chambre des comptes*; but some residual control still remained in the *Grand Conseil*, usually in conjunction with its independent offspring. 'Experiments' had been made with restricted councils. There were the *Conseil étroit* of 1316 and the *Conseil du mois* of

[1] Coquille, op. cit. p. 3.
[2] '... se pevent bien expedier aucunesfoys sans la presence du roy ...'; '... a veoir se elle luy plait' ('A, a, a, nescio loqui quia puer ego sum', fo. 42ʳ). Jean Juvenal's views on the council may be compared with profit with those of Claude de Seyssel (*La Monarchie de France*, ed. J. Poujol (1961) pp. 133–42).
[3] '... plus grant puissance prez du roy ...' ('A, a, a, nescio loqui quia puer ego sum', fo. 44ʳ); G. du Fresne de Beaucourt, *Hist. de Charles VII*, III (1885) 41 n2.

1318–19. There was the *Conseil secret* of Philippe VI's reign, which at times seemed almost identical with the *Chambre des comptes*.[1] But although there appear to have been similar small, sedentary councils under Jean II and Charles V, the idea of the restricted council or of the small council for special purposes does not seem to have caused much danger to the larger body. The only new offshoot which developed an institutional life was the restricted judicial *Grand Conseil*, which seems to have appeared at least by 1450–2. Its existence was not formal until the very end of the century, when it was confined to twenty members and other councillors were forbidden to have anything to do with it. Reduction in the numbers of the *Grand Conseil* had been the aim of reformers. The Estates of 1356 tried to get it down to twenty-eight; an attempt was made in 1380 to get it down to eleven and in 1410 to sixteen or seventeen; the Cabochian ordinance of 1413 tried to get it down to fifteen.[2] None, for various reasons, succeeded. There were too many interests involved; the body was too amorphous, too indefinite, too personal to the king to be regulated into a strict existence.

Beneath the council the administration divided. The administration of justice came under the Parlement; the administration of the finances in principle under the *Chambre des comptes*.[3] Some jurisdictions escaped the Parlement: the *Requêtes* of the Household[4] and the fifteenth-century judicial *Grand Conseil* were exempt from its attentions; but for the rest the Parlement of Paris and its later local offspring were the sovereign court of France. At least from 1278 (though they were not given a permanent form until much later) the business was divided between a

[1] R. Cazelles, *La Société politique et la crise de la royauté sous Philippe de Valois* (1958) pp. 122 ff.

[2] Valois, *Etude historique*, pp. c–cii.

[3] F. Aubert, *Le Parlement de Paris de Philippe le bel à Charles VII* (1887–90) and *Hist. du Parlement de Paris de l'origine à François Ier* (1894); G. Ducoudray, *Les Origines du Parlement de Paris et de la justice aux xiiie et xive siècles* (1902); E. Maugis, *Hist. du Parlement de Paris de l'avènement des rois Valois à la mort d'Henri IV* (1913–16); H. Jassemin, *La Chambre des comptes de Paris au xve siècle, précédé d'une étude sur ses origines* (1933); F. Lot and R. Fawtier, *Hist. des institutions françaises au Moyen âge*, II *Institutions royales* (1958) 332–71, 240–44.

[4] A. Guillois, *Recherches sur les maîtres des Requêtes de l'hôtel des origines à 1350* (1909); G. Bailhache, 'Les Maîtres des Requêtes de l'hôtel depuis l'avènement de Jean le bon jusqu'à l'édit de Compiègne (1350–1553)', in *Positions des thèses de l'Ec. Chartes* (1924) pp. 27–32; Lot and Fawtier, op. cit. pp. 82–4.

Grande Chambre, a *Chambre des enquêtes* and a *Chambre des requêtes*, each dealing with its own part of a mainly appellate jurisdiction. The development of the Parlement from the earlier *curia* is clearest gauged in the slow atrophy of aristocratic membership into dignity controlled by the king if never excluded. The body became the professional High Court: the representative element, which survived in the Parlement of Brittany[1] and the Parliament of England, was divorced from the judicial element of the old *curia* and lost by this a considerable part of its *raison d'être*. In the fifteenth century regional Parlements were set up (in Toulouse) or created out of the sovereign courts of annexed areas (in Dauphiné, in Bordeaux, in Burgundy, in Provence and in Normandy).[2] During the Anglo-Burgundian occupation of Paris a rival Parlement was set up at Poitiers; its members were integrated with that of Paris after the liberation.[3] Although the Parlement had some administrative functions its duties were primarily judicial; as a supreme court it could be an effective weapon in the defence of the crown; and its competence as the only court in which questions concerning the rights of the crown could be heard made it the scene for the semi-political legal battles against the greater magnates.

If the Parlement had its rivals — and 'all these jurisdictions', thought the ex-parliamentarian Jean Juvenal des Ursins, 'ought to be cut down'[4] — the *Chambre des comptes* had more. The extension of the financial resources of government to taxation as well as the revenue of the *domaine* seems to have posed an almost insoluble problem of control. First, asked the Questioner in the treatise *C'est le vestige des finances*,

> QUESTION: 'What are the finances of the kingdom?'
> ANSWER: 'There are two kinds of finance, to wit ordinary finances and extraordinary finances.'
> QUESTION: 'What are the ordinary finances?'
> ANSWER: 'They come from the king's *domaine*, which is ruled and administered by the four *trésoriers* of France, one in

---

[1] E. Texier, *Etude sur la Cour ducale et les origines du Parlement de Bretagne* (Rennes, 1905).

[2] A. Viala, *Le Parlement de Toulouse et l'admin. royale laïque, 1420–1525 environ* (Albi, 1953); Lot and Fawtier, op. cit. pp. 480–93, 497–502.

[3] Maugis, op. cit. I (1913) pp. 49 ff.

[4] '... toutes telles justices se doivent restraindre ...' ('Verba mea auribus percipe, Domine', Bibl. nat. MS fr. 2701, fo. 56ʳ).

control of Languedoil, one of Outre-Seine, one of Normandy and one of Languedoc . . .'

QUESTION: 'What are the extraordinary finances?'

ANSWER: 'These are the revenues of the *greniers*, the *aides* and the *tailles* of the kingdom.'[1]

The ordinary revenues were received in the *Trésor* by the *trésoriers* from the local accountants.[2] The extraordinary revenues were received, from the mid-fourteenth century, in their *Chambre* by the *généraux des finances*.[3] The relationship between these two administrations and that of the *Chambre des comptes* was far from precise; in the same way its relationship with the mint organisation of the *généraux-maîtres des monnaies*[4] was hard to define. The function of the *Chambre des comptes* according to the ordinance of Vivier-en-Brie in 1320 was essentially to deal with the accounting and the conservation of the *domaine*; this involved powers financial, administrative and judicial. The *Chambre*'s powers over expenditure were much more limited than its powers of receipt. Its apogee came essentially under Philippe VI — for personal as well as institutional reasons — but already, before it came under attack in the Estates of 1357, some control over the *Trésor*'s activities had escaped it, and with the crisis it lost the greater part of the administration of extraordinary finance to the nascent organisation of the *généraux*. Jurisdiction in cases arising out of taxation escaped it, ultimately to the *Cour des aides*, which began its chequered career in 1390.[5] The administration of the *domaine* and of its finances was shared by *Trésor* and

---

[1] *Docs relatifs à l'admin. financière en France de Charles VII à François Ier (1443–1523)*, ed. G. Jacqueton (Coll. de textes pour servir à l'étude et à l'enseignement de l'hist.: 1891) pp. 205, 225.

[2] Borrelli de Serres, *Recherches sur divers services publics du xiiie au xviie siècle*, III (1909) 1–243; M. Rey, *Le Domaine du roi et les finances extraordinaires sous Charles VI, 1388–1413* (1965) pp. 41–162.

[3] G. Dupont-Ferrier, *Études sur les institutions financières de la France à la fin du Moyen âge*, I *Les Élections et leur personnel* (1930), II *Les Finances extraordinaires et leur mécanisme* (1932); Rey, *Le Domaine du roi*, pp. 162–366.

[4] J. Bailhache, 'Chambre et cour des monnaies (xive, xve et xvie siècles). Aperçu hist.' in R. *numism.* ser. 4 XXXVII (1934) 63–99, 175–97, XXXVIII (1935) 67–89, XXXIX (1936) 157–79, 327–45.

[5] G. Dupont-Ferrier, *Nouvelles Études sur les institutions financières de la France à la fin du Moyen âge*, I *Les Origines et le premier siècle de la Chambre ou Cour des aides de Paris* (1933).

Chambre des comptes throughout the later fourteenth and fifteenth centuries; and again from 1390 a new court, the *Cour du Trésor*,[1] appeared to deal with cases arising from the *domaine* (though it never seems to have had as much éclat as its sister the *Cour des aides*, which produced offspring in Languedoc and in Normandy). And in matters concerning the currency its authority again was shared, this time with the *Chambre des monnaies*. Finance had become too complicated to be dealt with by the *Chambre des comptes* alone; new administrations and jurisdictions were necessary. These shared, in a way governed more by civil servants' influence and by convenience than by institutional nicety, the attributes which had at one time belonged to a body by the fifteenth century suffering, as we shall see, from an institutional sclerosis.

Restricted the *Chambre des comptes* was to remain, by the *Trésor*, the *Cour des aides*, the Household, the Parlement of Paris, the *Cour des monnaies*, the *Châtelet* and the new provincial *Chambres des comptes* whose beginnings are adumbrated in the fifteenth century; and the problem of the control of the finances remained too. There were some obscure experiments during the first half of the fifteenth century to create a unified system of administration for both ordinary and extraordinary finances; but they seem to have come to an end by 1445.[2] Almost as obscure were the government's means of creating the budget. The higher control of finance belonged essentially to the council. There is some evidence that *abrégés*, summaries of the expenses and receipts of the kingdom, were presented in the early 1330s for the king's guidance; but thereafter there is little evidence of formal control until taxation was firmly established in the 1430s and 1440s. From then on an *Etat général des finances* seems to have been drawn up by the financial departments in co-operation as an estimate of the coming year's expenditure on the basis of the year or years preceding. In the interval the king was probably advised in a more informal, *ad hoc* way.[3] But our knowledge of the mechanism of French royal finance in the later middle ages is pitifully limited.

[1] Ibid. II *Les Origines et le premier siècle de la Cour du Trésor* (Bibl. Ec. Hautes Etudes, 266: 1936).

[2] P. Viollet, *Hist. des institutions politiques et admin. de la France*, III (1903) 492–4; Dupont-Ferrier, *Les Elections*, pp. 168–70; Lot and Fawtier, op. cit. p. 247.

[3] Dupont-Ferrier, *Les Finances extraordinaires*, pp. 192–7.

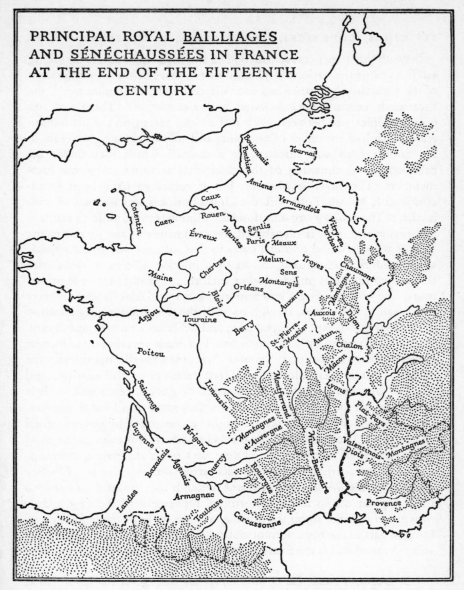

PRINCIPAL ROYAL BAILLIAGES AND SÉNÉCHAUSSÉES IN FRANCE AT THE END OF THE FIFTEENTH CENTURY

Boulonnais
Ponthieu
Tournai
Amiens
Vermandois
Caux
Vitry-en-Perthois
Cotentin
Caen
Rouen
Senlis
Évreux
Mantes
Paris
Meaux
Chaumont
Maine
Chartres
Melun
Sens
Troyes
Montagne
Dijon
Orléans
Montargis
Auxerre
Auxois
Anjou
Touraine
Berry
St-Pierre-le-Moutier
Autun
Chalon
Poitou
Limousin
Mâcon
Lyons
Saintonge
Montferrand
Plat-Pays
Guyenne
Périgord
Montagnes d'Auvergne
Nîmes-Beaucaire
Valentinois-Diois
Montagnes
Bazadais
Quercy
Rouergue
Agenais
Armagnac
Provence
Landes
Toulouse
Carcassonne

For further detail see G. Dupont-Ferrier, *Les Officiers royaux des bailliages et séné-chaussées et les institutions monarchiques locales en France à la fin du Moyen âge* (Bibl. Ec. Hautes Etudes, 145: 1902) *carte* no. 1; and for recent views on the problems of delimiting such areas, B. Guenée, 'La Géographie admin. de la France à la fin du Moyen âge: élections et bailliages', in *Moyen Age,* ser. 4 LXVII (1961) 293–323, and *Tribunaux et gens de justice dans le bailliage de Senlis à la fin du Moyen âge* (1963) p. 75 and *carte*.

Beneath the three great central bodies and their more or less unwilling satellites came the various local administrations. For the administration of the royal *domaine* France had been divided up by the beginning of the fourteenth century into *bailliages* and *sénéchaussées*.[1] There was no essential difference between *bailli* and *sénéchal* except on the promotion scale. Each had a number of assistants and subordinates to help him in his duties; each was directed by a council which met under his presidency and consisted of the chief civil servants and some local members. The body is obscure, but it seems to have been omni-competent; it dealt 'both with the king's business and affairs, and with justice'.[2] The *bailliage* organisation had administrative, judicial, military and financial duties. It distributed the commands of the government; it dealt with civil and criminal cases in first instance and heard appeals against inferior seigneurial and its own inferior officers; it dealt with the non-contentious jurisdiction of such things as dowries or legitima-tions. The *bailli* or *sénéchal* was responsible for the older 'feudal' military organisation in his area, though most of the new military organisation of the later middle ages escaped him, and *baillis* became very unmilitary. The administration only of the ordinary, *domaine* revenue came into its hands; for the extraordinary revenue there was a parallel organisation of *élections*. But in general the local civil servants of the *bailliages* and *sénéchaussées* were the maids of all work of government; and in their relations with the local political classes they acted as a kind of nervous system by which the body politic might be controlled by governmental cerebration. At times this control was imperfect; but even in the most weak-headed of moments the system was never destroyed. Adminis-tration of extraordinary revenues was carried out, over a part of France at least, by the *élus* in their *élections*.[3] Though they owed their name to their popular origin in the 'reforming' movement of the 1350s, their organisation, based upon the diocese, was almost from the beginning an integral part of the royal administration. They too had their proliferating subordinates; and as the financial officers of the *bailliages* were connected

---

[1] G. Dupont-Ferrier, *Les Officiers royaux des bailliages et sénéchaussées et les institutions monarchiques locales en France à la fin du Moyen âge* (Bibl. Ec. Hautes Etudes, 145: 1902).

[2] Ibid. p. 266.

[3] Dupont-Ferrier, *Les Elections* and *Les Finances extraordinaires*.

up with the *Trésor*, so they were in turn linked with the administration of the *généraux des finances*. And to the *généralités* accounted, too, a third local administration — that of the salt tax, the *gabelle*, with its organisation of *greniers* and *grenetiers*.

Different patterns imposed at various stages of its growth therefore created the complex of medieval administration. The king and his council presided over all. The final decision was always the king's; the final appeal always lay to him. An active ruler could with some measure of success cut through the tangle beneath; but routine matters still depended upon it. The Parlement of Paris had a very great control over the administration of justice; its enemies were the external jurisdictions which might escape it. The *Chambre des comptes*, though it still retained the power of audit over all finances, ordinary and extraordinary, was slowly being devoured by its own thankless children; but if this confounded the administrative confusion, arguably it allowed more vital administrations greater control of affairs — though perhaps the incompetences of the *Chambre* were the result of rather than an excuse for the process. But as well as the tangle of superimposed administrations there was the problem of the sheer size and weight of the administrative machine. This, too, affected the mechanism of effective control. The problem was not confined to war-time, though the difficulties of travel under war conditions enhanced it. A slow tendency towards decentralisation was apparent in the fifteenth century. Even the central financial bodies seemed to have succumbed to the temptation to think of themselves as a group of regional administrations, and when the Estates-general of 1484 split up, it split up consciously along lines of the six *généralités des finances*.[1] The confirmation of the regional Parlements and regional *Chambres des comptes* seems to recognise that a limit had been reached. The lieutenancies-general and governorships of provinces — the latter numbered some eleven at the end of the fifteenth century — were again possibly created as a result of this double pressure of convenience and particularism.[2] But from the attitude of the central

[1] Dupont-Ferrier, *Les Elections*, pp. 167–70, 179; J. Masselin, *Journal des Etats généraux de France tenus à Tours en 1484*, ed. A. Bernier (Docs inéd. sur l'hist. de France: 1835) pp. 66–8.

[2] P. Dognon, *Les Institutions politiques et admin. du pays de Languedoc, du xiii⁰ siècle aux guerres de Religion* (Toulouse, 1896) pp. 333, 345 *bis* ff. On the other

government towards the governors of the end of the fifteenth century it seems they were possibly more of a hindrance than a help to royal control — as, perhaps, they had always been.[1]

Civil servants

The civil service was not simply a dry, inhuman, mechanical structure: it, like all institutions, was made up of men, of human beings with all too human ambitions and temperaments. Did not Guillaume de Ste.-Maure, chancellor of France under Philippe VI, covet the wife of Angelin Baloce, 'who was very good-looking', and threaten to deprive her cousin, Perrin Chaufecire, of his office under the crown if he did not procure her for him?[2] They were all human; and it is of the civil service as a living organism that one must think, as an organism confused by human error. Who were the civil servants and what were they after? They came from all the sections of medieval society except the lowest: nobility, bourgeoisie, clergy, all provided civil servants from their ranks. Like that of the courtiers their aim was straightforward: they sought the rewards, material and immaterial, licit and illicit, public and private, of government service. In serving the king they were, reasonably enough, serving themselves. Their privileges and immunities made them almost a fourth order of the nation; and yet they remained in contact with the classes from which they came and to which their descendants might again return. They were engrained in the surface of local society; and since stability in office was remarkable, time made the grain run deep.

There were niches for all in the civil service. Magnates could become governors, *commissaires réformateurs* and even, in Languedoc, *viguiers*, local officers now subordinate to the *sénéchaux*.[3] Knights could become lieutenants to governors, *baillis* and *sénéchaux* themselves, *élus*, *généraux des aides*, *trésoriers de justice* and a number of other things: some even became lieutenants-general in *bailliages* or even became *grenetiers*, but in

---

hand, they could be disliked (ibid. pp. 360 *bis*-361; Dupont-Ferrier, *Les Officiers royaux*, p. 59 n 1).

[1] Dupont-Ferrier, *Les Officiers royaux*, p. 63; Dognon, op. cit. p. 360.

[2] Cazelles, op. cit. pp. 448–9.

[3] Dupont-Ferrier, *Les Officiers royaux*, pp. 55–8, 194; *Les Elections*, p. 191.

general they kept to the more honorific jobs in local or central administration.[1] Esquires were found lower in the scale: they filled offices from *baillis* or *généraux des aides* down to clerks of the *Trésor*.[2] The lower offices in Normandy were taken more often by the nobility than those elsewhere: this was yet another element in the peculiarity of *la langue de Normandie*.[3] The bourgeoisie tended to fill the financial jobs both in the central departments and in the country; prelates and clergy were scattered through the administration.[4] But this division into class is rather artificial and unreal: the offices were by no means confined to the rank from which the majority of their holders might have come; the officers themselves were by no means confined to the rank in which they might have been born. Tradition confined some offices — such as the southern *sénéchaussées* — to some ranks;[5] but tradition did not restrain the bourgeoisie from rising into the nobility and expanding into the clergy. Perhaps more remarkable is the growing importance of legal training for offices held by all three ranks.[6] Graduate nobles, graduate clergy, graduate bourgeois formed again almost a new class: a class in which the differences in background were slight. The civil service was a career to be prepared for; its posts were eagerly coveted. If one did not have favour one might have prowess to attract it or to obtain its rewards — the pleasures of office — by simple ability. If one was incompetent, one's opponents for the job would be quick to point it out;[7] and in the formal examination of newly appointed holders of the more important judicial offices horrible truths might emerge. When Jean Barton, sometime *général,* at the *Cour des aides,* aspired to become a

[1] Dupont-Ferrier, *Les Officiers royaux*, pp. 67, 71, 122; *Les Elections*, pp. 70, 143, 171; *Les Origines . . . Cour du Trésor*, p. 38.

[2] Dupont-Ferrier, *Les Officiers royaux*, pp. 71–2; *Les Elections*, p. 171; *Les Origines . . . Cour du Trésor*, p. 77.

[3] Dupont-Ferrier, *Les Officers royaux*, pp. 150, 160, 169, 184–5. For the term, see, for instance, H. Hervieu, *Recherches sur les premiers Etats généraux* (1879) pp. 244–5.

[4] See, for instance, Dupont-Ferrier, *Les Officers royaux*, pp. 66, 169, 218; *Les Elections*, pp. 69–71, 111–12, 170–1, 183; *Les Origines . . . Cour du Trésor*, pp. 38–9, 54, 69, 77; *Les Origines . . . Cour des aides*, p. 72.

[5] Viala, op. cit. I 126; cf. Dupont-Ferrier, *Les Officers royaux*, p. 71.

[6] See, for instance, ibid. pp. 75–6, 771–2; *Les Elections*, pp. 71, 183, 188; *Les Origines . . . Cour des aides*, p. 72.

[7] See, for instance, *Les Elections*, pp. 70–1, 100–1, 143.

counsellor at the Parlement of Paris, he was found, on 31 March 1443, to have an insufficient knowledge of procedure and had to spend two years more in study before he was received as a *conseiller clerc*.[1] Much the same thing seems to have been happening in the Parlement of Toulouse at the end of the fifteenth century.[2] The rush towards expertise was probably more characteristic of the end than of the beginning of our period;[3] but it was symptomatic of how far the civil service had, by 1500, become a mystery for which considerable qualification was necessary; qualification which in turn helped to give the caste its identity.

The development of the civil service as a distinct caste proceeded gradually if unevenly throughout the later middle ages.[4] Despite reformers' hankerings after election, the vast majority of offices was naturally in the king's gift.[5] So important was it to reach the king's ear before one's rivals did on the death of a royal officer that some unfortunates outstripped mortality and, as their opponents were careful to point out, received the succession before the previous office-holder had well and truly expired.[6] Such undexterous haste lost all. And when offices were given, like benefices, by the king 'at three o'clock after midnight', it was little wonder he got confused.[7] Charles VI might naturally be thought to have been the most confused of all; but litigation was incessant, and the checks imposed on royal grants of office by the departments which were bound to enregister his letters of appointment were very necessary.[8] The way to the king's ear was tortuous. In general outline it was clear to the critics of the government in 1413. 'It has come to our attention', the Cabochian ordinance made

---

[1] Dupont-Ferrier, *Les Origines . . . Cour des aides*, pp. 87–8.

[2] Viala, op. cit. 1 245–6.   [3] Cf. ibid. p. 242; and see below, pp. 150–1.

[4] Studies of local official groups may be found in B. Guenée, *Tribunaux et gens de justice dans le bailliage de Senlis à la fin du Moyen âge* (1963), and in R. Fédou, *Les Hommes de loi lyonnais à la fin du Moyen âge. Étude sur les origines de la classe de robe* (1964).

[5] Guenée, op. cit. pp. 168–9.

[6] G. Dupont-Ferrier, *Études sur les institutions financières de la France à la fin du Moyen âge*, 1 *Les Élections et leur personnel* (1930) 75.

[7] See above, p. 123.

[8] See, for instance, G. Dupont-Ferrier, *Les Officiers royaux des bailliages et sénéchaussées et les institutions monarchiques locales en France à la fin du Moyen âge* (Bibl. Ec. Hautes Etudes, 145: 1902) pp. 79–81.

Charles VI say, 'that many of the princes of the blood and also many of our household knights, servants and others, by putting in for them, ask and have each day offices from us, although they have no intention of holding them themselves or of exercising them in person, but of handing them over to their friends and servants, or of selling them for a profit...'[1] The members of the Estates of Languedoil in Paris in October 1356 thought much the same, though they were more trenchant in announcing it: 'they declared that many *baillis*, *sénéchaux*, *prévôts*, *contes*, receivers, keepers of ports and passages, *châtellains*, lieutenants to captains of particular *pays*, mint masters, *gardes* and counter-*gardes*, collectors of tenths and other officers, have been appointed by [the government]... without election, through friendships, through favours or through corruption...'[2] A century later Charles VII admitted that 'we are frequently bothered by many people... asking us for offices'; and the same thing happened under Louis XI.[3] 'Sums of money, beaver hats, wine and other things' could win over the king's secretaries;[4] the favour and intercession of the great could be solicited. It was because his wife had 'most lovingly begged and required' Philippe VI to give them their offices that Alexandre de Crèvecœur and Pierre d'Orgemont entered the Parlement of Paris;[5] the problem was thus hardly new in the reign of Charles VI; and there are enough general complaints and enough fragments of evidence at least to allow us to admit that 'favour' was widespread.

The movement towards the 'venality' seen in 1413 can be traced fairly consistently in the fourteenth and fifteenth centuries. It was a private venality, as opposed to the public venality of the sixteenth century and later. Those who held or had obtained offices could arrange to dispose of them to their relatives or to others. Resignations by an office-holder *in favorem* of a third party seem to have been practised

---

[1] *L'Ordonnance cabochienne*, ed. A. Coville (Coll. de textes pour servir à l'étude et à l'enseignement de l'hist.: 1891) p. 143.

[2] 'Journal des Etats généraux réunis à Paris au mois d'octobre 1356', ed. R. Delachenal, in *Nouvelle R. hist. Droit*, XXIV (1900) 433–4.

[3] Dupont-Ferrier, *Les Officiers royaux*, p. 79; cf. Dupont-Ferrier, 'Ignorances et distractions admin. en France aux xive et xve siècles', in *Bibl. Ec. Chartes*, C (1939) 148 ff.

[4] *L'Ordonnance cabochienne*, pp. 148–9.

[5] R. Cazelles, *La Société politique et la crise de la royauté sous Philippe de Valois* (1958) 336. Cf. pp. 267 ff, 312 ff.

in the smaller offices, like sergeantries, at least by the reign of Philippe VI;[1] and already in that reign a warm recommendation from the outgoing holder of an office rather higher in the *Chambre des enquêtes* ensured for Ysarn de St.-Astier the succession to it.[2] Resignations seem to have spread to the higher offices in the second half of the fourteenth century; in 1408 Charles VI stated clearly that *baillis*, *sénéchaux*, receivers, king's advocates and proctors had resigned their offices in favour of third persons, and accepted it under certain circumstances.[3] The process was informal; but it was current practice by the end of the fourteenth century and throughout the fifteenth.

Such resignations might be practised, as the Cabochian reformers alleged, for hard cash. From the beginning of the fourteenth century the king had given again minor offices as a favour to the recipient, who might exercise them or, explicitly, sell them for profit.[4] Again the process reached higher in the civil-service hierarchy. In 1387 Charles VI, for the first time, attempted to restrict the practice; given the silence of the Estates of 1357, it must have originated in the reign of Charles V. It was again condemned in 1408; and in 1413 the Cabochian ordinance provided a comprehensive list of officers both high and low who 'are accustomed to sell . . . [their] offices and in this way to abandon them to other people and to take a profit from the transaction by means of the sale or in some other way, so that those who buy them or in other ways provide that profit are more inclined and eager to have payments made to them in excess of what they should be and deny excuses, and to ask us through importunity or otherwise for gifts and benefits to recover what the offices cost them . . .'[5] But the same article allowed the king to dispense from it in the cases of those who because of 'illness, age or other occurrence' could not carry out their offices; and it was not until the 1490s that such venality was formally forbidden.[6] In the Midi it seems that resignations *in favorem* and their accompanying venality indeed developed strength from the end of the reign of Charles VII, with the significant difference that royal permission seemed now of

[1] O. Martin, 'La Nomination aux offices royaux au xive siècle', in *Mélanges P. Fournier* (1929) pp. 496–8.

[2] Cazelles, op. cit. pp. 342, 451–2.   [3] Guenée, op. cit. p. 170.

[4] O. Martin, op. cit. pp. 496–7; Guenée, op. cit. p. 172.

[5] *L'Ordonnance cabochienne*, pp. 128–9.   [6] Guenée, op. cit. p. 174.

overriding importance.[1] Probably elsewhere, as in the Midi, they still affected most of the inferior offices and, where higher offices were concerned, those of the *bailliages, sénéchaussées* and *élections* rather than of the central departments.[2] And if the king did not take a profit, he was ostensibly in control of the system. But when, in 1450–1, Nicolas de Louviers, receiver of *aides* in Paris, had from the king on the account of the *recette-générale* of Seine-Yonne '800 *livres* over four years . . . to help him to pay for his office' less favoured aspirants to place, as long as they could acquire the mere benevolence of the king, had little to fear.[3]

And there were other hopeful rules, too, they could break with impunity and profit. In general the formal wages of royal officers were pretty low.[4] At the end of the fifteenth century those of *baillis* and *sénéchaux* averaged some 350 *livres tournois*; if the *sénéchal* of Guyenne got 1200, the *bailli* of Gévaudan got only 50 *livres* a year.[5] The average for an *élu* was 100 *livres tournois*.[6] Governors, *généraux des finances*, receivers-general, presidents in the *Cour des aides* might get a substantial salary,[7] but the run of royal officers did not. How then did they live — and why were their offices so sought after? Extraordinary sources of income and plurality of office provide part of the answer. From many sources royal officers increased their meagre earnings. The king himself could be generous in ways which varied from grants of lordships, from the pensions which so much distressed the Estates-general of Tours in 1484 and from munificent gifts down to generous expense-accounts.[8] The

[1] A. Viala, *Le Parlement de Toulouse et l'admin. royale laïque, 1420–1525 environ*, I (Albi, 1953) 131 ff.

[2] Ibid. pp. 136, 198; but there are suspicions of venality in cases of advocates in the *Cour du Trésor* (G. Dupont-Ferrier, *Nouvelles Etudes sur les institutions financières de la France à la fin du Moyen âge*, II *Les Origines et le premier siècle de la Cour du Trésor* (Bibl. Ec. Hautes Etudes, 266: 1936) 71) and possibly of *généraux de justice* (ibid. I *Les Origines et le premier siècle de la Chambre ou Cour des aides de Paris* (1933) 86) before Louis XI's death.

[3] Dupont-Ferrier, *Les Elections*, p. 114. Cf. *Les Officiers royaux*, p. 81 nn 6–7.

[4] Guenée, op. cit. pp. 182–3.

[5] Dupont-Ferrier, *Les Officiers royaux*, pp. 86–8.

[6] Dupont-Ferrier, *Les Élections*, p. 78.

[7] Dupont-Ferrier, *Les Officiers royaux*, p. 60, and *Les Elections*, pp. 174, 184, and *Les Origines . . . Cour des aides*, p. 75.

[8] See, for instance, Dupont-Ferrier, *Les Officiers royaux*, pp. 60, 89, and *Les Elections*, pp. 116, 175, 184; Viala, op. cit. I 154–5; J. Masselin, *Journal des*

formal pickings of office — the *épices* of the north, the *especias* of the Midi — could be considerable; and between such old-established and regulated resources a whole gamut of 'presents' could stretch to outright bribery.[1] Again the Cabochian ordinance is instructive: royal officers concerned with justice were to swear

> that either directly or indirectly they would not receive . . .
> gold, silver, or any property or inheritance, for rent or for gift, or
> any revenue, perpetual or for a term; that they would not procure
> any gifts, rents or revenues to be given to their wives, children,
> brothers, sisters, nephews, cousins or relatives male or female, or
> their domestic servants, excepting only foodstuffs ready to eat and
> drink, without excess and without fraud . . . and that they would
> not take drink save in little kegs, bottles or pots, without fraud or
> corruption, and [only] from those who are rich and have enough,
> and without asking them for it; and that they will never sell
> what's left over, but that they will give it to charity; and also
> that . . . they will as far as they are able prevent their wives and
> [all] the other persons named above from taking the gifts
> enumerated above, and that, if they learn that they in fact have,
> they will force them to give up and hand back what they have
> thus taken, as soon as it comes to their notice.[2]

All this was far from new in 1413, and royal officers continued to take their illicit income as they found it. In 1462 the Estates of Rouergue had to raise the tariff from 'a fine horse' for the *sénéchal* to a wholesale tax for the bribery of him and others to avoid having to provide for *francs-archers*, which, with other expenses towards this purpose, came to a total of 1433 *livres* for the Alta Marcha of Rouergue alone.[3] And in plurality of office lay again a source of profit. There were few offices whose holders did not at one time or another hold them in plurality. In 1459 Jean d'Acy the elder was *juge-mage* of Beaucaire, president in the

Etats généraux de France tenus à Tours en 1484, ed. A. Bernier (Docs inéd. sur l'hist. de France: 1835) pp. 328–90.

[1] Dupont-Ferrier, *Les Officiers royaux*, pp. 89–90, and *Les Elections*, p. 116; Viala, op. cit. 1 155 ff, 206 ff; Fédou, op. cit. pp. 50 ff. For less licit takings, see *Les Officiers royaux*, pp. 129, 179, and *Les Elections*, pp. 82–3 (cf. G. Dupont-Ferrier, 'Les Elections financières en France sous Louis XI et les abus de leurs officiers', in *Mélanges . . . Nicolas Iorga* (1933) pp. 229–42) 116.

[2] *L'Ordonnance cabochienne*, p. 100.

[3] *Docs sur la ville de Millau*, ed. J. Artières (Arch. hist. Rouergue, 7: Millau, 1930) pp. 361–7.

Parlement of Toulouse and *général des aides*; in 1461 Jean I Bureau was a *trésorier de justice*, a *maître* in the *Chambre des comptes*, perpetual mayor of Bordeaux and captain of Meaux.[1] It had been the same in the fourteenth century. The *élu* and *vicomte* of Rouen in 1364, the *élu* and *vicomte* of Avranches in 1373, were the same persons; as were the *élu* of Séez and the *vicomte* of Falaise in 1366 and the *élu* of Bayeux and the *vicomte* of Caen in 1372. In 1374 one of the *élus* of Paris was lieutenant to the *prévôt des maréchaux*.[2] In the *sénéchaussée* of Carcassonne between 1430 and 1525 out of over five hundred promotions of civil servants over a hundred were to offices which were going to be held in plurality; in the *sénéchaussée* of Beaucaire seventy out of over seven hundred.[3] Plurality of office caused constant complaint.[4]

> I am here at Laon [wrote Jean Juvenal des Ursins in 1445] where is the head of the *bailliage* of Vermandois, which is, or ought to be, the most notable. But at the moment not the *bailli* nor his lieutenant nor the captain nor his lieutenant nor the *prévôt* is in the town. It is necessary that they reside; or, if they are prevented from doing so, that their lieutenants or vicegerents reside here; and that they should not have other charge or office of anyone save the king. We have [a *bailli*] here [who's] a most notable man, but he never stays in the town; he's sent on special commissions, and he's *bailli* to other lords. The *bailliage* of Vermandois is well worth the occupation of a man without other charge; and it's the same with all the others.[5]

This was Jamet du Tillay, councillor and *chambellan* to the king, servant of the duc d'Orléans, frequent royal commissioner.[6] The royal attitude throughout seems to have been that of Charles VIII's government in 1484: in reply to the standard complaint about accumulation of offices it replied that 'on the question of people holding several royal offices, the king will take advice and will not instruct them to do so without pressing reason'.[7] But the king had and would continue so to 'instruct',

---

[1] Viala, op. cit. 1 171; Dupont-Ferrier, *Les Origines . . . Cour du Trésor*, p. 42.
[2] Dupont-Ferrier, *Les Elections*, pp. 80–2.   [3] Viala, op. cit. 1 172.
[4] Guenée, op. cit. pp. 180 ff.
[5] P. S. Lewis, 'Jean Juvenal des Ursins and the Common Literary Attitude towards Tyranny in Fifteenth-century France', in *Medium Aevum*, XXXIV (1965) 117.
[6] G. Dupont-Ferrier, *Gallia regia* (1942–61) no. 22965.
[7] Masselin, op. cit. p. 707.

despite the proliferation of subordinates to do the work of the non-resident officers and the eloquence of Jean Masselin at the Estates-general of Tours.[1]

'There is nothing which so encourages an officer or servant most loyally and diligently to serve', thought those Estates-general, 'than to be secure in his position and in his livelihood in most loyally serving his master and carrying out his duties.'[2] Such natural quietism had, despite his own ordinance of 1467, allegedly been slighted by Louis XI throughout his life as king;[3] and when the mortally ill, mortally fearful old man hid himself away in Plessis-lès-Tours behind his iron fence, his mobile iron pill-boxes and his forty arbalesters, who at night were to shoot at sight,[4] 'he ordered bitter punishments so as to be feared and because he was afraid of losing people's obedience, for thus', said Commynes, 'he told me himself. He replaced officers and disbanded soldiery, he clipped pensions and cut them down entirely, and he told me a few days before his death that he spent his time making and unmaking people. And he made himself more talked about throughout the kingdom than he had ever been, and he did it for fear he would be thought dead . . .'[5] One of the signs of royal power was a king's control over his officers. In the fifteenth century, if not before, a strong feeling was apparent against the apparently arbitrary 'disappointment' of officers, either at will or at the accession of a new ruler. 'Offices', it was argued in Toulouse in the 1420s, 'are perpetual at the prince's will and he will never will that anyone should be deprived of his office without cause.'[6] Here the two interests were neatly conjoined. The reply of Charles VIII's government in 1484 was much the same: 'since [it] . . . is reasonable that no officer should be deprived of his office and position except by death, resignation or forfeiture after sentence by a competent judge and after the officer had been heard or at least duly summoned, the king was agreed and wishes that this practice should be maintained and observed in future'.[7] The ordinance of 1467 had in the

---

[1] Dupont-Ferrier, *Les Officiers royaux*, pp. 92 ff; Masselin, op. cit. pp. 366–8.
[2] Ibid. pp. 682–3.   [3] See, for instance, Viala, op. cit. 1 196 ff.
[4] P. de Commynes, *Mémoires*, ed. J. Calmette and G. Durville, 11 (Classiques de l'hist. de France au Moyen âge, 5: 1925) 291.
[5] Ibid. p. 297.   [6] Viala, op. cit. 1 193.
[7] Masselin, op. cit. p. 706.

interim made the question precise.[1] And in fact by the fifteenth century the stability in office of civil servants was remarkable.[2] The fifty-six years in office of Raoul Mallard as *général-maître des monnaies* which ended in 1395, the forty-three years in office of Nicolas Musart as *grenetier* of Reims were perhaps exceptional;[3] but examples could be drawn from most offices from those of governors, *baillis* and *sénéchaux*, *élus*, *généraux des finances* and *trésoriers de justice* down to those of *élus'* clerks and *greffiers* in the *Cour des aides* of over twenty years' service in the same function. There were, of course, cases of the untimely end of an official life.[4] There was that of Henri Boissereau, from June to September 1409 *général sur la justice des aides*, who retired from government employment altogether and set up as a provincial practitioner in Decize, where he was highly thought of thirty years later.[5] Others went with greater éclat. The rest hoped to stay; if possible to get rich; to make a career, to found a patrimony, to found the careers of their friends and relations. The case of Bernard I Lauret is perhaps not too much an untypical example which illustrates clearly how one could make good in the civil service.[6]

The Laurets lived in Pézenas in the mid-fifteenth century; they were of very minor noble stock, living off their lands and probably, like many meridional *petite-noblesse*, off a little trade on the side. But Bernard went in for the law at the university of Montpellier; he became assessor to the consuls of Montpellier; in 1453 he married the sister of a Montpelliérain lawyer, *noble* Ysabelle de St.-Félix; in 1453 and 1455 he represented Montpellier at the Estates of Languedoc; he did some pleading in the Parlement of Toulouse and in 1461 he became king's advocate at the court. From 1455 at least he was professor *in utroque jure* at Montpellier. As advocate he was particularly intransigent in the king's interests (though to be fair to him he did as lawyerly for his

---

[1] Viala, op. cit. 1 196; J. Kubler, *L'Origine de la perpétuité des offices royaux* (Nancy, 1958) pp. 151–7, 172 ff (but see Guenée, op. cit. p. 167 n364[bis]).

[2] Guenée, op. cit. pp. 166–8.

[3] M. Rey, *Le Domaine du roi et les finances extraordinaires sous Charles VI, 1388–1413* (1965) p. 130; Dupont-Ferrier, *Les Elections*, p. 149.

[4] Probably primarily at court or in the central departments (Guenée, op. cit. pp. 167–8).

[5] Dupont-Ferrier, *Les Origines . . . Cour des aides*, p. 87.

[6] Viala, op. cit. 1 179–85.

private clients). His brother, Bernard II, married in 1457 into a local noble family particularly 'devoted' to the monarchy; and in 1472, as well as acting as royal commissioner to the Estates of Languedoc, Bernard I was appointed *premier Président* of the Parlement of Toulouse. From then on his reign began. By 1479 they were calling the Parlement of Toulouse the Parlement of Lauret. He remained in royal favour — embassies, commissions, a seat on the *Grand Conseil* all fell to him. But never particularly honest (in 1466 he was caught out embezzling recognisances of debt entrusted to him as commissioner in a commercial case) he now began to pack the Parlement with his relations: there was no formal legislation against this at the time, but people began to get worried. Lauret was all very reasonable about it; nothing was done. His high-handedness was on a grand scale: he kept his 'servant and business administrator', Pierre de Villemur, in office as the captain of the watch at Toulouse despite the fact that the *capitouls* had sacked him for robbery and notorious pillage while on duty. He suppressed royal letters creating the fairs of Montpellier in order to safeguard those of Pézenas. He bullied his neighbours in the country (he went in for landed property of all kinds and in 1475 he bought — dishonestly — the seigneurie of Merville) in order to extend his property and build a great château. He got an exclusive royal grant to keep a mill on the Garonne at Merville, to have a port and keep boats on the river. He was accused of trying to appropriate part of the property of his ward, Denis de Beauvoir, one of the richest heirs in Toulousain. Finally he tried to create a dynasty by resigning his office (on his deathbed in 1494) to his son-in-law Jean Sarrat, whom he had already made resign his office of king's advocate in favour of another of his relations, his nephew Jean de Chavanhac, *juge-mage* of the *sénéchaussée* of Toulouse. But the Laurets did not become a great administrative line: Bernard's descendants, though well provided for, lived in dignified seclusion as gentlemen of Languedoc.

In the social structure of the Parlement of Toulouse Bernard I Lauret stands between the impoverished civil servants of the earlier period and the richer magistrates of the later.[1] For the development of a local judicial caste was affected by the external circumstances of politics. In the *bailliage* of Senlis[2] the peaceful generation of 1380–1420 was succeeded by the disturbed generation of 1420–50. In the first period it

[1] Ibid. p. 179.   [2] Guenée, op. cit. pp. 346–445.

comprised a restricted number of families, of no very remarkable learning; and numerous officers of justice were not legal practitioners. The war, by cutting down business, cut down the numbers of lawyers; a few families survived, but the lawyers of about 1450 were heavily weighted with old men even more unlearned than their fathers. The generation of the reconstruction, from 1450 to 1500, saw more work and some uneven increase in legal learning; its numbers increased, with new families, and in this period more and more practitioners held judicial office. It was not until the next two generations that the judicial society of the *bailliage* became more closed. Its members were certainly now more instructed; but with the development of stability offices changed hands slowly, with the development of venality they were open only to the rich, and finally with the development of hereditability of office — and this, in law if not in practice, post-dated 1550 — they were open only to the sons of officers. The development of the official caste thus lies long outside our period; but its prolegomenon is to be found in the mores of later medieval officialdom.

'The judicial society of France in modern times was born in the second half of the fifteenth century.'[1] But it was, at least partially — for some conditions became different for that society than they had been for its predecessors — a phoenix birth. Where royal officers had been able, from the reign of Philippe VI onwards,[2] one of their aims in life had been to increase or at least maintain their inherited estates or, if they were commoner in origin, like the merchants to found a noble line, if only to be able to invest in land. The prestige and dignity of office may have attracted some proud souls.[3] Others were clearly there to make a career — though a successful career brought other rewards than the pure joys of success. Since all offices above personal lieutenancies were crown appointments, medieval promotion was radically different from modern promotion: the fountain-head of honour had to be approached each time; there were no out-flowing gutters. But still careers could be made; there were even some well-trodden paths.[4] In the specialised

[1] Ibid. p. 445.   [2] Cazelles, op. cit. pp. 377, 389–90.
[3] Viala, op. cit. 1 216 ff; Guenée, op. cit. p. 183.
[4] Cazelles, op. cit. pp. 343–55; Dupont-Ferrier, *Les Officiers royaux*, pp. 67, 76, 98–9, 124 ff, 220; *Les Élections*, pp. 89, 150–1, 171–2, 179, 183, 189; *Les Origines . . . Cour du Trésor*, pp. 40, 44, 58, 63, 72, 74, 76, 77; *Les Origines . . . Cour des aides*, pp. 77. 80, 87, 90, 92, 104, 107; Viala, op. cit. 1 239.

legal and administrative offices non-civil-service candidates were probably rare.[1] And there was possibly a parallel development of the civil-service family. Though there were few dynasties there are many examples of family groups in the same or other departments.[2] Five out of seven *baillis* of Vitry from the mid-fifteenth century to 1515 belonged to the family of Lenoncourt; the Blancdraps at Avranches at the turn of the fourteenth century, the Le Vavasseurs at Evreux, the Aupers and the Gilberts at Mantes, the Maudoniers in Auvergne were only some of the fourteen-odd families which from then on provided two or more receivers of *élections*.[3] It was the same in the central departments throughout the fourteenth and fifteenth centuries: the families of *généraux des finances* stretched from the Braques in 1370 on to the Briçonnets from 1483; the families of *trésoriers de justice* were fewer, but they still included the d'Aunoys at the end of the fourteenth century, the Bureaus in the middle of the fifteenth century and the Bourrés at the end.[4] Between 1383 and 1483 the Chanteprimes, the Vaudetars, the Giffarts, the Bartons, the Brabans, the Compaigns, the Erlants, the Sabrevois and the Le Coqs all provided a number of officers in different central departments.[5] And as well as a vertical structure in time there was a horizontal structure through intermarriage. Bernard Lauret's case is an early and perhaps extreme example of a movement which, by the end of the fifteenth century, had created in the Parlement of Toulouse many unions of two families and some unions of three.[6] Such alliances were hardly new in the fifteenth century.[7] But though in the later middle ages their offices do not seem to have become too firmly mediatised, both forms of 'family' interest — as well as creating a tendency towards a

---

[1] Dupont-Ferrier, *Les Elections*, pp. 171–2, and *Les Origines . . . Cour du Trésor*, pp. 39–40.

[2] Guenée, op. cit. pp. 175–9; Cazelles, op. cit. p. 272; Dupont-Ferrier, *Les Officiers royaux*, pp. 73–4, 114, 117, 132–3, 145, 164, 173, 198, 212, 219–20; *Les Elections*, pp. 85, 90, 122–3, 134, 149, 178, 185; *Les Origines . . . Cour du Trésor*, p. 54; *Les Origines . . . Cour des aides*, p. 113.

[3] Dupont-Ferrier, *Les Officiers royaux*, p. 74, and *Les Elections*, pp. 122–3.

[4] Ibid. p. 178, and *Les Origines . . . Cour du Trésor*, p. 39.

[5] Dupont-Ferrier, *Les Origines . . . Cour des aides*, p. 81.

[6] Viala, op. cit. I 282. Cf. F. Leclercq, 'Le Personnel de la Chambre des comptes de Lille: sa place dans la société du xvᵉ siècle', in R. *Nord*, XLI (1959) 235.

[7] Cazelles, op. cit. pp. 121–2, 343.

closed group — cannot but have served to emphasise their interest in royal service. When Guillaume de Chanac, bishop of Paris, behaved towards Philippe VI and the government 'otherwise than as he should', 'many of the bishop's relatives and family, familiars, allies and friends' who had offices in the Parlement of Paris and elsewhere were deprived of them.[1] Rashness on the part of the leader of the group could ruin all. When the private war of patrons and their clients was comparatively stilled, when the turnover of civil servants was at its apparently normal very low rate, royal officers might well think of, as it were, their pensions — those preferably nice, quiet jobs which would see them out their days — and loyally serve the interests of the king rather than tempt protectors with promises of service to them and even of treachery to him.

Clientage

Yet it is clear that, perhaps in more troublous times, clientage could develop apace. Our knowledge is at the moment very slender. Even in the reign of Philippe VI, the 'political society' of which has been examined, the pattern of action is far from clear. Certainly the agents of the great territorial powers can be seen in the central administration: the Pyrenean Raymond Saquet in the Parlement and the *Requêtes* of the Household seems to have been the protégé of the comte de Foix; the Rouergat Guillaume de La Barrière, successively *sénéchal* of Agenais and of Périgord-Quercy, *maître des requêtes* of the Household, counsellor in the Parlement of Paris, governor of the *bailliage* of Vermandois and *sénéchal* of Poitou, the protégé of the comte d'Armagnac and Rodez. It is possible to see the clients of the duke of Lorraine, of the count of Savoy, of the king of Bavaria. 'This practice made the royal administration a cross-roads of different influences; it was useful to the king in keeping in touch with distant magnates and with foreign princes, but it also allowed them in turn to intrigue at court, to influence royal decisions and to bring about "leaks" which damaged the security of council sessions and led to cries of "treason" in the dark days of defeat.'[2]

The clearest example of external influence in the secret council, the

---

[1] Ibid. pp. 337, 353.   [2] Ibid. pp. 267–9.

core of the administration of Philippe VI, was that of Eudes IV of
Burgundy, whose party, increasingly from 1335, dominated it until at
least the early 1340s. But its hold was already weakening from about
1343, with the introduction into the council of westerners and of men
from the old royal *domaine* around Paris; and the defeat of Crécy
brought in, temporarily at least, new men whom any remaining
Burgundian agents seem to have been powerless to prevent from
depriving the duke of the county of Artois at the end of 1346. In the
last years of Philippe VI's reign it was his eldest son, Jean, who was
most influential; and he, the sometime protégé of Eudes IV, now
commanded the loyalty not only of the east but also of the west of the
kingdom. Most of the king's servants, indeed, seem to have come from
areas in the hands of the king; and one can derive little information
about their 'external' loyalties, if they had any.[1] But one should
perhaps be careful of seeing royal administration too consistently as a
nest of clients devoted irremediably to their patrons', rather than to the
king's or indeed their own interests. A client had his own career to
make: he would seek help where he found it, while trying, in the higher
traverses of his upward climb at least, to keep as much independence as
possible. The upper civil servants were themselves integers in the
patronage problem, to whom even a pope,[2] let alone a lesser magnate,
might become in turn a client. The balance of influence fell both ways.

The reign of Philippe VI's great-grandson Charles VI might be
thought to have offered greatest scope for the interplay of powerful
interests in the departments. A rather rough investigation shows that
his brother Louis d'Orléans, as regent of the kingdom after the king's
madness began, naturally provided a considerable number of his own
servants with royal places both in local and in central government.[3]
Open conflict with his uncle Philippe *le hardi* duke of Burgundy began
arguably in 1401–2; and it turned primarily upon such domestic
politics.[4] As early as 1397 there is evidence of Philippe's insertion of a

[1] Ibid. *passim*.

[2] G. Mollat, 'Le Saint-siège et la France sous le pontificat de Clément VI',
in R. *Hist. ecclés.* LV (1960) 9–12.

[3] Except, perhaps, in the Parlement of Paris (M. Nordberg, *Les Ducs et la
royauté. Études sur la rivalité des ducs d'Orléans et de Bourgogne, 1392–1407*
(Uppsala, 1964) pp. 39–60).

[4] Ibid. pp. 231 ff.

protégé into the college of the *généraux des finances*; but conflict over offices in the *Trésor* began essentially from 1402.[1] With Philippe *le hardi*'s death in 1404 there seems to have been almost a clean sweep of Burgundians from the financial departments of the *Trésor*, the *Aides* and the *Guerre*.[2] In 1406 Jean *sans peur*, Philippe's successor, succeeded in getting some headway with council appointments; but a *coup d'état* by Louis d'Orléans in 1407 placed him in an untenable position, from which he could extricate himself only by having his cousin assassinated.[3]

The struggle between Burgundy and Orléans thus had partly its roots and considerably its expression in appointment to office. And other magnates seem to have felt the need to secure their interests by making their clients royal officers or by making royal officers their clients. Jean duc de Berry put his *trésorier-général* Jean Courau into the college of *généraux des finances* in 1399, Gontier Col in 1401, and again his *trésorier*, Martin Gouge de Charpaignes, in 1404. Louis d'Anjou made his *trésorier* Jean du Puy a *général* in 1408; and in the same year Isabeau of Bavaria placed Pierre de Lesclat, her councillor and manager of her household, in the *Aides*.[4] The conflict continued after the death of Louis d'Orléans. But still some civil servants managed to keep their heads above water and some chopped happily from side to side. Jean des Hayes, for instance, *dit* Picquet, *général des finances*, was fundamentally a Burgundian sympathiser; but he was Orléanist when necessary, followed the duke of Guyenne during the anti-Cabochian reaction in 1413 and slipped from that position into the party of the constable Armagnac; but he found himself back with the victorious Burgundians after their capture of Paris in 1418.[5] The capacity of other men than Arnaud de Corbie to stay afloat was considerable: Macé Héron, in the service of Orléans, the king, Berry, whose *trésorier-général* he became, the king again during the anti-Cabochian reaction, Charles VII until after 1445; Jean Coignet, born a Burgundian, Orléanist by party, a refugee with Berry during the civil wars, *général-conseiller* at the *Aides* in the anti-Cabochian period and thenceforward a servant of successive

---

[1] Rey, *Le Domaine du roi*, pp. 295, 116. There is, of course, evidence of the presence of Philippe's agents in the *Trésor* before this (ibid. pp. 115–16).

[2] Ibid. p. 119, Nordberg, op. cit. p. 235.   [3] Ibid. pp. 215–24.

[4] Rey, *Le Domaine du roi*, pp. 295–7.   [5] Ibid. p. 288.

dauphins until 1436 at least.[1] The more able and influential of the civil servants — like, perhaps, that sea-green incorruptible Jean I Jouvenel, who could not, according to his son Jean II, bring himself to 'dissimulate', and that was his undoing — on their own ranked high in the in-fighting. Men like Blanchet Braque and Thibault de Chantemerle at the *Aides* were men who had to be 'acquired'.[2] The princes and the lords to whom the king granted, as we shall see, part of his taxation did not hesitate to bribe or pension a *général des finances* in order to hasten the payment of it; and there were other advantages in having a pensioner at court. But if an upper civil servant became too great, if he could not be seduced, he might have to be suppressed: Jean *sans peur* eliminated Jean de Montagu, *grand-maître* of the Household, as he had eliminated Jean de Montagu's old patron, Louis d'Orléans.

How exceptional was all this? Jean Juvenal des Ursins certainly thought in 1445 that magnates made their clients members of the king's council and that those clients regarded it their principal business to further their patrons' interests. Courtiers and local officers could still become the clients of magnates; or at least magnates might still rely upon courtiers to keep them in the good graces of their monarch. It would be unwise, perhaps, to over-assert the remarkableness of Charles VI's reign. It, again, has been the subject of studies touching adequately upon the personnel of government; it is, in fact, high-lit. It would be rash to compare it with periods more dark. But at least, it may be argued, it gives us a general idea of the quality of the patronage complex, even though it might give us exceptional data upon its size, and upon its operation in a time in which the king's personal authority was very far from robust.

And how much danger was clientage to 'government'? Philippe de Mézières thought it considerable.[3] Such violent assaults upon the offices as those practised from the turn of the fourteenth century seem certainly to have been disruptive of their normal working. Jean Juvenal's remedies against infiltration into the council seem to indicate the troublesomeness of clientage there. And 'justice' might well be thought

[1] M. Rey, *Les Finances royales sous Charles VI. Les Causes du déficit, 1388–1413* (1965) p. 391, and *Le Domaine du roi*, p. 116 n 2.

[2] Ibid. p. 309.

[3] D. M. Bell, *Etude sur Le Songe du vieil pèlerin de Philippe de Mézières* (Geneva, 1955) p. 165.

to suffer.[1] In the quarrel between Montferrand and Cusset over the exempt jurisdiction of Auvergne the consuls of Montferrand gave Guillaume Cousinot a hundred *écus d'or* 'for his trouble in getting royal letters making Montferrand the seat of the court dealing with the *exemptions d'Auvergne*'.[2] The consuls of Lyon spent a considerable amount of energy and money, as we shall see, in 'dealing' with the central departments.[3] But this was only, it may be argued, the way in which government worked. And retribution might still overcome a 'disloyal' royal officer who, like the unfortunate Jacques de Canlers, king's secretary and controller of the *Argenterie*, during the war of the Public Weal 'was double and wished to be in with all sides'.[4] One of the people attacked during the onslaught on Jean II duc de Bourbon in 1480 was Jean Cadier, royal *élu* in Bourbonnais, who was also a household servant of the duke and then auditor of accounts for him at Moulins. He was accused, as an 'officer of justice who should have known better', of not preventing a mildly high-handed action of Bourbon's in which he took part; and another accusation (which in fact showed him only over-zealous in the king's interest) gives one the impression that, in the last years of Louis XI at least, some royal officers were prepared to be pretty vicious to those of their colleagues whom they were minded to catch out.[5]

Control

But clientage was not the only hazard to the efficiency of government. A medieval administration could be a tangle. A medieval administration could be corrupt. Receivers had to be allowed to 'embezzle' because they were expected to advance to the crown.[6] The difficulties of the roads in war-time might give convenient excuses for malversating

[1] See, for instance, arts. 118–20 of the *ordonnance* of 1454 (*Ordonnances des rois de France de la troisième race*, XIV, ed. L. G. de Bréquigny (1790) p. 311).

[2] A. Bossuat, *Le Bailliage royal de Montferrand (1425–1556)* (1957) p. 66 n 19.

[3] See below, pp. 257–8.

[4] *Docs hist. inéd.* ed. A. Champollion-Figeac (Docs inéd. sur l'hist. de France) II (1843) 383.

[5] H. de Surirey de St.-Rémy, *Jean II de Bourbon* (1944) pp. 188–90.

[6] H. Jassemin, *La Chambre des comptes de Paris au xvᵉ siècle, précédé d'un étude sur ses origines* (1933) pp. 320–1; Dupont-Ferrier, *Les Elections*, pp. 111, 117.

accountants. The misdeeds of local officers of all kinds were hardly conducive towards efficiency of government simply in a mechanical sense. And a central department like the *Chambre des comptes* of Paris exhibited, for instance, in the fifteenth century a number of radical hindrances to effective administration. From the fourteenth century the *Comptes* people tended to abandon the boring business of audit for the more exciting matters such as hearing law suits: it was little wonder that in the fifteenth century there was laxity in examining accounts.[1] The prevailing financial practices of the time added their weakening effect to that simply of the constitution of the *Chambre*: like other great medieval institutions it was an *ad hoc* body with a vague universal competence, legislative, judicial, fiscal. Because its officers were competent to do anything they tended to be incompetent at everything.[2] The lacunae and uncertainties both of central and of local departments might allegedly be remarkable.[3] And the names and quality of royal officers were often unknown: a king could give 'sometimes the same office to two or three people'. Although there was ostensibly some record of the appointment of officers, the only effective check on such an oversight was when the sitting tenant forced his advertent or inadvertent usurper to law. In the face of all this it was little wonder that the king, at least from 1318 onwards, expected the central departments to keep a check on his actions lest, 'by inadvertence, importunity or otherwise' they might indeed be pernicious.[4]

One way to avoid this first problem of mechanical control was obvious. *Ad hoc* commissioners for *ad hoc* purposes could be used to cut through the administrative tangle. Anything abnormal, diplomatic, ecclesiastical, legal came their way; as *commissaires réformateurs* they were found from 1315 on almost all over France (though their aim at least in the mid-fifteenth century may have been primarily a fiscal one);[5] as *commissaires* delegated to hold *Grands Jours* they attempted to check the

---

[1] Jassemin, op. cit. p. 315.   [2] Ibid. pp. 323–4.

[3] Dupont-Ferrier, 'Ignorances et distractions admin.'; *Les Officiers royaux*, pp. 3–20; *Les Elections*, pp. 48 ff. But see B. Guenée, 'La Géographie admin. de la France à la fin du Moyen âge: élections et bailliages', in *Moyen Age*, LXVII (1961) 293–323, for an important new view of the problem.

[4] Dupont-Ferrier, 'Ignorances et distractions admin.'.

[5] H. Gilles, 'Authorité royale et résistances urbaines. Un Exemple languedocien: l'échec de la réformation générale de 1434–1435', in *B. philol.*

misdeeds of royal officers, as *commissaires* to sessions of Estates they received substantial presents in the pious hope that they would recommend the region to the king. Political cases, from that of Enguerrand de Marigny in 1315 to that of the 'tough old man' Semblançay in 1527, were extracted from the ordinary courts and dealt with by commissioners. Not only judicial functions, but also financial and military and 'police' administration, from presiding at the *Cour des aides* to acting as *élus* or receivers, visiting castles, raising *francs-archers* and inspecting the quality and price of bread, came their way. Already in 1303 they were under one another's feet; already in 1327 there were commissioners appointed to investigate the misdeeds of other commissioners; in the 1460s Jean de Bueil thought even 'the courtier . . . is always under the thumb of the *commissaires*'.[1]

Significant amongst the commissioners were the members of the immediate royal entourage: of the Household as opposed to the government (though the distinction, as we have seen, is a tenuous one), of the Household, which, even though it could be influenced from outside, even Philippe VI was careful to retain his own.[2] In the fifteenth century, possibly from the reign of Charles V, the commissioners were often chosen from amongst the *maîtres des requêtes* of the Household.[3] But members or ex-members of the Household were not confined in other office to that of *commissaire*. Take, for instance, the official career of Jean IV de Bar, son of Jean III de Bar seigneur de Baugy.[4] By 1420 he was a *valet de chambre* of Charles VII. In 1435 he was receiver of the *aide au lieu des aides* in Berry; in 1440 he acted as royal commissioner to the Estates of Languedoc; in 1444 he became a *général des finances*. Commissions

hist. Com. Travaux hist. sci. (1961) pp. 142–4. Cf. J. Richard, 'Finances princières et banquiers au xive siècle. L'Affaire des Bourgeoise et la réformation de 1343 en Bourgogne', in *A. Bourgogne*, xxvii (1955) 30–1.

[1] G. Dupont-Ferrier, 'Le Rôle des commissaires royaux dans le gouvernement de la France spécialement du xive au xvie siècle', in *Mélanges P. Fournier* (1929) pp. 171–84; J. de Bueil, *Le Jouvencel*, ed. L. Lecestre (Soc. Hist. France) I (1887) 44; cf. Jassemin, op. cit. p. 324.

[2] Cazelles, op. cit. pp. 415–16.

[3] Dupont-Ferrier, 'Le Rôle des commissaires royaux', p. 182. See also A. Petracchi, 'I "Maîtres des requêtes". Genesi dell'amministrazione periferica di tipo moderno nella monarchia francese tardo-medioevale e rinascimentale', in *A. Fondazione ital. Stor. amministrativa*, I (1964) 190–241.

[4] *Dict. de biog. française*, v (1951) cols 127–8.

sions to meetings of Estates in central France and to lodge soldiery there came his way in the later 1440s; and he was concerned with the business, financial, military and diplomatic, of the recovery of Normandy. Disgraced at the same time as Jacques Cœur, he was rehabilitated by Louis XI: in 1461 he became again *général des finances*, *bailli* of Touraine, captain of Tours and Amboise. Commissions continued; and in 1464 he was appointed *maître clerc* in the *Chambre des comptes*. The war of the Public Weal brought him under a cloud; in 1466 he abandoned his office of *général* to Jean de Reilhac. He died four years later and was buried in the Jacobin church in Bourges. His brother, 'Pion' de Bar, who followed him as a *valet de chambre* probably by 1436, seems to have had a similar, though much less successful, life.[1] But this was the sort of career one could make in the Household; and these were the uses to which Household officers could be put. The same kind of career and use could be found in the fourteenth century.[2] By the end of the fifteenth century the number of *baillis* and *sénéchaux* who held Household office as well was remarkable; and it was the Household office they were permitted to 'neglect', not that of being in a special way the king's servants in the country.[3]

In the same way it was remarkable how, throughout the reign of Charles VII and through most of that of Louis XI, the preponderant element in the Parlement of Toulouse was chosen from amongst this group in which the king might have personal confidence.[4] Jean Dauvet, for instance, *premier Président*, who, like so many of Charles VII's intimate servants, began his career in the service of the Anjou family, was perhaps an extreme example.[5] His time in Toulouse from 1461 to

[1] Ibid. col. 139. Jean IV's children profited by his advancement: his son Denis became bishop of St.-Papoul, then bishop of Tulle, then again bishop of St.-Papoul and finally resigned his bishopric in favour of his brother Charles; his son Jean became bishop of Beauvais; his son Robert was an *échanson* of Charles VIII; and his daughter Charlotte married Pierre d'Oriole (ibid. cols 113–15, 128–30).

[2] See, for instance, A. Coville, *Les Etats de Normandie. Leurs Origines et leur développement au xiv⁰ siècle* (1894) pp. 272–5, 278–81, 283–7, 303–7.

[3] Dupont-Ferrier, *Les Officiers royaux*, pp. 92–4.

[4] A. Viala, *Le Parlement de Toulouse et l'admin. royale laïque, 1420–1525 environ*, 1 (Albi, 1953) 121 ff.

[5] Ibid. pp. 122–3; *Les Affaires de Jacques Cœur. Journal du Procureur Dauvet* ed. M. Mollat, 1 (1952) viii–x.

1465 was possibly an honourable exile during the period of Louis XI's onslaught on his father's officers; in 1465 he returned northward to become *premier Président* of the Parlement of Paris and, as in Charles VII's reign, continued constantly to be involved in important affairs. But lesser members of his class were fairly common in Toulouse. To them were added local magnates with possibly an equal interest in devotedly serving the crown; such as Garsias du Faur, chancellor from 1468 of the remarkable and incestuous Jean V d'Armagnac, who was stolen from Armagnac by Louis XI when he came in 1472 to negotiate the surrender of Lectoure and was made president in the Parlement of Toulouse.[1]

The *baillis* of Montferrand in the fifteenth century were derived from both groups.[2] Hervé du Mesnil (*bailli* from 1425, when the *bailliage* was formed, to 1455) was the son of the 'gouverneresse' and *première demoiselle d'honneur* of the infant Charles VII, who later went into the service of the queen, Marie d'Anjou. Her eldest son, Jean, was councillor, *chambellan* and ambassador for the king; Hervé from 1420 was *premier panetier* and then *premier maître d'hôtel*. His successor, Estevenot de Thalauresse (1455–65), was an *écuyer de l'écurie du roi* and a nephew of La Hire, with whom his military exploits were hardly *sans reproche*. Poncet de Rivière (1465–8), councillor and *chambellan*, was a mistake: intriguing with Charles *le téméraire*, he felt it prudent to go on pilgrimage to Jerusalem and Mount Sinai almost as soon as he was appointed; but contemplation of the Holy Places and the monastery of St. Catherine did not cure him, because he got mixed up with the Burgundians again and, after Péronne, had to abandon his *bailliage*. His three successors to 1480 were obscure; but Jean de Doyat (1480–2), son of the *greffier* of the *bailliage*, was very different.[3] His devotion to the crown (or his dislike of the duc de Bourbon) and his capacity for extremes of action were to bring about an unpleasant end to his career after Louis XI's death. It was these men and their subordinates, and others like them throughout the kingdom, who, in pursuit of their own profit — for their extension of their powers in the name of the crown increased their own importance

[1] Viala, op. cit. 1 124–5.
[2] A. Bossuat, *Le Bailliage royal de Montferrand (1425–1556)* (1957) pp. 121–3.
[3] A. Bardoux, 'Les Grands Baillis au quinzième siècle. Jean de Doyat', in R. *hist. Droit*, IX (1863) 5–44.

and income — could make great assertions of royal authority. Often they and the officers of the central departments went further than the king might wish — or might find it politic to wish. They appeared more eager for his sovereignty than the ruler himself: it was his officers, local and central, who created in theory and in practice his absolutism for him.

What could they do? The case of Montferrand and the duc de Bourbon provides an excellent if perhaps extreme example.[1] The *bailliage* was created in 1425, when the Bourbons were allowed to have Auvergne under the terms of the settlement made by Jean duc de Berry in 1400, in order to provide a local jurisdiction for the exempt areas of Montferrand and Usson. In much the same way the exempt churches of Auvergne had under the duc de Berry come under the royal *bailliage* of St.-Pierre-le-Moutier and its lieutenancy at Cusset. There were thus two rival royal jurisdictions in Auvergne: and the attempts of Montferrand to oust Cusset had a violence which bordered on *lèse-majesté*. The third major jurisdiction in Auvergne was that of the ducal *sénéchal* at Riom; and it was against Riom that the particularly 'political' quarrel took place. It began immediately in 1425 — when Charles VII was almost at the nadir of his power; perhaps, indeed, his weakness encouraged both Riom and Cusset to complain against Montferrand. The case was not heard in the Parlement until 1430; and it was to go on until after the death of Louis XI. It became intimately linked with the political fortunes of Jean II duc de Bourbon. The evidence on which the Montferrand case for an extensive competence was based was thin, to say the least; but, although the contentions of the Riom people were on the whole correct, they had still to prove them; and it was undoubted that any concession of immunity such as that granted to the Bourbons in 1425 was 'prejudicial' to a crown which did not necessarily think itself bound by its own former actions. The case dragged on; and meanwhile the local war of jurisdictions, of summonses and intimidations on both sides was fought out grimly on the legal beach-heads. The king had need to be grateful to the duc de Bourbon, who had led the French delegation at Arras; but if Montferrand was ceded wholesale, the Parlement of Paris was watching in the high échelons, for the project was abandoned. Jean II did loyal service in the reconquest of Normandy and of Guyenne; but this did not stop the lawsuit with

[1] Bossuat, op. cit. pp. 39-57.

Montferrand. Both sides had their servants grubbing in archives for precious evidence. The royal archives at Montferrand were certainly not all they should have been. Previous officers of the duc de Berry had taken some home with them — to Riom. Others had been put away in far too safe a place because of the war. About 1452 the Montferrand commandos had made a notable thrust forward into the territory of the dauphin of Auvergne, the barony of Mercœur and the seigneurie of Canillac; this case, too, was sent down from the council to the Parlement in 1458. The fictitious arguments on the Montferrand side became more and more detailed. Even the lieutenancy of the duc de Bourbon — that dangerous concession of royal powers to a local magnate already possessed of considerable immunities — could be turned to advantage. When the duc de Berry or the duc de Bourbon himself had taken certain notable homages, had they taken them as ducs d'Auvergne or as lieutenants of the king? The Parlement was in no hurry to decide; for the case turned far more on politics than on justice and justice itself became political.

The lawsuit with Montferrand was not the only conflict with a royal jurisdiction to provide at least some part of the background for the duc de Bourbon's participation in the war of the Public Weal.[1] The Parlement of Paris had quarrelled in 1464 with the use of the word 'sovereignty' and with the duke's granting amortisation in Forez and Beaujolais, evidence of which had been found in ducal documents brought to Paris apparently on another matter. The question of whether Jean II could exempt his subjects in Forez and Beaujolais from the payment of *franc-fief* and *nouveaux acquêts* dues was lingering on in the Parlement in 1464. It was little wonder the duke complained, in his letter notifying Louis XI of his participation in the league of 1465, of 'some of the members of your entourage who, as far as one can tell from their behaviour, knew almost nothing about the way in which things are done in your kingdom'.[2] But although his part in the war brought Jean II very considerable advantages indeed, it did not mean an end of his tribulations at the hands of royal officers. Worse was to follow.[3]

[1] H. de Surirey de St.-Rémy, *Jean II de Bourbon* (1944) pp. 109 ff.
[2] J. du Clercq, 'Mémoires', ed. J. A. C. Buchon, in *Chron. d'E. de Monstrelet*, xiv (Coll. des chron. nationales françaises: 1826) 404.
[3] Surirey, op. cit. pp. 134 ff.

Other jurisdictions than that of Montferrand were affected by Louis XI's 'surrender' to the duc de Bourbon. Since parts of Forez were in Languedoc, the *bailli* of Velay, the *sénéchal* of Beaucaire and even the Parlement of Toulouse were involved. In 1466 Jean II staved off a citation to Toulouse by appealing to the king; in 1469 he complained to the king personally that the *Chambre des comptes* of Paris had prevented the *grenetiers* of Bourbonnais and Clermontois from giving him the profits of their fines and confiscations and his proctor had had to appeal (again successfully) against the *prévôts* of Xaincoins and Issoudun. In 1470 the old affair of the *nouveaux acquêts* was heated up again; and in 1473 the case of Montferrand was reopened. The formidable Jean de Doyat was in command in the country from 1477 as *bailli* and captain of Cusset and from 1480 as *bailli* of Montferrand. The political background was favourable to the civil servants; the final attack was mounted in the Parlement of Paris.[1]

The ducal chancellor, Jean Pelletier, called de St.-Haon, and other ducal officers — including the unfortunate royal *élu* Jean Cadier — were cited on a number of counts, which came under a general heading of encroaching on the power of the crown. Royal support was clear: Louis XI would in any case allow Jean II de Bourbon only the rights he had enjoyed at the death of Charles VII. But the king's advocate in the Parlement, maître François Hallé, would allow him much less. The question of 'truth' was begged from the beginning: the whole case was presented, in the usual way of the *gens du roi*, at an exalted level of pure political theory. 'The question before us', he began, was one concerning 'the highest rights that could possibly be and the highest enterprise [against them] that has been made since the kingdom was *in esse* [since the kingdom was in being]'; and Hallé's essential argument was that no-one was allowed to obstruct 'the rights of the king'. It was little wonder that in this and parallel cases in the Parlement the duke's cause lost. The king's attitude remained slightly ambivalent; between 1480 and 1483 the royal officers continued to be more royalist than he. With Louis' death in 1483 the judgements of 1480 were reversed and Jean de Doyat was condemned to humiliation, mutilation, deprivation of his goods and office for ever and banishment from the kingdom. Undismayed, the officers of the crown struggled on; unmoved by the

[1] Ibid. pp. 179 ff.

exigencies of politics they continued to fight for the rights of an ideal, all-powerful ruler. Not until 1486 was the 1483 decision confirmed. Two years later Jean II de Bourbon incontinently died. He had not enjoyed for very long the fruits of such a victory.

The role of the *gens du roi* in the Parlement as an aggressor against those who challenged or usurped the king's rights was hardly a new one; nor were the guerrilla activities of local royal officers confined to tormenting the duc de Bourbon. The quarrel of the 'enclaves' between the ducal officers of Burgundy and those of the crown[1] was another example from the fifteenth century of the way in which they could afflict an over-mighty subject. But it would perhaps be wrong to imagine that the process was perpetual or necessarily widespread. In the fourteenth and at the beginning of the fifteenth century the Parlement had hardly a systematic attitude of hostility to the duc de Bourbon.[2] The relations of the duke of Burgundy and the duke of Brittany with the last Capetians do not seem to have been as fraught as those of the duke of Aquitaine with them.[3] The essential origin of the conflict at a local level was arguably far from political: it sprang primarily from the pressure of litigants choosing their court with little respect for propriety and it endured with passion primarily because of lawyers' eagerness to inflate their costs. The conflict between the seigneurial jurisdiction of the bishop of Beauvais and the royal jurisdiction of the *prévôté* of Angy in the fifteenth century should not be seen wholly as part of a political struggle between king and immunist, nor as the result even of a feud between officers, but simply as a result of the fact that judges and lawyers found it more convenient to hold their court in Beauvais and thus for their own convenience endangered, in a fit of absence of mind, the episcopal jurisdiction.[4] One is hardly justified in

[1] J. Richard, ' "Enclaves" royales et limites des provinces. Les Elections bourguignonnes', in *A. Bourgogne*, XX (1948) 89–113.

[2] A. Leguai, *Les Ducs de Bourbon pendant la crise monarchique du xvᵉ siècle* (1962) pp. 21–9, and 'De La Seigneurie à l'état. Le Bourbonnais pendant la guerre de Cent ans', in *B. Soc. Emulation Bourbonnais*, LIV (1966–7) 146–53.

[3] J. Richard, *Les Ducs de Bourgogne et la formation du duché du xiᵉ au xivᵉ siècle* (1954) p. 228; J. Le Patourel, 'The King and the Princes in Fourteenth-century France', in *Europe in the Late Middle Ages*, ed. J.R. Hale, J.R.L. Highfield and B. Smalley (1965) p. 166.

[4] B. Guenée, *Tribunaux et gens de justice dans le bailliage de Senlis à la fin du Moyen âge* (1963) pp. 333–4.

seeing conflicts of jurisdiction as wholly 'inspired' by an aggressive monarchy or even by an aggressive civil service — though some of them may well have been.[1] Yet even inadvertent conflict did in the end become political; and naturally the exigencies of politics came into play. A king unsure of himself might be forced to balm the wounds his dogs had made. But by letting them loose at convenient moments he gained, if he wanted it, a perfectly legitimate advantage. Even if their full rigour could rarely be enforced, the extended theoretical rights of the crown could have a practical sting. It was in this way, as well as in the mere mechanics of administration, that the king's servants took their place in the structure of power in later medieval France.

[1] Richard, op. cit. pp. 101 ff; Surirey, op. cit. pp. 177 ff.

3

Nobles, *Peuple gras, Menu peuple,* Churchmen

I. DEFINITION AND MOBILITY

WE are, perhaps, almost too familiar with the hierarchic conception of later medieval society.[1] Admittedly the idea that God had made people for their proper stations was at least a cliché.

> As . . . God has created men with different faces [thought Georges Chastellain], so he has created them with different conditions, with different natures and influences, and has given them diverse separate qualities: some he has had born to labour and servile work, others to the government of towns and cities, others to dignities and rule over people, others to trade and the exchange of goods, others to serve the Church at different levels, and others to maintain the estate of nobility in its diversity of ranks, as bachelors, as knights, as barons and as great princes, kings and dukes . . .[2]

No-one could read dame Aliénor de Poitiers' *Honneurs de la cour* without being impressed with her capacity for snobbishness at least.[3] Others, too, were anguished by the niceties of precedence; and insistence upon rank was hardly confined to the nobility.[4] And that diversity of function did not mean conflict of interest was again a common idea.

> Everyone [said Philippe de Poitiers at the Estates-general of 1484] knows how the commonwealth is divided into members

[1] J. Huizinga, *Le Déclin du Moyen âge* (1932) pp. 68–77.
[2] *Œuvres*, ed. Kervyn de Lettenhove, VI (Brussels, 1864) 416–17.
[3] ed. La Curne de Ste.-Palaye, in *Mémoires sur l'ancienne chevalerie*, nouv. éd. II (1781) 183–267.
[4] See below, p. 184.

and estates: the clergy to pray for the others, to counsel, to exhort; the nobility to protect the others by arms; and the people to nourish and sustain the nobles and clergy with payments and produce. But this division was not made for private profit . . . it was made for the single end of a single commonwealth, which each person, in doing his duty, must prosecute, working not for himself alone, but for the whole community . . .[1]

The idea of the divine ordering of society had thus an inevitable parallel in the idea of the *corpus mysticum*. The place of each group in society was natural as well as willed by God. Christine de Pisan produced from her *corps de policie* much the same argument as Philippe de Poitiers eighty years later.[2] Gerson thought 'that the people should be content with its estate, and that it should suffer itself to be led and conducted by the head, and by the two sovereign estates; or otherwise the order of the *corps mystique* of the commonwealth should be utterly subverted. . . .'[3] The theory of the *corpus mysticum* again weighed against a justification of social conflict based upon class interests. This is not to say that conflict between various privileged groups did not occur. But such conflict was not inevitable: the clergy of Troyes, for instance, lived on the whole in complete harmony with the bourgeoisie of the town.[4] And rivalry between privileged persons within the same order could be as acute: the grant of taxation taken upon their lands to lesser nobles of his duchy clearly cut across the interests of René d'Anjou.[5] Nor is it to deny the existence of conflict between great and small: the Jacquerie, 'the commotions of the non-nobles against the nobles',[6] was a general expression of a resentment which was the counterpart of the scorn with which some of the upper classes regarded their inferiors, both on paper and in practice. But class conflict was not perpetual: there were

[1] J. Masselin, *Journal des Etats généraux de France tenus à Tours en 1484*, ed. A. Bernier (Docs inéd. sur l'hist. de France: 1835) p. 504.

[2] 'Le Livre du corps de policie', British Museum, Harleian MS 4410, folios 55ʳ ff.

[3] *Opera*, ed. E. du Pin, IV (Antwerp, 1706) col. 676.

[4] F. Bibolet, 'La Participation du clergé aux affaires municipales de la ville de Troyes aux xive et xve siècles', in *M. Soc. acad. Aube*, C (1943–5) 51–70.

[5] See above, pp. 15–16.

[6] S. Luce, *Hist. de la Jacquerie*, 2nd ed. (1894) p. 177.

members of the lower orders who did not wish to change the nature of things; and there were members of the upper orders who, like René d'Anjou, though they might admit their own interest, still might find 'the charges and oppressions upon . . . [their] subjects displeasing with all . . . [their] hearts' and who might wish 'to labour to the extent of . . . [their] power for their relief, as . . . [they] are obliged to do and as reason and justice require'.[1]

There was, thought Claude de Seyssel, so little social conflict in France because the hope of rising in the world 'makes each person content in his estate and without cause to machinate against the other estates, since he knows that by proper and lawful means he may rise into them and that it is risky to attempt to do so in any other way'. The possibility of social mobility thus forestalled revolution: one's aim was not to change the system, but to advance one's self within it. 'Every day', wrote Seyssel, 'one sees members of the popular estate rise by degrees into that of the nobility; and they flock without number into that of the middle class.' For Seyssel the particular members of each order — though of course not the order itself — were not prepared to remain in their divinely ordained and natural stations. It was right, he thought, that the *menu peuple* should not have too much liberty or become too rich, or be too much exercised in arms, because then its natural desire to rise might urge it successfully to revolution; but it was equally right that individual members of the *menu peuple* should rise into the higher orders.[2] The structure of society remained the same as before; but the structure did not inhibit movement within it.

The social hierarchy thus exists; but it does not prevent the individual's rising. And in other ways, too, Claude de Seyssel's discussion of society betrays perhaps more sophistication than Georges Chastellain's. For Seyssel it divided into laity and clergy. The laity itself divided into three: the nobility, the middle class of well-off non-nobles, and the lowest class of the *menu peuple*, in towns or in the country. Seyssel, like Chastellain, was very conscious that, in the clergy and nobility, there were within the order a number of degrees. In the Church a member of the lower or middle classes might rise even to the cardinalate or the papacy. But there is here not only a sense of great and small; there is

---

[1] P. Marchegay, *Arch. d'Anjou*, II (Angers, 1853) 317.
[2] *La Monarchie de France*, ed. J. Poujol (1961) pp. 125, 124.

also a sense of the integration of the Church into society.[1] 'The estate of the Church . . . is common to the three others.'

Men living clergily

'There are two kinds of men', thought the canonists: 'the laity and the clergy'.[2] But at times it might in later medieval France in practice be difficult to distinguish the one from the other. Jacques Cœur, born a bourgeois, ennobled in 1441, claimed himself a clerk at his trial in 1453.[3] Merchants of Toulouse had done the same thing in the fourteenth century; and indeed the case was far from uncommon. Farther north Jacques de Basquehem, alleged by Maroie Tasquete to have moved her boundary marks, beat her; during a delay of two years in his trial he got himself tonsured, took the habit of a clerk and purged himself in the episcopal court of Arras.[4] An abbot of Déols, inserted by Louis XI, was, his convent claimed in 1484, a 'soldier who had never worn the long robe [of a clerk] until he pretended title to the abbey, nor a hat with a short point, and he has had his face burned by artillery or by fire in the war, and he has lost several fingers and cannot work because of it'.[5] A peaceful monastery on the Indre must have been a change for him. But his case, like the others, illustrates the difficulty of defining a cleric in France in the fourteenth and fifteenth centuries.

Essentially a clerk was a man who at some time or another had taken

[1] Ibid. pp. 120–7. For Christine de Pisan, society divided into the nobles and chivalrous, and 'luniversite de tout le peuple'; and 'en la communite du peuple sont compriz troiz estas, cestassavoir, par especial en la cite de Paris et ainsi en autres citez, le clergie, les bourgois & marchans & puis le commun, comme gent de mestier & laboureurs' ('Le Livre du corps de policie', British Museum, Harleian MS 4410, folios 55^r, 59^r).

[2] *Questiones Johannis Galli*, ed. M. Boulet (Bibl. Ec. fr. Athènes Rome, 156: 1944) pp. 468–9.

[3] G. du Fresne de Beaucourt, *Hist. de Charles VII*, v (1890) 99, 123.

[4] P. Wolff, *Commerces et marchands de Toulouse (vers 1350–vers 1450)* (1954) p. 607; J. Lestocquoy, *Les Dynasties bourgeoises d'Arras du xie au xve siècle* (Arras, 1945) p. 54. Cf. O. Martin, *L'Assemblée de Vincennes de 1329 et ses conséquences. Etude sur les conflits entre la juridiction laïque et la juridiction ecclésiastique au xive siècle* (Rennes, 1909) pp. 288 ff.

[5] P. Ourliac, 'Le Concordat de 1472. Etude sur les rapports de Louis XI et de Sixte IV (Suite et fin)', in R. *hist. Droit*, ser. 4 xxii (1943) 136–7.

the tonsure.[1] In principle he should not have been permitted to have done so unless he was literate (in perhaps rather a broad sense), unless he was over seven (the age of reason), unless he was of free status, legitimate and unmarried. In practice some, if not all, of these canonical rules could be avoided by dispensation and all seem sometimes to have been overlooked. But as tonsure given irregularly was as valid as any: 'although an illiterate man should not be ordained clerk,' said the knight in the *Songe du verger* to his interlocutor, the clerk, 'all the same, if he is in fact ordained, his orders are valid; and according to the opinion of your canon law doctors, if a bishop tonsures a child he is at once a clerk'.[2] As such he shared in the power Christ left to His disciples; and this initial privilege was fortified by more mundane privileges accorded him by the society from which he was thus set apart. He was in principle immune from lay violence, in principle immune from lay jurisdiction, in principle immune from lay taxation; and these privileges he shared with those who were assimilated into his status, primarily with members of religious orders.[3] It was this web of privilege, as well as his religious functions, which distinguished him from a layman.

Apart from in certain cases covered, from the later fourteenth century, by the theory of the *cas privilegié* — and these were perhaps not very many[4] — no-one disputed the immunity of the clerk who behaved indubitably as a clerk. But difficulties did arise out of the cases of clerks who did not. For the fringe of clerks who were assimilated into the world and whose behaviour was partly or wholly mundane was considerable; and so was the number of those essential laymen who had made themselves clerks in order to enjoy the immunities of the status. It was a problem for the royal courts to decide precisely how far a clerk

[1] R. Génestal, *Le Privilegium* Fori *en France du décret de Gratien a la fin du xiv⁰ siècle*, I (Bibl. Ec. Hautes Etudes, Sci. religieuses, 35: 1921) 3 ff.

[2] ed. J. L. Brunet, in *Traitez des droits et libertez de l'Eglise gallicane*, II, part 2 (1731) 41–2; cf. Génestal, op. cit. pp. 9 ff. There was, however, a financial penalty in the *fructus male percepte* (W. E. Lunt, *Papal Revenues in the Middle Ages*, I (Columbia, 1934) 101–2; C. Samaran and G. Mollat, *La Fiscalité pontificale en France au xiv⁰ siècle* (Bibl. Ec. fr. Athènes Rome, 96: 1905) p. 65.

[3] G. Dupont-Ferrier, *Etudes sur les institutions financières de la France à la fin du Moyen âge*, II *Les Finances extraordinaires et leur mécanisme* (1932) 164–8; Génestal, op. cit. pp. 21 ff.

[4] Martin, op. cit. pp. 267 ff; B. Guenée, *Tribunaux et gens de justice dans le bailliage de Senlis à la fin du Moyen âge* (1963) pp. 111–13.

could go before he lost his immunity from lay jurisdiction; and the line that they drew provides us with a convenient boundary for the legal definition of the class.

Essentially the courts were concerned to apply the common doctrine of the Church.[1] This might be opposed in argument before them by advocates ecclesiastical or lay, who might seek, in aberrant doctrine or in aberrant custom, a ruling more favourable to their principals. Two groups of questions had to be decided. The first concerned married clerks; for clerical marriage was licit below the grade of sub-deacon. Bigamous clerks — those unfortunate enough not to have married *cum unica et virgine* — on the whole clearly lost their immunity. The position of clerks legitimately married *cum unica et virgine* had been decided by Boniface VIII by 1298. Provided he retained his tonsure and his sober and single-coloured habit, a married clerk retained his immunity in criminal cases, but lost it in civil ones; and this was the doctrine which the royal courts succeeded by the end of the fourteenth century in enforcing.[2] The second group of questions concerned 'apostate' clerks: those who had gone out into the world, who had abandoned the tonsure and the habit, who lived far from 'clergily'[3] in secular professions or royal office, who wore arms, who went to the wars and indulged in military violence or who, worst of all, indulged as 'goliards' in the most mundane of pleasures. Towards such anomalous members of the Church ecclesiastical common law became indulgent in the fourteenth century; and the royal courts became indulgent with it. Only the goliard and perhaps the brigand clerk lost his privileges *ipso facto*; and the royal courts accepted the doctrine that the other apostates lost them only after three episcopal warnings — episcopal warnings that might never be given. But the crown developed means of control over its own clerk officers;[4] and from the end of the fourteenth century onwards the royal courts began to derive, from canonical texts themselves, the framework for a more severe attitude towards the more delinquent of the apostate.[5]

[1] Génestal, op. cit. pp. xi–xviii, 174–244.
[2] O. Martin, op. cit. pp. 287–8; Guenée, op. cit. pp. 109–10.
[3] 'Sauvegarde pour ung clerc non marie. Charles &c. a tous noz justiciers &c. salut. A la supplication de tel &c. clerc non marie vivant clergeaument...' (Bibl. nat. MS fr. 5909, fo. 11ʳ).
[4] Génestal, op. cit. pp. 203 ff; Martin, op. cit. p. 270.
[5] Génestal, op. cit. p. 244; Guenée, op. cit. p. 111.

Yet it still remained that the definition 'clerk' could be a wide one; and 'clerks' remarkable in their malefactions[1] — as well as 'clerks' far from clerkly — might still be accepted by the Church as its own.

Men living nobly

If the distinction between the first order of society and the other two was blurred, was the distinction between the nobility and the bourgeoisie any clearer? How did the nobility identify itself? That it should be visibly identifiable by its manner of dress, that it should not be aped by the lower orders, was a norm of later medieval social thinking.[2] 'There isn't a working man however wretched', wrote Jean Juvenal des Ursins in 1445, 'who doesn't want to wear marten's fur, and their wives squirrel of various sorts, even the public women selling sex wholesale or retail; and you can't tell a woman of ill fame from an honest one.'[3] That noble extravagance on dress should be deplored was equally normal. Jean de Venette's description of the nobility in 1356, when its 'luxury and dissoluteness ... became still more deeply rooted', was seized upon by Jean Juvenal ninety years later; the author of the complaint upon the army before Poitiers listed angrily the

> Junketing and vain glory, improper dress,
> Gilded belts and feathers for the head,
> Billy-goats' big beards ...

of the nobility.[4] The excesses of court ladies was a subject to which Jean Juvenal returned most willingly, and with a considerable amount of

[1] See, for instance, ibid. p. 112 n 111; and cf. G. Boyer, 'Notes sur la jurisprudence toulousaine du xve siècle en matière de *privilegium fori*', in *Mélanges P. Fournier* (1929) pp. 25–39.

[2] See, for instance, F.E. Baldwin, *Sumptuary Legislation and Personal Regulation in England* (Baltimore, 1926).

[3] 'Il ny a si meschant homme mescanique qui ne veullent porter martres et leurs femmes gris ou menu ver, voire les fillettes vendans amourettes en gros et en detail; et ne congnoit on une paillarde dune preudefemme' ('A, a, a, nescio loqui quia puer ego sum', Bibl. nat. MS fr. 2701, fo. 55^v).

[4] *Chronicle*, ed. J. Birdsall and R.A. Newhall (New York, 1953) p. 62; J. Juvenal des Ursins, 'Traictie compendieux de la querelle de France contre les Anglois', Bibl. nat. MS fr. 17512, fo. 29^r–v; 'Complainte sur la bataille de Poitiers', ed. C. de Beaurepaire, in *Bibl. Ec. Chartes*, ser. 3 ii (1851) 261.

graphic realism.[1] His diatribes were hardly likely to have appealed to Charles VII in the 1450s. But that the appearance and manners of the nobility gave the class its identity is clear. To be a noble one must behave like one.

The claim to nobility of these courtiers, of the upper aristocracy, was obviously unquestionable. It was at the bottom end of the class that criteria had to be found to separate the elect from the rejected. Opposed by a king's proctor determined to prevent unauthorised insinuation into the nobility, how did one prove one's case? In the mid-fifteenth century maître Jean Barbin argued that his father, 'the late Nicolas Barbin, was in his lifetime a nobleman, born and descended of a noble line, and as such held and reputed publicly and to the knowledge of all', that he 'lived like a nobleman', that his elder son, Gillet, 'behaved . . . like a noble all his life', that both Nicolas and Gillet had served as nobles in the army, and that his and Gillet's sisters married nobles of old stock.[2] The public reputation of one's family in a difficult case like this, in which the putative noble was not himself living particularly nobly, was clearly all-important.[3] Maître Jean Bontaud, a priest, *licencié* in civil and canon law and dean of Bressuire, produced half a dozen elderly witnesses in 1475 who testified that his relatives had always behaved like nobles, that his father had served the king in every *arrière-ban* raised of the nobles of Poitou, and that the family had observed the customary rules of noble succession in the *pays*. His rights were upheld.[4] The essential noble was, then, it might be argued, of noble stock; and whether he was indeed of noble stock was decided by the witness of aged men or by the evidence, if it was available, of documents. Maître Jean Barbin, for instance, asserted that 'the aforesaid Nicolas Barbin in his lifetime behaved like a noble and styled himself noble in his letters, including contracts'.[5] In this sense lineage was prescriptive;[6] and some hopeful lineages were at least allegedly pretty shaky.

[1] Beaucourt, op. cit. IV (1888) 175 n 2.

[2] R. Favreau, 'La Preuve de noblesse en Poitou au xve siècle', in B. Soc. Antiq. Ouest, ser. 4 v (1960) 619–22.

[3] Guenée, op. cit. pp. 412–13.   [4] Favreau, op. cit. p. 619.   [5] Ibid. p. 622.

[6] The acquisition of noble fiefs gave still, at the end of the fifteenth century, only a dubious title to nobility. See, for instance, H. Sée, *Louis XI et les villes* (1891) pp. 356–7; Guenée, op. cit. p. 414; J. Bartier, *Légistes et gens de finances au xve siècle. Les Conseillers des ducs de Bourgogne Philippe le bon et Charles le téméraire* (Brussels, 1955) pp. 191–4.

But that birth conferred nobility might be denied by an opposing advocate.[1] Essential nobility, it might be argued, showed in a noble way of life. The essential noble lived nobly; and he lived in the practice of arms. The concept of a fiscal *dérogeance* appeared by the last quarter of the fourteenth century if not before.[2] It derived from the general immunity of nobles of 'noble descent' who 'frequent the wars' or who, if they were prevented from doing so by age or infirmity, at least lived nobly, from direct taxation in principle taken for the war and originally taken in lieu of military service.[3] Such exemption was not wholly unchallenged; taxpayers had a ready eye for nobles or alleged nobles living less than nobly; and it was this financial consideration which dominated the jurisprudence of the Parlement of Paris and of the *Chambre des comptes* in the matter of *dérogeance*.[4] 'It is not proper for a noble to be an innkeeper', declared Charles VI in 1393, in an attempt to decide under what conditions the noble proprietor of a vineyard might sell his produce.[5] In the *bailliage* of Senlis it was clear that in the fifteenth century to be an advocate or a proctor was derogatory to nobility, however much it might be asserted that 'nobles are advocates'; for there was no *noblesse de robe* in the later middle ages.[6] Though on the lower fringes of the nobility, as we shall see, curious things could occur, it was on the whole quite clear that 'a noble who lives at home does not live nobly unless he frequents the wars'.[7]

The clearest and safest method of entry into the nobility was the acquisition of *lettres d'anoblissement* from the crown or, still in the fifteenth century, from a great magnate.[8] This could be costly;[9] hence

[1] At least in 1505 (E. Dravasa, ' "Vivre noblement". Recherches sur la dérogeance de noblesse du xive au xvie siècles', in *R. jurid. écon. Sud-Ouest*, *Sér. jurid.* XVII (1966) 33–4).

[2] Ibid. XVI (1965) 135–93, XVII (1966) 23–129.

[3] Dupont-Ferrier, op. cit. pp. 175 ff.   [4] Dravasa, op. cit.

[5] *Ordonnances des rois de France de la troisième race*, VII, ed. D. Secousse (1745) 526; Dravasa, op. cit. XVII 51 ff.

[6] Guenée, op. cit. p. 413 (but cf. R. Favreau, 'La Condition sociale des maires de Poitiers au xve siècle', in *B. philol. hist. Com. Travaux hist. sci.* (1961) pp. 166–7); Bartier, op. cit. p. 287.

[7] Guenée, op. cit. p. 413.

[8] J. R. Bloch, *L'Anoblissement en France au temps de François Ier* (1934) pp. 130–2; Dupont-Ferrier, op. cit. p. 178; Guenée, op. cit. p. 414.

[9] Dupont-Ferrier, op. cit. p. 178; P. Viollet, *Hist. des institutions politiques et admin. de la France*, III (1903) p. 410.

the desire of the less than wealthy to slip unnoticed into the promised land. Their neighbours, eager enough to restrict, if possible, advantages accruing to those who bought *lettres d'anoblissement*,[1] stood watchdog on the frontier. Pierre Daillencourt, fortified by the possession of 10,000 or 12,000 *écus*, proclaimed himself noble in 1467; the inhabitants of Chaumont-en-Bassigny, where he lived, maintained that he was a serf and the son of a serf and the grandson of a serf.[2] But the neighbours of a would-be noble did relax. Social mobility in Forez in the fourteenth century was hindered neither by legal nicety nor by neighbourly prejudice.[3] Here acceptance by the group, conformity to its mores, was the essential thing which made a noble. Hence, perhaps, the dislike with which the false noble was regarded by his old and his new peers elsewhere. How far indeed did such social pressures force the transformation of the ex-bourgeois family into the truly noble family? The sons of the ennobled money-changer of Toulouse, Raymond Ysalguier, went on being merchants as well as nobles; his grandsons abandoned trade and the house in the rue des Changeurs in Toulouse for the uncertain fortunes of the fourteenth-century nobility.[4] Here was a family which conformed; and it was far from untypical.

Clearly the crown had its fiscal interest, the *droit de franc-fief*, the payment for *lettres d'anoblissement*, in restricting at least informal social mobility; clearly the prejudice of noble and non-noble could contribute towards lessening the convection of the peasant or bourgeois towards the nobility. Equally clearly that convection occurred. Without it, the nobility would have vanished away as a class: the old lines were by nature unable to maintain its numbers. In Forez, of the families recorded in the thirteenth century, some 30 per cent had vanished before 1300; between 1300 and 1400 some 50 per cent of the remaining families disappeared; and another 50-odd per cent of the survivors had vanished

---

[1] Cf. Bartier, op. cit. p. 199 ff.

[2] Dupont-Ferrier, op. cit. p. 178.

[3] E. Perroy, 'Social Mobility among the French *Noblesse* in the Later Middle Ages', in *Past & Present*, XXI (1962) 25–38. But see E. Fournial, *Les Villes et l'économie d'échange en Forez aux xiiie et xive siècles* (1967) pp. 261–2.

[4] P. Wolff, 'Une Famille, du xiiie au xvie siècle: les Ysalguier de Toulouse', in *Mél. Hist. sociale*, I (1942) 35–58; but see below, pp. 180–1. Cf. R. Fédou, 'Une Famille aux xive et xve siècles: les Jossard de Lyon', in *Annales*, IX (1954) 461–80.

by 1500.[1] 50 per cent per century seems in fact a reasonable disappearance
rate for the members of an average noble group of *lignages*.[2] This erosion
was due partly to the disappearance of noble families into the lower
classes, and partly to the failure of the family to produce a male heir.
The class was in a constant state of flux.[3] But the nature of the nobility,
though it was revivified, did not change. The new families, living
nobly and in the practice of arms, could decline as rapidly as ever the
old ones had. By the mid-fifteenth century there were five Ysalguier
lignages. Only the Ysalguier-Mérenvielle lasted until at least the
eighteenth century; another line survived the sixteenth century; another
ran into the female line during it; a fourth disappeared by 1542; and the
fifth had been finished effectively by 1518.[4]

Anoblis

Over and over again the successful bourgeois family rose and fled
into its apotheosis in the minor nobility. The Jouvenel family, for
instance, may or may not have been descended from an obscure member
of the Roman family of Orsini;[5] but the author of its successful line
was a Pierre Jouvenel, who was possibly a cloth-merchant of Troyes in
1360.[6] His son Jean I he sent 'a young student to Orléans', where of his
university year 'he came out top in the *licence* in *Décret*';[7] 'and afterwards
he came to Paris, and I've heard him say', wrote his son Jean II in 1445,
'that if he'd known almost any other town in the world where he'd have
been able to learn more of worth and of honour than in Paris he'd have
gone there; and he spent some time in canon law and studied hard. And

[1] Perroy, op. cit. p. 31.
[2] Cf. L. Genicot, *L'Econ. rurale Namuroise au Bas moyen âge*, II *Les Hommes —
la noblesse* (Louvain, 1960) 137 ff.
[3] Cf. Bartier, op. cit. p. 246.
[4] Wolff, 'Une Famille', pp. 50–4.
[5] Even the most recent view, that of A. de Boüard and C. Hirschauer,
'Les Jouvenel des Ursins et les Orsini', in *Mél. Archéol. Hist. Ecole franç. Rome*,
XXXII (1912) 49–67, does not provide the last word on the subject.
[6] This, unfortunately, is far from proven.
[7] '. . . josne estudiant a Orleans . . .' ('Verba mea auribus percipe, Domine'
Bibl. nat. MS fr. 2701, fo. 46ʳ); A. Coville, *Jean Petit. La Question du tyrannicide
au commencement du xvᵉ siècle* (1932) p. 5.

because he talked boldly and had some property from his mother, monsieur de Noviant, who was *grand-maître* of the king's Household, wanted him for his niece . . . and though he'd wanted to be a church-man, all the same he got married.'[1] His career as a royal lawyer more than on the fringes of politics was restricted, Jean II thought, by a bluff reluctance to wink at the political peccadilloes of the great: 'and when people warned him of it, saying it was very detrimental to him and his children, and that it would be better to let things go on as they were', he replied 'that he wasn't worried that he and his children wouldn't be sufficiently provided for'.[2] And indeed those of the sixteen children[3] of the reluctant husband who survived did far from badly. His purchases of property had been capped with the barony of Trainel; and despite the vicissitudes of the family and of its estates during the civil war and the English invasion three of the sixteen rose through the law and royal service to remarkable eminence. Jean Juvenal des Ursins became successively bishop of Beauvais, bishop of Laon, archbishop of Reims, in interminable treatises the scourge of the morals of his time;[4] Guillaume Jouvenel des Ursins, soldier as well as lawyer, who succeeded Jean I as baron de Trainel, became chancellor of France; Jacques Jouvenel des Ursins resigned his archbishopric of Reims to his elder brother Jean and became bishop of Poitiers and titular patriarch of Antioch. Their brother Michel, blessed (or cursed) with six sons and four daughters, became *bailli* of Troyes; their sister Marie prioress of

[1] '. . . et aprez sen vint a Paris, et luy ay ouy dire que se il eut sceu ville a peine ou monde ou il eust peu aprendre plus de bien et de honneur que a Paris il y feust ale; et fut par aucun temps en droit canon et fort estudioit. Et pourceque il estoit bien en langage et avoit du sien de par sa mere, monsr. de Noviant, qui estoit grant maistre dostel du roy, desira a lavoir pour sa niepce . . . et combien que il eust voulente destre homme desglise toutevoye il se maria.' ('A, a, a, nescio loqui quia puer ego sum', fo. 46r.) For Jean I Jouvenel, see L. Battifol, *Jean Jouvenel, prévôt des marchands de la ville de Paris (1360–1431)* (1894); for the all-powerful Jean Le Mercier, seigneur de Noviant, see H. Moranvillé, 'Etude sur la vie de Jean Le Mercier, 13 . . –1397', in *Mém. présentées par divers savants à l'Acad. Inscript.* ser. 2 VI (1888) part 2.

[2] '. . . et quant on le advertissoit en disant que il y avoit grant dommage et ses enffans, et que il valoit mieulx que il laissast passer le temps tel comme il estoit . . .'; '. . . que il ne avoit point de doubte que luy et ses enffans neussent assez' ('A, a, a, nescio loquia quia puer ego sum', fo. 46r).

[3] Battifol, op. cit. pp. 317–24.

[4] P. L. Péchenard, *Jean Juvénal des Ursins* (1876).

the royal house of Poissy. The grandchildren of Pierre Jouvenel of Troyes, however noble and Roman his ancestors may have been, had come a long way from their father's provincial origins. Yet as two of Jean Juvenal's letters — and his will — show, Michel's branch of the family was not without its material worries.[1] However splendid his brothers' positions, the preoccupations of the minor seigneur with the large family seems to have dogged him to his death.

Example after example could be given of the breakthrough of the successful bourgeois family into the nobility through wealth derived from business or from office-holding. Yet perhaps one should not overestimate the number or the importance of the new *lignages*. In the area around Paris in which many of the upper civil servants found their estates the development of the landed fortune of the new families lagged clearly behind that of their political fortune — as, indeed, in the case of the Jouvenels.[2] Only the Orgemonts, perhaps, stand out as a line which succeeded rapidly in acquiring its patrimony.[3] And the resistance of the older seigneurial families to decline and consequent expropriation was considerable: provided, possibly in most cases, that they too basked, to however small an extent, in the favour of the crown. The same resistance, for the same reason, may be seen in a number of Burgundian *bailliages*. The administration of the dukes of Burgundy had, like that of the crown, its bourgeois careerists heading towards the nobility; but their impact upon the seigneurial world was less than one might suppose.[4] The same resistance could be seen, at least in the third quarter of the fourteenth century, in the area around Montauban.[5] The rise of the bourgeois family into the nobility was a perpetual process; but it will not do to over-emphasise its intensity.

Fame might be spur enough for some proud souls in seeking nobility, for 'the knight and the noble look to acquire renown and praise in the world'. 'The bourgeois', according to the same authority,

---

[1] Bibl. nat. MS Dupuy 673, folios 51, 56, 63–6.

[2] G. Fourquin, *Les Campagnes de la région parisienne à la fin du Moyen âge* (1964) p. 343.

[3] L. Mirot, *Une Grande Famille parlementaire aux xive et xve siècles. Les d'Orgemont* (1913); Fourquin, op. cit. pp. 341–3.

[4] Bartier, op. cit. pp. 242 ff.

[5] C. Cugnasse, 'Activité écon. et milieu humain à Montauban au xive siècle d'après le reg. de Barthélémy Bonis', in *A. Midi*, LXIX (1957) 226.

looked rather 'to acquire wealth for himself and his children'.[1] In pursuing this laudable end it was still possible to reap the benefits of noble status without its drawbacks, though at some price: an *anobli* could live bourgeoisly — provided he paid bourgeois taxes;[2] a non-ennobled bourgeois could acquire noble land under a general privilege; both could acquire exemption from military service. In the same way a noble could acquire a 'congé de marchander' which allowed him to indulge in trade without danger of derogation.[3] Louis XI was possibly more wholesale in his concessions than his predecessors; but most of these practices went back to the beginning of our period and beyond; and the general *anoblissement* of some urban oligarchies again had a respectable ancestry.[4] Equally respectable, therefore, was the ancestry of a median class of men who were effectively privileged bourgeois: scorned formally by such prophets of gentility as Olivier de La Marche, who argued that only the heirs of an *anobli* could call themselves gentlemen, and then only if he had observed 'the upkeep of free conditions' and led an 'honest life of a nobleman';[5] constantly the object of the malevolence of their less fortunate fellow-citizens and of those responsible for collecting the revenues of the crown. Even Odet d'Ysalguier, the great-great-grandson of Raymond, was ordered in April 1459 to submit a list of his goods in Toulouse for taxation. In vain did he argue that he lived nobly as seigneur de Clermont, that he lived in a house at Odars crenellated like a castle, that he descended from a number of valiant ancestors living in the practice of arms, notably a lieutenant of the *sénéchal* of Toulouse, that he himself had served in the army and that if he had acted as a *capitoul* of the city it was in the city's interest and not in his own: if the *capitoulat* was an honour for base-born people, it was not for a *chevalier*. The *capitouls* replied that his status (in a *pays de taille réelle*) did not exempt his non-noble possessions from

---

[1] *Le Ménagier de Paris*, ed. J. Pichon (Soc. des bibliophiles fr.) 1 (1846) 57.

[2] R. Gandilhon, *Politique écon. de Louis XI* (Rennes, 1940) pp. 116–18.

[3] Bloch, op. cit. pp. 42 ff; Gandilhon, op. cit. pp. 115–20; Sée, op. cit. pp. 354 ff.

[4] Bloch, op. cit. pp. 27, 37 ff, 46, 107 ff; G. Dupont-Ferrier, *Les Officiers royaux des bailliages et sénéchaussées et les institutions monarchiques locales en France à la fin du Moyen âge* (Bibl. Ec. Hautes Etudes, 145: 1902) pp. 484 ff, 569–70; Wolff, *Commerces et marchands*, pp. 616 ff.

[5] Bartier, op. cit. pp. 205–6.

taxation and they added that it was hardly Odet's place to be snobbish about the *capitoulat* when his family had become nobles only as members of it.[1] If a family which had so clearly risen as the Ysalguiers could by its members' official connection with the town and by the mendacious memory of its Toulousain peers still, however properly, be brought down, the medial position of those more clearly involved in the bourgeois life was indeed uncertain. The frontier between the bourgeoisie and the nobility may have been elastic;[2] but that elasticity might make the final breakthrough even more difficult. To have the best of both worlds required considerable ingenuity. The watchdogs on the frontiers of the social groups lay ready to snarl at those who tried to avoid their rules: the no-man's-land of the frontiers was hazardous for the hesitant and even for the determined. The bogus ancestries with which families supplied themselves — and even the Jouvenel des Ursins were suspect — demonstrate their social anxieties.[3] That families did succeed is indisputable; but beyond the mere acquisition of 'wealth for himself and his children' the hopeful bourgeois in later medieval France had many problems on his mind.

But it was not only Claude de Seyssel's *peuple gras*, rich men, who, however formally, might escape their origins. Members of the *menu peuple*, too, might rise. In the fourteenth century, if not so much in the fifteenth, a peasant's son might become at least a bishop. Jean d'Arsonval, bishop of Chalon from 1413 to 1416, was a serf and the son of a serf.[4] Pierre Gouin, called de Mortemart after his village in Limousin, bishop of Viviers from 1322 to 1325 and then bishop of Auxerre, was made a cardinal in 1327.[5] Jean Charlier, called de Gerson after his village in Champagne, was of 'low and plebeian' origin, the

---

[1] E. Roschach, *Inv.-sommaire des arch. com. Toulouse*, I (Toulouse, 1891) 90; Wolff, *Commerces et marchands*, p. 618 (but cf. p. 574 n 6).

[2] Bloch, op. cit. pp. 213, 215.

[3] Bartier, op. cit. p. 202; Fourquin, op. cit. p. 343. For the Jouvenels, see above, p. 177 n 5. A clerk drawing up quittances for Guillaume Jouvenel des Ursins in 1456–7 styled him 'dit des Ursins' (Bibl. nat. Pièces orig. 1593, doss. Jouvenel, nos. 39, 41; MS Clairambault 170, no. 90. In the first of these documents the 'dit' was erased).

[4] P. Gras, 'Les Evêques de Chalon de 1302 à 1416', in *M. Soc. Droit Pays bourguignons*, xv (1953) 40–6.

[5] R. Limouzin-Lamothe, *Le Diocèse de Limoges des origines à la fin du Moyen âge* (Strasbourg, 1951) pp. 144–5.

son of labourers. Nicolas de Baye, *curé*, canon, archdeacon, like Jean d'Arsonval a humanist and like Jean d'Arsonval of servile background, was *greffier* of the Parlement of Paris.[1] University training, especially in law, and the Church could, as Seyssel said, bring members of the lowest estate to considerable dignity; dignity in which they might, like Gerson, prefer to forget their origins. In Normandy the period 1380–1480 saw the rise of the Perrote family from well-off labourers to country gentry.[2] In Forez over half a dozen peasant families were accepted by their peers in the fourteenth century: the du Bost, the Champuljan, the Chassain, the Contenson, the La Coste, the Lignères, the Murcent, the Villette lines all ran back to non-nobles.[3] But the dividing line between a poor noble and a peasant was hardly sharp, as far as their economic situations, as opposed to their attitudes, were concerned. The ancestors of Perrin Blondel were in 1315 very poor; at the end of the century Perrin was one of the largest tenants of the grand prior of St.-Denis at Garges-lès-Gonesse.[4] In Bordelais, even through the troubles of the fourteenth century, fortune smiled upon the Gaubanh family.[5] In Sologne there were at the turn of the century apparently numerous labourers who, like Etienne Gaveau, with his manor of Le Plessis, held their properties in fief; and it was the same in Forez.[6]

Clearly the peasantry as a group had as much social distinction within it as any other. In parts of France, as we have seen, serfdom still survived;[7] but even amongst serfs, as for instance in Sologne, there

[1] E. Delaruelle *et al.*, *L'Eglise au temps du Grand schisme et de la crise conciliaire* (Hist. de l'Eglise . . . fondée par A. Fliche et V. Martin, 14: 1962) pp. 327–8.

[2] M. Boudin, 'Du Laboureur aisé au gentilhomme campagnard. Les Perrote de Cairon, de Bretteville-l'Orgueilleuse (1380–1480)', in *A. Normandie*, XIII (1963) 237–68.

[3] E. Perroy, 'Social Mobility among the French *Noblesse* in the Later Middle Ages', in *Past & Present*, XXI (1962) 38 n 32.

[4] G. Fourquin, *Les Campagnes de la région parisienne à la fin du Moyen âge* (1964) p. 350.

[5] R. Boutruche, *La Crise d'une société. Seigneurs et paysans du Bordelais pendant la guerre de Cent ans* (1947) p. 314.

[6] I. Guérin, *La Vie rurale en Sologne aux xive et xve siècles* (1960) p. 191; Perroy, op. cit. p. 34.

[7] Primarily in the east and south. See P. Petot, 'Les Fluctuations numériques de la classe servile en France du ixe au xive siècle', in *Comitato Internazionale di Scienze Storiche, X Congresso Internazionale di Scienze Storiche, Roma . . . 1955, Riassunti delle Comunicazioni* (Florence, 1955) pp. 189–90 (cf. ibid. *Atti* (Rome,

could be considerable variety in wealth.[1] In Nivernais in the mid-fifteenth century it was alleged that some serfs possessed 2000 *écus* and 'do not deign to marry their daughters to serfs like them [but] ... wish to marry them into nobilities and bourgeoisies'; but the serfs who, in the fifteenth century, were unable to purchase their enfranchisement must be counted amongst the poorest members of society.[2] From them the gamut ran upwards to the rich peasant thinking of living nobly. Ability and luck naturally enabled some village families slowly to prosper at the expense of their less able and less fortunate neighbours; and the demographic disasters of the fourteenth century helped them in the process. In a period of 'reconstruction' the advantages lay with the tenant, not with the land-owner.[3] But one is warned against over-estimating the number of large peasant holdings. The process which at Garges made Perrin Blondel an important man in his village did not continue.[4] Around Paris at the end of the fifteenth century peasant tenures were generally as small as they had been two centuries earlier. But too little is known for generalisation on the subject to be profitable; though it may well be that the heyday in France of the prosperous peasant was a short-lived one; as may have been in France the heyday of the building labourer.[5]

Other distinctions

The extent of social mobility in later medieval France should not therefore be underestimated; and neither should the overlapping and

1957) pp. 327–8); P. Ourliac, 'Le Servage dans la région toulousaine', in ibid. *Riassunti*, pp. 191–3.

[1] Guérin, op. cit. p. 231.

[2] A. Bossuat, 'Le Servage en Nivernais au xve siècle', in *Bibl. Ec. Chartes*, CXVII (1959) 110–13.

[3] See, for a rapid generalisation, J. Heers, *L'Occident aux xive et xve siècles. Aspects économiques et sociaux* (Nouvelle Clio, 23: 2nd ed. 1966) pp. 113–17.

[4] Fourquin, op. cit. p. 525. In Le Neubourg, on the other hand, there was a clear if gentle movement between 1397 and 1496 towards concentration of property A. Plaisse, *La Baronnie du Neubourg* (1961) p. 346).

[5] G. Duby, *L'Econ. rurale et la vie des campagnes dans l'Occident médiévale* (1962) pp. 590–1; E. H. Phelps Brown and S. V. Hopkins, 'Wage-rates and Prices: Evidence for Population Pressure in the Sixteenth Century', in *Economica*, NS XXIV (1957) 289–306.

the mingling of those far-too-simplified abstractions, the 'clergy', the 'nobility' and the *'tiers état'*. And the variation in actual status within each of these abstract groups was if anything more significant socially than the famous variation in function. From the very bottom of society to the very top the finest of distinctions separated those below from those above. Serfs had their statuses; so did the free peasantry. In towns there could be not only as at Le Puy[1] a distinction between mere 'inhabitants', 'citizens', 'bourgeois' graced with the title of *sen* and graduates graced with the title of *messier*; there could be as well as at Nîmes[2] a division of urban society into ten degrees, as at Le Puy into twenty-two; and these *échelles* did not exhaust the capacity of the Ponots for social distinction: the order of precedence amongst the *métiers*, the guilds, was regulated formally by the Parlement of Toulouse. The Church was an abstraction which covered not only a very clearly defined variation in hierarchical position from goliard clerk to cardinal; it covered a considerable variation in actual status between clergy formally of the same rank and it covered, as well, a considerable variation of clerical opinion. Within the nobility some members might be very poor, like the unfortunate Guichard Vert in Forez, who died in 1287 possessed to mark his gentility only of a chess-board.[3] Some might be very rich, like Jean III de Chalon, who died in 1418 possessed *inter alia* of a box of precious stones five knights could not lift.[4] Some might be barely of the class; some might be princes of the fleurs-de-lis. Within the class there was infinite variation of status and wealth and actual influence. At its head stood the princes of the blood and the peers of France, members of a privileged and dignified but not entirely closed circle.[5] Below them came the territorial titles, a gamut from duke to mere seigneur; cutting across them titles essentially military, knight, esquire, with their further complications of banneret rank. But questions of status and precedence did not end here. There were those rather

[1] E. Delcambre, *Le Consulat du Puy en Velay des origines à 1610* (Le Puy, 1933) pp. 47 ff.

[2] A. Angelras, *Le Consulat nîmois* (Nîmes, 1912) pp. 90 ff.

[3] Perroy, op. cit. pp. 28–9.

[4] F. Barbey, *Louis de Chalon, prince d'Orange . . . 1390–1463* (Lausanne, 1926) p. 77.

[5] P. Viollet, *Hist. des institutions politiques et admin. de la France*, III (1903) 303–8.

undignified squabbles over the seating order which disturbed the formalities of public life in Brittany or in Béarn[1] and which could disturb even the Estates-general of the kingdom. When at Tours in 1468 'Charles, monsieur d'Armagnac came in — he had just arrived and had not been at the . . . assembly before — . . . in order to decide where he should sit the . . . seigneurs got up and discussed the matter between them and because they could not assess his place very clearly they had monsieur de Dammartin tell him to go away until tomorrow, when the king would decide his position; and this was done'.[2] A meeting of the Estates was in some sense a formal image of the political community; its physical appearance and *assiette* were recorded carefully by eye-witnesses; it was important that one's proper position was recognised. Here, when people as important as Charles d'Armagnac or the comte d'Eu or the comte de Nevers were involved in a possible 'debat de lassiette',[3] argument about the seating-plan, the question of status became political.

With those pieces of living political iconography, the great formal sessions of Estates, we shall be concerned later; and with the problem of status to the nobility. For the moment it is enough to stress that 'the Church, the nobility, the *tiers état*, are not "people whom one meets on the road"'.[4] Society in later medieval France was much too human to be comprehended so simply. And already we have seen in the civil service — a new abstraction which might include the officers of clerks and nobles as well as the king's — effectively a fourth 'order', a *mélange* of men from noble, bourgeois and clerical backgrounds, extracted at least temporarily from their cadres, physically and mentally. Increasingly in the fourteenth and fifteenth centuries the lawyers

---

[1] Dom H. Morice, *Mémoires pour servir de preuves à l'hist. ecclés. et civile de Bretagne*, II (1744) cols 1564 ff, 1670 ff; L. Flourac, 'Une Querelle de préséance à la Cour majour de Béarn, in *R. Béarn, Navarre et Lannes*, v (1887) 351–83.

[2] '. . . vint Charles monsr. dArmaignac lequel venoit tout de noveau qui navoit encourres point este oudit conseil . . . pour li donner lieu se levarent lesdits seigneurs et parlarent ensemble et pourcequilz ne veoient pas bien son lieu luy fuirent dire par monsr. de Dampmartin quil sen allast jusques a lendemain que le roy luy donret siege et ainsi fu fait' (Arch. com. Rodez, BB 3, fo. 55ᵛ).

[3] Ibid.

[4] B. Guenée, 'L'Hist. de l'Etat en France à la fin du Moyen âge vue par les historiens français depuis cent ans', in *R. hist.* CCXXXII (1964) 352.

formed another possible abstraction, a group of men of a particular training and attitude, more and more important in the civil services, in the Church, in the oligarchies of the towns, even amongst simple land-owners running their estates. Jean I Jouvenel was possibly an *anobli* and a knight when he sat, just before his death in 1431, in the Parlement of Poitiers as *deuxième Président*. His son Jean II Juvenal was a clerk, king's advocate there since 2 June 1429; his son Guillaume Jouvenel was perhaps more clearly noble, a knight, *conseiller lai* in the court; his son Jacques Jouvenel, a clerk, was soon to enter it as a private advocate. Noble, *anobli*, clerk; but it was to the law that this remarkable family belonged, the law that enabled its members to rise in 'this court', to succeed in government and to reap the rewards of the Church.

But if one does not regard them as rigid and exclusive, if one does not regard them as single-minded, there is some point in respecting the old categories. If we regard them simply as conveniences, as large and unwieldy abstractions, based upon the gradual legal definition of forces in society which might strain against the restrictions which that definition might, as that society developed, impose, they have their use. In the 'Church' were problems which, though they affected others than churchmen, were clearly primarily clerical. In towns there were problems which, though they affected others than the bourgeoisie, were clearly primarily urban and bourgeois. In the 'nobility' were problems which, though others than nobles might face them too, were in some way primarily noble. And though in political action in representative institutions the French exhibited their taste for localism, in their less formal relations with the government they dealt with a single organism. With regional feeling in politics we will deal when we come to discuss the Estates of France. When as individuals or in small groups the inhabitants of the country in the later middle ages faced the problems of their condition or the king's government they faced problems and forces generally common to all those in their position in France. Thus, for convenience, and having been warned, we may discuss the preoccupations and problems of those who belonged to the Church, of those who lived in towns, of those who were not noble outside them and of those who were.

II. Nobles

Honour and status

To begin with the nobility. A noble, it will be remembered, was a man who behaved like a noble, ideally and essentially 'noble . . . living nobly and in the practice of arms'.[1] As such the class identified itself. It had its privileges; its sections in each *pays* might have their separate privileges;[2] it had its obligations. Its members were readily identifiable, if only by their 'clothes' or by their 'dogs and birds'.[3] Honour in principle infused the class; though honour was not, of course, confined to the nobility, even to the 'nobility of arms'.[4] 'Let Honour be your dear master always,' François Garin, bourgeois of Lyon, told his son in 1460.[5] But honour was the essence of chivalry. That there should be honour amongst soldiers, as amongst the members of any profession, even thieves, was reasonable enough; and for those who prided themselves on their honour, the conscience of knighthood might have been enough to control their conduct. But the laws of war, in taking into account practices based upon chivalric ideas, gave some sanction for their non-observance. And the laws of war were concerned primarily with the regulation of the material side of war; a soldier might have a strong material interest in being honourable. In this sense the code of chivalry did have some reality in the later middle ages. The military did, on the whole, treat one another properly. Their treatment of mere civilians was, if the civilians' complaints are to be believed, very different. Honour as a motive outside the army was perhaps a more questionable matter. Clearly those important enough to have their honour damaged were concerned with it: the question of prestige was highly important to the later medieval aristocrat. How far

---

[1] J. Bartier, *Légistes et gens de finances au xve siècle. Les Conseillers des ducs de Bourgogne Philippe le bon et Charles le téméraire* (Brussels, 1955) p. 199 n 2.

[2] See, for instance, A. Artonne, *Le Mouvement de 1314 et les chartes provinciales de 1315* (1912).

[3] B. Guenée, *Tribunaux et gens de justice dans le bailliage de Senlis à la fin du Moyen âge* (1963) p. 412.

[4] M. H. Keen, *The Laws of War in the Late Middle Ages* (1965) pp. 254–7.

[5] *Complainte et enseignements*, ed. D[urand] de L[ancon] (1832) fo. xj^v.

in their politics were men governed by the dictates of honour? The word was often enough on their lips; and consideration of it could give bias to their actions. Negotiating with Huntingdon herald his treachery to Charles VII in 1455, Jean duc d'Alençon declined to become Henry VI's liege man at that moment 'but when the king of England has invaded France', he said, 'and taken part of my lands, he can send to summon me to go and live on them or to surrender them. In this way I shall have a good reason and an excuse to ask the king [Charles VII] to give me leave of absence and to go and live on my lands. If I should do things in any other way it would be a charge against me and dishonour for ever, seeing that my predecessors have always served the king of France and have died in his service.'[1] The letter of the law was observed; and one would be rash to ignore this fact. Men might succeed in circumventing the code by which they lived; but the very manœuvres of circumvention gave a particular obliquity to their actions.

The members of the nobility were acutely conscious of their status within the order; and the connection between status and politics could be abundantly clear. When François II duke of Brittany — perhaps an extreme example — declared in 1480 that 'since time immemorial the estate, honour and magnificence of our seigneury and principality has by our predecessors, sometimes kings, sometimes dukes and princes of it, been conducted, ruled and governed in order and regulation by nine prelates and nine barons, besides the bannerets, bachelors and other members of the Estates of this our lordship',[2] he was intent upon emphasising the status and the independence of his duchy. From Jean IV on, the dukes of Brittany were intent on reinforcing the 'royal' tradition. From 1417 they ruled by the grace of God.[3] The invention of the Nine Ancient Baronies was an attempt both to prove the antiquity of the duchy and to assert its equality with the kingdom of France. The existence and importance of the Parlement of Brittany, very much part of the duke's royal dignity, was stressed both in 1384 and in 1455.[4] The struggle for status and the struggle for independence were almost synonymous. In 1443 'because [of the fact that] no temporal

[1] G. du Fresne de Beaucourt, *Hist. de Charles VII*, VI (1891) 49.

[2] Morice, op. cit. III (1746) col. 368.

[3] B. A. Pocquet du Haut-Jussé, 'Les Faux Etats de Bretagne de 1315 et les premiers Etats de Bretagne', in *Bibl. Ec. Chartes*, LXXXVI (1925) 391–2, 396.

[4] Morice, op. cit. II (1744) cols 457–8, 1651–68.

lord, unless he is a sovereign prince, should use [the] . . . title "by the
grace of God" the king, since he is sovereign in his kingdom and allows
no subject of his to be his peer, has forbidden . . . the comte de Foix,
unless he wishes to commit a crime against him, to use from henceforth that title "by the grace of God". And in the same way, a little
time ago, it was forbidden the comtes d'Armagnac, de Comminges
and d'Astarac.' Gaston IV de Foix, though he maintained that 'very
long prescription is good and sufficient title', admitted that 'he did not
intend to deny that the king was his sovereign'.[1]

For Charles VII sovereignty was not mocked: Philippe *le bon*'s title
to *par la grâce de Dieu* was challenged as well in 1446.[2] Given the more
material causes of conflict between the king and the duke of Burgundy
or the comte de Foix such contention may seem rather unreal. But the
question of dignity had itself a certain reality; and that dignity itself
might be the justification for a number of those material acts which
provided the contents of the lists of *gravamina* drawn up by indignant
king or indignant magnate.[3] The struggle for status was not wholly a
struggle for prestige; but that prestige was a thing worth seeking for
itself is abundantly clear. Dignity and political position rose and fell
together, though some titles might be empty and some without title in
fact, if only temporarily, more powerful than the great in name. But it
was the great, essentially, who in their relationship with the king
provided political movement in later medieval France. 'In the realm of
France', thought Sir John Fortescue, 'was never change of their king,
since it was first inhabited by Frenchmen, but by the rebellion of such
mighty subjects';[4] and on the whole he was right, about their intentions
if not about their effectiveness.

[1] G. Leseur, *Hist. de Gaston IV, comte de Foix*, ed. H. Courteault (Soc. Hist.
France) II (1896) 293–4, 299. For the part played by the chroniclers Michel du
Bernis and Arnaud Esquerrier in discovering evidence for the title, see
H. Courteault, 'Un Archiviste des comtes de Foix au quinzième siècle. Le
Chroniqueur Michel du Bernis', in *A. Midi*, VI (1894) 281–300. The existence
of chronicles of seigneurial houses — such as those of Foix and Armagnac
(C. Samaran, 'Un Texte historiographe à retrouver: les chroniques de la
maison d'Armagnac (xive siècle)' in *Rec. . . . Clovis Brunel*, II (1955) 501–6) and
Brittany — is arguably at least a reflection of the same kind of pretension.
[2] Beaucourt, op. cit. IV (1888) 335.
[3] See, for instance, Leseur, op. cit. pp. 293–305.
[4] *The Governance of England*, ed. C. Plummer (Oxford, 1885) p. 129.

Families

Who were these princes? The simplest course is probably to take an arbitrary point — say 1400 — and examine the past and the future of each *lignage*; and to begin with those closest to the crown and to work outwards from them. Nearest to the king was his brother, Louis duc d'Orléans, whose children were to continue in three lines, the main Orléans branch (to Louis' grandson, Louis XII king of France), the cadet Angoulême branch (to Louis' great-grandson François I king of France) and the bastard branch of Jean d'Orléans, comte de Dunois. Next were Charles VI's uncles, dukes of Anjou, Berry and Burgundy. The main line of Louis I d'Anjou produced in the third generation a cadet branch of Maine; but the family died out in 1481 with the death of Charles comte du Maine, who had succeeded his uncle René, the grandson of Louis I, the year before. The title of Berry did not survive Charles VI's uncle Jean; but it was revived for his second grandson, Charles, brother of Louis XI, afterwards duke of Normandy and duke of Guyenne. The house of Burgundy continued in the male main line for three generations after Philippe *le hardi*, acquiring a number of imperial counties and duchies, and in the cadet line of Brabant and Nevers. From Charles VI's great-great-grandfather, Charles de Valois, the founder of the Valois line, sprang the branch of the comtes and later ducs d'Alençon.

From Charles de Valois' father, Philippe III, king of France, came, as well as the cadet line of Valois, that of Evreux, in the second generation kings of Navarre, which was to die out in the male line in 1425. And from Philippe III's father, Louis IX, came the proliferating Bourbon *lignage*, with its offshoot in the third generation of La Marche (which in turn produced its own third-generation cadet line of Vendôme) and in the sixth generation of Montpensier. Older still as offshoots of the Capetians was the Eu family, a cadet line of the Artois family, itself a cadet branch from Louis VIII and of which the heir was now the son of Philippe *le hardi* duke of Burgundy. The house of Dreux went back to Louis VI; and from a cadet line of Dreux came the male main line of Brittany. From Robert II king of France came the Capetian house of Burgundy, which had died out in 1361, and from it in turn the line of dauphins of Viennois, which, too, ended in the mid-century with its property in Valois hands.

The dukes of Brittany were clearly remote as relatives; and there were many great houses which had little or no connection with the Capetians and their cadets the Valois, except, perhaps, by marriage.[1] These are best, perhaps, grouped regionally. In the north the greatest county was that of Flanders, now in the hands of Philippe *le hardi* duke of Burgundy through his marriage with the Dampierre heiress. The county of St.-Pol was in the hands of the Luxembourg-Ligny family; it was to escape to a younger branch of the Valois-Burgundy cadet line of Brabant between 1415 and 1430; but it was to return thereafter to the Luxembourg-Ligny line, a family which attempted to play an equivocal frontier role and suffered for it. The line of the comtes de Guines had died out in 1350; it was to be snatched thereafter between the crown, the Burgundy family and that of the Croys before it finally reverted to the crown in 1504. The county of Boulogne had long been in the hands of the comtes d'Auvergne; but it, too, was to be acquired by the crown in 1478.

In the west, great princes not immediately of the royal blood were few. But in the north-east, that part of the duchy of Bar in the kingdom of France, the *Barrois mouvant*, was not to come into the possession of the Valois until René d'Anjou became duke in 1419. In the centre the county of Auxerre had been sold to the king of France in 1371; the county of Nevers had come to the Valois house of Burgundy via the Dampierre counts of Flanders, as had the county of Rethel; the county of Blois had come to that of Orléans in 1391, and with it the county of Dunois, sold in 1382 to Guy II de Blois. The Orléans family had also, from 1400, the barony of Coucy and from 1404 a claim to the county of Soissons; but the lawsuit between Louis d'Orléans and his heirs, and the other claimants and theirs was to last out the century.[2] The county of Dreux had come to the crown in 1377 and 1378 (though it was given out in apanage later); and that of Montfort had long been in the possession of the Montfort dukes of Brittany.

Greater principalities were to be found in the south-west. The vicomté of Bearn, *de facto* sovereign, had been since 1290 in the possession of the house of Foix. In 1425 it was to acquire Bigorre, in the

[1] Cf. G. A. de La Roque, *Traité de la noblesse* (Rouen, 1735) pp. 265 ff.
[2] H. Lacaille, 'La Vente de la baronnie de Coucy', in *Bibl. Ec. Chartes*, LV (1894) pp. 573–97.

possession of the crown since 1292. Its great rival line of Armagnac
had by the end of the fourteenth century three groups of property, a
western group around Armagnac, an eastern group around Rodez, and
a smaller southern group in the Pyrenees. But the Armagnacs failed
permanently to keep the county of Comminges as they had failed to
acquire that of Bigorre; between 1419 and 1453 it was in the hands of
Mathieu, brother of Jean I de Foix, and thereafter reverted to the crown
until 1461. In third place, in the west, came the house of Albret, linked by
marriage to the Valois. Farther east, in Languedoc, there were no houses
approaching princely status. To the north, the county of Périgord had
been confiscated in 1399 from Archambaud VI and given to Louis
d'Orléans; in 1437 it was sold to the Blois-Penthièvre family, comtes de
Limoges, and it went with the heiress of the line to the Albrets at the end
of the century. The branches of the line of the old family of comtes
d'Auvergne ran out successively into daughters; in 1400 the county was
in the hands of Jean duc de Berry as husband of Jeanne II d'Auvergne;
and it was eventually to settle in the hands of the La Tour family. The
line of the dauphins of Auvergne was to run out to a daughter in 1426,
who took the dauphiné to Louis de Bourbon comte de Montpensier.

In the south-east, the princes of Orange were vassals of the count of
Provence. The last comte de Valentinois-Diois was to cede his territory
in 1419 to the future Charles VII. Farther north, the county of Forez
had gone to Louis II de Bourbon by his marriage to Anne d'Auvergne
in 1371; and in 1400 Edouard II de Beaujeu sold him his barony of
Beaujeu and his part of Dombes.

Below the princes in rank — and they themselves, as we have seen,
had their own hierarchy — came a hierarchy of lesser magnates, each of
whom might be of considerable local importance. Some were themselves
cadets of princely lines: the Ligny and Fiennes branches of the St.-Pol
family at the end of the fifteenth century, for instance, the Penthièvre
branch of the Breton line, the Fezensaguet cadet line of the Armagnac
family, whose property returned to the main line in 1403, the Pardiac
cadet line created by Bernard III d'Armagnac, which acquired the duchy
of Nemours in 1462, the Kendal and Lautrec cadet lines of the house of
Foix. Some had an independent ancestry: in the south-west, for instance
(for now we must limit our field), the captals de Buch, whose inheritance
fell to the Foix family, the comtes d'Astarac, the vicomtes de Couserans,

the vicomtes de Narbonne, whose vicomté also went to the Foixs, the seigneurs de Lévis-Mirepoix. Beneath them again were less notable men, but still, in the south-west, of houses of sufficient local importance to be wooed by the greater nobles in their quarrels:[1] the houses of Montferrand, Durfort and Caumont in Guyenne, for instance; and beneath them again lesser families, still of importance in their immediate areas: the Lamothes of Roquetaillade, for instance, the Lamothes of Castelnau de Mesmes and Noaillan, the Ferrans of Mauvezin. The list for each area of France would be endless; but never without its fascination. For these were the men who completed the group of the most important protagonists in the politics of later medieval France.

Was there much movement within the class as a whole? Is it possible to discern trends of change in the nobility, parallel to those found in England in the later middle ages? There, it is argued, the development during the fifteenth century of tail male and, paradoxically, of enfeoff-ment to uses had tended to create out of an undifferentiated mass of 'nobility', headed by a dozen earls, the possibility of a larger noble caste, distinct from its inferiors, the 'gentry', now denied that quality.[2] In the seventeenth century La Roque appreciated the English distinction: 'the nobility of England', he wrote, 'is differentiated in several degrees, by the princes of the royal house, by the dukes [and other ranks down to] . . . the *milords*, and by the simple gentlemen. . . . The lords or *milords* are the seigneurs who take their rank amongst the upper nobility, which, with the clergy . . . makes up the upper chamber'.[3] But he could make no such division for France; for he could have no criterion of parliamentary place. In England a sharp dividing line between 'nobility' and 'gentry' was provided by their place in Parliament. Had the French Estates-general ever achieved a permanent existence, it, too, might have made possible a distinction between the greater nobles, who had their place physically in an assembly apart from the ruck of lesser nobles, and a 'gentry'; especially when, as at the Estates-general at least of 1484, the latter were elected — and elected as representatives of all three orders

[1] P. S. Lewis, 'Decayed and Non-feudalism in Later Medieval France', in *B. Inst. hist. Research*, XXXVII (1964) 161 ff.

[2] K. B. McFarlane, 'The English Nobility in the Later Middle Ages', in *Comité international des sciences historiques, xiie Congrès international . . . Vienne . . . 1965, Rapports*, I *Grands Thèmes* (Vienna, [1965]) 337–45.

[3] Op. cit. p. 394.

of their circumscription. But the Estates-general did not achieve that permanent existence; and for La Roque the terms 'noble' and 'gentle' were synonymous.[1]

Not that the French nobility, as we have seen, was an undifferentiated mass; nor was it ignorant of the dangers of a divided inheritance. At least in the Albret family, as we shall see, some attempt was made by juggling with local customs in the south-west to exclude daughters and younger sons.[2] It would be of some importance to know if other magnates, too (as well as the crown in its dealing with apanages in the fourteenth and fifteenth centuries),[3] had thought of doing the same. But as a subject the French nobility in the later middle ages is hardly an overworked field. Enough lines do seem to have run out to daughters; ancient *lignages* fell, as we have seen, in the fourteenth and fifteenth centuries to the crown or the greater princes; the crown and the greater princes created new cadet lines — though this process may have served, in the same paradoxical way as in England, to reinforce the caste of the princes. But the practice of providing younger sons with apanages was not new: Louis VIII had created, as well as that of Artois for his second son, Robert, others in Poitou and Auvergne, and in Anjou and Maine, for his son Alphonse and (eventually) for his son Charles, which had returned to the crown before the succession of the Valois. St.-Louis had created three apanages, of which only the Bourbon line survived. The apanage of Valois created by Philippe III came to the crown with Philippe III's grandson Philippe VI; as had those created by Philippe IV for his younger sons as they in turn succeeded their elder brother. Nor was the process of the extinction of old *lignages* a new one: Vermandois, for instance, had fallen to the crown in 1183, Valois in 1214, Alençon in 1219, Perche in 1226, and Clermont in 1258.

But the result of the process in the later middle ages was clearly to limit the number of princes not with some immediacy of royal blood, and even in the male line. It is difficult to find a duke created who was not of that stock; Archibald earl of Douglas, created duke of Touraine by Charles VII, is perhaps an exception; and Jacques comte de Pardiac,

---

[1] See below, pp. 332–45; La Roque, op. cit. pp. 3, 4.

[2] See below, p. 213.

[3] F. Lot and R. Fawtier, *Hist. des institutions françaises au Moyen âge*, II *Institutions royales* (1958) 125 ff. Cf. C. T. Wood, *The French Apanages and the Capetian Monarchy, 1224–1328* (Harvard, 1966) pp. 37–66.

a nephew of Jean IV d'Armagnac, had a claim to the duchy of Nemours by inheritance. But marriage, as in England, could raise men to comital status: Charles de La Rivière became comte de Dammartin by marriage at the end of the fourteenth century, Antoine de Chabannes comte de Dammartin by marriage in the mid-fifteenth. Service, too, could raise a man to comital status. The barony of Guillaume Roger II de Beaufort, brother of pope Clement VI, was turned into a county by Philippe VI; Jean de Melun's barony of Tancarville was turned into a county by Jean II. Bertrand du Guesclin under Charles V became comte de Longueville; Pierre de Brézé, under Charles VII, comte de Maulévrier[1] and John Stuart comte d'Evreux. Under Louis XI Odet d'Aydie became comte de Comminges, Boffile de Juge comte de Castres, Philippe de Commynes prince de Talmont; and Louis, bastard of Bourbon, admiral of France, had his barony of Roussillon in Dauphiné turned into a county when he married Louis XI's bastard daughter. But the number of such fortunates does not seem to have been very large; nor were their counties singularly important ones.

Noble power and noble administrations

The princes of the fleurs-de-lis and the surviving magnates not immediately of the royal blood in a direct male line retained their pre-eminence. What precisely was the nature of their power? It was in the first place more obviously territorial than that of their contemporaries in England. The judicial and fiscal rights of French magnates were much greater.[2] The development of the administration of the greater princes has been seen as a process roughly parallel to that of royal administration, providing from the fourteenth century a foundation for an independence which might not finally be claimed.[3] The process was an

[1] The title admittedly was given him by the duke of Savoy (P. Bernus, 'Louis XI et Pierre de Brézé (1440 à 1465)', in R. *Anjou*, NS LXIII (1911) 245); but there is some evidence of his holding, perhaps briefly, the titles of comte d'Evreux and de Tonnerre (G. Dupont-Ferrier, *Gallia regia* (Paris, 1942–61) nos. 17603, 19710).

[2] See, for instance, those given Jean duc de Berry with his apanage in 1360 (R. Lacour, *Le Gouvernement de l'apanage de Jean, duc de Berry* (1934) pp. 5–9).

[3] J. Le Patourel, 'The King and the Princes in Fourteenth-century France' in *Europe in the Late Middle Ages*, ed. J. R. Hale, J. R. L. Highfield and

uneven one; in the earlier fourteenth century, for instance, comparatively unimportant Forez was administratively more sophisticated than the duchy of Burgundy under its last Capetian duke.[1] But the development of these principalities 'from the seigneurie to the state'[2] has been emphasised, not only for Aquitaine and for Béarn,[3] but for Brittany, for Flanders, for Burgundy[4] and for Bourbonnais.[5] The use of the word 'state' for these principalities 'for want of a better one'[6] is perhaps a little unfortunate; but the stress that has been placed upon the development of their administrations in providing a *sine qua non* for the attitudes of princes *vis-à-vis* the king is clearly far from misplaced — though noble administrations may well have developed as much because of various pressures internal and external beyond their control as because of seigneurial ambition.[7] Naturally these administrations varied from prince to prince. The administration of the royal and imperial possessions of the Valois house of Burgundy was almost as complex as that of a kingdom. The administration of the comtes de Comminges was, to say the least, rudimentary in comparison. But even lesser seigneurs in Comminges had some kind of administrative machine, based upon that

B. Smalley (1965) pp. 155–83; see also Lot and Fawtier, op. cit. 1 *Institutions seigneuriales* (1957).

[1] E. Perroy, 'Feudalism or Principalities in Fifteenth-century France', in *B. Inst. hist. Research*, xx (1945) 182–3. For Forez, see E. Fournial, *Les Mémoriaux de la Chambre des comptes de Forez. Restitution du reg. des années 1349–1356* (Macon, 1964); for Burgundy, J. Richard, *Les Ducs de Bourgogne et la formation du duché du xie au xive siècle* (Dijon, 1954) pp. 523–5.

[2] A. Leguai, 'De La Seigneurie à l'état. Le Bourbonnais pendant la guerre de Cent ans', in *B. Soc. Emulation Bourbonnais*, LIII (1964–5) 155–75, 246–69, 313–47, 494–523, 577–90, LIV (1966–7) 37–53, 76–89, 138–54, 252–76, 365–83, 423–47 (still in progress).

[3] P. Tucoo-Chala, *Gaston Fébus et la vicomté de Béarn (1343–1391)* (Bordeaux, 1960).

[4] The most convenient work on Valois Burgundy is that still in progress of Professor Richard Vaughan — *Philip the Bold: The Formation of the Burgundian State* (1962); *John the Fearless: The Growth of Burgundian Power* (1966).

[5] Leguai, op. cit. and 'Un Aspect de la formation des Etats princiers en France à la fin du Moyen âge: les réformes admin. de Louis II, duc de Bourbon', in *Moyen Age*, LXX (1964) 49–72.

[6] Ibid. p. 70; Vaughan, *John the Fearless*, p. 287.

[7] A. Leguai, *Les Ducs de Bourbon pendant la crise monarchique du xve siècle* (1962) p. 184; M. Mollat, 'Recherches sur les finances des ducs Valois de Bourgogne', in *R. hist.*, CCXIX (1958) 287–8.

of the counts.[1] Each magnate moved in a more or less pompous household; each was the head of a more or less complex administration; each had a following and a clientage which brought him prestige, power and a considerable amount of trouble. As an example we may take an administration which did not 'develop', but which was created, as it were, of one piece: that of Jean duc de Berry at the end of the fourteenth and the beginning of the fifteenth centuries.

In October 1360 Jean, third son of Jean II king of France, was given by his father in apanage the *bailliages* of Berry, of Auvergne and of the Montagnes d'Auvergne; the county of Poitou was added by Charles V in 1374. The administration[2] which he employed to deal with this complex of rights had, like that of other princes, a marked affinity with that of the king. Like his, it divided into 'central' and 'local'. At the very centre was the ducal household. In its midst was the duke, surrounded by his *chambellans*, seventeen in 1370, twenty-one in 1413–15. Lower in status was the score and more of *valets de chambre* (who included in 1370 Jean's tailor, his goldsmiths, his painter, in 1398 his butcher and his minstrel, in 1413 his principal barber). After the *chambre* came the six principal services of the household, which saw to its material needs; the lesser services; the keeper of the duke's remarkable collections; the chapel; the *gens d'armes* of the household; the household accountants and other lesser functionaries. At 'court', too, at least while the duke was in his apanage, were the 'central' administrators. Most important were the councillors: some ducal civil servants, some magnates local or not so local, lay and ecclesiastic, some permanent members and others not, summoned *ad hoc* as business arose, omni-competent. Most important on the council was the chancellor, head of the chancery and its secretaries, head of the judicial organisation, president (unlike his colleague in the kingdom) of the ducal *Chambre des comptes* and superior of the *trésorier-général* and his underlings. Like the king, the duc de Berry had his proctor-general; like the king he had his *maîtres des requêtes*; like the king he had his *réformateurs généraux*, immediate ducal plenipotentiaries to check upon the local civil servants. These officers and their offices again were modelled closely upon the

[1] C. Higounet, *Le Comté de Comminges de ses origines à son annexion à la couronne*, I (Toulouse, 1949) 205–32, 311.

[2] Lacour, op. cit.

royal organisations which they succeeded. The *sénéchaux* of Berry, Auvergne and Poitou had beneath them a complex of administrative, judicial and financial subordinates; but like their colleagues in the kingdom they were incompetent to deal with certain important judicial cases (which were reserved for the equivalent of Parlement, the ducal *Grands Jours*, or for the ducal council) and they were incompetent to deal with extraordinary finance; taxation, as in the kingdom, had its own organisation. But all finance went eventually into the hands of the *trésorier-général*; and the *Chambre des comptes* had from its inauguration in 1379 ultimate overall financial competence.

Such a dry enumeration of offices cannot animate the seigneurial administration of Jean duc de Berry; but it can give some idea of the complex hierarchy of which he was head, of the administrative pyramid which made, in a very real sense, his territorial power. This great apanagist had essentially taken over a part of the royal administration for his own uses: in so far as it alone went, he was king. But there was much of government which escaped this part of the royal administration. Hence the eagerness with which Jean and others of his equals acquired the royal rights inherent in the office of lieutenant-general: an eagerness which, as we have seen, might bring its own punishment for seigneurial ambition.[1] Fortified with these a magnate might be considerable indeed.

A military organisation was also inherent in Jean duc de Berry's apanage. The greater part of his forces was still supplied by the feudal *ban* and *arrière-ban*. This, in principle, should not have served the duke against the king: but in fact it did.[2] Purely 'feudal' support for an independent magnate should, therefore, not be underestimated. Until Charles *le téméraire* replaced it with *compagnies d'ordonnance* from 1471 the dukes of Burgundy seem to have relied heavily upon it; Jean II duc de Bourbon still thought it worth-while calling out his subjects in Forez during the magnate revolt of the Public Weal in 1465.[3] But, naturally, such service could be relied upon only for brief periods at a time. The necessities of normal life imposed themselves upon the conscripts: there was a truce sought to bring in the vintage in Mâconnais in 1430; in 1465 the Milanese ambassador thought the war would be short

---

[1] See above, p. 163.　　　　　　[2] Lacour, op. cit. pp. 313–14.

[3] J. Bartier, *Charles le téméraire* (Brussels, 1944) pp. 182 ff; Arch. nat. P 1402[1], cote 1225.

'especially seeing that the crops are coming on in the country'.[1] For the longer campaigns of the Hundred Years War new forms of recruitment had developed: the paid companies were equally available to those magnates who could afford them. In 1412, for instance, Jean de Berry raised eight to defend Poitou; Jean V of Brittany had his permanent 'retinue' in 1419 and his *francs-archers* in 1425; and François II in the second half of the century had six permanent *compagnies d'ordonnance* containing a total of 200 men at arms and 400 archers.[2] But we know all too little about the way in which the magnates of the civil war raised their forces.[3] In 1465, again, Malletta thought 'all these seigneurs are short of cash or have no men except their gentlemen and subjects under their command'.[4] Clearly the logistical problems of rebellion were considerable.

Clientage

But the problem of military power was intimately bound up with that of political influence as a whole: the larger question of old 'feudal' following and new 'non-feudal' clientage includes that of military support. Clearly a magnate hoped to rely on his vassals for political as well as military support. Equally clearly he looked beyond them in the hope of wider influence. Methods of creating that wider influence varied. The nucleus of the household provided the most intimate opportunity. Amongst the *chambellans* of Jean duc de Berry were nobles from areas beyond his apanage; amongst men retained of the household of the first two Valois dukes of Burgundy were neighbouring seigneurs of considerable importance.[5] Most spectacular of the means of creating

[1] Barbey, op. cit. p. 157; *Dépêches des ambassadeurs milanais en France sous Louis XI et François Sforza*, ed. B. de Mandrot and C. Samaran (Soc. Hist. France) III (1920) 161.

[2] Lacour, op. cit. pp. 275–6; B. A. Pocquet du Haut-Jussé, 'Le Grand Fief breton', in Lot and Fawtier, op. cit. I 284.

[3] But see above, p. 198 n 3, and C. Brusten, *L'Armée bourguignonne de 1465 à 1468* (Brussels, 1953); J. Richard, 'L'Armée des ducs de Bourgogne', in *R. hist. Armée*, XII (1956) 25–31.

[4] *Dépêches des ambassadeurs milanais*, p. 161.

[5] Lacour, op. cit. p. 144; B. A. Pocquet du Haut-Jussé, 'Les Pensionnaires fieffés des ducs de Bourgogne de 1352 à 1419', in *M. Soc. Droit Pays bourguignons*, VIII (1942) 146.

influence possibly was the chivalric order: but while Louis d'Orléans' *Porc-épic*, the Breton *Hermine* and the Burgundian *Toison d'or* had fairly clearly some political content it is more difficult to ascribe one to a number of these exercises in an eccentric social convention. The marshal Boucicaut's *Ecu vert à la dame blanche*, Jean I de Bourbon's *Fer de prisonnier* and the highly obscure Foix 'devise' of the *Dragon*, for instance, seem all to have had a highly limited purpose of a purely chivalric character.[1] There were other and less cumbersome ways by which a magnate could collect clients and *alliés*.

A form of contract still provided the method used by magnates in south-west France and to a certain extent elsewhere in the century before 1450.[2] The transition from the feudal to the non-feudal contract for life service occurred with hardly a jolt in France. The step from the money fee for term of life, reinforced by an oath of homage, to the contract of *alliance* for term of life, reinforced by a different oath, was an easy one to take in practical if not in moral terms. Why the idea of homage should have palled is not at all clear; but that there was a flight from the 'feudal' form in the administrations of the comte de Foix, of the duc d'Orléans and of the duke of Burgundy towards the end of the fourteenth century is plainly apparent. The history of the new form of contract is most clearly at the moment seen in the south-west. A considerable number of contracts of *alliance* survives for the reigns of Jean I and of Gaston IV comte de Foix; and an analysis of their *alliés* may be attempted. These supporters were drawn with a fine and Gascon impartiality from both 'English' and 'French' sides of that uncertain frontier of sovereignty in the south-west. They included local magnates so important as Jean *par la grâce de Dieu* comte d'Astarac; they included royal officers from both sides; they included less important men. That some of the attached houses could display considerable fidelity, in the sense that their members provided *alliés* for the counts over a considerable period, does not seem to be doubtful. Clearly it would be rash to assert the complete irrefrangibility of the non-feudal contract, any more than of the feudal contract; but in so far as they remained loyal the local *alliés* of the comtes de Foix, as well as enhancing their military strength,

---

[1] P. S. Lewis, 'Une Devise de chevalerie inconnue, créée par un comte de Foix? Le *Dragon*', in *A. Midi*, LXXVI (1964) 77–84.

[2] Lewis, 'Decayed and Non-feudalism in Later Medieval France', pp. 157–184.

carried the counts' political influence westward into the Landes and Bordelais, northward to the Garonne and beyond into Quercy and Périgord, eastward into the plain of Languedoc, even over the mountains into Spain. *Alliances* could also be made with clients at court: but in what sense such confidantes of the dauphin Louis as Aymerigon seigneur d'Estissac or Jean de Daillon seigneur de Fontaines were 'clients' of Gaston IV de Foix is a complex matter. With courtiers, magnates probably contracted more often on more equal terms than with local seigneurs in their *pays*. But with such contracts we exceed the boundary of a single magnate's power: it was by such *alliances* between equals that the magnates of the later fourteenth and fifteenth centuries bound themselves to each other in their rebellious coalitions.

Dispendiousness

What were the preoccupations of the nobility? Dignity and status we have seen obsessed them. They could be far from uncultured. Not all might have the literary flair of Charles d'Orléans or even of René d'Anjou or of Gaston III Fébus, but such a comparatively minor seigneur as Nompar II de Caumont could exhibit a literary turn of mind;[1] many of the nobility were patrons of the arts and many more had the conventional tastes of the age for moral treatises, stirring histories and gentle romances, tapestries, beds, clothes, jewellery and plate. In ability they varied as much as any social class ever does; in personality as much as men do one from another. Generalisation is thus dangerous: but some of the conditions of the class as a whole did apply pretty generally. And it was the conditions of the class which provided the motive force for their political action: it was what the nobility was that made it act as it did.

The impoverished Guichard Vert at least possessed when he died in 1287 a chess-board to mark his gentility. A noble living nobly lived with a proper degree of magnificence: a noble must dispend. Admittedly the careful noble did exist: Louis de Chalon was alleged to have said

[1] P. Champion, *Vie de Charles d'Orléans* (1911) *passim*; A. Lecoy de La Marche, *Le Roi René*, II (1875) 153 ff (but see V. Chichmaref, 'Notes sur quelques œuvres attribuées au roi René', in *Romania*, LV (1929) 214–50); Tucoo-Chala, op. cit. pp. 18–20; *Voyaige d'oultremer ou Jhérusalem par le seigneur de Caumont, l'an mccccxviii*, ed. A. E. L. de La Grange (1858).

'a man who had as big an income as he did didn't manage his affairs properly unless he saved 10,000 *francs* a year': but still he paid the Lucchese merchant Barthélémy Bertin 600 *couronnes d'or* in April 1415 for a Cyprus material shining with gold; his reputation for opulence (both in spending and in saving) was considerable; and, although he expired obsessed with the fear of losing his treasure, he was clearly far from non-conformist in his attitude towards the noble way of life.[1] To visit the treasures of the great for over long would rapidly dull one's senses with sad satiety of so many diamonds, rubies, balas, pearls, sapphires, emeralds, gold, gilt, silver, enamel; so many reliquaries, so many crosses, chalices, pyxes, patens; so many collars, rings, brooches; so many flagons, cups, plates, pots, spoons and fantastic salts. The inventories of Jean duc de Berry, who 'delighted greatly in precious stones', alone overwhelm one in utter magnificence;[2] but that omnivorous collector of the world's wonders did not confine himself to these. When he died in 1416 his tapestries were valued at 28,000 *livres tournois*; his jewels, manuscripts and other treasures at 130,000 *livres tournois*; his executors valued his great psalter painted by Jacquemart de Hesdin alone at 4000 *livres*. As a patron, as a builder, he was equally notable; and the magnificence which one can see in the *Très Riches Heures* is faithful to its owner's way of life.[3]

Expenditure on building, on tapestries, on furniture, on plate, on clothing, on jewellery, on manuscripts, on pictures, on patronage, all, of course, in principle might amount to so much conspicuous waste. The more convertible treasures might represent hoarding against a rainy day; but even so the cost of the goldsmith's work could add some three or four times to the price of an object above the value of the precious metal.[4] Magnificence might have a hidden value in enhancing the prestige of a magnate, especially of a magnate like the duke of

[1] Barbey, op. cit. pp. 240, 36, 85, 209, 224, 226, 236 ff.

[2] *Inventaires de Jean, duc de Berry (1401–16)*, ed. J.J. Guiffrey (1894–6); J. Juvenal des Ursins, *Hist. de Charles VI*, ed. Michaud and Poujoulat (Nouv. Coll. des mém. 2: 1857) p. 532.

[3] For a remarkable account of Jean duc de Berry, see J.H. Wylie and W.T. Waugh, *The Reign of Henry the Fifth*, II (Cambridge, 1919) 391–447.

[4] M. Rey, 'Les Emissions d'écus à la couronne à l'Hôtel des monnaies de Paris vers la fin du xive siècle et dans les premières années du xve (1385–1413)', in *Mélanges . . . Halphen* (1951) pp. 602–3.

Burgundy eager to impress his independence upon the world; but in general it remains clear that a great noble's standard of living led to the need for a considerable income to support it. Jean duc de Berry had, indeed, a considerable income: but it was not enough for his dispendious tastes.[1]

And as well as seigneurial magnificence seigneurial piety could be costly. In the first place one's interment must be suitably pompous. The cost of burying Catherine de l'Isle-Bouchard, widow of Georges de La Trémoille, on 30 July 1472 came to 1364*l*. 14*s*. 6*d*. *tournois*.[2] The cost of cloth at Louis I de La Trémoille's funeral in 1483 came to 563 *livres* odd; the cost of 'the litter in the church of Sully' to 277 *livres* odd; and with other expenses the total rose again to over 1000 *livres*.[3] The tomb of Guy de La Trémoille cost 200 *francs*; and on top of this were the expenses of his servants hunting for his mortal remains in Hungary, in Italy, on Lesbos, in Turkey, and at the court of the Sultan.[4] Others expired in less picaresque situations than he: but all, according to their means, conformed to the rules of noble burial. They also conformed to the rules which demanded their commemoration upon a monumental scale. The foundation of high and of low masses to pray for a noble's soul and for those of his family, friends and deceased comrades in arms, the foundation of annual and perpetual services, the foundation of perpetual chaplainries, could be expensive. In Bordelais in 1374 low masses cost 2 *sous* each; the amount left per mass by members of the Polignac family in the fourteenth and fifteenth centuries varied around that figure.[5] Jean de Grailly captal de Buch in his will in 1369 left enough at this rate for 50,000 masses in the year which followed his death, as well as for sixty-one anniversaries, eighteen chaplainries, a

[1] F. Lehoux, 'Le Duc de Berri, les Juifs et les Lombards', in R. *hist*. CCXV (1956) 38–57.

[2] *Le Chartrier de Thouars*, ed. C.L. de La Trémoille (1877) pp. 22–4.

[3] *Les La Trémoille pendant cinq siècles*, ed. C.L. de La Trémoille II (Nantes, 1892) 5–8.

[4] *Guy de La Trémoille et Marie de Sully, Livre de comptes, 1395–1406*, ed. C.L. de La Trémoille (Nantes, 1887) pp. 54 ff, 127.

[5] R. Boutruche, *La Crise d'une société. Seigneurs et paysans du Bordelais pendant la guerre de Cent ans* (1947) p. 276 n 3. In Velay in 1343 and in 1363 the rate was 12 *d.t.* (*Preuves de la Maison de Polignac*, ed. A. Jacotin, II (1899) 6, IV (1905) 240) and in 1407 2 *s.t.* (ibid. II 195).

number of perpetual lamps and innumerable prayers; but Bernard Ezi II sire d'Albret in 1358 founded 100,000 masses for the pardon of his sins.[1] A lesser seigneur, Bernard d'Ecoussans, was more moderate (or less guilty) in 1338 with 25,000 for his own soul and 10,000 for those of his ancestors; the lower *noblesse* in Bordelais confined themselves to 1500–5000 masses, four to eight anniversaries, one or two chaplainries.[2] On this scale the mere 3000 masses of Armand VII de Polignac in Velay in 1343 were modest; but still, with 20 *sous tournois* on the *péage* of Colet and the mill of Bouzols a week left to the Preachers of Le Puy for various services, and with another 1000 *livres tournois* left for his tomb, a chapel and other building purposes, and with other pious legacies, the cost of his soul to his heirs came to very nearly 3000 *livres tournois*.[3] The list of pious uses could be extended: building operations, crusading funds, innumerable charities: Amanieu VII d'Albret left 1000 *livres bordelais* for the marriage of the daughters of poor labourers.[4] Conscience awoke at the approach of death: all debts unpaid and oppressions unremedied were provided for by the moribund with guilt in his soul.[5] It could all be very costly. Jean de Grailly burdened his estate with pious legacies amounting to 40,000 *écus d'or*; 1500–3000 *livres bordelais* was a fair average for a modest seigneur in the south-west.[6] It was left to their executors to find the money; and however much they delayed finding it, it had to be paid in the end. In Bordelais at least, as in the case of Armand VII de Polignac farther north, revenue could be found in fixed seigneurial dues; in the south-west the greater part of pious donations was paid from this source. But still, in some cases, heirs found it necessary to pare away the patrimony with royal licence.[7]

From the point of view of the principal heir, the claims of his father's soul must have seemed on a line with the claims of the other bereaved members of the family. Their interest in the estate was controlled first by custom and second by the testamentary dispositions of the defunct. In the former, elements of Roman and of customary law became inextricably mingled: in the north, the later middle ages saw a rigorous

---

[1] Boutruche, op. cit. pp. 276, 515. [2] Ibid. p. 276.
[3] *Preuves de la maison de Polignac*, II 1–11.
[4] P. Raymond, *Inv.-sommaire des arch. dép. Basses-Pyrénées*, IV (1867) 6 [E 21].
[5] Boutruche, op. cit. pp. 279–80. Cf. *Le Chartrier de Thouars*, p. 234.
[6] Boutruche, op. cit. p. 280. [7] Ibid. pp. 281–3.

practice of primogeniture weaken before the interest of the younger children; in the Midi, a régime of equitable partition weaken before the interest of the eldest son.[1] It seems certain that testators were prepared to manipulate the law as far as they could to suit their own needs. Political and paternal emotions warred in the seigneurial breast: the line must be maintained; dowagers and cadets must be provided for. Paternal emotion could, of course, go awry: Louis de Chalon disliked his eldest son and gave him as little as he could by custom get away with: to his beloved benjamin, Hugues, his son by his second wife, he is alleged to have said on top of the Tour du Meix south of Lons-le-Saunier, 'In fact, my son, I don't leave you anything like as much land or seigneuries as I leave your brothers; but I shall leave you so well provided for with money that you will have enough to buy them and have as much as any of the others.'[2] Cadets had to be maintained in their status: and there could be all too many cadets. The twenty-two sons of André de Budos are probably legendary; but Jean de Creney, who died in 1349, reposes on his tomb with his wife, his six daughters and his eleven sons; Amadée de Saluces vicomtesse de Polignac provided in her will in 1473 for five sons and six daughters; and Jean de Croy and Marguerite de Craon are alleged to have had at the beginning of the century seven sons (three of which died young) and nine daughters (four of which died young).[3] Death, of course, could compensate for irrepressible fecundity; but still the survivors could be numerous, and there was also the problem of one's bastards. 'Charles by the grace of God comte d'Armagnac' declared towards the end of the fifteenth century that 'because of the good and praiseworthy report that has been given to us of the person of Pierre, the son of Marguerite de Claux . . . with whom, both before and also after the conception and birth of . . . Pierre, we several times had intercourse, and . . . because . . . Marguerite has told . . . us several times since that she conceived him naturally by us; and also because of the good habits, virtues, sense,

[1] Ibid. p. 286 n 1.
[2] F. Barbey, *Louis de Chalon, prince d'Orange . . . 1390–1463* (Lausanne, 1926) p. 224.
[3] Boutruche, op. cit. p. 289; E. Mâle, *L'Art religieux de la fin du Moyen âge en France*, 5th ed. (1949) p. 411; *Preuves de la maison de Polignac*, II 319; M.R. Thielemans, 'Les Croÿ, conseillers des ducs de Bourgogne', in *B. Comm. hist. Belgique*, CXXIV (1959) 8 n2.

sufficiency, valiance, experience and true diligence with which they have said . . . Pierre is provided . . . we avow . . . [him] our bastard son'; and he also granted him 15,000 *écus d'or* on the barony of Caussade.[1] It was natural, as Georges de La Trémoille pointed out, to help one's illegitimate children 'to live and maintain [their] . . . estate'; in the 1340s Roger Bernard vicomte de Castelbon left 150 *livres morlaas* to each of his born or to be born.[2] The share for the legitimate was proportionally reduced.

But though some fathers might hand out property liberally to their younger sons and daughters, it was possible to buy them out with lump sums; it was possible to deposit them in holy orders, though even this could be expensive: it cost over 200 *écus* to fit Katherine de La Trémoille out as a Benedictine nun in 1471, with another 200-odd on her ring, the dinner and the bishop at her profession.[3] The nunnery of Comps was left 100 *livres tournois* by Armand VII de Polignac in 1343 in final quittance for his daughter Beatrice, immured there. Armand VII was clearly strong-minded: his eldest son was to inherit all that remained after incidental legacies, save 4000 *livres tournois* to the eldest daughter for her marriage; all other daughters were to follow Beatrice into orders.[4] Though for some more lucky their indulgent fathers priced up their marriage-portions in order to get them an heir or a cadet well provided for in turn by his indulgent parent (and that prestige was at stake here came out clearly when Marguerite d'Amboise refused to marry the eldest son of the seigneur de Chaumont on 5 April 1445),[5] the joys of legitimate parenthood at least were denied these unfortunates. One claim on the estate was more difficult to avoid: the interest of the dowager was protected by custom or by the marriage contract. Marguerite de Craon's dowry, 'which by justice and by custom can and should pertain and belong to her, that is half of the fiefs and a third of the non-noble properties in the inheritance', came to 400 *livres* a year.[6] The dowry, like the marriage-portion, varied with the status of families: but it was inescapable.

One should probably not overestimate the effect of their own

---

[1] P. Raymond, *Inv.-sommaire des arch. dép. Basses-Pyrénées*, IV (1867) 67–8 [E 274]. See C. Samaran, *La Maison d'Armagnac au xv⁵ siècle* (1908) pp. 359 ff.

[2] *Le Chartier de Thouars*, p. 304; Raymond, op. cit. p. 76 [E 299].

[3] *Le Chartrier de Thouars*, pp. 240–1.   [4] *Preuves de la maison de Polignac*, II 2, 4.

[5] *Le Chartrier de Thouars*, pp. 28–9.   [6] Thielemans, op. cit. pp. 54, 56.

practices in bringing about the decline of noble houses. It has been argued that in Bordelais it was 'for a number of families a cause at times primary, at times secondary, of decline'.[1] But it was possible to restrict the interest of others than the principal heir; dowries returned to the main line; cadet lines might expire; and in the portions brought to the family with the brides of the principal heir much might be recouped. An untrammelled heiress was a rich prize; but others, too, might be profitable. A daughter of Arnaud Amanieu sire d'Albret brought her fortunate husband 50,000 *florins d'Aragon*; Jeanne, the eldest daughter of Bernard-Ezi II d'Albret, 31,000 *écus d'or*; Rose, another daughter, took Jean de Grailly captal de Buch 15,000 *réaux d'or*.[2] The figure was proportional to the status of the family and to the status of the prospective son-in-law (when Marguerite de Chabannes, for instance, married Pierre de Cornier in 1421, her *dot* consisted of 400 *livres tournois* from her brother and 30 *livres tournois* rent from her aunt); one marriage-portion at least was not paid until seventy years after the original contract;[3] but still it was clear that one man's daughter was another man's wife. It was a matter of intelligently playing the marriage market; and of luck.

But it was not only a matter of negotiating marriage-portions, dowries and settlements; it was as well a matter of paying them and of enforcing their payment. Litigation in the bosom of the family could be endemic.[4] Successions, marriage-portions, dowries, pious donations, all could involve beneficiaries, counter-beneficiaries and those who had acquired however remotely an interest from them in the trammels of the law. The beginning of the interminable case of the Chabannes family against Astorge seigneur de Peyre began when Astorge, in order to pay a considerable number of obligations on the estate of his daughter-in-law Ysabeau de Saignes, sold the *terre* of La Dailhe to Jacques I de Chabannes for 4000 *écus d'or* on 30 December 1444. The

[1] Boutruche, op. cit. p. 294.

[2] Ibid. p. 356; Raymond, op. cit. p. 10 [E 36].

[3] H. de Chabannes, *Hist. de la maison de Chabannes, Supplément* (Dijon, 1901) pp. 593–7, and *Preuves pour servir à l'hist. de la maison de Chabannes,* 1 (Dijon, 1892) 302, 315.

[4] See, for instance, A. Bossuat, 'Une Scandaleuse Affaire. Richard de Chancey et la succession d'Hugues Moreau doyen de Dijon', in *Cah. Hist.* VII (1962) 301–17.

interests of Astorge de Peyre's son, Astorge, of his wife and of the will
of her father were all entangled in the arrangement: Astorge the elder
promised Chabannes to let him have a copy of the will and of the
marriage contract.[1] The purchase of a title to property in dispute might
be a form of speculation: three years later Jacques de Chabannes
bought up such a claim from Annette de Chauvigny for 675 *livres
tournois*, together with the documents and the lawsuit hanging in the
Parlement; two months later he sold out to Jacques Cœur for 621 *livres
tournois*.[2] It might be not only the unfortunate who found themselves at
law. But whether litigation was voluntary or involuntary it could still
be costly;[3] and it became more protracted and more expensive as one
moved up the courts. It had been reckoned that 10 per cent per annum
of income is a fair figure for the expenditure on litigation (for those who
could afford it) in the *bailliage* of Senlis in the later fourteenth and the
fifteenth centuries.[4] Many might litigate happily well within their
means; but great losses might lead to the paring away of the patrimony
and the weakening of the resources of the line. In 1462 Louis de Chalon
is alleged to have told the seigneur de Charny 'that he had a million in
gold coinage, without the cash he had from his father', and that he'd
spend it all in the attempt to recover the county of Neufchâtel; and
twelve years after his death, his sons, less competent than he, had lost
the house its precious Vaudois lands.[5]

'Ordinary' revenues

All these expenditures, all these losses must be seen against the
background of more or less profound dislocation in the basic source of
seigneurial revenue: the yield from the estates. A general picture is

[1] Chabannes, *Preuves*, I 176 ff.

[2] Ibid. pp. 193–7; and see M. Mollat, 'Jacques Cœur', in *Città mercanti
dottrine nell'econ. Europea dal iv al xviii secolo. Saggi in memoria di G. Luzzatto*,
ed. A. Fanfani (Milan, 1964) pp. 198–99.

[3] See, for instance, H. Courteault, *Gaston IV comte de Foix* (Toulouse, 1895)
pp. 130 ff, 397–8; C. Samaran, *La Maison d'Armagnac au xve siècle* (1907) pp.
7 ff; *Le Chartrier de Thouars*, p. 237.

[4] B. Guenée, *Tribunaux et gens de justice dans le bailliage de Senlis à la fin du
Moyen âge* (1963) pp. 252 ff.

[5] Barbey, op. cit. pp. 224, 265.

drawn of a shrinking of profits from such 'ordinary' sources, beginning certainly with the first epidemic of the Black Death, staved off perhaps until the last decades of the fourteenth century, thereafter more rapid until a new level of depressed stability was reached some time about the second quarter of the fifteenth century. The precise consequences of such dislocation are rather harder to determine, since documents in a sufficiently long run are generally lacking (the barony of Le Neubourg, for instance, is one of the best-documented as well as one of the best-studied of lay estates:[1] its series begin well after the first waves of the crisis were over) and since the particular elements in the *conjoncture de crise* naturally varied in importance from particular seigneur to particular seigneur. The value of impressionistic evidence concerning any particular noble becomes perhaps even more uncertain. And one should perhaps above all avoid the inference of political motive from general evidence of secular decline in seigneurial income from ordinary sources. But that particular crises, each one an element in that, in this context, essentially unreal concept of general conjuncture, could have a disastrous or depressing effect for particular members of a noble house need not be doubted; and though the nobility's search for extra profits from crown sources might well have occurred even if their revenues from land had been untroubled, that search, for a noble suddenly embarrassed by some disaster, was naturally all the more acute.

The basic cause of the diminishing of seigneurial incomes was, probably, the dislocation caused by the shortage and the increased price of labour following the epidemics of plague. The most spectacular cause was the war. The fall in revenues in Le Neubourg, for instance, from the beginning of the fifteenth century is ostensibly due to warfare in Normandy;[2] the fall in yields from the various sources of revenue in the barony could at certain times be spectacular enough. But one has learned, if only from the example of Gascony, a theatre of war *par excellence*, that such military devastation affected variably different areas and within them different families and estates; and that the pressure of destruction itself was naturally variable in its chronology. But still, in Bordelais, and if only from the example of the archbishopric of Bordeaux, it is clear that in times of crises landlords could certainly

---

[1] A. Plaisse, *La Baronnie du Neubourg* (1961).   [2] Ibid. pp. 76, 321–43.

suffer.[1] One must make the inevitable allowances for incompetent administrators and highly inefficient land-owners; not everything was to be blamed upon external pressures; but still it stands to reason that, with a troubled labour-supply, with soldiery devastating his crops and with monetary instability threatening periodically to play havoc with his fixed rents, even the most prudent landlord might suffer at times. But certain reservations must still be maintained: the incidence of pressure was variable and it was met with variable competence.

The fortune of war

The wholesale confiscation of his property for infidelity[2] was, of course, quite another matter for a land-owner than the temporary requisition of his produce by the military, its destruction or even its absence over a longer period. Yet the effects even of this misfortune could be mitigated; the wrath of the betrayed was not necessarily unassuageable. The houses that suffered in the final débâcle in Gascony in 1453 were comparatively few;[3] though a further number may have suffered from time to time throughout the long centuries on that wavering frontier in the south-west. Loyalty in later medieval France was, as we have seen, a complicated matter: when the civil war set father against son, and brother against brother, this may well have been in a large number of cases because the family was in all agreement looking after its property on both sides of the battle-line.[4] In 1453 François de Montferrand seigneur d'Uza and de Belin in the Landes went with his son Jeannot to England; his son Bernard remained in possession of the French properties.[5] Yet perhaps one should not over-estimate the number of such prudent families. Confiscation and spoliation was a very real threat to a noble caught with divided property and forced into a single loyalty; and even when the troubles were over, there was still the litigation to which they had given rise.

But upon this hazard of the seigneurial way of life we have already

---

[1] Boutruche, op. cit. pp. 247–64.   [2] See, for instance, ibid. pp. 235 ff.
[3] A. Peyrègne, 'Les Emigrés gascons en Angleterre (1453–1485)', in *A. Midi*, LXVI (1954) 115.
[4] See above, p. 68.   [5] *Arch. hist. Gironde*, XIII (1871–2) 85–94.

touched. Confiscation did not end the catalogue of the possible miseries of war for the noble. Extravagant possessions were a ready lure for the enemy (or, for that matter, for marauding soldiery on any side); and, indeed, a number of the campaigns of the war were mounted with the plunder of goods movable as the major military objective.[1] Where, for instance, did Sir John Fastolf get his 'two high candlesticks for altars, on the base of each two gilt knobs, with the king of France's arms'?[2] Certainly his profits of war were very far from negligible.[3] A prudent noble might try to keep his treasures out of harm's way: Charles d'Orléans in 1427 had the books, pictures and tapestries in his château of Blois moved to Saumur before the English advance, and then off again to La Rochelle.[4] Lesser people might try to hide their more portable goods in holes in the ground: but informers were especially zealous in revealing their whereabouts[5] and marauding troops themselves had a sharp nose for buried treasure. To escape the plunderer, enemy, friendly or free, was on the whole difficult in those areas in which the soldiery roamed unhindered.

But perhaps even more disastrous for a seigneur was the capture of his person. His captor was naturally eager to wring every drop of ransom he could out of him; and since his obligation to pay, with its sureties and its penalties, was essentially like any normal, legally enforceable obligation for debt, interminable lawsuits for himself and his friends lay ahead, as well as the pains of payment.[6] Ready cash was pathetically hard to raise: the cases of the Rodemack and the Châteauvillain ransoms give overwhelming evidence of the ultimately disastrous effect an accident of war might have upon the whole *lignage*; however much litigation might stave off the inevitable end, dismemberment of

[1] See, for instance, H. J. Hewitt, *The Black Prince's Expedition of 1355–1357* (Manchester, 1958) pp. 68–73, 100 ff.

[2] Magdalen College Oxford Muniment Room, Fastolf Paper 78 (2) m. 1.

[3] K. B. McFarlane, 'The Investment of Sir John Fastolf's Profits of War', in *Trans. Roy. hist. Soc.* ser. 5 VII (1957) 91–116.

[4] He was, admittedly, thinking of selling them up to pay his ransom (Champion, op. cit. pp. 186–7).

[5] A. Bossuat, 'Le Rétablissement de la paix sociale sous le règne de Charles VII', in *Moyen Age*, ser. 4 LX (1954) 144.

[6] P. C. Timbal, *La Guerre de Cent ans vue à travers les reg. du Parlement (1337–1369)* (1961) pp. 305–74; M. H. Keen, *The Laws of War in the Late Middle Ages* (1965) pp. 156–85.

the patrimony was the only answer to the exigencies of creditors.[1] Since the figure of the ransom was naturally calculated by his captor upon an at times rather rosy impression of the prisoner's ability to pay, the pressure of ransoms, though those figures varied from person to person, was equally great on all levels of the nobility: it was as difficult for the duchesse de Bourbon to raise the ransom of Jean I, captured at Agincourt,[2] as it was for the relatives of Jean de Rodemack or of Guillaume de Châteauvillain to raise theirs. Jean I de Bourbon died, still in captivity, twenty years after his capture. And the longer one stayed in captivity the more, naturally, one had to pay one's captor for one's keep, if only, as Rénier Le Coutelier *vicomte* of Bayeux, captured by the Navarrais Michel de Villeneuve in 1363, 'to escape the danger of death, from torture or from imprisonment'.[3] Other captors were, of course, more courtly.

It was possible to get help with one's ransom from one's lord: from the king or from one's commander. Jean de Rodemack appealed to René d'Anjou, who had his own ransom to pay, but who promised him 10,000 florins and in fact paid 6000. In 1426 Georges de La Trémoille got the seigneurie of Melle in Poitou from Charles VII in recompense for 10,000 *écus* promised him to deliver him from Perrinet Gressart and not paid; at the same time he was supporting others in the payment of their ransoms.[4] For the upper magnates at least a balance in this ransom trade would be hard to strike. But even though the Rodemacks were subvented by king René they were still unable to avoid disaster. Such reinsurance might help some; but it could not save all.

How to survive

The web of his own existence was thus something that every seigneur had to come to terms with. He could never escape from it; its conditions

[1] A. Bossuat, 'Les Prisonniers de guerre au xve siècle: la rançon de Jean, seigneur de Rodemack', in *A. Est*, ser. 5 II (1951) 145–62, and 'la rançon de Guillaume, seigneur de Châteauvillain', in *A. Bourgogne*, XXIII (1951) 7–35.

[2] A. Leguai, 'Le Problème des rançons au xve siècle: la captivité de Jean Ier, duc de Bourbon', in *Cah. Hist.* VI (1961) 41–58.

[3] A. Coville, *Les Etats de Normandie. Leurs Origines et leur développement au xive siècle* (1894) p. 312.

[4] *Les La Trémoille*, I 134–6, 165–7.

were dominant. And yet disaster was not necessarily at hand at every move: with luck, prudence and ability a family might come through. The senior line of the Albrets is, for instance, an excellent example of such survival.[1] War ruined its territory in the south-west, confiscations by both French and English governments ruined its patrimony. The sires d'Albret were far from diligent administrators, far from parsimonious in their tastes, far from misoprogenitive. Quarrels between husbands and wives and between elder and younger sons upset family unity; lawsuits swallowed up its ready cash. In their wills the sires d'Albret were especially generous to the Church: heaven rang with prayers for their souls, and if any family should have crashed it was the Albrets. But it survived. The line never failed; the family was strong enough to impose rigid succession practices, which it maintained in the face of customary law by every legal weapon or illegal subterfuge; its lawyers juggled with the customs of Gascony for its advantage. The favouring of the eldest Albret son, the virtual exclusion of younger sons and the complete exclusion of daughters from the inheritance went a long way towards saving the main line: the only cadet line to establish itself died out in 1379. The marriages of the Albret heirs were skilfully made: Marguerite de Bourbon brought Arnaud-Amanieu 30,000 *francs*; Marie de Sully brought Charles I a number of seigneuries of her own and of her late husband, Guy de La Trémoille; Anne d'Armagnac brought Charles II 40,000 *livres tournois*. In this fortunate family even the daughters were useful: it was through two of them that the inheritance of Foix-Grailly fell to the Albrets. The family's original patrimony was a useful sheet-anchor; it was well administered by efficient civil servants who got the best revenue they could from this failing source. But the main Albret revenue came from outside. Pillage and commerce brought in profits; the politics of the south-west, handled with tact, produced as a net result honours, fat pensions and several seigneuries. Disaster did not necessarily lie at every turn for the later medieval noble.

Antoine de Chabannes comte de Dammartin, for instance, according to an early-sixteenth-century genealogy,

> when he died, had 20,000 *francs tournois* rent, and 100,000 gold coins, of which the least in value was an *écu* . . . and he had built

[1] Boutruche, op. cit. pp. 377–95.

three or four fine grand places, well equipped, and with grand furniture, and a very great number of silver vessels, and on top a sideboard filled with silver gilt, and a kitchen service all in silver gilt, in which there were several fine big gilded plates, and many others; [and he had] six cups of pure gold, with a flagon, an ewer and a basin and so much jewellery. And his way of life was always grand and magnificent, and he kept state almost like a prince, which was a remarkable thing; and seeing all this he had saved a great deal; but he came at a good time, and he had begun early, and he was the *mignon* of king Charles.[1]

Thus, to someone in 1527, did someone — admittedly a parvenu — succeed a century earlier. The constable de Clisson stored away at the château of Josselin 109,053 *francs*, 11,857 *écus*, 9539 *moutons*, 993 *guyennois*, 866 florins, 611 *nobles*, 404 *réaux* and 17 *pavillons*.[2] The 14,272 *écus*, 1200 *lyons*, 93 *florins d'or* and other miscellaneous coins in the bedroom of the defunct Louis de Chalon, 'in the coffer next to the table with the books on', are pale in comparison to this remarkable hoard; but still Louis could be a considerable lender to his peers: Nicolas Floret said that he once saw a letter from René d'Anjou to him about a loan of 15,000 *francs*.[3] Other noble money-lenders are not hard to find.[4] If there is ample evidence of nobles in distress there is also evidence of those who were very far from disaster.

'Extraordinary' revenues

It would be simple-minded to suggest that there was a single cause of salvation. But clearly external or 'extraordinary' sources of revenue

[1] Chabannes, *Preuves, Supplément*, 1 (Dijon, 1915) 49–50.

[2] Raymond, op. cit. p. 33 [E 134]; F.L. Bruel, 'Inventaire de meubles et de titres trouvés au château de Josselin à la mort du connétable de Clisson (1407)', in *Bibl. Ec. Chartes*, LXVI (1905) 193–245 (cf. M. Rey, *Les Finances royales sous Charles VI. Les Causes du déficit, 1388–1413* (1965) pp. 576–7).

[3] J. Gauthier, 'Inventaire de l'argenterie et de l'argent monnayé trouvés au château de Nozeroy (Jura) à la mort de Louis de Chalon-Arlay III, prince d'Orange (14 décembre 1463)', in *B. archéol.* (1885) pp. 270–3; Barbey, op. cit. pp. 189–90, 238; Lecoy de La Marche, op. cit. 1 (1875) 120.

[4] See, for instance, Lehoux, op. cit. pp. 49, 56; *Les La Trémoille*, 1 136 ff, 230 J-N; Theilemans, op. cit. pp. 62–3; R. Lacour, *Le Gouvernement de l'apanage de Jean duc de Berry 1360–1416* (1934) pp. 238 ff.

could be as important to a seigneur as they were to the king.

> Alas, poor *aides* [it will be remembered Jean Juvenal des Ursins
> wrote in 1445],[1] go you to the war! But the allowances and
> pensions of the lords of the blood of France and the officers ...
> I can't think what the reason is why they should have them:
> they're relatives of the king, *ergo* they should have that with
> which the king should make war against his enemies. There isn't
> anyone nowadays who doesn't want to have a pension — the
> constable, the marshals, the *sénéchaux*, the *baillis*, the captains of
> particular places — above their ordinary wages. If every seigneur
> in his *pays* wanted to take the taxes levied on his lands and have
> pensions there'd be nothing left for the king.

Jean Juvenal was, as we have seen, not alone in his aversion to such
grants. But Claude de Seyssel's attitude was rather different: it was clear
to him that the nobility had to be maintained and that the king and the
greater lords had the means to do so.[2]

Seyssel laid most stress upon office, in the Household and in the
country. In the king's service, he wrote, there were in the Household
'a very large number [of nobles], serving in different offices, not all at
one time, but quarterly; things would be in confusion otherwise, given
the multitude of the offices, and also so that each one of them can have
the time to deal with his domestic businesses.[3] And in serving their
time, they all have ordinary wages upon which they can live, and they
can always hope to do better.' Nobles could also find a living with the
princes of the blood and other magnates, 'who all have some *état*, some
allowance and revenue from the king', and who maintained a great
number of them; and the system descended the scale of nobility, 'from
degree to degree: the counts, barons and other rich and powerful
gentlemen maintain lesser nobles, each one according to his means'.
There was also the army as a career for the nobility; and there was also
the civil service, with an 'almost incredible' number of offices for it:
'governorships of *pays* and provinces, *bailliages*, *sénéchaussées*, *châtellenies*,
captaincies of towns and castles and many others — not to mention the
principal offices [of state] which are given to great personages for life,

[1] See above, p. 108.
[2] *La Monarchie de France*, ed. J. Poujol (1961) pp. 121–3.
[3] Cf. Rey, *Les Finances royales*, pp. 23 ff.

like the office of constable, that of the marshals, that of the admiral and others like them, and not to mention the pensions which the king gives upon his establishment, at will, to many others who have neither office nor position, nor are attached to his Household'. Seyssel might have mentioned too the prospect of seigneurial pensions in return for less domestic service. Of the accuracy of his remarks we have already seen some evidence. But Jean Juvenal des Ursins' were no less accurate. The crown was only too eager to support its supporters. But perhaps we should look at its actions in closer detail. The general history of this kind of crown patronage in later medieval France is, except for some brightly lit passages, rather unclear. But even a cursory glance at some of the material may allow one to make some tentative conclusions.

Gifts from the crown to the great and to its servants antedate our period. Royal generosity is already marked under Philippe VI; cash, lands and houses (generally confiscated from the criminal or the politically unfortunate), grants of wardship, remission of dues to the crown, all found their way into the hands of the favoured.[1] Royal generosity continued under Philippe VI's successors. But having secured his gift the happy recipient was not necessarily secure in his enjoyment of it. The constable Richmond, for instance, had acquired the lands of the sire de Parthenay from Charles VII in 1425 and had taken possession of them at the end of 1427.[2] Almost immediately he found himself in the Parlement of Poitiers up against not only Marie de Parthenay comtesse de Tonnerre, but also the king's proctor, arguing (through Jean Juvenal des Ursins, king's advocate, two years later) that the estate was 'properly the king's *domaine* . . . and for this reason he cannot alienate it . . . the king cannot alienate his *domaine* in whole or in part, and this he swore at his coronation . . .' Richmond's grant was supposedly 'by the king in council'; but

> when the king in his council had been told of it all had been amazed; and the king asked Villebresme [the secretary who had signed the donation] what had happened. And then Villebresme said that at the end of a council Richmond had made his request

[1] R. Cazelles, *La Société politique et la crise de la royauté sous Philippe de Valois* (1958) pp. 367–76.

[2] E. Cosneau, *Le Connétable de Richemont (Artur de Bretagne) (1393–1458)* (1886) p. 151. For the whole affair, see ibid. pp. 485–93.

by a certain clerk; the king had granted it and ordered Villebresme to make out the letters. The king might have said that Villebresme was telling the truth; but none of his council had heard of it, and one can only say that it was importunity and worthless, and such things are revoked every day: the king is powerless to make such alienation, and it is null . . .[1]

The case, and Jean Juvenal's arguments, were more complicated than this; but it illustrates what could happen to a magnate's gifts from the crown.

Rentes — annuities — upon the *Trésor* had an added difficulty: the *Trésor* might be unable to pay them.[2] But in any case *rentes* — at least hereditable ones — seem to have been on the way out under Philippe VI; and pensions at will seem to have become more popular. It was the pension that was more and more to dominate this side of royal patronage; though the life rent was to survive for a considerable time. Pensions for life or at will again antedated our period; and by its end, it will be remembered,[3] the pensions of the princes of the blood (without such things as the grant of revenues of *greniers*) came to 326,000-odd *livres*; the pensions of the members of the order of St.-Michel and of courtiers to 221,000; and other miscellaneous pensions and gifts to 94,000. Given the deficit that year — 1470 — of some 147,000 *livres tournois*, it is not surprising to find some pensioners at least suffering from 'retrenchments'.[4] 1480 was another bad year for the pensioners: monsieur d'Angoulême's pension was cut from 6000 livres to 4500; monsieur de Concressault's from 1200 to 1000.[5] Jean du Plessis was docked 100 *livres* on the receiver-general of Normandy;

---

[1] '. . . le propre dommaine du roy . . . parquoy ne le peut alienner . . . le roy . . . ne peut alienner de son dommaine ne tout ne partie & ainsi le jure a son sacre . . .'; '. . . quant le roy en son conseil en a este adverti touz en ont este esmerveilliez; & advint que le roy demanda a Villebresme comment en estoit ale. Adonc Villebresme dist que a lissue dun conseil Richemont par certain clerc fist fere sa requeste; le roy lottroya & commanda a Villebresme la lettre. Le roy dist bien que Villebresme disoit voir; mais ny avoit celui du conseil qui en eust ouy parler, et doit on dire que ce ne fut que une importunite et ne vault, et teles choses se revoquent aussi de jour en jour; et nest en puissance de faire tele alienacion, mais est tout nul . . .' (Arch. nat. X¹ᴬ9199, fos 212ᵛ, 213ʳ.)

[2] Cazelles, op. cit. p. 374.
[3] See above, pp. 109–10.
[4] Bibl. nat. MS fr. 20683, no. 53.
[5] Bibl. nat. MS fr. 2906, fo. 8ʳ.

but he was reimbursed the following year and so was one of those who had suffered ten years before.[1] But difficulties about one's pension may have been endemic: Guillaume Cousinot, for instance, was having trouble in the 1460s.[2] On the other hand, regular series of quittances seem to show some magnates in peaceful enjoyment of their stipends. But pensions at will naturally terminated with the grantor. Georges de La Trémoille in 1440 was getting a pension of 9000 *francs* from Charles VII and the profits of the *grenier* of Sully-sur-Loire; he thought it prudent to get the promise of the future Louis XI that his pension and gift of the *grenier* would be maintained;[3] and his was not the only case of anxiety about this form of income. As we shall see, it could be an important motive in stirring up a noble to confront the crown.

Gifts of *aides* — the grant to a magnate of a proportion of royal taxation taken in his territory — had an equally respectable history. The practice had begun with the beginning of taxation itself; it was the *quid pro quo* to the important for their assent to a subvention, the king's right to which was to say the least ill-defined.[4] It could be argued on behalf of Louis II d'Anjou king of Sicily in the *Cour des aides* in 1406 that 'when the *aides* were put on, it was ordered that the seigneurs should take part of them, and this was well founded upon justice, seeing that it came from their subjects'.[5] Gifts of *aides* can be found under Philippe VI; by the reign of Jean II the proportion normally granted seems to have settled at a third.[6] During the last decade of the fourteenth and the first decade of the fifteenth century the proportion — at least for the princes of the blood — rose rapidly to reach the whole of the taxes taken upon their lands — though the comtes d'Eu, at least, had trouble from local royal officers in collecting their share in 1385 and 1387–9.[7] And in the first decade of the fifteenth

[1] Bibl. nat. MS fr. 20683, no. 53.

[2] Bibl. nat. MS Clairambault 1075, folios 196^r ff.

[3] *Le Chartrier de Thouars*, p. 20.   [4] See above, p. 104.

[5] G. Dupont-Ferrier, *Etudes sur les institutions financières de la France à la fin du Moyen âge*, II *Les Finances extraordinaires et leur mécanisme* (1932) 33 n 44.

[6] Cazelles, op. cit. p. 369; see, for instance, Bibl. nat. MSS fr. 26003, no. 1055, fr. 25700, nos. 124, 129, 134.

[7] M. Rey, *Le Domaine du roi et les finances extraordinaires sous Charles VI, 1388–1413* (1965) pp. 269 ff; Bibl. nat. MS fr. 20398, nos. 78, 85, 92.

century, too, even *hobereaux* in Languedoc were pretending to take a third or even a half of the impositions upon their tenants.[1]

But this hey-day could not last. If in the second half of the fifteenth century Jean II de Bourbon had the gift of *aides*, he had it only partially and temporarily as the reward for successful revolt in the war of the Public Weal.[2] And the gift of *aides* may primarily have been confined — save for those disastrous decades at the turn of the century — to the very great; though René d'Anjou was anxious enough about grants to lesser nobles which cut into his grant in Anjou in the mid-fifteenth century.[3] The greatest pensions went, on the whole, again to the magnates; the astronomical numbers in the 1480s were made up primarily of courtiers and civil servants.[4] And, again, the greatest gifts went probably to the princes — who had, after all, the greatest need. For they in turn had gifts to give, officers to pay, servants to reward. Wages, gifts, allowances and rewards cost Jean II de Bourbon 38,000 *livres* in 1472, and 30,000 in 1482.[5] In the later 1360s Charles V gave Arnaud-Amanieu d'Albret a money fee of 4000 *livres* a year when he came over (half-way) from the English; in the same years Arnaud-Amanieu gave a life rent of 100 *livres* to Pierre-Arnaud de 'Leysshirie', to make him change sides too.[6]

The upkeep of one's estate was probably the most common expressed reason of the crown for its subvention of nobility great and small. Jean d'Artois comte d'Eu received his third of the *aides* in 1361 partly to maintain his *état* around the king and dauphin;[7] and this was still the common phrase at the end of the fifteenth century. But his grant of 2000 *francs* on the receipt-general of Normandy was made in 1365 with the proviso that he should allow the *aides* to be taken unhindered on his lands; in 1378 it was to provide for the upkeep of his châteaux.[8] Under Charles VI, grants to magnates seem to have been made professedly for military expenses — as, for instance, were those granted to

---

[1] Rey, *Le Domaine du roi*, p. 313.
[2] H. de Surirey de St.-Rémy, *Jean II de Bourbon* (1944) p. 94 n 3.
[3] See above, p. 15.   [4] Bibl. nat. MS fr. 2900, folios 7ʳ ff.
[5] Surirey, op. cit. pp. 93–4.
[6] R. Delachenal, *Hist. de Charles V*, IV (1928) 84–5; Raymond, op. cit. p. 11 [E 42].
[7] Bibl. nat., MS fr. 25700, no. 129.
[8] Bibl. nat., MS fr. 20398, nos. 64, 75.

Louis II de Bourbon and out of which he can be found authorising payments for military expenses, say in 1385.[1] Pensions, too, could be a reward for service. In the reign of Charles VII, Jean I de Foix took his pension as king's lieutenant in Languedoc; Pierre de Foix, cardinal of St.-Stephen, his as a king's councillor and agent at the Curia; Mathieu de Foix comte de Comminges his for service in the war and on other business of the king.[2] In 1467 Jean de Foix comte de Kendal's pension was given him to cover his expenses as king's lieutenant in Roussillon and Cerdagne.[3] Guillaume Cousinot's anxiety about his pension in 1465–6 was due to the fact that it had been granted partly to him as captain of Cabrières; he was anxious, having ceased to be captain, lest his pension cease to be paid, and got letters from Louis XI to say that it should not.[4] The open grant for the upkeep of one's estate, for one's maintenance generally in the king's service, was clearly the safest.

Pensions, patronage and politics

Political motive clearly entered into the matter of royal gifts and grants. Arnaud-Amanieu's *fief-rente* is an obvious example; and other Gascon seigneurs than he, however much they excepted their loyalty to the king of England, had such fees from the king in the 1360s.[5] The hazards of abolishing or reducing pensions were obvious to the chancellor of France at the Estates-general of 1484;[6] even though retrenchment or abolition was at times necessary. Pierre de Foix was alarmed by the prospect that his pension in Languedoc would be affected by a general stoppage of novel ones there in 1438.[7] But the king's original motive was, at least partially, it may be argued, not political; it was simply to assist in the maintenance of his relatives — Charles VII's grant of a pension of 6000 *livres tournois* at will to Charles d'Artois comte d'Eu in 1441 was made at least ostensibly

[1] Rey, *Le Domaine du roi*, p. 198; Bibl. nat. MS fr. 20389, no. 52.
[2] Bibl. nat. Pièces orig. 1172, doss. Foix, nos. 45, 25, 56.
[3] Bibl. nat. Pièces orig. 1173, doss. Foix, no. 141.
[4] Bibl. nat. MS Clairambault 1075, folios 196r–197v.
[5] Delachenal, op. cit. III (1916) 51.   [6] See above, p. 109.
[7] Bibl. nat. Pièces orig. 1173, doss. Foix, no. 95.

with regard to his proximity of lineage to the king[1] — and of his officers. This clearly was the opinion of Jean Juvenal des Ursins in 1445. One must not see in this kind of crown patronage necessarily a deliberate political weapon. But, on the other hand, the way in which it was exercised became very clearly a political matter.

In 1396 the firm of Rapondi brothers was handling the financial affairs of Guy VI de La Trémoille, and the 'estat' of his revenues with which Guy provided them survives.[2] 5500 *francs* were to come in in life pensions from the pope, the king, the duke of Burgundy and an assortment of foreign rulers. 8000 *francs* were to come from pensions at will from the king, from the duke of Burgundy and the queen of Sicily. 15,560 *francs* were to come from the gift of *aides*. In this year Guy de La Trémoille anticipated, therefore, an 'extraordinary' receipt of 29,060 *francs*. The revenue (as Guy estimated it) from his lands and heritages should have been only 11,295 *francs*. Admittedly the year of the Nicopolis crusade may have been exceptional; but still it may be argued that Guy VI could not have lived upon his ordinary revenues. It was upon the 'favour of the crown' and of others that his way of life depended. If one lived by one's lands alone one lived, to say the least, more modestly than one need. If one was able, if one was lucky, if one 'came at a good time, and had begun early', and, above all, if one 'was the *mignon*' of king or magnate, it was possible to advance oneself in the world of dispendiousness so essential to medieval seigneurial mores. Not that the declining courtier does not appear; but office and reward were essentially the *sine qua non* for even the survival of the minor nobility, say in Sologne, say in Burgundy;[3] and, from the budgets of the very great, it is equally clear that crown subvention was essential to their way of life too. Up to half the revenue of the dukes of Burgundy

[1] Bibl. nat. MS fr. 20398, no. 95.

[2] *Les La Trémoille pendant cinq siècles*, ed. C. L. de La Trémoille, I (Nantes, 1890) 6–10.

[3] I. Guérin, *La Vie rurale en Sologne aux xiv*e *et xv*e *siècles* (1960) pp. 181–3; J. Bartier, *Légistes et gens de finances au xv*e *siècle. Les Conseillers des ducs de Bourgogne Philippe le bon et Charles le téméraire* (Brussels, 1955) pp. 229 ff. It has been argued that a diminution in the number of places in the army and around the king between 1453 and the Italian wars produced a crop of seigneurial victims in the area around Paris at the end of the fifteenth century (G. Fourquin, *Les Campagnes de la région parisienne à la fin du Moyen âge* (1964) pp. 465–6).

at the beginning of the fifteenth century and up to half the revenue of the
ducs de Bourbon at the end of it came from royal sources;[1] and there
was nothing unique in their position,[2] or in that of Guy VI de La
Trémoille. It becomes in fact at times impossible to understand their
relationship with the king unless one understands this aspect of it —
and this hold, this ultimately dangerous hold, that he had over them.

For pensions at will need not be renewed at the year's end; gift
of *aides* was annual; simple gifts need not be made. The comte de
Nevers was deprived of his pension and other benefits for displeasing
Louis XI in 1463: 'above all things', it was thought, he 'must fear to
incur the indignation of the king, from whom and from the crown of
France all honour, nobility and worldly goods that he has and may
honourably have are derived and upon which they depend, as is well
known'.[3] Through his participation in the war of the Public Weal the
comte de Dunois, thought Malletta, the Milanese ambassador, 'has
lost an excellent *stato* and 18,000 *francs,* which he had from the king of
France between offices and pension'.[4] In March 1468 Charles
d'Armagnac vicomte de Creissels was deprived of his pension by
Louis XI 'seeing the great acts of force and disobedience to justice
which [he] . . . and his men employ'.[5] The fortunes of the great were
in the king's hand. He had made them; he had made them, of his own
volition, because (*pace* Jean Juvenal) the great had to be 'maintained';[6]
and maintained perhaps far beyond the level from which the revenues
of their estates — if they had indeed ever lived upon them alone — had
fallen because of the manifold disasters of the later fourteenth and
earlier fifteenth centuries.

Yet perhaps some *caveat* is desirable here. Though the dukes of
Brittany did receive gifts from the king of France, the most important

---

[1] M. Mollat, 'Recherches sur les finances des ducs Valois de Bourgogne', in
R. *hist.* CCXIX (1958) 314–15; H. de Surirey de St.-Rémy, *Jean II de Bourbon*
(1944) pp. 94–7.
[2] See, for instance (until his third volume appears), M. Rey, *Les Finances
royales sous Charles VI. Les Causes du déficit, 1388–1413* (1965) pp. 589 ff.
[3] P. de Commynes, *Mémoires*, ed. Lenglet-du Fresnoy, II (1747) 409–10.
[4] *Dépêches des ambassadeurs milanais en France sous Louis XI et François Sforza,*
ed. B. de Mandrot and C. Samaran (Soc. Hist. France) III (1920) 90–1.
[5] C. Samaran, *La Maison d'Armagnac au xve siècle* (1908) p. 214.
[6] Cf. Rey, *Les Finances royales*, p. 589.

was apparently the grant of the *traite des vins* at Les Ponts-de-Cé; and though François II did receive a pension of 80,000 *francs* from Louis XI it was paid for only two and a half years.[1] The revenue of Philippe *le bon* duke of Burgundy from royal sources Plantagenet or Valois was, it has been argued, negligible, and indeed non-existent from the earlier 1430s.[2] His recourse and that of his son Charles *le téméraire* was first to taxation. This, admittedly, had been in principle a royal gift. But it had been taken without permission from 1399; and, whereas it had been occasional, under Philippe *le bon* it became 'a normal resource of the state'. Under Charles *le téméraire* it increased considerably; but it was still insufficient. A further recourse was necessary. Philippe *le bon*'s predecessors had had resort to borrowing; but under his rule again credit dealings became 'institutionalised, for they could . . . provide the balance previously taken from royal generosity'. Philippe *le bon*'s moderation kept his credit high; Charles *le téméraire*'s abuses ruined his, both with the great towns of the Low Countries and with the Italian banks.

The last two Valois dukes of Burgundy, however uneasily,[3] thus succeeded in existing without 'royal' sources of revenue. But one has to take into account the income they derived from the Low Countries. The advantages of 'commercial' over 'agricultural' revenue showed clearly in their ordinary income. The ducal *domaine* was a solid foundation for their finances. Alienations were probably outweighed by acquisitions; and even under Charles *le téméraire,* taking his reign as a whole, ordinary revenue exceeded extraordinary revenue. Its distribution shows the increasing value of the Low Countries over the duchy and county of Burgundy, from the reign of the first Valois duke. The two Burgundies under Jean *sans peur* provided only a third of the revenue taken from Flanders and Artois; and under Philippe *le bon*, above all after the acquisition of Holland and Brabant, the proportion fell further. Under Charles *le téméraire* the duchy and county of Burgundy

---

[1] B. A. Pocquet du Haut-Jussé, 'Le Grand Fief breton', in F. Lot and R. Fawtier, *Hist. des institutions françaises au Moyen âge*, 1 *Institutions seigneuriales* (1957) 282–3.

[2] Mollat, op. cit. pp. 314–15; but cf. C. A. J. Armstrong, 'La Double Monarchie France-Angleterre et la maison de Bourgogne (1420–1435). Le Déclin d'une alliance', in *A. Bourgogne*, XXXVII (1965) 109.

[3] Mollat, op. cit. pp. 309–10.

provided only five per cent of the duke's ordinary revenue. That from Flanders and Artois alone, between 1384 and 1477, provided almost a quarter of the total revenue, ordinary and extraordinary, of the Valois dukes of Burgundy. For it was the same with the extraordinary revenue of the *aides*. Under Philippe *le bon* the Low Countries provided three-quarters of the total; and the proportion was the same under Charles *le téméraire*.

The dukes of Brittany, too, from the reign of Jean IV in the later fourteenth century, had had recourse to a system of taxation; and though our information is scanty indeed compared with that which survives for the Valois dukes of Burgundy it seems clear, at least about 1481, that taxes provided an overwhelming part of Breton revenue.[1] The residual hold of the kings of France through the subsidies they provided for the great could thus vary; for Brittany it seems never to have existed, for the Burgundian dominions it could be shaken off. But Brittany — like Burgundy and Flanders — was, it might be argued, exceptionally placed. Other princes might not have the opportunities of their rulers. But other princes, too, might take taxes on their estates. The duc de Bourbon in Beaujolais from 1420, for instance, began to take direct seigneurial taxes and apparently to neglect the search for grants of royal taxes.[2] The little material which survives for the finances of the comtes d'Armagnac shows that they, too, profited from the taxes on their estates.[3] As we have seen, the royal claim to a monopoly of taxation was not fully enforced until the sixteenth century.[4] But after the ordinance of 1439, which forbade seigneurial taxation, the comtes d'Armagnac seem to have come under pressure.[5] The comtes de Foix, too, took taxes, from Foix as well as from Béarn. But Gaston IV de Foix's grants from the crown in the form of pensions and gifts were very considerable from about 1445–7.[6] And that the principal motive of the ducs de Bourbon was to gain

[1] A. de La Borderie and B. Pocquet, *Hist. de Bretagne*, IV (Rennes, 1906) 609; Pocquet du Haut-Jussé, op. cit. p. 283.

[2] E. Perroy, 'La Fiscalité royale en Beaujolais aux xive et xve siècles', in *Moyen Age*, XXXVIII (1928) 17–19.

[3] Samaran, op. cit. p. 37.   [4] See above, p. 107.

[5] A. Viala, *Le Parlement de Toulouse et l'administration royale laïque, 1420–1525 environ*, II (Albi, 1953) 24–5. And see below, p. 355.

[6] H. Courteault, *Gaston IV comte de Foix* (Toulouse, 1895) p. 392.

control of government for financial reasons has been emphasised.[1]
Our knowledge of the chronological development of royal *largesse* is,
except in a few cases, too slender to plot with accuracy the relationship
between its ups and downs and magnate disaffection; but there are
enough pieces of impressionistic evidence, at least, to allow one to
argue that it was often enough in the minds of its recipients.

There was as well the question of patronage. Desire to safeguard
one's interest with the financial departments was, as we have seen, a
motive in the princes' 'placing' their men there in the reign of Charles
VI.[2] But the clients had interests as well as the patrons. It is clear that
the relationships of the greater seigneurs with the crown were complicated by the interests of their supporters. Not only their civil
servants but lesser nobles who looked to them rather than to the crown
for office and pension in return for their local loyalty might press them
from behind. This complication of interests would bear very much
closer investigation:[3] how far was a magnate in politics not a one-man
firm but a joint-stock enterprise? Certainly there were pickings for
the lesser noble to find in following his master: the Gascons who
came to court with Jean I de Foix in 1425, for instance,[4] had little to
complain of on this score. But we know all too little.

The political interests of the lesser nobility thus interweave, it may
be argued, with those of the great.[5] It was possible to rise in court by
the direct patronage of the crown, to become the *mignon* of the king and
so, for the brief moment of one's favour, at the very fountain-head of
profit and influence. Then one might indeed be courted by the great;

---

[1] E. Perroy, 'L'Etat bourbonnais', in Lot and Fawtier, op. cit. 1 316–17;
A. Leguai, *Les Ducs de Bourbon pendant la crise monarchique du xv⁰ siècle* (1962)
pp. 184–5.

[2] See above, pp. 155–6.

[3] Even, perhaps, than it gets from M. Nordberg (*Les Ducs et la royauté.
Etude sur la rivalité des ducs d'Orléans et de Bourgogne, 1392–1407* (Uppsala,
1964)) and M. Rey (*Le Domaine du roi et les finances extraordinaires sous Charles VI,
1388–1413* (1965); *Les Finances royales*). For later evidence of the connection
between seigneurial and royal office, see, for instance, N. Valois, *Le Conseil du
roi aux xiv⁰, xv⁰ et xvi⁰ siècles* (1888) pp. 156–9; A. Thomas, *Les Etats
provinciaux de la France centrale sous Charles VII*, 1 (1879) 273–365 *passim*.

[4] P. S. Lewis, 'Decayed and Non-feudalism in Later Medieval France', in
B. Inst. hist. Research, XXXVII (1964) 165.

[5] Cf. Leguai, op. cit. p. 183.

one's interest might be solicited. One might equally become the object of their loathing; one's political demise, if not one's actual demise, might eagerly be pursued. But such men apart, the political interests of the local nobilities were bound up with those of their patrons, their feudal lord, their regional magnate. The structure of politics was a vertical, not a horizontal, one. The leagues of 1314–16 arguably were those of a regional class; their divisions followed the divisions of the *pays*; group homogeneity was particularly strong in them.[1] But, their privileges secured, their immunity from taxation normal, what interest had the regional nobility in politics except in seeking its own advantage and in following its leaders on ostensibly a virtuous crusade against 'insufficient counsel' or the alleged mismanagement of a king? In magnate politics were bound up the interests of the whole group.

Magnates and the king

What were magnate politics about? Magnate insurrection was endemic throughout our period. Princes could plot and conspire on their own; they could plot and conspire in groups; and their leagues might include members of other sections of society. The more powerful leagues provided the only effective 'opposition' to the crown in later medieval France. But what were the motives of their members? Certainly 'reform' came often enough into their arguments. The war of the *Bien public,* the Public Weal, for instance, in 1465, took its name from the expressed desires of the rebel leaders.

> We have been duly warned and informed by the princes of the blood of France and other nobles and counsellors of our late most dear lord and father [wrote Charles de France, Louis XI's brother, in a propaganda letter to his *sénéchal* of Berry], who demonstrated to us the great calamity which has befallen the common weal of this kingdom by the means of some enemies of it who are around the king, to whose desire justice is wounded and damaged to an extreme, to such an extent that it is necessary both in the court of Parlement and elsewhere to decide cases as they will; the great and excessive exactions of the proctors, by which the people of

[1] A. Artonne, *Le Mouvement de 1314 et les chartes provinciaux de 1315* (1912).

this kingdom is very much damaged, so that it can hardly support
them; the churchmen oppressed, molested and deprived of their
livings and benefices; and, what is worse, they have arranged
marriages against the will and without the consent of the fathers
and mothers, and other relatives, which things are against the
whole character of justice, productive of dishonour and shame of
the kingdom, the confusion of the commonwealth and scorn in all
the neighbouring kingdoms.[1]

Other leaders of the revolt were less specific. But all agreed upon the
need 'to give order, provision and police to the government and
régime of the . . . kingdom, to the conservation of the public weal and
the relief of its poor people'.[2] General misgovernment, a refusal to
listen to complaint, government by those around the king against the
interests, not only of the great, but also of the whole commonwealth
were the things the princes wished to reform.[3]

Such demands by the king's great relatives were hardly new. Much
the same kind of remonstration had been made by the princes of the
blood assembled at Nevers in 1442.[4] They were the stock complaints
about government found on the lips of all those discontented with it
at any time in the later middle ages, an inheritance from the thirteenth
century, 'an exigence of public opinion since St.-Louis'.[5] But did this,
in the later fourteenth and fifteenth centuries, provide the true spirit
of the opposition of his descendants to their royal kinsmen? 'The prime
reason why the duc de Bourbon and his adherents and accomplices
have . . . risen up in rebellion against the king', Louis XI declared to
the three estates of Auvergne in 1465, 'was and is because they wanted
to have most excessive pensions and benefits from the king, much
bigger ones than they had in the time of . . . his father.'[6] Certainly

[1] Commynes, ed. Lenglet-du Fresnoy, II 438–9.
[2] Docs hist. inéd. ed. A. Champollion Figeac (Docs inéd. sur l'hist. de France)
II (1843) part II, p. 352.
[3] See, for instance, Commynes, ed. Lenglet-du Fresnoy, II 440, 443–5.
[4] M. d'Escouchy, Chron. ed. G. du Fresne de Beaucourt (Soc. Hist. France)
III (1864) 70 ff.
[5] P. S. Lewis, 'Jean Juvenal des Ursins and the Common Literary Attitude
towards Tyranny in Fifteenth-century France', in Medium Aevum, XXXIV
(1965) 103–21; R. Cazelles, 'Une Exigence de l'opinion depuis St.-Louis: la
réformation du royaume', in Annu.-B. Soc. Hist. France (1962–3) pp. 90–9.
[6] Docs hist. inéd. p. 214.

private gain and the 'particular matters of ... [the] lords' came very strongly into the question in 1465 as in 1442.[1] It is only too clear that their personal interests weighed very heavily with a magnate tempted to revolt. Whether a noble revolted or remained loyal, he needed to be bribed or rewarded. Jean II de Bourbon got *inter alia* 100,000 *écus d'or* for his marriage, the grant perhaps of part of the *aides* on his estates, the lieutenancy-general of a wide area south of the Loire to Albigeois and later of Languedoc, and a gift of another 20,000 *livres* beyond his pension as his reward for rebellion in the Public Weal.[2] Gaston IV de Foix had his pension increased by 4000 *livres* and a gift of 10,000 *écus* as a bribe to him in April and May 1465 not to rebel.[3]

Why did Alençon rebel in 1455?[4] After Verneuil this paragon of a prisoner at the age of nineteen told the duke of Bedford that 'I am unshakeable in my purpose never in all my life to take an oath against my rightful sovereign lord Charles, king of France'. But he had been involved in plot after plot against his rightful sovereign lord since 1440, when, 'deprived by the fortune of war of his fathers' property, so that after he was released he was forced to live less refulgently, the poorest of France', he had thought by joining the Praguerie to gain the wherewithal to live more comfortably. With the failure of the Praguerie he had lost his lieutenancy-general, had been deprived temporarily of his pension of 12,000 *livres* and had lost Niort, which he held in pledge for 22,500 *écus* due to him from the crown (which was in fact repaid by 1444). In the meantime he had developed an intense dislike for the comte du Maine and a persecution complex. 'I've certainly heard him say often publicly before his servants', one of them deposed later on, 'that he had served the king well and loyally, but that he had been poorly recompensed, and that the king did not recognise the services he had done him.' His pension, he said, had been cut from 12,000 to 6000 *livres*; but here rancour had forced him into complete untruth: it was never cut. From the 1440s he appeared rarely at court; from the early

[1] See, for instance, ibid. pp. 361–2, 384–5; Escouchy, op. cit. pp. 78 ff.

[2] Surirey, op. cit. pp. 127 ff. Other rebels, on the other hand, may have received little (P. de Commynes, *Mémoires*, ed. J. Calmette and G. Durville, I (Classiques de l'hist. de France au Moyen âge, 3: 1924) 86; but see below, p. 236).

[3] Courteault, op. cit. pp. 288–9.

[4] G. du Fresne de Beaucourt, *Hist. de Charles VII*, VI (1891) 38 ff.

1450s his loathing of Charles VII became fully vocal; his rebellion, to us, does not come as very much of a surprise.

Both Thomas Basin and Jean V d'Armagnac had been involved in the Public Weal; and both complained that some at least of its members came with its name on their lips and their private interests in their hearts.[1] Jean V, whose private interests had allegedly been thwarted by his allies, may have had a clear motive for such self-righteousness. But yet Thomas Basin thought it would be too easy to condemn outright the nobles who formed the league of the Public Weal of simple self-seeking.[2] Charles *le téméraire* accused the chancellor of France and his 'adherents having influence and authority around . . . the king' of protecting their particular interests against the just retribution of the leaguers.[3] Everybody had their private interests. It would have been perhaps unnatural if they had not in the end triumphed over thoughts of a more public weal. But perhaps one should not be over-cynical about a magnate's protestations of concern for the public interest of the *menu peuple*. René d'Anjou, in remonstrating with Charles VII over the miseries of his duchy in the middle of the fifteenth century, freely admitted that his particular interest was bound up with the general interest of his subjects; but he had thought of them.[4] The leaguers of 1465, in the moment of their partial triumph, set up a reforming committee of thirty-six, which included Jean Juvenal des Ursins, a reformer enough, even though he did think a rebellion like the Public Weal treason.[5] Though, as Louis XI perceived,[6] the promise of reform of taxation was a hallowed temptation to political support, one cannot dismiss the cry for reform as pure propaganda.

In any case, even Louis XI could perceive that his government had given offence reasonable enough to some of those who leagued against

---

[1] T. Basin, *Hist. de Louis XI*, ed. C. Samaran, I (Classiques de l'hist. de France au Moyen âge, 26: 1963) 168; *Dépêches des ambassadeurs milanais*, IV (1923) 12.

[2] Basin, op. cit. p. 168.   [3] *Docs hist. inéd.* p. 316.

[4] P. Marchegay, *Arch. d'Anjou*, II (Angers, 1853) 317; H. Bellugou, *Le Roi René et la réforme fiscale dans le duché d'Anjou au milieu du xve siècle* (Angers, 1962).

[5] Commynes, ed. Lenglet-du Fresnoy, II 519; Lewis, 'Jean Juvenal des Ursins', p. 113.

[6] *Docs hist. inéd.* p. 214.

him. The abolition of the Pragmatic Sanction, he told the pope at the end of 1465, had been a cause of the Public Weal.[1] In 1482 Louis demonstrated to his son 'the great evils and irreparable harms which occurred to us a short while after our accession to the throne, for not having kept the . . . seigneurs [of the blood and others] and officers of our kingdom in their estates, functions and offices, which lasted a long time to the greatest harm, damage and destruction of many of our *pays* and subjects, and which still endure without an end and peace, although, as is said, we have not "lost anything of the crown" '.[2] Certainly discontented clergy and discontented courtier-officers can be found in the league of 1465 — though one should probably not overestimate their importance, nor the extent of the 'oppression' caused by either the 'abolition of the Pragmatic' or the alleged *épuration* of 1461.[3] The Public Weal, like the Praguerie, like the war of Armagnacs and Burgundians, was primarily magnate rebellion: it was the most extreme manifestation — short, perhaps, of diffidation — of the disaffection of the princes of the blood of France, disaffection that was if anything more characteristic of their policy than love of country or their cousin the king.

We have seen the way in which the Hundred Years War could be characterised as a civil war; it is only hindsight that can justify the mission of the king of France to 'centralise' his country. But the degree of princely disaffection naturally varied from time to time and from prince to prince. It would go far beyond the scope of this study fully to account for each relationship. The disaffection of the dukes of Aquitaine was clearly an extreme case, if not in the end the most successful; and so was that of the seigneurs of Béarn.[4] More notorious, perhaps, is the case of the last two Valois dukes of Burgundy, counts of Flanders — another 'principality' heading towards 'sub-state'-hood some time before Philippe *le hardi* inherited it in 1384 — and lords ultimately of a much greater territory between the kingdom and the empire. Their story has

[1] Ibid. p. 406.

[2] Commynes, ed. Lenglet-du Fresnoy, IV (1747) 91.

[3] The war of the Public Weal still awaits its historian. For strictures on the *épuration* of 1461, see B. Guenée, *Tribunaux et gens de justice dans le bailliage de Senlis à la fin du Moyen âge* (1963) p. 167.

[4] P. Tucoo-Chala, *La Vicomté de Béarn et le problème de sa souveraineté des origines à 1620* (Bordeaux, 1961).

often been told,[1] and will soon be told again.[2] We have seen something of their relationship with the English down to the treaty of Arras in 1435.[3] Philippe *le bon* had from the beginning of his alliance with them made gestures of independence; and having found the duke of Bedford too good a defender of the French crown, and the Parlement of Paris acting in the name of Henry VI perhaps less agreeable to him than it had been to his father and grandfather, Philippe had made his peace with Charles VII.[4] But despite the fact that he received the privilege of nominating twelve counsellors in the Parlement his hopes of its favours were to be disappointed under Charles VII.[5] And in general Philippe seems to have been thwarted of his desire, if indeed it was such, to take once more the place *vis-à-vis* the Valois kings of France his grandfather had held; and he found his position in a number of ways under pressure from the king, his courts and his officers.[6] With the accession of Louis XI he may again have hoped to gain his proper place in French politics.[7] Personally exempt by the treaty of Arras from homage to Charles VII, Philippe *le bon* did homage to the new king at Reims and set foot once more in Paris. But once more he was deceived; and already in his lifetime his heir had developed reasons for disliking his cousin of France.

Charles *le téméraire*, it has been argued, was 'the first to have broken completely with the French tradition of his line'.[8] But the old problems of the relationship of the Valois dukes with the kings of France remained. Some Charles tried to settle after the war of the Public Weal, in the treaty of Conflans. When he had the king at his mercy at Péronne in 1468 Louis had perforce to give in on every point of litigious difference between France and Burgundy — the powers of the Parlement of Paris in Flanders, for instance, were limited; and in 1471 Charles used Louis' violation of the treaty of Péronne to abstract the Burgundians

---

[1] See, for instance, P. Bonenfant, *Philippe le bon*, 3rd ed. (Brussels, 1955); J. Bartier, *Charles le téméraire* (Brussels, 1944).

[2] By Professor Richard Vaughan.   [3] See above, pp. 45–6.

[4] Armstrong, op. cit. pp. 81–112.   [5] Ibid. p. 100 n 5.

[6] Bonenfant, op. cit. pp. 70 ff. See, for example, J. Richard, 'Enclaves "royales" et limites des provinces. Les Elections bourguignonnes', in *A. Bourgogne*, xx (1948) 89–113.

[7] Bonenfant, op. cit. pp. 102 ff.   [8] Bartier, op. cit. p. 169.

from the jurisdiction of the Parlement.[1] The conflict continued upon an
international scale as Louis and Charles sought to encircle each other,
and involved once more the disaffected princes of France.[2] From 1473
Charles, it has been argued, became completely obsessed with the
Lotharingian dream, with the dream of a great 'Burgundian' kingdom
that had once been his father's.[3] But despite an English invasion in
1475, headed by Edward IV in search of his rightful French throne —
a pursuit from which he was easily turned by Louis XI — Charles,
fatally embroiled in the east and with crisis developing at home,[4] was
defeated at Nancy in January 1477 by René II duke of Lorraine and
killed. With him died the dream of 'the old kingdom of Burgundy,
which the French have longtime usurped and made a duchy'.[5] That
cloud-kingdom was once more clearly what the French had made of it.

But to the west was another dream of ancient royalty. We have
already seen something of the views of the dukes of Brittany in the
fifteenth century.[6] No-one, it has been argued, could have suspected in
the time of Philippe III and Philippe IV, and for a while afterwards, the
degree of independence the Bretons achieved after the succession war
between Montfort and Penthièvre claimants to the duchy which began
in 1341.[7] Twenty-four years of warfare seem to have given the Bretons a
clear dislike of external interference either English or French. Too
much collusion with Edward III (to whom he owed his victory at Auray
in 1364) led a number of Breton seigneurs to demand the expulsion of
Jean IV de Montfort in 1373; the annexation of the duchy by Charles V
in 1378, in the face of the rights not only of Jean IV but also of the
Penthièvre claimant to the ducal throne, seems to have led his subjects,
including Jeanne de Penthièvre (whose husband he had defeated at

---

[1] Ibid. pp. 132–3, 181.   [2] Ibid. pp. 147 ff.

[3] Ibid. pp. 168 ff, 279 ff. A Burgundian advocate argued in 1451 that
'le pays et nacion de Bourgoingne a eu de grande ancienneté royaume
excellent qui contenoit et s'extendoit en long dès la rivière de Rin, qu'est ès
parties d'Alemainne, jusques à Arles le Blanc qu'est ès parties de la mer
devers Marseilles et duroit de large dès les pays de Provence, qu'est ès parties
des Ytalies, jusques ès fluves et rivières de Marne et de Seine et juxques à la
ville de Sens en Bourgoingne inclusivement'. The king's proctor 'respond...
qu'il ne croit pas le fait de l'article'. (Richard, op. cit. p. 107 n 4.)

[4] Bartier, op. cit. pp. 201 ff.   [5] Ibid. p. 175.   [6] See above, p. 188.

[7] B. A. Pocquet du Haut-Jussé, 'Une Idée politique de Louis XI: la sujétion
éclipse la vassalité', in R. hist. CCXXVI (1961) 398.

Auray) to clamour for his return a year later. The aim of subsequent dukes seems to have been as far as possible to balance between Valois and Plantagenets in an attempt to ward off the danger of either.[1] Claimed by both sides, Brittany remained ambiguous to the end of the war; and a complicated English attempt to seduce François I in 1449 has been seen as the real motive for the French occupation of Normandy.[2]

The problem of the position of the duke of Brittany *vis-à-vis* the king of France survived the war. The question of his 'subjection' to France, already posed in 1449, came up again in a cognate situation in 1463–4; and it came up again in the question of regalian right in Brittany about the same time.[3] And during the second affair more longstanding grievances were aired.[4] The dukes of Brittany refused to admit that their homage to the king of France should be liege. The duke and his officers refused to admit in Brittany other *cas royaux* and *de souveraineté* than appeal of false judgement and of denial of justice. The duke pretended to the *garde* of churches. The recent dukes of Brittany had refused to admit the *baillis* of Touraine and Cotentin to take cognisance of certain *cas royaux* and *privilegiés*; they had refused to allow the execution of royal letters and of Parlement sentences. The duke called himself a sovereign seigneur; he employed the formulas 'by our royal and ducal power and authority' and 'by the grace of God'. Recent dukes had given their obedience to popes contrary to the king's wishes. They and Bretons at Rome had acquired bulls which made a separation and difference between France and Brittany. There was a crown on the shield of the present duke's arms rather than a ducal chaplet, and crowned banners of Brittany had been seen at Rome during the canonisation of St.-Vincent Ferrer. The duke levied *tailles* and *aides* at will. He minted coins. And this did not exhaust the list of grievances raked up over the past century of Franco-Breton relations.

It was little wonder François II remained a *mécontent*. A founder of the Public Weal in 1465, a leader in subsequent princely manœuvres,

---

[1] See, for instance, G. A. Knowlson, *Jean V, duc de Bretagne et l'Angleterre (1399–1442)* (Arch. hist. Bretagne, 2: Rennes, 1964).

[2] A. Bossuat, *Perrinet Gressart et François de Surienne agents de l'Angleterre* (1936) pp. 330 ff.

[3] Pocquet du Haut-Jussé, 'Une Idée politique', pp. 386 ff.

[4] Dom H. Morice, *Mémoires pour servir de preuves à l'hist. ecclés. et civile de Bretagne*, III (1746) cols 46–7.

like Charles *le téméraire* an ally of Edward IV of England, François had — as indeed had the Valois dukes of Burgundy — a 'pro-French' as well as an 'independent' party amongst his administration and his subjects.[1] Intrigues and negotiations continued. François II refused to become a member of Louis XI's order of St.-Michel in 1470, partly because it would be contrary to his dignity and authority as duke of Brittany. He was again a founder of the princely coalition backed by a restored Edward IV a year later. Louis' reaction in part was to provoke appeals from Brittany to the Parlement of Paris. But the coalition collapsed; and François II seems to have been unwilling to support the English venture of 1475, despite the views of his 'pro-English' or 'independent' councillors. 'He was not and did not wish to be English', he said, 'and . . . never would he wear the red cross or be English, if it were not by force.'[2] On the other hand, he was at least neutral; and Edward seems to have been loyal enough to his Breton attachment. After the defeats of Charles *le téméraire* in 1476, François seems to have been glad enough to return to the English alliance of 1468, though the conflict of 'French' and 'English' parties in his government helped to confuse the issue. An effective neutrality was still the aim of François II in the war between Louis XI, and Charles *le téméraire*'s daughter Marie and her husband, Maximilian of Austria. In 1480 Louis XI bought the thoroughly dubious[3] reversionary interest of the Penthièvres to the ducal throne. Once more François made an English alliance. The following year his *trésorier* Pierre Landais brought down his old rival, the 'pro-French' chancellor, Guillaume Chauvin; and Brittany survived Louis XI. The 'subjection' of the western duchy was in the end brought about only by the marriage of François II's daughter Anne to Louis XI's son Charles VIII.[4]

And in the south-west, too, there were those who might have high pretensions. We have already seen something of them.[5] The right of the comte d'Armagnac to coronation *qua* comte de Rodez was still claimed at the beginning of the fifteenth century; and the iron crown of Rodez was still in the archive-room at Montauban at the end of the seventeenth

[1] La Borderie and Pocquet, op. cit. pp. 467 ff.
[2] Morice, op. cit. III col. 274.
[3] Pocquet du Haut-Jussé, 'Une Idée politique', pp. 394 ff.   [4] Ibid.
[5] See above, p. 189; C. Samaran, 'Les Institutions féodales en Gascogne au Moyen âge', in Lot and Fawtier, op. cit. I 185–207.

century.[1] Jean IV d'Armagnac still argued in the 1440s in defence of his title 'by the grace of God' that the land of Armagnac was older than the kingdom of France.[2] In the south-west, too, tension grew again in the course of the fifteenth century.[3] Charles VII listed his grievances against Gaston IV de Foix in thirty-one articles in 1443.[4] First came the complaint about the title 'by the grace of God'; a number of articles listed usurpations of ancient *domaine*; Gaston IV minted a currency called 'morlans' and gave it course improperly within the kingdom; he refused to allow the king's taxes to be taken on his lands; he had usurped the right of safeguard and made war on the king's subjects. Two years later, Jean IV d'Armagnac, Charles complained, had, as well as ruled by the grace of God, kept a mint, impeded royal officers, usurped royal prerogatives, occupied royal property, protected pro-English *routiers* and taken down royal arms to replace them with his own.[5] The fall of the house of Armagnac was the most spectacular manifestation of royal pressure in the south-west. Jean IV had, like Jean V duke of Brittany, attempted willy-nilly to balance between England and France.[6] In the 1440s, while his eldest son, Jean vicomte de Lomagne, was in the service of Charles VII, he entered into negotiation for the marriage of his daughter to Henry VI. Like Jean V of Brittany he found the game of balancing difficult. After the English defeat in Gascony and from 1442 French activity against him developed.[7] A brief assertion of Armagnac independence failed miserably the following year; and Jean IV did not receive his pardon until 1445.

But a spirit of resistance remained in Rouergue; and it was not only that of the counts themselves. The Montcalms of Millau could argue *c.* 1440 that Charles VII 'the son of a barber, was a madman who would destroy the kingdom of France, and that that kingdom should be divided up amongst the comte d'Armagnac and other lords of the kingdom'.[8] Jean V d'Armagnac began again to 'usurp' regalian rights;

---

[1] Viala, op. cit. pp. 11–12; Samaran, 'Les Institutions féodales', p. 199.

[2] Viala, op. cit. p. 12.

[3] Ibid. pp. 10–46; Samaran, 'Les Institutions féodales', p. 200.

[4] G. Leseur, *Hist. de Gaston IV, comte de Foix*, ed. H. Courteault (Soc. Hist. France) II (1896) pp. 293–8.

[5] Escouchy, op. cit. pp. 125–39.

[6] Samaran, *La Maison d'Armagnac*, pp. 72 ff.   [7] Ibid. pp. 90 ff.

[8] Ibid. p. 108.

the question of the succession to the county of Comminges and the archbishopric of Auch caused more friction; these and other peccadilloes, let alone Jean V's incestuous relationship with his sister Isabelle, led ultimately once more to humiliation, banishment and confiscation in 1460.[1] Returning with the accession of Louis XI, Jean V was not long in entering once more into obscure conflict with the crown, which led 'almost naturally' to his part in the Public Weal.[2] His reward was the full recovery of his estates, the annulment of previous sentences against him and 16,000 *livres* pension. But he continued to foment, or at least to tolerate, disorders against royal officers, and trouble continued. The re-creation of the duchy of Guyenne for Charles de France in 1469 enhanced the danger of Armagnac pretensions in the south-west. In the same year Jean V married one of the daughters of Gaston IV de Foix. The question of their dealings in Spain — always a complicating factor in Pyrenean politics — made matters worse. A case of treasonable dealings with England seems to have been forged against Jean V by Louis XI; but it led to his condemnation in 1470, to his conspiracies with Charles de France and François II of Brittany in 1470, and his final downfall and fortuitous murder at Lectoure in 1473. His wife's unborn son was aborted by Louis' agents.[3] His brother Charles, imprisoned since 1472 after accusations of sodomy, counterfeiting, styling himself 'by the grace of God' and offending in other ways against royal rights, and many other miscellaneous disorders,[4] emerged from prison in 1483 and succeeded him as at least titular count of Armagnac; but the great days of the house were over.

These examples of princely disaffection must suffice us. The causes of friction exhibited in them existed in the relationship of every magnate with the king, from the duke of Aquitaine and the duke of Brittany downwards. We have seen, for instance, how the duc de Bourbon found his 'rights' restricted in the fifteenth century.[5] In 1464 he had mentioned his sovereignty. The king's proctor in the Parlement of Paris was ready immediately to argue that 'the king is emperor in his kingdom and there is no-one who has sufficient authority to be able to employ sovereignty'.[6] Twelve years later Louis de La Trémoille

---

[1] Ibid. pp. 114–30.   [2] Ibid. pp. 142 ff.   [3] Ibid. p. 221.
[4] Ibid. pp. 423–7.   [5] See above, pp. 162–5.
[6] A. Bossuat, 'La Formule "Le Roi est empereur en son royaume". Son

objected to Louis XI's attaching to his *domaine* the vicomté of Thouars, to which his children had title through their mother.

> The king [said the king's advocate] is very emperor in his kingdom and has the conditions of the good emperor and the true Augustus and wishes always to increase his lordship . . . in pursuing the name *most Christian* which he possesses, and which was attributed to the emperors, even to Octavian who governed the commonwealth fourteen years peaceably at the time of the birth of Jesus Christ . . . also the king is universal lord in all his kingdom and all the inhabitants are his subjects. . . . He can therefore attach the lordships as he pleases in the interest of the commonwealth . . . [1]

With this as the working political theory of the *gens du roi* there was not much the advocates of the king's opponents could say. And if this was indeed the view of kings they were as well to beware lest, as the unfortunate René d'Anjou found in 1474, they were in danger of being deprived of their prerogatives.[2] In defence of these, and in the search to acquire subvention from the crown, the princes of France found themselves time and time again in temporary coalitions with each other — or in temporary coalition with the crown against their fellows. Prestige and status and the income which maintained them were at stake. Each was a simple *ad hoc* alliance in which each magnate fought for his own ends; and when he had achieved them his interest in alliance and opposition was over until the next rebellion. Each noble was for the king essentially a problem in himself; and when the formula for dealing with him had been found, in bullying or in bribing, in *douceur* or in threats, the problem, at least temporarily, was over. It was in discovering the formula that government lay at this rarified level. The princes of France cannot be blamed for the eagerness with which they attempted to keep their footing in French later medieval politics. Many were men of considerable sensibility. But, given their condition, their political action was inevitable. Nor can they be blamed for the eagerness with which they accepted the opportunities offered by the disputed title to the throne, opportunities which, by alliance with the English claimant, they might seem to have enhanced.

Emploi au xve siècle devant le Parlement de Paris', in R. *hist. Droit*, ser. 4 XXXIX 376.

[1] Ibid. p. 378.   [2] A. Lecoy de La Marche, *Le Roi René*, 1 (1875) 394 ff.

III. PEUPLE

The urban world

The urban world had its own screen of privileges, its own hierarchies, its own political life. It was essentially that web of privilege which created a town and set it apart from the countryside.[1] Those privileges might extend outside the urban agglomeration into the surrounding area, the *banlieu*:[2] but the essential dichotomy remained valid. A town thus defined could vary in size from that of Paris or Lyon to that of a remarkably small village — for example in Toulousain and Lauragais.[3] And as size varied so did the amount of privilege and immunity conceded to the town by the seigneur vary. Was the town governed by a seigneurial *prévôt* or by its own municipality? Did the municipality possess powers of jurisdiction over those whom it governed and how extensive were those powers? What were the immunities of the town from seigneurial fiscal exaction and what its powers of raising money itself for its own purposes? What were its military privileges?

Upon the origin of these liberties and immunities we need not dwell. The distinction which earlier historians of French municipal liberties saw between the commune and the *ville franche* has been reduced to the moral question of the common oath taken in the former:[4] the nature and extent of the other franchises enjoyed by each could be the same; and there were *villes franches* with very extensive liberties and communes with very restricted ones. As far as the later middle ages are concerned it is simpler to ignore the distinction altogether and to regard all towns, as they were coming to be thought of at the beginning of the fourteenth

---

[1] M. Boulet-Sautel, 'L'Emancipation urbaine dans les villes du Centre de la France', in *Rec. Soc. Jean Bodin*, VI (1954) 403–4.

[2] As, for instance, around Eu (S. Deck, *La Ville d'Eu (1151–1475)* (Bibl. Ec. Hautes Etudes, 243 : 1924) pp. 85 ff).

[3] P. C. Timbal, 'Les Villes de consulat dans le Midi de la France', in *Rec. Soc. Jean Bodin*, VI (1954) 347.

[4] But cf. ibid. pp. 343–6. See, however, A. Vermeesch, *Essai sur les origines et la signification de la commune dans le nord de la France (xie et xiie siècles)* (Heule, 1966) pp. 169 ff.

century, as they were clearly at its end, as *bonnes villes*.[1] But an enormous variety in the extent of their franchises in principle could still exist within the group; and although the development of urban liberties had come almost to a standstill compared with its efflorescence in the earlier period, there was still a considerable movement up and down.[2]

But a town was not only a web of privilege: it was a place its inhabitants could (if perhaps with some ulterior motive) feel proud of. Expatriate in Tours in 1477, Francesco Florio, for instance, could exclaim that his adopted city 'not so much for its size as for its dignity exceeds even the most notable and beautiful cities'.[3] The same kind of eulogy could be found on the lips of the prelates, barons and communities of Agenais some hundred years earlier, as they attempted to persuade Edward III to establish his appeal court in Agen: the town, they thought, 'is amongst other cities and towns of the duchy of Aquitaine delectable . . .'[4] Its lawyers, its virtues and its geographical position would, the Estates of Agenais considered, make it an ideal legal centre. No-one could fail to be blandished by the mild air, the varied comestibles and the peaceable and erudite conversation of the capital of the middle Garonne valley.

Much of the physical aspect of a later medieval town may still be apprehended today. Difficult perhaps in Paris or in Lyon, which in the fifteenth century claimed its periphery as large as the capital's,[5] apprehension becomes easier in a town, like Beaune, like Avallon, in which part of the medieval *enceinte* survives; and it becomes easy indeed in cities frozen in their past, like Aigues-Mortes, like Carcassonne. The *cité* of Carcassonne, much restored, still bears resemblance to a drawing of it which survives from 1462.[6] The long, low grey city crouching on its hill provides a type for the greater town. Less perfect, less preserved, smaller, the *bastide* of Cordes in Albigeois, with its alleys winding

---

[1] Boulet-Sautel, op. cit. pp. 398 ff.

[2] C. Petit-Dutaillis, *Les Communes françaises* (1947) pp. 169 ff.

[3] 'Description de la ville de Tours sous le règne de Louis XI', ed. A. Salmon, in *M. Soc. archéol. Touraine*, VII (1855) 92.

[4] *Arch. hist. Gironde*, XXXIV (1899) 181.

[5] L. Caillet, *Etude sur les relations de la commune de Lyon avec Charles VII et Louis XI* (Lyon, 1909) p. 331.

[6] Bibl. nat. Estampes, Va 17 — reproduced in P. Embry, *Carcassonne* (Paris, 1958) p. 5.

through multiple *enceintes*, gives us a physical image of a small meridional town; and less preserved, less perfect and smaller again the tiny ruined, fortified village of Montjoie-en-Couserans, clustered around the massive west end of its castellated church, gives us the image perhaps of the smallest meridional community. The list could be extended almost indefinitely; and it could be amplified by the reconstructions on paper of cities long buried, like Lyon, like Bordeaux,[1] beneath their wider future.

The way of life of the bourgeoisie

But a town was not only a place: it was a community of bourgeois whose interests might coincide or might collide. Naturally those bourgeois had, like the clergy, like the nobility, like all men, their mundane problems. The family imposed its burdens upon them too. The old had to be maintained and eventually buried. When Jaquemin du Puy, who belonged to a consular family in Lyon in the earlier fourteenth century, buried his mother Tevena in the autumn of 1316, it cost him 40 *sous viennois* on the day of burial to chaplains, clerks and *clergeons*; 20 *sous* each to the Preachers, the Minors, the Augustines and Carmelites; 16 *sous* to the hermit of St.-Sebastien; 7 *livres* 9 *sous* to the candlemakers and 8 *sous* to the bell-ringers. The burial itself cost 40 *sous*, winding in the sheet 15; two chalices for different churches cost 4 *livres* 5 *sous* each; cloth cost 25 *sous*, forty-one robes for the poor 14 *livres* and forty shirts 4 *livres*. Tevena's perse robe he sold for 10 *livres*, her green robe for 5; but the proceeds of her diamond, her emerald, her beryls, her agates, her silk belts with silver ornaments, her garlands (one good and two small), her purses, her five gold rings and her long sapphire, silver-mounted and good for swellings, are, if Jaquemin du Puy sold them too, unknown.[2]

His passage to heaven was as important to a bourgeois as to a noble and was, *mutatis mutandis*, as suitably commemorated. Antoine de

[1] J. Déniau, *La Commune de Lyon et la guerre bourguignonne, 1417–1435* (Lyon, 1934), pp. 51–8; L. Drouyn, *Bordeaux vers 1450* (Arch. mun. Bordeaux. Tome complémentaire: Bordeaux, 1874).

[2] *Le Livre de raison d'un bourgeois de Lyon au xive siècle*, ed. G. Guigue (Lyon, 1882) pp. 17–20.

Chapponay, bourgeois of Lyon, reserved funds in 1434 for 300 masses after his death; Janette de Bames, daughter and wife of citizens of Lyon, left 50 *écus d'or* for her obsequies in 1436; Guichard Bastier, doctor in laws and citizen of Lyon, had in 1475 built a new chapel in Ste.-Croix in which to be buried.[1] Some eighty years earlier Henry Chevrier, formerly a draper, citizen of Lyon, had left funds for 1200 masses at 15 *deniers tournois* each to be said in the three months after his demise.[2] In devotion, as far as their finances allowed, the upper bourgeoisie pursued the mores of the aristocracy. Henry Chevrier had his 'silver cross with base, in which there was a piece of the True Cross and several other relics',[3] which even Jean duc de Berry, that omnivorous collector of wonders, his contemporary, might well have coveted.

He also shared Berry's delight in jewels: his 'biggest and best sapphire' might have tempted Berry too. In so far as their finances allowed, the upper bourgeoisie of Lyon would follow the nobility again in dispendious magnificence.[4] And there were other, family, problems which the bourgeoisie shared with the nobility. The costs of his mother's burial in 1316 were for Jaquemin du Puy nothing to the costs of his daughter Raymonde's marriage and his son Humbert's pilgrimage to Compostella in 1343.[5] An education, too, say in the law, could be costly.[6] The problem of acquiring husbands for one's daughters, wives for one's sons, or honourable places in convents for either was not confined to the nobility.[7] Dowries and the costs of dispatching suitably one's offspring into orders were not the end of trouble: the spectre of the lawsuit might follow. When Guy de Grolée tried to get his son Jean

---

[1] *Les Masures de L'Ile Barbe*, ed. C. Le Laboureur (Lyon, 1887), I 434, 397, 398.

[2] Ibid. p. 450.   [3] Ibid. p. 450–1.

[4] Déniau, op. cit. pp. 127–98 *passim*. For the tastes of the upper bourgeoisie of Paris at the same time, see A. Coville, *Les Cabochiens et l'ordonnance de 1413* (1888) pp. 94–5; for those of the upper bourgeoisie of Arras, G. Bigwood, 'Les Financiers d'Arras. Contribution à l'étude des origines du capitalisme moderne', in R. *belge Philol. Hist.* III (1924) 501 ff; for those of the upper bourgeoisie of Toulouse, P. Wolff, *Commerces et marchands de Toulouse (vers 1350–vers 1450)* (1954) pp. 598 ff.

[5] *Le Livre de raison d'un bourgeois de Lyon*, pp. 26 ff.

[6] R. Fédou, *Les Hommes de loi lyonnais de la fin du Moyen âge. Etude sur les origines de la classe de robe* (1964) pp. 300–3.

[7] Déniau, op. cit. pp. 152 ff.

into the noble chapter of St.-Jean in Lyon, the canons, disdaining his grandmother's ancestry, fought him for seven years, even though he had the pope on his side.[1] And the sheer size of families, as for the aristocracy, aggravated the problem. With Jean I Jouvenel's we have already dealt; between 1318 and 1340 Jaquemin du Puy seems to have fathered three sons and four daughters, but two of each did not survive infancy, though all were born 'en la bon ura'.[2] Later Lyon consular families were luckier — or unluckier. Guillaume Jullian had eight children living; Guillaume de Varey seven, of whom four sons and two daughters had been safely deposited in the Church. Henry Chevrier had eight children, his son Pierre six, his son André seven. But it would be otiose to continue the list of the philoprogenitive. It may be brought to a term by the commemoration of Huart Walois of Arras, who died in 1414, and of Barthélémy I Bellièvre of Lyon, who died in 1483, the sires each of twenty-two offspring.[3]

Yet if the upper bourgeoisie so clearly shared some of the social mores of the aristocracy, in others they might still seem distinct. In 1460 François Garin, merchant of Lyon, put together a 'complainte et enseignemens' for his son.[4] His ambitions for him were hardly great.[5] Security above all was Garin's preoccupation; his own confidence had been badly sapped by failure and the torments of the Limousin who had 'undone' him,[6] and some of his obsessions might well lead one to speculate upon some deeper disorders. Parts of his saner advice were rather curious — he disapproved of the acquisition of new knowledge, for instance[7] — and on the whole a rather dull and sober bourgeois emerges from his moral programme. The infant Garin was, for instance, to avoid sartorial excess:

[1] Ibid. pp. 115–16.   [2] *Le Livre de raison d'un bourgeois de Lyon*, pp. 21–5.

[3] Déniau, op. cit. p. 153 n 51; J. Lestocquoy, *Les Dynasties bourgeoises d'Arras du xie au xve siècle* (Arras, 1945) p. 48; C. Bellièvre, *Souvenirs de voyages en Italie et en Orient, notes historiques, pièces en vers*, ed. C. Perrat (Travaux d'humanisme et renaissance, 23: Geneva, 1956) p. 49. For an example of the consequences of fecundity, see A. Higounet-Nadal, 'Une Famille de marchands de Périgueux au xive siècle: les Giraudoux', in *Annales*. xx (1965) 116–17.

[4] ed. D[urand] de L[ancon] (1832). Cf. the views of a fourteenth-century Etienne Benoist in Limoges ('Le Livre de raison d'Etienne Benoist (1426–54)', ed. L. Guibert, in *B. Soc. archéol. hist. Limousin*, xxix (1881) 250 ff).

[5] folios xix^v–xx^r.   [6] fo. v^r.   [7] folios xj^r, xij^v–xiij^r.

Wear the dress of a merchant,
Or of a clerk if you wish to be one
And don't look like a trouble-maker;
Let Honour be always your dear master.
Never wear too long a robe like a priest,
And never one too short;
Dress according to your rank:
Reason provides for the mean.[1]

Physical exertions were to be left to the aristocracy; the young Garin should concentrate upon his work.[2] He was warned of the pitfalls which lay before the merchant:

Don't let your goods out on credit,
When you don't know clearly how you're doing it,
Without good security or to a person you trust:
The borrower borrows most lightly;
Repayment's another matter.
Sometimes one has to lend;
One must think how to do it safely . . .

and he was advised, too, to avoid the law and the 'et cetera' of the notary.[3] But it was not only the bourgeois who had need to watch out for that.

Difficulties

François Garin, after all his troubles, took a rather low view of his fellows. Nobles, he thought, were ready to help their friends and relations; not so bourgeois.[4] But Garin was clear also about their tribulations:

Often they venture abroad
By sea, by land through the country;
God knows what the merchant endures.[5]

---

[1] fo. xj^v.   [2] folios xiij^r, xj^r, xix^r.

[3] fo. xix^v. Cf. A. Dumas, 'Dieu nous garde et l'*et caetera* du notaire', in *Mélanges P. Fournier* (1929) p. 155.

[4] folios iv^v, ix^v.   [5] fo. x^v.

The bourgeois was, with the possible exception of the labourer living in the undefended countryside, the most liable to damage by marauding armies: that *routiers* licked their lips at the mere thought of a rich merchant moving through the countryside is all too well known. The military hazard was added to the merely commercial hazards of being a merchant at all.[1] For manufacturers and entrepreneurs the fall in demand for ordinary — as opposed to luxury — consumer goods as a result of population movement must have been very considerable — though the problem of being at all precise is a considerable one.[2] The manifold elements which contributed to the general *conjoncture de crise* each had their individual and local impact upon particular bourgeois. There were those who profited from the continued demand for luxury goods, even from the war;[3] but very many must have been hard put to make a profit. At the height of crises bourgeois opinion of life became gloomy indeed. The assessor of the *capitouls* of Toulouse opened the session of 20 April 1419 with an eloquent recital of the clichés of despair: 'Work has totally ceased. . . . Merchants no longer buy and sell, and send their goods about the country. Bourgeois can no longer take or levy their *oblies* and other rents. Artisans have nothing to work on; or, if they do succeed in manufacturing something, they can get only a miserable price for it.'[4] That such a recital of woe might have an ulterior motive, the reduction of taxation, cannot be denied: towns, like clergy, were adept at describing their fortunes in the blackest possible terms. But some element of truth had still to lie in their complaints; and the sense of insecurity so marked for personal reasons in those of François Garin was clearly shared by the bourgeoisie of Toulouse.[5]

The search for security contributed to the bourgeois' search for landed property. However much its revenues might have been depleted, however much its possession laid one open to all the tribulations of the land-owner, it might still in the end be the safest investment. In Montauban in the mid-fourteenth century Barthélémy Bonis turned first from trade to money-lending, and from money-lending by foreclosure

[1] See, for instance, Wolff, op. cit. p. 61.
[2] See for instance, E. Coonaert, 'Draperies rurales, draperies urbaines. L'Evolution de l'industrie flamande au Moyen âge et au xvie', in R. *belge Philol. Hist.* xxviii (1950) 59–96.
[3] Wolff, op. cit. p. 62.   [4] Ibid. p. 63.   [5] Ibid. p. 64.

to the acquisition of property, and then by purchase and exchange to building up a compact little estate around Villemade, in the Poncha d'Aveyro between the Aveyron and the Tarn.[1] This attitude of mind amongst the bourgeois of France long outlasted the fifteenth century: 'the traditional concept of wealth remained, of wealth founded in land, and liquid capital was regarded as property risked until the profits came in': one should perhaps not overestimate the part of the *conjoncture de crise* in the creation of this aspect of the bourgeois mentality.[2] The risks of commerce remained formidable: between 1522 and 1537 the adventurous Jean Ango of Normandy lost 650,000 *écus* in ships captured by the Spaniards and the Portuguese; and his inheritance when he died in 1551 was encumbered with debts and lawsuits. The prudence of the more traditionally minded Le Pelletiers (though an heir could deplete the family's capital in noble dispendiousness) was still perhaps the safer course for a Norman bourgeois to follow at the turn of the fifteenth century.[3] But both for those traditionally minded or adventurous, the opportunities perhaps seemed far more tempting in the half-century after 1450 than in the century before it.[4]

Urban government and urban politics

In his search for advancement or his search for security the bourgeois naturally came into conflict with those who might prey on him — like the Limousin who 'undid' poor François Garin — and with those upon whom he might prey. Inside the town itself such activity might in principle be restricted by the social organisations created within it: by systems of commercial organisation and regulation, by systems of urban government. But these, however much they might provide in principle for good and popular administration — or at least the administration of the *maior et sanior pars*[5] — and however much they might in principle

[1] C. Cugnasse, 'Activité écon. et milieu humain à Montauban au xive siècle d'après le reg. de Barthélémy Bonis', in *A. Midi*, LXIX (1957) 219 ff.
[2] M. Mollat, *Le Commerce maritime normand à la fin du Moyen âge* (1952) p. 545
[3] Ibid. pp. 483–97, 503, 507.
[4] One must again make allowances for contradictory patterns. See, for instance, R. van Uytven, 'La Flandre et le Brabant, "Terres de promission" sous les ducs de Bourgogne', in *R. Nord*, XLIII (1961) 281–317.
[5] See below, pp. 249–50.

provide for equity and a fair share for all, were in fact conditioned by the nature and structure of each urban society. The politics of each town were what the most powerful interests made them; and very often the *voie de fait*, force, was all that was left for those whom the powerful interests oppressed, slighted or ignored.

Each urban society was very much a hierarchy.[1] Most of the bourgeois whom we have already met belonged to the group at its summit: to the urban oligarchy which effectively ran each town. The composition of these oligarchies naturally varied from town to town and within a single town from generation to generation. Within each generation their influence might fluctuate under the pressure of groups outside their ranks; over two centuries the human politics of even a single town are nuanced beyond hope of generalisation. The oligarchies of each town must be seen as groups of families, as groups at any moment of individual members of those families. 'Bourgeois', thought Christine de Pisan, 'are those who are of ancient descent, belonging to the families of the cities, and have their own surname and ancient arms, and are the principal dwellers and inhabitants in the towns, with rents and heritages in houses and manors upon which they live alone ... and in some places some of the ancient families call themselves noble, when they have been for long people of great property and renown.'[2] In 1526 Claude Bellièvre asked his eighty-year-old father, 'Which do you think are the oldest of the existing families of Lyon?' 'Of those whom we have at present', wrote his father in reply, 'I believe the oldest are the Dodieu, the Baronnats, the Paterins, the Guerriers, the Chapponay, the Palmiers, the Thomassins. There used to be others who have now almost died out, but who used to be very notable, the Juliens, the

---

[1] From the discussion which follows, the towns of Flanders have been omitted, because their economic and social structure, and political position — in the case of the three great towns of Bruges, Ghent and Ypres, comparable only with those of the great towns of Italy — would tend perhaps to distort the general pattern shown by the towns of later medieval France.

[2] 'Bourgois sont ceulx qui sont de nation ancienne, enlignagiez es citez, et ont propre sournom et armes antiques, et sont les principaulx demourans et habitans es villes, rentez & heritez de maisons et de manoirs de quoy ilz se vivent purement ... & en aucuns lieux sappellent les lignages anciens daucuns deulx nobles, quant ilz ont este de longtemps gens de bel estat & de renommee.' ('Le Livre du corps de policie', British Museum, Harleian MS 4410, fo. 61ᵛ.)

Nyevre, the Villeneuve, the Varey, the Pompierre and the Dulchy.'[1] The old man's memory did not fail him far: those names, and others, had dominated the history of Lyon since the foundation of the commune early in the fourteenth century.[2] But even though the families might show remarkable power of survival, the interests of their members in successive generations might alter; the oligarchs might belong to the same background, but their notions might change.

The rise of new families was, of course, inevitable; a group which did not recruit from outside failed naturally from mere mortality. The two oligarchies of thirteenth-century Nîmes, the nobles of the Arena and the bourgeois of the *Place*, were, it could be argued, reduced by the mid-fourteenth century to numbers which no longer justified their formal position in urban government.[3] New groups appeared to break into the closed circle of urban administration: in Nîmes the lawyers, in the fourteenth century a depressed class, produced in the years 1403–76 twenty-five out of the fifty-six consuls in office.[4] The same apparent rise of the lawyers can be seen in fifteenth-century Lyon, in fifteenth-century Amiens, in fifteenth-century Poitiers and to some extent in fifteenth-century Le Puy.[5] In Lyon in the fifteenth century the old families appear to become bored with urban administration: their members turn more towards royal or seigneurial service; the Villeneuves and the Vareys, still active in Lyon, accumulated royal and archiepiscopal office; and it was the same in Poitiers.[6] Thus though the family structure of an urban oligarchy might exhibit some elements of continuity the interests of the members of the family in successive generations might shift; it might

[1] Bellièvre, op. cit. p. 69.

[2] J. Déniau, *La Commune de Lyon et la guerre bourguignonne, 1417–1435* (Lyon, 1934) pp. 79–98.

[3] F. Ménard, *Hist. . . . de la ville de Nismes*, II (1751) 'Preuves', p. 155.

[4] A. Angelras, *Le Consulat nîmois* (Nîmes, 1912) p. 129.

[5] R. Fédou, *Les Hommes de loi lyonnais à la fin du Moyen âge. Etude sur les origines de la classe de robe* (1964) pp. 279–90; E. Maugis, *Recherches sur les transformations du régime politique et sociale de la ville d'Amiens des origines de la commune à la fin du xvie siècle* (1906) pp. 25 ff; E. Delcambre, *Le Consulat du Puy en Velay des origines à 1610* (Le Puy, 1933) pp. 49, 67; R. Favreau, 'La Condition sociale des maires de Poitiers au xve siècle', in *B. philol. hist. Com. Travaux hist. sci.* (1961) pp. 166–7.

[6] A. J. Kleinclausz, *Hist. de Lyon*, I (Lyon, 1939) p. 318 (cf. P. Dognon, *Les Institutions politiques et admin. du pays de Languedoc du xiiie siècle aux guerres de Religion* (Toulouse, 1895) pp. 492–3); Favreau, op. cit. pp. 167 ff.

need a particularly strong-minded, or a particularly hidebound, old oligarch to swim against the tide.

How the tide ran will interest us later; first we must investigate the interests of the oligarchy. One should perhaps be careful of overestimating the cynicism of a later medieval urban magnate; as one should perhaps be careful of overestimating the disinterestedness of virulent complaint against his probity. That complaint might be indeed virulent there can be no doubt. 'The rule and governance of the consulate', said an alleged group of *populares* of Nîmes in 1390 in their attack upon every element of urban government, 'has turned into tyranny, and there were intrigues and conspiracies and other things from which the people would suffer' unless there was reform.[1] More longwinded, and more circumstantial, were the complaints of Bernard Gros, commander of the Temple of Breuil in Agenais in 1480.

> The towns which have certain taxes on goods entering them each year [he wrote], which were given by the king [Louis XI] and his predecessors for the repair of the walls and ditches of the towns and the bad bits of the roads — well, they're not used for that, but there are seven, or eight, or twelve people in the town who, when they are consuls, embezzle the lot [to the destruction of the poor people and the dilapidation of the town] ... and they refuse to pay *tailles* on their rural property and charge everything upon the poor people, and they take more in *tailles* than they're authorised to in their commission; and those who do this sort of thing in the town are all in one conspiracy, and anybody who doesn't belong to it doesn't become consul or *jurat*, and they won't let anyone of the *menu peuple* be, so that they can do as they please against them; and so the entry taxes don't profit the public interest at all.[2]

The same kind of consular behaviour is alleged endemic in Le Puy in the fourteenth and fifteenth centuries.[3]

But it was not only by sheer dishonesty that an oligarchy could do

[1] Ménard, op. cit. III (1752) 'Preuves', p. 100.

[2] 'Le Livre de raison de Bernard Gros, commandeur du Temple de Breuil, en Agenais, sous Louis XI et Charles VIII', ed. M. Tholin, in *B. philol. hist. Com. Travaux hist. sci.* (1889) pp. 124–5.

[3] Delcambre, op. cit. pp. 172 ff. For the same sort of allegation in Carcassonne in 1390, see C. Devic and J. Vaissete, *Hist. gén. de Languedoc*, x (Toulouse, 1885) 'Preuves', cols 1799–1808.

well out of the town it ruled. The legitimate exemptions afforded by nobility and by royal office were, as we have seen, very considerable. 'A very large number of the richest people are exempt and don't pay anything', it was complained at Dijon in 1452, '. . . and the merchants and the *menu peuple* pay all.'[1] 'There are', thought Louis XI in 1463–4, 'in our . . . town [of Amiens] many people who allege themselves noble, and others who are officers, who are the richest there, numbering up to seven score or two hundred people, who refuse to pay anything, and thus the poor and simple folk have to take the whole burden upon themselves.'[2] The effect of all this was naturally, it was thought by foul means or fair, to force the burden of taxation onto the lower classes; alleged pressure towards indirect taxes,[3] which hit everyone in proportion to his consumption of, say, salt or wine, rather than towards direct taxes, which might hit the wealthy disproportionately, especially if the rich were thought obliged to 'carry' the poor by contributing even in a head tax more heavily;[4] perhaps, too, a lack of preoccupation with the horrors of government fiscality. Did the bourgeoisie deserve to allege itself the protector of the poor, on the grounds it shared its burden of taxation? asked the knight Philippe de Poitiers at the Estates-general of 1484. 'They are normally exempt from *tailles*, either because they've just got themselves ennobled, or because they're bourgeois of some commune exempt from taxation, or because of the privileges of their offices, or because people are simply afraid of them';[5] and if the detractors of the bourgeoisie were to be believed he was not so very far from wrong.

How did the oligarchy get away with it? In the first place, later

---

[1] F. Humbert, *Les Finances municipales de Dijon du milieu du xive siècle à 1477* (1961) p. 247.

[2] Maugis, op. cit. p. 34.

[3] As at Amiens (E. Maugis, 'Essai sur le régime financier de la ville d'Amiens du xive à la fin du xvie siècle (1356–1588)', in *M. Soc. Antiq. Picardie*, ser. 4 III (1899) 150 ff) and in Languedoc (Dognon, op. cit. p. 164). In Amiens it seems clear that the lower groups would have preferred *tailles*; in Languedoc, on the other hand, they seem themselves to have preferred indirect taxation.

[4] See, for instance, L. Caillet, *Etude sur les relations de la commune de Lyon avec Charles VII et Louis XI* (Lyon, 1909), p. 470.

[5] J. Masselin, *Journal des Etats généraux de France tenus à Tours en 1484*, ed. A. Bernier (Docs inéd. sur l'hist. de France: 1835) p. 500.

medieval town-government was dominated by the concept of the 'plus grant & seine partie'. What did this mean? 'If the majority of people in general doesn't agree, nevertheless if a majority of notable bourgeois and men of worth consent this will be enough', ran a note in a fifteenth-century formulary after a stock letter of 'permission to raise a tax for towns' of Charles VII's time.[1] The bias of urban politics was thus towards quality rather than towards quantity. And however much part might be given formally to popular consent in the choice of urban governors and in the control of their actions, in practice this could too often be overlooked.

The balance between oligarchical domination and popular consent naturally varied from town to town; and within a single town apparently from period to period. In Le Puy, for instance, the consulate was elected effectively, as at Nîmes, by co-option. Between 1384 and 1427 at least, the 'bourgeois', perhaps already in the fourteenth century a comparatively closed caste, identified perhaps by birth, perhaps by wealth, but most often by living 'bourgeoisly' in the avoidance of manual labour and of retail trade, almost always predominated over the 'citizens', the mass of native-born taxpayers; in the fifteenth century their predominance was less, because the caste was getting smaller; but the consulate was still in the hands of the comparatively rich.[2] And within the consulate itself, it has been argued, any consuls of comparatively low rank were men of straw before their richer colleagues. The oligarchy, it was complained in 1446, saw to it that 'each year consuls were elected who were suitable to them, since the group from which consuls were elected didn't number over fifty; and they rendered their account one to another and were acquitted by themselves, turn and turn about balancing fraud with fraud'. Examples of such fraud were provided; but the decision of the lieutenant of the *sénéchal* of Nîmes-Beaucaire, sitting in judgement on the consuls, was that there was no case to answer.[3] But agitation seems to have continued in Le Puy; in 1469 the oligarchy was widened; in 1473 it was forced to capitulate.

---

[1] '. . . se la plus grant partie de tous en general ne se y consent au moins que la plus grant partie des notables bourgeois & gens de raison se y consente & souffira' (Bibl. nat. MS fr. 5909, fo. 35ʳ). Cf. P. Viollet, *Hist. des institutions politiques et admin. de la France*, III (1903) 109.

[2] Delcambre, op. cit. pp. 47 ff.   [3] Ibid. pp. [37] ff.

A new system of election was devised in which the twenty-one non-'bourgeois' *échelles*, the formal groupings of the *métiers*, the trades of the town, predominated. But there were still restrictions which gave advantage to the oligarchs, and there was a rapid oligarchical *révanche*. By 1477 the *échelles* had ceased to take any part in the election, and the town had once more, according to an allegedly 'popular' party, 'the worst government one has ever known'. The oligarchs were accused of undoing the people: 'the poor would be destroyed', it was complained, 'because there is a certain number of rich men who have leagued against them'. But still the consuls had the support of royal officers; and the final fling of the 'popular' party was a riot of 800 inhabitants of Le Puy against them. Some even went so far as to complain, with some irreverence, to the king in person. But Louis XI, like his courtiers — and his father's for that matter — had a short way with agitators. One of them escaped being thrown into the river only through the intervention of the Auvergnat Gilbert de La Fayette.[1] It was not until the end of the century that 'democracy' triumphed in Le Puy. But we should perhaps be careful in our use of the word. Those who triumphed were the *maîtres* of the *métiers*; and those who held power by their election were the old oligarchs. The agitation against them was thus less simple than it might seem. It was not the lower 'citizens' who won in Le Puy, and it was certainly not the simple 'inhabitants', strangers to the town or too poor to pay taxes. The apparent victory lay to the median group of the leaders of the trades.[2]

The development of guild organisations, of *communautés de métier*, began effectively in France towards the mid-twelfth century.[3] Geographically, chronologically and institutionally it was an uneven one. In Paris and in a small number of towns on the royal *domaine* it developed rapidly into a strict form, the *métier juré*; by the 1260s, when Etienne Boileau's *Livre des métiers de Paris* was compiled, the regulations of some hundred *métiers* could be codified.[4] In the North and in the Midi development was slower. These, it has been argued, were the areas of

---

[1] Ibid. pp. 62–70.   [2] Ibid. pp. 47, 70–2.

[3] E. Coornaert, *Les Corporations en France avant 1789* (1941) p. 57; A. Gouron, *La Réglementation des métiers en Languedoc au Moyen âge* (Geneva, 1958) p. 38.

[4] *Réglemens sur les arts et métiers de Paris rédigés au xiiie siècle*, ed. G. B. Depping (Docs inéd. sur l'hist. de France: 1837) pp. 1–274.

the *métier réglé*, the trade regulated in the public interest by the municipality, but freer in its internal organisation and above all in its rules concerning recruitment. But as in the parallel case of the definition of communes and *villes franches*, it is probably wise to avoid too doctrinaire an identification of one type of *métier* or another.[1]

But it does seem evident that the freer *métiers* of the Midi hardened progressively during the fourteenth and fifteenth centuries.[2] The restrictive and oligarchic tendencies already apparent in those of Paris before the beginning of the period developed in the south. The social differentiation between *maîtres* and their workmen increased from the fourteenth century. Dues and formalities for entry into the *métier*, non-existent in thirteenth-century Languedoc, became more frequent and, as their tariff rose, more discouraging for the workman hoping to rise in the world. Hostility to these *compagnons* was underlined by the exemptions offered to the sons of *maîtres*. The *métiers* closed in upon themselves; and at the same time they developed greater control over their own members. The *maître*'s oath to the town succumbed in importance to his oath to the *métier*; the *métier réglé* — though the meridional consuls might still play a part in its regulation — succumbed before the *métier juré*. In Toulouse in 1446 a group of workman tailors, having been refused work by the *maîtres* of their *métier* after they had brought (and lost) a lawsuit against its officers, the *bailes*, tried to open a shop of their own. The *bailes* objected; the workmen argued that formerly new *maîtres* had only to pay 2 *livres tournois* as an entry fee and provide a collateral of 40 *livres tournois*. The *capitouls* of Toulouse intervened and re-wrote the statutes of the tailors and *juponniers* to make them more severe for those who wished to become *maîtres*.[3] This attitude seems to have been a general one.[4]

[1] Coornaert, op. cit. pp. 27 ff; Gouron, op. cit. pp. 10, 367.

[2] Ibid. pp. 367 ff. Cf. P. Wolff, 'Les Bouchers de Toulouse du xiie au xve siècle', in *A. Midi*, LXV (1953) 375–93.

[3] Wolff, *Commerces et marchands de Toulouse (vers 1350–vers 1450)* (1954) pp. 551–4.

[4] R. Gandilhon, *Politique écon. de Louis XI* (Rennes, 1940) pp. 165 ff; P. Imbart de La Tour, *Les Origines de la Réforme*, 2nd ed. 1 (Melun, 1948) pp. 415–21. But one is warned against accepting the regulation for the reality (cf. J. P. Sosson, 'La Structure sociale de la corporation médiévale. L'Exemple des tonneliers de Bruges de 1350 à 1500', in *R. belge Philol. Hist.* XLIV (1966) 457–78). And it was, of course, possible for the king to sell

Yet a *métier* might protect the interests of the workmen — in their place; and the workmen might be inclined to follow their *maîtres* in the in-fighting of urban politics.[1] A *métier* might protect the interests of the weaker *maître* against the stronger, 'lest the power of the rich damage the commonwealth and oppress the poor members of the mystery'.[2] The *confréries*, the devotional and charitable organisations, which more or less precisely doubled the *métiers*, might provide some moral link which bound all its members together.[3] It is difficult to generalise the balance of social cohesion and disintegration that the *métiers* provided. But certainly in some towns and on some occasions they could provide an effective political body. In Paris they furnished the only urban administrative cadre. In Amiens in the fourteenth century they seem to have provided the same kind of opposition to the oligarchy as did the *métiers* of Le Puy in the fifteenth century — until the *maieurs des bannières*, their *maîtres*, were suppressed in the royal repression of a popular revolt in 1382.[4] In Nîmes their organisation into nine *échelles*, which dated from 1272, came under attack with those of the nobles of the Arena and the bourgeois of the *Place* in 1390, apparently from below; in the reforms which led apparently to the advancement of the lawyers (who had occupied in the fourteenth century the ninth and lowest *échelle*), they lost their direct share in the nomination of consuls and councillors.[5] In Lyon (where the development of an oligarchy may have been more backward than elsewhere) they retained a considerable part in the election of the consulate and some control over its actions; in Poitiers in the fifteenth century the *métiers* were completely excluded from municipal administration.[6] Too much generalisation on this matter, too, is probably unwise.

And there could be political divisions other than those dictated by

would-be *maîtres lettres de maîtrise* (see especially Gandilhon, op. cit. pp. 171–172).

[1] As, for instance, in Lyon during the Rebeyne in 1436 (R. Fédou, 'Une Révolte populaire à Lyon au xve siècle: la Rebeyne de 1436', in *Cah. Hist.* III (1958) 134).

[2] Wolff, *Commerces et marchands* p. 554.

[3] A. Coville, *Les Cabochiens et l'ordonnance de 1413* (1888) pp. 97–100.

[4] Maugis, 'Essai sur le régime financier de la ville d'Amiens', pp. 166 ff.

[5] Angelras, op. cit. pp. 95–123.

[6] Kleinclausz, op. cit. pp. 291–2; Déniau, op. cit. pp. 223–6; Favreau, op. cit. p. 169.

the dichotomy between rich and poor, between one type of institution in a town and another. In Toulouse the system of taxation consistently favoured those in possession of property, rich or poor, at the expense of those, poor or rich, whose fortune lay in movable goods. This distinction between 'landlords' and 'businessmen' was even clearer in Bayonne: the 'popular' party and the 'aristocratic' party both contained elements both rich and poor; wealthy merchants joined sailors, fishermen and boat-builders in their opposition to the land-owning upper bourgeoisie.[1] That other divisions broke across the barriers of wealth is apparent elsewhere; interests were not necessarily of one kind. And even the test of apparent group-interest may betray us; we should be careful of allowing too little weight in urban politics to personal factors — though a divergence of views amongst the members of a single social group might effectively betray an old attitude in conflict with a new one. The internal rivalries of Lyon in 1423–4, for instance, seem to reveal on the one side younger members of the patrician class in alliance with royal officers, on the other older members of it, some from the same families as their opponents, in alliance with urban officers and the median group;[2] but the alliance of patricians and the crown in the diminishing of urban liberties and the maintaining of the patricians' own advantages might be seen as prodromic of developments twenty years later.[3] The structure of politics within each town was very far from simple. Appearances were not necessarily what they seemed. Even the apparent generalisation about the rapacity of the oligarchy may seem a treacherous one. And a town was not a society in a vacuum. It was open to the elements at many points. Most important of these was the declared interest of the community at large: the interest of government. It was this that brought the royal officers into the towns.

Towns and civil servants

In their impact upon the towns the government and its officers

---

[1] P. Wolff, 'Les Luttes sociales dans les villes du midi français, xiiie–xve siècles', in *Annales*, II (1947) 453.

[2] Déniau, op. cit. pp. 475–8; Kleinclausz, op. cit. p. 258.

[3] Déniau, op. cit. pp. 229–30.

followed much the same pattern as they did in their impact upon other immunists, clerical and lay. The pattern was a far from simple one. It would be utterly anachronistic to imagine a consistent royal policy, even the consistent policy of one king, towards the towns of his kingdom;[1] any more than it would be to expect a consistent royal policy towards the 'nobility' or the 'clergy', or even to a single magnate, lay or ecclesiastical. The king's — or the government's — attitude was compounded of the interest of the moment, of the 'kingdom' or of the members of the government, and confounded by the interests of all the inferior administrations with which any particular magnate, or any particular town, happened at that moment to be dealing.

A town might have dealings with local royal officers; it might have dealings with the central departments; it might have dealings with the king himself and with his immediate entourage. A considerable amount of manœuvre was possible for a municipality eager, say, to avoid the interference of one set of royal officers in its affairs or to avoid taxation. As in their dealings with magnates, local royal officers might appear — or at least seem to appear — more royal than the king himself. In Tours in 1379 a local receiver refused to recognise Charles V's letters remitting a third of the *fouage*.[2] The problem was the same for towns on a magnate's *domaine*: the officers of the *bailliage* of Dijon in the 1440s refused to recognise a decision of Philippe *le bon* concerning the town's jurisdiction. In conflict with his officers, Dijon appealed to the duke; in conflict with the duke, the municipality appealed to the Parlement.[3] Wrangles with local officers may be taken as endemic in the towns of later medieval France. Some towns may have had the infection in a milder form: Poitiers, for instance, where the town council seems to have been recruited considerably from the royal officers themselves; Lyon, which in the fifteenth century had for a considerable time *baillis* tactful in their management of the key to the eastern frontier of the kingdom of

---

[1] Dognon, op. cit. pp. 168–9; Wolff, 'Les Luttes sociales', p. 452. But see B. Chevalier, 'La Politique de Louis XI à l'égard des bonnes villes. Le Cas de Tours', in *Moyen Age*, LXX (1964) 473–504.

[2] *Reg. des comptes municipaux de la ville de Tours* [1367–1380], ed. J. Delaville Le Roulx (1881) pp. 205–7.

[3] C. Bertucat, *La Juridiction municipale de Dijon* (Dijon, 1911) pp. 63, 70; G. Chevrier, 'Les Villes du duché de Bourgogne du xiiie à la fin du xve siècle', in *Rec. Soc. Jean Bodin*, VI (Brussels, 1954) 439.

Bourges;[1] but the generalisation seems to stand.[2] Appeal against the king's local agents naturally lay to the central departments of government: Tours in 1379 appealed to the *généraux*. But the central departments — and especially, perhaps, the new regional Parlements of the fifteenth century[3] — were quite prepared to intervene upon their own account; and to conflict with one another. The resistance of Le Puy to the appointment of the notorious Pierre de Louvain as captain of the town in the 1440s put the *Grand Conseil* (which supported him) against the Parlements of Paris and Toulouse (which supported the municipality) and the case threatened to drag on interminably. The possible way out was to attempt to deal with the king directly — as indeed the Ponots appear to have done, perhaps with final success.[4] In 'defending his interests' the king's officers were quite prepared to contradict his apparent wishes;[5] and the king himself might be far from single-minded.

A visit by the king in person, as to Rouen after the revolt of the Harelle in 1382 or to Lyon after the revolt of the Rebeyne in 1436,[6] led perhaps to the most untrammelled manifestation of royal decision. If, as it was argued by a member of the Lyon oligarchy during the Rebeyne, 'the king could, when he pleased, turn the town of Lyon or a bigger town than it into a garden, if it didn't do its duty by him at every turn',[7] there was little to do under such circumstances but beg for mercy. In Montpellier in 1380, under similar circumstances, they set all the children under fourteen to cry 'Misericorde' to the duke of Anjou.[8] The means of pressure which the king's officers normally could exert were less radical than those exerted by the king himself or by his lieutenant.

---

[1] A. Giry, *Les Etablissements de Rouen* (Bibl. Ec. Hautes Etudes, 55: 1883) p. 406; Favreau, *op. cit.* pp. 167–8; Kleinclausz, *op. cit.* pp. 289–90.

[2] Though again successive generations of a town's rulers might adopt different attitudes to royal officers — see below, pp. 269–70, and Fédou, *Les Hommes de loi lyonnais*, pp. 385 ff.

[3] Dognon, op. cit. pp. 477–80; H. Sée, *Louis XI et les villes* (1891), pp. 68–70.

[4] Delcambre, op. cit. pp. 125–6.

[5] Sée, op. cit. pp. 66–72.

[6] G. Lecarpentier, 'La Harelle, révolte rouennaise de 1382', in *Moyen Age*, XVI (1903) 31–2, 89 ff; Fédou, 'Une Révolte populaire à Lyon', pp. 147–8.

[7] C. Bellièvre, *Souvenirs de voyages en Italie et en Orient, notes historiques, pièces en vers*, ed. C. Perrat (Travaux d'humanisme et renaissance, 23: Geneva, 1956) p. 90.

[8] R. Delachenal, *Hist. de Charles V*, v (1931) 310.

In Lyon in the fifteenth century the consuls trooped off regularly to formal 'arrest' in the *maison de Roanne*.[1] The consuls of Agde found themselves in the prison of *la Malapague* in Béziers for having failed to produce the town's taxation in 1360.[2] In 1462 the inhabitants of Millau were threatened with the penalty of 'a hundred marks of silver and with the seizure and sale of our goods and with the arrest of our persons and on top of that with the penalty of being rebels and disobedient to the king our lord'; undismayed, they resisted, on the grounds that the *pays* had already sent an embassy to appeal to the king.[3]

In the tangled web of the administration which stretched upwards towards the king, the opportunities for resistance were increased by careful corruption. The royal officers themselves were far from immune from collusion;[4] and from the most local official up to the king himself the *douceur* brought its own reward. The bribe to the local officer 'so that he should feel more favourable towards the town'[5] was so frequent as to be almost normal. The greater towns at least sought their patrons farther afield. Rising members of their oligarchies might find themselves in a position to help their families' towns: from Lyon Mathieu Thomassin, Guillaume Becey, Jean de Chapponay and, above all, Pierre du Nyèvre, who became Louis' *échanson*, were in the dauphin's circle in the 1440s and 1450s; Pierre Varinier was the duc d'Orléans' chancellor.[6] But it was not only to local loyalty that anxious towns might appeal. Monsieur d'Argenton, the chronicler Philippe de Commynes, was wooed by the municipalities of Tournai and of Dijon as well as by that of Lyon, which felt that he 'can be very much of service to the town *vis-à-vis* the king, as he has been before'.[7] If the court was as corrupt as Alain Chartier bewailed,[8] there was plenty of scope for the shy advances of towns seeking favour or defence.

[1] Caillet, op. cit. pp. 265–6.

[2] J. Picheire, 'Le Livre de Clavaria d'Agde (1360)', in *XXVIIe et XXVIIIe Congrès Fédér. hist. Languedoc* (1953–4) p. 102.

[3] *Docs sur la ville de Millau*, ed. J. Artières (Arch. hist. Rouergue, 7: Millau, 1930) p. 359.

[4] See, for instance, above, p. 146; and, for another attractive example, see *Reg. de l'échevinage de St.-Jean-d'Angély*, ed. D. d'Aussy, III (Arch. hist. Saintonge Aunis, 32: Saintes, 1902) 352–3.

[5] Caillet, op. cit. p. 56. [6] Kleinclausz, op. cit. p. 309–10.

[7] Sée, op. cit. p. 174. [8] See above, p. 120.

But intrigue around the king had its own torments. Not only did a town's ambassadors to court have to be 'notable people and of some rank who will be bold enough to talk'[1] to the ruler; they had also to be at least fairly expert in the in-fighting of the court and the central government departments. Four letters which Rolin de Mâcon, the *procureur* of Lyon, wrote back to the town in 1425 illustrate the mechanisms and hazards which lay open to and threatened a suppliant at court.[2] Approach to the king himself might be far from easy;[3] and although rapid action might follow a *démarche* to the king in person, even a direct royal promise might threaten to get trammelled in the entanglements of government. When Pierre Thomassin, preceded by a wave of bribery, some of which appears to have been absorbed by the king himself, succeeded in getting remissions of the *taille* for Lyon out of Louis XI in 1462, he feared that the king's verbal agreement was not enough, for 'the financial officers had refused to give the grant in writing'. Though the town obtained its remissions in the end, it was not without further anxiety.[4] Yet the direct approach might be still the most fruitful.

The reasons for the intervention of royal officers and of the king himself divide more easily into categories. First, their administrative duties necessarily created a more or less close connection with the towns in the areas of their authority. For the *villes franches* under a royal *prévôt* this connection was obviously a close one; but a considerable opportunity for interference still remained to the king's agents *vis-à-vis* the communes and the consulates. Residual control over trade regulation, over the 'policing' of the towns, remained in their hands; and over a whole gamut of other matters they might or might not intervene.[5]

---

[1] *Reg. consulaires de la ville de Lyon*, ed. M.C. and G. Guigue, I (Lyon, 1882) 331.

[2] Déniau, op. cit. p. 509.

[3] G. du Fresne de Beaucourt, *Hist. de Charles VII*, v (1890) 336–7.

[4] Caillet, op. cit. pp. 170–2. For a similar effort by Tours at the beginning of the century, see M. Rey, *Le Domaine du roi et les finances extraordinaires sous Charles VI, 1388–1413* (1965) p. 338.

[5] Coornaert, op. cit. pp. 95 ff; Gouron, op. cit. pp. 152–63; Gandilhon, op. cit. pp. 161–72; G. Dupont-Ferrier, *Les Officiers royaux des bailliages et sénéchaussées et les institutions monarchiques locales en France à la fin du Moyen âge* (Bibl. Ec. Hautes Etudes, 145: 1902) pp. 280 ff; Sée, op. cit. pp. 66–72.

Problems of the defence of towns in the areas of war brought them again to deal with the municipalities.[1] At this local level the relationship between a town and the government interpreted itself as a complex of institutional and personal relationships with the local *bailli*, the local *élus*, their subordinate officers, and *ad hoc commissaires*; for each town the pattern of the political kaleidoscope was different, though the elements which made it up might be common ones.

A perpetual element in the relationship, for those towns which possessed it, was the question of jurisdiction.[2] Conflict of jurisdiction occurred as naturally between that of a town and that of a local royal officer as it did between the latter's and that of a magnate. But it was not only with royal jurisdiction that a town's might conflict; its quarrels with other immunists might also be endemic — if not perhaps of everyday occurrence. And it was not only about jurisdiction that a municipality might quarrel with a local noble or a local cleric. A town like Le Puy, recently snatched from beneath the wing of an ecclesiastical seigneur, might find itself involved in an interminable lawsuit about other privileges as well.[3] As taxation developed and became permanent the struggle of a town to submit the exempted in its midst — nobles, clerics, royal officers, mint-masters, those of its own citizens exempt *ad hoc* — might again lead to the intervention of the king's courts and the king's officers.[4] These conflicts of interest — and the question of who had jurisdiction over whom and what was essentially a question of interest — thus led to the perpetual interference of the agents of government local and central in a town's affairs. Some might even give them a whip-hand over the town: the willingness of the Parlement of Paris to perpetuate the lawsuit between the town of Le Puy and its successive bishops might not wholly have been due to the complications of later medieval litigation.[5]

Such opportunities were not, of course, confined to royal officers' dealings with the towns; they were endemic in their dealings with any immunist, and their danger to him rested primarily upon the willingness

---

[1] See, for instance, Dupont-Ferrier, op. cit. pp. 441 ff.

[2] G. Testaud, *Des Juridictions municipales en France (des origines jusqu'à l'ordonnance de Moulins)* (1901).

[3] Delcambre, op. cit. pp. 32 ff. [4] Ibid. pp. 168 ff.

[5] E. Delcambre, 'Le Paréage du Puy', in *Bibl. Ec. Chartes*, XCII (1931) 331–2.

of the central departments and of the king and his entourage to support their local agents.[1] The patterns of interference were created: governments with a taste for arbitrary behaviour had only to follow and emphasise them. But in two aspects of their relationship with the government the towns differed from other immunists. A magnate might have some negotiations with the administration about finance; a town's relationship with the crown turned almost primarily upon questions of finance. A magnate could not be divided against himself; social conflict within a town too often led to royal intervention. And social conflict in turn found its roots primarily in the question of taxation.

Taxes were taken in towns for two purposes. There were the taxes that went to the king; there were the taxes that were spent upon the town's affairs. Both the taxes themselves and indeed their purposes might confound. Both might be raised together;[2] part of the king's taxes might be remitted to a town for its own purposes; a town might have to delegate part of its own funds to the king for his immediate needs. Some distinction is possible between urban and royal taxes: different kinds of taxes might be appropriated to the one purpose or the other, might have separate receivers and be accounted for separately.[3] But in their impact upon the taxpayer the confusion is possibly more important than the distinction: the fact of payment was more important than the identification of the payee.

The crown had naturally some interest in the restriction of the taxes taken for the town's own purposes — or those of its oligarchy. On the other hand, some of those purposes might be in some sense more widely laudable. A principle of restriction was clearly useful to the government, if it might be relaxed in practice. In 1401 a king's proctor in the Parlement announced that ' "in the kingdom no town may put on a tax without the consent of the king", even in order to pay for the fortifications'.[4] In the same way as the king captured in theory and more or less in fact the right of veto upon seigneurial taxation, so he captured the right of veto over urban taxation. General prohibitions were still

---

[1] Cf. A. Leguai, *Les Ducs de Bourbon pendant la crise monarchique du xve siècle* (1962) pp. 21–33.

[2] As, for instance, at Lyon under Charles VII (Caillet, op. cit. p. 265).

[3] Delcambre, op. cit. pp. 180–1; Caillet, op. cit. pp. 263–9.

[4] Maugis, 'Essai sur le régime financier de la ville d'Amiens', p. 247.

necessary; and exemptions and concessions were constant.[1] The patterns of influence which might lead to concession were naturally complicated: the clear virtue of urban defence was only amongst the simplest. Fear and favour might play their part here too. A town on the frontiers could hardly be prevented from protecting itself; influential bourgeois might need to be wooed. The need to get royal consent to urban taxation might even strengthen their hand *vis-à-vis* their taxpayers: the need to get royal permission was, it has been argued, more of a hedge for the oligarchs of Amiens against the multitude in the period up to 1471, when the town was dispensed from it, than a restriction upon their powers.[2]

But if the king might restrict urban taxation the towns themselves did their best to restrict royal taxation. Cries of poverty rang to Heaven and to the king. Although an oligarchy might seem to have an interest in the continuation of royal taxation as an excuse and a cover for its own peculations, it could still manage to find its profit in other ways; and there were further hard reasons for bargaining with the crown other than the mere protection of the right of consent and of the town's liberties against prejudice. The question of consent naturally provided the terrain over which the battle was fought. Naturally, too, it might involve a wider front than that on which a single town might face the government: it involved in turn the whole question of representative institutions. With the attitude of towns to the Estates which might exist in the areas in which they were situated we will deal later. For the moment it is enough to say that in general the municipalities of later medieval France were prepared in their own interests to hinder the free and proper working of representative institutions as far as they were able and as far as they dared. They restricted with the *mandat impératif* the capacities of their delegates to the assemblies; and they indulged after them in backstairs negotiations with the government for modification of the assemblies' decisions. The attitude of Tours, whose representatives, arriving too late for a general assembly at Poitiers, refused to grant a tax without a further general meeting, was exceptional.[3] More

---

[1] See, for instance, Delcambre, op. cit. pp. 160 ff.

[2] Maugis, 'Essai sur le régime financier de la ville d'Amiens', pp. 160–1, 408.

[3] A. Thomas, 'Les Etats généraux sous Charles VII. Notes et docs nouveaux', in R. *hist.* XL (1889) 82–3. Exceptional, too — at least to a certain

typical was the direct approach, the direct negotiation with the king and with the members of his entourage in the hope of favour and remission.[1]

Each town thus developed its own pattern of behaviour in dealing with the government. But it was not only the question of consent that might bring it up against the administration. Though they might have consented to a tax upon the town there was still room for those who ruled it to manœuvre. There was, it will be remembered, the question of the nature of the tax. Should it be direct or indirect, a tax upon persons or property or a tax on consumables? It has been argued that the oligarchs of Le Puy negotiated for royal permission to convert direct taxes into indirect ones consistently from 1353 in order, as we have seen, allegedly to off-load a greater burden of taxation upon the poor; that indirect taxes hit the poor more than the rich, and that direct taxes hit the rich more than the poor, has been regarded as axiomatic.[2] Then there was the question of the assessment of the tax. Here again, as we have seen, the conflict of interests provided ample scope for controversy and the intervention of the king's officers and the king's courts. In Le Puy, for instance, the *anoblis* found themselves, amongst those with some claim to exemption from taxation, as elsewhere upon the weakest ground. It was they who cracked first; but although the *taille réelle* concept that non-noble land held by nobles should be taxed seems to have developed only slowly in the town by 1420 there was a general order that the Vellave nobility should contribute upon non-noble holdings in Le Puy; and this was generally accepted by the mid-century. The clergy were harder nuts to crack: they disobeyed royal injunctions, they entered in 1434 upon an interminable lawsuit with the consulate which involved excommunication, interdict and papal intervention, and which died out apparently only in the early years of Louis XI's reign with an apparent victory for the consuls. By the end of the century it

---

extent — was the attitude of the great towns of Languedoc in the early years of Charles VII (B. Gilles, 'Autorité royale et resistances urbaines. Un Exemple languedocien: l'échec de la réformation générale de 1434–1435', in *B. philol. hist. Com. Travaux hist. sci.* (1961) pp. 115–46, and *Les États de Languedoc* (Toulouse, 1965) pp. 29 ff).

[1] Cf. Gilles, 'Autorité royale et resistances urbaines', pp. 126 ff; A. M. Tattegrain, 'Le Vexin français sous la domination anglaise', in *Positions des thèses de l'Ec. Chartes* (1937) pp. 161–2.

[2] Delcambre, op. cit. pp. 162 ff (but see above, p. 249 n 3).

was only the royal sergeants who retained their immunity in the town. But the question of assessment involved also one of the equitable — or inequitable — distribution of its burdens amongst those indisputably liable to taxation. The revision of the tax-lists again provided ample scope for litigation in Le Puy from 1387 onwards.[1] The problem was again a general one; and both the taxpayer and the administration had an interest in the detection of evasion.

In the same way the collection and the audit of accounts, in so far as they were carried out by a municipality, could lead to controversy between oligarchs and their inferiors, oligarchs and royal officers. The possibilities of fraud in the collection and the concealment of fraud in the accounting were eagerly exhibited by the inhabitants of Le Puy to the officers of the *sénéchaussée* of Nîmes-Beaucaire in 1446. Between 1374 and 1466 royal officers of one kind or another made constant attempts to get at the consuls' papers.[2] In the same way the local officers in Lyon laid siege to the financial archives of the Lyon consulate in the 1440s and 1450s.[3] The involvement of the king's servants and the social groups of a town in conflict was thus a close one.

Some royal officers were prepared to help the *menu peuple*. When Bertrand de Ribérac was *réformateur général* in the Midi between 1340 and 1355 the lower classes of Béziers formed a '*réformateurs*' party'; and the willingness of *réformateurs* to act in the interests of the *peuple* may be found elsewhere.[4] Local officers might support their claims against the oligarchies, as the king's proctor in the *sénéchaussée* of Nîmes-Beaucaire seems to have supported the claims of the opposition in Le Puy in 1446.[5] Private and public interest might lead them to take the side of the people. Inequitable assessment of taxation and its embezzlement reduced the profits of the crown; a constant tyranny meant constant trouble. The administration may thus have helped the cause of the *peuple* more than has sometimes been argued; and certainly one should not see the royal officers completely in the pockets of the oligarchs.[6] But it would be anachronistic to see a government even preponderantly in opposition to the *maior et sanior pars* of its bourgeoisie. The attitude of local royal

---

[1] Ibid. pp. 168 ff.   [2] Ibid. pp. [37], 184–6.   [3] Kleinclausz, op. cit. p. 317.

[4] Dognon, op. cit. p. 168; Angelras, op. cit. pp. 114 ff; Delcambre, op. cit. p. 60.

[5] Ibid. p. [36].   [6] Wolff, 'Les Luttes sociales', p. 452.

officers of course might vary; but it may well have been in the company of the oligarchs that one would have found them most frequently. Conversation with them brought a bourgeois under suspicion: during the Rebeyne in Lyon in 1436, according to the town's *procureur*, Rolin de Mâcon, 'the merchants, whether rich or not, were suspicious of him because he talked willingly with . . . the *bailli* and other royal officers inside the town . . . and out'.[1] Oligarchs and officers were, it was felt, all tarred with the same brush.

Urban revolt

As such they might be attacked together when violence broke loose. This was perhaps always not very far below the surface. Each town had its quota of men like Pascal Balmas in Nîmes in 1364, allegedly 'a brutal and riotous man, who all his life was disobedient and rebel to the consuls, and captains, and royal officers, and who committed many enormous crimes and malefactions and was never punished for them'.[2] Certain trades were thought especially bloody-minded: 'butchers', wrote a sixteenth-century chronicler of Le Puy, 'are men of blood and easily moved [to violence]'.[3] In so far as any generalisation is possible or even wise the principal motive for manifestations of violence was resentment of the burden of taxation, heavily spiced with resentment of upper-class fraud. Jean de Condeyssie, interrogated upon the causes of the Rebeyne in 1436, could suggest no further motive other than that 'the bourgeois and other magnates of the town (of Lyon) always refused to pay their *cottes* and shares of the *tailles* and subsidies which the king imposed in the town and other taxes, about which the *menu peuple* has always grumbled and been discontent. And he . . . believed that this [was] . . . one of the principal causes of the . . . assemblies and commotions.'[4] Conflict could manifest itself in many ways, as we have seen, from mere grumbling through a more or less acrimonious lawsuit to an open revolt. In the actual *conjoncture* of events which led finally to the last a considerable number of elements may be distinguished.

[1] Bellièvre, op. cit. p. 88.   [2] Ménard, op. cit. II 'Preuves', pp. 286–7.
[3] E. Médicis, *Chron.* ed. A. Chassaing, I (Le Puy, 1869) 213.
[4] Bellièvre, op. cit. p. 100.

Synchronisms apparent in waves of urban revolt might lead one to suspect broad movements of wages, food-prices and disease. Some of the revolts were tinged with the acrimony of wider political struggles.[1] Some of the revolts were inspired: by politicians for political motives, as the Burgundians inspired the Cabochian revolt in Paris in 1413,[2] or by oligarchs as a means of frightening royal officers into tax-remission. In Montpellier in 1379, in Lyon in 1436,[3] in Bourges in 1474 it was possible for the administration to suspect their intervention in apparently spontaneous outbreaks of wrath against the king's taxes and the king's officers. 'The poor', thought Louis XI in 1474, 'didn't do it on their own.' He may well have been wrong; but his suspicion is salutary.[4] The apparent simplicity of complaint before a revolt and of confession after it should not delude us into believing in expressed motivation or in expressed justification. Jean de Condeyssie said 'that he did not know by hearsay, presumption or otherwise that any of the magnates of the ... town [of Lyon] or others from outside had been either secretly or openly the cause by deed or word of the assemblies' in 1436.[5] But the consulate seems to have got into the habit of summoning large assemblies in the years before; the Rebeyne was, perhaps, such an assembly which got out of hand.[6]

Louis XI forbade the *échevins* of Arras in 1481 to summon a general assembly without the consent or in the absence of royal officers, for, he thought, 'all general assemblies of large communities are sometimes of dangerous consequence, and malevolent people may in their wickedness seduce many simple folk'.[7] A whole gamut of private motive might lie

---

[1] Wolff, 'Les Luttes sociales', pp. 449–50.   [2] Coville, op. cit. pp. 179 ff.

[3] R. Delachenal, *Hist. de Charles V*, v (1931) 302 (cf. pp. 323 ff); C. Bellièvre, *Souvenirs de voyages en Italie et en Orient, notes historiques, pièces en vers*, ed. C. Perrat (Travaux d'humanisme et renaissance, 23: Geneva, 1956) p. 100.

[4] H. Sée, *Louis XI et les villes* (1891) p. 180 (cf. p. 142).

[5] Bellièvre, op. cit. p. 100.

[6] J. Déniau, *La Commune de Lyon et la guerre bourguignonne, 1417–1435* (Lyon, 1934) pp. 218–22; R. Fédou, 'Une Révolte populaire à Lyon au xve siècle: la Rebeyne de 1436', in *Cah. Hist.* III (1958) 131.

[7] Sée, op. cit. p. 31. Although in some towns the general assembly appears to have played some part in urban affairs — see, for instance, P. Dognon, *Les Institutions politiques et admin. du pays de Languedoc du xiiie siècle aux guerres de Religion* (Toulouse, 1895) pp. 87, 171 ff; A. Giry, *Les Etablissements de Rouen* (Bibl. Ec. Hautes Etudes, 55: 1883) pp. 213, 311–12; Sée, op. cit. pp. 29 ff —

behind even the most partisan of group motives. Why did Jean de Condeyssie, a notary, appear to support the revolt of 1436? Was it, as he claimed, 'with good intention and to pacify the people, whom he saw so incensed, and to prevent greater trouble happening, such as murder' because 'the town was in great danger and in the way that some massacre would take place like happened in Paris' and because 'things were dangerous and they came about because of the *tailles* which the magnates of the town refused to pay'?[1] Was it because this defender of the people thought the attitude of those oligarchs unjust?[2] Or was it because he wanted to get down Rolin de Mâcon and make Barthélémy Dalmès *procureur* of Lyon in his place?[3] Or were his motives a complication of all three? In any case their obvious complexity must warn us against the simple answer. The predisposing causes and the immediate causes of urban insurrection were both full of local nuances: too much generalisation clearly is unwise.

Though the fundamental cause of insurrection might lie in the pressures of urban society itself, almost inevitably the royal officers, agents of the taxing power, came under attack during a revolt, perhaps even before the oligarchs themselves. Equally inevitably their revenge was terrible. Many years after the bloodless Rebeyne the heads of its leaders decorated the Pont de Saône.[4] It was little wonder that the oligarchies of a town had in the fifteenth century developed a general tendency to regard as 'wise and noteworthy words' a suggestion that the king's wrath should not be tempted and that his 'ill-will' should be held off at all costs.[5] It was a far cry from the bright days of the 1350s, when the ruling groups in a number of towns thought that insurrection

it seems in general to have had very little influence. How many members of the lower social groups were, like Jean Oudot in Senlis in 1446, too shy to speak in an assembly? (J. Flammermont, *Hist. des institutions municipales de Senlis* (Bibl. Ec. Hautes Etudes, 45: 1881) p. 90). Louis' hostility to general assemblies was hardly new: the government of Charles VI had the same view in 1414 (C. Petit-Dutaillis, *Les Communes françaises* (1947) p. 236 n 1).

[1] Bellièvre, op. cit. pp. 98–101.

[2] Fédou, 'Une Révolte populaire à Lyon', pp. 137–8. He had as a receiver in 1428 pursued an under-assessed oligarch (R. Fédou, *Les Hommes de loi lyonnais de la fin du Moyen âge. Etude sur les origines de la classe de robe* (1964) pp. 242, 273 ff).

[3] Bellièvre, op. cit. p. 94.   [4] Ibid. p. 72.   [5] Ibid. pp. 90–1.

could be profitable.[1] In the fifteenth century insurrection was more clearly foolish.

Peuple gras *and the king*

That *lèse-majesté* brought its own reward was one of the clearer political opinions of later medieval government. Oligarchies might well be advised to follow the advice of Christine de Pisan: 'because the *menu peuple* never has usually much prudence either in word or even in deeds which concern administration — so that they should never interfere in the ordinances drawn up for it by the princes — the bourgeois and the substantial people in the towns should take care that the common people should not put itself in the way of anything done concerning it, or make any evil conspiracy against the prince or the council. The reason for this is that such conspiracies or machinations of the common people always rebound to the prejudice of those who can only lose . . .' Urban rulers should present the interests of the common people humbly to the princes and the council, and never allow them to use violence: 'for that is the destruction of towns and of *pays*'.[2] And if the gradual and uneven restriction of urban liberties is any guide, the government had little desire to encourage the more peacable aspirations of the bourgeoisie it ruled — or perhaps little capacity. As in the case of Tours under

[1] Delachenal, op. cit. 1 (1909) 395 ff. For the attitude, for example, of the upper bourgeoisie of Amiens, see E. Maugis, 'Essai sur le régime financier de la ville d'Amiens du xive à la fin du xvie siècle (1356–1588)', in *M. Soc. Antiq. Picardie*, ser. 4 III (1899) 174 ff.

[2] '. . . pourceque le menu peuple na mie communement grant prudence en parole ne meismes en faiz qui touche policie — dont ne se doivent mesler des ordenances dicelle establiez par les princes — doivent prendre garde les bourgois et les gros que pour chose qui en soit faicte le commun ne sen empesche ne nen face aucune conspiration mauvaise contre le prince ou le conseil. La cause si est pourceque teles conspirations ou machinations de commun revertissent tousjours en prejudice a ceulx qui ont que perdre . . .'; 'car cest la destruction de villes & de pais' ('Le Livre du corps de policie', British Museum, Harleian MS 4410, folios 61ᵛ–62ʳ). The attitude of the great towns of the Low Countries was perhaps different (H. Pirenne, *Hist. de Belgique*, II (Brussels, 1908) 347 ff; cf. E. Coornaert, 'L'Etat et les villes à la fin du Moyen âge. La Politique d'Anvers', in *R. hist.* CCVII (1952) 185–201).

Louis XI, a town might (at least in the later fifteenth century) have less high aspirations than its monarch.[1] The communal movement in the north was moribund at the beginning of the fourteenth century. Many communes survived, some were created; the trials of the war gave to Troyes and a number of other towns considerable impetus towards a communal self-consciousness.[2] Towns on vulnerable frontier lines, like Tournai, like Lyon, could not when those frontiers were threatened be too much restricted.[3] A whole complex of reasons might lead towards a gentle attitude towards the towns. Yet the fourteenth and fifteenth centuries saw the development it has been argued of pressure upon them. Many communes disappeared, especially in the fourteenth century, as a result of revolts provoked by royal taxation, as a result of conflicts between the town and local royal or ecclesiastical officers, as a result of internal dissensions.[4] For some towns the suppression of their commune was a happy release from the torments of self-government;[5] as for Tours, what was one town's privilege was another's duty. The control of royal officers over all aspects of communal administration developed.[6] It was the same in the Midi from at least the 1380s onwards.[7] Again there are exceptions to the rules: Le Puy was favoured with privileges to the mid-sixteenth century:[8] its docile tax-embezzling and tax-collecting oligarchy was a useful royal outpost in the Massif. Again there are the suicides: in 1349 the consuls of Montesquieu-Lauragais bought part of the rights of justice in the town for the king rather than for themselves in return for confirmation of their customs, liberties

[1] B. Chevalier, 'La Politique de Louis XI à l'égard des bonnes villes. Le Cas de Tours', in *Moyen Age*, LXX (1964) 473–504.

[2] Petit-Dutaillis, op. cit. pp. 169 ff; F. Bibolet, 'Le Rôle de la guerre de Cent ans dans le développement des libertés municipales à Troyes', in *M. Soc. acad. Aube*, XCIX (1939–42) pp. 295–320.

[3] Petit-Dutaillis, op. cit. pp. 191–3; Sée, op. cit. pp. 188–90; A. J. Kleinclausz, *Hist. de Lyon*, I (Lyon, 1939) pp. 289 ff. The same kind of tenderness was shown at times to La Rochelle, Oléron and St.-Jean-d'Angély (Giry, op. cit. pp. 72, 93, 298 ff).

[4] Petit-Dutaillis, op. cit. p. 197.   [5] Ibid. pp. 178 ff.

[6] As, for instance, in Amiens (Maugis, 'Essai sur le régime financier de la ville d'Amiens', pp. 201 ff).

[7] Dognon, op. cit. pp. 469 ff.

[8] E. Delcambre, *Le Consulat du Puy en Velay des origines à 1610* (Le Puy, 1933) pp. 197 ff.

and franchises.[1] Lassitude and decadence have been seen as general tendencies from the fourteenth century on.

When the war was over, even a town like Lyon, so adept at resistance of all kinds, began to feel the pinch. From about 1436, with the end, temporarily, of the Burgundian threat on the Saône–Rhône line, the tone of royal letters to the town changed: 'they command, they require, and they no longer explain'.[2] The privileges of the town were over-looked. The financial autonomy of the town was damaged. In 1455 Charles VII replied to the town's standard plea for a reduction in its quota of taxation that 'when he gave a remission he would give it to everybody, and not otherwise'.[3] It needed the involvements of Louis XI with the dukes of Burgundy, Bourbon and Savoy for the town to recover its lost position. Even Louis, arbitrary — in his words at least — in his attitude to the towns of his kingdom could not, under those circumstances, bully Lyon too much.[4]

But even in Lyon the development of a submissive attitude in the oligarchy has been seen. The increasing control of the government and its officers over the towns was balanced by an increasing lack of interest on the part of urban rulers in the true breath of communal or consular liberties. The basis of this shift in attitudes has been analysed: the development of the precedence of private over public privilege in the minds of the oligarchs, which led eventually to the disintegration of the oligarchies, an increasing reliance by the rulers of the towns upon the support of those who exploited them.[5] The concept of the honour of the town, so dear to a Bernard de Varey in Lyon in 1423, went down before the concept of private honour: in their search for nobility and for office and for profit, the members of the old families were prepared to neglect the profit of the city.[6] From 1430–50 to the 1490s Lyon was run by lawyers in alliance with a new generation of merchants; and,

---

[1] P. C. Timbal, 'Les Villes de consulat dans le Midi de la France', in *Rec. Soc. Jean Bodin*, VI (1954) 351.

[2] Kleinclausz, op. cit. p. 316.   [3] Ibid. p. 317.

[4] Ibid. pp. 324 ff.

[5] See, for instance, Sée, op. cit. pp. 77 ff; R. Gandilhon, *Politique écon. de Louis XI* (Rennes, 1940) pp. 113 ff; E. Maugis, *Recherches sur les transformations du régime politique et sociale de la ville d'Amiens des origines de la commune à la fin du xvie siècle* (1906) pp. 44, 212.

[6] Déniau, op. cit. p. 479.

though some resistance was made to Charles VII and Louis XI, they were by their training and their desire for office inclined towards submission. An earlier generation of lawyers in the town had perhaps been troubled with more regard for its honour; but the later generation — though they might still reject 'tyranny' — fell more easily prey to the materialism bewailed by François Garin in 1460.[1] 'No-one is as eager or attentive to spend time on something that's unprofitable as he is on something which is' thought the *maîtres des métiers* of Lyon in 1447, deciding that the consuls should be paid;[2] but the profit lay elsewhere than in the pursuit and defence of the honour of the town.

When the constitution of Le Puy became more democratic in the fifteenth century, the town's resistance to taxation increased.[3] There was a direct connection between the attitude of the town's rulers and the impact of government upon its inhabitants. How far the government was conscious in its seduction of the oligarchs is another matter:[4] the oligarchs themselves were anxious enough, in their pursuit of worldly advancement, to be seduced. Tarnished virtue could be found in every town in France. But the control a determined monarch could exercise had other methods than the acceptance of the timid advances of ambitious oligarchs. Charles VII seems not to have interfered very much with the internal workings of towns; Louis XI's interference was incessant.[5] 'Because of our sovereignty and royal majesty', he announced in 1464, 'the general government and administration of our kingdom belongs and pertains to us alone, in matter of offices, or jurisdictions, or otherwise; and also of all our *bonnes villes* and cities, and *mairies, lois* and *échevinages*; which *mairies, lois* and *échevinages* we may renew, create and ordain at our simple pleasure and will; and all anyone can do about it is simply to take notice of the fact.'[6] But there were limits to what even Louis might want to do; and, as in the case of Tours, he might embarrass a town with offers of unwanted liberty.[7]

Towards the question of finance Louis XI was as flexible in his

[1] Fédou, *Les Hommes de loi lyonnais*, pp. 279 ff, 381 ff.

[2] Déniau, op. cit. p. 608.   [3] Delcambre, op. cit. p. 155.

[4] Chevalier, op. cit. pp. 475 ff.

[5] Petit-Dutaillis, op. cit. pp. 230, 237 ff; Sée, op. cit. *passim*.

[6] *Rec. des monuments inéd. de l'hist. du Tiers état*, ed. A. Thierry (Docs inéd. sur l'hist. de France) ser. 1 II (1853) 271–2.

[7] Chevalier, op. cit. pp. 480 ff.

attitude as he was in his attitude towards urban administration. The problem for the government was to extract from the towns as much money as it needed, taking into consideration the needs and exigencies of the town itself. The pattern of bargaining was thus a complicated one. Remission for poverty, remission for good service or for abandoning the enemy, remission for urban fortification[1] had to be off-set against a perhaps rather hazy notion of the total needs of the government receipt. The question was further complicated by the acrimonious discussion of the relative capacity to pay at any time of a town and its neighbouring countryside. Lyon, for instance, complained that the ratio ran unfairly against it in the 1460s; and in the Estates of Velay the conflict over the apportioning of taxation between the countryside and the town of Le Puy went on well into the sixteenth century.[2]

As the arguments of Lyon in the 1460s show, the elements of the general economic *conjoncture* had their part in influencing the relationship of town and administration: a town might be driven to ask for remission because of sheer economic misfortune. But in the same way as the pressures which might drive a noble to seek the favour of a pension may perhaps not have been wholly those of his economic situation, so the pressures which might drive a municipality to seek the favour of a tax-remission were perhaps not wholly those of theirs. Certainly the search for remission upon whatever pretext was incessant. Very frequently that search was successful.[3] During the Burgundian war Lyon profited very considerably. Exemption after exemption was granted to Le Puy.[4] Louis XI in his wilder moments thought of exempting towns generally at the expense of the countryside; he was told that if he did so 'it would be a disaster for his people and would hazard his revenue'.[5] Still a very

---

[1] See, for instance, L. Caillet, *Etude sur les relations de la commune de Lyon avec Charles VII et Louis XI* (Lyon, 1909) *passim*; Déniau, op. cit. *passim*; *Docs sur la ville de Millau*, ed. J. Artières (Arch. hist. Rouergue, 7: Millau, 1930) pp. 183, 188, 203; *Reg. des comptes municipaux de la ville de Tours* [1367–1380], ed. J. Delaville-Le Roulx (1881) *passim*; *Reg. de l'échevinage de St.-Jean d'Angély*, ed. D. d'Aussy (Arch. hist. Saintonge Aunis, 24, 26, 32: 1895, 1897, 1902) *passim*.

[2] Caillet, op. cit. pp. 542–4; Delcambre, op. cit. pp. 150 ff.

[3] See, for instance, G. du Fresne de Beaucourt, *Hist. de Charles VII*, I (1881) 381–2, II (1882) 611–12, III (1885) 461, IV (1888) 424, V (1890) 334, VI (1891) 378, and the evidence cited above, n 1.

[4] Delcambre, op. cit. p. 146.

[5] A. de Reilhac, *Jean de Reilhac*, I (1886) 232–3.

considerable number of towns profited from individual exemption.[1] But one should be careful of seeing such favours as purely *actes gratuites*. They could become quite expensive, though not perhaps as expensive as the taxation they replaced;[2] and favour given might be balanced by favour asked. The towns were one of the more convenient sources of immediate ready cash. If the town was unable to raise sums rapidly by its own internal taxation, it might well have wealthy merchants prepared to advance considerable sums to it as a loan. Though they were by no means the sole source of royal credit[3] towns thus found themselves throughout the period asked to lend to the crown; Lyon, anxious for its fairs in the 1460s, went so far as to argue that the king could 'in case of need . . . be able to find there quickly by means of a loan 100,000 or 200,000 *francs* . . . through the merchants and foreign bankers who live and will come to live in the town'.[4] An element of compulsion entered early into royal arguments: refusal might be regarded as disloyalty.[5] A number of the methods of extraction used with such éclat by Louis XI had been used by his predecessors.[6] Louis used them with perhaps more obvious heartlessness; he seems to have used them more; but — at least in Tours — the weight of taxation now fell more on the countryside and, though the town naturally protested, it protested without the acrimony which had characterised its dealings with Charles VII.[7]

And it would indeed be wrong to imagine that Louis aimed at the 'destruction' of the towns. He was indeed prepared to allow them considerable fiscal and judicial liberties. His 'interference' aimed at the

[1] Gandilhon, op. cit. pp. 286–7.

[2] Delcambre, op. cit. p. 149; Gandilhon, op. cit. p. 288 n 4; Chevalier, op. cit. pp. 493–5.

[3] M. M. Postan and H. J. Habakkuk, *The Cambridge Econ. Hist. of Europe*, III *Econ. Organization and Policies in the Middle Ages* (Cambridge, 1963) 472–92; A. Bossuat, 'Etude sur les emprunts royaux au début du xvᵉ siècle', in R. *hist. Droit*, ser. 4 XXVIII (1950) 351–71; Gandilhon, op. cit. pp. 343–64.

[4] Gandilhon, op. cit. p. 228.

[5] L. Mirot, *Les Insurrections urbaines au début du règne de Charles VI (1380–1383)* (1905) p. 19 n 1.

[6] See, for instance, Maugis, 'Essai sur le régime financier de la ville d'Amiens', pp. 271 ff; Caillet, op. cit. *passim*.

[7] Sée, op. cit. pp. 126 ff; Gandilhon, op. cit. pp. 286 ff; Chevalier, op. cit. p. 495.

maintenance of secure oligarchical rule in the towns; at the maintenance of the peace; at the maintenance of urban defences. Partly, as in the matter of taxation, it was a question of providing ready reservoirs of resources: as well as money, towns could be called upon, for instance, to furnish transport, victuals and arms for the soldiery. But there was also the question of security; and it was this that led to Louis' notorious interventions in municipal elections. Occasionally these came about because of importunity from below. But in those which clearly emanated from Louis' own will the need to get into urban office those loyal to him seems to have been paramount. Louis does not seem to have had a particular preference for the oligarchs. He was perfectly prepared to see 'mechanics' in urban government. But the burdens of urban office were too great for them, and the prejudices of the oligarchs themselves were too much for anyone to overcome.[1]

Given the interests the oligarchies of the towns of later medieval France had in playing in with the government, it is not surprising that they provided on the whole very little political trouble for its kings. Apart from those of the 1350s, urban revolt — though possibly covertly sympathised with or even fomented by the upper bourgeoisie — was carried out by the *menu peuple*. The upper bourgeoisie had too much to lose. 'Certainly', thought the *Ménagier de Paris* on the subject of bourgeois comforts, such things 'make a man anxious to get home, and see his lady wife, and avoid other people.[2] The attitude of the bourgeoisie of Angers, who tried to hold out against Louis XI's reorganisation of the town's administration after its confiscation from king René, was again exceptional.[3] On the whole the intervention of royal officers protected the upper bourgeoisie from its inferiors; the interference of the administration in the towns of Languedoc has been seen as the principal force in the restriction in them of social change.[4] Nor were the towns to be seduced by a king's magnate opponents. Again there

---

[1] Chevalier, op. cit. pp. 473–504.
[2] ed. J. Pichon (Soc. des bibliophiles fr.) 1 (1846) 169. Cf. A. Coville, *Les Cabochiens et l'ordonnance de 1413* (1888) p. 95.
[3] Sée, op. cit. pp. 259 ff.
[4] See, for instance, Fédou, *Les Hommes de loi lyonnais*, p. 389; Dognon, op. cit. p. 170.

are exceptions: Bordeaux was seduced by the English in 1452, the charms of the dukes of Burgundy might tempt towns — Amiens, for instance — on the north-eastern periphery;[1] it was still necessary for Louis XI to make a considerable effort to affirm the possible waverers.[2] Social conflict within a town might take on a political form: the *menu peuple* of Le Puy appeared to support the duc de Bourbon, the *menu peuple* of a number of Burgundian towns appeared to support Marie of Burgundy after the death of her father and Louis' occupation of the duchy, and so did those of Arras.[3] In Angers the Tricoterie broke out in support of king René.[4] But during the war of the Public Weal and during the crisis of 1472, despite valiant attempts by the magnates to woo towns away from the king, despite their success in winning the towns of Normandy for their duke, despite some obvious anxiety on Louis' part, the towns of the kingdom in general kept their faith due to the king. In a letter to Langres, Thibaut de Neufchâtel told the town that the 'princes wish and intend to see that all the *aides* and subsidies with which the people of this kingdom have to put up are abolished and never put on again . . . and that you shall be upheld and maintained in your privileges, franchises and liberties'.[5] The inhabitants of Langres were not to be seduced.

The oligarchies had too much to lose not to be loyal. Loyalty they might keep alight in devious ways. In January 1439 the council of Troyes begged the friar Liénart Breton to stay on in their town 'so that by his preaching the people may be encouraged to devotion and prayer, saying that he was the most commendable preacher, who had done more good to the people than any one of their order who had preached there for years before friar Liénart came to Troyes; and what was more, he commended the cause of the king our lord and of his lordship most notably in all his preachings, and exhorted the people to love him and

---

[1] T. Basin, *Hist. de Charles VII*, ed. C. Samaran, II (Classiques de l'hist. de France au Moyen âge, 21: 1944), pp. 182–6; Maugis, 'Essai sur le régime financier de la ville d'Amiens', pp. 388 ff. It is possible Niort was less than wholeheartedly royal during the *Praguerie* (Giry, op. cit. p. 259).

[2] See, for instance, Sée, op. cit. pp. 209 ff. Cf. Chevalier, op. cit. pp. 496 ff.

[3] Delcambre, op. cit. p. 200; Sée, op. cit. pp. 269, 278, 285.

[4] Sée, op. cit. pp. 259–63; P. Marchegay, 'Sédition à Angers en 1461 dite la Tricotterie', in R. *Anjou*, II (1853) 268–70.

[5] Sée, op. cit. pp. 209–21.

to remain in good and true obedience to him'.[1] But it was the oligarchs of Lyon who produced perhaps the highest paean of praise for loyal submission.

> The ... councillors [they wrote in 1423] and inhabitants of the ... town of Lyon have always been, are and will be, please God, truly and loyally obedient to the king our ... lord and to his predecessors, without any fault; and to such an extent that it seems to these councillors and inhabitants that the loyalty and entire obedience should be everywhere public knowledge and perpetually to be remembered; and that because of them the greater part of the *pays* in the obedience of that lord remained on his side, because if they had failed to do their loyal duty like some other people in some of the biggest towns in this kingdom, God knows what would have happened to the cause and lordship of that lord; and these councillors have not been ashamed often to remind their sovereign lord of their ... loyalty, so that he shall always favour them especially, for good and for better.[2]

For the councillors and inhabitants of Lyon loyalty certainly brought its own rewards.

Rural communities

It was essentially a web of privilege which created a town and set it apart from the countryside. In Toulousain and Lauragais, if not elsewhere, a village could become a town thus defined.[3] But rural society elsewhere was not wholly without organisation; and communes and consulates were, in fact, essentially sophisticated and exceptional manifestations of the innate impulse towards it.[4] The rural 'communities of inhabitants' were among the most basic and least formalised of associations. Since they were customary they had no formal charter, no definition; few kept, in the middle ages, much in the way of records; but nevertheless some idea of them may be gleaned from their impact upon parts of society more articulate.

[1] F. Bibolet, 'La Participation du clergé aux affaires municipales de la ville de Troyes aux xive et xve siècles', in *M. Soc. acad. Aube*, C (1943–5) 68–9.

[2] Caillet, op. cit. p. 331.   [3] See above, p. 238.

[4] P. Duparc, 'Confréries du Saint-esprit et communautés d'habitants au Moyen âge', in *R. hist. Droit*, ser. 4 xxxvi (1958), p. 367.

The essential bond was of the locality: common labour, common worship, intermarriage formed its elements. The rhythm of the agricultural year in that particular area created common interest and common habits; natural disasters, common tribulations. War, though it might destroy whole communities as it destroyed together with 'the mortalities' the parish of Vignolles near Cognac, could have ultimately little effect upon so fundamental a form of social organisation. The religious unit, the parish, doubled the community. In the death-throes of Vignolles the five survivors carried off to Bordeaux the silver cross 'which belonged to their church, in the time when they lived there'. When they had settled in Bordeaux, in different parishes, 'they assembled together, and had a council and deliberation between themselves' in 1417; and they decided to give the cross to the *confrérie* of Notre-Dame in the parish of St.-Seurin in Bordeaux, on condition that the *confrères* should celebrate two solemn general anniversaries, with sung mass of requiem, each year in perpetuity for them and for the souls of those who had paid for the cross in the parish church of Vignolles.[1] The village might, at least temporarily, have died; but the obligations of its community towards those who had provided their cross continued to be observed some fifty miles away in Bordeaux.

Simple membership of the Christian community was reinforced on occasion by membership of that community's *confrérie*, obscure organisations 'à ras de terre', at earth-level; *confréries* with the principal aim of mutual support and the provision of an annual banquet. 'It was before a table, preferably well provided, that the community became, materially and spiritually, conscious of itself.' One village in the mountains behind Nice remained conscious of itself in this way, at least until the last war.[2] But it was not only in a moral or convivial sense that the Church helped to create the community. Problems of parish administration — the upkeep of the 'fabric' of the church — might bring the parishioners together in consultation.[3] Up to the thirteenth century the repair of the building and its ornaments and the administration of the funds left by

[1] R. Boutruche, *La Crise d'une société. Seigneurs et paysans du Bordelais pendant la guerre de Cent ans* (1947) pp. 517–18.

[2] Duparc, op. cit. pp. 351, 352, 361–2.

[3] P. Adam, *La Vie paroissiale en France au xive siècle* (1964) pp. 80–6; V. Chomel, 'Droit de patronage et pratique religieuse dans l'archevêché de Narbonne au début du xve siècle', in *Bibl. Éc. Chartes*, cxv (1957) 112 ff.

testators for pious purposes had been the duty of the parish priest. In the fourteenth century the parishioners, suspicious of maladministration if not of malversation, got permission from their bishop to deal with the 'fabric' themselves in a number of dioceses. The duty was delegated to the churchwardens, whose precise title varied from diocese to diocese; they were chosen in some places by the *curé*, in others by the notables of the parish; their number varied: in the diocese of Bourges there were one or two of them, in the diocese of Dax two, elsewhere 'several'. The property which they administered could be considerable. The donations of deceased villagers might on the whole have been small, but at least they were numerous; and some legacies might entail the administration not only of money or of liturgical objects, but also of fields, woods, vineyards or houses. The local hospital, alms-house, or leper-house might be under their control. And for the repair of the church itself it might be necessary for them to tax, with the consent of the *maior et sanior pars* of the village, their co-parishioners.

The churchwardens were ideally 'well-advised, discreet, wealthy and honest'; but naturally, in some villages, their social status was well down on earth-level. In the parish of Solers near Tournon in the fourteenth century there was a poor 'varlet', a manual labourer, who was churchwarden of his parish and kept the accounts; he could thus presumably read, write and count, despite his social situation.[1] Though some churchwardens were negligent — for instance those in Cérisy in 1321, who were ordered to provide a bag for the vestments, a key for the font, binding for the books and a number of church ornaments on pain of a fine — others were only too active in defence of their parish and its property in the church.[2] They could compel their neighbours to subscribe to it; in Bizanet, near Narbonne, at the end of the fourteenth century they threatened to disinter the recently entombed ward of a recalcitrant noble from the church and re-bury him in the churchyard unless his guardian paid up.[3] They could in turn bully the clergy: at Littry, near Cérisy, in 1315 the official had decided in a dispute between the *curé* and the churchwardens about the hay grown in the cemetery that it should be cut for the horse of the priest who visited the sick. In

[1] M. Mollat, *La Vie et la pratique religieuses au xive siècle et dans la première partie du xve principalement en France*, I (1963) 84.

[2] Ibid. pp. 87–8.   [3] Chomel, op. cit. pp. 118–19.

1333 the churchwardens returned to the attack and had the hay appropriated to the 'fabric'.[1] And in the diocese of Narbonne, if not elsewhere, it was they who should be given the credit for the upkeep of their churches throughout the troubles of the fourteenth century: through their efforts the 'désolation des églises' was not as much as it might have been if the churches had been left in the tender care of their *curés*.[2]

The churchwardens were not afraid to litigate in defence of their charges.[3] In principle the judge competent to deal with the cases they brought was the bishop or his official. But in the fourteenth century, through the use of the plea of *novelleté* in a case of seizin, which, by *prévention*, belonged to the crown, such cases began to be heard in the Parlement of Paris; and an ordinance of 1385 gave the court formal competence effectively over the innumerable conflicts between *curés*, churchwardens and parishioners. In 1380, for instance, the church-wardens of Mareuil, near Abbeville, complained that their *curé* had objected to the digging of a grave in the nave of his church and accused him of removing earth from the cemetery. Not that the laity in that essentially just court necessarily always won: in 1400 the *curé* of Montromant, near Lyon, was maintained in rights which his parishioners hoped to abstract from him. But the competence of the Parlement of Paris not only allowed royal officers to interfere in the minor details of parish life and to make inroads into questions of jurisdiction at least arguably spiritual: it also brought the churchwardens out of their parishes, away from earth-level, to the central departments and the hierarchy of government.

But officers of the Parlement of Paris were not the only representatives of the central power with whom the village parishioner came into contact. The parish was the penultimate unit in the assessment and the ultimate unit in the collection of direct taxes.[4] The villagers had to deal with the *élu* and his subordinates. They had to assemble before them when they came on circuit to deal with the apportionment of the *taille*

---

[1] Adam, op. cit. p. 86.   [2] Chomel, op. cit. pp. 79–84, 123.

[3] G. Mollat, 'Les Origines du gallicanisme parlementaire aux xive et xve siècles', in R. *Hist. ecclés.* XLIII (1948) 101 ff.

[4] G. Dupont-Ferrier, *Etudes sur les institutions financières de la France à la fin du Moyen âge*, II *Les Finances extraordinaires et leur mécanisme* (1932) 56 ff.

amongst the parishes; the 'larger and better part of the taxpayers' in each parish had to assemble to choose assessors; the parishioners had to assemble again to discuss complaints against the assessment. Villagers, 'powerful' in status, 'middling' and 'small' had to act as assessors; villagers 'sufficient and solvent' had — albeit, like the assessors, reluctantly — to act as collectors.[1] These multiple contacts with the wider world served effectively, not only to emphasise the sense of community in the locality: they also gave a body 'juridically amorphous'[2] from time to time, however temporarily, a juridical personality, and a body in principle institutionally and socially amorphous again both a concept of majority rule and a recognition, in deciding the majority, of hierarchy in the precedence of the *maior et sanior pars*.

In 1365 the peasants of a group of Champenois villages which formed a single parish, litigating before the Parlement of Paris, got into trouble for using the words *corps* and *commune* of themselves; they explained that they had not intended to use them as terms of art, but merely in order to explain that they were not present as individuals to be taken 'one by one'.[3] *Communauté* was the term which eventually described such bodies as theirs. On specific occasions communities could elect proctors to act in their name, thus acquiring, for the moment, the qualities of a person at law.[4] In 1358, for instance, the parishioners and *confrères* of St.-Jean-d'Illac pleaded by proctor against their *curé* before the *officialité* of Bordeaux on the question of his fees.[5] The authority for this form of common action was naturally again that of the *maior et sanior pars*. The procuration of the inhabitants of the parish of St.-Corneille, near Le Mans, in litigation with their *curé* over his tithes was passed by the *plus grant et saine partie* of them; and that this form of consent was, as in towns, necessary was clear to the royal chancery in the later fourteenth century.[6]

But procurations could be given by groups on a larger scale. The

---

[1] *Documents relatifs à l'admin. financière en France de Charles VII à François Ier (1443–1523)*, ed. G. Jacqueton (Coll. de textes pour servir à l'étude et à l'enseignement de l'hist.: 1891) pp. 104–6.

[2] F. L. Cheyette, 'Procurations by large-scale communities in fourteenth-century France', in *Speculum*, XXXVII (1962) 18.

[3] M. Bloch, *Les Caractères originaux de l'hist. rurale française*, I (1955) 179.

[4] Cheyette, op. cit. p. 18.   [5] Boutruche, op. cit. p. 123 n4.

[6] Cheyette, op. cit. p. 18 n3.

villages in Champagne, in litigation in 1365, at least formed one parish and (though in this case they perhaps did not) they were all accustomed to act in common. But litigation by larger-scale communities can be found in fourteenth-century France: by the 'noble bourgeois and inhabitants of Anjou, Touraine and Maine'; by the 'clergy, nobles, bourgeois and inhabitants of the duchy of Burgundy'; and by the inhabitants of the *châtellenie* of Craon. In the last case the inhabitants of the *plat-pays*, the countryside, complained against the assessment upon them by Isabelle, dame de Sully and de Craon, of part of a subsidy of 1200 *francs* which she claimed had been granted her by the clergy, the nobles and 'others' of the *châtellenie*. Arguing 'no taxation without consultation', the 'poor labourers and inhabitants' had taken the case to the king's court. In 1386 they obtained royal letters instructing the *bailli* of Chartres to order dame Isabelle to allow them to draw up a procuration in order to tax themselves for the cost of the case.[1]

We have come a long way from the simple conviviality of parish *confréries*: the community of Craonnais in the later 1380s may even have omitted the parish as an intermediate unit towards the whole and formed a single group from the men in the district regarded as individuals. Here the 'inhabitants' and 'poor labourers' of some thirty parishes were acting in joint defiance of at least an alleged decision of the three estates of the *pays*. If these men can be regarded as villagers, as peasants, they were very different from the impoverished, powerless, cowed individuals, the ravaged sheep of moralists. And, if anything, it was, according to Jean Juvenal des Ursins, the upper classes who were on the run. 'No-one', he wrote in 1445, 'is poor nowadays except the clergy and the gentlemen.' Partly this was due to the fall in the income of their estates; 'but another thing is the merchants and the labourers, for they have everything. If a churchman had only one *franc* a labourer or a merchant would have to have it; and townsfolk and villagers tax them

1 Ibid. pp. 19, 22. For further light on the activities of *communautés d'habitants*, see, for instance, L. Delisle, *Etudes sur la condition de la classe agricole et de l'état de l'agriculture en Normandie au Moyen âge* (Evreux, 1851) pp. 137 ff; F. Dumont and P. C. Timbal, 'Gouvernés et gouvernants en France. Périodes du Moyen âge et du xvie siècle', in *Rec. Soc. Jean Bodin*, XXIV (1966) 231–3; E. Dravasa, ' "Vivre noblement". Recherches sur la dérogeance de noblesse du xive au xvie siècles', in *R. jurid. écon. Sud-Ouest, Sér. jurid.* XVII (1966) 23 ff.

and put unjust charges upon them.'[1] Alain Chartier, too, allowed the
knight in his *Quadrilogue invectif* to argue that 'if the people . . . complains
and it is trampled and wounded, I call upon God to witness that we,
too, are not undamaged and that we have quite enough of our share of
it. And since it's necessary to match evil with evil, the populars have
this advantage, that their purse is like the cistern which has collected
and is collecting the waters and the drains of all the riches in this
kingdom, which have been drained from the coffers of the nobles and
the clergy . . .'[2] One should not, perhaps, overestimate this redistribution of wealth;[3] but there was at least something to be said on the side
of the gentry. That land-owners were forced in a period of 'reconstruction' to lighten the burdens of their tenants has been emphasised for
many parts of France.[4] 'The people always . . . complain and they
always pay', said, according to Jean Juvenal in another mood, a royal
councillor in council before Charles VII; and this may in fact have been
only too true.[5]

Rural revolt

Was it then misery which caused peasant revolt? There were, as we
have just seen, other means than force with which to resist 'oppression'.
And one's lord was, after all, one's natural protector. The clergy and
the nobility, thought Philippe de Poitiers at the Estates-general of

[1] 'Ny a aujourduy povrete si non en gens desglise et gentilzhommes . . .
mais aultre chose est des marchans et laboureux, car ilz ont tout. Se ung
homme desglise na que ung franc il fault que ung labeureur ou ung marchant
layent; et encores les gens des villes et des villages les taillent et mettent a
charges non raisonnables . . .' ('A, a, a, nescio loqui quia puer ego sum',
Bibl. nat. MS fr 2701, fo. 50ʳ.)

[2] ed. E. Droz (Classiques français du Moyen âge: 2nd ed. 1950) pp. 33–4.

[3] See above, p. 183.

[4] See, for instance, Boutruche, op. cit. pp. 295–331; I. Guérin, *La Vie rurale
en Sologne aux xivᵉ et xvᵉ siècles* (1960) pp. 202–88; A. Plaisse, *La Baronnie du
Neubourg* (1961) pp. 337 ff; G. Fourquin, *Les Campagnes de la région parisienne à
la fin du Moyen âge* (1964) pp. 377 ff, 437 ff.

[5] P.S. Lewis, 'Jean Juvenal des Ursins and the Common Literary Attitude
towards Tyranny in Fifteenth-century France', in *Medium Aevum*, xxxiv
(1965) 117; Fourquin, op. cit. pp. 514–15.

1484, were far more the defenders of the people than the *tiers état*. 'Who', he demanded, 'have made clear the miseries of the people in discourses befor the king and the princes? The clergy. By which deputies' influence have the burdens of the people most been lightened? By the deputies of the Church and the nobility.... Who, finally, after the people share in the misfortunes of the people, and must thus have the common weal most at heart? I dare to affirm the clergy and the nobility, whose whole position depends upon their revenue from the people ...'[1] Interest and sentiment joined to make the upper classes, rather than the *peuple gras*, who were interested only in fleecing it, the natural defenders of the *menu peuple*. Certainly a churchman such as Jean Juvenal could be vocal enough in its defence; to reveal the miseries of the populars was at least a literary and predicatory convention.[2] The *cahier de doléances*, the petitions, of the Estates-general contained a considerable section upon 'the persecutions, poverties and miseries' which the *menu peuple* suffered;[3] and it was drawn up by the assembly divided not into three orders but into six regional groups. Regional particularism and some general inefficiency was noticed by Jean Masselin in his journal of the assembly; but not class particularism.[4] The regional orders, who had, after all, in 1484 been elected, as Philippe de Poitiers pointed out, as the deputies each of all three orders of the region,[5] may well, as he argued, have regarded themselves as concerned with a common, albeit regional, good. And certainly the *mélange* of interest and sentiment which he discussed provided the ostensible motive for René d'Anjou's interventions on behalf of his Angevin subjects in the mid-fifteenth century.[6] Admittedly, except in such manœuvres as that of the poor labourers and inhabitants of the *châtellenie* of Craon, the *peuple* never acquired very much of a formal political attribute. In France, only, possibly, in minuscule Franc-Alleu on the boundary of Auvergne and

---

[1] J. Masselin, *Journal des Etats généraux de France tenus à Tours en 1484*, ed. A. Bernier (Docs inéd. sur l'hist. de France: 1835) pp. 498–500.

[2] J. Huizinga, *Le Déclin du Moyen âge* (1932) pp. 73 ff.

[3] Masselin, op. cit. pp. 672 ff.   [4] Ibid. pp. 68–74.

[5] P. Viollet, 'Elections des députés aux Etats généraux réunis à Tours en 1468 et en 1484', in *Bibl. Ec. Chartes*, ser. 6 II (1866) 31 ff.

[6] P. Marchegay, *Arch. d'Anjou*, II (Angers, 1853) 317, 322; H. Bellugou, *Le Roi René et la réforme fiscale dans le duché d'Anjou au milieu du xve siècle* (Angers, 1962).

Limousin were the peasantry admitted to a representative assembly directly.[1] Admittedly peasant insurrection was endemic. 'How many serfs', declaimed a thirteenth-century preacher quoted by Marc Bloch, 'have killed their lords or burned their castles!'[2] But perhaps we should look at their motives for creating the holocaust more closely.

In the mass of peasant insurrection in later medieval France the Jacquerie which broke out on 28 May 1358 in areas to the north and east of Paris[3] stands out as the nearest thing to coherent social protest. The most completely organised group was found in the Compiègne district, with a peasant from Mello, Guillaume Cale, as captain; he was in contact with Etienne Marcel, the leader of the Parisians in their resistance to the regent; and his group was annihilated by Charles *le mauvais* king of Navarre at Mello on 9 June. Although the peasantry continued to support the Parisian bourgeoisie in the field, the peasant movement was over; and the massacre of the Parisians and their supporters before the *Marché*, the fortified suburb-market of Meaux, by Gaston III Fébus comte de Foix and the captal de Buch, who had arrived unexpectedly with a small company, brought the whole episode to a term. But there was a considerable amount of more or less disorganised insurrection in other districts. The most important of these was south-west of Amiens, on the edges of Beauvaisis; a large company of Jacques was massacred by a group of Norman and Picard men-at-arms, whose captain, Guillaume de Picquigny, had been murdered by one of them during a parley near Lignières. A host of peasant rebels could not withstand even a small company of trained soldiers. When the upper classes, against whom the revolt was directed, had had time to gather their wits and their troops, popular protest was easily dealt with. Peasant movements were not, in the later middle ages, serious political things.

In the material concerning the Jacquerie the phrase 'the commotions

---

[1] A. Thomas, *Les Etats provinciaux de la France centrale sous Charles VII*, I (1879) 36. For an assembly composed entirely of peasant *alleutiers* (in Drenthe in the Netherlands), see R. Petit, 'Bulletin bibliographique', in *Anciens Pays et assemblées d'Etats*, II (Louvain, 1951) 100–1.

[2] Op. cit. p. 174.

[3] S. Luce, *Hist. de la Jacquerie*, 2nd ed. (1894); R. Delachenal, *Hist. de Charles V*, I (1909) 394–416; G. Fourquin, *Les Campagnes de la région parisienne à la fin du Moyen âge* (1964) pp. 229–40.

of the non-nobles against the nobles' occurs over and over again.[1] It may well be argued that hatred of the nobility was the prime cause of the revolt:[2] a hatred engendered by the failure of the nobility to do its social duty and protect the people from the miseries of warfare.[3] The authors of the *Complainte sur la bataille de Poitiers*[4] and of the *Tragicum argumentum de miserabili statu regni Francie*[5] both accept what the second, François de Monte-Belluna, described as the popular view that the nobility had failed Jean II at Poitiers — though François de Monte-Belluna thought the people were as much to blame for fleeing the field. In Arcy-Ste.-Restitue, near Soissons, during the Jacquerie the local seigneur decided to flee the village. One of the inhabitants, Robert du Jardin, allegedly tried to persuade him of the villagers' affection for him and complained that there would be no-one to protect them if he went. His seigneur took no notice. 'All right,' said Robert du Jardin, 'we must just let everything go hang, or we must all be masters.' For this unwitting sedition he was hanged by a neighbouring noble.[6] The counter-Jacquerie of the nobility was as terrible as the Jacquerie of the Jacques. The whole affair revealed a moral crisis of lordship, an acute crisis: the same sentiment appeared again, in the Tuchinat in the Midi, in the 1380s, amongst the brigands around Paris after the English invasion in the fifteenth century,[7] amongst the brigands in the mountains of Forez and Lyonnais in the 1420s. In 1422 Humbert de Grolée, *bailli* of Mâcon, examined the 'principal captain' of the brigands, who explained that they had had the intention of destroying all the nobility, then all the priests except for one for each parish, and then all the bourgeois, merchants, lawyers and other notables of the towns.[8] Dislike of the

---

[1] See, for instance, Luce, op. cit. p. 177. Cf. Delachenal, op. cit. p. 395.

[2] Fourquin, op. cit. p. 232.

[3] 'Aucunesfois', wrote Christine de Pisan, 'chieent des murmurations entre les trois estaz... cestassavoir les princes, la chevalerie & le peuple, parcequil semble aux uns que les autres ne facent mie bien leur devoir en leurs offices.' ('Le Livre du corps de policie', British Museum, Harleian MS 4410, fo. 56r.)

[4] ed. C. de Beaurepaire, *Bibl. Ec. Chartes*, ser. 3 II (1851) 260 ff.

[5] ed. A. Vernet, *Annu.-B. Soc. Hist. France* (1962–3) pp. 150–1.

[6] Luce, op. cit. pp. 274–6.

[7] See below, p. 288; Fourquin, op. cit. p. 232 n 50.

[8] L. Caillet, *Etude sur les relations de la commune de Lyon avec Charles VII et Louis XI* (Lyon, 1909) pp. 26, 324–5. Cf. E. Fournial, *Les Villes et l'économie d'échange en Forez aux xiiie et xive siècles* (1967) pp. 472 ff.

nobility can be found in individual cases at other times. In 1420 Pierre Lasnier, 'who was, so it's said, a man riotous and seditious enough', told two squires, Anthoine du Preel and Robert Gontier, 'that they were worthless and not worthy of riding a horse, and that he and other people in the district of the same rank as he was should rise up to attack and kill such men as they were'. A third gentleman, Aubert du Mez, 'told him politely that he shouldn't say such things, which smacked, perhaps, a little of Jacquerie'. Lasnier 'replied most arrogantly' that he wouldn't. 'And then . . . Aubert told him, laughing, that he must be blind drunk and that when he *did* stir up his insurrection he'd willingly be his captain. "Some captain of brigands you'd make", said . . . Anthoine du Preel to . . . Aubert, for fun . . .' But Pierre Lasnier went on insulting Antoine and Robert Gontier, and eventually they lost their tempers and killed him.[1] ' "You gentlemen behave too much like bosses", said the farrier of Signy-l'Abbaye, near Mézières, to Jacquemin Aubry on his way to the wars in 1382, "and believe me, it won't always be so", or words to that effect. The . . . squire replied, in a friendly enough way, "Somebody'll clout you if you go on saying things like that"; and the farrier said, "Where's your mother's son brave enough for that?" And then Jacquemin clouted him'; and eventually, in self-defence, after the farrier, a *conversus* of the abbey, had gone for him with an iron bar, killed him too.[2] But rage against the nobility was never as consistent, never as organised as in the Jacquerie *eo nomine* of 1358.

Rage against the clergy is equally apparent. In 1358 the clergy in Perthois thought they would be held traitors by the Jacques because they regarded favourably and submitted to the nobility of the *pays*.[3] But any connection between simple popular heresy and sedition seems impossible to find; heretics do not seem to have been seditious, and the seditious do not seem to have been heretical. There is no breath of it in the material concerning the Jacquerie, no evidence of it in the Tuchinat in the Midi[4]; though the account of the brigand captain in Lyonnais may be some frail indication of the connection of the two

---

[1] *Choix de pièces inéd. relatives au règne de Charles VI*, ed. L. Douët-d'Arcq (Soc. Hist. France) II (1864) 41–2. A reflection of the tensions between *chevalerie* and *peuple* in the early 1420s may be seen very clearly in Alain Chartier's *Quadrilogue invectif*.

[2] *Choix de pièces*, II 63–4.   [3] Luce, op. cit. p. 270.

[4] *Pace* M. Boudet, *La Jacquerie des Tuchins, 1363–1384* (Riom, 1895) pp. 77 ff.

forms of protest. As difficult to find, in the Jacquerie at least, is real
misery as a prime cause of revolt.[1] The insurrection occurred, not in the
poorest areas around Paris, nor in those hardest hit by war. The revolt,
in one view, was 'against the consequences of the corn crisis of the
beginning of the century': from 1315 the price of corn had fallen in
relation to the price of industrial products; it was the price scissors in
'the rich cornfields' that was a considerable cause of discontent. But
the pillaging around Paris by English, Navarrese and French *routiers*
was clearly the secondary cause of the Jacquerie; and the immediate
cause was perhaps the behaviour of the regent's troops in the areas
engaged in blockading Paris and taking prises in the countryside. As
a result, thought the author of the *Chronique normande*, 'the peasants said
that the knights, who ought to protect them, had agreed to deprive
them of all their goods. And for this reason, the peasants rose up most
marvellously, and attacked the knights and all nobles and even their
own lords.'[2]

In 1358 the failure of the nobility of France in arms at Poitiers two
years earlier gave its particular flavour to the Jacquerie. But peasant disorder was endemic wherever there was military disorder. Its causes were
simple enough. In 1427 Jean de Bonval, tailor of Noyant in Vermandois,
got letters of remission from Henry VI king of France and England

> containing how that in consequence of the wars and divisions . . .
> in our kingdom of France, and of the oppressions done to the
> labourers, of the captures, ransoms, and imprisonments by the
> enemies of our . . . kingdom . . . many good and honest men,
> seeing that everyone had retreated from the countryside and had
> gone to live in the towns or moved to another district, and that
> no-one knew what to do, what to take up, or what to work at to
> gain his living, and that they had no . . . refuge in a fortress or
> place to which they could retire, except to the woods, the rocks,
> the quarries or the caverns, because of the places occupied by
> our . . . enemies — this suppliant, through the pressure and
> urgency of hunger and many other necessities, and in order to
> provide for his livelihood and his poor humanity, applied himself
> to making war upon our enemies, always sticking to our side. . . .

[1] Fourquin, op. cit. pp. 232 ff.
[2] ed. A. and E. Molinier (Soc. Hist. France: 1882) pp. 127–8. Cf. the background to the revolt in the Pays de Caux in 1435 (see above, p. 71).

And because it happened that four years ago or thereabouts the
... suppliant saw that he could get work, he entirely gave up
going to the wars, and set himself to his work and trade, and
nothing else.

But the *prévôt-forain* of Laon persecuted him because of his brigand-like
military activities, and Jean de Bonval had to get his pardon.[1]

Such desperation can be found everywhere the armies ravaged: it
drove a poor labourer of La Villette-St.-Ladre, near St.-Denis, to lose
most of his hair and his wits and slander the king; it drove a butcher
of Sarcelles, near Pontoise, two of whose children had been killed before
his eyes and who was unable, because of pillage, to provide for the
remainder of his family, to suicide.[2] Many men, like Jean de Bonval,
took to the woods or became pillagers themselves out of sheer
necessity. Some may have gone into the *maquis* for patriotic reasons;
but many of those who were executed by Bedford's government in
Normandy as brigands 'were just that and nothing more'.[3] Brigandage
was far too common all over France for the word to be synonymous
with fervent patriotism. Thomas Basin was quite clear about the criminal
elements in the *maquis*.[4] Some of the Tuchins in Haut-Auvergne might,
because they attacked the English, be styled patriots; but it is only too
clear that patriotism was hardly in the minds[5] of the more or less
organised bands which intermittently terrorised Auvergne from 1363 to
1384 and which were also active in Languedoc. And the Tuchins are
only among the best known of the brigands. They were in Nivernais
in 1365, 'a familiar feature in northern France' at least from the turn
of the century, rife around Béziers in 1431.[6] Patriotism is an element
which one need not deny; but it was very far from being the only one.

Social protest, too, was an element one need not deny, in the Tuchins,
in the brigandage around Paris; but again one must not overestimate

[1] *Letters and Papers Illustrative of the Wars of the English in France during the
Reign of Henry the Sixth*, ed. J. Stevenson (Rolls Series) 1 (1861) 23–31.

[2] Fourquin, op. cit. p. 300.

[3] B. J. H. Rowe, 'John Duke of Bedford and the Norman "Brigands" ', in
Engl. hist. R. XLVII (1932) 599.

[4] *Hist. de Charles VII*, ed. C. Samaran, 1 (Classiques de l'hist. de France au
Moyen âge, 15: 1964) 106 ff.

[5] Boudet, op. cit. p. 35.

[6] *Choix de pièces*, 1 (1863) 29–30; Rowe, op. cit. pp. 584–5, 598.

its importance.[1] If people might become 'patriots' because they attacked out of fury a legitimate government apparently unable to protect them from 'eternal misery as long as they lived under . . . [its] domination',[2] so people might become social rebels when it was a matter of singling out those rich enough to rob. Destruction of nobility and clergy and rich bourgeoisie was not only a rallying cry for the oppressed poor; it was an invitation to assist in seeking out the richest opportunities for pillage.

How many villagers, like Robert du Jardin in Arcy-Ste.-Restitue, in fact might have been alleged to have had even some affection for their seigneur? How many accused their lords, not for mere existence, but for failing in the duty for which they existed? It would, it may be argued, be anachronistic to assume, except perhaps in a number of exceptional cases, that the secret aim of the 'non-nobles' was to do away with all nobility. This, it may be argued, was not the way in which the mind of the *menu peuple*, in the town or in the country, worked in the later middle ages. The revolutionary mentality was not, perhaps, the mentality of the workman in the workshop, or the labourer in the fields, in the fourteenth and fifteenth centuries in France. Few, if any, seem to have pursued the millennium.[3] More significant ultimately, perhaps, than the rather crazy attitude of the renegade nephew of Hugue Aubert, bishop of Albi, Pierre de Brugère, captain of the Tuchin army in 1384, who, according to the annalist of Mauriac, had set 'all the *pays*, Haute- and Basse-Auvergne . . . against the gentlemen and churchmen of the *pays*, no-one knew why', was the conformist, legalistic attitude of the 'inhabitants' and 'poor labourers' of the *châtellenie* of Craon about the same time; an attitude they shared with even serfs in Nivernais in the fifteenth century.[4]

This is not to scorn, as so many people in the later middle ages

[1] Cf. Boudet, op. cit. pp. 80 ff. [2] Basin, op. cit. p. 206.
[3] N. Cohn, *The Pursuit of the Millennium* (1962) p. 236 (ultimately from *Sacrorum conciliorum . . . amplissima collectio*, ed. J.D. Mansi, xxix (Venice, 1788) col. 402). The groups mentioned by the French clergy may be those referred to above, pp. 19, 284.
[4] Boudet, op. cit. pp. 68–76; A. Bossuat, 'Le Servage en Nivernais au xve siècle', in *Bibl. Ec. Chartes*, cxvii (1959) 113 ff. For the same attitude in Bordelais, see Boutruche, op. cit. pp. 321 ff. This is not, of course, to argue that the serfs did not wish to escape from the condition of serfdom.

scorned, the *menu peuple* in their distress. That distress intermittently could be very great; and, if there was a redistribution of wealth in favour of the lower classes in the later middle ages — and the result of the Black Death in a number of meridional towns, if not elsewhere, was to raise the lowest urban class out of its extreme of misery[1]— that redistribution was in France perhaps more delayed than in England,[2] and may well have been less. But this is a dangerous subject. It is perhaps enough to attempt to convey an absolute sympathy with the *menu peuple* in their tribulations — a sympathy clearly felt by Christine de Pisan[3] and by Jean Juvenal des Ursins — together with the doubts expressed about both the motives of the peasantry in apparent revolt and the efficacy of direct action in a haphazard way against powers capable, after the first shock had passed, of suppressing revolt with insolent ease.

IV. CHURCHMEN

Within the fringe of 'clerks' far from clerkly lay the mass of religious living 'clergily'. Its size has not been estimated, though such an estimate might be attempted.[4] Its principal cadres — as far as the secular clergy at least were concerned — were the archdiocese and the diocese. The number of these varied, in the period after 1317, primarily with variations in the boundaries of the kingdom. The northern archdioceses were Reims, with eleven suffragans, Rouen with six, and Sens

[1] G. Prat, 'Albi et la Peste noire', in *A. Midi*, LXIV (1952) 15–26; P. Wolff, 'Trois Etudes de démographie médiévale en France méridionale', in *Studi . . . A. Sapori*, I (Milan, 1957) 493–503.

[2] E. Perroy, 'Wage Labour in France in the Later Middle Ages', in *Econ. Hist. R.* ser. 2 VIII (1955–6) 232– . (cf. E. H. Phelps Brown and S. V. Hopkins, 'Wage-rates and Prices: Evidence for Population Pressure in the Sixteenth Century', in *Economica*, NS XXIV (1957) 289–305). For early examples of 'seigneurial reaction', see Boutruche, op. cit. pp. 338–9; L. Musset, 'Y-Eut-Il Une Reaction seigneuriale dans le nord du Cotentin sous l'occupation anglaise ?', in *A. Normandie*, XIII (1963) 205–6.

[3] See, for instance, 'Le Livre du corps de policie', British Museum, Harleian MS 4410, folios 11^{r-v}, 65^r ff.

[4] B. Guillemain, 'Chiffres et statistiques pour l'hist. ecclés. du Moyen âge', in *Moyen Age*, LIX (1953) 346–7.

with seven. In the west were the archdioceses of Tours, with eleven suffragans, Bordeaux with nine, and Auch with ten. The central archdiocese of Bourges had ten suffragans; the bishopric of Le Puy, in its territory, depended immediately upon the Holy See. In the south the archdiocese of Toulouse possessed seven suffragans, and the archdiocese of Narbonne (after the occupation of Roussillon in 1463) ten. On the eastern frontier were the archdioceses of Lyon, with four suffragans, and Vienne, with (after the cession of Valentinois-Diois by 1434) three. The three Provençal archdioceses of Arles, Aix and Embrun were added to the list in 1481.

The size of the diocese naturally varied; a bishopric like Agde, perched uncomfortably upon the Mediterranean, was not to be compared with one of the greater northern bishoprics. But *mutatis mutandis* the composition of the medieval dioceses followed the same pattern. The territory of each contained benefices both secular and regular. A benefice represented both spiritual duty and material reward: it was a sacred function and a source of revenue, bestowed by ecclesiastical authority upon its possessor for life.[1] Bishoprics and abbacies, places — dignities and prebends — in cathedral and collegiate churches, chaplainries, offices in monasteries, the incumbency of priories and parish churches were all comprehended under the term 'benefice'. A rough estimate of the number of these in any particular diocese may be derived from the surviving *pouillés*, the inventories established for the purposes of ecclesiastical taxation 'taken', as was that of the diocese of Langres somewhere around 1436, 'from old and authentic books and registers' of the bishop,[2] and from surviving accounts for that taxation. The parochial benefices of Langres in the mid-fifteenth century, for instance, numbered some 600, grouped under 17 deaneries, in turn grouped under 6 archdeaconries.[3] The diocese of Laon had, about the same time, some 350 parishes divided under 11 deaneries and 2 archdeaconries; and it included, according to its *pouillé*, some 200 prebends and 275 chaplainries.[4] This information is lacking on the Langres

---

[1] *Dict. d'hist. et de géog. ecclés.* VII (1934) col. 1238.

[2] *Pouillés de la province de Lyon*, ed. A. Longnon (Rec. des historiens de la France, Pouillés, 1: 1904) p. 145.

[3] Ibid. pp. 145–62.

[4] *Pouillés de la province de Reims*, ed. A. Longnon (Rec. des historiens de la France, Pouillés, 6: 1908) pp. 680–708.

pouillé; but the diocese possessed in the fifteenth century, as well as its cathedral chapter, some 18 collegiate churches and several communities of chaplains. Regular houses in Langres included 11 Benedictine abbeys (7 of men and 4 of women), 1 Cluniac abbey, 14 Cistercian abbeys (11 of men and 3 of women) and 4 communities of canons regular. The diocese had well over a hundred priories and a considerable number of Hospitaller establishments; and the friars, Dominican, Franciscan, Carmelite, Trinitarian and Minim, had founded between them 12 houses in it.[1]

The organisation of the secular clergy was in principle clearly hierarchical. Some archbishops had a claim to primacies, primacies which the increase in the number of degrees of appellate jurisdiction provided for by the Pragmatic Sanction of Bourges in 1438 — with which we will deal later — should have strengthened. But the primate of Lyon could not subdue the archbishops of Tours, Rouen and Sens, nor the primate of Bourges the archbishop of Bordeaux.[2] Metropolitans fared perhaps better *vis-à-vis* their suffragans; but still, as we shall see, their control, both in the question of appointments to benefices and in jurisdiction, was more or less radically weakened.[3] And within the diocese itself the bishop was faced with further conflict: with his chapter,[4] with his archdeacons,[5] with those that had any claim to be exempt from him.[6] The organisation of the regular clergy, centralised upon their orders, cut across the diocesan organisation; and the regular houses were persistent in their resistance to bishops. And conflict

[1] J. Laurent and F. Claudon, *Abbayes et prieurés de l'ancienne France*, XII *Province ecclés. de Lyon*, III *Diocèses de Langres et de Dijon* (Arch. France monastique, 45: 1941).

[2] N. Valois, *Hist. de la Pragmatique Sanction de Bourges sous Charles VII* (1906) p. cxxiii.

[3] F. Lot and R. Fawtier, *Hist. des institutions françaises au Moyen âge*, iii *Institutions ecclés.* (1962) 339–40.

[4] See, for instance, ibid. pp. 342 ff; P. Imbart de La Tour, *Les Origines de la Réforme*, 2nd ed. II (Melun, 1946) 193–5. For an example of a bishop on the other hand on good terms with his canons, see A. Bossuat, 'Jacques de Comborn, évêque de Clermont, et son secrétaire. Notes sur l'humanisme en Auvergne au xve siècle', in *Rec. . . . Clovis Brunel*, I (1955) 153.

[5] See, for instance, G. Mollat, 'Conflits entre archidiacres et évêques aux xive et xve siècles', in *R. hist. Droit*, ser. 4 XXXV (1957) 549–60; Imbart, op. cit. pp. 195–6; Lot and Fawtier, op. cit. pp. 352–5.

[6] Ibid. pp. 362 ff.

within the diocese was not limited to quarrels of religious with their bishop: the religious could quarrel amongst themselves as happily. From within the Church itself, from the conflict of interest of its members, arose the pressures which conditioned its political behaviour; and since its members could have recourse not only to their own superiors, but also directly to the Holy See or to the king's courts — or the king's court — the game was considerably quickened.

Motives and means

What were those interests? The question is impossible to answer with anything like statistical precision. We know too little about that vast army of later medieval French churchmen; the individuals about whom we may be reasonably certain may be bad representatives of their fellows. We cannot be sure of very much; less sure, perhaps, than were the later medieval critics of the French Church of their contemporaries. Why did men enter the Church? 'Anyone nowadays who is lazy, anyone who shrinks from work, anyone who wishes to luxuriate in leisure hastens into the priesthood', thought Nicolas de Clamanges at the beginning of the fifteenth century.[1] That men entered the Church in order to serve God was not, in the opinion of the later medieval reformers, a popular later medieval view. Men were in the Church for what they could get out of it. 'Not a single word nowadays', wrote Clamanges, 'when people assume the pastoral burden and take upon themselves the cure of souls, of the divine service, of the salvation and edification of their subjects; all they ask about is the size of the revenue . . .'[2] 'Where can one find nowadays', asked Gerson about the same time, 'a bishop who hasn't moved to that noble from an ignoble station out of ambition or avarice?'[3] But Clamanges was at least prepared to accept that there were exceptions to those whose regular sins he catalogued.

> I do not wish, however [he wrote], that anyone should think from what has been said about the vices of clerics, that I should wish

[1] Le Traité de la ruine de l'église et la traduction française de 1564, ed. A. Coville (1936) p. 131.
[2] Ibid. p. 115.   [3] Gersonii opera, ed. E. du Pin, II (Antwerp, 1706) col. 315.

all ecclesiastics utterly to be included in their number without exception ... For I am not unmindful that in particular stations there are some, even many, good, just and innocent men, stranger to those crimes that have been rehearsed ... Far be it from me to wish to brand many men preferred to title in the Church, whom to name particularly would achieve nothing, and whom I believe unaffected by crimes of this kind, along with those whose imperfections I have demonstrated. But so great is the abundance of the wicked in each profession, that scarcely one in a thousand will be found who performs sincerely what his profession demands of him. And so, because of the overwhelming amount of wickedness, the good men should not be mentioned who, in the whole mass of churchmen, are excessively few in number and importance ...[1]

To the cataloguer of the sinners, the virtuous were uninteresting.

This habit of mind will return to dog us. But it is clear that for those who sought anything like a normal life in the Church the Church was a career like any other. Even the reformers accepted promotion. And the Church, as a whole, like the civil services which drew a considerable number of their members from it, could offer a career to the sons of men of all groups in society. The sons of the upper nobility could do well in it, like the two fifteenth-century cardinals of Foix. The sons of the minor nobility could do well in it, like the Limousin Pierre Roger, who became pope Clement VI, or Guillaume de Grimoard, son of the seigneur de Grisac in Gévaudan, who became pope Urban V. The sons of the bourgeoisie could do well in it, like Etienne Aubert, son of a bourgeois of the village of Les Monts, in Beyssac parish in Limousin, who became pope Innocent VI,[2] or Pierre d'Ailly, son of a bourgeois of Compiègne, who became cardinal of Cambrai. The sons of the peasantry could do well in it,[3] like Jean Charlier, called Gerson from his native village in Champagne, who became chancellor of the university of Paris. Even the sons of the clergy, albeit illegitimate, could do well in it, like Jean de Lescun-Armagnac, one of the bastards of Arnaud-

[1] Op. cit. pp. 144–5.

[2] R. Limouzin-Lamothe, *Le Diocèse de Limoges des origines à la fin du Moyen âge* (1951) pp. 137–41.

[3] At least in the fourteenth century (E. Delaruelle *et al.*, *L'Eglise au temps du Grand schisme et de la crise conciliaire* (Hist. de l'Eglise fondée par A. Fliche et V. Martin, 14: 1962–4) pp. 327–8).

Guillaume de Lescun, bishop of Aire, who became archbishop of Auch in the mid-fifteenth century.[1]

But to assess the relative importance of the members of each group in the recruitment of the clergy as a whole is a far more difficult matter. Even of so relatively small a section of the Church as the later medieval French episcopate an over-all analysis is at the moment impracticable; we know too little about the men. And in the same way it is impossible to assess the relative importance of the different patterns of success within the Church; the information has not been collated. The critics of the Church naturally took a gloomy view of its members' techniques of securing promotion. 'No-one', thought Clamanges, 'accedes to the clericature or to holy orders or to any ecclesiastical rank except by paying for it.'

> No learned men [he wrote], and by learned I mean learned in holy writ, no upright men, no just men, no virtuous men, who are not in the habit of frequenting courts, arrive at the supreme heights of dignities, but ambitious men, fawning men, hypocritical men, men saturated in every vice, such as we see frequent the halls of princes. . . . Pontificates are held either by ignorant and illiterate men or by men who, if they are lettered, are lettered only in the temporal rules of civil law, which are forbidden study to priests; and they pursue the lucrative sorts of knowledge, thinking absolutely nothing of divine law or of spiritual erudition, by which the people is instructed.[2]

Expertise in the 'lucrative sorts of knowledge' and patronage — apart from simony — were thus in Clamanges' view the keys to a prelacy. A university training — especially in civil or indeed in canon law — and pull were the means of success. 'Now the study of holy eloquence

---

[1] R. Génestal, *Le Privilegium Fori en France du décret de Gratien à la fin du xive siècle*, I (Bibl. Ec. Hautes Etudes, Sci. religieuses, 35: 1921) 8–9; J. de Jaurgain, *Deux Comtes de Comminges béarnais au xve siècle. Jean de Lescun bâtard d'Armagnac et Odet d'Aydie seigneur de Lescun* (1919) pp. 27–30. Marriage was, of course, licit for clerks below the grade of sub-deacon; and one should not overestimate the uncontrolled lusts of those above it (Adam, op. cit. pp. 151–63; cf. J. Epinat, 'La Situation religieuse dans le diocèse de Lyon d'après la visite pastorale de J. de Talaru, 1378–1379', in *Cah. Hist.* VI (1961) 228 ff; V. Chomel, 'Notes sur l'activité disciplinaire des officialités du diocèse de Grenoble (1418–1449)', in *Etudes . . . N. Didier* (1960) pp. 52 ff).

[2] Op. cit. pp. 130, 127.

and its professors suffer the laughter and derision of all.'[1] Given that the Church was no longer in its primitive state of pristine and immaterial innocence — and it was essentially the loss of this innocence that Clamanges bewailed — the mockery of the saintly was perhaps not unjustified. 'Utterly unsuitable and unworthy of priesthood', clamoured his *bêtes-noires*, the clergy learned in the law, 'is the man who, ignorant of earthly law, is not qualified to defend his rights, doesn't know how by canonical censures to rule, mulct and coerce his subjects, and has learned nothing except to exert himself in slothful repose or sermonising, which is clearly now the job of the mendicants . . .'[2]. Given that the modern bishopric was a complex of temporal and judicial rights, as well as a cure of souls, there was much to be said for their view. The age of the saints could not be recalled.

It is impossible at the moment to demonstrate in any quantitative way the importance of the lawyers in the Church. But example after example can be given of lawyers successful in the Church. Jean Juvenal des Ursins was a lawyer; Jacques Jouvenel des Ursins was a lawyer. In the diocese of Limoges — not a particularly attractive one from the point of view of revenue — lawyer bishops preponderated in the fourteenth and fifteenth centuries.[3] At the university of Toulouse — the second most notable of the French universities for civil law in the later fourteenth century[4] — the largest number of Limousin clerks, graduates or undergraduates, in 1378 were reading canon law; the next largest grammar; the next largest civil law; the artists came fourth.[5] When, at the age of twelve, the infant Thomas Basin's 'disposition inclined towards the acquisition of letters', his Norman bourgeois parents, 'not wishing to divert or impair our desire in this', sent him to the university of Paris; and later they sent him to Louvain and Pavia for civil law and back to Louvain for canon law.[6] They had set him upon one of the safest tracks to preferment in the later medieval Church.

But if the universities provided the individual with his qualifications,

---

[1] Ibid. p. 128.   [2] Ibid.   [3] Limouzin-Lamothe, op. cit. pp. 137–54.

[4] H. Rashdall, *The Universities of Europe in the Middle Ages*, ed. F. M. Powicke and A. B. Emden, II (Oxford, 1936) 168.

[5] R. Fage, 'Les Etudiants limousins à l'université de Toulouse en 1378', in *B. Soc. archéol. hist. Limousin*, LXX (1923) 148–56.

[6] *Hist. des règnes de Charles VII et de Louis XI*, ed. J. Quicherat (Soc. Hist. France) IV (1859) 13–14.

they also, as concentrations of qualified men ambitious for promotion, provided the Church with pressure-groups eager to assert the interests of their members. The graduates had to be got jobs.

> It is expedient [wrote Pierre d'Ailly in his *Tractatus de reformatione seu canones reformandi Ecclesiam* in 1416] that the ordinaries, who can and should have a good appreciation of the worthy persons in their localities, should confer benefices [upon them] according to their merit; that their collation should not be taken away from them wholly, at least as long, however, as the power of the ordinaries is limited to lessen their abuses. For example, they should not be able to confer dignities and major benefices, except upon doctors in theology or in law, whenever there are any such men in their own or neighbouring dioceses; and they should not be able to confer cure of souls, or parsonages, or other benefices of 100 *livres* income or over, except upon graduates, or noblemen, or others who well deserve them. And the same with many like provisions; by which the worthy may be promoted, and many nobles and talented men provoked to the study of letters, and the universities may flourish, and, what is much to be desired, the importunate and vehement petitions of temporal lords for unworthy men may cease. That they are today most dangerous, experience teaches.[1]

The attempt to create in the name of Reform a vested interest for graduates in the more lucrative benefices was not wholly unsuccessful and perhaps not wholly unlaudable. But though the interests of the ordinary collators — primarily, in France in the later middle ages, bishops and religious houses — waned, the interests of the lords of this world did not; neither did the interests of that principal target of all reformers, the pope.

For how did one get a benefice in the later middle ages? One might still apply to an ordinary collator; but one was, as we shall see, far more likely to apply to the Holy See. And the Curia might be approached directly;[2] or via a powerful patron. 'If a bishop dies,' wrote Clamanges, 'or a dean, or a prior or some other ecclesiastical personage, whoever, seeking to be appointed to the place of the defunct, does not go first to

---

[1] *Gersonii opera*, II, col. 913.

[2] See, for instance, C. Tihon, 'Les Expectatives in forma pauperum particulièrement au xive siècle', in *B. Inst. hist. belge Rome*, v (1925) 51–118 (but cf. E. F. Jacob, *Essays in the Conciliar Epoch* (Manchester, 1953) p. 225).

the king rather than the pope; indeed, who is crazy enough to approach the pope as a petitioner without royal letters?'[1] The king had his own interests to serve; but with the problem of patronage from his point of view we will deal later. From the point of view of the ambitious clerk it was a question of securing the favour of the king or of a magnate lay or ecclesiastical;[2] and one of the ways of securing his favour was to enter his service: to rise, as Clamanges put it, 'from the service of secular powers ... by importunate petitions'.[3] As a lawyer one did well in this world too. Take, for instance, the career of Jacques Jouvenel des Ursins.[4] By July 1437, at the age of twenty-six, he was counsellor and advocate of the king in the Parlement of Paris. In 1441 he got his first benefice, the archdeaconry of Paris. In 1443 he became *trésorier* of the Ste.-Chapelle; in July 1444 a king's councillor; in September 1444 archbishop of Reims; and in January 1445 *président-clerc* in the *Chambre des comptes*.[5] In the later 1440s he was active in diplomatic negotiations. In 1449 Reims went to his brother Jean in a complicated reshuffle of prelacies; Jacques received the bishopric of Poitiers and was compensated with the title of patriarch of Antioch and with the privilege of retaining his pallium; and in the autumn of 1449 he added the bishopric of Fréjus in plurality with Poitiers. Fréjus he soon exchanged for the priory of St.-Martin-des-Champs in Paris; but financially he had probably not lost very much on the original transaction.[6] After 1453 he may have faded out of major politics; but he remained president in the *Chambre des comptes* until his death in 1457, at the age of forty-six. Compared with his brothers Jean and Guillaume (who remained a layman and became chancellor of France) he died young; but in his twenty-odd years' career as a royal servant his rewards matched theirs. And those rewards, like his brother Jean's, were the rewards of the Church.

[1] Op. cit. p. 126.

[2] Universities and bodies like the Parlement of Paris could, of course, submit their own rolls of petitions.

[3] Op. cit. p. 124.

[4] J. Salvini, 'Un Evêque de Poitiers: Jacques Jouvenel des Ursins (1410–1457)', in *B. Soc. Antiq. Ouest*, ser. 4 VI (1961) 85–107.

[5] Bibl. nat. MS fr. 7706, fo. 258ʳ.

[6] In 1449 Reims was taxed at 1/2 × 4000 fl., Poitiers at 1/2 × 2800 and Fréjus at 1400 (H. Hoberg, *Taxae pro communibus servitiis ex libris obligationum ab anno 1295 usque ad annum 1455 confectis* (Studi e testi, 144: Vatican, 1949) pp. 55, 95, 101).

It was little wonder that those who had for whatever reason laboured more assiduously in the vineyard howled to see the vintage delivered to the unworthy; and to the unworthy who still neglected to labour in it. The civil services of king and magnates still beckoned those who had risen through them in the Church.[1] 'Is it not so', asked Gerson with some hyperbole, 'that bishops today, and abbots, and monks, are the officials more of the fisc than of Christ, struggling tooth and claw in the world in the courts of princes, and of secular jurisdictions, or of the Parlement?'[2] 'Mercenaries,' cried Clamanges, pointing out quite accurately that the service that they actually did was to the king, who paid them less, rather than to the Church, which paid them more.[3] But ecclesiastical civil servants from the rank of cardinal downwards had the same attitude towards the benefices upon which they lived. For the emphasis, in the minds of most churchmen in the later middle ages, was far more upon the benefice, the property, than upon the office for the performance of which it was in principle the reward. Though popes might complain of the execrable ambition, greed, wicked explanations and pernicious subtlety of their petitioners, there was little they did — or perhaps could do — about them.[4] The accumulation of benefices — plurality — and the failure to perform an office in person — non-residence — remained characteristic of the period.

Benefices, income and taxation

The pressure of petitioners upon the pope was very considerable.

> It might be utterly unbelievable [wrote Clamanges] how rudely, how mightily, how with hand, if I may so term it, sword-bearing, the lords of the world, under the pressure of their men, beset the pope with daily letters, if it were not, made public by continuous use, a certainty. The matter is dealt with in communications

[1] See, for instance, P. Gras, 'Un Siège épiscopal au temps des papes d'Avignon et du Grand schisme d'Occident. Les Evêques de Chalon de 1302 à 1416. Leurs Origines, leurs modes de nomination', in *M. Soc. Droit Pays bourguignons*, xv (1953) 7–50.

[2] Op. cit. col. 316. Cf. (for 1445) Valois, op. cit. p. 153.

[3] Op. cit. pp. 133–4.

[4] G. Barraclough, *Papal Provisions* (Oxford, 1935) p. 73.

containing instructions and threats rather than commendations and petitions; and if the popes refuse to conform with them and confer the benefice upon someone other than the person for whom they petition, it is certain they won't accept him.[1]

But it was not only the lords of the world who put pressure on the pope; the lords of the Church could be as assiduous upon their own or their clients' behalf; and the lesser petitioners themselves were innumerable.[2] For though ordinary collators or electors might still have some control over benefices, and though the king of France had a considerable right of collation *pleno jure*, it was inevitably to the pope, in the period before the liberties of the Gallican Church were seized upon by those interested in wresting away from him some part of his control over the distribution of benefices, that one had ultimately, directly or indirectly, to turn if one sought advancement in the Church.

For that control had been considerably increased during the period of the papal residence at Avignon. But the practice of papal provision to benefices and of papal reservation of benefices to the pope's provision preceded the fourteenth century. Papal interference in appointments to benefices developed naturally with the development of the medieval Church; it was, indeed, forced upon the papacy by the importunity of petitioners.[3] There was much, as Gerson pointed out, to be said for a system of central, rather than of local, collation; but there was also much, as Gerson also pointed out, to be said against it.[4] Essentially it was a question of use and abuse; both forms had their uses, both their abuses. But if they coincided with their interests, those affected by papal provisions appreciated their virtues; if they diverged from those interests they condemned their vices. The curious ambivalence with which powers lay and ecclesiastical appeared to regard the question of provisions is resolved by an understanding of this dichotomy; what suited their interests was overlooked, what contradicted them was condemned.

From the practice of provision developed others: of giving 'expectatives', provisions in anticipation to a benefice not yet vacant, above all to 'poor' clerks; of giving benefices 'in commendation', to hold

[1] Op. cit. p. 126.   [2] Barraclough, op. cit. pp. 31, 105–6.   [3] Ibid. pp. 153 ff.
[4] *Gersonii opera*, ed. E. du Pin, II (Antwerp, 1706) cols 63–4.

legitimately with one's titular benefice, above all to the magnates of the church.[1] From before the mid-thirteenth century the practice automatically of reserving certain benefices to papal collation had developed: those which became vacant in the Curia, those which devolved upon the pope through some misdemeanour of their holder.[2] The categories of 'general' reservations grew broader as the fourteenth century went on; and they, and the instances of 'special' reservations, reached their greatest extension under the last popes of Avignon.[3] It was over such practices and over the whole question of papal provision that, in so far as it concerned the question of appointment to benefices and of the dues taken by those who appointed to them, that curiously unreal battle for the liberties of the Gallican Church was to be fought.

For Nicolas de Clamanges, its control of benefices was one of the principal sins of the central government of the Church.[4] But we should perhaps beware of overestimating its efficiency. Of a total of 196 provisions made by Clement VII between October 1387 and October 1392 in those parts of the dioceses of Cambrai, Tournai and Thérouanne under his obedience, only 88 were clearly effective; 11 more may have been; 97 were clearly valueless. In some cases the beneficiary of a provision no longer wanted the benefice; in some the ordinary had already collated; in some there was a fault in the details of the provision; in some the church was abandoned because of the war. In a number of cases the provision was ineffective because of the conflict between competitors for the same benefice.[5] For a provision or an expectative gave its recipient only a claim to the living he sought; a claim that might be contested by an ordinary collatee or by an alternative papal provisor. A provision was in some sense an *ex parte* statement in an inevitable

[1] G. Mollat, *La Collation des bénéfices ecclés. sous les papes d'Avignon* (1921) pp. 69 ff, 79 ff; C. Tihon, 'Les Expectatives in forma pauperum particulièrement au xive siècle', in *B. Inst. hist. belge Rome*, v (1925) 51–118.

[2] Mollat, *La Collation des bénéfices*, pp. 21 ff, 149 ff.

[3] *Dict. d'hist. et de géog. ecclés.* VII (1934) col. 1266. For detailed evidence upon the extent of papal intervention in France in the years 1334–42, see B. Guillemain, *La Politique bénéficiale du pape Benoît XII* (Bibl. Ec. Hautes Etudes, 199: 1952) pp. 35–74.

[4] Op. cit. pp. 117 ff.

[5] F. Baix, 'De La Valeur historique des actes pontificaux de collation des bénéfices', in *Hommage à dom U. Berlière* (Brussels, 1931) pp. 57–66.

lawsuit to decide the proper holder of the benefice.[1] The system may
have given full play to the rights of the various parties;[2] but it also gave
full play to conflict at law and even to more open conflict by the *voie de
fait*.[3] 'There are indeed very few', thought Clamanges, 'by whatever
title they may claim, who may obtain their benefice without a counter-
claimant and a lawsuit'; and in his eyes the complication and expense of
litigation at the Curia made up another major sin of papal government.[4]

Having secured their benefices, how well did the clergy do out of
them? If Clamanges was to be believed, prelates exhibited considerable
agitation about their income: 'they quarrel for it, they struggle, they
brawl, they litigate, they'd much rather put up with the loss of ten
thousand souls than with the loss of ten or a dozen *sous*'.[5] Such agitation
was perhaps not the product merely of illimitable clerical avarice. As
land-owners the clergy had suffered along with the laity from the
economic difficulties of the later middle ages; that churches were
desolate was the constant plea of those who hoped to get off papal
taxation. It would be otiose to dwell over-long upon an interminable
catalogue of misery; but it might well be considered that the alleged
rapacity of later medieval churchmen was a function of economic
depression.[6] Yet perhaps one should avoid — as in the case of lay
magnates — under-much blaming of the clergy on this account.
Accused by Clamanges of accumulating clerical and lay office, his
prelates were prompt with their answer: 'although what they get from
the Church is more than what they get from the ruler, still the lesser

---

[1] Barraclough, op. cit. p. 97.   [2] Ibid. pp. 97–8.

[3] See, for instance, N. Valois, *Hist. de la Pragmatique Sanction de Bourges sous
Charles VII* (1906) p. xlix. But one is warned against overestimating the
number of such cases (E. Delaruelle *et al.*, *L'Eglise au temps du Grand schisme
et de la crise conciliaire* (Hist. de l'Eglise fondée par A. Fliche et V. Martin,
14: 1962–4) p. 364).

[4] Op. cit. p. 121.   [5] Ibid. p. 127.

[6] See, for instance, H. S. Denifle, *La Désolation des églises, monastères et
hôpitaux en France pendant la guerre de Cent ans* (1897–9); R. Boutruche, *La Crise
d'une société. Seigneurs et paysans du Bordelais pendant la guerre de Cent ans* (1947)
especially pp. 249–64; G. Fourquin, *Les Campagnes de la région parisienne à la fin
du Moyen âge* (1964); A. d'Haenens, *L'Abbaye St.-Martin de Tournai de 1290 à
1350. Origines, évolution et dénouement d'une crise* (Louvain, 1961); J. Favier, *Les
Finances pontificales à l'époque du Grand schisme d'Occident, 1378–1409* (Bibl. Ec.
fr. Athènes Rome, 211: 1966) pp. 385 ff.

added to the greater produces a larger sum, and two good things are better than one'.[1] Extra income was attractive at any time.

A very considerable variation existed between the richer of the major benefices and the poorer. In 1471 the archbishopric of Rouen was taxed at 12,000 florins, the bishoprics of Langres and Narbonne at 9000; the bishopric of Dax was taxed at 500 florins, the bishopric of Le Puy at 300 and the bishopric of Bayonne at 100. The abbey of Cluny paid 9000 florins, the abbeys of St.-Germain-des-Prés and Fécamp 8000; the abbey of St.-Savin paid 150 florins, the abbey of St.-Allyre de Clermont 100, the abbey of Ressons 73⅓.[2] But however great — or however small — that income did not remain wholly to the holder of the benefice. He had not only to meet his ordinary expenses, not only (if he were a prelate) to meet the expenses of an allegedly luxurious way of life;[3] the taxation of his superiors might deprive him of a considerable part of his income.

First there might be the dues a clerk paid on receiving his living.[4] The holders of the major benefices — patriarchs, archbishops, bishops and abbots — if they had a revenue of over a hundred florins a year and if they had been appointed or confirmed by the pope, might pay in 'common' and 'petty services' and in other minor fees a sum which could amount to about half their annual income. The holders of other benefices subject to papal reservation, and later those subject to papal confirmation, with a revenue of over six marks a year, might pay again in 'annates' a part of their first year's income. Then there might be the taxes a clerk paid during his tenure of his benefice.[5] In principle he was

[1] Op. cit. p. 134.

[2] P. Ourliac, 'Le Concordat de 1472. Etude sur les rapports de Louis XI et de Sixte IV (1er article)', in R. hist. Droit, ser. 4 xxi (1942) 196–8 (cf. the figures given by Hoberg, op. cit.). For the difficulties in assessing their real incomes, see J. Favier, 'Temporels ecclés. et taxation fiscale: le poids de la fiscalité pontificale au xive siècle', in J. Savants (1964) pp. 106 ff.

[3] Gersonii opera, II, col. 635.

[4] C. Samaran and G. Mollat, La Fiscalité pontificale en France au xive siècle (Bibl. Ec. fr. Athènes Rome, 96: 1905) pp. 23–34; W.E. Lunt, Papal Revenues in the Middle Ages, I (Columbia, 1934) 81–91, 93–9; A. Clergeac, La Curie et les bénéficiers consistoriaux. Etude sur les communs et menus services, 1300–1600 (1911); Favier, 'Temporels ecclés.' pp. 102–27; Favier, Les Finances pontificales, pp. 205–8, 341–96.

[5] Samaran and Mollat, op. cit. pp. 56–60, 12–22, 11; Lunt, op. cit. pp. 77–81, 71–7, 91–3; Favier, 'Temporels ecclés.'; Favier, Les Finances pontificales, pp. 208–17, 221–32.

exempt from lay taxation. But a lay ruler might with papal permission take a 'charitable subsidy' — of the kind taken by the pope himself; and part — or indeed the whole — of the more regular papal tax of a 'tenth' of a clerk's annual income might also find its way into a royal treasury. If the clerk were a prelate, he might, if he were unlucky, have to pay a 'visitation tax' on some of his stipulated visits to the Curia. If he were an inferior clerk he might have to contribute to some more or less irregular taxation instituted by his diocesan; and he might have to pay the 'procuration' tax due to the visitor of his benefice.[1] And finally, after his death, a clerk's personal property might be seized as 'spoils' by the pope or by the clerk's bishop.[2] But of this, at least, he himself would be unaware.

The question of taxation, like that of the provision to benefices, was hard fought over in the years following the Schism. The conduct of the papacy in this also was bitterly attacked. The extension during the fourteenth century of papal reservation naturally extended the number of cases in which services or annates could be taken; for a critic like Nicolas de Clamanges the aim of the practice of reservation was that income itself.[3] Subsidies had increased, tenths were taken regularly. The papacy acquired a considerable interest in procurations.[4] From early in the century, increasingly from the middle of it, prelates composed with 'voluntary gifts' of a part of their procurations for papal permission not to visit in person; and from the pontificate of Urban V (1362–70) the papacy developed the practice of reserving part, and in some cases the whole, of procurations to itself, even if the visitor in fact made his visitations. Prelates complained bitterly of this blow to ecclesiastical discipline; 'I do not know', wrote Clamanges in a much-quoted lament, 'a greater wound the Church has sustained.'[5] The papal right of spoils, too, was extended in the fourteenth century from special cases to general

---

[1] F. Lot and R. Fawtier, *Hist. des institutions françaises au Moyen âge*, III *Institutions ecclés.* (1962) 378–9; P. Imbart de la Tour, *Les Origines de la Réforme*, 2nd ed. II (Melun, 1946) 244 ff; Favier, 'Temporels ecclés.'

[2] Samaran and Mollat, op. cit. pp. 47–55; Lunt, op. cit. pp. 103–7; Favier, 'Temporels ecclés.'; Favier, *Les Finances pontificales*, pp. 250–91.

[3] Op. cit. p. 118.

[4] Samaran and Mollat, op. cit. pp. 35–47; Lunt, op. cit. pp. 107–11; Favier, 'Temporels ecclés.'; Favier, *Les Finances pontificales*, pp. 217–21.

[5] Op. cit. p. 120.

ones, again in the wake of extended reservation; and again in the face of complaint and resistance, and of slanders such as that upon the papal collector who 'had a priest stripped who was lying dead in the church waiting to be buried, dressed in a chasuble, saying that the chasuble was [perfectly] good, and took it off him. Such a thing had never been seen in France.'[1] The general oppressions of the collectors were bewailed;[2] and some seem to have deserved their reputation.[3] But despite their fulminating excommunication and ecclesiastical censure, resistance against them seems, with some help from royal officers, to have stiffened towards the end of the century.[4]

And within the diocese there was resistance against episcopal taxation from those who claimed themselves exempt from it or who claimed themselves unable to pay. Here it was the diocesan that suffered. Like other members of the clergy he looked around for new sources of income or for ways of increasing old ones — or at least of preserving them. The fiscal aspect of episcopal jurisdiction, indeed of all ecclesiastical jurisdiction, at least retained its importance; it brought those that possessed it into conflict with each other and, as we shall see, with lay jurisdictions in that inevitable tangle of later medieval French justice. In creating new sources of income, prelates seem in the end to have been unsuccessful.[5] But their revenues could be maintained by the licit plurality of the commendation system: the great need not suffer too much.[6]

'The mistress of the world is widowed'

In all this clash of interest, what was left of the bride of Christ? 'What shall I say of churches?' asked Nicolas de Clamanges at the end

---

[1] Favier, 'Temporels ecclés.' p. 117.

[2] As, for instance, by Clamanges (*Le Traité de la ruine de l'église et la traduction française de 1564*, ed. A. Coville (1936) pp. 120–1). But cf. Favier, 'Temporels ecclés.' pp. 116 ff.

[3] Samaran and Mollat, op. cit. pp. 117 ff.

[4] Ibid. p. 115; Favier, *Les Finances pontificales*, pp. 205–396 *passim*, 694.

[5] Lot and Fawtier, op. cit. pp. 378–9; Imbart, op. cit. pp. 246 ff.

[6] See, for instance, the case of Jean Balue (H. Forgeot, *Jean Balue, cardinal d'Angers (1421?–1491)* (Bibl. Ec. Hautes Etudes, 106: 1895) pp. 12–13).

of his life, 'by ruin and calamity and unworthy oppression the mistress
of the world is widowed'.[1] We have already heard something of the
complaints of the critics of the later medieval French Church. To
rehearse them over-long would be, though enlivening, hardly fruitful.
No-one was safe from the rebarbative pen of a reformer. Throughout
the later middle ages, with interminable repetition,[2] those pens were
busy in condemnation of the church. From top to bottom they described
in a fascinated — though often formal — detail the sins of its members.
Prelates, thought Clamanges, were addicted to 'Sensuality, which
denoted the delights of wine, of slumber, of feasts, of music, of games,
of effeminate panders and prostitutes; Pride, which required high
houses, castles, citadels, palaces, splendid and most abundant furnish-
ings, the most expensive hangings and the processional display of the
horses of the household; and Avarice, which eagerly stored up the huge
hoards for this, so that they might suffice to pay for the first two . . .'[3]
Jean de Cardaillac, patriarch of Alexandria, had said much the same
thing twenty-five years before — and so had Guillaume Durand, bishop
of Mende, early in the century.[4] Fifty years later Jean Juvenal des Ursins,
archbishop of Reims, too, had his doubts about his peers; although, he
said prudently, 'I don't want to imply that there are not many prelates
who are worthy men and who do their duty largely and notably, in
preaching as in other things, edifying their people for the safety of their
souls; and who have, by proper means and without doing anything
worthy of blame, enough with which humbly to maintain their estate,
observing a mean, without superfluity . . .'[5] Nicolas de Clamanges also,
as we have seen, had made some exceptions;[6] but the rule ran the other
way. At the other end of the ecclesiastical social scale were the parish
priests, to Clamanges 'everywhere wicked and miserable men who are
subject to ruin and scandal by their dishonest way of life. Thence [he
argued] such contempt for the priesthood expressed by the vulgar, such
despite, thence the dishonour, disgrace, opprobrium of the whole
ecclesiastical order. . . .'[7] For Clamanges, too, his fellow canons were

---

[1] Op. cit. p. 104.   [2] Ibid. pp. 33–4.   [3] Ibid. p. 116.
[4] G. Mollat, 'Jean de Cardaillac, un prelat réformateur du clergé au xive
siècle', in R. *Hist. ecclés.* XLVIII (1953) 74–121; *Hist. Litt. France*, XXXV (1921)
79–129.
[5] Valois, *Hist. de la Pragmatique Sanction*, p. 218.   [6] See above, pp. 292–3.
[7] Op. cit. p. 119.

sinful and quarrelsome, monks were mundane, mendicants vainglorious and hypocritical; the tribulations of the clergy were the punishment for their sins, and only divine intervention could bring 'reparation'.[1]

It is impossible here to discuss adequately the justice of such later medieval onslaughts upon the Church.[1] But it is clear that the golden age to which a Clamanges looked back with such intense yearning had never existed; that the centralising system of the papacy can find its modern defenders — and that its medieval critics were sometimes less than impartial in their onslaughts upon it; that as far as anything like statistical material is available upon the morals of the clergy, it shows frequently a virtuous mediocrity, rather than a sinful eccentricity; and that attempts at reform were far from uncommon. Still less is it possible here to deal with those measures of reform or with the ideas and forces which lay behind them; or to discuss the reactions of the laity to the Church or to the religion the Church professed. Our concern is with a simpler clash of interests on a material plane amongst those who might have some say in the Church's ruling. The word 'reform' certainly came into their arguments. A sensibility towards the sins of the Church lay frequently behind that demand; but so did a sensibility towards papal cornering of benefices and papal taxation. The demand for reform as it was propounded in the councils of the Gallican Church from the end of the fourteenth century had behind it those mundane clerical interests which we have already examined; and it is with the interplay of those interests with others outside the church that we must now deal.

Interests in the Church

First of these was the interest of 'government': of the king, of the court, of the civil service, and of those who put pressure upon them.[2] The king, it will be remembered, was himself a charismatic figure. 'The king our lord has not only temporality but divinity too', argued Pierre Masuyer bishop of Arras, 'loftily and elegantly' and with some partisan

[1] Ibid. pp. 135–46.
[2] See, for an instance of papal pressure, G. Mollat, 'Le Saint-Siège et la France sous le pontificat de Clément VI', in R. *Hist. ecclés.* LV (1960) 5–24.

fervour in the Parlement in 1380, 'because he is *iniunctus*, anointed, and gives benefices *en régale* and has, moreover, the administration of the temporalities of bishoprics during vacancies, until new bishops are appointed. He has also the wardship of all the churches in his kingdom. . . .'[1] A king had a considerable collation *pleno jure* to benefices,[2] over which another litigant claimed in the Parlement at the end of the fourteenth century he possessed 'the same kind of right . . . as the Supreme Pontiff has in those which are recognised as belonging to his collation'.[3] Certainly he too dabbled in reservations and expectatives,[4] took annates, dispensed for plurality and non-residence. He had, as Pierre Masuyer claimed, the right of presentation to benefices becoming vacant during the vacancy of a bishopric *en régale*; and in other ways, too, he possessed direct or indirect control over benefices.[5] But the king had also a more protean role in the Church. At his coronation a king promised his bishops to defend their canonical privileges and immunities.[6] All the churches of his kingdom were, as Pierre Masuyer pointed out, in his safeguard.[7] And he had, it might be argued, a duty to reform the Church in his kingdom. 'I should like to conclude', argued Jean I Jouvenel at the Paris council in 1406, 'that the king, and especially he who is *unctus puer*, may very properly assemble the prelates of his kingdom, to consult with them about what is to be done in the question of this present schism; and he can, it would seem, do so more properly

[1] F. L. Cheyette, 'La Justice et le pouvoir royal à la fin du Moyen âge français', in R. *hist. Droit*, ser. 4 XL (1962) 390–1.

[2] G. Mollat, 'Le Roi de France et la collation plénière (*pleno jure*) des bénéfices ecclés.' in *Mémoires présentées par divers savants à l'Acad. Inscript.* XIV, part 2 (1951) 107–286.

[3] Ibid. p. 126 n 5.

[4] Ibid. pp. 130–45; J. Salvini, 'L'Application de la Pragmatique Sanction sous Charles VII et Louis XI au chapitre cathédrale de Paris', in R. *Hist. Eglise France*, III (1912) 427.

[5] G. Mollat, 'L'Application du droit de régale spirituelle en France, du xiie au xive siècle', in R. *Hist. ecclés.* XXV (1929) 425–46, 645–76; J. Gaudemet, *La Collation par le roi des bénéfices vacants en régale* (Bibl. Ec. Hautes Etudes, Sci. religieuses, 51: 1935); G. Mollat, 'Le Droit de patronage en Normandie, du xie au xve siècle', in R. *Hist. ecclés.* XXXIII (1937) 463–84, 725–88, XXXIV (1938) 21–69.

[6] See, for instance, *The Coronation Book of Charles V of France*, ed. E. S. Dewick (H. Bradshaw Soc. 16: 1899) col. 12.

[7] V. Martin, *Les Origines du Gallicanisme*, I (1939) 58–61.

than a primate might, or a simple prelate or chapter'; and his arguments were recalled by his son Jean II in the 1450s.[1]

That he had a duty to God did not escape a king like Charles VII; it is at times difficult to explain his behaviour *vis-à-vis* the Church except in terms of conscience.[2] But the Church was not an island; to rephrase Pierre Masuyer, it had not only divinity, but temporality too. The magnates of the Church were great land-owners. They had temporal and spiritual jurisdiction. Naturally on these mundane matters they were brought into conflict, as lay owners of lands and of courts were brought into conflict, with the crown and its officers. It was of little help for Jean Juvenal des Ursins to argue that there were 'some prelates whose lordships were founded, and they were both spiritual and temporal lords before ever Christ suffered death and passion and they were called Druids or *archiflamines* . . . and when the faith was granted us, in place of these Druids (who were pagans) bishops and archbishops were created, who had complete jurisdiction spiritual and temporal, principalities, rights and lordships, as the Druids had had them'.[3] The inheritors of the Druids, in his view, were hardly accorded their due. Their patrimony and temporal jurisdiction were damaged by the actions of the government and of its minor officials; their subjects were grievously taxed and 'are unable to pay the seigneurial dues of their ecclesiastical lords';[4] their temporalities were in danger if they did not give benefices to royal nominees. 'By all the kings whom God has helped in time past', Jean Juvenal told Charles VII in the 1450s,

---

[1] Bourgeois du Chastenet, *Nouvelle hist. du concile de Constance* (1718) 'Preuves', pp. 230ᵛ–231ʳ; J. Juvenal des Ursins, 'Verba mea auribus percipe, Domine', Bibl. nat. MS fr. 2701, fo. 114ʳ.

[2] Cf. Delaruelle *et al.*, op. cit. pp. 347–8.

[3] '. . . aucuns prelats dont les seignouries sont fondees et estoient seigneurs temporelz et spirituelx avant que oncques Jesus Crist souffrist mort et passion et se appelloient Druides ou archiflamines . . . et quant ce vint que la foy fut exaussee, en lieu de ces Druides (qui estoient payens) furent ordonnes evesques et arcevesques, qui eurent toute juridiction sp[irit]uelle et temporelle, principaultes, drois et seignouries comme avoient les Druides' ('Verba mea auribus percipe, Domine', folios 107ᵛ–108ʳ). The Druids (who were derived from *De bello gallico*, VI, cc. 13–14) also appealed to François de Monte-Belluna ('Tragicum argumentum de miserabili statu regni Francie', ed. A. Vernet, in *Annu.-B. Soc. Hist. France* (1962–3) pp. 146–7).

[4] Valois, *Hist. de la Pragmatique Sanction*, p. 211.

'neither ecclesiastical persons nor ecclesiastical jurisdiction was so trampled on, and is so trampled on, as in your time.'[1]

But collision between lay and ecclesiastical jurisdiction was hardly new under Charles VII. The two were allegedly in perpetual conflict in the thirteenth century.[2] In 1329 a council of prelates and barons was held by the king at Paris — the 'assembly of Vincennes' — ostensibly to arrive at a remedy for their mutual recriminations and to conserve between them in future 'the indissoluble bonds of love and charity'.[3] The fundamental onslaught upon ecclesiastical jurisdiction made in it by the legist Pierre de Cuignières did not bear immediate fruit. Indeed, the ecclesiastical myth of the council was that ecclesiastical liberties were upheld by Philippe VI. 'When the king had heard everything', wrote Jean Juvenal some hundred and twenty years later, 'his reply and decision was that everyone should carry on as they had before and that they should correct the abuses themselves.'[4] But the assembly marked a stage in the hardening of the attitude of the Parlement towards ecclesiastical jurisdiction. As the fourteenth century went on the sovereign court not only eliminated gradually most of the sixty-six 'abuses' listed by Pierre de Cuignières; it also began gradually to acquire cognisance of cases which might be thought purely spiritual.[5]

This development was produced not by a doctrinaire view of royal sovereignty — though such a view existed — nor by the deliberate desire of the crown or its advocates to extend royal power or to do down the liberties of the Church.[6] The Parlement had both clerical and lay members; its learning in ecclesiastical law was far from imperfect;[7]

---

[1] Ibid. p. 210.

[2] O. Martin, *L'Assemblée de Vincennes de 1329 et ses conséquences. Etude sur les conflits entre la juridiction laïque et la juridiction ecclés. au xive siècle* (Rennes, 1909) p. 26.

[3] Ibid. p. 72.

[4] 'Quant le roy eust tout ouy, la responce et conclusion du roy fut que chacun usast comme on avoit accoustume et que de eulx mesmes ilz corrigassent les abbus' ('Verba mea auribus percipe, Domine', fo. 110[r]). Cf. O. Martin, op. cit. pp. 204 ff.

[5] Ibid. p. 384; G. Mollat, 'Les Origines du gallicanisme parlementaire aux xive et xve siècles', in R. *Hist. ecclés.* XLIII (1948) 89–147.

[6] Cheyette, op. cit.

[7] Cf. R. Delachenal, *Hist. des avocats au Parlement de Paris, 1300–1600* (1885) pp. 6 ff.

it could pretend with considerable justification to its control over ecclesiastical affairs. It had, its members told Louis XI in 1480, been instituted as a mixed body 'for the conservation of your rights and privileges of the Church, for, amongst all the princes of this world, you alone are held and reputed a mixed person, taking cognisance of matters ecclesiastical and temporal, as most Christian king and principal restorer of the Holy Apostolic See, and founder of the Church of France, which is called the Gallican Church'.[1] The essential pressures, as always, came primarily from below: from the clerical litigants themselves, who saw in litigation before a royal court the most advantageous way of settling their legal quarrels with each other.[2] The jurisprudence of the Parlement gave them what they asked for; and at the same time it created a title to legitimate control by the crown's highest court over matters hitherto 'spiritual'. Thus, through the careful working of the Parlement, the image of the divine king acquired reality. And at the same time the defences of royal officers hardened against ecclesiastical sanctions imposed upon them for their interference in the affairs of the Church.[3] Excommunication ceased to have its terrors when the Parlement developed the practice of examining its regularity and of forcing its revocation by the seizure of the offender's temporalities. The Church thus lost a principal means of its own defence. But the conscience of the Parlement was, though perhaps arrogant, at least a high one; it defended its concept of the law against all who sought to derogate it; arguably, its actions tended in the later middle ages more to limit than to increase arbitrary rule. In its dealings with the Church it was driven by the internal dynamic of its jurisprudence; it was not the weapon of government, though the development of that jurisprudence might in later centuries provide one. Nor in

[1] *Lettres de Louis XI*, ed. J. Vaesen and E. Charavay (Soc. Hist. France) ix (1905) 360–1.

[2] 'Est en lelection du demandeur de poursuivre ou il vouldra', wrote Jean Juvenal on the question of litigation on contracts, 'car toutes lesdictes deux juridictions [ecclesiastic and secular] sont cappables et chacune dicelles de en avoir la congnoissance; et en ce nest fait prejudice en lune ne en laultre' ('Verba mea auribus percipe, Domine', fo. 111r).

[3] O. Martin, op. cit. pp. 366–78; M. Morel, *L'Excommunication et le pouvoir civil en France du droit canonique classique au commencement du xvᵉ siècle* (1926) pp. 115 ff.

its Gallican sentiments — such as those of its lengthy manifesto of 1465[1] — was it intent upon ensnaring the Church; it was intent only upon the maintenance of what it considered the truth. Although it could be silenced by the sheer exercise of royal will, it continued under Louis XI to express those sentiments when it had a chance; but the Parlement did not come into its vocal own until the 'Gallican reaction' which followed Louis' death.[2]

But the king's interest in the Church had a more mundane aspect than that imposed upon it by charismatic tradition or even by the development of legal precedent in the Parlement. First there was the question of appointment to benefices. Not only did the king need a steady supply of benefices of the higher grades to provide for the upkeep in office and in retirement of his civil servants;[3] but he needed also to have some say in the appointment to the highest of them in the Church in France.

> After the civil war of the Public Weal [for instance, as an advocate told the Parlement of Paris in 1484], the king was in great fear and perplexity . . . he had his eye on the bishoprics and archbishoprics of this kingdom, and well he had cause to have, because they have great temporalities, fine fat towns, [fortified] places and castles; and he wished that when they became vacant, persons sure, loyal and agreeable to him were provided to them. . . . For this reason the king begged the pope to provide to these bishoprics and archbishoprics at his nomination and request; this the pope readily granted him, and since then he has always given the bishoprics and archbishoprics that have become vacant at the nomination and request of the king.[4]

But such an *entente* was hardly a new thing. In the period up to 1378 a 'tacit concordat' is alleged to have existed between the papacy and the French crown over the appointments to benefices, even, until at least the mid-century, a 'close alliance'.[5] The pressures evinced by Charles V in the election of his cousin the Dominican Charles d'Alençon to the

---

[1] *Rec. gén. des anciennes lois françaises*, ed. F. A. Isambert *et al.* x (n.d.) 396–416.

[2] Ourliac, op. cit. pp. 175, 203 n 3; ibid. '(Suite et fin)', in R. *hist. Droit*, ser. 4 XXII (1943) 136 ff.

[3] See, for instance, R. Cazelles, *La Société politique et la crise de la royauté sous Philippe de Valois* (1958) pp. 383–7.

[4] Ourliac, op. cit. '(Suite et fin)', p. 148.

[5] Mollat, *La Collation des bénéfices*, pp. 199, 206, 297.

archbishopric of Lyon and the complicity in it of Urban V, for instance, seem evident.[1] Certainly Nicolas de Clamanges, as we have seen, at the end of the century thought it madness to approach the pope without a royal recommendation.[2]

Second there was the question of ecclesiastical taxation. In general principle the churchmen and clerics were thought 'free of *aides* and subventions'; and in practice the clergy, while not exempt from lay indirect taxes, was (except in a period from 1383 to about 1416) more or less exempt from direct lay taxes.[3] But in practice, too, ecclesiastical tenths seem to have been, up to 1378 at least, royal things. Clerical tenths were taken at least once without consent; they were taken on occasion with the consent of the clergy itself; but usually, it seems, they were taken with the consent of the pope, who, until the pontificate of Clement VII, seems to have renounced them completely to the king of France. The popes of the Schism were less generous — if the French clergy perforce was not. But while the protector of the liberties of the Gallican Church might be prepared not to wince at oppression if it turned to his profit, his conscience might be aroused if it turned to someone else's; and a feeling against papal taxes seems to have developed at the end of the century.[4]

But there were other interests in what was effectively the property of the Church than those of the government, however broadly the term 'government' might be interpreted — for instance, to include those civil servants who entered into a backstairs relationship with the papacy upon their own account.[5] The magnates of the world had their own relatives[6] and servants to provide for; and so did the magnates of the

[1] Ibid. p. 207.   [2] See above, p. 297.

[3] G. Dupont-Ferrier, *Etudes sur les institutions financières de la France à la fin du Moyen âge*, II *Les Finances extraordinaires et leur mécanisme* (1932) 165 n27.

[4] Samaran and Mollat, op. cit. pp. 20, 165; Favier, *Les Finances pontificales*, pp. 209–11; M. Rey, *Le Domaine du roi et les finances extraordinaires sous Charles VI, 1388–1413* (1965) pp. 341 ff.

[5] Mollat, 'Le Saint-Siège et la France', pp. 9–12.

[6] Charles II d'Albret, for instance, left in his will nothing to his third son, Louis, because, he said, 'il lui a procuré, par son crédit et savoir-faire, la dignité de protonotaire du Saint-Siége, l'évêché d'Aire, il lui a donné beaucoup d'argent aux ambassades où il a été employé par le roi de France, en Italie, en Aragon et en Castille, et qu'enfin il a été fait cardinal' (P. Raymond, *Inv.-Sommaire des Arch. dep. Basses-Pyrénées*, IV (1867) 18 [E 71]).

Church. As early as 1307 the archbishop of Bordeaux found himself with an insufficient number of benefices with which to reward his servants; he was granted a clutch in perpetuity by Clement V.[1] But it was, of course, the ordinary collator whom reservation and a royal-papal *entente* primarily hit; and he lost, as well as the patronage, the first-fruits when he was thus deprived of a benefice. Any increase in taxation, royal or papal, might, in theory at least, reduce the amount which a prelate might in turn hope to extract from his reluctant and complaining clergy. Apart from his own direct relationship with the Church as an individual, he had as well almost an exterior political interest in it as a source of patronage and income. And in the interplay of these external interests others, which might have no direct relationship with ecclesiastical matters, might influence those who were affected by them in their attitude to the Church. The tidal movements and sudden storms of wider politics, inside or outside France, might redound upon the inland sea of domestic ecclesiastical politics. Thus the interplay of those politics in the fifteenth century demonstrates an apparent confusion, perhaps even greater than that visible in the politics of other social groups. There are so many strands that the pattern is naturally more complicated. Yet some pattern does appear.

The Schism and the Gallican Church

On 8 April 1378 sixteen cardinals elected at Rome Bartolomeo Prignano pope as Urban VI.[2] On 20 September eleven of them (one had died, and three abstained) together with a twelfth cardinal, who had not been present in April, elected at Fondi the last of their number, Robert de Génève, pope as Clement VII. Urban's insane denunciation of their 'sins' had not taken long to drive his electors into revolt. The remaining six of the old cardinals at Avignon joined them in renouncing him; only Francesco Tebaldeschi, who had died, might have remained on his side. Urban's creation of twenty-nine new cardinals two days before was of

[1] *Cartulaire de l'évêché de Poitiers ou Grand-Gauthier*, ed. M. Redet (Arch. hist. Poitou, 10: Poitiers, 1881) pp. 107–14.
[2] E. Delaruelle *et al.*, *L'Eglise au temps du Grand schisme et de la crise conciliare* (Hist. de l'Eglise fondée par A. Fliche et V. Martin, 14: 1962–4) pp. 6 ff.

little use. The Church was in a state of schism, between the pope at Rome, Urban, and the pope at Avignon, Clement.

The essential question was how to end it. The problem took fifty years to solve. Urban VI was succeeded by Boniface IX, by Innocent VII and by Gregory XII; Clement VII by Benedict XIII. Gregory and Benedict were deposed by the council of Pisa in 1409 and Alexander V elected; but Gregory did not abdicate until 1415 and Benedict died pope of a tiny obedience in 1423. He was succeeded by Clement VIII (who himself may have had a rival in Benedict XIV); but with Clement's renunciation in 1429 this schism finally ended. But the problem of removing one — or two — superfluous heads from the Church had long been outstripped in the heady days of the later councils by the problem of 'reform'. From the beginning the question of reform had entered into the arguments about the means to end the schism; and with the question of reform had entered the question of reform-in-whose-interest. The Gallican Church was much involved in the arguments that led up to the council of Pisa; and it was against the background manœuvres of pope and councils over the following thirty years that the more domestic manœuvres of that Church were played out.

How was the schism to be brought to an end? Force was contemplated and at times even employed; but it did not provide the answer. The abstainers of 1378 had already thought on 5 August of a council as a means of settling the problems developing around the election of Urban VI. They persevered in their view for a short while after the schism; in 1381 a clerk of the university of Paris celebrated its cause in verse; and it remained in the air. But there were other possibilities: the way of compromise and the way of cession. In 1394 the university of Paris adopted the latter: the abdication of both popes and the election by both their colleges of cardinals of a new one. But already in the minds of some of the promoters of the way of cession the evils of the Curia appear to have loomed more largely than the mere evil of a broken Church. On 6 June 1394 the university addressed an epistle, *Quanquam majorum nostrorum*, composed by Clamanges, Ailly and Gilles Deschamps, to Charles VI on the subject of its 'destroyed liberties'; and the liberties of the Church — of the Gallican Church — became more and more obsessive at its councils from 1395 onwards.[1] It was argued

[1] *Chron. du religieux de St.-Denis*, ed. L. Bellaguet (Docs inéd. sur l'hist. de

that the pope supported by the French — Benedict XIII — should be deprived of his control over benefices and of taxation as a means of forcing him to accept cession; but this argument turned by the third council of 1398 into pressure for the end in itself. Gilles Deschamps maintained that even if there had been no schism still the pope should be deprived of the things he had 'usurped'.[1] It was not the means to end the schism that essentially was now discussed; it was the means of immunising the Gallican Church.

But the views of Gilles Deschamps and his colleagues were not necessarily shared by all French churchmen or by all those who shared in the government of the country. From the left wing of those who wished for the total subtraction of the Church in France from papal obedience, clerical attitudes ran to the right wing of those who wished dutifully to obey him.[2] The strongest motive of the clergy remained naturally their own advantage; however much conscience might obfuscate it and opinion rationalise it. But that advantage was not at all clear. Submission might be profitable if the pope bribed the leaders of the faithful with benefices and reduced taxes; subtraction, if in an autocephalic paradise that right arm of the Church, the king, did so. The clergy was uncertain about its advantage and divided about its advantage; and as experience taught the truth about both Gallican liberties and submissive obedience, a virtuous steadfastness of opinion was hardly to be expected.

In the ten years after 1398 the papalists had the support of the duc d'Orléans; their enemies the support of his enemies.[3] In 1398 the left wing won; on 27 July a royal ordinance proclaimed total subtraction.[4] No taxes were to be paid to Benedict XIII; benefices were to be in the hands of collators and electors. But the autocephalic régime was not wholly paradise. The pressure of the great fell upon the electors and collators; bishops and universities snarled at one another over the pickings of benefices now ultimately under the control of the government; taxation continued to be paid to it. Churchmen naturally began

France) II (1840) 136–82; V. Martin, *Les Origines du Gallicanisme*, I (1939) 243 ff; Delaruelle *et al.* op. cit. pp. 335 ff.
  [1] V. Martin, op. cit. p. 286.   [2] Delaruelle *et al.* pp. 339–40.
  [3] N. Valois, *La France et le Grand schisme d'Occident*, III (1901) 239 ff.
  [4] V. Martin, op. cit. pp. 287 ff; Delaruelle *et al.* op. cit. pp. 335 ff.

to long for the sweeter days of submission. In 1403 the right wing won; on 30 May submission to Benedict was announced; and it was finally secured by June 1404. But submission, too, had for some its bitterness. The left wing of the university of Paris led the campaign for subtraction; but in 1406 it was a compromise that won. It was enshrined in two royal ordinances made on 18 February 1407. Their publication, over a year later, has been seen to mark the official birth of Gallicanism.[1]

The ordinances gave the Church in France much the same 'liberties' as had that of 1398. From 1408 the essential question remained to what degree those new-found — or re-found — 'liberties' should be preserved. The question was, and is, very difficult to answer simply. The attitude of the government is at first sight comparatively straightforward. From the council of Pisa onwards it apparently wavered between the liberties in some form or another and an *entente* with the papacy. Anglo-Burgundian France accepted a quasi-concordat with Martin V in 1418, after the council of Constance; and French France remained under a régime of liberties imposed by the Armagnac administration in March 1418. But the years after 1419 saw in the kingdom of Bourges a slow and unsteady movement towards agreement with the papacy; discussion about a concordat was broken in 1422 by a confirmation of liberties; but eventually, in 1425, the government made a complete submission to Martin V.[2] A year later a quasi-concordat of Genazzano, a modified version of that of 1418, established a régime which lasted until Martin's death in 1431. From 1432 the situation was confused by the activities of the council of Basle; the eventual outcome of a period in which there appear to have been no rules, or if there were no-one knew what they were, was, in 1438, the Pragmatic Sanction of Bourges, a measure on the whole left-wing, but moderate, which gave the Gallican Church liberties less than those of 1408 and 1418 and less than those decreed by the council of Basle itself. Despite negotiations for a new agreement, the Pragmatic Sanction, to Eugenius IV 'iniquitous, impious, liable to compromise the king's salvation',[3] remained in force formally until Charles VII's death. In 1461 it was formally abolished by Louis XI; and eleven years later a concordat of Amboise

---

[1] V. Martin, op. cit. p. 333.   [2] Ibid. II (1939) p. 255.
[3] N. Valois, *Hist. de la Pragmatique Sanction de Bourges sous Charles VII* (1906) p. xcvi.

established a régime which, with some modifications, lasted until the end of his reign and beyond.

But such a bare description expresses far less than the realities of the question. Not only were the periods of apparent 'agreement' and 'disagreement' with the papacy broken by moves towards *'entente'* or 'hostility'; but the game the government played was at times willy-nilly far more subtle again. A government divided against itself tended naturally towards tergiversations; those of the 1420s, for instance, may well have been the product of opposing groups in government backing opposing attitudes towards Gallican liberties, as were, more obviously, those of 1413–18. Political situations inside and outside the kingdom might influence even a single-minded government's attitude towards the pope; the liberties might become, at least formally, a bargaining weapon as in, for instance, the in-fighting of Italian politics from the mid-century.[1] At the time of the council of Basle it might be difficult for the government to resist the lunar pull of its left-wing fervour; and the motives even of a Charles VII alone, when he was more apparently in control of government, might be far from unmixed. A duty of devotion to the papacy might be inhibited by a duty to the Gallican Church of his kingdom;[2] and a royal eye for profit might turn both ways (and so indeed might an eye for duty) when other pressures made it advisable. But the pressures for the liberties came also from below;[3] neither the mind nor the hands of 'government' was wholly free, even in the reign of Louis XI;[4] even in periods formally of rapprochement — as for instance in 1461 — the liberties might still effectively be in force. The actions of the clergy were not wholly under the control of either the crown or the papacy. The reality was what the clergy could get away with, not what its heads in collusion or in rivalry decreed.[5]

A king had still to try to rule his Church. Even a king conscious of his duty could not abandon the profit. Even the submission of 1425

[1] Ibid. p. cxxviii; J. Combet, *Louis XI et le Saint-Siège* (1903) pp. 1 ff; P. Ourliac, 'Le Concordat de 1472. Etude sur les rapports de Louis XI et de Sixte IV (1er article)', in R. *hist. Droit*, ser. 4 XXI (1942) 212 ff.

[2] Delaruelle *et al.* op. cit. pp. 347–8.

[3] See, for instance, V. Martin, op. cit. II 281 n 5.

[4] Ourliac, op. cit. pp. 198 ff.

[5] Cf. (on a different matter) Y. Perotin, 'Les Chapitres bordelais contre Charles VII', in *A. Midi*, LXXIII (1951) 33–42.

was accompanied by a demand for five hundred benefices.[1] The old game of accepting in practice favourable provisions and of protesting in principle against unfavourable ones continued in the period before the Pragmatic Sanction.[2] Under the régime of the Pragmatic the principal ecclesiastical person in the kingdom after the pope was quite prepared, in order to get his own way with the bishoprics, either as such to bully electors directly or to train the pope upon them; it was at this time, too, that translations of bishops by the pope at the king's request became a general practice.[3] But there might still be resistance;[4] and the king's control over collative benefices seems to have been much weaker than his control over elective ones. From 1438 the royal attitude seems to have been to invoke the Pragmatic if it was profitable; to ignore it if it was not. Within an effective uncertainty the kings acted as far as they could to achieve their own purposes; whatever they themselves might have said, whatever laws they may have made said, whatever the papacy or the Gallican Church itself clamoured for.

This effective uncertainty was reflected in anarchy in the law of benefices. The Parlement of Paris, despite an attitude less than whole-hearted in the period up to 1418, and perhaps less than pure on occasion later,[5] became the palladium of the Gallicans. It lectured Charles VII on the evils of expectatives, of reservations, of commendations and pensions, of appeals to Rome, of the promotion of the unworthy.[6] It resisted attempts against the liberties: the Parlement of Paris was forced to enregister the Burgundian submission in 1419; the Parlement of Poitiers refused to enregister Charles VII's submission in 1425 and

---

[1] V. Martin, op. cit. II 257.   [2] Delaruelle et al., op. cit. p. 353.

[3] Ibid. p. 362. The practice had some antiquity (A. Artonne, 'Transferts d'évêques sous Jean XXII', in R. Hist. Église France, XL (1954) 242–3).

[4] See, for instance, J. Salvini, 'L'Application de la Pragmatique Sanction sous Charles VII et Louis XI au chapitre cathédrale de Paris', in R. Hist. Église France, III (1912) 125 ff; G. Plique, 'Etude sur le chapitre cathédrale de Mende de 1123 à 1516', in Chron. et Mél. Soc. Lettres Sci. et Arts Lozère, V (1930–4) 13–14, 110–11; G. de Valous, Jean de Bourbon, évêque du Puy, lieutenant-général de Languedoc et de Forez, abbé de Cluny, serviteur et adversaire de Louis XI (?1413–1485) (St.-Wandrille, 1949) pp. 8–9, 13 ff.

[5] V. Martin, op. cit. II 175–9, 188–90, 280 n 1.

[6] M. Jusselin, 'Remontrances du Parlement au roi sur la situation de l'église de France (1430 a.st. [1431])', in Bibl. Ec. Chartes, LXXIV (1913) 516–24.

protested against the 'concordat' of Genazzano; this attitude persisted
and was to some extent shared by the Parlement of Toulouse.[1] Under
the régime of Genazzano the jurisprudence of the Parlement on
beneficial matters seems to have developed rapidly; and in the confusion
of the 1430s, to which the development of its jurisprudence in fact
contributed and in which rival candidates for an elective benefice might
be supported by electors, by pope, by king, or by council, its prestige
grew. The Pragmatic Sanction tried to cut down the number of cases
formally allowed on appeal to Rome and re-established the authority of
an hierarchy of ecclesiastical courts; but the Parlement, if less exuberant
in its ideas than before, still kept its grip upon the Church.[2] From 1448
the procedure of the *appel comme d'abus* replaced that of the *cas privilegié*
as a means of restricting ecclesiastical authority.[3]

Attitudes towards Gallican liberties

Litigious disorder was perhaps greater under the régime of the
Pragmatic Sanction than before 1438, and perhaps greater under the
régime of the concordat of Amboise than under that of the Pragmatic.[4]
The conflict of possible courts to which inevitable rivals might appeal
was in fact fundamental; and the ambiguous attitude of the king of
France towards papacy and Gallican Church might enhance an ambiguous attitude of litigants towards them. But general attitudes towards the
liberties of the Church do seem to have evolved amongst the interested
groups of churchmen. The university of Paris, disappointed of its
benefices after 1408, returned to the papal fold after the council of Pisa
and never again effectively emerged from it; mere graduates did better

[1] V. Martin, op. cit. II 227–30, 259–61, 265; A. Viala, *Le Parlement de
Toulouse et l'admin. royale laïque, 1420–1525 environ*, II (Albi, 1953) 420–1.

[2] Delaruelle *et al.* op. cit. pp. 359, 363–4. For a picaresque case of the 1440s,
see A. Bossuat, 'Une application particulière de la Pragmatique Sanction de
Bourges devant le Parlement de Paris', in *Moyen Âge*, LXIX (1963) 829–44.

[3] R. Génestal, *Les Origines de l'appel comme d'abus* (Bibl. Ec. Hautes Etudes,
Sci. religieuses, 63 : 1951).

[4] [M. Martin-Chabot, 'Nicolas V, Charles VII et la Pragmatique Sanction.
Essai sur le régime des bénéfices ecclés. de France de 1447 à 1455'], in
C. R. Acad. Inscript. (1906) pp. 382–3; Delaruelle *et al.* op. cit. pp. 364–5.

out of papal provision than out of collations made with or without royal or seigneurial pressures — though graduates could solicit the favour of king or lords.[1] At the council of Constance the split between prelates hastening, according to Nicolas de Clamanges, to recover their patronage,[2] and academics eager to deprive them of it for the council's and graduates' benefit was clearly marked. It was at this time that Pierre d'Ailly stressed their interests in his *Tractatus de reformatione seu canones reformandi Ecclesiam*.[3] Suffering under the Armagnacs for their dexterous haste in recognising Martin V and in sending him their roll in 1417, the university of Paris the following year sank gratefully into the comfort of Burgundian ultramontanism.[4] The Pragmatic Sanction gave the universities of the kingdom a very considerable share of collative benefices; but though there is some evidence of the university of Paris's affection for the Pragmatic, there is also evidence of its distaste for it; and there is evidence, as for other periods of Gallican liberties, that graduates without patronage at court got less than they had been promised.[5] The university seems to have remained torn between liberties and advantages, and in the pursuit of the latter hardly active in defence of the former.

Prelates in principle had much to gain from the liberties of the Gallican Church. But though they gave them their patronage they laid them open to the pressure of patrons in a looser sense, seigneurs and kings. A considerable grievance of the time of Charles VII, thought Jean Juvenal des Ursins when archbishop of Reims, in the 1450s, 'is the way the prelates of your kingdom are constrained by seizure of their temporalities to give benefices to people you want: a method most damnable and unjust, and dangerous for the souls of those who take the benefices. And to this complaint ... may be assimilated the sort of threats offered when elections are made by you ...'[6] The prelates of the Pragmatic were not wholly loth to keep elections out of the hands of

[1] V. Martin, op. cit. II 162 ff; *Chartularium universitatis Parisiensis*, ed. H. Denifle and E. Chatelain, IV (Paris, 1897) 404.

[2] *Opera omnia* (Liège, 1613) p. 292.

[3] See above, p. 296.

[4] V. Martin, op. cit. II 203 ff.

[5] Ibid. II 295 n5; Delaruelle *et al.* op. cit. pp. 366–7; P. Imbart de La Tour, *Les Origines de la Réforme*, 2nd ed. II (Melun, 1946) 124–5, 226.

[6] Valois, *Hist. de la Pragmatique Sanction*, p. 211.

electors;[1] but certainly both electors and collators (who had their own intestine quarrels)[2] found themselves faced during the periods of liberties both with direct royal pressure and with papal provisions in principle improper:[3] if the word 'improper' had any meaning.

In mid-century the liberties of the Gallican Church still had prelates to defend them. It was Gérard Machet, bishop of Castres, perhaps, who went so far as piously to forge the Pragmatic Sanction of St.-Louis in their defence.[4] The real Pragmatic of 1438 was in Jean Juvenal's eyes 'just and holy',[5] representing an ancient propriety. But even Jean Juvenal had been prepared to see some modification in the Pragmatic, because, as he wrote about 1452,

> given the choice of two evils the lesser is the one to choose and, all in all, it is less evil to alter it and change it . . . than to use it as it is used. For the way and manner in which it was used was uncivil and unjust (at present things are stopping); and the prelates, at least some of them, did not do their duty according to it, nor in the matter of conferring benefices. And I believe with a true conscience one should obey the rule of law . . . That is that the king's reply [to papal advances for the abolition of the Pragmatic] should be that our Holy Father should summon a general council, as he has promised, so it's said, and that the king should send deputies to it; and that what was there discussed and decided the king should observe.[6]

For however politic Jean Juvenal and Gérard Machet may have been, the ultimate appeal for liberties and the Pragmatic lay to the future council.[7] Some prelates, Amédée de Talaru, archbishop of Lyon, and Philippe de Coëtquis, archbishop of Tours, were farther left in support of a council than they; others, Guillaume de Montjoie, bishop of Béziers, Bernard de Rozier, archbishop of Toulouse, and Hélie de Bourdeilles, archbishop of Tours (who wrote treatises against the

---

[1] Delaruelle et al., op. cit. p. 357. Jean Juvenal echoed the arguments of the Bourges assembly (Valois, Hist. de la Pragmatique Sanction, p. 206).

[2] Imbart, op. cit. pp. 223–4.

[3] Valois, Hist. de la Pragmatique Sanction, pp. xcvi ff; Salvini, op. cit. pp. 125 ff.

[4] Valois, Hist. de la Pragmatique Sanction, pp. clix–clxxiv.   [5] Ibid. p. 206.

[6] Ibid. p. 209.

[7] See, for instance, ibid. p. 228; Lettres de Louis XI, ed. J. Vaesen and E. Charavay (Soc. Hist. France) II (1885) p. 122.

Pragmatic), much farther to the right in support of the pope.[1] In the mid-century a majority of bishops may have been on the side of the abrogation of the Pragmatic.[2]

How far the political structure of the group had already changed is difficult to say; but it became increasingly clear in the reign of Louis XI that the bishops were the king's men and their views his.[3] François Hallé, sometime king's advocate, 'the greatest Pragmatician, who upheld more of the king's rights against the pope than anyone else in the kingdom', under this régime became archbishop of Narbonne, especially absolved from all the sentences of excommunication he had incurred in his Gallican fury; as archbishop he upheld the candidates of the pope.[4] To the sturdy Gallicans of the Estates-general of Tours in 1484 the bishops 'save for very few' were all enemies of the Pragmatic Sanction; headed by the cardinals and those hopeful of that honour (who had the backing of the great) and having for the most part obtained their sees 'by the king's nomination and against the tenor of the Pragmatic', they saw more advantage in a régime of concordat than in one of liberties under which they were forced to give a third of their benefices to graduates.[5] Certainly a number of the 'bishops of king Louis' suffered in the Gallican reaction after his death; and François Hallé found himself hoist by his rival for Narbonne, Georges d'Amboise, with the principles he himself had upheld in his long years as king's advocate in the Parlement.[6]

Gallican liberties may have been cherished most dearly in the breasts of members of chapters.[7] Their rights of election had suffered from the

---

[1] Valois, *Hist. de la Pragmatique Sanction*, pp. lxxvi, lxxxii, cxxviii, cxxxiv n2, and *La Crise religieuse du xve siècle. Le Pape et le Concile (1418–1450)* II (1909) 228–9; P. Ourliac, 'La Pragmatique Sanction et la légation en France du cardinal d'Estouteville (1451–1453)', in *Mél. Archéol. Hist. Ecole franç. Rome,* LV (1938) 405 ff; Imbart, op. cit. II 108–9.

[2] Delaruelle *et al.* op. cit. p. 368.

[3] Imbart, op. cit. II 110; Ourliac, 'Le Concordat de 1472 . . . (Suite et fin)', in R. *hist. Droit,* ser. 4 XXII (1943) 134.

[4] Ibid. pp. 129 n2, 137; Imbart, op. cit. II 110 n2.

[5] J. Masselin, *Journal des Etats généraux de France tenus à Tours en 1484* (Docs inéd. sur l'hist. de France: 1835) pp. 516–18.

[6] Ourliac, 'Le Concordat de 1472 . . . (Suite et fin)', pp. 149, 137; R. Delachenal, *Hist. des avocats au Parlement de Paris, 1300–1600* (1885) p. 180 n1.

[7] Imbart, op. cit. II 115–21.

manœuvres of the great; and the Pragmatic (at least in principle) preserved them. It preserved them also from the provision by pope or legates to their number; it preserved them from taxation. Their feelings may to a certain extent have been shared by the inhabitants of monasteries. But the conflicts which might develop in chapters and houses led their members, at least on the question of litigation, still to rely on Rome. Dispute with bishops over exemptions,[1] dispute between rival parties in elections, dispute over accession to their own membership, all might lead an ecclesiastical college temporarily to swallow its feeling for the liberties of the Gallican Church.

The attitudes of the influential groups in that Church on the questions of benefices and of litigation were thus, like that of 'government', far from clear-cut. So, too, seem their attitudes to have been upon the question of taxation. Clergy who had resort to the pope for their benefices could hardly refuse him the taxes he took at the time of their provision; this was as difficult after 1409 as it was after 1438.[2] And even the Pragmatic Sanction allowed Eugenius IV, for his life and without prejudice to the liberties of the Gallican Church, a form of first-fruit. Though procurations seem to have been abandoned, at least formally, by the papacy after Constance,[3] spoils certainly could still have to be forbidden in France in 1464, and the revenues of vacant benefices could still be a matter for discussion in 1436.[4] But the question seems still rather an obscure one; as, indeed, is to some extent the question of tenths. These were taken after Constance as before by both pope and king: the clergy in Languedoc at the Estates of Chinon in 1428 (which granted the king a tenth) added 'provided, however, that the king gets remission from the pope of a tenth which he has recently imposed upon the clergy for the Faith' arguing that 'the king has the

[1] Cf. G. Hubrecht, 'Juridictions et compétences en Guyenne recouvrée', in *A. Fac. Droit. Bordeaux, Sér. jurid.* III (1952) 76 ff.

[2] Delaruelle *et al.* op. cit. pp. 343, 363; [Martin-Chabot], op. cit. p. 382; [P. Bourdon, 'Etude sur le régime de la Pragmatique Sanction d'après les registres d'Eugène IV'], in *C. R. Acad. Inscript.* (1909) pp. 561–3; Ourliac, 'Le Concordat de 1472 ... (1er article)', p. 195.

[3] C. Samaran and G. Mollat, *La Fiscalité pontificale en France au xive siècle* (Bibl. Ec. fr. Athènes Rome, 96: 1905) p. 47; but see W. E. Lunt, *Papal Revenues in the Middle Ages*, I (Columbia, 1934) 111, II (Columbia, 1934) 447–8.

[4] *Ordonnances des rois de France de la troisième race*, XVI, ed. C. E. de Pastoret (1814) pp. 217–19; V. Martin, op. cit. II 278.

privilege that no apostolic tenth should be put on in his kingdom without his express consent'. The same avoidance of double taxation was stressed in 1432.[1] But though ecclesiastical assemblies could, as in 1440, still grant the king his tenth, he could also turn to the pope for permission to raise it: in 1442, when both Charles VII and Charles d'Orléans, who had his ransom to pay, had asked for one, the papal legate was to protest the poverty of the clergy, to argue that if the duke of Burgundy had had a tenth his clergy were less burdened, and to emphasise the exceptional character of the tax, intended above all for crusade against the infidel (the duke of Burgundy had sent three ships to Rhodes); in the last resort he could grant them one between them.[2] Papal tenths appear to have continued to have been taken, perhaps intermittently: in 1447 the Estates of Languedoc complained that one was against the holy canons and the Pragmatic Sanction, and without the previous assent of the clergy.[3] Ten years later the virulence of the province of Rouen was even greater: Charles VII was forced to admit that if, at the request of the pope, he had authorised the levy of a tenth without the consent of the clergy, it was without prejudice to the liberties of the Church in France.[4] The crusading tenth provided a leitmotive throughout the reign of Louis XI; even on his deathbed he was anguished about it by St. Francis of Paula;[5] but information about his own exactions upon the clergy — if they took this form — seems to be lacking.

Churchmen and the king

'In becoming a procedure, Gallicanism ceased to be a conviction.'[6]

[1] C. Devic and J. Vaissete, *Hist. gén. de Languedoc*, IX (Toulouse, 1885) 1098–9; Valois, *Hist. de la Pragmatique Sanction*, p. lix n 3.
[2] *Ordonnances*, XIII, ed. L. G. de Vilevault and L. G. de Bréquigny (1782) 326–7; Valois, *Hist. de la Pragmatique Sanction*, pp. cxxxii–cxxxiii. In Berry at least, after 1406, 'les décimes deviennent infiment plus rares et ne sont plus perçus que pour le roi' (J. de Font-Réaulx, 'La Fiscalité pontificale en Berry, spécialement au xive siècle', in *M. Antiq. Centre*, XLV (1931–3) 134).
[3] Devic and Vaissete, op. cit. XI (Toulouse, 1889) 16.
[4] Valois, *Hist. de la Pragmatique Sanction*, pp. clxxxv–clxxxvi.
[5] Ourliac, 'Le Concordat de 1472 ... (Suite et fin)', pp. 127 ff.
[6] Imbart, op. cit. p. 121.

Gallicanism had more than one form.[1] There was a theological Gallicanism which restricted papal power; there was a royal-ecclesiastical
Gallicanism which arrogated the 'ancient liberties' of a Church in which
the king was, after the pope, the first ecclesiastical person; there was a
parliamentary Gallicanism. All had their doctrines, all their theoretical
commonplaces. They had their literature; and the last had a jurisprudence which might inculcate loyalty to it. That conviction of the
rectitude of Gallican ideas could arise is hardly to be doubted; it would
be foolish to deny that men, even kings, might act because of an idea.
But the essential thing about those ideas was that they justified interest;
and when interest failed, ideas fell to earth; the most eager Pragmatician
might abandon them. But, while it lasted, men could hardly be blamed
if they flew them high. Interested motive was not the whole of
Gallicanism; but in part Gallicanism consecrated it. Should one then
blame those who saw in Gallicanism only a means to their immediate
end, an argument they need not believe?

The confusion thus apparent throughout the fifteenth century in
France at every level of the Church, from the king at its head to the
merest clerk after a benefice at its base, thus sprang from a confusion
about the best means, at any particular moment, to achieve for each
particular person his own particular ends. For the government the
liberties complicated its immediate political problem: the control of the
greater churchmen. Admittedly other members of the Church could
interfere in mundane political affairs: members of the university of
Paris, for instance, could provide the theoretical arguments behind the
Cabochian movement of 1413.[2] But individual prelates were, as we have
seen Louis XI alleged to perceive them, powerful political integers.
Xenophobia, mercantilism[3] and the interests of security might unite in
opposition to alien provisors; in 1432 Charles VII, reserving all
benefices in the kingdom to denizens, complained that the pope
regularly gave major benefices to 'persons unknown to us, who are
complete strangers to our kingdom, and to others in the obedience and
on the side of our enemies' and that as a result not only were 'moneys

[1] Delaruelle *et al.* op. cit. p. 329.
[2] A. Coville, *Les Cabochiens et l'ordonnance de 1413* (1888) pp. 124 ff.
[3] Cf. Valois, *Hist. de la Pragmatique Sanction*, p. 145; Thomas Basin, *Hist. des
règnes de Charles VII et de Louis XI*, ed. J. Quicherat (Soc. Hist. France) IV
(1859) 74, 79, 86.

emptied and taken out of our kingdom and obedience, and turned to the profit of our . . . enemies', but 'our enemies and adversaries may know the secrets of the government and state of our . . . kingdom'.[1] The danger was ever-present: 'the old archbishop' of Toulouse, Bernard de Rozier, was, according to Louis XI in 1482, 'for the comte d'Armagnac, and all the Rozier family, and the nephew [to whom he had hoped to resign his archbishopric] was a strong Armagnac, and that's not what's needed at Toulouse, which is too close to Armagnac'.[2]

The list of bishops prepared to play politics was a long one. But *semel pastor, semper pastor*. What could be done with those who 'betrayed' the king? The pope might be persuaded to transfer them to a safer diocese; but this was difficult, even for Louis XI.[3] Even Geoffroy Hébert, bishop of Coutances, according to Louis given to the invocation of devils, 'in Latin, in Greek, and that in public, and who has served monsieur de Bourbon and has advanced him further than he was', was only exiled from his diocese.[4] Some bishops, like Bernard de Rozier, like Philippe de Lévis, archbishop of Auch, could be forced into resignation; some, like Thomas Basin, into voluntary exile. In the last resort one could brave the 'great ecclesiastical censures'[5] and boldly incarcerate the delinquent. The scandal might be considerable; but Jean Juvenal des Ursins, who catalogued such misdeeds, recognised in his advice to his brother the chancellor of France that 'where one can't win, the most expedient thing to do is for you to dissimulate and mitigate and soften the prince's will'.[6] In 1469 Louis XI arrested and imprisoned Jean Balue, cardinal bishop of Angers, and Guillaume de Haraucourt, bishop of Verdun.[7] Although Balue remained in possession of his diocese he was saved from a worse fate only by papal intervention; and although he may

[1] *Ordonnances*, XIII 177–9.   [2] Basin, op. cit. p. 398.

[3] Ourliac, 'Le Concordat de 1472 . . . (Suite et fin)', pp. 130 ff.

[4] Basin, op. cit. p. 402. M. Ourliac ('Le Concordat de 1472 . . . (Suite et fin)', p. 131) reads 'punicque' for 'publicque' in this text, which is derived from F. Pinsson, *Caroli septimi francorum regis Pragmatica Sanctio* (Paris, 1666) p. 998.

[5] '. . . grans censures ecclesiastiques . . .' (J. Juvenal des Ursins, 'Verba mea auribus percipe, Domine', Bibl. nat.MS fr. 2701, fo. 109ᵛ).

[6] '. . . la ou ne pourroit pourfiter le plus expedient seroit pour vous de dissimuler en mittigant et adoulcissant le plaisir du prince' ('À, a, a, nescio loqui quia puer ego sum', Bibl. nat. MS fr. 2701, fo. 47ᵛ).

[7] H. Forgeot, *Jean Balue, cardinal d'Angers (1421?–1491)* (Bibl. Ec. Hautes Etudes, 106: 1895) pp. 80 ff.

have spent only a short time in it, the notorious cage in which he was confined at least caught the public imagination. Nearly fifty years later alleged fragments of it could be pointed out beneath the stairs leading from the courtyard to the council-chamber of the *hôtel commun* of Lyon.[1]

His predecessors, kings of France, thought Charles VII in 1432, had always been concerned that 'notable men, natives of the kingdom, nobles, clerks and other people of great merit' should be provided to benefices, 'so that the [fortified] places, of which there are many belonging to the Church, should be administered and inhabited by people loyal to them, and not by others, in order to obviate the great misfortunes which might have come about, and which were really to be feared, if those benefices got into the hands of foreigners'.[2] The dukes of Brittany and the dukes of Burgundy, and the English rulers of the *pays de conquête*, shared their view. The concordat of Redon in 1441 conceded to Jean V of Brittany the provision only of bishops 'faithful and agreeable' to him.[3] The last two dukes of Burgundy had effectively the same privilege.[4] All rulers had the same problems: concerning the political control of the greater benefices, concerning the supply of the lesser ones, concerning ecclesiastical taxation, concerning ecclesiastical jurisdiction. But the dukes of Brittany and Burgundy and the English regent in the north[5] did not feel it necessary for whatever reasons to bow to the Pragmaticians[6] — though they might for tactical reasons wave the flag of liberties. Charles VII did feel it necessary to bow to them. Their interests, those interests which were the very nature of later medieval career-churchmanship, in the form they took were too much for him to suppress.

[1] C. Bellièvre, *Souvenirs de voyages en Italie et en Orient, notes historiques, pièces en vers*, ed. C. Perrat (Travaux d'humanisme et renaissance, 23: Geneva, 1956) p. 33.

[2] *Ordonnances*, XIII 177.

[3] B. A. Pocquet du Haut-Jussé, *Les Papes et les ducs de Bretagne. Essai sur les rapports du Saint-Siège avec un état* (Bibl. Ec. fr. Athènes Rome, 133: 1928) pp. 577 ff.

[4] See, for instance, P. Gras, 'Les Evêques de Chalon de 1302 à 1416', in *M. Soc. Droit Pays bourguignons*, XV (1953) 49–50.

[5] C. T. Allmand, 'Normandy and the Council of Basel', in *Speculum*, XL (1965) 1–14.

[6] But see A. G. Jongkees, 'Philippe le Bon et la Pragmatique Sanction de Bourges', in *A. Bourgogne*, XXXVIII (1966) 161–71.

4

Representative Institutions

As individuals, each churchman, each noble, each town might conduct a private political relationship with the crown. Their fortune in this, as we have seen, and their success might vary. But was there no way in which they could unite against royal importunity — other than by the open leagues and alliances for military action, other than in a Praguerie or a war of the Public Weal? Could no more peaceable means be devised for settlement of the frictions of public life?

Some banding together was almost instinctive. There had been leagues of clergy, nobles and non-nobles long before the Valois. Local charters of privilege which concerned all three orders of society had been granted in the reign of Philippe *le bel* in return for grants of taxation; to Rouergue in 1297, to Auvergne in 1304. General ordinances had been made which concerned the privileges of land-owners in general.[1] After the death of Philippe *le bel* a general movement of provincial insurrection against a theoretically unjustifiable war-tax spread throughout France. In some areas leagues were formed. A grand assembly at Dijon in November 1314 was composed of 110 nobles led by Jean de Chalon comte d'Auxerre, 18 abbeys, 11 chapters, and deputies of the *commun* of 11 Burgundian towns. In Auvergne, Normandy and Languedoc there were no such unions; but still, in the following year, charters were granted to their inhabitants and to those of Burgundy, Picardy, Champagne, the *basses-marches* of the west, Berry and Nevers.[2]

Forms of such co-operation had developed all over western Europe in the thirteenth and fourteenth centuries. Attempts have been made to

[1] E. Lavisse, *Hist. de France*, III, part 2 (1901) 256 ff.
[2] A. Artonne, *Le Mouvement de 1314 et les chartes provinciales de 1315* (1912).

generalise about their nature.[1] But too much rigidity in such generalisation should be avoided. Each in its different way was the product of a search for a mechanism through which the forces of a medieval society as each developed might agree about the government of that society. In all the matters — financial, administrative, judicial and political — which fell within the competence of various institutions two elements emerge. One is the prince's need for assistance: a need expressed in his vassals' duty of aid and counsel, and descending, as the financial and administrative complexity of the later middle ages developed, into many more meticulous matters. The other is the subjects' need to advertise to the government their interests, whether already recognised in charters of privileges or newly developed. Both needs probably existed everywhere simultaneously, in varying proportions. And the nature of each assembly naturally varied with the social composition of the area it was drawn from and with that area's political past. Its existence also depended on the area's political present. None of these bodies was immutable; each changed with the political development of the region concerned. Around the crude political realities might be woven an integument of political theory, of law, of custom; but as the realities changed so was the virtuous husk shattered or itself transformed.

The beginning of royal Estates

A convenient starting-point of the more general assemblies in France is the reign of Philippe IV. Two kinds of royal motive are apparent; both had possibly a common ground in 'the legal fictions of the period'. The first was a need for support — or agreement — in a difficult matter which affected the king and kingdom. The legal consent of the community was necessary to the king before he could act, in a theory which was backed up in practice, not because the government might be too

[1] Corporatist comment on parliamentary opinion, with a useful if incomplete bibliography and résumé of both views, is given by E. Lousse, *La Société d'Ancien régime. Organisation et représentation corporatives*, 1 (Louvain, 1943). Cf. also H. M. Cam *et al.* 'Recent Work and Present Views on the Origins and Development of Representative Assemblies', in *Comitato Internazionale di Scienze Storiche, X Congresso Internazionale di Scienze Storiche, Roma ... 1955, Relazioni*, 1 (Florence, 1955) 15–21.

weak to act without it, but because an apparently solid support of the
Estates of the kingdom served to intimidate the pope, who ultimately
suffered. There were consultations about the king's relations with the
papacy in 1290 and 1302; there was a more important consultation in
1303 about the question of appealing to a general council against
Boniface VIII; there was a consultation in 1308 about the king's
measures to suppress the Templars.[1] No trouble was encountered from
any of them, and indeed some urban deputies to the last assembly went
according to their procurations 'to see and to know about the constitutions and the ordinances of our lord the king and to obey them,
according to the order of our said lord the king and of his officers' as
that of the deputies of Montiéramey put it.[2] But the government could
not be so sure of support in assemblies summoned for the second motive:
taxation. Only once in Philippe IV's reign was a general assembly
summoned, at the end of the reign at Paris in 1314, when the 'proposition'
was made by Enguerrand de Marigny and a tax was 'granted'.[3] But it
was granted only in principle and (especially since the assembly seems
to have been limited to the bourgeoisie of cathedral cities) was regarded
by nobody, not even the government, as finally binding on the taxpayers
of the kingdom.[4] The business of getting consent was not as simple as
that in France.

Opposition to taxation was apparent from the very beginning. There
was open resistance to taxation in the *bailliage* of Chaumont in 1296, and
it could be taken in the bishopric of Langres only 'by violence and by
force of arms'.[5] The government's difficulty was not in swallowing its
pride and asking for consent; it lay in the sheer mechanics of getting
that consent. About 1304 the assent of the king's council, of regional
assemblies, of local assemblies beneath them, was often not enough;
individuals had to be asked as well.[6] A period of experiment followed;
of attempts by the government to influence the taxpayer into giving his

[1] Lavisse, op. cit. III, part 2, 260 ff.
[2] *Docs relatifs aux Etats généraux et assemblées réunis sous Philippe le bel*, ed.
G. Picot (Docs inéd. sur l'hist. de France: 1901) p. 564.
[3] *Les Grandes Chron. de France*, ed. J. Viard (Soc. Hist. France) VIII (1934)
299–301.
[4] J. R. Strayer and C. H. Taylor, *Studies in Early French Taxation* (Harvard,
1939) pp. 82 ff.
[5] Ibid. p. 49.   [6] Ibid. pp. 67 ff.

consent and to create adequate machinery to obtain it. Assemblies of towns met, of varying composition and size, with varying powers demanded of their delegates by the government. By 1316 it had gathered enough information about the towns of the kingdom to be able to make quite a comprehensive assembly.[1] But this it failed to do consistently; and it failed also to use the larger meetings finally to grant taxes on behalf of the towns represented. The larger meetings were therefore simply to persuade, to negotiate and to facilitate the granting of taxes by more local urban bodies. The government could not get delegates to the larger meetings sufficiently instructed by their towns to grant a tax unless the town had first been fully informed of the government's purpose. Although an attempt was possibly made to inform the towns locally before the central meeting, the normal pattern was the opposite; their delegates heard the government's plans and reported back to them, and they later negotiated separately with the royal commissioners.[2]

Assemblies of nobles also met in the period before 1320, again of varying composition and size. There appears to have been a core-group of about three hundred barons on whom the government relied both for military service and for these meetings; sometimes the government took advice of smaller groups of barons and prelates, and sometimes the core-group was reinforced by other barons and by bannerets. Again there seems to have been a failure on the part of the government to persuade a central meeting to commit the whole class to taxation. Again this may have led to the prevailing use in the next decades of local rather than central assemblies of nobles when subsidies were in the air.[3] Assemblies of the clergy, too, were summoned to consent to taxation taken directly from them without consulting the pope; here again the natural unit seems to have been the council of the ecclesiastical province and there is again evidence that those nominally represented at the meeting refused to recognise grants made by it.[4] A general assembly of the kingdom was prepared, therefore, to endorse the dissolution of an

[1] C. H. Taylor, 'Assemblies of French Towns in 1316', in *Speculum*, XIV (1939) 289.

[2] C. H. Taylor, 'An Assembly of French Towns in March 1318', in *Speculum*, XIII (1938) 295–303; Strayer and Taylor, op. cit. pp. 109–74.

[3] C. H. Taylor, 'The Composition of Baronial Assemblies in France, 1315–1320', in *Speculum*, XXIX (1954) 433–59.

[4] Strayer and Taylor, op. cit. pp. 24–43.

old and honourable military order; but it was not prepared to endorse the government's actions when it came to that far sharper sting, the possibility of losing money to it.

So sharp was the sting that the struggle against the royal commissioners was carried to every last local ditch. As a result the *quid pro quo* for taxation — 'redress of grievances' — was also made locally. In the period before 1320 the administrative gravamina of the governed were channelled to the government in as many different ways as the administrative needs of the government were channelled down to them. Grievances were presented sometimes by the regional unit, sometimes by the class unit, sometimes by units even smaller. The aim was those acts conferring or confirming privilege; acts such as those obtained by the three orders of Rouergue in 1297 and by those of Auvergne in 1304; such as those protecting the privileges of the nobility of the kingdom in general from 1287 onwards.[1] The amount of resistance offered, the extent of the concessions claimed and the formality with which they were granted naturally varied. The movement for the charters of 1314–16 was simply an accumulation of local resistances which gathered most naturally, when such agglomeration was necessary, at a regional level. Some of the leaders of these movements received their training in the central royal administration, but they put regional loyalty first.[2] But if the *pays* imposed its allegiance, so did the town, the locality, the class, the local group, the family; even the individual felt he must make his separate bargain with the government. By the third decade of the fourteenth century some vague and imprecise forms of representative institutions had emerged; they were tentative, experimental, institutionally inchoate; and they were almost wholly the product of a government's attempt, in its own interests, to impose a form of 'liberty' upon the kingdom which it seems it did not want.

General assemblies

The attempts continued; but the necessity of appealing to regional assemblies remained. Throughout the reign of Philippe VI difficulties with privileged bodies and with privileged individuals continued.

[1] Lavisse, op. cit. III, part 2, 256–7.   [2] Artonne, op. cit. pp. 51 ff.

Commissioners went round the *bailliages* and *sénéchaussées*, taking their taxes as they could find them; in return, local exemptions and privileges were granted.[1] In 1339 a memorandum headed 'These are the ways by which it seems the king may raise money' was drafted in the *Chambre des comptes* in Paris. 'First [it ran], by asking his people, great, middling and small, and the clergy, and he has a good reason for doing so, which will be told them. And the way to ask them is this: the king should summon them to Paris before him on a certain day, as has been done before. But if this way does not have his approval, then he should talk first to those of the town of Paris and of the *vicomté* of Paris and those of the *bailliages* of Senlis, of Vermandois and of Amiens.' Other meetings were to be held at Chartres for the southern part of the *domaine* and for the west, at Melun for Sens, Mâcon and Auvergne, and at Provins or Meaux for Champagne. 'Then, that in his presence the requests that he thinks useful to make should be made. Or the king should send some sure persons to the places named to make the requests; but this seems the less appropriate method. Then it would seem a good idea if the king should speak to the prelates of the places named and to those who would be near the places, and in those places named in which they would be nearest. Then in the same way he should summon the deans and chapters, abbots and priors of black and white monks.'[2] Admittedly about this time in England Edward III was thinking about much the same kind of expedient;[3] but this in England was exceptional, whereas in France it was the norm.

Already in 1316 in Languedoc there were complaints of the distance to travel to a central meeting from 'a region so remote': and Midi deputies did not come to a projected general assembly two years

[1] J. Viard, 'Un Chapitre d'histoire admin. Les Ressources extraordinaires de la royauté sous Philippe VI de Valois', in R. *Questions hist.* XLIV (1888) 167–218.

[2] M. Jusselin, 'Comment la France se préparait à la guerre de Cent ans', in *Bibl. Ec. Chartes*, LXXIII (1912) 229–30. For the government's manœuvres in raising taxes the following year, see J. B. Henneman, Jr, 'Financing the Hundred Years War: Royal Taxation in France in 1340', in *Speculum*, XLII (1967) 275–98.

[3] J. F. Willard, 'Edward III's Negotiations for a Grant in 1337', in *Engl. hist. R.* XXI (1906) 727–31; J. G. Edwards, 'Taxation and Consent in the Court of Common Pleas, 1338', in *Engl. hist. R.* LVII (1942) 473–82.

later.[1] By 1345 Philippe VI could tell his son that 'the inhabitants of the *sénéchaussées* . . . can be assembled more speedily and with less trouble, less cost and less expense before you than before us'; after this there were no general assemblies of the whole kingdom until the 1420s.[2] But if at the last such general assembly, in 1343, a general grant had been made it was still necessary to send commissioners down into the country: separate agreements were made with, for instance, Jeanne de Navarre in May 1343; with Rouen in September; with the archbishop of Reims and with the comte de Blois.[3] In 1345 commissioners went around without a preliminary meeting. They had very little success in the south: except on the lands of the comte de Vendôme and of his brother, the communities of Carcassonne *sénéchaussée* refused to pay; only part of Rouergue contributed; in Beaucaire, Montpellier paid up only after a long discussion and Nîmes, having disgorged 600 *livres* owing on the 1338 subsidy, protested so much that the king had to give it back to them. In the north things were better: summoned to consult the king directly, the deputies of Reims gave a subsidy; but it was still necessary to make a grant of non-prejudice of the town's liberties and franchises and to say that their consent conferred no new right upon the king.[4] At the Estates of Languedoil at Paris in 1346 each province voted separately; but it was still necessary for the Vermandois Estates to meet afterwards to confirm the grant.[5] The same thing happened again in 1347 and again in 1351.[6] Similarly in the Midi the independent position of the *sénéchaussées* changed only slowly; even in a general assembly of the Estates of Languedoc each at this time deliberated separately, handed in separate lists of grievances and made separate grants.[7]

In the north general meetings were in abeyance between 1351 and 1355. By this time it seems as if a blanket grant by a general assembly

[1] P. Dognon, *Les Institutions politiques et admin. du pays de Languedoc du xiii* *siècle aux guerres de Religion* (Toulouse, 1895) p. 207.

[2] C. Devic and J. Vaissete, *Hist. gén. de Languedoc*, x (Toulouse, 1885) 'Preuves', col. 977; Dognon, op. cit. pp. 209–11.

[3] Strayer and Taylor, op. cit. p. 171; Viard, op. cit. pp. 192–3.

[4] Ibid. pp. 194–5.   [5] Ibid. pp. 195–7.

[6] Ibid. pp. 201–4; *Ordonnances des rois de France de la troisième race*, ii, ed. E. J. de Laurière (1729) 393–6, 400–10, 439–41, iii, ed. D. Secousse (1732) 677.

[7] Dognon, op. cit. p. 213.

had become sufficient to cover a multitude of subsequent specific grants by a local assembly. The letters to the commissioners to hold the Estates of Anjou and Maine in 1352 recite the proceedings of the 1351 general assembly and ask for a renewal of the tax then granted. Unfortunately these Estates were not held before the end of August, if they were held at all; but the nobles and the towns (and possibly the clergy) of Vermandois and Beauvaisis renewed the grant and renewed it again in 1353.[1] Letters to the commissioners to hold the Estates of the *bailliage* of Senlis in 1354 again refer to the 1351 grant; Senlis was to grant a tax for another year as they had the year before (but again there is no evidence that the Estates were held).[2] The 1353 grant of Vermandois was renewed in 1354, and in 1355 the Estates of the *bailliages* of Auvergne and the Montagnes d'Auvergne made a similar grant; and the same kind of yearly grant was made in Normandy in this period.[3] Each was repaid with an ordinance against 'abuses'. Not until November 1355, under pressure of the war, did the government try again to get a large grant out of a general assembly of Languedoil — and with ultimately disastrous consequences.[4]

The Estates, after the débâcle of Poitiers, showed, under the influence of the friends of the imprisoned Charles de Navarre and of Robert Le Coq, bishop of Laon, a clear hostility to the court and a passion for reform of the administration. The session of October 1356 demanded *inter alia* the dauphin's consent to their nominating a reforming council or at least to their close surveillance of military and financial matters. Charles succeeded in fending off the assembly; but his need to raise the money he had hoped to obtain from it led to unpopular monetary mutations and a rising in Paris under Etienne Marcel, *prévôt des marchands*, which demanded the return of the Estates. A second session early in 1357 demanded an *épuration* of the civil service on a far grander scale than its predecessor and a greater reforming ordinance. The crisis continued into 1358, after the escape of Charles de Navarre at the end of

[1] *Ordonnances*, II 503–8, 529–32, III xxv–xxvij; *Arch. admin. de la ville de Reims*, ed. P. Varin (Docs inéd. sur l'hist. de France) III (1848) 32, 43.
[2] *Ordonnances*, II 557–8, III xxix.
[3] Ibid. II 567–70, III 678–82; *Arch. admin. . . . Reims*, III 59; H. Prentout, *Les Etats provinciaux de Normandie*, I (M. Acad. nat. Sci. Arts Caen, NS I: Caen, 1925) 102–4.
[4] R. Delachenal, *Hist. de Charles V*, I (1909) 119 ff.

the previous year. The session of the Estates of February 1358 attempted to resuscitate the ordinance of 1357 and the *épuration* of the civil service, both of which were hardly being executed; and it demanded full meetings of the Estates of Languedoil at Paris. Violence grew worse, and the dauphin was forced once more to submit. In March he left Paris and began military operations against the city; in May he summoned the Estates of Languedoil to Compiègne. The assembly, though far from subservient, proved clearly that a reaction had occurred against the activities of the Estates of the previous years. Robert Le Coq lost all influence. But it was not until after the convulsions of the Jacquerie, and after the collapse of Marcel's authority in Paris had produced a revolt against him which led to his death, that the Parisian revolution ended. It was it, rather than the reforming fervour of the Estates of Languedoil, that had provided the real danger. The Estates themselves continued to exhibit the tendencies which made them of so little value to a ruler. Even in the session of October 1356 the question of referring back was in the air;[1] both sides — or at least the administration — made appeals to regional assemblies;[2] there is evidence that their constituents disapproved of some of the things that the Estates in Paris did, both because they were too radical[3] and because they were not radical enough (for the latter reason Normandy boycotted the session of March 1356).[4]

In the Midi the pressure of the war tended to reinforce the links of the *sénéchaussées*; large general assemblies of more than the three great *sénéchaussées* of Toulouse, Carcassonne and Beaucaire were held, but many more were of the three alone or of a smaller number — even of a single *sénéchaussée*. But before the battle of Poitiers some common sense was emerging; in that very year the *sénéchaussées* of Périgord-Quercy, Rouergue, Carcassonne and Toulouse gave a subsidy, wrote out their conditions together, and asserted that no tax should be taken until the whole of Languedoc agreed. But when, eventually, the *pays* of the west and north-west returned from the English sovereignty imposed on them

---

[1] 'Journal des Etats généraux réunis à Paris au mois d'octobre 1356', ed. R. Delachenal, in *Nouvelle R. hist. Droit*, XXIV (1900) 439–40.

[2] Delachenal, op. cit. I 265 nn 1–2, 299.

[3] G. Picot, *Hist. des Etats généraux*, 2nd ed. I (1888) 58 n 2.

[4] Delachenal, op. cit. I 139; *Chron. des règnes de Jean II et de Charles V*, ed. R. Delachenal (Soc. Hist. France) I (1910) 58.

by the treaty of Brétigny, they refused to renew this co-operation with areas now heavily taxed, since part of the bribe to win them into accepting liberation had been temporary release from taxation.[1] The Estates of Languedoc from now on fall awkwardly between the categories of general and regional assemblies; and simply because of their vitality and survival power it becomes more reasonable to deal with them as the latter. The only general assembly which remained was therefore the Estates of Languedoil, very occasionally indeed reinforced by deputies from the Midi into a simulacrum of a general assembly of the kingdom.

The aid for the ransom of Jean II did not in theory need to be agreed to; though a number of local assemblies may have 'regulated' it and so to some extent 'consented'.[2] A further tax for the war seems to have been put on by some kind of assembly at Amiens in 1363,[3] and this again seems to have covered a number of later local grants. Certainly an ordinance issued in 1367 after a meeting at Sens of the Estates of southern and eastern Languedoil referred for authority for a tax to the Amiens grant; and it was still current in 1369 when, after a general meeting in Paris in May to whip up enthusiasm for a campaign against the English, a general assembly at Rouen in August put on a year's tax and another at Paris in December put one on indefinitely at a higher rate than the Amiens grant.[4] After 1369 Charles V found general meetings unnecessary; and he had not found them very necessary since the rather peculiarly composed meeting of 1363. It is possible that the Sens meeting of 1367 was part of a larger complex, since there seem to have been meetings of some importance at Chartres and Compiègne about the same time;[5] but otherwise only the matter of renewing the war with England, with its legal and financial problems, seems to have provoked him into dealing with them. And towards the end of his reign 'royal'

---

[1] Dognon, op. cit. pp. 213–17.

[2] A. Vuitry, *Études sur le régime financier de la France avant la Révolution de 1789*, NS II *Les Trois Premiers Valois, 1328–1380* (1883) 108 ff.

[3] Ibid. pp. 115–18.

[4] *Ordonnances*, v, ed. D. Secousse (1736) p. 20; *Chron. ... de Jean II et ... Charles V*, II (1916) 72–6; *Mandements et actes divers de Charles V (1364–1380)*, ed. L. Delisle (Docs inéd. sur l'hist. de France: 1874) pp. 277–80, 311–15, 319–20, 342–3; Vuitry, op. cit. pp. 125–9.

[5] *Ordonnances*, v 15–22; *Arch. admin. ... Reims*, III 318–21; Vuitry, op. cit. pp. 119–20.

regional assemblies too were feeling the pinch. From 1360, except under pressing war conditions, the Norman Estates or fragments of them met rarely.[1] In Languedoc opposition is evident at least in the 1370s; it is possible the Estates of Auvergne and Limousin suffered at the same period and an administrative reaction to the Estates of Dauphiné again began in 1370.[2]

But popular reaction followed Charles' abolition of the *fouages* and his death in 1380. A meeting of the Estates of Languedoil forced, again with the assistance of a Paris mob, an ordinance abolishing all taxation; but it seems also to have granted a tax in principle, the details of which were to be decided on by local assemblies.[3] These seem to have refused a tax at all; the Norman Estates replied 'that there should be a meeting at Paris, and that the province of Normandy should do what the other provinces did', and Laon refused on the interesting grounds that its deputies 'to assemblies and convocations sent in the past' had not been provided with 'proxies and powers to grant what would be there discussed, but only to hear and report, and sometimes to do what the deputies of Paris did, and [those of] the . . . inhabitants of the other *bonnes villes* of the . . . kingdom, and not what those of the . . . province to which they belonged did'.[4] In Sens a merchant called Pierre Chasserat stirred up a riot; and he said to the deputy Pierre Le Peletier 'You were at the assembly and you granted the tax. God's blood, it won't go through. The fur hats [the urban magnates] will pay.' Peletier tried to tell him that grant was reasonable; but to no avail.[5]

At a new general assembly in Paris in December the deputies (who seem to have retained their regional groupings) failed to agree; though the ordinance of November abolishing taxes was slightly extended, nothing was done about a new grant. In February 1381 a number of

[1] Prentout, op. cit. I 120 ff.

[2] Dognon, op. cit. pp. 236 ff; H. Gilles, *Les Etats de Languedoc au xve siècle* (Toulouse, 1965) pp. 26–27; A. Thomas, *Les Etats provinciaux de la France centrale sous Charles VII*, I (1879) 22–4; A. Dussert, *Les Etats du Dauphiné aux xive et xve siècles* (B. Acad. delphinale, ser. 5 VIII: Grenoble, 1914) pp. 71–96.

[3] L. Mirot, *Les Insurrections urbaines au début du règne de Charles VI (1380–1383)* (1905) pp. 28 ff.

[4] *Chron. des quatres premiers Valois (1327–1393)*, ed. S. Luce (Soc. Hist. France: 1862) p. 293; Mirot, op. cit. pp. 19 n 1, 40–1.

[5] Ibid. pp. 42–3.

regions granted a tax; and in March possibly a prorogued session of the Estates of Languedoil made this general. Local increments were put on by further local assemblies; and at the same time there was local resistance and refusal to pay even the original tax already granted by local and central assemblies. In 1382 the crown took more control of taxes via the local meetings; by this time some of the major urban revolts which characterised the early 1380s had been suppressed. There was still some resistance from local assemblies in some areas; but more and more the resistance seems to have been outside the Estates. Towards the end of 1382 arbitrary increments were taken without the authority of any assembly in Normandy and elsewhere; and the opposition was now entirely disorganised.[1] The whole system of Estates, both general and regional, seems to have broken down; and if the ordinances of November 1380, and of January and March 1381, had reduced the government as far as taxation was concerned beyond even the position of Philippe IV, the Estates' inability to act had reduced them equally to the level of their primitive forebears of the early fourteenth century. With an army in being and a victory to its reputation, the administration of Charles VI had little trouble in suppressing such disorganised revolt in the months after the battle of Roosebeke; thereafter general meetings were in abeyance and local assemblies again came under pressure.

With the English invasion in 1412 a new meeting of the Estates of Languedoil was summoned.[2] Reform was again very much in the air; the political background again was favourable and there was again an intervention by a Paris mob. But at least as far as taxation was concerned, the Estates of 1413 proved as unco-operative as their predecessors; the deputies of Normandy said, for instance, that 'as for the aid and comfort which the king requires, that the king has not at all made clear what aid and what comfort he does require, and that they, present for the *bonnes villes* of the province, are and always will be ready to serve him and obey him, and they think that those who are not there will be too; and, as far as the *aide* is concerned, that they have power only to hear and report'.[3]

---

[1] Ibid. *passim.*
[2] A. Coville, *Les Cabochiens et l'ordonnance de 1413* (1888) pp. 137 ff.
[3] 'Rapport adressé au roi, sur les doléances du clergé, aux Etats généraux de 1413', ed. J. Marion, in *Bibl. Ec. Chartes*, ser. 2 1 (1844) 284.

M

The abolitions of taxation in 1417–18 were quickly dealt with. In English France a meeting of the Estates at Paris in 1420 put back 'the spawn of the devil of hell, that is, impositions, *quatriesmes* and *maltotes*'.[1] In French France an assembly of those of the Estates of Languedoil which remained un-Englished, together with a few deputies from Languedoc, granted a *fouage* of 800,000 *livres*.[2] But whereas in the north there was only to be under the duke of Bedford one further general assembly of the Estates of the English possessions as a whole,[3] in the south a second period of general meetings was beginning.[4] The idea now seems on the whole to have been more acceptable; even the Midi made (if only in 1421) some attempt to attend, and when its deputies were not there the government at first pretended that they were, but this helpful fiction seems soon to have been abandoned.[5] But though Tours, at least, believed in the virtues of common action,[6] it was uncommonly difficult to impose upon the kingdom. In the first twenty years of Charles VII's reign six attempts were made to get a plenary assembly of the three estates of the kingdom; only one was successful, after four or five prorogations, at Chinon in September and October 1428, and even now the deputies of Languedoc deliberated apart from those of Languedoil. Possibly they made a joint vote; but certainly they presented separate lists of grievances and asked (in fact unsuccessfully) for an assurance that they would not in future be summoned outside the *pays*. The deputies of Rouergue at the assembly made their notorious

---

[1] *Journal d'un bourgeois de Paris, 1405–1449*, ed. A. Tuétey (Soc. Hist. Paris: 1881) p. 149.

[2] A. Thomas, 'Les Etats généraux sous Charles VII. Etude chronologique d'après des docs inéd.' in *Cabinet hist.* XXIV (1878) 124–5; 'Les Etats généraux sous Charles VII. Notes et docs nouveaux', in R. *hist.* XL (1889) 56–7; *Reg. consulaires de la ville de Lyon*, ed. M.C. and G. Guigue, I (Lyon, 1882) p. 303.

[3] B. J. H. Rowe, 'The Estates of Normandy under the Duke of Bedford', in *Engl. hist. R.* XLVI (1931) 553–4.

[4] The most recent general discussion may be found in J.R. Major, *Representative Institutions in Renaissance France, 1421–1559* (Madison, 1960) pp. 25 ff.

[5] Thomas, 'Les Etats généraux ... Notes', pp. 56–8; 'Le Midi et les Etats généraux sous Charles VII', in *A. Midi*, I (1889) 292 ff.

[6] See below, p. 364.

declaration of independence.[1] But between 1420 and 1440 a general assembly of Languedoil met fairly frequently. It was sometimes necessary to split the assembly into two, for the east and the west; but general grants were made and, on the whole, deputies seem to have come with sufficient powers.[2] Yet throughout the period ran a leitmotive of provincial consent: their quota of taxation had still to be granted by local assemblies;[3] local assemblies still granted taxes not apparently authorised by a general assembly;[4] local representations, from bodies even beneath the level of local assemblies, were made and, in response to this pressure, general or specific relaxations and rebates were made by the government.[5]

As early as 1425 a tax was raised by the government in anticipation of a grant by the Estates of Languedoil; but there was difficulty in raising it.[6] After the Estates of Chinon in 1428 the general assembly in the north is clouded in an obscurity due possibly only to lack of evidence; but there is evidence that in both 1429 and 1430 the king by-passed any central assembly 'as much by his right and authority after his recent coronation at Reims as otherwise' and dealt with local assemblies directly.[7] Again victory brought its own rewards. In 1435 the Estates of western Languedoil at Poitiers granted the old *aides* for the war of Charles VI for four years.[8] In Poitiers the following year the Estates of

[1] Thomas, 'Le Midi et les Etats généraux', in *A. Midi*, IV (1892) 8; 'Les Etats généraux ... Etude', pp. 167–9; 'Les Etats généraux ... Notes', pp. 66–8.

[2] Thomas, 'Les Etats généraux ... Etude', pp. 158–60, 163–6, 167; 'Les Etats généraux ... Notes', pp. 63–5. For the powers demanded and given, see ibid. p. 80; 'Nouveaux docs sur les Etats généraux du xve siècle', ed. C. de Grandmaison, in *B. Soc. archéol. Touraine*, IV (1877–9) 144–6; *Reg. consulaires ... Lyon*, I 301.

[3] Thomas, 'Les Etats généraux ... Etude', pp. 156, 164 n3, 205–6; 'Les Etats généraux ... Notes', pp. 63–5, 85 n 2; *Les Etats provinciaux*, I 69–81, 128–34; G. du Fresne de Beaucourt, *Hist. de Charles VII*, II (1882) 581, 600, III (1885) 435.

[4] *Reg. consulaires ... Lyon*, I 349 ff; Thomas, *Les Etats provinciaux*, I 74 ff.

[5] Ibid. pp. 70–2; 'Les Etats généraux ... Etude', pp. 201, 204; 'Les Etats généraux ... Notes', pp. 59–60, 62–3, 71; Beaucourt, op. cit. II 277–8, 598.

[6] Thomas, 'Les Etats généraux ... Etude', pp. 160–2, 215–16; Beaucourt, op. cit. II 584–5.

[7] Thomas, 'Les Etats généraux ... Notes', pp. 68–71.

[8] Thomas, 'Les Etats généraux ... Etude', pp. 205–6.

Languedoil granted them indefinitely; if others were not so certain, the government certainly considered *aides* permanent.[1] The end was in sight; and from 1436 Charles VII began to behave as if the *tailles*, previously granted annually, were indefinite too. If a general session of the Estates of the kingdom was held at Bourges in 1440, its members were few and its acts are unknown;[2] a last grant of taxation was made by the Estates of Languedoil at Orléans in the autumn of 1439.[3] If the number of prorogations of the assemblies for lack of attendance is any guide, not many shared the affection for general meetings displayed by the deputies of Tours or possibly by the Auvergnats in 1442.[4] Their being abandoned seems to have caused little consternation. Thereafter they were merely the armament of politicians,[5] the battle-cry of satirists and the hope of honest reformers. The only Estates-general of Louis XI's reign, the session at Tours in 1468, begged, 'because they cannot easily assemble', not to be summoned again.[6]

Pretension and inanition

Since the general assembly of the kingdom never became permanent, it could not acquire precise 'attributions'. Broad theories of the Estates' powers did, of course, exist. A general principle that 'whosoever wishes to make a law or constitution must summon those whom it affects' had been used as an argument by Guillaume Erard in a Parlement

[1] Ibid. pp. 207–8; 'Les Etats généraux... Notes', pp. 84–8.

[2] Beaucourt, op. cit. III 442–3; J. Garillot, *Les Etats généraux de 1439* (Nancy, 1947) pp. 17–18; Thomas, 'Le Midi et les Etats généraux', IV 17.

[3] Thomas, 'Les Etats généraux... Etude', pp. 208–10; Beaucourt, op. cit. III 63–6, 441–3, 528–9; A. Marchadier, *Les Etats généraux sous Charles VII* (Bordeaux, 1904) pp. 104 ff; Garillot, op. cit. pp. 9 ff; Thomas, 'Le Midi et les Etats généraux', IV 15–16.

[4] Beaucourt, op. cit. II 588–9; Thomas, 'Les Etats généraux... Etude', pp. 166–7, 200, 205–6, 217–18; 'Les Etats généraux... Notes', pp. 79–82; *Les Etats provinciaux*, I 118–20.

[5] Beaucourt, op. cit. III 129, 220, 227; M. d'Escouchy, *Chron.* ed. Beaucourt (Soc. Hist. France) III (1864) 75; E. de Monstrelet, *Chron.* ed. L. Douët-d'Arcq (Soc. Hist. France) VI (1862) 39.

[6] C. J. de Mayer, *Des Etats généraux et autres assemblées nationales*, IX (1789) 222.

lawsuit in 1433; and in the following February in the *Cour des aides* Jacques Jouvenel des Ursins argued from 'the ordinance recently made at the three estates at Tours, that is that because of the great burdens and oppressions which were upon the people no *aides* or subsidies would be imposed in future without summoning the three estates'.[1] In the general Estates of 1439, it will be remembered, Jacques Jouvenel again maintained 'with a great deal of vigour that since the king was only a simple usufructuary of the crown he could not alienate the least part of his *domaine* without the consent of his Estates'.[2] The question of the regency during the minority of Charles VIII, thought Philippe Pot in 1484, 'should be examined first by the Estates-general, not that they should undertake it themselves, but so that some most worthy people may be appointed by the decision of the Estates'. Philippe VI, he argued, had submitted the question of the succession to the throne at the beginning of the war with England to the assembly. When Jean II was captured, 'did not the Estates assume the government and administration of the kingdom . . .'? Charles V had received his powers from the Estates; at his death 'the kingdom was regulated and administered by the advice of the Estates'.[3] These instances will hardly bear examination; though Charles VI was thought, at least by Monstrelet, to have promulgated an ordinance which provided for government by the three estates during the minority of his heir in 1407.[4] But Jean de Terre-Vermeille some thirteen years later denied the Estates (along with the pope and the 'civil body of the kingdom') any right to change the fundamental law of primogenitary right.[5]

For the trouble with these arguments was that any examples which could be given of the principles' being put into practice were some of the rather rare occasions when they were being honoured more in the observance than in the breach. The assembly had admittedly ratified treaties and partitionings of the kingdom; but in a very random way.[6] And in the view

[1] P. Viollet, *Hist. des institutions politiques et admin. de la France*, III (1903) 221–2; Thomas, 'Les Etats généraux . . . Etude', p. 203.

[2] See above, pp. 95–6.

[3] J. Masselin, *Journal des Etats généraux de France tenus à Tours en 1484*, ed. A. Bernier (Docs inéd. sur l'hist. de France: 1835) pp. 146, 152.

[4] Op. cit. I (1857) 170; *Ordonnances*, IX, ed. D. Secousse (1755) p. 269 n (b).

[5] *Joannes de Terra Rubea contra rebelles suorum regum* (Lyon, 1526) fo. 30ʳ.

[6] Garillot, op. cit. pp. 55–8.

of Pierre d'Oriole at the Estates of 1468 the assembly should be grateful to the king for letting it deal with the affair of Normandy at all: 'We are bound to thank him when it pleases him to tell us of such a great and weighty matter; and we see the good and high desire which he has to preserve the rights of his crown and of his kingdom.'[1] This was very much the view of those whom Philippe Pot took some trouble to attack in his speech in 1484; of those who thought 'the consent of the Estates has not legally to be sought except in raising taxes; if it is granted otherwise, it is a favour of the princes, and their courteousness'.[2] And though, admittedly, the assembly presented grievances, some of which might end up in ameliorative ordinances, that Erard's principle of the consent of those interested to 'une loy ou constitucion' should be generally observed was too much to hope. The assembly could not therefore acquire a share in the process of law-making. Except at certain great and rather *ad hoc* moments the general Estates were not concerned with the business of justice. The law remained the king's own; and the question of a statute law to oppose the king's law by ordinance never arose. However many grievances might actually be redressed in an assembly, it lacked the essential permanence of an institution. Even if it did acquire some 'constitutional significance' when it met, this soon faded away when it was in abeyance; and, because it was infrequent, such attributions as it did possess could not develop from session to session. Because of this the actions of the general Estates of France, and their apologists' account of their powers, are largely irrelevant.

Even their brief moments of glory are irrelevant. The Estates could give political support when appealed to and as a result could assume a political role. An assembly could be captured by political parties or by an honest reforming movement. Both in 1355–8 and in 1413 worthy desire for reform mingled with less virtuous motives. The power of both Estates was not their own, but that of a Parisian mob; the initial submission of the government on both occasions was brought about by

---

[1] '. . . nous luy sommez tenu de mercier quant luy plet nous communiquer si grande et pondereuse matiere et voions le bon et ault vouloir quil a a guarder les droiz de ca couronne et de son royaume' (Arch. com. Rodez, BB 3, fo. 57ᵛ).

[2] Masselin, op. cit. p. 140.

its intervention. The far from disinterested role of Robert Le Coq in the Estates of the first period has been very much emphasised; behind the Estates' complaints about the iniquities of royal officers lay Le Coq's determination to oust his civil-service rivals and become chancellor.[1] The motives of Etienne Marcel, too, were equally far from disinterested;[2] and in the background lurked the sinister figure of Charles de Navarre. The Cabochian movement of 1413 had a Burgundian overtone; it was brought to an end when in August the upper-class Parisians revolted against the butchers and the Burgundians. The duc d'Orléans was admitted into Paris and on 5 September the ordinance of 26 May was revoked. The Religieux de St.-Denis asked several councillors who had praised it why they had consented to its abrogation. ' "By thus favouring the lords [they said], we'll get through our time"; and I rejoined at once [said the Religieux], "Then I may compare you to the weathercocks on church belfries, turning to every wind." '[3] But the great ordinance, the most comprehensive attempt by a general assembly to reform French royal administration in the later middle ages, was not so easily brought back.

Regional assemblies

The king was left, like his greater princes, to confront regional[4] assemblies. These had developed in most areas of the country during the fourteenth century. They have been defined as 'the meeting of the three orders of a province in an assembly regularly constituted, periodically convened and in the possession of certain political and administrative attributions of which the most important is the vote of taxation'.[5] But so narrow a definition is perhaps unwise.

[1] A. L. Funk, 'Robert Le Coq and Etienne Marcel', in *Speculum*, XIX (1944) 470–87; R. Cazelles, *La Société politique et la crise de la royauté sous Philippe de Valois* (1958) pp. 253–61.

[2] R. Cazelles, 'Etienne Marcel au sein de la haute bourgeoisie d'affaires', in *J. Savants* (1965) pp. 413–27.

[3] *Chron. du religieux de St.-Denis*, ed. L. Bellaguet (Docs inéd. sur. l'hist. de France) v (1844) 154.

[4] For the nomenclature of medieval French Estates, see G. Dupont-Ferrier, *Etudes sur les institutions financières de la France à la fin du Moyen âge*, II *Les Finances extraordinaires et leur mécanisme* (1932) 24, 27–8.

[5] L. Cadier, *Les Etats de Béarn depuis leurs origines jusqu'au commencement du xvie siècle* (1888) p. 1.

The origin of these regional assemblies varied. Some had emerged insensibly out of a princely council. The origins of the Estates of Brittany, for instance, are obscure. If the assembly is defined as a 'meeting of the three orders' then it developed late in the fourteenth century and existed pretty sporadically throughout the fifteenth. If the Breton Parlement is taken as the true assembly of Brittany (as indeed it should be) then the origins of that aristocratic and clerical body, like other *curiae*, lie much farther back. Before duke Pierre *mauclerc* in the earlier thirteenth century, vassals or representatives appear not to have been summoned to the duke's court; it consisted entirely of officers, civil-service councillors and a few lords. Not until the end of the thirteenth century did 'the session of the highest law court in Brittany coincide with the meeting of the Estates';[1] but from then on it seems clear that the sovereign court of Brittany, the highest appellate juris-diction, was firmly attached to and derived its authority from the larger Parlement of Breton seigneurs, prelates and clerks. It seems as im-possible to give many examples of the meeting of this body in the thirteenth and early fourteenth centuries as it is to compile an accurate list of sessions of the Parlement or of the Estates under either name in the fourteenth and fifteenth centuries.[2] But it seems clear that in Brittany, at least, possibly because of the comparatively small population of the duchy and the comparative insignificance of its towns, the process of development of the Estates from an enlarged *curia* was a slow and comparatively incomplete one.

The origins of the Estates of Béarn are even more obscure. The long reign of the powerful Gaston Fébus seems to have obfuscated the development of a single representative body out of the fragmentary *cours* in existence in Béarn in the early fourteenth century. The full *curia* of the vicomte had been weakened from the twelfth century by the development of a small council of *barons-jurats* which effectively became the sovereign court; the *cour majour* of all the nobles of the vicomté was

---

[1] E. Texier, *Etude sur la Cour ducale et les origines du Parlement de Bretagne* (Rennes, 1905) p. 70.

[2] Ibid. pp. 70 ff; B.-A. Pocquet du Haut-Jussé, 'Les Faux Etats de Bretagne de 1315 et les premiers Etats de Bretagne', in *Bibl. Ec. Chartes*, LXXXVI (1925) 401 n 1. J. de La Martinière, 'Le Parlement de Bretagne sous les rois de France, 1491–1554 [iii]', in *A. Bretagne*, XXXIX (1930–1) 219–22, gives a list of Breton assemblies from 1384 to 1462, but it is not complete.

summoned only for great matters like difficult successions. Alongside the *cour majour* developed, by 1270, a *cour des communautés*, which ratified matters concerning the bourgeoisie and which, in the early fourteenth century, increased in importance to parallel the *cour majour*. Under Gaston Fébus all these *cours* were ignored; legislation became the work of the seigneur alone; justice, already in the early fourteenth century slipping into the hands of the *sénéchal* of Béarn, became entirely his province and that of new and (if such a thing were possible) even more absolute courts.[1] But if the liberties of the Béarnais were trampled under their intemperate lord, their determination to resist as soon as possible seems to have developed almost as much; in 1391 the three estates of Béarn sprung fully armed into autonomous existence, and by 1440 they had acquired a comprehensive collection of attributions.[2] But sovereign jurisdiction returned into the hands of a resuscitated *cour* of barons, now given, since that body had disappeared with the *cour des communautés* into the Estates of Béarn, the name of *cour majour*.[3] It is possible to argue that the autonomous and sudden origin of the Estates of Béarn in 1391 is to a great extent illusory; though there seems to be very little evidence indeed of any fusion of the already existing bodies of the orders in the reign of Gaston Fébus, this was primarily due to the formidable character of Fébus himself. His reign was an interregnum in the history of the Béarnais assembly; and the assembly's powers, when that body did form, were inherited from the fragments of the *curia* (though other powers might develop later). The power of sovereign justice, which had broken off early, never returned to the ultimate heir of the early *curia*; but the fact that the meeting of 1391 did not deal with taxation, but with the question of succession, of the status of the vicomté and of the status of the Estates[4] adds weight to the curial argument.

In Dauphiné, too, there is a certain amount of evidence that the

---

[1] P. Tucoo-Chala, 'Les Institutions de la vicomté de Béarn', in F. Lot and R. Fawtier, *Hist. des institutions françaises au Moyen âge*, 1 *Institutions seigneuriales* (1957) 326 ff; Tucoo-Chala, *Gaston Fébus et la vicomté de Béarn* (Bordeaux, 1960) pp. 161–6.

[2] Tucoo-Chala, 'Les Institutions . . . de Béarn', pp. 335 ff; Cadier, op. cit. pp. 299 ff.

[3] Tucoo-Chala, 'Les Institutions . . . de Béarn', p. 338.

[4] Ibid. p. 335; Tucoo-Chala, *Gaston Fébus*, p. 339. The Estates of Provence provide a third example of an assembly which emerged out of a princely

delphinal *curia* might have developed into a representative body; but the cession of Dauphiné to France intervened, and the delphinal Estates were the creation of the French kings-dauphins in imitation of the French Estates.[1] For in a certain number of areas seigneurial initiative was much more clearly marked than in others: whatever the nature of their prodromes, some assemblies had been created specifically to deal with the matter of consent to new taxation. In Languedoc, for instance, there had by 1300 been considerable experience of representation and of assemblies.[2] There had been 'feudal' assemblies; there had been in the north diocesan peace assemblies; there had been assemblies summoned by royal officers to deal with such things as fealties or the regulation of the export of corn under the ordinances of 1254. But there had been little or no institutional continuity between the anterior non-royal assemblies and the later royal assemblies; and the quarter-century before 1302–3 saw less progress in the use of the latter than did the era of Alphonse and Louis IX. The effect of the experiments of Guillaume de Cohardon, *sénéchal* of Carcassonne, and his lieutenant, Barthélémy de Pennautier, with largish assemblies may indeed have been to impress upon their successors the need to avoid them. But assemblies had occurred, had perhaps even 'assumed a place in tradition'. There is some evidence of a formal summons procedure. There is some evidence of representation. It was all very inchoate; and all very human. The assemblies were intended to serve the purposes of those who summoned them; and the primary purpose before, perhaps, the last decades of the century was not so much to obtain consent to taxation (though the question of consent was raised in Agenais and in Quercy), but to deal with political and administrative matters. But when the 'Estates of Languedoc' as a whole was created it was created to deal with the business of consent and effectively as a fragment of the general assembly of the kingdom.[3]

council (J. Denizet, 'Les Etats de Provence depuis l'origine jusqu'à la réunion de la Provence à la France, 1481', in *Positions des thèses de l'Ec. Chartes* (1920) p. 6).

[1] A. Dussert, *Les Etats du Dauphiné aux xive et xve siècles* (B. Acad. delphinale, ser. 5 VIII: Grenoble, 1914) pp. 37–9.

[2] T. N. Bisson, *Assemblies and Representation in Languedoc in the Thirteenth Century* (Princeton, 1964).

[3] H. Gilles, *Les Etats de Languedoc au xve siècle* (Toulouse, 1965) pp. 23 ff;

And in the areas more homogeneous than Languedoc, too, the financial needs of king or ruler were again the dynamic force in forming a representative assembly which had little connection with any pre-existing institution. In Burgundy, for example, at the end of the thirteenth century it appears to have been the custom to summon members of the three estates to the *Grands Jours* of Beaune (which included all members of the *curia ducis* together with some inferior judges) when important matters arose; but by the mid-fourteenth century they no longer appeared. And it is precisely in the mid-fourteenth century — in 1352 — that the first Burgundian assembly was summoned, by the king of France, the temporary possessor of the duchy, to grant a tax to him.[1] Again, as in Dauphiné at much the same time, a foreign idea gave a boost to the development of an institution apparently ignored by a native ruler. Eudes IV of Burgundy was probably content to collect local consent.[2] In Artois the assembly of the three estates, after a precursory assembly in 1340, effectively began in 1361 under the pressure of the *aide* for the ransom of Jean II, which could not be taken by the government except from the king's own vassals. An assembly in that year granted it for one year only in the form of a composition for the *aides* by which it was to be raised; and the *composition d'Artois* was levied annually in an annual assembly.[3] In Normandy there was a gap too great to be bridged between the last *curia ducis* before the English loss of Normandy and the first Estates in the mid-fourteenth century. There is little evidence of *bailliage* courts. The earliest negotiations for extraordinary taxation appear to have been with *ad hoc* groups, for most of which there is little evidence and all of which are obscure. In 1333 the duchy of Normandy was revived for the king's eldest son; and the revival of a political identity for an area which could in 1346 be called 'la langue de Normandie' may have contributed, in this turbulent and independent area, towards the formation of the

P. Dognon, *Les Institutions politiques et admin. du pays de Languedoc du xiiie siècle aux guerres de Religion* (Toulouse, 1895) pp. 205 ff.

[1] J. Billioud, *Les Etats de Bourgogne aux xive et xve siècles* (M. Acad. Dijon, ser. 5 IV: Dijon, 1922) pp. 7–23.

[2] Ibid. p. 14. Cf. J. Richard, 'Les Etats de Bourgogne', in *Rec. Soc. Jean Bodin*, XXIV (1966) 299–302.

[3] C. Hirschauer, *Les Etats d'Artois de leurs origines à l'occupation française*, I (1923) 12 ff.

first meeting of the Norman Estates in 1337.[1] The assembly, though firmly rooted on the charter of 1315, was sporadic until the late 1340s; in 1347 the duke of Normandy was authorised to assemble 'whenever and as often as he wants to all his subjects, both those of the *pays* of Normandy and those of his other lands ... be they prelates, religious, clerks, barons, nobles and non-nobles and all others of whatsoever estate or condition they may be, all together or in sections, in one place, town or castle or in several, and to require of them counsel and all kinds of *aides* for the wars ...'[2] Despite the *pays'* antiquity of independence and its notorious charter, the Estates of Normandy were again an artificial creation.

The direct action of the war which had caused such taxation or other more peaceable external pressure, too, could provoke the *ad hoc* creation of assemblies. In Normandy, from the 1350s on, smaller assemblies developed beneath the larger meeting in order to deal with the immediate local problems of the Breton war;[3] and such subordinate assemblies remained in Normandy until the end of the Hundred Years War.[4] The needs of local defence gave a boost to the development of the Estates of Dauphiné;[5] and in northern Languedoc they provoked the formation of autonomous assemblies in the period between 1350 and 1380. The three Cevenol dioceses of Gévaudan, Vivarais and Velay met together or apart in order to arrange for their protection, especially against the companies.[6] General political pressure could be a motive in a ruler's first summoning an assembly for support; the Estates of Lorraine appear first to have been called for counsel rather than for aid, in 1435, with a form possibly borrowed from the kingdom of France. But even in Lorraine the grant of an aid as a form of political support appeared

[1] H. Prentout, *Les Etats provinciaux de Normandie*, I (M. Acad. nat. Sci. Arts Caen, NS 1: Caen, 1925) 35–92.

[2] Ibid. pp. 92 ff; A. Coville, *Les Etats de Normandie. Leurs Origines et leur développement au xive siècle* (1894) p. 344.

[3] Ibid. pp. 144–7; Prentout, op. cit. I 103 ff.

[4] B. J. H. Rowe, 'The Estates of Normandy under the Duke of Bedford', in *Engl. hist. R.* XLVI (1931) 558–9.

[5] Dussert, op. cit. pp. 97 ff.

[6] A. Le Sourd, *Essai sur les Etats de Vivarais* (1926) pp. 40 ff; E. Delcambre, *Les Etats du Velay des origines à 1642* (St.-Etienne, 1938) pp. 61 ff. But the support these examples, and other odd autonomous meetings elsewhere, give to corporatist theses is minimal (cf. ibid. pp. 452–4).

incontinently upon the heels of the political motive; the Estates were dealing with the matter of consent to taxation in 1437. The most vital motive for the summoning of assemblies, both in response to local disturbance and, essentially, in response to external political pressure, was the need to raise money for these purposes.[1]

In some areas of France, then, especially on the wilder fringes of the country, the development of a ruler's *curia* to include the politically important men of the *pays* had effectively created an assembly when other pressures intervened; and the newest and possibly greatest pressure was the pressure of taxation, with all its implications for the 'liberties' of the region. In other areas, assemblies had to be formed in order to deal with the novelties. Though the motives might be common (and they, too, might vary in emphasis with the region), the actual emergence of an assembly was conditioned by the structure of politics in the *pays* concerned. The institution was formed by the men of that region as they required it; in the group of institutions as a whole there is infinite variety. And the nature of the institution during its existence was again conditioned by local social and political factors. In Flanders, for instance, the overwhelming preponderance of the three great towns of Bruges, Ghent and Ypres almost completely begged the question of representation by the 'orders' of the county.[2] The composition of the Estates varied with the social composition of the region. It is extremely difficult to deal with the personnel of the local assemblies in other than general terms: *procès-verbaux* are scanty and often non-existent; and it is clear from the better-known areas that the proportions of the Estates' composition could vary from period to period and from meeting to meeting. But none seems so nicely balanced as to be affected by such shifts; and it is possible to generalise about their social structure.

Structure and function

Most were aristocratic. In Burgundy the nobility roughly equalled

[1] E. Duvernoy, *Les Etats généraux des duchés de Lorraine et de Bar jusqu'à la majorité de Charles III (1559)* (1904) pp. 113 ff.
[2] J. Dhondt, ' "Ordres" ou "puissances": l'exemple des Etats de Flandre', in *Annales*, v (1950) 289–305.

the clergy and the *tiers état* put together;[1] and the same seems to be true of the Breton Estates. The Norman assembly may have had a preponderance of nobles in the fourteenth century; but the first clear evidence comes from 1443, when a few Norman nobles were with Charles VII, more (including the new English possessors of French titles, who had presumably in principle at least to attend the Estates) were on English service, and many seem inexplicably to have stayed away out of inertia: there were twenty-four clerical members present (and nine proctors), thirty urban deputies and only nine noble representatives. Such conditions were clearly exceptional.[2] In Artois the nobility clearly outnumbered the other two orders; in the Estates of central France they were again preponderant, and in those of Velay they were for a long time almost the only members.[3] In other areas the proportion was not perhaps so high: the *tiers* of Béarn was possibly more in evidence than elsewhere.[4] One great assembly was dominated by the bourgeoisie, that of Languedoc; only in those wilder areas in the *sénéchaussée* of Beaucaire-Nîmes was the part of the nobility at all active.[5] But in France none was dominated by the clergy and none by the peasantry, as were those of the allodial Drenthe in the Netherlands where, because of the peculiar structure of Drentois society, 'the Estates which appeared [in 1402] . . . with a regular constitution were confined to the single order of peasants holding allods'.[6] It is clear that the liberties of the subject were mainly in the hands of the minor nobility.

The size of the assembly naturally varied with the size of the area

---

[1] Billioud, op. cit. pp. 26 ff.

[2] Coville, op. cit. pp. 155–9; Prentout, op. cit. II (M. Acad. nat. Sci. Arts Caen, NS 2: Caen, 1926) 91 ff.

[3] Hirschauer, op. cit. I 36 ff; A. Thomas, *Les Etats provinciaux de la France centrale sous Charles VII*, I (1879) 29–36; Delcambre, op. cit. pp. 66 ff, 88 ff, 133 ff, 143 ff.

[4] Cadier, op. cit. pp. 225 ff.

[5] Dognon, op. cit. pp. 217–33; Gilles, op. cit. pp. 81–111. The determination of the assembly to protect the economic interests of the meridional towns has been stressed by J. Favier, 'La Defense des intérêts provinciaux: les Etats de Languedoc au xve siècle', in *J. Savants* (1966) pp. 183–92.

[6] R. Petit, 'Bulletin bibliographique', in *Anciens Pays et assemblées d'Etats*, II (1951) 100–1. Only in Normandy and in Velay was the peasantry in some sense directly represented (M. Baudot, 'La Représentation du tiers état aux Etats provinciaux de Normandie', in *M. Acad. nat. Sci. arts Caen*, NS V (1929) 129–47; Delcambre, op. cit. pp. 69–70, 90–2, 135–6, 159 ff); though it

concerned. It might also vary with the development of methods of representation from area to area, with the local political situation, and with a developing inertia.[1] In appearance an assembly might vary from the pomps and splendours of the Breton Parlement to the little group of people who met in the courtyard of the Auberge de la Pomme in Villeneuve-de-Berg in April 1422 as the three estates of Vivarais, or to the possibly even smaller group of people who met in Tulle in September 1419 as the three estates of Bas-Limousin.[2] Yet, whatever the size and formality of the assembly, all could claim a title of a representative institution, and all could, in some way, act as mediator between a ruler and his subjects.

All could be useful to their prince and to themselves. In the first place, they could act as the protectors of the liberties, privileges and interests of the regional orders.[3] In this they continued a tradition established by the leagues of 1314–16, if not before; but some appear to have been more active in this than others. Control in Brittany was, in theory, very close. During an enquiry into the royal rights and ancient customs of the *pays* of Brittany in 1455 the extremely elderly Jean de Breil, who said he had known the institution since 1384, deposed that 'when there is need the ... princes have the prelates, barons and other people representing the estates of the ... *pays* convened and assembled, and by their advice or by that of the majority, make in their Parlements constitutions and establishments for the activity, regulation and govern-ment of the *pays*, including the matter of justice, and they also make corrections in and interpretations of the ... customs, and what is established and ordained there has the force of law and constitution'; but in fact, as we shall see, the initiative lay elsewhere.[4] Nevertheless the

is possible that in Franc-Alleu the *tiers* was admitted on a larger franchise (see Thomas, *Les Etats provinciaux*, 1 36).

[1] Prentout, op. cit. II 91 ff; Dognon, op. cit. pp. 250–1; Gilles, op. cit. pp. 81–111.

[2] *Procès-verbaux*, in dom H. Morice, *Mémoires pour servir de preuves à l'hist. ecclés. et civile de Bretagne*, II (1744) cols 513, 557, 649, 686–7, 1564 ff, 1670–5, III (1746) cols 1–9; Le Sourd, op. cit. pp. 512–15; Thomas, *Les Etats provinciaux*, II (1879) 1–12.

[3] O. Martin, *Hist. du droit français* (1948) pp. 388–90, 397–9.

[4] Morice, op. cit. II col. 1654 (corrected by J. de La Martinière, 'Vannes, siège du Parlement de Bretagne', in *A. Bretagne*, XXXV (1921–3) 72–3). See below, p. 357.

machinery existed for remonstrance, and the care taken, for instance, by
François II to apologise for anticipating the grant of taxes seems to
show that he, if not others, was aware of it.[1] Most Estates presented
cahiers of *doléances* to be remedied in return for taxation; though it
depended on the area how extensive these were and how much notice
was taken of them by the sovereign.[2]

In the second place, they might be the ultimate grantors of taxation.
Consent to and the power of haggling over taxes remained, it might be
argued, probably the most vital function of most regional assembly as
long as it existed: Estates which were deprived of it, as were the royal
regional assemblies of central France in the 1450s, incontinently
disappeared as political bodies. Some areas were more exercised about
their right than others. In Brittany the business of consent seems to have
caused little fuss.[3] In Dauphiné and in Languedoc it caused a great deal.[4]
But again the efficacy of the 'liberty' varied. It was, in theory, preserved
by an assembly effectively in tutelage: there was very little the Estates of
Normandy or of Languedoc, for instance, could do about the demands
made of them by Louis XI.[5] In Dauphiné the Estates in this period did
rather better;[6] but everywhere where it was necessary and possible to
extract larger taxes from an assembly unable to resist such importunity,
but where it was not possible to ignore the assembly altogether, such
pressure was found. It was evident both on the Estates of Burgundy
and on those of Artois under Charles *le téméraire*; and these were areas in
which assemblies had taken firm root.[7] In those areas where the roots
were too frail to stand the blasts of seigneurial exigence the right of
consent was swept away with the assembly itself. If it was the prime and
basic factor in the life of an assembly it was also the most fragile; and

---

[1] A. de La Borderie and B. Pocquet, *Hist. de Bretagne*, IV (Rennes, 1906) 609.

[2] Considerable notice seems to have been taken of them, for instance, in
Béarn (Cadier, op. cit. p. 357). The efforts of the Estates of Languedoc to gain
control over the economic affairs of the *pays* has again been stressed by
J. Favier, 'La Défense'.

[3] See the document cited above, p. 353 n4.

[4] Dussert, op. cit. and *Les Etats du Dauphiné de la guerre de Cent ans aux guerres
de Réligion* (B. Acad. delphinale, ser. 5 XIII, part 2: Grenoble, 1922) *passim*;
Dognon, op. cit. pp. 233–48; Gilles, op. cit. pp. 29 ff.

[5] Prentout, op. cit. I 181–203; Gilles, op. cit. pp. 59–70.

[6] Dussert, *Les Etats du Dauphiné de la guerre de Cent ans*, pp. 59 ff.

[7] Billioud, op. cit. pp. 335–6; Hirschauer, op. cit. I 209–14.

assemblies to which the power of consent alone remained had the marks of political death upon them. In Vermandois in the fourteenth century, in Saintonge in the fifteenth and in Poitou[1], such Estates appeared and soon faded wraithlike away.

Local Estates also met for local purposes such as raising local taxes, especially to keep the local peace. In this they might again be useful to the government, in the suppression of the English, the companies or the *Ecorcheurs*; and over such local subventions the assemblies seem to have had rather greater control than over royal taxes. Even in the tiny assemblies of Velay and of Vivarais, firmly from the 1420s subordinated to the Estates of Languedoc, local taxes for the diocese were raised and audited by the assembly, as well as others for the greater province.[2] But on the right to raise and control local taxes, royal pressure, in the more generally peaceable mid-fifteenth century, was clearly apparent, not only on 'royal' assemblies, but also on those of seigneurs whose right to levy taxes was at last under effective attack.[3] The watchful eye of the *Chambre des comptes* was evidently cast over the Estates of Haut- and Bas-Limousin from 1440 and over those of Auvergne from 1443.[4] Local taxes in Dauphiné had to be authorised by the dauphin king of France or squared with the governor of the *pays*.[5] Little right remained in the matter, and little usefulness in such local taxation to the ruler.

Third, an assembly might take over in part or in whole the administration of the taxes it had granted. If consent was a function of all assemblies and at times a fragile claim to life, administration of taxation was a function of few and possibly a stronger one. Once more the extent of an assembly's powers might fluctuate. There is little evidence in France for the modest reluctance shown by the Estates of the Palatinate, which, in 1517, refused to undertake the administrative control of taxation; though it could be pointed out by the government in 1484, in reply to Limousin and Languedocien pressure for the right of administration, that an experiment along the lines they wanted had

[1] J. M. Tyrrell, 'Financial Activities of the Estates of Poitou', in *Medieval Studies*, XXVI (1964) 186–209.

[2] Delcambre, op. cit. pp. 131–3; Le Sourd, op. cit. pp. 191 ff.

[3] Delcambre, op. cit. pp. 131–2; H. de Surirey de St.-Rémy, *Jean II de Bourbon* (1944) p. 84.

[4] Thomas, *Les Etats provinciaux*, I 106, 109–13. Cf. Tyrrell, op. cit. pp. 193 ff.

[5] Dussert, *Les Etats du Dauphiné aux xive et xve siècles*, p. 330.

failed in Normandy (in the 1460s).[1] Both Limousin and Languedoc had had extensive rights; Languedoc had preserved some of them; and the memory of the liberty remained.[2] An assembly could gain control over the assessment, the collection and the audit of taxation. It could even claim to have some control over the way in which the money was spent. There was again a great deal of local variation. The Estates of Burgundy had by the fifteenth century acquired the greatest liberties of all; but in Artois, which was under Burgundian rule, the Estates had little influence even over assessment until 1536.[3] But, save those of Brittany (where there is no evidence of any control whatsoever), the Estates of the 'independent' areas probably achieved more than those of regions more directly under royal control. In seigneurial Béarn and Beaujolais considerable rights were maintained;[4] but in areas under royal influence in the fifteenth century old privileges disappeared. In Languedoc and in Dauphiné too much control by the Estates was avoided, though those of Languedoc kept more than most royal Estates.[5] Those of central France lost all influence in the 1450s.[6] Those of Normandy had already lost their considerable rights in Charles VI's reign, and administration of taxation, a privilege unknown in England, was not amongst those given it under the English occupation; it may have been for the same reason that financial control seems to have been unknown to the Estates of English Guyenne.[7]

There were two things with which regional assemblies were in

[1] F. Carsten, *Princes and Parliaments in Germany from the Fifteenth to the Eighteenth Century* (Oxford, 1959) p. 344; Masselin, op. cit. pp. 632–4; Prentout, op. cit. I 181–7, II 176.

[2] Thomas, *Les Etats provinciaux*, I 98 ff, 104 ff; Dognon, op. cit. pp. 275–83, 313–14; Gilles, op. cit. pp. 167 ff.

[3] Billioud, op. cit. pp. 159 ff (Provence probably came second — see Denizet, op. cit. pp. 12–14); Hirschauer, op. cit. I 97 ff.

[4] Cadier, op. cit. pp. 331–47; E. Perroy, 'La Fiscalité royale en Beaujolais aux xiv⁰ et xv⁰ siècles', in *Moyen Age*, XXXVIII (1928) 32–3.

[5] See above, n2; Dussert, *Les Etats du Dauphiné aux xiv⁰ et xv⁰ siècles*, pp. 331–2.

[6] Thomas, *Les Etats provinciaux*, I 171–3. The Estates of Poitou seem never to have been concerned with financial administration (Tyrrell, op. cit. pp. 197 ff).

[7] Prentout, op. cit. II 172–5; Rowe, op. cit. pp. 569–70. Little is known of Estates in Guyenne; but cf. L. Cadier, 'La Sénéchaussée des Lannes sous Charles VII. Admin. royale et Etats provinciaux', in R. *Béarn, Navarre et Lannes, partie hist.* III (1885) 435 ff.

general not concerned. The first was to act as a law court or a legislative body. In this they were like the central assemblies. Only in Brittany had a later medieval French Estates inherited these functions from its predecessor, the *curia* of its ruler. The actual judicial work was done from the last years of the fourteenth century by a committee of the Estates; but too close a connection with the ducal council was avoided, and until 1492, despite attacks, the Parlement of Brittany kept its rights as a final court.[1] On the other hand, any connection it may have been thought to have in the process of legislation had been weakened: those who effectively took part in it were an *élite* partly selected by the Breton government; the place of the general assembly was, on the whole, simply to accept what they were told.[2] Yet such 'consent' at least survived; though at the end of the fifteenth century the Parlement, purely as a law court, broke away from the Estates of Brittany,[3] until that time fusion of the two protected and encouraged the Breton representative assembly. Such encouragement was not the only factor in the strength of the Estates; but the frequency of the assembly's sessions was largely governed by the judicial necessities of a court with which most of the assembly's members had little directly to do, if they were pleased to think that it derived its authority from the larger body of which they were part. When the duchy lost its independence, its Estates had partly for this reason become too firmly rooted to be ignored by the kings of France. But such encouragement, and such a powerful *raison d'être*, did not exist elsewhere; presumably because so few French regional assemblies had developed directly from a seigneurial *curia* with judicial powers.

The second field unexploited by regional assemblies was that of politics (in a narrow sense). If the local assemblies of western Germany found in the support of insecure princes a powerful reason why they should enjoy princely favour, those of France, except in a few cases, did not. Admittedly ratification of changes in the political status of an area

---

[1] La Martinière, 'Vannes', pp. 69–79, and 'Le Parlement de Bretagne [i]', in *A. Bretagne*, XXXVI (1924–5) p. 270, '[iii]', pp. 207–18; Pocquet du Haut-Jussé, op. cit. pp. 400 ff, and 'Le Conseil du duc en Bretagne d'après ses procès-verbaux (1459–1463)', in *Bibl. Ec. Chartes*, CXVI (1958) 157 ff.

[2] Pocquet du Haut-Jussé, 'La Genèse du législatif dans le duché de Bretagne', in *R. hist. Droit*, ser. 4 XL (1962) 351–72.

[3] La Martinière, 'Le Parlement de Bretagne [i]', pp. 270–98.

through the fortunes of war, recognition of the sovereignty of a new ruler, were well-established attributions of regional Estates which one or two, at least, had inherited from a conciliar past;[1] and these, in fourteenth and fifteenth century France, too often entailed some decision by the Estates and often their support for one side or another in a political duel. In Brittany, in Artois and in Béarn the insecurity of princes beset by pretenders to their thrones or by the importunities of sovereigns abetted the growth of the regional assembly.[2] They could be a reservoir of casual political assistance: it was to the Estates of Agenais that the dauphin appealed unsuccessfully for help in 1446; and to the Estates of Auvergne that he and the coalition magnates, the duc de Bourbon and the dauphin of Auvergne included, had appealed equally unsuccessfully during the Praguerie of 1440.[3] But the local rulers of France, unlike those of Germany, of Lorraine and of the Netherlands,[4] were not too often in a state of open warfare. Direct political support can be seen clearly as a motive of their princes summoning Estates only in Brittany and in the Burgundian group of territories — and, perhaps, with a different nuance, in the vicomté of Turenne under Louis XI. There in 1477 the Estates subvented the vicomte's defence of the exemption of the vicomté from royal taxation; and when Louis XI's commissioners appear to have tried to object on the ground that the subvention had not been taken with the consent of the assembly, it was little wonder that the Estates in 1486 could be persuaded to declare, at least, 'that they never knew that' the vicomte 'had ever taken any tax in the vicomté without the consent of the members of the Estates'.[5]

[1] See, for instance, Cadier, op. cit. pp. 312–13; A. Rebillon, *Les Etats de Bretagne de 1661 à 1789* (1932) p. 21; Billioud, op. cit. pp. 292–6; Hirschauer, op. cit. 1 171; Denizet, op. cit. pp. 8–11, 17.

[2] Rebillon, op. cit. p. 21; Hirschauer, op. cit. 1 26–8; Cadier, op. cit. p. 371.

[3] 'Comptes des consuls de Montréal-du-Gers [iii], 1439–50', in *Arch. hist. Gironde*, XXXII (1897) 46–61; A. Breuils, 'La Campagne de Charles VII en Gascogne. Une Conspiration du dauphin en 1446', in R. *Questions hist.* LVII (1895) 132 ff; Thomas, *Les Etats provinciaux*, 1 121–3.

[4] Carsten, op. cit. pp. 426–7; Duvernoy, op. cit. pp. 122, 145–8, 189–91; C. Bocage, 'Les Etats de Hainaut (des origines à la maison de Bourgogne)', in *Anciens Pays et assemblées d'Etats*, II (1951) 71 ff; Petit, op. cit. pp. 98–9; J. Muller, 'La Représentation populaire dans le comté de Namur au début du XVe siècle', in *Etudes . . . F. Courtoy*, I (Gembloux, 1952) 490–5.

[5] R. Fage, *Les Etats de la vicomté de Turenne*, II (1894) 52–62.

Failure and survival

The regional assemblies of later medieval France thus exhibited varying degrees of institutional cohesion. The assemblies of some areas were remarkably robust. The assemblies of other areas were, like the Estates of the kingdom, remarkably frail. Why, in those areas, and in the kingdom as a whole, did the idea of the Estates fail?

We have already seen something of the causes of the failure of the Estates of the kingdom. Regional particularism provides an obvious *prima facie* explanation of their inanition. In 1379 the *pays* of Rouergue, not long recovered from a brief period of English occupation and still a frontier province, promised a force of 100 *lances* to the comte d'Armagnac, allegedly 'so that the country should be safe from French and English'.[1] The attitude of Rouergue towards the general assemblies of the kingdom also betrays an independent dislike of the outside world. The deputies of the *pays* to the general Estates of Chinon in 1428 said that 'they did not wish to come into or to have anything to do with a general assembly of Languedoc and Languedoil, because they were not accustomed to be in assemblies with them, but the *pays* of Rouergue was accustomed to have an assembly on its own';[2] and certainly after the province's recovery by France in 1369 its deputies rarely attended general assemblies either of the kingdom or of Languedoc. But Rouergue's proud assertion was only a voicing of the general tacit attitude of the *pays* of France towards general assemblies in the period.

There were clearly simple physical difficulties in summoning the three estates of the kingdom. Halls that were large enough had to be found. The constituents of distant regions had to be prepared to pay large expense-accounts for their deputies.[3] France was, comparatively,

[1] *Docs sur la ville de Millau*, ed. J. Artières (Arch. hist. Rouergue, 7: Millau, 1930) p. 209.
[2] A. Thomas, 'Le Midi et les Etats généraux sous Charles VII', in *A. Midi*, IV (1892) 8.
[3] J. Masselin, *Journal des Etats généraux de France tenus à Tours en 1484*, ed. A. Bernier (Docs inéd. sur l'hist. de France: 1835) pp. 508–10; 'Docs inéd. sur les Etats de Tours, 1484', ed. F. Bourquelot, in *M. Soc. royale des antiquaires de France*, NS VI (1842) 506–7; P. Viollet, 'Elections des députés aux Etats généraux réunis à Tours en 1468 et en 1484', in *Bibl. Ec. Chartes*, ser. 6 II (1866) 36–7.

a large country, and again for men of the distant regions that size was made bigger by the difficulties of having to talk French to those who apparently could not even read romance.[1] The insecurity of the roads due to endemic warfare was the commonest excuse offered by defaulting deputies. 'England men made such war in France, that the three Estates dared not come together,'[2] wrote Sir John Fortescue; and many harassed Frenchmen might agree with him. In 1427 the inhabitants of Orléans excused themselves from sending deputies to an assembly of the Estates of Languedoil at Poitiers, saying that 'no-one dared go, for fear of the soldiery who were about in the *pays*'; and in 1420 those of Bordeaux were doubtful whether they should send representatives to the Estates of Dax: the provost of Bordeaux 'was of the opinion that the journey should be put off, if it could be done in due form, seeing the great perils, damages and misfortunes which could ensue from the king's enemies . . . and, if postponement could not be got, that power should be given to . . . the constable [to represent the town at the assembly] . . .'[3] Certainly the perils of encountering soldiery were pretty great. When the Estates of the kingdom were looking for the king in 1440, they were ambushed on the way under the conduct of a royal *bailli* from Bourges to St.-Pourçain by Arnaud de Martres, captain of Montfaucon, whose men fell upon them, crying, apparently, 'Sort them out, sort them out, those who come from Languedoc! Cut their throats! Kill them!' Some were indeed killed; and a lawyer of Carcassonne was so terrified that he suddenly went off his head and had to be taken back to Bourges.[4]

But some large meetings of general assemblies,[5] as we have seen,

[1] See above, p. 4.

[2] *The Governance of England*, ed. C. Plummer (Oxford, 1885) p. 113.

[3] G. du Fresne de Beaucourt, *Hist. de Charles VII*, II (1882) 591 n6; *Reg. de la Jurade* [1414–16, 1420–2] (Arch. mun. Bordeaux, 4: Bordeaux, 1883) p. 374.

[4] Thomas, 'Le Midi et les Etats généraux', IV 21.

[5] *Procès-verbaux* survive for the sessions of the Estates of Languedoil at Paris in October 1356 ('Journal des Etats généraux réunis à Paris au mois d'octobre 1356', ed. R. Delachenal, in *Nouvelle R. hist. Droit*, XXIV (1900) 429–59) and of the Estates-general of the kingdom in 1468 (Arch. com. Rodez, BB 3, folios 50ᵛ–66ʳ; *Docs hist. inéd.* ed. A. Champollion-Figeac (Docs inéd. sur l'hist. de France) III (1847) 494–9; C. J. de Mayer, *Des Etats généraux et autres assemblées nationales*, IX (1789) 204–26) and in 1484 (Masselin, op. cit.;

were vocal enough; and there seems to have been no physical reason why such an assembly should not have been able, had it ever been allowed by its deputies' constituents to develop into an institution, to produce views which might curtail too arbitrary action on the part of the government. None of the difficulties was finally insuperable. The hall of the archbishop at Tours was large enough to contain the deputies to the Estates-general of 1484, who numbered, without counting anyone summoned directly, at least 250; and the difficulty of making such a cumbersome meeting work could be overcome with practice and the development of procedure or by a committee system, which was used in the Estates of Paris in 1356 and in the Tours meeting of 1484.[1] Towns deep in the Midi were prepared to pay the expenses of their delegates to Paris when their interests demanded it; and, until the establishment of the regional Parlements, lawsuit business meant, as we have seen, a constant trail of litigants and messengers northward.[2] And if the dauphin could not understand 'nostra lenga' in 1443, the deputies of Rouergue in 1468 could, as we have seen, certainly understand his.[3] If those who attended or sent deputies to the general assemblies of the three estates of France had thought it in their interest to clamour for representative institutions, they would have done so; irksome difficulties would have been forgotten. But in general it seems clear that they did not.

Evidence of the popularity of representative institutions is admittedly not hard to find. From Artois to Gascony, from Normandy to Dauphiné and from Brittany to Languedoc, in guises more or less familiar, the doctrine that what touched all should be approved by all was at one time or another proclaimed. When the duke of Burgundy tried to raise taxes without the consent of the Artesian Estates in 1450, the town of St.-Omer refused to pay, saying that no Estates had been held as they usually were.[4] In 1420 the Bordelais deputies to an insufficiently attended assembly at Dax refused to grant a tax because 'what touches all should be commended, approved and confirmed by all, according to law'.[5] A

Docs hist. inéd. II, part 2 (1843) 473–7; *Preuves de la maison de Polignac*, ed. A. Jacotin, IV (1905) 326–31).

[1] 'Journal des Etats généraux . . . 1356', pp. 429 ff; Masselin, op. cit.

[2] See, for instance, above, p. 10.   [3] See above, p. 5.

[4] C. Hirschauer, *Les Etats d'Artois de leurs origines à l'occupation française, 1340–1640*, I (1923) 204 n 6.

[5] *Reg. de la Jurade*, p. 382.

year before, Toulouse had demanded of the comte de Foix that the town should be represented before it was taxed; and in Dauphiné in 1473 complaints about taxes not granted by the Estates received a soft answer from Louis XI and an on the whole effective promise that they would not occur again.[1] Guarantees against excessive taxation were written into the only charter of 1315 which survived: the Norman charter was renewed by Philippe VI and Jean duke of Normandy in 1339, by Charles VI in 1381, by the duke of Bedford in 1423, by Charles VII in 1458, and by Louis XI in 1462: it was the battle-cry of the Normans, even if it was at times ignored.[2] In Brittany it was simply assumed that the Breton Parlement saw to the raising of subsidies; and it was only the slightest of grievances tactfully anticipated by duke François II in 1459 which brought from him an immediate declaration that the principle of consent was firmly enthroned in the western duchy.[3]

Reformers dinned it into the ears of the government. 'I've seen a book talking about the past, the present and the future (and I don't at all say one should believe it)', wrote Jean Juvenal des Ursins to Charles VII about 1452, 'which says that at the end of these wars such exactions would be made and that the nobles, the churchmen and the people, who will be as if completely impoverished of their goods, will band together to do something about it, and that, in the end, the taxes taken in the kingdom for the war and for public business, will be managed . . . by the deputies of those that pay them.'[4] Politicians adopted assemblies as party policy: the duke of Burgundy 'wanted the kingdom to be governed by the three estates, as it used to be', thought the Norman chronicler Pierre Cochon in 1405, 'and that the duc

---

[1] P. Dognon, *Quomodo tres Status Linguae Occitanae ineunte quinto decimo saeculo inter se convenire assueverint* (Toulouse, 1896) pp. 30–1; A. Dussert, *Les Etats du Dauphiné de la guerre de Cent ans aux guerres de Religion* (B. Acad. delphinale, ser. 5 XIII, part 2: Grenoble, 1922) pp. 59–61.

[2] A. Artonne, *Le Mouvement de 1314 et les chartes provinciales de 1315* (1912) pp. 44–5, 105, 151–2; H. Prentout, *Les Etats provinciaux de Normandie*, I (M. Acad. nat. Sci. Arts Caen, NS I: Caen, 1925) 94 ff.

[3] Dom H. Morice, *Mémoires pour servir de preuves à l'hist. ecclés. et civile de Bretagne*, II (1744) cols 456–9, 1651–68; A. de La Borderie and B. Pocquet, *Hist. de Bretagne*, IV (Rennes, 1906) 422.

[4] P. Viollet, *Hist. des institutions politiques et admin. de la France*, III (1903) 466.

d'Orléans should render account of the revenue of the kingdom, which
he had governed for three years'; and the constable Richmond clamoured
for them in 1425 and 1428.[1] Versifiers extolled their virtues hopefully to
partisan princes and anyone else who would listen: a ballad of very
respectable prosody, alleged to have been sent in 1465, before the battle
of Montlhéry, into the army of Charles comte de Charolais, the son of
the duke of Burgundy, begged him

> that you remember their administration
> Who can give good counsel readily?
> Who? Yes, who? the three estates of France![2]

Such striving was not without practical results. The rights of some
regions to their Estates were enshrined in charters and privileges and
were dear to the hearts of at least some of their inhabitants. In 1355 the
king had recognised that no taxes should be taken in Anjou and Maine
without the express consent of the regional Estates.[3] In Béarn the
vicomte made an oath to this effect at his accession which was settled by
1398; in Foix a comital charter granted the right of consent in 1391; in
Guyenne it had been recognised by the Black Prince as prince of
Aquitaine in 1368 and by John of Gaunt as duke of Guyenne in 1395.[4]
In Languedoc the right of consent had been explicitly granted by
Charles VII at the Estates of Chinon in 1428, and it was generally
maintained, though it was not confirmed until the Estates-general of
Tours in 1484.[5] And in some areas the Estates were clearly regarded

[1] P. Cochon, *Chronique normande*, ed. C. de Beaurepaire (Soc. Hist.
Normandie: Rouen, 1870) p. 214; A. Thomas, 'Les Etats généraux sous
Charles VII. Etude chronologique d'après des docs inéd.' in *Cabinet hist.*
XXIV (1878) 160–2, 167–9.

[2] J. du Clercq, 'Mémoires', ed. J. A. C. Buchon, in *Chron. d'E. de Monstrelet*,
xv (Coll. des chroniques nationales françaises: 1827) p. 10.

[3] *Ordonnances des rois de France de la troisième race*, III, ed. D. Secousse (1732)
7–8, 683.

[4] L. Cadier, *Les Etats de Béarn depuis leurs origines jusqu'au commencement du
xvie siècle* (1888) p. 299; F. Pasquier, 'Privilèges et libertés des trois états du
comté de Foix à la fin du xive et au commencement du xve siècle', in *B. philol.
hist. Com. Travaux hist. sci.* (1896) pp. 348–51; *Livre des Bouillons* (Arch. mun.
Bordeaux, 1: Bordeaux, 1867) pp. 173–6, 263.

[5] P. Dognon, *Les Institutions politiques et admin. du pays de Languedoc du xiiie
siècle aux guerres de Religion* (Toulouse, 1895) p. 247; H. Gilles, *Les Etats de
Languedoc au xve siècle* (Toulouse, 1965) pp. 46–73.

highly. When, in the English south-west, at the Estates of Dax in 1420, the deputies from the Landes insisted on deliberating apart the deputies from Bordelais were furious; they thought that the affair 'is and was a very bad example, and the reason why . . . that parliament came to no good and due conclusion'.[1] Such virtue was not confined to English France: Tours warned its deputies, summoned to a meeting at Issoudun in 1426, that they should see that 'a single *pays* on its own does not do, without the three estates of the other *pays* anything it cannot do'; and in 1435 its representatives, arriving too late for a general assembly at Poitiers, refused to grant a tax without a further general meeting.[2]

Representative assemblies were therefore not wholly unappreciated in later medieval France. But even in Burgundy and in Brittany — which possessed two of the most vital assemblies — it was necessary at least once to threaten deputies with fines for non-attendance; and in the mid-fifteenth century the members of the former obtained letters patent from the duke 'by which he granted them that in future the . . . members of the three estates should no longer be assembled, except by authority of his letters patent and for most necessary and urgent affairs which would be declared in his . . . letters patent'.[3] There was not much eagerness for assemblies here. In areas in which absenteeism was disregarded, or in which proctors were allowed, the level of vitality of the assembly cannot have been very high.[4] Inertia of this kind could be a practical means of defence against a ruler: an insufficiently attended assembly could 'constitutionally' refuse to grant a tax.[5] But a simple, unaggressive inertia was apparently more common.

Nor was the system of representation which emerged in later

---

[1] *Reg. de la Jurade*, p. 382.

[2] Beaucourt, op. cit. II 589; A. Thomas, 'Les Etats généraux sous Charles VII. Notes et docs nouveaux', in *R. hist.* XL (1889) 82–3. Tours seems to have had the same kind of affection for local Estates (ibid. p. 69).

[3] Morice, op. cit. II, col. 1568; J. Billioud, *Les Etats de Bourgogne aux xive et xve siècles* (M. Acad. Dijon, ser. 5 IV: Dijon, 1922) p. 445.

[4] Dauphiné seems to provide an exception (A. Dussert, *Les Etats du Dauphiné aux xive et xve siècles* (B. Acad. delphinale, ser. 5 VIII: Grenoble, 1914) p. 295 n3).

[5] In 1446, for instance, 'lo pays part dessa Guarona no autreyen re a causa que no eran mandatz los tres Estats ne totz los locs cum estar deben' ('Comptes des consuls de Montréal-du-Gers [iii], 1439–50', in *Arch. hist. Gironde*, XXXII (1897) 53).

medieval France at all well formed.[1] In England everyone in each shire except the peers, the clergy and the burgesses was prepared to be represented by a pair of country gentlemen. Whatever reason made this possible in England it does not seem to have been possible in France. As far as urban representation went, there were close analogies. But proper representation of the order of the nobility seems to have been achieved only in Normandy, where the influence of English ideas under the occupation is perhaps apparent;[2] elsewhere the most important men of the *pays* would expect to be summoned. The same difficulties seem to have been apparent in the matter of representation of a locality (either a *pays* or a *bailliage*) at a central assembly. In one or two areas — such as Vivarais and Gévaudan — a rota system for attendance at the general meetings based on importance was eventually established.[3] In other areas the deputy was not necessarily chosen by a regional assembly: he might be chosen by the regional orders or simply by the government.[4] Eventually the government tried to generalise a system of election by *bailliage*:[5] but by this time central assemblies were effectively dead, and so artificial a system was a recognition of this. And however he was chosen, a feeling that he could not fully represent his constituents seems in many areas to have remained. They still wished to have their personal say in a smaller assembly. Many might refuse to accept the decisions of a local assembly at which they were not present or directly represented. In 1365 Regnaut de Pons vicomte de Carlat in Auvergne refused to

[1] Theories of representation were of course clearly known in France as elsewhere; see, for instance G. Post, 'Plena Potestas and Consent in Medieval Assemblies. A Study in Romano-Canonical Procedure and the Rise of Representation, 1150–1325', in *Traditio*, 1 (1943) 355–408. But see also T. N. Bisson, *Assemblies and Representation in Languedoc in the Thirteenth Century* (Princeton, 1964) 223 ff, 274, 277, 290 ff.

[2] H. Prentout, *Les Etats provinciaux de Normandie* (M. Acad. nat. Sci. Arts Caen, NS 2: Caen, 1926) pp. 58–9, corrected by B. J. H. Rowe, 'The Estates of Normandy under the Duke of Bedford', in *Engl. hist. R.* XLVI (1931) 560. But even here the system of direct summons was not wholly destroyed. For this and for a few other examples of 'representation' of the nobility, see Viollet, *Hist. des institutions*, III 187, 190.

[3] A. Le Sourd, *Essai sur les Etats de Vivarais* (1926) pp. 71–3, 182.

[4] J. Cadart, *Le Régime électoral des Etats généraux de 1789 et ses origines (1302–1614)* (1952) pp. 38–42; Viollet, *Hist. des institutions*, III 187–97; Thomas, 'Le Midi et les Etats généraux', in *A. Midi*, I (1889) 292–315, IV 1–16.

[5] Viollet, 'Elections des députés', pp. 22–58.

contribute to a tax granted by the three estates of the Montagnes d'Auvergne on the pretext that neither he, nor any delegate of his, nor any representative of any of his subjects had been present; and the comte de Boulogne and Auvergne did the same in 1376. Both were, however, finally constrained to do so by the duc de Berry, to whom the taxes had been voted: superior power could overcome a too precisely held legal fiction.[1] Even when members of the Estates were present in person or directly represented, a suspicion (when the ruler was not strong enough to override it) of even the smaller assemblies seems to have been apparent, at least in the early days in the less homogeneous areas. At this stage legal nicety and self-interest are seen most clearly in their true confounded form. The means of resistance were manifold. Magnates could simply refuse taxes and have to be dealt with individually. The *tiers'* weapon was the *mandat impératif*: urban deputies, as we have seen, were tied as tightly as possible to their instructions, if possible they were sent only *ad audiendum et referendum*. From the beginning of the fourteenth century, it will be remembered, the government in France struggled for some ample deputies' powers and for large, fully representative assemblies: for that plenitude of power which, with a single session of the kingdom, had been achieved so easily in England. But not till 1343, if then, did the French government actually get a definite commitment from a central assembly;[2] and the problem, as we have seen, remained.

But if there were pressures towards individualism in men's attitudes towards their public obligations, there were also pressures towards individual indifference. Each class represented in an assembly had, in principle, some interest in the assembly's actions; but for many members of each class that interest must have been minimal. The protection by the Estates of regional liberties was theoretically of interest to all; common protection of general privilege could become a shibboleth; but there were private liberties which were more important privately. In the Estates-general of 1484 the knight Philippe de Poitiers claimed that the clergy and the nobility, despite the fact that they did not pay taxes, were more active in the defence of the taxpayer than the bourgeoisie, who did. But this was special pleading on their behalf; the

[1] R. Lacour, *Le Gouvernement de l'apanage de Jean duc de Berry* (1934) pp. 380–1.
[2] See above, p. 334.

exemption of the first two orders must have tended towards indifference. And as Philippe de Poitiers pointed out, members of the bourgeoisie, either in their towns or as individuals, could become exempt too.[1] For many, therefore, the sharpest spur to action was missing.

The privilege of administering taxes could possibly become a matter of local pride protected equally by all the orders; but it was again only those of the bourgeoisie who paid the taxes who were affected at all nearly. Yet one of the few possible causes of weakness that was not very apparent was class conflict. Although the obvious attempts were made to exacerbate the differences of the orders, to play off class against class,[2] the three estates could at times show remarkable solidarity. In Artois in 1476 an attempt to make a grant of taxation agreed to by the first two orders binding on the third (which had refused to grant) was met by a flat refusal on the grounds that 'if all the . . . estates were not assembled together and of common accord, nothing should emerge', and the government had to give in.[3] In the stresses of the 1390s in Dauphiné the nobles and clergy demanded to be united with the *tiers état*. This dangerous liaison was allowed only once.[4] Class divergence seems to have led in most cases to a lack of support for each other on the part of the orders rather than an open clash in the assembly. That much-riven body, the Estates-general of 1484, showed few divisions along class lines. But private interests must, it may be argued, have led to indifference. Backstairs representations and bargaining with the government by towns were, as we have seen, a perpetual theme throughout the period. Clearly such a relationship might be thought to weaken the assembly of which these towns were a part.[5] At the beginning of the reign of Charles VII, remission of taxation was habitually made to the greater towns of Languedoc, whose delegates opened the discussions at the Estates of Languedoc, 'so that', as the comte de Foix confessed openly in 1429, 'they may be more voluntarious and inclined towards granting the . . . tax'.[6]

[1] Masselin, op. cit. pp. 500–2.
[2] For instance in Auvergne (Lacour, op. cit. p. 384).
[3] Hirschauer, op. cit. I 66–7.
[4] Dussert, *Les États du Dauphiné aux xive et xve siècles*, pp. 111 ff, 312.
[5] Cf. J. M. Tyrrell, 'Financial Activities of the Estates of Poitou', in *Medieval Studies*, XXVI (1964) 206 ff.
[6] Gilles, op. cit. pp. 187–8.

The question of patronage in medieval France is still, as we have seen, largely unexplored. It is impossible to say how far such interests cut across those of an assembly. Sometimes an assembly seemed clearly strong enough to survive them. The Estates of Burgundy had a reputation for independence in the fifteenth century, and the session of June 1448 is regarded as one in which they were, on a matter of principle, more intransigent than usual. The duke was particularly anxious to influence this meeting. The governor of the *vierie* of Autun was summoned to Dijon with other ducal officers to talk to members of the duke's council and others 'concerning some requests which . . . were to be made to the members of the three estates, so that [they] . . . should induce the inhabitants of Autun and other members of the . . . Estates to acquiesce to those requests'.[1] Letters were written to several nobles whose influence over the Estates might be counted on.[2] It was all to no avail. Yet a cursory glance at the sixteen members of the most important order, the nobility, reveals them closely interrelated (though this at times might bring more discord than harmony), and amongst their number nine ducal officers (one the husband of an illegitimate daughter of Philippe *le bon*) and at least two debtors about whose financial, if not political, independence there might be some doubt.[3] Could it be that in Burgundy there was somehow a tacit agreement about the lengths to which the duke could expect a seigneur's loyalty to stretch? Was it in fact that the patronage relationship did not affect the political relationship of a member of the Estates and the ruler? It is difficult to build much on such slender knowledge of the working of the Burgundian assembly as we have; but clearly one must be careful with generalisations based on interest. Clientage was very much in the air in the Estates-general of 1484; Commynes said that the seigneurs of France consented to arbitrary taxation 'for certain pensions which were promised them for the money which was raised on their lands';[4] yet the political patronage-groupings arranged for a struggle over the composition of the council seem to have been ineffective for a struggle over taxation.

[1] Billioud, op. cit. p. 140.
[2] P. S. Lewis, 'The Failure of the French Medieval Estates', in *Past & Present*, XXIII (1962) 24.
[3] Ibid.
[4] *Mémoires*, ed. J. Calmette and G. Durville, II (Classiques de l'hist. de France au Moyen âge, 5: 1925) p. 289.

Noble and some clerical deputies to regional and to the earlier general assemblies were chosen by the government; but its choice was limited to the important seigneuries of the *pays* and its hand was not entirely free. Where there were elections to an assembly — as to the Estates-general of 1468 and 1484 — there is some evidence of possible interference in the method of election, but it is very inconclusive; and there is some evidence of direct instruction to an elective body to choose a particular deputy in 1484. The Beaujeu were careful to get their able partisan Philippe Pot elected by the three estates of Burgundy.[1] But it is impossible to assess accurately the extent of such control. There was possibly more scope, as in England, for 'management' of the assembly in session. At some assemblies royal or seigneurial officers were present and clearly influenced the discussion; but one is woefully hampered from knowing how widespread this practice was by the lack of such *procès-verbaux* as those surviving for the Estates-general of 1468 and 1484.[2] In 1484 the president of the Estates was controlled by the government, and there were government men amongst the members as well as partisans of the conflicting parties. Every kind of pressure, according to Masselin, was put on the independent deputies to submit; and eventually they did so.

But there were more open forms of coercion of a reluctant assembly. It could be kept in session or threatened with a further meeting under troublesome circumstances with a personal summons for its members, as was the Estates of Rouergue at Sauveterre in 1377; this assembly eventually gave in, 'to avoid greater troubles and expenses'.[3] In the last resort the Estates could be by-passed and commissioners sent to make a local levy. When Agenais tried to avoid giving any aid to the dauphin in 1446, 'because the three estates were not summoned, nor all the places that should be', his commissioners 'not content with the reply

[1] Viollet, 'Elections des députés', pp. 22–58; P. Pélicier, 'Voyage des députés de Bourgogne à Blois (1483). Election des députés de la Bourgogne aux Etats généraux de 1484. La Bourgogne aux Etats généraux de 1484', in *Bibl. Ec. Chartes*, XLVII (1886) 357–69; H. Bouchard, 'Philippe Pot et la démocratie aux Etats généraux de 1484', in *A. Bourgogne*, XXII (1950) 33–40.

[2] See, for instance, Billioud, op. cit. pp. 52–4, 140; but cf. Gilles, op. cit. p. 145.

[3] *Comptes consulaires de la cité et du bourg de Rodez*, ed. H. Bousquet, part 1, *Cité*, II (Arch. hist. Rouergue, 17: Rodez, 1943) 165–6.

then made' came, 'so it's said, another time, to make a particular demand' at Montréal-du-Gers.[1] In 1462 the Millavois, it will be remembered, were threatened with a fine of 'a hundred marks of silver and with the seizure and sale of our goods and with the arrest of our persons and on top of that with the penalty of being rebels and disobedient to the king our lord' if they did not accede to such a demand; bravely, they held out, since the *pays* had appealed to the king.[2] Others might not have been so temerarious. And if it was necessary at an awkward moment for a government to give in to an importunate assembly, the Estates' decisions could only too often simply be ignored when normal conditions returned. Jean Masselin was eloquent about the shame and mockery of this procedure.[3] Under such circumstances it would have been little wonder if many people regarded assemblies simply as a convenient device for extracting taxation with little offered in return. This, at least, was what some Norman deputies thought of regional Estates in 1484.[4]

And yet some assemblies did survive. At the death of Louis XI there were still Estates under royal control in Normandy, Rouergue, Languedoc, Dauphiné, Provence and Burgundy; under seigneurial control in Brittany, south-west France, Bourbonnais, Beaujolais and elsewhere. By 1484 it had become accepted — at times with envy — that these areas had assemblies.[5] Although some of them showed a tendency towards the development of fragmentary Estates, so destructive elsewhere, many felt a sentimental attachment to and pride in their full assembly.[6] As far as their social structure was concerned, they had little in common to mark them out from other areas, except, perhaps, in the case of Languedoc. And again except, perhaps, in the case of Languedoc, they did not find common ground in the possession of

---

[1] 'Comptes des consuls de Montréal-du-Gers [iii], 1439–50', p. 53.
[2] *Docs sur la ville de Millau*, p. 359.   [3] Masselin, op. cit. pp. 432–4.
[4] Ibid. pp. 636–8.   [5] Ibid. pp. 486–8.
[6] See, for instance, R. Fage, *Les Etats de la vicomté de Turenne*, 1 (1894) 52; Prentout, op. cit. 1 103 ff; A. Coville, *Les Etats de Normandie. Leurs Origines et leur développement au xive siècle* (1894) pp. 144–7; Billioud, op. cit. pp. 21–3. When the government in 1484 demanded deputies to the Estates-general from *bailliages* and *sénéchaussées* rather than from the whole region, there was resistance in Burgundy, Provence, Dauphiné and Bourbonnais, and the government had to give in; but not for long (Viollet, *Hist. des institutions*, III 194–6).

administrative functions marginally useful to the government: if Languedoc had retained some administration of taxation, Normandy had tried it again under Louis XI and seems to have abandoned its rights.[1] Nor did their secret lie in the absence of a *mandat imperatif* or in a refusal to allow proctors.[2] Their common characteristic lay rather in the fact that all had for longer than the rest of France enjoyed a greater or less degree of independent political life. Amongst areas whose assemblies were summoned by the king, Provence, Burgundy and Artois were very recently under royal control; Dauphiné was not in this period properly a part of the kingdom; the Normans had in the matter of assemblies found encouragement under the English occupation; the meridionals were furthest from the centre — though the Estates of Languedoc was itself threatened with extinction in 1442.[3] Guyenne, which might have been expected to be a member of this group, had never had an effective assembly under English rule.

Other areas — Auvergne and Limousin, for example — may have seen their assemblies go with some regret; and if the Estates of Auvergne lost its right to grant royal taxes it continued in existence in order to grant them to the duc de Bourbon.[4] The need of the princes to consult assemblies seems clear enough; it took perhaps the exceptional toughness of Gaston III Fébus to take taxes arbitrarily in Béarn in the later fourteenth century. And it was primarily the princes who found — in Brittany, in Béarn, in Turenne, for example — assemblies useful for political purposes, as a mark of status and independence; and the members of such assemblies too might find an interest in uniting with

[1] Prentout, op. cit. 1 181–7; R. Gandilhon, *Politique écon. de Louis XI* (Rennes, 1940) pp. 282–4. Some modifications made in Languedoc were also received without much enthusiasm (ibid. pp. 276–80). But see above, pp. 355–6.

[2] The *mandat* flourished in Artois and in Languedoc, at least up to about 1440 (Hirschauer, op. cit. 1 45; Dognon, *Institutions politiques*, pp. 263–5; Gilles, op. cit. pp. 105–6, 151) if not in Burgundy (Billioud, op. cit. p. 340); proctors were allowed in Artois and in Dauphiné (Hirschauer, op. cit. 1 43 ff; Dussert, *Les Etats du Dauphiné aux xiv⁰ et xv⁰ siècles*, p. 295 n 3) if not in Béarn (Cadier, op. cit. pp. 242–3) and absenteeism seems to have been common in Dauphiné (Dussert, loc. cit.) if not in Brittany (for reasons for absence acceptable there, see Morice, op. cit. II, cols 1564–71, 1670–5; III (1746) cols 1–9).

[3] Gilles, op. cit. p. 55.

[4] A. Thomas, *Les Etats provinciaux de la France centrale sous Charles VII*, 1 (1879) 169–71; H. de Surirey de St.-Rémy, *Jean II de Bourbon* (1944) pp. 83–5.

the ruler, as the Estates of Turenne united with its vicomte, in the common defence of the *pays*. But if Philippe *le bon* might (or might not) have dreamed of an Estates-general of Burgundy as a coagulating force amongst his disparate dominions,[1] there is little evidence that any king of France felt the same. Yet it was possibly essentially a simple political motive which lay behind the attempts of the kings of France to create assemblies in the kingdom.

Assemblies and the king

For why had rulers wanted assemblies at all? It was they who summoned them to meet: only in one small area in the northern mountains of Languedoc did an autonomous assembly make a fleeting appearance before it was taken over by the government.[2] Clearly they and their entourages could find the idea of representative institutions distasteful. 'Above all things, be sure that no great assemblies of nobles or of communes take place in your . . . kingdom,' wrote Pierre Salmon to Charles VI in 1408, 'but take all questions and discords which have arisen and will arise into your own hands, and, as king and sovereign, leave them to law and justice.'[3] In 1442 Charles VII is alleged to have said that to deal with those who thought to 'govern the kingdom through the three estates', 'he would leave aside all other business to attack them and would treat them [like] the English his ancient enemies'.[4] In the same year certainly he told the Estates of Languedoc that he 'did not wish such assemblies to meet in future', for, as he told the lords assembled at Nevers, 'there is now no need to assemble the three estates to put on the . . . *tailles*, because it is only a cost and expense for the poor common people, who have to pay the expenses of those who come

---

[1] Billioud, op. cit. pp. 351–3; H. G. Koenigsberger, 'The States General of the Netherlands before the Revolt', in *Études présentées à la Commission internationale pour l'hist. des assemblées d'Etats*, XVIII (Louvain, 1958) 144–5.

[2] See above, p. 350.

[3] *Les Demandes faites par le roi Charles VI . . . avec les réponses de Pierre Salmon*, ed. G. A. Crapelet (1833) p. 101.

[4] E. de Monstrelet, *Chron.* ed. L. Douët-d'Arcq (Soc. Hist. France) VI (1862) 49–50.

there'.[1] Jean Juvenal des Ursins' account of Charles' behaviour to the Estates of Languedoil at Orléans in 1439 seems to show at least that he preferred not to get too closely involved with an assembly.[2] In 1484 some of the old servants of Louis XI thought 'it is treason to talk of assembling Estates; it is to diminish the power of the crown'.[3] Princes could feel the same. Jean duc de Berry imprisoned six members of the Estates of Auvergne which, in 1373, had complained to the *conseillers généraux des aides* about a local tax the assembly had not granted; they were in the Grosse Tour of Riom for a week, and the towns had to give in to the imposition. This was not the only way which Berry tried to avoid the importunities of an assembly.[4] Though on the whole he was successful, he was not as successful as the government of the kingdom of which he was intermittently part. The dukes of Burgundy seem to have put pressure on their assemblies in the duchy as often as they could; it is evident from 1382, under the latter years of Philippe *le hardi* and under Jean *sans peur*; and it was evident again under Charles *le téméraire*. Though the periodicity is different, their pressure was felt by the Estates of Artois too.[5]

Essentially rulers would put up with assemblies only when they had to; essentially again when they could not get their taxes without them. From the government's attitude towards general assemblies in the kingdom it seems clear that they felt them necessary in order to influence opinion in time primarily of defeat. It was partly because 'of his right and authority after his recent coronation at Reims' that Charles VII in 1429 and 1430 by-passed a central assembly.[6] The fortunes of the Estates of Languedoc waxed and waned inversely with the fortunes of the Valois.[7] And only, it seems, in the larger regions conscious of their own identity did assemblies become sufficiently rooted to weather the destructive forces to which they were exposed. Only there was the desire for an assembly permanently kindled; elsewhere the material would not catch alight; elsewhere the necessary political conjuncture did not exist. In place of a sentimental attachment to assemblies and out

[1] Gilles, op. cit. p. 55; Monstrelet, op. cit. VI 39.
[2] G. du Fresne de Beaucourt, *Hist. de Charles VII*, III (1885) 136–7.
[3] Commynes, op. cit. II 219.   [4] Lacour, op. cit. pp. 384–5.
[5] Billioud, op. cit. pp. 327 ff; Hirschauer, op. cit. I 193 ff.
[6] See above, p. 341.   [7] Gilles, op. cit. pp. 23–70.

of the trials of the country in the Hundred Years War came a sentimental attachment to a strong ruler. The readiness of Frenchmen to submit was extolled, not only by Commynes, but also by Chancellor Rochefort in the Estates-general of 1484. If Sir John Fortescue could complain of French lack of rebelliousness, Guillaume de Rochefort could allege that the English had had twenty-six changes of dynasty since the foundation of their monarchy. 'No-one,' he added, 'no-one will descry such inconstancy amongst the faithful French, such stigmata of crime.'[1] Almost the same thing was said by a spokesman of the assembly itself, Jean de Rély; and the formidable Masselin, too, echoed Commynes in his plea that the government should not oppress a people so willing to support it body and soul.[2] 'Is it then', asked Commynes, 'over such subjects that the king should claim the privilege of being able to take as he pleases, who give to him so liberally? Would it not be more just towards God and the world to take taxes [by consent] . . . than by uncontrolled will?'[3] More just indeed; but over subjects 'so good and loyal' why should a king bother?

[1] *The Governance of England*, ed. C. Plummer (Oxford, 1885) p. 114; Masselin, op. cit. p. 38.
[2] Ibid. pp. 252, 400.   [3] Op. cit. II 222.

5

Conclusion

'Crisis'

WE have come a long way, morally if not chronologically, from the kind of doubt about the duty of loyalty expressed by Jean Batiffol of Bialon or the abbot of St.-Michel. If there had been a 'crisis' in French society in the later middle ages, what had been its nature? Admittedly there had been economic misfortune. Admittedly there had been social tension. But a 'crisis', it may be argued, was political, and its roots were to be found in the disputed successions to the last Capetian kings of France. It was the Plantagenet claim that gave the secular conflict of the period its peculiar configuration. Behind all the manœuvres, all the tergiversations and the treacheries of the conflict, military and diplomatic, lay the appeal or the recourse of an alternative dynasty; an appeal exercised in a state whose elements were not yet wholly fused.

The claim and the war were themselves not essentially 'disruptive'; for what was there to disrupt? A moral authority, it may be argued; a claim to sovereignty; an exercise of supreme jurisdiction. But that authority might seem frail; that sovereignty might be challenged; that claim to *dernier ressort* ignored. We are now familiar with the separatist tendencies of the sub-'states', the great princely administrations. In the later middle ages the hopeful sub-'sovereigns' saw their chance. Some — the duke of Aquitaine and Gaston III Fébus vicomte de Béarn, for instance — asserted their full sovereignty. Others might attempt to achieve at least an effective independence. There is no reason to condemn them for moral turpitude except an anachronistic belief in the ultimate virtues of the unity of the French nation; no reason to condemn them for flying in the face of History except hindsight.

But it was not only the sub-'states' on the periphery of the kingdom which, under their rulers, might tend, in that centrifugal society, to break away from the centre. The more central mass itself was hardly whole. The southern shore of the English Channel, it may be argued, indeed the whole land-mass from Gascony through Saintonge and Poitou, Brittany, Normandy and the littoral to Flanders, was liable to feel its affinity with the northern shore;[1] an affinity not only in geographical situation and in old political organisation but also in intermittent reoccupation.

The crisis of the title was thus fundamental. From it derived a number of other effective subjections of the crown in later medieval France. But the king of France, despite the fact that the natural resources of his country were so much greater than those of the king of England, was basically in a politically weaker position, before ever the Valois came to the throne, than the king of England. The last Capetians, unlike the Plantagenets, could not extract taxes from a single general assembly with full powers. They could not tax their nobles. And the over-mightiness of the magnates of France of the older lines was apparent before the weakness of the Valois title made it even more necessary for the kings of France to placate them and their newer colleagues.

It might in fact be seen as aggression for a king to attempt to assert a greater unity; aggression even in the name of an idea, of a concept only in the later middle ages being created. It was the creation of the king's lawyers and the king's propagandists; it was they who created the myth which the king's armies realised. By a combination of good management and good fortune Aquitaine was defeated; Burgundy and Anjou died out in the direct male line, as had Berry; the line of Orléans was apparently sterilised by Louis XI's marriage of Louis II d'Orléans to his deformed daughter Jeanne de France. Louis exulted over his enemies. 'His joy was very great', wrote Commynes, 'to see himself on top of all those whom he hated and his adversaries. On some he was avenged, like the constable of France, the duc de Nemours and several others; the duke of Guyenne, his brother, was dead, and he had his succession; all the house of Anjou was dead, René king of Sicily, Jean and Nicolas dukes of Calabria, and then their cousin the comte du Maine, who was

[1] R. Cazelles, *La Société politique et la crise de la royauté sous Philippe de Valois* (1958) pp. 143–5.

later comte de Provence, the comte d'Armagnac, who had been killed at Lectoure, and of all of them the king had collected the inheritance and the property.' He had also collected part of those of the duke of Burgundy and might have collected the rest if he could have married the heiress of Charles *le téméraire* to the dauphin or to some rather older seigneur who would be in his pocket.[1] But Flanders remained beyond Louis' grasp; and the houses of Brittany, Bourbon, Orléans and Foix remained. And, though the senior branches of the first and last of these ran out into a female line in 1488 and 1483, the problem of the very great was to remain for later kings to deal with — if their families may have been different.

But the rebellion of the duke of Aquitaine and the war for the throne of France was, in 1453, effectively over. The Valois had won. Yet the crisis of the war had produced a number of problems. The hatreds it had engendered took a generation to die down. The bribes made, out of weakness, to the great for their loyalty — and that this was what pensions were was clear enough to Thomas Basin — had to be continued, despite Basin's views in 1461 that they were now unnecessary.[2] Charles VIII, according to Guillaume de Rochefort, chancellor of France in 1484, was as weak in this as ever his predecessors were; and pensions long outlived the fifteenth century. The control of the civil service, the control of the army, remained a problem; and so did the control of the higher clergy and their property. The towns, with their social tensions and their *populaires'* liability to accept too readily the promises of rebels, remained dangerous in Louis XI's eyes; and even their oligarchies might need to be watched closely. The effects of the crisis of confidence, of the crisis of control, remained to the end of his reign.

'Absolutism'

Is it then realistic to think of the crown in France by the end of the

---

[1] *Mémoires*, ed. J. Calmette and G. Durville, II (Classiques de l'hist. de France au Moyen âge, 5 : 1925) 166–9.

[2] *Histoire des règnes de Charles VII et de Louis XI*, ed. J. Quicherat (Soc. Hist. France) III (1857) 253–7.

middle ages as 'absolute'? First of all we must be careful in our use of
the term. Although Claude de Seyssel might equate absolutism with
despotism, by the 1530s the term was beginning to be used to describe a
true monarchy precisely of his own definition: a rule bridled by God's
laws, by natural law, by fundamental laws. It was only, it has been
maintained, in the arguments of seventeenth-century aristocrats and
their supporters that the word became once more pejorative. But one is
warned against taking the formal position for the real one.[1] Clearly
there were many things a king was powerless to do in the face of his
subjects of all estates, in practice as well as in principle. His courts might
effectively protect his subjects' rights against his immediate whim; and
his courts and his central departments might effectively protect his own
'rights', as an abstract entity, against his personal volition. The true
bridles of the king of France lay in his entourage, in his agents, and
in the power of those who effectively resisted them. Some, like the
resistance of the Parlements or of the departments to royal actions, were
formal. Some, like the backstairs intrigues and pressures of princes,
great clerics and great towns, were informal. In the interplay of the
forces of this political society true power was to be found and the true
position of the king to be ascertained. And it is upon this complex that
the effect of the crisis of confidence should be assessed.

The tyranny which men like Jean Juvenal des Ursins saw in France in
the fifteenth century was the tyranny of royal ineffectiveness within that
complex. That ineffectiveness, admittedly, preceded the Valois crisis;
but the crisis, let alone the incapacity of Charles VI, clearly enhanced it.
The king of Bourges could do little but be ineffective, given his political
situation. The libel 'tyranny' came easily into the polemic of the critical
then and later. The Englishman Sir John Fortescue, for instance, who
spent eight impoverished years on the Meuse, was chilled to the marrow
by the governance of France for much the same reasons in part as it
displeased French men of letters: for the burden of the army, of the
gabelle, of other taxation, and for the arbitrary nature of that taxation.
But Fortescue disapproved also of the procedures of civil law and of the
power of the king under civil law. Yet

---

[1] R. Mousnier, 'Réflexions critiques sur la notion d'absolutisme', in *B. Soc.
Hist. moderne*, LIV (1955) 2–8.

those things which ... are seen to be a reproach to the power of a king holding sway simply regally [a king under civil law] do not proceed from a defect of his law, but from the carelessness and negligence of someone holding sway in such a way. Therefore these powers do not diminish that dignity from that of a king ruling politically [as under English law]; both kings [are] equal in power.... But ... the power of a king holding sway simply regally [is] ... more difficult in practice and of less safety for himself and his people, so that it would not be desirable for a prudent king to exchange a political rule for one simply regal.[1]

It was the opportunity for tyranny offered by the civil law as he conceived it that Fortescue abhorred. Many heads were better than one; and for Fortescue the salvation of England lay in parliamentary control of taxation and the statute law. Admittedly 'representation stabilizes power structure by providing a mean between extremes of concentration and dispersion of power ...'[2] But what part in reality did the English Parliament play in the fifteenth century in creating that mean? How far, indeed, was Fortescue in defence of the English system *parti pris* or at the most prophetic? The activities of Parliament were hardly the whole of politics. Nor was the existence of Parliament incontrovertible. Fortescue himself seems to have been very much afraid of a 'reception' of civil law; and, in the next century and later, England was not without its theorists of 'absolutism' *à la française*. And Fortescue would still be forced to admit that the whole question turned essentially upon what the king ruling simply regally did with his powers. The absence of effective representative institutions cannot be seen in Fortescue's terms as creating an absolutism in the non-pejorative sense. Neither can it be seen as creating a despotism; for this was created by the misuse of the unfettered will, both for Fortescue and for Seyssel. For both of them tyranny was created by the negligence of such governance; Parliament was simply Fortescue's bridle for the monarch. It was the accident of the development of the English polity that it existed; and it continued to exist only because the structure of that polity allowed it to.

It is thus to a certain extent with the advantage of hindsight that one sees the French Estates and their failure as important. But the liberty of

[1] *De Laudibus Legum Anglie*, ed. S.B. Chrimes (Cambridge, 1942) p. 90.
[2] H.D. Lasswell and A. Kaplan, *Power and Society. A Framework for Political Enquiry* (Yale, 1950) p. 166.

those who were politically important under the Valois kings need not
have suffered unless they became the king's enemies; the oligarchs of
the towns, the greater clergy, the greater nobility had their own place in
the scheme of tensions and resistances that was the power complex in
later medieval France. It was the more minute changes in that scheme
which made political movement in the fourteenth and fifteenth centuries,
not the protection of a poor taxpayer — however much his interests
may have been paraded by the men of letters and their near kin, the
compilers of the *cahier de doléances* of 1484.

For that society, including perhaps even its lowest members, did not,
perhaps, any more than Sir John Fortescue, believe in progress. From
top to bottom its members might be rebels; but they were hardly
revolutionary. Even Gerson could be ashamed of his peasant origins.
Nor was there much social change willy-nilly. There was a constant
movement between the classes, but this does not constitute social
change. There is perhaps some evidence that peasant fortunes improved
with the shortage of labour from the first plague onwards; but there is
also evidence that this improvement may have been short-lived. There
is also evidence of the capacity of the old families to survive the
misfortunes of the fourteenth and fifteenth centuries. The social realities
of the period matched its general political theory. Out of the long
decades of tribulation had emerged a sentimental attachment to a strong
ruler, whose

safety is our safety
And his ruin is our loss.

Nobles, churchmen, oligarchs effectively accepted the myths of
monarchy. In this sense at least there was an absolute monarchy in
France, an absolute monarchy by 'right divine'. This was the essential
'recovery of France' at the end of the middle ages: the arrogation of the
idea of Valois monarchy over its opponent theories to some extent in
practice. The process was far from wholly deliberate, far from wholly
without the intervention if not of God at least of Fortune. It was the
result in part of a series of accidents, and it was in part to dominate the
history of the French people to the present day.

Bibliographical Indications

No more than in the footnotes would it have been possible here to give anything like a complete bibliographical guide to the material, published and unpublished, which is available to the student of each topic raised in this book. These notes are limited, therefore, to general works (themselves containing useful general bibliographies), to major monographs (which normally contain a complete bibliography of the material available to each author) and to those shorter papers which seem at the moment most useful guides in the trackless wastes. A brief indication of bibliographies themselves has been given, and of guides in turn to the source material.

§1. *Society in general.* There is no general survey of French society in the later middle ages, though much information may be derived from the general works cited below, §8. But there is a number of studies of the societies of particular regions and of their economies. Among them may be cited L. Delisle, *Etudes sur la condition de la classe agricole et l'état de l'agriculture en Normandie au Moyen âge* (Evreux, 1851); A. Plaisse, *La Baronnie du Neubourg* (1961); M. Mollat, *Le Commerce maritime normand à la fin du Moyen âge* (1952); G. Fourquin, *Les Campagnes de la région parisienne à la fin du Moyen âge* (1964); Y. Bézard, *La Vie rurale dans le sud de la région parisienne de 1450 à 1560* (1929); I. Guérin, *La Vie rurale en Sologne aux xive et xve siècles* (1960); E. Fournial, *Les Villes et l'économie d'échange en Forez aux xiiie et xive siècles* (1967); P. Wolff, *Commerces et marchands de Toulouse (vers 1350–vers 1450)* (1954); R. Boutruche, *La Crise d'une société. Seigneurs et paysans du Bordelais pendant la guerre de Cent ans* (1947).

For demographic problems see R. Mols, *Introduction à la démographie historique des villes d'Europe du xive au xviiie siècle* (Louvain, 1954–6); E. Carpentier and J. Glénisson, 'La Démographie française au xive siècle', in *Annales*, XVII (1962) 109–29; E. Baratier, *La Démographie provençale du xiiie au xvie siècle* (1961); for problems concerning war damage, R. Boutruche, 'La Dévastation des campagnes pendant la guerre de Cent ans et la reconstruction agricole de la France', in

Mélanges 1945, III *Etudes historiques* (1947) 127–63; and for problems concerning money and prices, M. Bloch, *Esquisse d'une histoire monétaire de l'Europe* (1954); H. A. Miskimin, *Money, Prices and Foreign Exchange in Fourteenth-century France* (Yale, 1963).

For religious attitudes, see below, §4; for attitudes towards the heretical and the occult, J. Hansen, *Quellen und Untersuchungen zur Geschichte des Hexenwahns und der Hexenverfolgung im Mittelalter* (Bonn, 1901); J. Marx, *L'Inquisition en Dauphiné. Etude sur le développement et la répression de l'hérésie et de la sorcellerie du xive siècle au début du règne de François 1er* (Bibl. Ec. Hautes Etudes, 206: 1914). J. Huizinga, *Le Déclin du Moyen âge* (1932) (English translation, without footnotes, *The Waning of the Middle Ages* (1924)) remains a remarkable contribution to the literature of the period; and it is to be hoped that the last volume of F. Lot and R. Fawtier, *Hist. des institutions françaises au Moyen âge*, V *Institutions sociales*, ed. G. Duby (in preparation) will contain material upon attitudes towards these and *devant la vie*. For attitudes towards the English and 'national sentiment' (again still very much a thorny problem) see C. V. Langlois, 'Les Anglais du Moyen âge d'après les sources françaises', in *R. hist.* LII (1893) 298–315; G. Ascoli, *La Grande-Bretagne devant l'opinion française depuis la guerre de Cent ans jusqu'à la fin du xvie siècle* (1927); D. Kirkland, 'The Growth of National Sentiment in France before the Fifteenth Century', in *History*, XXIII (1938) 12–24; B. Guenée, 'Etat et nation en France au Moyen âge', in *R. hist.* CCXXXVII (1967) 17–30; P. S. Lewis, 'War-propaganda and Historiography in Fifteenth-century France and England', in *Trans. Roy. hist. Soc.* ser. 5 XV (1965) 1–21; A. Bossuat, 'L'Idée de nation et la jurisprudence du Parlement de Paris au xve siècle', in *R. hist.* CCIV (1950) 54–61; G. Lefèvre-Pontalis, 'La Guerre de partisans dans la Haute-Normandie (1424–1429)', in *Bibl. Ec. Chartes*, LIV (1893) 475–521, LV (1894) 295–305, LVI (1895) 433–508, LVII (1896) 5–54, XCVII (1936) 102–30; A. Bossuat, 'Le Rétablissement de la paix sociale sous le règne de Charles VII', in *Moyen Age*, LX (1954) 138–62.

§2. *Peuple.* (*a*) Countrymen. Apart from the regional studies cited above, §1, see, for the conditions of serfs, A. Bossuat, 'Le Servage en Nivernais au xve siècle', in *Bibl. Ec. Chartes*, CXVII (1959) 89–134, and for rural insurrection, S. Luce, *Hist. de la Jacquerie*, 2nd ed. (1894); M. Boudet, *La Jacquerie des Tuchins, 1363–1384* (Riom, 1895).

(*b*) Townsmen. The most recent and most convenient bibliography of urban history is that of P. Dollinger, P. Wolff and S. Guenée, *Bibliographie d'hist. des villes de France* (1967); the most convenient general work is that of C. Petit-Dutaillis, *Les Communes françaises* (1947), but see also *Rec. Soc. Jean Bodin*, VI (1954). F. Lot and R. Fawtier, *Hist. des institutions françaises au Moyen âge*, IV *Institutions urbaines*, ed. J. Schneider, is in preparation.

Institutional studies of towns abound; rarer are those which deal with men and how they dealt with their problems. But see J. Lestocquoy, *Les Dynasties bourgeoises d'Arras du xie au xve siècle* (Arras, 1945); E. Maugis, *Recherches sur les transformations du régime politique et sociale de la ville d'Amiens des origines de la commune à la fin du xvie siècle* (1906); M. Mollat, *Le Commerce maritime normand* . . . cited above, §1; J. Déniau, *La Commune de Lyon et la guerre bourguignonne, 1417–1435* (Lyon, 1934); E. Delcambre, *Le Consulat du Puy en Velay des origines à 1610* (Le Puy, 1933); P. Wolff, *Commerces et marchands de Toulouse*, cited above, §1. *Métiers* are discussed by O. Martin, *L'Organisation corporative de la France d'Ancien régime* (1938); E. Coornaert, *Les Corporations en France avant 1789*, 4th ed. (1941); A. Gouron, *La Réglementation des métiers en Languedoc au Moyen âge* (Geneva, 1958). P. Wolff, 'Les Luttes sociales dans les villes du Midi français, xiiie–xve siècles', in *Annales*, II (1947) 443–54, provides a useful general *aperçu* of social conflict. For problems concerning urban finances, see, for instance, E. Maugis, 'Essai sur le régime financier de la ville d'Amiens du xive à la fin du xvie siècle', in *M. Soc. Antiq. Picardie*, ser. 4 III (1899) 133–656; F. Humbert, *Les Finances municipales de Dijon du milieu du xive siècle à 1477* (1961); and concerning urban jurisdiction, G. Testaud, *Des Juridictions municipales en France (des origines jusqu'à l'ordonnance de Moulins)* (1901). For material on the relations of towns with the government, see L. Caillet, *Etude sur les relations de la commune de Lyon avec Charles VII et Louis XI (1417–1483)* (Lyon, 1909); H. Sée, *Louis XI et les villes* (1891) (but for an important corrective to outlook, see B. Chevalier, 'La Politique de Louis XI à l'égard des bonnes villes. Le Cas de Tours', in *Moyen Age*, LXX (1964) 473–504); R. Gandilhon, *Politique économique de Louis XI* (Rennes, 1940).

§3. *Nobles*. No over-all study exists. For the question of definition,

see J. Bloch, *L'Anoblissement en France au temps de François I*er* (1934);
E. Dravasa, ' "Vivre noblement". Recherches sur la dérogeance de
noblesse du xiv*e* au xvi*e* siècles', in R. *jurid. écon. Sud-Ouest, Sér. jurid.*
XVI (1965) 135–93, XVII (1966) 23–119; E. Perroy, 'Social Mobility
among the French *Noblesse* in the Later Middle Ages', in *Past & Present,*
XXI (1962) 25–38. A number of the problems involved in the noble way
of life is discussed by R. Boutruche, *La Crise d'une société,* cited above, §1;
and for those involved in the creation of clientages, see B.A. Pocquet
du Haut-Jussé, 'Les Pensionnaires fieffés des ducs de Bourgogne de
1352 à 1419', in *M. Soc. Droit Pays bourguignons,* VIII (1942) 127–50;
M. Nordberg, *Les Ducs et la royauté. Etudes sur la rivalité des ducs d'Orléans
et de Bourgogne, 1392–1407* (Uppsala, 1964); P.S. Lewis, 'Decayed and
Non-feudalism in Later Medieval France', in *B. Inst. hist. Research,*
XXXVII (1964) 157–84.

For particular princely houses and their administrations, see F. Lot
and R. Fawtier, *Hist. des institutions françaises au Moyen âge,* I *Institutions
seigneuriales* (1957), with chapters by F.L. Ganshof (on Flanders), B.A.
Pocquet du Haut-Jussé (on Brittany), J. Richard (on Burgundy),
E. Perroy (on Bourbonnais), A. Bossuat (on Auvergne), Y. Renouard
(on Aquitaine), C. Samaran (on Gascony) and P. Tucoo-Chala (on
Béarn). Flanders has a considerable literature; for the period before the
Valois, see as well R. Monier, *Les Institutions centrales du comté de Flandre
de la fin du ix*e* siècle à 1384* (1943) and *Les Institutions financières du comté de
Flandre du xi*e* siècle à 1384* (1948). Much, again, has been written on
Brittany; see as well C. Bellier Dumaine, 'L'Administration du duché de
Bretagne sous le règne de Jean V', in *A. Bretagne,* XIV (1898–9) 562–90,
XV (1899–1900) 162–88, 468–89, XVI (1900–1) 112–29, 246–78, 477–514;
B.A. Pocquet du Haut-Jussé, 'Le Conseil du duc en Bretagne d'après
ses procès-verbaux (1459–1463)', in *Bibl. Ec. Chartes,* CXVI (1958) 136–
169, and 'La Genèse du législatif dans le duché de Bretagne', in R. *hist.
Droit,* ser. 4 XL (1962) 351–72. Burgundy, too, has a considerable
literature: for the earlier period, see J. Richard, *Les Ducs de Bourgogne et
la formation du duché du xi*e* au xiv*e* siècle* (1954). The most convenient
recent general work on Valois Burgundy is that of R. Vaughan, *Philip
the Bold* (1962); *John the Fearless* (1966); but until the last two volumes
appear see P. Bonenfant, *Philippe-le-bon,* 3rd ed. (Brussels, 1955);
J. Bartier, *Charles le téméraire* (Brussels, 1944); M. Mollat, 'Recherches

sur les finances des ducs Valois de Bourgogne', in R. *hist.* CCXIX (1958) 285–321.

For Anjou, see A. Lecoy de La Marche, *Le Roi René* (1875); H. Bellugou, *Le Roi René et la réforme fiscale dans le duché d'Anjou au milieu du xvᵉ siècle* (Angers, 1962); for Berry, F. Lehoux, *Jean de France, duc de Berri* (1966–); R. Lacour, *Le Gouvernement de l'apanage de Jean, duc de Berry, 1360–1416* (1934); for Bourbonnais, A. Leguai, 'De La Seigneurie à l'état. Le Bourbonnais pendant la guerre de Cent ans', in *B. Soc. Emulation Bourbonnais,* LIII (1964–5) 155–75, 246–69, 313–47, 494–523, 577–90, LIV (1966–7) 37–53, 76–89, 138–54, 252–76, 365–83, 423–47 (in progress), 'Un Aspect de la formation des états princiers en France à la fin du Moyen âge: les réformes administratives de Louis II duc de Bourbon', in *Moyen Age,* LXX (1964) 49–72, and *Les Ducs de Bourbon pendant la crise monarchique du xvᵉ siècle* (1962). For Aquitaine, see E. Lodge, *Gascony under English Rule* (1926); H. Stein, *Charles de France, frère de Louis XI* (1921); for Albret, A. Luchaire, *Alain le grand sire d'Albret: l'administration royale et la féodalité du Midi (1440–1522)* (1877); for Armagnac, C. Samaran, *La Maison d'Armagnac au xvᵉ siècle et les dernières luttes de la féodalité dans le Midi de la France* (1907); for Comminges, C. Higounet, *Le Comté de Comminges de ses origines à son annexion à la couronne* (Toulouse, 1949); and for Foix-Béarn, P. Tucoo-Chala, *La Vicomté de Béarn et le problème de sa souveraineté des origines à 1620* (Bordeaux, 1961) and *Gaston Fébus et la vicomté de Béarn, 1343–1391* (Bordeaux, 1960); L. Flourac, *Jean I comte de Foix* (1884); H. Courteault, *Gaston IV comte de Foix* (Toulouse, 1895).

§4. *Churchmen.* The most convenient general work is that of E. Delaruelle, E.R. Labande and P. Ourliac, *L'Eglise au temps du Grand schisme et de la crise conciliaire (1378–1449)* (Hist. de l'Eglise ... fondée par A. Fliche et V. Martin, 14: 1962–4); see also F. Lot and R. Fawtier, *Hist. des institutions françaises au Moyen âge,* III *Institutions ecclésiastiques* (1962). For religious practice and sentiment, see P. Adam, *La Vie paroissiale en France au xivᵉ siècle* (1964); J. Toussaert, *Le Sentiment religieux en Flandre à la fin du Moyen âge* (1963); J. Epinat, 'La Situation religieuse dans le diocèse de Lyon d'après la visite pastorale de J. de Talaru, 1378–1379', in *Cah. Hist.* VI (1961) 217–43; V. Chomel, 'Droit de patronage et pratique religieuse dans l'archevêché de Narbonne au début du xve siècle', in *Bibl. Ec. Chartes*, cxv (1957) 58–137.

For problems involved in the ecclesiastical way of life, see R. Génestal, *Le Privilegium Fori en France du décret de Gratien à la fin du xive siècle* (1921); M. Mollat, *La Collation des bénéfices ecclésiastiques sous les papes d'Avignon* (1921); B. Guillemain, *La Politique bénéficiale du pape Benoit XII, 1334–1342* (Bibl. Ec. Hautes Etudes, 299: 1952); F. Baix, 'De La Valeur historique des actes pontificaux de collation des bénéfices', in *Hommage à dom Ursmer Berlière* (Brussels, 1931) pp. 57–66; C. Samaran and G. Mollat, *La Fiscalité pontificale en France au xive siècle* (Bibl. Ec. fr. Athènes Rome, 96: 1905); W.E. Lunt, *Papal Revenues in the Middle Ages* (Columbia, 1934); J. Favier, 'Temporels ecclésiastiques et taxation fiscale: le poids de la fiscalité pontificale au xive siècle', in *J. Savants* (1964) pp. 102–27, and *Les Finances pontificales à l'époque du Grand schisme d'Occident, 1378–1409* (Bibl. Ec. fr. Athènes Rome, 211: 1966); H.S. Denifle, *La Désolation des églises, monastères et hôpitaux en France pendant la guerre de Cent ans* (1897–9); A. d'Haenens, *L'Abbaye Saint-Martin de Tournai de 1290 à 1350. Origines, évolution et dénouement d'une crise* (Louvain, 1961). For questions concerning conflicts of jurisdiction, see O. Martin, *L'Assemblée de Vincennes de 1329 et ses conséquences* (Rennes, 1909); B. Guenée, *Tribunaux et gens de justice*, cited below, §6. For the development of a Gallican Church, see J. Gaudemet, *La Collation par le roi de France des bénéfices vacants en régale des origines à la fin du xive siècle* (Bibl. Ec. Hautes Etudes, Sci. religieuses, 51: 1935); G. Mollat, 'Le Roi de France et la collation plénière (*pleno jure*) des bénéfices ecclésiastiques', in *Mémoires présentées par divers savants à l'Acad. Inscript.* XIV, part 2 (1952) 107–252; M. Morel, *L'Excommunication et le pouvoir civil en France du droit canonique classique au commencement du xve siècle* (1926); G. Mollat, 'Les Origines du gallicanisme parlementaire aux xive et xve siècles', in *R. Hist. ecclés.* XLIII (1948) 90–147; F.L. Cheyette, 'La Justice et le pouvoir royal à la fin du Moyen âge français', in *R. hist. Droit*, ser. 4 XL (1962) 373–94; V. Martin, *Les Origines du Gallicanisme* (1939); N. Valois, *Hist. de la Pragmatique Sanction de Bourges sous Charles VII* (1906); R. Génestal, *Les Origines de l'appel comme d'abus* (Bibl. Ec. Hautes Etudes, Sci. religieuses, 63: 1951); P. Ourliac, 'Le Concordat de 1472. Etude sur les rapports de Louis XI et de Sixte IV', in *R. hist. Droit*, ser. 4 XXI (1942) 124–223, XXII (1943) 117–49; J. Salvini, 'L'Application de la Pragmatique Sanction sous Charles VII et Louis XI au chapitre cathédrale de Paris', in R. *hist. Eglise France*, III (1912) 121–48, 276–96, 421–31, 550–61.

§5. *Representative institutions* have excited an almost disproportionate amount of literature. For a general view, see P. S. Lewis, 'The Failure of the French Medieval Estates', in *Past & Present*, XXIII (1962) 3–14; and upon ideas of representation in general, G. Post, '*Plena Potestas* and Consent in Medieval Assemblies: A Study in Romano-Canonical Procedure and the Rise of Representation, 1150–1325', in *Traditio*, I (1943) 355–408 (but see Bisson, cited below); J. Cadart, *Le Régime électoral des Etats généraux de 1789 et ses origines, 1302–1614* (1952); P. Viollet, 'Elections des députés aux Etats généraux de Tours en 1468 et en 1484', in *Bibl. Ec. Chartes*, ser. 6 II (1866) 22–58.

There is no adequate over-all work on the central assemblies of the fourteenth century. For the fifteenth, see J. R. Major, *Representative Institutions in Renaissance France, 1421–1559* (Madison, 1960). Specific notorious assemblies are dealt with by R. Delachenal, *Hist. de Charles V*, cited below, §8 (for the 1350s); L. Mirot, *Les Insurrections urbaines au début du règne de Charles VI (1380–83), leurs causes, leurs conséquences* (1905); A. Coville, *Les Cabochiens et l'ordonnance de 1413* (1888); there is no adequate work on the Estates-general of 1484. Upon the more important regional assemblies the following works, for the most part institutional rather than social studies, may be cited: for Flanders, J. Dhondt, 'Les Origines des Etats de Flandre', in *Anciens pays et assemblées d'Etats: Standen en Landen*, I (1950) 1–52, and '"Ordres" ou "puissances": l'exemple des Etats de Flandre', in *Annales*, V (1950) 289–305; for Artois, C. Hirschauer, *Les Etats d'Artois de leurs origines à l'occupation française, 1340–1640* (1923). For Normandy, see A. Coville, *Les Etats de Normandie, leurs origines et leur développement au xiv*e *siècle* (1894); H. Prentout, *Les Etats provinciaux de Normandie* (M. Acad. nat. Sci. Arts Caen, NS 1–3: Caen, 1925–7); B. J. H. Rowe, 'The Estates of Normandy under the Duke of Bedford', in *Engl. hist. R.* XLVI (1931) 551–78. For Brittany, see A. Rebillon, *Les Etats de Bretagne de 1661 à 1789* (1932); B. A. Pocquet du Haut-Jussé, 'Les Faux Etats de Bretagne de 1315 et les premiers Etats de Bretagne', in *Bibl. Ec. Chartes*, LXXXVI (1925) 388–406, and 'La Genèse du législatif', cited above, §3; J. de La Martinière, 'Vannes, siège du Parlement de Bretagne', in *A. Bretagne*, XXXV (1921–3) 69–80, and 'Le Parlement de Bretagne sous les rois de France', in *A. Bretagne,* XXXVI (1924–5) 270–98, XXXVII (1926) 102–30, XXXIX (1930–1) 217–78.

For the Estates of central France, see A. Thomas, *Les Etats provinciaux de la France centrale sous Charles VII* (1879); J.M. Tyrrell, 'Financial Activities of the Estates of Poitou', in *Medieval Stud.* XXVI (1964) 186–209; for those of Burgundy, J. Billioud, *Les Etats de Bourgogne aux xive et xve siècles* (M. Acad. Dijon, ser. 5 IV: Dijon, 1922). For Languedoc, see T.N. Bisson, *Assemblies and Representation in Languedoc in the Thirteenth Century* (Princeton, 1964); Dognon, cited below, §6; H. Gilles, *Les Etats de Languedoc au xve siècle* (Toulouse, 1965); A. Le Sourd, *Essai sur les Etats de Vivarais* (1926); E. Delcambre, *Les Etats du Velay des origines à 1642* (St.-Etienne, 1938); for Dauphiné, A. Dussert, *Les Etats du Dauphiné aux xive et xve siècles* (B. Acad. delphinale, ser. 5 VIII: Grenoble, 1914), and *Les Etats du Dauphiné de la guerre de Cent ans aux guerres de Religion* (ibid. 13 part 2: Grenoble, 1922); and for Béarn, L. Cadier, *Les Etats de Béarn depuis leurs origines jusqu'au commencement du xvie siècle* (1888).

§6. *Government*. Institutional studies again abound. The most convenient general work on royal administration is that of F. Lot and R. Fawtier, *Hist. des institutions françaises au Moyen âge,* II *Institutions royales* (1958). Still useful are P. Viollet, *Hist. des institutions politiques et admin. de la France* (1890–1903); P. Dognon, *Les Institutions politiques et admin. du pays de Languedoc du xiiie siècle aux guerres de Religion* (Toulouse, 1895).

For civil servants royal or seigneurial — groups now rapidly emerging from institutional obscurity — and their problems, see O. Martin, 'La Nomination aux offices royaux au xive siècle', in *Mélanges Paul Fournier* (1929) pp. 486–98; G. Dupont-Ferrier, *Gallia regia ou état des officiers royaux des bailliages et des sénéchaussées de 1328 à 1515* (1942–61); R. Cazelles, *La Société politique et la crise de la royauté sous Philippe de Valois* (1958); Rey, cited below; R. Delachenal, *Hist. des avocats au Parlement de Paris, 1300–1600* (1885); A. Bossuat, *Le Bailliage royal de Montferrand (1425–1556)* (1957); B. Guenée, *Tribunaux et gens de justice dans le bailliage de Senlis à la fin du Moyen âge* (1963); R. Fédou, *Les Hommes de loi lyonnais à la fin du Moyen âge. Etude sur les origines de la classe de robe* (1964); J. Bartier, *Légistes et gens de finances au xve siècle. Les Conseillers des ducs de Bourgogne Philippe le bon et Charles le téméraire* (Brussels, 1955–7).

For the mechanism of local administration, see G. Dupont-Ferrier, *Les Officiers royaux des bailliages et sénéchaussées et les institutions monarchiques locales en France à la fin du Moyen âge* (Bibl. Ec. Hautes Etudes, 145: 1902) and *Les Elections*, cited next. A considerable amount has been written about financial administration: G. Dupont-Ferrier, *Etudes sur les institutions financières de la France à la fin du Moyen âge*, I *Les Elections et leur personnel* (1930), II *Les Finances extraordinaires et leur mécanisme* (1932), and *Nouvelles Etudes sur les institutions financières de la France à la fin du Moyen âge*, I *Les Origines et le premier siècle de la Chambre ou Cour des aides de Paris* (1933), II *Les Origines et le premier siècle de la Cour du Trésor* (Bibl. Ec. Hautes Etudes, 266: 1936); H. Jassemin, *La Chambre des comptes de Paris au xve siècle* (1933). Since most of the material for the financial history of later medieval France does not survive, the actual working of royal finances is more difficult to perceive. But see M. Rey, *Le Domaine du roi et les finances extraordinaires sous Charles VI, 1388–1413* (1965) and *Les Finances royales sous Charles VI. Les Causes du déficit, 1388–1413* (1965).

For the Parlement of Paris, see G. Ducoudray, *Les Origines du Parlement de Paris et de la justice aux xiiie et xive siècles* (1902); E. Maugis, *Hist. du Parlement de Paris de l'avènement des rois Valois à la mort d'Henri IV* (1913–16); for the Parlement of Toulouse, A. Viala, *Le Parlement de Toulouse et l'admin. royale laïque, 1420–1525 environ* (Albi, 1953). For the problems involved in making government work, see G. Dupont-Ferrier, 'Ignorances et distractions admin. en France aux xive et xve siècles', in *Bibl. Ec. Chartes*, C (1939) 145–56 — but see B. Guenée, 'La Géographie admin. de la France à la fin du Moyen âge: élections et bailliages', in *Moyen Age*, ser. 4 LXVII (1961) 293–323; G. Dupont-Ferrier, 'Le rôle des commissaires royaux dans le gouvernement de la France, spécialement du xive au xvie siècle', in *Mélanges Paul Fournier* (1929) pp. 171–84 — but see H. Gilles, 'Autorité royale et résistances urbaines, un exemple languedocien: l'échec de la réformation générale de 1434–1435', in *B. philol. hist. Com. Travaux hist. sci.* (1961) pp. 115–46. The royal Council has been examined by N. Valois, *Etude hist. sur le Conseil du roi* (1886) and *Le Conseil du roi aux xive, xve et xvie siècles* (1888). The court as a political institution has not received the attention it deserves.

§7. *The king.* For the ideal, see D. M. Bell, *L'Idéal éthique de la royauté en France au Moyen âge* (Geneva, 1962); for the charisma, see M. Bloch, *Les Rois thaumaturges. Etude sur le caractère surnaturel attribué à la puissance royale, particulièrement en France et en Angleterre* (1961); R. E. Giesey, *The Royal Funerary Ceremony in Renaissance France* (Geneva, 1960). For ideas concerning the position of the king, see A. Lemaire, *Les Lois fondamentales de la monarchie française d'après les théoriciens de l'Ancien régime* (1907); P. Viollet, 'Comment les femmes ont été exclues, en France, de la succession à la couronne', in *Mémoires de l'Acad. Inscript.* XXXIV, part 2 (1895) 125–78; R. E. Giesey, 'The Juristic Basis of Dynastic Right to the French Throne', in *Trans. Am. philosophical Soc.* NS LI (1961) part 5; M. David, 'Le Serment du sacre du ixe au xve siècle. Contribution à l'étude des limites juridiques de la souveraineté', in R. *Moyen Age latin*, VI (1950) 5–272, and *La Souveraineté et les limites juridiques du pouvoir monarchique du ixe au xve siècle* (1954); A. Bossuat, 'La Formule, "Le Roi est empereur en son royaume". Son Emploi au xve siècle devant le Parlement de Paris', in *R. hist. Droit*, ser. 4 XXXIX (1961) 371–81; R. E. Giesey, 'The French Estates and the Corpus Mysticum Regni', in *Album Helen Maud Cam*, I (Etudes presentées à la Commission internationale pour l'hist. des assemblées d'Etats, 23: Louvain, 1960) 153–72; P. S. Lewis, 'Jean Juvenal des Ursins and the Common Literary Attitude towards Tyranny in Fifteenth-century France', in *Medium Aevum*, XXXIV (1965) 103–21. For the persons of the kings, apart from the general studies cited below, §8, see A. Brachet, *La Pathologie mentale des rois de France: Louis XI et ses ascendants* (1903) — to be treated with prudence.

§8. *Political narratives* do not exist for the reigns of the first two Valois kings. For Charles V, see R. Delachenal, *Hist. de Charles V* (1909–31). There is again no modern work on the reign of Charles VI as a whole. For Charles VII, see G. du Fresne de Beaucourt, *Hist. de Charles VII* (1881–91) and for Louis XI, P. Champion, *Louis XI* (Paris, 1927) (English tr. without footnotes (n.d.)). For a general political narrative (and much more besides), see A. Lavisse, *Hist. de France*, III (1901). The Hundred Years War is dealt with by E. Perroy, *La Guerre de Cent ans* (1945) (English tr., *The Hundred Years War* (1951)); material on recent views on the origins of the war may be found in G. P. Cuttino,

'Historical Revision: the Causes of the Hundred Years War', in *Speculum*, XXXI (1956) 463–77.

§9. *Bibliographies*. Apart from those in works already indicated, J. Calmette, *L'Elaboration du monde moderne* (Clio, 5) 3rd ed. (1949) provides a most useful guide both to monographs and to printed source materials. Reference to those published since 1955 may be found in the *Bibliographie annuelle de l'hist. de France du cinquième siècle à 1939, 1955–* (1956–); a retrospective series — of which one volume, *1953–54* (1964), has been published — is designed to close the gap between the recent series and the *Répertoire bibliographique de l'hist. de France, 1920–31* (1923–38). A valuable guide to work in periodicals published by learned societies is the *Bibliographie générale des travaux hist. et archéol. publiés par les Sociétés savantes de la France, –1900* (1888–1904); *Bibliographie annuelle des travaux . . . 1901–10* (1906–14); *Bibliographie générale . . . 1910–40* (1944–1951). For the literature of later medieval France, one should consult R. Bossuat, *Manuel bibliographique de la littérature française du Moyen âge* (1951–); and for its sources in print, as well as Calmette and the *Bibliographie annuelle*, A. Molinier, *Les Sources de l'hist. de France*, IV–VI (1904–6), a new edition of which is in preparation.

§10. *Orientation*. No better guide can be found than B. Guenée, 'L'Hist. de l'Etat en France à la fin du Moyen âge, vue par les historiens français depuis cent ans', in R. *hist.* CCXXXII (1964) 331–60.

Index

Abbeville, 278
abrégés, 136
absolutism, meaning of term, 378
Acy, Jean d', 146-7
Agde: consuls of, 257; bishopric of, 290
Agen, 239
Agenais, 239, 248, 348; effect of war on, 53; *sénéchal* of, 153
  Estates of, 239, 358; bypassed, 369-70
Agincourt, battle of, 45, 212
aides, 105-8 *passim*, 135, 215, 349, 350; meaning of term, 105 n; gift of, 218-22 *passim*, 228; abolition of, 106, 274; *de facto* permanent, 341-2
Aigues-Mortes, 1, 239
Ailly, Pierre d', 293, 314; on benefices for graduates, 296, 320; and astrology, 25
Aire, bishop of, (Arnaud-Guillaume de Lescun) 293-4, (Louis d'Albret) 312 n
Aix, archbishopric of, 290
Albi, 2; population movement in, 29-30, 289 n; bishop of, 288
Albigeois, 228, 239
Albret, house of, 192, 213; piety of, 213; family custom of, 194, 213; survival of, 213
  Amanieu VII sire d' (1298-1324), 204
  Bernard-Ezi II sire d' (1324-58), 204, 207
  Arnaud Amanieu sire d' (1358-1401), 207, 213, 219, 220; wife of (Marguerite de Bourbon), 213
  Charles I sire d' (1401-15), 213; wife of (Marie de Sully), 213
  Charles II sire d' (1415-71), 129, 213, 312 n; wife of (Anne d'Armagnac), 213
  Louis d', 312 n
  Jeanne d', 207
  Rose d', 207
Alençon, 45, 194
Alençon, cadet line of Valois, 190
  Jean II duc d' (1415-76), 48; pension of, 228; intrigues with English, 41, 188, 228-9; and astrologers, 25, 26
  Charles d', 311-12
alliances, 200-1
ambassadors, Italian: on the court, 122-4 *passim*; on the war of the Public Weal, 198-9, 222; and Louis XI, 116-19, 121

Amboise, 160; concordat of, 316-17, 319
Amboise: Georges d', 322; Marguerite d', 206
Amiens, 6, 21, 113, 249 n, 274, 283, 337; rise of lawyers in, 247; *métiers* of, in politics, 253; revolt in, 253, 267 n; *bailliage* of, 333; control of royal officers in, 268 n
  oligarchy of, 261; exemption of, 249; shift in attitudes of, 269 and n
Angers: bourgeoisie of, and Louis XI, 273; revolt of Tricoterie in, 274; university of, 10; bishop of, 326
Anglure, Ogier VIII seigneur d', 12
Ango, Jean, 245
Angoulême, cadet line of Orléans, 190; Jean d'Orléans comte d' (1407-67), 9, 217
Angy, *prévôté* of, 165
Anjou, 14, 15, 168, 219, 280; *sénéchal* of, 125; English rights in, 33, 39; occupied by English, 45
Anjou, house of, 160; extinction in male line, 376
  Charles I comte d' (1246-85), 194
  Louis I duc d' (1356-84), 11, 92, 190, 256; wife of (Marie de Blois), 221
  Louis II duc d' (1384-1417), 190, 218; *trésorier* of, 155
  René duc d' (1434-80), 168, 190, 191, 214, 219, 376; multilingual, 4; literary capacity of, 201 and n; *Livre du Cuer d'Amours espris* of, 76; defends interests of Angevin subjects, 14, 15-16, 169, 229, 282; ransom of, 212; in danger of losing prerogatives, 237; loses Angers, 273; revolt of Tricoterie in support of, 274
  Jean d', duke of Calabria, 376
  Nicolas d', duke of Calabria, 376
  [Marie duchesse d'] (queen of Sicily), 221
  Marie d' (queen of France), 161
Anjou and Maine, Estates of, 335, 363
annates, 302, 303, 323; taken by king, 307
anoblissement, 175-6; *lettres d'*, 175-6; of urban oligarchies, 180
apanages, 194
appeal to king of France: from Aquitaine, 33, 34; from Brittany, 234

O

DATE DUE

NOV 1 2 1991			